DATE DUE

DEMCO 38-296

INDEX

History of the Modern World

Volume 10

Index

Marshall Cavendish
New York • London • Toronto • Sydney

Marshall Cavendish Corporation
99 White Plains Road
Tarrytown, NY 10591-9001

Consultants

Professor Charles Ingrao, Purdue University
Professor Ronald J. Ross, University of Wisconsin–Milwaukee

Created by Brown Partworks Ltd
Editor: Timothy Cooke
Associate Editors: Robert Anderson, David Scott-Macnab, Casey Horton
Design: Wilson Design Associates
Picture Research: Jenny Speller, Adrian Bentley
Maps: Bill Lebihan
Index Editor: Kay Ollerenshaw

Library of Congress Cataloging-in-Publication Data

History of the modern world / [editor, Timothy Cooke].
    p. cm.
    Contents: v. 1. Origins of the modern world—v. 2. Religion and change in Europe—v. 3. Old and new worlds—v. 4. The Age of the Enlightenment—
v. 5. Revolution and change—v. 6. The changing balance of power—v. 7. World War I and its consequences—v. 8. World War II and the Cold War—
v. 9. The world today—v. 10. Index
    Includes bibliographical references and index.
    ISBN 0-7614-7147-2 (set).—ISBN 0-7614-7148-0 (v. 1).—ISBN 0-7614-7149-9 (v. 2).—ISBN 0-7614-7150-2 (v. 3).—ISBN 0-7614-7151-0 (v. 4).—
ISBN 0-7614-7152-9 (v. 5).—ISBN 0-7614-7153-7 (v. 6).—ISBN 0-7614-7154-5 (v. 7).—ISBN 0-7614-7155-3 (v. 8).—ISBN 0-7614-7156-1 (v. 9).
ISBN 0-7614-7157-X (v. 10).
    1. World history Juvenile literature. I. Cooke, Timothy, 1961- .
D20.h544 1999
909.08—dc21
                                  99-14780
                                    CIP

ISBN 0-7614-7155-3 (set)
ISBN 0-7614-7157-X (v. 10)

Printed and bound in Italy

07 06 05 04 03 02 01 00 7 6 5 4 3 2 1

CONTENTS

1302 Chronicles

1314 Time Line

1329 Glossary

1344 Further Resources

1359 Thematic Indexes
   Arts and Culture
   Customs and Everyday Life
   Geographical Locations
     Africa
     Europe
     Far East
     Middle East
     North America
     South America
   Government and Politics
   Religion
   Trade and Economy
   Wars and Battles

1391 Comprehensive A–Z Index

Chronicles

Albania

First Secretaries of the Albanian (Communist)
Party of Labor
1948–1985 Enver Hoxha
1985–1991 Ramiz Alia

Presidents
1991–1992 Ramiz Alia
1992–1997 Sali Berisha

Angola

Presidents
1975–1979 Agostinho Neto
1979–   José Eduardo dos Santos

Argentina

Presidents
1862–1868 Bartolomé Mitre
1868–1874 Domingo Faustino Sarmiento
1874–1880 Nicolás Avellaneda
1880–1886 Julio A. Roca
1886–1890 Miguel Juárez Celman
1890–1892 Carlos Pellegrini
1892–1895 Luis Sáenz Peña
1895–1898 José Evaristo Uriburu
1898–1904 Julio A. Roca
1904–1906 Manuel A. Quintana
1906–1910 José Figueroa Alcorta
1910–1914 Roque Sáenz Peña
1914–1916 Victorino de la Plaza
1916–1922 Hipólito Irigoyen
1922–1928 Marcelo T. de Alvear
1928–1930 Hipólito Irigoyen
1930–1932 José Félix Uriburu
1932–1938 Agustín Pedro Justo
1938–1942 Roberto M. Ortiz
1940–1943 Ramón S. Castillo
1943–1943 Arturo Rawson Corvalán
1943–1944 Pedro Pablo Ramírez Machuca
1944–1946 Edelmiro J. Farrell
1946–1955 Juan Perón
1955–1955 José Domingo Molina Gómez
1955–1955 Eduardo A. Lonardi
1955–1958 Pedro Eugenio Aramburu Cilveti
1958–1962 Arturo Frondizi
1962–1963 José María Guido
1963–1966 Arturo Umberto Illia
1966–1966 Revolutionary Junta
1966–1970 Juan Carlos Onganía
1970–1970 Pedro Alberto José Gnavi
1970–1971 Roberto Marcelo Levingston
1971–1973 Alejandro Agustín Lanusse
1973–1973 Héctor José Cámpora
1973–1973 Raúl Alberto Lastiri
1973–1974 Juan Perón
1974–1976 Isabel Perón
1976–1976 Military junta
1976–1981 Jorge Rafael Videla
1981–1981 Roberto Eduardo Viola
1981–1982 Leopoldo Galtieri
1982–1983 Reynaldo Bignone
1983–1989 Raúl Alfonsín
1989–   Carlos Saúl Menem

Australia

Prime ministers
1901–1903 Edmund Barton
1903–1904 Alfred Deakin
1904–1904 John Christian Watson
1904–1905 George Houston Reid
1905–1908 Alfred Deakin
1908–1909 Andrew Fisher
1909–1910 Alfred Deakin
1910–1913 Andrew Fisher
1913–1914 Joseph Cook
1914–1915 Andrew Fisher
1915–1923 William Morris Hughes
1923–1929 Stanley Melbourne Bruce
1929–1932 James Henry Scullin
1932–1939 Joseph Aloysius Lyons
1939–1941 Robert Gordon Menzies
1941–1941 Arthur William Fadden
1941–1945 John Joseph Curtin
1945–1945 Francis Michael Forde
1945–1949 Joseph Benedict Chifley
1949–1966 Robert Gordon Menzies
1966–1967 Harold Holt
1967–1968 John McEwen
1968–1971 John Grey Gorton
1971–1972 William McMahon
1972–1975 Gough Whitlam
1975–1983 Malcolm Fraser
1983–1991 Robert J. Hawke
1991–1996 Paul Keating
1996–   John Howard

Austria

Emperors
1804–1835 Francis (II)
1835–1848 Ferdinand
1848–1916 Franz Joseph I
1916–1918 Charles

Presidents
1919–1920 Karl Seitz
1920–1928 Michael Hainisch
1928–1938 Wilhelm Miklas
1945–1950 Karl Renner
1950–1951 Leopold Figl
1951–1957 Theodor Körner
1957–1957 Julius Raab
1957–1965 Adolf Schärf
1965–1965 Josef Klaus (acting)
1965–1974 Franz Jonas
1974–1974 Bruno Kreisky
1974–1986 Rudolf Kirchschläger
1986–1992 Kurt Waldheim
1992–   Thomas Klestil

Belgium

Monarchs
1831–1865 Leopold I
1865–1909 Leopold II
1909–1934 Albert I
1934–1951 Leopold III
1944–1950 Charles (regent)
1950–1951 Baudouin (regent)
1951–1993 Baudouin I
1993–   Albert II

Bolivia

Liberators
1825–1826 Simón Bolívar
1826–1826 Antonio José de Sucre

Presidents since 1943
1943–1946 Gualberto Villarroel
1946–1946 Néstor Guillén
1946–1947 Tomás Monje Gutiérrez
1947–1949 Enrique Hertzog
1949–1951 Mamerto Urriolagoitia
1951–1952 Hugo Ballivián Rojas
1952–1952 Hernán Siles Zuazo
1952–1956 Víctor Paz Estenssoro
1956–1960 Hernán Siles Zuazo
1960–1964 Víctor Paz Estenssoro
1964–1966 Military junta
1966–1969 René Barrientos Ortuño
1969–1969 Luis Adolfo Siles Salinas
1969–1970 Alfredo Ovando Candía
1970–1971 Juan José Torres González
1971–1978 Hugo Banzer Suárez
1978–1978 Juan Pereda Asbún
1978–1979 David Padilla Arancibia
1980–1981 Luis García Meza Tejada
1981–1981 Junta of Commanders
1981–1982 Celso Torrelio Villa
1982–1982 Junta of Commanders
1982–1982 Guido Vildoso Calderón
1982–1985 Hernán Siles Zuazo
1985–1989 Víctor Paz Estenssoro
1989–1993 Jaime Paz Zamora
1993–1997 Gonzalo Sánchez de Lozada
1997–   Hugo Banzer Suárez

Bosnia-Herzegovina

Chairman of the State Presidency
1990–1996 Alija Izetbegovic

Chairmen of the Presidency of the Republic
1996–1998 Alija Izetbegovic
1998–   Zivko Radisic

Federation of Bosnia and Herzegovina
Presidents
1994–1997 Kresimir Zubak
1997–1997 Vladimir Soljic
1997–1999 Ejup Ganic
1999–   Ivo Andric-Luzanski

Brazil

Monarchs
1815–1816 Maria I
1815–1816 João (regent)
1816–1822 João VI
1822–1822 Pedro (regent)

Emperors
1822–1831 Pedro I
1831–1889 Pedro II

Presidents since 1930
1930–1945 Getúlio Vargas
1945–1946 José Linhares

1946–1951 Eurico Gaspar Dutra
1951–1954 Getúlio Vargas
1954–1956 João Café Filho
1956–1961 Juscelino Kubitschek de Oliveira
1961–1961 Jânio da Silva Quadros
1961–1961 Pascoal Ranieri Mazzilli
1961–1964 João Belchior Marques Goulart
1964–1964 Pascoal Ranieri Mazzilli
1964–1967 Humberto de Alencar Castelo Branco
1967–1969 Artur da Costa e Silva
1969–1969 Military junta
1969–1974 Emílio Garrastazú Médici
1974–1979 Ernesto Geisel
1979–1985 João Baptista de Oliveira Figueiredo
1985–1990 José Sarney
1990–1992 Fernando Collor de Mello
1992–1995 Itamar Franco
1995–   Fernando Henrique Cardoso

Bulgaria

General secretaries of the Communist Party
1948–1949 Georgi Dimitrov
1949–1950 Vasil Petrov Kolarov
1950–1954 Vulko Chervenkov
1954–1989 Todor Zhivkov
1989–1990 Petur Mladenov

Presidents
1990–1990 Petur Mladenov
1990–1990 Stanko Todorov
1990–1990 Nikolay Todorov
1990–1997 Zhelyu Zhelev
1997–   Petur Stoyanov

Burgundy, Duchy of

1364–1404 Philip the Bold
1404–1419 John the Fearless
1419–1467 Philip the Good
1467–1477 Charles the Bold
1477–1482 Mary of Burgundy

Cambodia

Monarchs
1860–1904 Norodom
1904–1927 Sisovath
1927–1941 Sisovath Monivong
1941–1955 Norodom Sihanouk
1955–1960 Norodom Suramarit

Heads of state
1960–1960 Chuop Hell
1960–1960 Prince Sisovath Monireth
1960–1960 Chuop Hell
1960–1970 Prince Norodom Sihanouk
1970–1972 Cheng Heng
1972–1972 Lon Nol

Presidents
1972–1975 Lon Nol
1975–1975 Saukham Khoy

Head of state
1975–1976 Prince Norodom Sihanouk

Chairman of the State Presidium
1976–1979 Khieu Samphan

President of the People's Revolutionary Council
1979–1981 Heng Samrin

Chairmen of the Council of State
1981–1992 Heng Samrin
1992–1993 Chea Sim

Chairman of the Supreme National Council
1991–1993 Prince Norodom Sihanouk

Head of state
1993–1993 Prince Norodom Sihanouk

Monarch
1993–   Norodom Sihanouk

Canada

Prime ministers
1867–1873 John Alexander Macdonald
1873–1878 Alexander Mackenzie
1878–1891 John Alexander Macdonald
1891–1892 John Abbott
1892–1894 John Thompson
1894–1896 Mackenzie Bowell
1896–1896 Charles Tupper
1896–1911 Wilfrid Laurier
1911–1920 Robert Laird Borden
1920–1921 Arthur Meighen
1921–1926 W.L. Mackenzie King
1926–1926 Arthur Meighen
1926–1930 W.L. Mackenzie King
1930–1935 Richard Bedford Bennett
1935–1948 W.L. Mackenzie King
1948–1957 Louis Saint Laurent
1957–1963 John G. Diefenbaker
1963–1968 Lester B. Pearson
1968–1979 Pierre Elliott Trudeau
1979–1980 Joe Clark
1980–1984 Pierre Elliott Trudeau
1984–1984 John Turner
1984–1993 Brian Mulroney
1993–1993 Kim Campbell
1993–   Jean Chrétien

Chile

Supreme Directors
1818–1823 Bernardo O'Higgins
1823–1823 Agustín de Eyzaguirre
1823–1823 Congress of Plenipotentiaries
1823–1823 Ramón Freire
1823–1823 Deputy Supreme Junta
1823–1826 Ramón Freire

Presidents since 1946
1946–1946 Alfredo Duhalde Vásquez
1946–1946 Vicente Merino Bielich
1946–1946 Juan Antonio Iribarren Cabezas
1946–1952 Gabriel González Videla
1952–1958 Carlos Ibáñez del Campo
1958–1964 Jorge Alessandri Rodríguez
1964–1970 Eduardo Frei Montalva
1970–1973 Salvador Allende
1973–1974 Military Junta
1974–1990 Augusto Pinochet Ugarte
1990–1994 Patricio Aylwin Azócar
1994–   Eduardo Frei Ruiz-Tagle

China

Emperors
1644–1661 Shunzhi
1661–1722 K'ang-hsi
1722–1736 Yung-cheng
1736–1796 Ch'ien-lung
1796–1820 Chia-ch'ing
1821–1850 Tao-kuang
1851–1861 Hsien-feng
1862–1875 T'ung-chi
1875–1908 Kuang-hsü
1908–1912 Hsüan-t'ung (P'u-i)

Presidents
1912–1912 Sun Yat-sen (provisional)
1912–1915 Yuan Shikai
1916–1916 Yuan Shikai
1916–1917 Li Yuanhong
1918–1922 Xu Shichang
1922–1923 Li Yuanhong
1923–1924 Cao Kun
1924–1926 Duan Qirui
1927–1928 Zhang Zuolin

Chairmen of the National Government
1928–1931 Chiang Kai-shek
1931–1943 Lin Sen
1943–1948 Chiang Kai-shek

Presidents
1948–1949 Chiang Kai-shek
1949–1950 Li Zongren

Chairmen of the Communist Party of China
1943–1976 Mao Tse-tung
1976–1981 Hua Guofeng
1981–1987 Hu Yaobang
1987–1989 Zhao Ziyang
1989–   Jiang Zemin

Premiers
1949–1976 Zhou Enlai
1976–1980 Hua Guofeng
1980–1987 Zhao Ziyang
1987–1998 Li Peng
1998–   Zhu Rongji

Croatia

President
1990–   Franjo Tudjman

Cuba

Presidents since 1936
1936–1940 Federico Laredo Brú
1940–1944 Fulgencio Batista
1944–1948 Ramón Grau San Martín
1948–1952 Carlos Prío Socarrás
1952–1959 Fulgencio Batista
1959–1959 Anselmo Alliegro y Milá
1959–1959 Manuel Urrutia Lleó
1959–1976 Osvaldo Dorticós Torrado

President of the Council of State
1976–   Fidel Castro

Premiers
1959–1959 José Miro Cardona
1959–1976 Fidel Castro

Czechoslovakia

First/General Secretaries of the Communist
Party
1946–1953 Klement Gottwald
1953–1968 Antonín Novotní
1968–1969 Alexander Dubcek
1969–1987 Gustav Husák
1987–1989 Milos Jakes
1989–1989 Karel Urbánek
1989–1990 Ladislav Adamec

Presidents
1918–1935 Tomás Masaryk
1935–1938 Edvard Benes
1938–1945 Emil Hácha
1945–1948 Edvard Benes
1948–1953 Klement Gottwald
1953–1957 Antonín Zápotocky
1957–1968 Antonín Novotny
1968–1975 Ludvík Svoboda
1975–1989 Gustáv Husák
1989–1992 Václav Havel

Czech Republic
Presidents
1993–1993 Václav Klaus (acting)
1993–   Václav Havel

Denmark

Monarchs
1863–1906 Christian IX
1906–1912 Frederik VIII
1912–1947 Christian X
1947–1972 Frederik IX
1972–   Margrethe II (queen)

Ecuador

Presidents since 1940
1940–1944 Carlos Alberto Arroyo del Río
1944–1944 Julio Teodoro Salem Gallegos
1944–1947 José María Velasco Ibarra
1947–1947 Carlos Mancheno Cajas
1947–1947 Mariano Suárez Veintimilla
1947–1948 Carlos Julio Arosemena Tola
1948–1952 Galo Plaza Lasso
1952–1956 José María Velasco Ibarra
1956–1960 Camilo Ponce Enríquez
1960–1961 José María Velasco Ibarra
1961–1963 Carlos Julio Arosemena Monroy
1963–1966 Ramón Castro Jijón
1966–1966 Clemente Yerovi Indaburu
1966–1968 Otto Arosemena Gómez
1968–1972 José María Velasco Ibarra
1972–1976 Guillermo A. Rodríguez Lara
1976–1979 Alfredo Ernesto Poveda Burbano
1979–1981 Jaime Roldós Aguilera
1981–1984 Osvaldo Hurtado Larrea
1984–1988 León Febres Cordero Rivadeneira
1988–1992 Rodrigo Borja Cevallos
1992–1996 Sixto Durán Ballén
1996–1997 Abdalá Bucaram Ortiz
1997–1998 Fabián Alarcón
1998–   Jamil Mahuad

Egypt

Khedives
1867–1879 Isma`il Pasha
1879–1892 Muhammad Tawfiq Pasha
1892–1914 `Abbas Hilmi Pasha

Sultans
1914–1917 Hussein Kamil
1917–1922 Ahmad Fuad

Kings
1922–1936 Fuad I
1936–1952 Faruq I
1952–1953 Fuad II

Presidents
1953–1954 Muhammad Naguib
1954–1954 Gamal Abdel Nasser
1954–1954 Muhammad Naguib
1954–1970 Gamal Abdel Nasser
1970–1981 Anwar as-Sadat
1981–   Hosni Mubarak

Ethiopia

Emperors
1872–1889 Yohannes IV
1889–1913 Menelik II
1913–1916 Iyasu V
1916–1930 Zauditu (empress)
1930–1974 Haile Selassie

Heads of state and chairmen of the
Provisional Military Administrative Council
1974–1977 Tafari Benti
1977–1987 Mengistu Haile Mariam

Presidents
1987–1991 Mengistu Haile Mariam
1991–1991 Tesfaye Gebre Kidan
1991–1995 Meles Zenawi
1995–   Negasso Gidada

Finland

Presidents
1919–1925 Kaarlo Juho Ståhlberg
1925–1931 Lauri Kristian Relander
1931–1937 Pehr Evind Svinhufvud
1937–1940 Kyösti Kallio
1940–1944 Risto Heikki Ryti
1944–1946 Carl Gustaf Mannerheim
1946–1956 Juho Kusti Paasikivi
1956–1981 Urho Kekkonen
1981–1994 Mauno Koivisto
1994–   Martti Ahtisaari

France

Kings since 1380
1380–1422 Charles VI
1422–1461 Charles VII
1461–1483 Louis XI
1483–1498 Charles VIII
1498–1515 Louis XII
1515–1547 Francis I
1547–1559 Henry II
1559–1560 Francis II
1560–1574 Charles IX

1574–1589 Henry III
1589–1610 Henry IV
1610–1643 Louis XIII
1643–1715 Louis XIV
1715–1774 Louis XV
1774–1792 Louis XVI

First Republic
1792–1795 The Convention
1795–1799 The Directory
1799–1804 The Consulate

Emperor (First Empire)
1804–1814 Napoleon I

Kings
1814–1824 Louis XVIII
1824–1830 Charles I
1830–1848 Louis-Philippe

President of the Second Republic
1848–1852 Louis-Napoleon Bonaparte

Emperor of the Second Empire
1852–1870 Napoleon III (Louis-Napoleon
          Bonaparte)

Presidents of the Third Republic
1871–1873 Adolphe Thiers
1873–1879 Patrice Maurice de Mac-Mahon
1879–1887 Jules Grévy
1887–1894 Sadi Carnot
1894–1895 Jean Casimir-Périer
1895–1899 Félix Faure
1899–1906 Émile Loubet
1906–1913 Armand Fallières
1913–1920 Raymond Poincaré
1920–1920 Paul Deschanel
1920–1924 Alexandre Millerand
1924–1931 Gaston Doumergue
1931–1932 Paul Doumer
1932–1940 Albert Lebrun

Head of State
1940–1944 Philippe Pétain

Presidents
1947–1954 Vincent Auriol
1954–1959 René Coty
1959–1969 Charles de Gaulle
1969–1974 Georges Pompidou
1974–1981 Valéry Giscard d'Estaing
1981–1995 François Mitterrand
1995–   Jacques Chirac

Prime ministers
Notable among the 88 prime ministers of the
Third Republic:
1881–1882 Léon Gambetta
1906–1909 Georges Clemenceau
1909–1911 Aristide Briand
1912–1913 Raymond Poincaré
1913–1913 Aristide Briand
1915–1917 Aristide Briand
1917–1920 Georges Clemenceau
1921–1922 Aristide Briand
1922–1924 Raymond Poincaré
1924–1925 Édouard Herriot
1925–1926 Aristide Briand
1926–1926 Édouard Herriot
1926–1929 Raymond Poincaré
1929–1929 Aristide Briand
1931–1932 Pierre Laval
1932–1932 Édouard Herriot
1933–1933 Édouard Daladier
1934–1934 Édouard Daladier

1935–1936 Pierre Laval
1936–1937 Léon Blum
1938–1938 Léon Blum
1938–1940 Édouard Daladier
1940–1942 Philippe Pétain
1942–1944 Pierre Laval

Chairmen of the Provisional Government
1944–1946 Charles de Gaulle
1946–1946 Félix Gouin
1946–1946 Georges Bidault
1946–1947 Léon Blum

Prime ministers of the Fourth Republic
1947–1947 Paul Ramadier
1947–1948 Robert Schuman
1948–1948 André Marie
1948–1948 Robert Schuman
1948–1949 Henri Queuille
1949–1950 Georges Bidault
1950–1950 Henri Queuille
1950–1951 René Pleven
1951–1951 Henri Queuille
1951–1952 René Pleven
1952–1952 Edgar Faure
1952–1953 Antoine Pinay
1953–1953 René Mayer
1953–1954 Joseph Laniel
1954–1955 Pierre Mendès-France
1955–1955 Christian Pineau
1955–1956 Edgar Faure
1956–1957 Guy Mollet
1957–1957 Maurice Bourgès-Maunoury
1957–1958 Félix Gaillard
1958–1958 Pierre Pflimlin
1958–1959 Charles de Gaulle
1959–1962 Michel Debré
1962–1968 Georges Pompidou
1968–1969 Maurice Couve de Murville
1969–1973 Jacques Chaban-Delmas
1973–1974 Pierre Messmer
1974–1976 Jacques Chirac
1976–1981 Raymond Barre
1981–1984 Pierre Mauroy
1984–1986 Laurent Fabius
1986–1988 Jacques Chirac
1988–1991 Michel Rocard
1991–1992 Edith Cresson
1992–1993 Pierre Bérégovoy
1993–1995 Édouard Balladur
1995–1997 Alain Juppé
1997–   Lionel Jospin

Germany

Kings of Prussia
1701–1713 Frederick I
1713–1740 Frederick William
1740–1786 Frederick II the Great
1786–1797 Frederick William II
1797–1840 Frederick William III
1840–1861 Frederick William IV
1861–1871 Wilhelm I

Emperors of Germany
1871–1888 Wilhelm I
1888–1888 Frederick III
1888–1918 Wilhelm II

Presidents
1918–1919 Provisional government
1919–1919 Eduard David
1919–1925 Friedrich Ebert
1925–1934 Paul von Hindenburg

1934–1945 Adolf Hitler (Führer)
1945–1945 Karl Dönitz

Chancellors of the Empire
1871–1890 Otto von Bismarck
1890–1894 Leo von Caprivi
1894–1900 Chlodwig zu Hohenlohe-
         Schillingsfürst
1900–1909 Bernhard von Bülow
1909–1917 Theobald von Bethmann Hollweg
1917–1917 Georg Michaelis
1917–1918 Georg von Hertling
1918–1918 Max, Prince of Baden
1918–1918 Friedrich Ebert

Chancellors of the Republic
1919–1919 Philipp Scheidemann
1919–1920 Gustav Bauer
1920–1920 Hermann Müller
1920–1921 Konstantin Fehrenbach
1921–1922 Joseph Wirth
1922–1923 Wilhelm Cuno
1923–1923 Gustav Stresemann
1923–1925 Wilhelm Marx
1925–1926 Hans Luther
1926–1928 Wilhelm Marx
1928–1930 Hermann Müller
1930–1932 Heinrich Brüning
1932–1932 Franz von Papen
1932–1933 Kurt von Schleicher
1933–1934 Adolf Hitler

German Democratic Republic
General secretaries of the Socialist Unity
(Communist) Party
1946–1950 Wilhelm Pieck/Otto Grotewohl
1950–1971 Walter Ulbricht
1971–1989 Erich Honecker
1989–1989 Egon Krenz

Federal Republic of Germany
Chancellors
1949–1963 Konrad Adenauer
1963–1966 Ludwig Erhard
1966–1969 Kurt Georg Kiesinger
1969–1974 Willy Brandt
1974–1982 Helmut Schmidt
1982–1998 Helmut Kohl
1998–   Gerhard Schröder

Greece

Kings
1863–1913 Georgios I
1913–1917 Konstantinos I
1917–1920 Alexandros
1920–1922 Konstantinos I (restored)
1922–1924 Georgios II

Presidents of the Hellenic Republic
1925–1926 Pavlos Koundouriotis
1926–1926 Theodoros Pangalos
1926–1929 Pavlos Koundouriotis
1929–1935 Alexandros Zaimis

Kings
1935–1947 Georgios II (restored)
1947–1964 Pavlos I
1964–1973 Konstantinos II

Presidents
1973–1973 Georgios Papadopoulos
1973–1974 Phaidon Gizikis
1974–1975 Michael Stasinopoulos

1975–1980 Konstantinos Tsatsos
1980–1985 Konstantinos Karamanlis
1985–1990 Christos Sartzetakis
1990–1995 Konstantinos Karamanlis
1995–   Kostis Stephanopoulos

Holy Roman Empire

Emperors
1438–1439 Albert II
1440–1493 Frederick III
1493–1519 Maximilian I
1519–1556 Charles V
1556–1564 Ferdinand I
1564–1576 Maximilian II
1576–1612 Rudolf II
1612–1619 Matthias
1619–1637 Ferdinand II
1637–1657 Ferdinand III
1658–1705 Leopold I
1705–1711 Joseph I
1711–1740 Charles VI
1742–1745 Charles VII of Bavaria
1745–1765 Francis I of Lorraine
1765–1790 Joseph II
1790–1792 Leopold II
1792–1806 Francis II of Austria

Hungary

General secretaries of the Hungarian Workers'
Party
1945–1956 Mátyás Rákosi
1956–1956 Ernö Gerö
1956–1988 János Kádár
1988–1989 Károly Grosz

Kings (also emperors of Austria)
1849–1916 Ferenc József I
1916–1918 Károly IV

Presidents
1946–1948 Zoltán Tildy
1948–1949 Árpád Szákasits
1949–1950 Árpád Szákasits
1950–1952 Sándor Rónai
1952–1967 István Dobi
1967–1987 Pál Losonczi
1987–1988 Károly Németh
1988–1989 Brunó Ferenc Straub

Presidents
1989–1990 Mátyás Szürös
1990–   Árpád Göncz (b. 1922)

India

Mogul Emperors
1526–1530 Babur
1530–1539 Humayun
1539–1555 Interregnum (usurpers)
1555–1556 Humayun (restored)
1556–1605 Akbar
1605–1627 Jahangir
1627–1628 Dawar Bakhsh
1628–1658 Shah Jahan
1658–1707 Aurangzeb Alamgir I
1707–1712 Bahadur Shah
1713–1719 Farrukhsiyar
1719–1719 Rafi-ud-Daulat

1719–1719 Shah Jahan II
1719–1719 Nikusiyar
1719–1720 Muhammad Shah
1720–1720 Muhammad Ibrahim
1720–1748 Muhammad Shah (restored)
1748–1754 Ahmad Shah
1754–1759 Alamgir II
1759–1760 Shah Jahan III
1759–1802 Shah Alam II

Presidents
1950–1962 Rajendra Prasad
1962–1967 Sarvapalli Radhakrishnan
1967–1969 Zakir Husain
1969–1974 Varahagiri Venkata Giri
1974–1977 Fakhruddin Ali Ahmed
1977–1982 N. Sanjiva Reddy
1982–1987 Zail Singh
1987–1992 Ramaswamy Venkataraman
1992–1997 Shankar Dayal Sharma
1997–   K. R. Narayanan

Prime ministers
1947–1964 Jawaharlal Nehru
1964–1964 Gulzarilal Nanda
1964–1966 Lal Bahadur Shastri
1966–1966 Gulzarilal Nanda
1966–1977 Indira Gandhi
1977–1979 Morarji Desai
1979–1980 Charan Singh
1980–1984 Indira Gandhi
1984–1989 Rajiv Gandhi
1989–1990 Vishwanath Pratap Singh
1990–1991 Chandra Shekhar
1991–1996 P. V. Narasimha Rao
1996–1996 Atal Bihari Vajpayee
1996–1997 H. D. Deve Gowda
1997–1998 Inder Kumar Gujral
1998–   Atal Bihari Vajpayee

Indonesia

Presidents
1949–1967 Muhammad Achmed Sukarno
1967–1998 T. N. I. Suharto

Iran (*formerly* **Persia**)

Shahs
1501–1524 Isma'il I
1524–1576 Tahmasp
1576–1577 Isma'il II
1577–1587 Sultan Mohammad
1588–1629 Shah Abbas
1629–1642 Safi I
1642–1666 Abbas II
1666–1694 Sulayman
1694–1722 Husayn
1722–1725 Mahmud
1725–1729 Ashraf
1732–1736 Abbas III
1737–1747 Nadir Shah
1747–1748 Ali-quli Khan
1748–1749 Ibrahim
1749–1750 Sulayman II
1751–1794 Karim Khan
1796–1797 Aqa Mohammad Shah
1797–1834 Fath Ali Shah
1834–1848 Mohammad Shah
1848–1896 Naser od-Din Shah
1896–1907 Mozaffar od-Din Qajar
1907–1909 Mohammad Ali Qajar

1909–1925 Soltan Ahmad Qajar
1925–1941 Reza Pahlavi
1941–1979 Mohammad Reza Pahlavi

Leader of the Revolution
1979–1980 Ayatollah Ruhollah Khomeini

Presidents
1980–1981 Abolhassan Bani-Sadr
1981–1981 Provisional Presidential Council
1981–1981 Mohammad Ali Raja´i
1981–1989 Sayyed Ali Khamenei
1989–1997 Hojatolislam Ali Akbar Hashemi
   Rafsanjani
1997–   Mohammad Khatami

Iraq

Kings
1921–1933 Faisal I
1933–1939 Ghazi I
1939–1958 Faisal II
1958–1963 Muhammad Najib ar-Ruba`i

Presidents
1963–1966 `Abd as-Salam `Arif
1966–1968 `Abd ar-Rahman `Arif
1968–1979 Ahmad Hassan al-Bakr
1979–   Saddam Hussein

Ireland

Presidents
1919–1922 Eamon de Valera
1922–1922 Arthur Griffith
1922–1922 William Thomas Cosgrave

Governors-general
1922–1928 T.M. Healy
1928–1932 James McNeill
1932–1936 Donal Buckley
1936–1937 Frank Fahy/Eamon de Valera

Presidents
1937–1938 Presidential Commission
1938–1945 Douglas Hyde
1945–1959 Sean T. O'Kelly
1959–1973 Eamon de Valera
1973–1974 Erskine H. Childers
1974–1976 Cearbhall O Dalaigh
1976–1990 Patrick J. Hillery
1990–1997 Mary Robinson
1997–   Mary McAleese

Chairmen of the Provisional Government
1922–1922 Michael Collins
1922–1922 William Thomas Cosgrave

Prime ministers
1922–1932 William Thomas Cosgrave
1932–1948 Eamon de Valera
1948–1951 John A. Costello
1951–1954 Eamon de Valera
1954–1957 John A. Costello
1957–1959 Eamon de Valera
1959–1966 Sean F. Lemass
1966–1973 John Lynch
1973–1977 Liam Cosgrave
1977–1979 John Lynch
1979–1981 Charles Haughey
1981–1982 Garret FitzGerald
1982–1982 Charles Haughey

1982–1987 Garret FitzGerald
1987–1992 Charles Haughey
1992–1994 Albert Reynolds
1994–1997 John Bruton
1997–   Bertie Ahern

Israel

Presidents
1948–1948 David Ben-Gurion
1948–1952 Chaim Weizmann
1952–1963 Itzhak Ben Zvi
1963–1973 Zalman Shazar
1973–1978 Ephraim Katzir
1978–1983 Yitzhak Navon
1983–1993 Chaim Herzog
1993–   Ezer Weizman

Prime ministers
1948–1953 David Ben-Gurion
1953–1955 Moshe Sharett
1955–1963 David Ben-Gurion
1963–1969 Levi Eshkol
1969–1974 Golda Meir
1974–1977 Yitzhak Rabin
1977–1977 Shimon Peres
1977–1983 Menachem Begin
1983–1984 Yitzhak Shamir
1984–1986 Shimon Peres
1986–1992 Yitzhak Shamir
1992–1995 Yitzhak Rabin
1995–1996 Shimon Peres
1996–1999 Benjamin Netanyahu
1999–   Ehud Barak

Italy

Kings
1861–1878 Victor Emmanuel II
1878–1900 Humbert I
1900–1946 Victor Emmanuel III
1946–1946 Humbert II

Provisional Heads of State
1946–1946 Alcide De Gasperi
1946–1948 Enrico De Nicola

Presidents
1948–1948 Enrico De Nicola
1948–1955 Luigi Einaudi
1955–1962 Giovanni Gronchi
1962–1964 Antonio Segni
1964–1971 Giuseppe Saragat
1971–1978 Giovanni Leone
1978–1985 Alessandro Pertini
1985–1992 Francesco Cossiga
1992–   Oscar Luigi Scalfaro

Prime ministers
1887–1891 Francesco Crispi
1891–1892 Antonio Starabba, marchese di
   Rudinì
1892–1893 Giovanni Giolitti
1893–1896 Francesco Crispi
1896–1898 Antonio Starabba, marchese di
   Rudinì
1898–1900 Luigi Pelloux
1900–1901 Giuseppe Saracco
1901–1903 Giuseppe Zanardelli
1903–1905 Giovanni Giolitti
1905–1906 Alessandro Fortis
1906–1906 Sidney Sonnino

1906–1909 Giovanni Giolitti
1909–1910 Sidney Sonnino
1910–1911 Luigi Luzzatti
1911–1914 Giovanni Giolitti
1914–1916 Antonio Salandra
1916–1917 Paolo Boselli
1917–1919 Vittorio Emanuele Orlando
1919–1920 Francesco Saverio Nitti
1920–1921 Giovanni Giolitti
1921–1922 Ivanoe Bonomi
1922–1922 Luigi Facta
1922–1943 Benito Mussolini
1943–1944 Pietro Badoglio
(1943–April 1945 Benito Mussolini, counter-government at Lake Garda)
1944–1945 Ivanoe Bonomi
1945–1945 Ferruccio Parri
1945–1953 Alcide De Gasperi
1953–1954 Giuseppe Pella
1954–1954 Amintore Fanfani
1954–1955 Mario Scelba
1955–1957 Antonio Segni
1957–1958 Adone Zoli
1958–1959 Amintore Fanfani
1959–1960 Antonio Segni
1960–1960 Fernando Tambroni-Armaroli
1960–1963 Amintore Fanfani
1963–1963 Giovanni Leone
1963–1968 Aldo Moro
1968–1968 Giovanni Leone
1968–1970 Mariano Rumor
1970–1972 Emilio Colombo
1972–1973 Giulio Andreotti
1973–1974 Mariano Rumor
1974–1976 Aldo Moro
1976–1979 Giulio Andreotti
1979–1980 Francesco Cossiga
1980–1981 Arnaldo Forlani
1981–1982 Giovanni Spadolini
1982–1983 Amintore Fanfani
1983–1987 Bettino Craxi
1987–1987 Amintore Fanfani
1987–1988 Giovanni Goria
1988–1989 Ciriaco De Mita
1989–1992 Giulio Andreotti
1992–1993 Giuliano Amato
1993–1994 Carlo Azeglio Ciampi
1994–1995 Silvio Berlusconi
1995–1996 Lamberto Dini
1996–1998 Romano Prodi
1998– Massimo D'Alema

Japan

Emperors
1867–1912 Mutsuhito (Meiji-tenno)
1912–1921 Yoshihito (Taisho-tenno)
1921–1926 Prince Hirohito (regent)
1926–1989 Hirohito (Showa-tenno)
1989– Akihito

Jordan

Emir
1921–1946 Abdullah I

Kings
1946–1951 Abdullah I
1951–1951 Naif (regent)
1951–1952 Talal
1952–1999 Hussein
1999– Abdullah II

Kenya

Presidents
1964–1978 Jomo Kenyatta
1978– Daniel arap Moi

Korea

North Korea
General secretaries of the Central Committee
of the Communist Party of Korea
1948–1994 Kim Il Sung
1994–1997 vacant
1997– Kim Jong Il

South Korea
Presidents
1948–1960 Syngman Rhee
1960–1962 Yun Po Sun
1962–1979 Park Chung Hee
1979–1980 Choi Kyu Hah
1980–1988 Chun Doo Hwan
1988–1993 Roh Tae Woo
1993–1998 Kim Young Sam
1998– Kim Dae Jung

Latvia

Presidents
1918–1922 Janis Cakste
1918–1919 Peteris Stucka
1919–1919 Fricis Rozins-Azis
1922–1927 Janis Cakste
1927–1930 Gustavs Zemgals
1930–1936 Alberts Kviesis
1936–1940 Karlis Ulmanis
1940–1940 Augusts Kirchensteins
1988–1993 Anatolijs Gorbunovs
1993– Guntis Ulmanis

Lithuania

Presidents
1918–1920 Antanas Smetona
1918–1919 Vincas Kapsukas
1919–1919 Kazimieras Cihovskis
1920–1926 Aleksandras Stulginskis
1920–1921 Lucjan Zeilgowski
1921–1922 Aleksander Michal Marian
  Meysztowicz
1926–1926 Kazys Grinius
1926–1940 Antanas Smetona
1940–1940 Justas Paleckis
1990–1992 Vytautas Landsbergis
1992–1998 Algirdas Brazauskas
1998– Valdas Adamkus

Luxembourg

Grand Dukes
1890–1905 Adolf
1905–1912 Wilhelm IV Alexander
1908–1912 Maria Anna of Braganza (regent)
1912–1919 Marie-Adélaïde (grand duchess)
1919–1964 Charlotte (grand duchess)
1961–1964 Jean (regent)
1964– Jean

Macedonia

President
1991– Kiri Gligorov

Prime ministers
1991–1992 Nikola Kljusev
1992–1998 Branko Crvenkovski
1998– Ljupco Georgievski

Mexico

Of more than 80 presidents of Mexico, the
more notable before 1924 included:
1833–1837 Antonio López de Santa Anna
1841–1844 Antonio López de Santa Anna
1844–1845 Antonio López de Santa Anna
1847–1847 Antonio López de Santa Anna
1853–1855 Antonio López de Santa Anna
1858–1858 Benito Juárez
1859–1861 Benito Juárez
1864–1867 Maximilian I (emperor)
1867–1872 Benito Juárez
1876–1880 Porfirio Díaz
1884–1911 Porfirio Díaz
1911–1913 Francisco Indalécio Madero
1913–1914 Victoriano Huerta
1914–1914 Venustiano Carranza
1915–1920 Venustiano Carranza
1920–1924 Alvaro Obregón

Presidents since 1924
1924–1928 Plutarco Elías Calles
1928–1930 Emilio Portes Gil
1930–1932 Pascual Ortiz Rubio
1932–1934 Abelardo Luján Rodríguez
1934–1940 Lázaro Cárdenas
1940–1946 Manuel Ávila Camacho
1946–1952 Miguel Alemán
1952–1958 Adolfo Ruíz Cortines
1958–1964 Adolfo López Mateos
1964–1970 Gustavo Díaz Ordaz
1970–1976 Luis Echeverría Álvarez
1976–1982 José López Portillo
1982–1988 Miguel de la Madrid
1988–1994 Carlos Salinas de Gortari
1994– Ernesto Zedillo

Morocco

Sultans
1894–1908 'Abd al-'Aziz
1908–1912 'Abd al-Hafiz
1912–1927 Yusuf
1927–1953 Muhammad V
1953–1955 Muhammad VI
1955–1955 Council of Throne Guardians
1955–1957 Muhammad V

Kings
1957–1961 Muhammad V
1961– Hassan II 1929)

Mozambique

Presidents
1975–1986 Samora Machel
1986– Joaquim Chissanó

Prime ministers
1986–1994 Mário da Graça Machungo
1994– Pascoal Mocumbi

Myanmar (*formerly* **Burma**)

Presidents
1948–1952 Saw Shwe Thaik
1952–1957 Ba U
1957–1962 Win Maung
1962–1981 Ne Win
1981–1988 San Yu
1988–1988 Sein Lwin
1988–1988 Aye Ko (acting)
1988–1988 Maung Maung

Chairmen of the State Law and Order
Restoration Council
1988–1992 Saw Maung
1992–1997 Than Shwe

Chairman of the State Peace and
Development Council
1997– Than Shwe

Namibia

President
1990– Sam Nujoma

Prime minister
1990– Hage Geingob

The Netherlands

Monarchs
1815–1840 Willem I
1840–1849 Willem II
1849–1890 Willem III
1890–1948 Wilhelmina
1948–1980 Juliana
1980– Beatrix

Prime ministers since 1945
1945–1946 Willem Schermerhorn
1946–1948 Louis J. M. Beel
1948–1958 Willem Drees
1958–1959 Louis J. M. Beel
1959–1963 Jan Eduard de Quay
1963–1965 Victor Marijnen
1965–1966 Jo Cals
1966–1967 Jelle Zijlstra
1967–1971 Piet de Jong
1971–1973 Barend Willem Biesheuvel
1973–1977 Joop den Uyl
1977–1982 Andreas van Agt
1982–1994 Ruud Lubbers
1994– Wim Kok

New Zealand

Prime ministers
1893–1906 Richard John Seddon
1906–1912 Joseph Ward
1912–1912 Thomas Mackenzie
1912–1925 William Ferguson Massey
1925–1925 Francis Henry Dillon Bell
1925–1928 Joseph Gordon Coates

1928–1930 Joseph Ward
1930–1935 George William Forbes
1935–1940 Michael Joseph Savage
1940–1949 Peter Fraser
1949–1957 Sidney Holland
1957–1957 Keith Jacka Holyoake
1957–1960 Walter Nash
1960–1972 Keith Jacka Holyoake
1972–1972 John Ross Marshall
1972–1974 Norman Eric Kirk
1974–1975 Wallace Edward Rowling
1975–1984 Robert David Muldoon
1984–1989 David Russell Lange
1989–1990 Geoffrey Palmer
1990–1990 Mike Moore
1990–1997 Jim Bolger
1997– Jenny Shipley

Nigeria

Presidents
1963–1966 Benjamin Nnamdi Azikiwe
1966–1966 Johnson Aguiyi-Ironsi
1966–1975 Yakubu Gowon
1975–1976 Murtala R. Muhammad
1976–1979 Olusegun Obasanjo
1979–1983 Alhaji Shehu Shagari
1983–1985 Mohammed Buhari
1985–1993 Ibrahim Babangida
1993–1993 Ernest Shonekan
1993–1998 Sani Abacha
1998– Abdulsalami Abubakar

Norway

Kings since independence
1905–1957 Haakon VII
1951–1991 Olav V
1991– Harald V

Prime ministers since 1945
1945–1951 Einar Henry Gerhardsen
1951–1955 Oscar Fredrik Torp
1955–1963 Einar Henry Gerhardsen
1963–1963 John Daniel Fyrstenberg Lyng
1963–1965 Einar Henry Gerhardsen
1965–1971 Per Borten
1971–1972 Trygve Martin Bratteli
1972–1973 Lars Korvald
1973–1976 Trygve Martin Bratteli
1976–1981 Odvar Nordli
1981–1981 Gro Harlem Brundtland
1981–1986 Kåre Isaachsen Willoch
1986–1989 Gro Harlem Brundtland
1989–1990 Jan Peder Syse
1990–1996 Gro Harlem Brundtland
1996–1997 Thorbjørn Jagland
1997– Kjell Magne Bondevik

Ottoman Empire

Emperors
1290–1326 Osman I
1326–1359 Orxan
1359–1389 Murad I
1389–1402 Bayezid I
1402–1421 Mehmed I
1421–1451 Murad II
1451–1481 Mehmed II Fatih
1481–1512 Bayezid II
1512–1520 Selîm I Yavuz

1520–1566 Süleyman I, the Magnificent
1566–1574 Selim II
1574–1595 Murad III
1595–1603 Mehmed III
1603–1617 Ahmed I
1617–1618 Mustafa I
1618–1623 Osman II
1622–1623 Ahmed I (restored)
1623–1640 Murad IV
1640–1648 Ibrahim
1648–1687 Mehmed IV
1687–1691 Süleyman II
1691–1695 Ahmed II
1695–1703 Mustafa II
1703–1730 Ahmed III
1730–1754 Mahmud I
1754–1757 Osman III
1757–1774 Mustafa III
1774–1789 Abdülhamid I
1789–1807 Selim III
1807–1808 Mustafa IV
1808–1839 Mahmud II
1839–1861 Abdülmecid I
1861–1876 Abdülaziz
1876–1876 Murad V
1876–1909 Abdülhamid II
1909–1918 Mehmed V
1918–1922 Mehmed VI

Pakistan

Governors-general
1947–1948 Mohammad Ali Jinnah
1948–1951 Hwaja Nazim ad-Din
1951–1955 Ghulam Mohammad
1955–1956 Iskandar Ali Mirza

Presidents
1956–1958 Iskandar Ali Mirza
1958–1969 Mohammad Ayub Khan
1969–1971 Agha Mohammad Yahya Khan
1971–1973 Zulfikar Ali Bhutto
1973–1978 Fazal Elahi Chaudhri
1978–1988 Mohammad Zia-ul-Haq
1988–1993 Ghulam Ishaq Khan
1993–1993 Wasim Sajjad
1993–1997 Farooq Ahmed Leghari
1997–1998 Wasim Sajjad
1998– Mohammad Rafiq Tarar

Prime ministers
1947–1951 Liaquat Ali Khan
1951–1953 Hwaja Nazim ad-Din
1953–1955 Mohammad Ali Bogra
1955–1956 Chaudhri Mohammad Ali
1956–1957 Husayn Sahid Suhrawardi
1957–1957 Ismail Ibrahim Chundrigar
1957–1958 Malik Firuz Khan Nun
1958–1969 Mohammad Ayub Khan
1969–1971 Agha Mohammad Yahya Khan
1971–1971 Nurul Amin
1971–1977 Zulfikar Ali Bhutto
1977–1985 Mohammad Zia-ul-Haq
1985–1988 Mohammad Khan Junejo
1988–1988 Mohammad Zia-ul-Haq
1988–1990 Benazir Bhutto
1990–1990 Ghulam Mustafa Jatoi
1990–1993 Nawaz Sharif
1993–1993 Balakh Sher Mazari
1993–1993 Nawaz Sharif
1993–1993 Moeen Qureshi
1993–1996 Benazir Bhutto
1996–1997 Miraj Khalid
1997– Nawaz Sharif

Palestine

President of the Palestinian Authority
1996– Yasir Arafat

Poland

Chairmen of the Provisional Council of State
1917–1917 Waclaw Niemojowski
1917–1917 Józef Mikulowski Pomorski
1917–1918 Regency Council

Head of State
1918–1922 Józef Pilsudsk

Presidents
1922–1922 Gabriel Narutowicz
1922–1926 Stanislaw Wojciechowski
1926–1939 Ignacy Móscicki

Secretaries-general of the Polish Workers'
(Communist) Party
1943–1948 Wladyslaw Gomulka
1948–1956 Boleslaw Bierut
1956–1956 Edward Ochab
1956–1970 Wladyslaw Gomulka
1970–1980 Edward Gierek
1980–1981 Stanislaw Kania
1981–1989 Wojciech Jaruzelski
1989–1990 Mieczyslaw Rakowski

Chairmen of the Council of State
1944–1952 Boleslaw Bierut
1952–1964 Aleksander Zawadzki
1964–1968 Edward Ochab
1968–1970 Marian Spychalski
1970–1972 Józef Cyrankiewicz
1972–1985 Henryk Jablonski
1985–1989 Wojciech Jaruzelski

Presidents
1989–1990 Wojciech Jaruzelski
1990–1995 Lech Walesa
1995– Aleksander Kwasniewski

Popes

1404–1406 Innocent VII
1406–1415 Gregory XII
[1409–1410 Alexander V]
[1410–1415 John XXIII]
1417–1431 Martin V
[1423–1429 Clement VIII]
[1425–1425 Benedict XIV]
1431–1447 Eugene IV
[1439–1449 Felix V]
1447–1455 Nicholas V
1455–1458 Callistus III
1458–1464 Pius II
1464–1471 Paul II
1471–1484 Sixtus IV
1484–1492 Innocent VIII
1492–1503 Alexander VI
1503–1503 Pius III
1503–1513 Julius II
1513–1521 Leo X
1522–1523 Hadrian VI
1523–1534 Clement VII
1534–1539 Paul III
1550–1555 Julius III
1555–1555 Marcellus II
1555–1559 Paul IV

1559–1565 Pius IV
1566–1572 Gregory XIII
1585–1590 Sixtus V
1590–1590 Urban VII
1590–1591 Gregory XIV
1591–1591 Innocent IX
1592–1605 Clement VIII
1605–1605 Leo XI
1605–1621 Paul V
1621–1623 Gregory XV
1623–1644 Urban VIII
1644–1655 Innocent X
1655–1667 Alexander VII
1667–1669 Clement IX
1670–1676 Clement X
1676–1689 Innocent XI
1689–1691 Alexander VIII
1691–1700 Innocent XII
1700–1721 Clement XI
1721–1724 Innocent XIII
1724–1730 Benedict XIII
1730–1740 Clement XII
1740–1758 Benedict XIV
1758–1769 Clement XIII
1769–1774 Clement XIV
1775–1799 Pius VI
1800–1823 Pius VII
1823–1829 Leo XII
1831–1846 Pius VIII
1846–1878 Pius IX
1878–1903 Leo XIII
1903–1914 Pius X
1914–1922 Benedict XV
1922–1939 Pius XI
1939–1958 Pius XII
1958–1963 John XXIII
1963–1978 Paul VI
1978–1978 John Paul I
1978– John Paul II
[indicates antipopes]

Portugal

Monarchs
1889–1908 Carlos I
1908–1910 Manuel II

Presidents
1910–1911 Joaquim Teófilo Fernandes Braga
1911–1915 Manuel José de Arriaga Brum da
  Silveira e Peyrelongue
1915–1915 Joaquim Teófilo Fernandes Braga
1915–1917 Bernardino Luís Machado
  Guimarães
1917–1918 Sidónio Bernardino Cardoso da
  Silva Pais
1918–1918 Council of Ministers
1918–1919 João do Canto e Castro Silva
  Antunes
1919–1923 António José de Almeida
1923–1925 Manuel Teixeira Gomes
1925–1926 Bernardino Luís Machado
  Guimarães
1926–1926 Manuel de Oliveira Gomes da
  Costa
1926–1951 António Óscar de Fragoso
  Carmona
1951–1951 António de Oliveira Salazar
1951–1958 Francisco Higino Craveiro Lopes
1958–1974 Américo de Deus Rodrigues Tomás
1974–1974 António de Spínola
1974–1976 Francisco da Costa Gomes
1976–1986 António dos Santos Ramalho
  Eanes

1986–1996 Mário Soares
1996– Jorge Sampaio

Prime ministers since 1932
1932–1968 António de Oliveira Salazar
1968–1974 Marcelo Caetano
1974–1974 Adelino da Palma Carlos
1974–1975 Vasco dos Santos Gonçalves
1975–1976 José Batista Pinheiro de Azevedo
1976–1978 Mário Soares
1978–1978 Alfredo Nobre da Costa
1978–1979 Carlos Mota Pinto
1979–1980 Maria de Lurdes Pintassilgo
1980–1980 Francisco Sá Carneiro
1981–1983 Francisco Pinto Balsemão
1983–1985 Mário Soares
1985–1995 Aníbal Cavaço Silva
1995– António Guterres

Romania

General secretaries of the Romanian
Communist Party
1945–1954 Gheorghe Gheorghiu-Dej
1954–1955 Gheorghe Apostol
1955–1965 Gheorghe Gheorghiu-Dej
1965–1989 Nicolae Ceausescu
1989–1996 Ion Iliescu
1996– Emil Constantinescu

Kings
1881–1914 Carol I
1914–1927 Ferdinand I
1927–1930 Michael I
1930–1940 Carol II
1940–1947 Michael I (restored)

Russia/Soviet Union

Czars from 1328
1328–1341 Ivan I
1341–1353 Simeon
1353–1359 Ivan II
1359–1389 Demetrius Donski
1389–1425 Basil I
1425–1462 Basil II
1462–1505 Ivan III, the Great
1505–1533 Basil III
1533–1584 Ivan IV
1584–1598 Fyodor I
1598–1605 Boris Godunov
1605–1605 Fyodor II
1605–1606 Dmitry
1606–1610 Basil IV Shiusky
1613–1645 Michael
1645–1676 Alexis
1676–1682 Fyodor III
1682–1696 Ivan V (co-czar)
1682–1725 Peter I
1725–1727 Catherine I
1727–1730 Peter II
1730–1740 Anna
1740–1741 Ivan VI
1741–1762 Elizabeth
1762–1796 Catherine the Great
1796–1801 Paul
1801–1825 Alexander I
1825–1855 Nicholas I
1855–1881 Alexander II
1881–1894 Alexander III
1894–1917 Nicholas II

Chairmen of the All-Russian Central
Executive Committee
1917–1917 Lev Borisovich Kamenev
1917–1919 Yakov Mikhailovich Sverdlov
1919–1938 Mikhail Kalinin

Prime ministers (1917–1992)
1917–1917 Prince Nikolay Dmitryevich
1917–1917 Prince Georgy Yevgenyevich
 Lvov
1917–1917 Aleksandr Kerensky
1917–1924 Vladimir Ilich Lenin

Soviet Union

General secretaries of the Communist Party
1922–1953 Joseph Stalin
1953–1953 Georgy Malenkov
1953–1964 Nikita Khrushchev
1964–1982 Leonid Brezhnev
1982–1984 Yuri Andropov
1984–1985 Konstantin Chernenko
1985–1991 Mikhail Gorbachev

Chairmen of the Central Executive Committee
(presidents)
1922–1938 Mikhail Kalinin
1922–1938 Grigory Petrovsky
1922–1937 Aleksandr Chervyakov
1922–1925 Nariman Narimanov
1925–1925 Gazanfar Musabekov
1925–1937 Nedirbay Aytakov
1925–1937 Fayzulla Khodzhayev
1931–1934 Nusratulla Lutfullayev
1934–1937 Abdullo Rakhimbayev
1938–1946 Mikhail Kalinin
1946–1953 Nikolay Shvernik
1953–1960 Kliment Voroshilov
1960–1964 Leonid Brezhnev
1964–1965 Anastas Mikoyan
1965–1977 Nikolay Podgorny
1977–1982 Leonid Brezhnev
1983–1984 Yuri Andropov
1984–1985 Konstantin Chernenko
1985–1985 Vasily Kuznetsov
1985–1988 Andrey Gromyko
1988–1991 Mikhail Gorbachev

Chairmen of the Council of People's
Commissars (Prime Ministers)
1923–1924 Vladimir Ilich Lenin
1924–1930 Aleksey Rykov
1930–1941 Vyacheslav Molotov
1941–1953 Joseph Stalin
1953–1955 Georgy Malenkov
1955–1958 Nikolay Bulganin
1958–1964 Nikita Khrushchev
1964–1980 Aleksey Kosygin
1980–1985 Nikolay Tikhonov
1985–1991 Nikolay Ryzhkov
1991–1991 Valentin Pavlov
1991–1991 Ivan Silayev

Russia since 1991

President
1991– Boris Yeltsin

Prime ministers
1991–1992 Boris Yeltsin
1992–1992 Yegor Gaidar (acting)
1992–1998 Viktor Chernomyrdin
1998–1998 Sergey Kiriyenko
1998–1998 Viktor Chernomyrdin
1998– Yevgeny Primakov

Saudi Arabia

Kings
1916–1924 al-Husayn ibn `Ali al-Hashimi
1924–1925 `Ali ibn al-Husayn al-Hashimi
1926–1932 Ibn Sa`ud
1932–1953 Ibn Sa`ud
1953–1964 Sa`ud
1964–1975 Faisal
1975–1982 Khalid
1982– Fahd

Singapore

Prime ministers
1959–1990 Lee Kuan Yew
1990– Goh Chok Tong

Slovakia

Presidents
1939–1945 Jozef Tiso
1993–1998 Michal Kovác
1998–1998 Vladimír Meciar
1998– Mikulás Dzurinda

Prime ministers
1939–1944 Vojtech Tuka
1944–1945 Stefan Tiso
1993–1994 Vladimír Meciar
1994–1994 Jozef Moravcik
1994–1998 Vladimír Meciar
1998– Mikulás Dzurinda

South Africa

Presidents
1961–1967 Charles Robberts Swart
1967–1968 Jozua François Naudé
1968–1975 Jacobus Johannes Fouché
1975–1978 Nicolaas Diederich
1978–1979 Balthazar John Vorster
1979–1984 Marais Viljoen
1984–1989 Pieter Willem Botha
1989–1994 Frederick Willem de Klerk
1994–1999 Nelson Mandela
1999– Thabo Mvuyelwa Mbeki

Prime Ministers
1910–1919 Louis Botha
1919–1924 Jan Christiaan Smuts
1924–1939 James Barry Munik Herzog
1939–1948 Jan Christiaan Smuts
1948–1954 Daniel François Malan
1954–1958 Johannes Gerhardhus Strijdom
1958–1966 Hendrik Verwoerd
1966–1978 Balthazar John Vorster
1978–1984 Pieter Willem Botha

Spain

Monarchs
1474–1516 Ferdinand V
1474–1504 Isabella I
1504–1555 Juana
1504–1506 Philip I
1516–1556 Charles V
1556–1598 Philip II

1598–1621 Philip III
1621–1665 Philip IV
1665–1700 Charles II
1700–1724 Philip V
1724–1724 Luis
1724–1746 Philip V (restored)
1746–1759 Ferdinand VI
1759–1788 Charles III
1788–1808 Charles IV
1808–1808 Ferdinand VII
1808–1808 Charles IV (restored)
1808–1813 Joseph Bonaparte
1813–1833 Ferdinand VII (restored)
1833–1868 Isabella II
1870–1873 Amadeo
1874–1885 Alfonso XII
1886–1931 Alfonso XIII

Presidents
1931–1936 Niceto Alcalá-Zamora y Torres
1936–1936 Manuel Azaña y Díaz

Head of state
1936–1975 Francisco Franco

King
1975– Juan Carlos I

Prime ministers since 1936
1936–1973 Francisco Franco y Bahamonde
1973–1973 Luis Carrero Blanco
1973–1976 Carlos Arias Navarro
1976–1981 Adolfo Suárez González
1981–1982 Leopoldo Calvo Sotelo y Bustelo
1982–1996 Felipe González Márquez
1996– José María Aznar

Sudan

Presidents
1956–1958 Sovereignty Council
1958–1964 Ibrahim Abboud
1964–1965 Committee of Sovereignty
1965–1969 Isma`il al-Azhari
1969–1971 Gaafar Nimeiry
1971–1971 Abu Bakr an-Nur `Uthman
1971–1985 Gaafar Nimeiry
1985–1986 `Abd ar-Rahman Siwar ad-Dahab
1986–1989 Ahmad al-Mirghani
1989– Omar Hassan Ahmad al-Bashir

Sweden

Kings
1523–1560 Gustav I Adolf
1560–1568 Eric XIV
1568–1592 Johann III
1592–1599 Sigismund
1599–1611 Carl IX
1611–1632 Gustavus Adolphus
1632–1654 Christina
1654–1660 Carl X Gustav
1660–1697 Carl XI
1697–1718 Carl XII
1718–1726 Ulrika Eleonora
1726–1751 Fredrik
1751–1771 Adolf Fredrik
1771–1792 Gustav III
1792–1809 Gustav IV Adolf
1809–1818 Carl XIII
1818–1844 Carl XIV Johan
1844–1859 Oscar I

1859–1872 Carl XV
1872–1907 Oscar II
1907–1950 Gustav V
1950–1973 Gustav VI Adolf
1973– Carl XVI Gustav

Prime ministers since 1932
1932–1936 Per Albin Hansson
1936–1936 Axel Pehrsson-Branstorp
1936–1946 Per Albin Hansson
1946–1969 Tage Fritiof Erlander
1969–1976 Olof Palme
1976–1978 Thorbjörn Fälldin
1978–1979 Ola Ullsten
1979–1982 Thorbjörn Fälldin
1982–1986 Olof Palme
1986–1991 Ingvar Carlsson
1991–1994 Carl Bildt
1994–1996 Ingvar Carlsson
1996– Göran Persson

Syria

Head of Government
1918–1920 Faisal ibn al-Husayn al-Hashimi

King
1920–1920 Faisal ibn al-Husayn al-Hashimii

Heads of State
1922–1925 Subhi Bay Barakat al-Khalidi
1926–1928 Damad-i Shahriyari Ahmad Nami
  Bay

Presidents
1932–1936 Muhammad `Ali Bay al-`Abid
1936–1939 Hashim al-Atassi
1939–1941 Bahij ad-Din al-Khatib
1941–1941 Khalid al-`Azm
1941–1943 Shaykh Taj ad-Din al-Hasani
1943–1943 `Ata´ Bay al-Ayyubi
1943–1949 Shukri al-Kuwatli
1949–1949 Husni az-Zaim
1949–1949 Muhammad Sami Hilmi al-
  Hinnawi
1949–1951 Hashim al-Atassi
1951–1951 Adib ash-Shishakli
1951–1953 Fawzi as-Salu
1953–1954 Adib ash-Shishakli
1954–1955 Hashim al-Atassi
1955–1958 Shukri al-Kuwatli
1961–1963 Nazim al-Kudsi
1963–1963 Louai al-Atassi
1963–1966 Amin al-Hafez
1966–1970 Nureddin al-Atassi
1970–1971 Ahmed Khatib
1971– Hafez al-Assad

Taiwan

Presidents
1950–1975 Chiang Kai-shek
1975–1978 Yen Chia-kan
1978–1988 Chiang Ching-kuo
1988– Lee Teng-hui

Tanzania

Presidents
1962–1985 Julius Nyerere

1985–1995 Ali Hassan Mwinyi
1995– Benjamin Mkapa

Chief minister
1960–1961 Julius Nyerere

Prime ministers
1961–1962 Julius Nyerere
1962–1962 Rashid Kawawa
1972–1977 Rashid Kawawa
1977–1980 Edward Moringe Sokoine
1980–1983 Cleopa David Msuya
1983–1984 Edward Moringe Sokoine
1984–1985 Salim Ahmed Salim
1985–1990 Joseph Warioba
1990–1994 John Malecela
1994–1995 Cleopa David Msuya
1995– Frederick Sumaye

Thailand

Kings
1868–1910 Chulalongkorn
1910–1925 Vajiravudh
1925–1935 Prajadhipok
1935–1946 Ananda Mahidol
1946– Bhumibol Adulyadej

Turkey

Sultans
1876–1909 Abdülhamid II
1909–1918 Mehmed V Reshat
1918–1922 Mehmed VI Vahidettin

Presidents
1923–1938 Mustafa Kemal (Kemal Atatürk)
1938–1950 Ismet Inönü
1950–1960 Mahmud Celâl Bayar
1960–1966 Cemâl Gürsel
1966–1973 Cevdet Sunay
1973–1980 Fahri Korutürk
1980–1989 Kenan Evren
1989–1993 Turgut Özal
1993– Süleyman Demirel

Uganda

Presidents
1963–1966 Edward Mutesa
1966–1971 Milton Obote
1971–1979 Idi Amin
1979–1979 Yusufu K. Lule
1979–1980 Godfrey L. Binaisa
1980–1980 Paulo Muwanga
1980–1980 Presidential Commission
1980–1985 Milton Obote
1985–1985 Basilio Olara Okello
1985–1986 Tito Okello
1986– Yoweri Museveni

Prime ministers
1962–1966 Milton Obote
1980–1985 Erifasi Otema Allimadi
1985–1985 Paulo Muwanga
1985–1986 Abraham Waligo
1986–1991 Samson Kisekka
1991–1994 George Cosmas Adyebo
1994– Kintu Musoke

Ukraine

Presidents
1991–1994 Leonid Kravchuk
1994– Leonid Kuchma

Prime ministers
1990–1992 Vitold Fokin
1992–1992 Valentyn Symonenko
1992–1993 Leonid Kuchma
1994–1995 Vitaly Masol
1995–1996 Yevhen Marchuk
1996–1997 Pavlo Lazarenko
1997–1997 Vasyl Durdynets
1997– Valery Pustovoitenko

United Kingdom

Monarchs
1483–1485 Richard III
1485–1509 Henry VII
1509–1547 Henry VIII
1547–1553 Edward VI
1553–1553 Jane Grey
1553–1558 Mary I
1558–1603 Elizabeth I
1603–1625 James I
1625–1649 Charles I
1660–1685 Charles II
1685–1688 James II
1689–1702 William III
1689–1694 Mary II
1702–1714 Anne
1714–1727 George I
1727–1760 George II
1760–1820 George III
1820–1830 George IV
1830–1837 William IV
1837–1901 Victoria
1901–1910 Edward VII
1910–1936 George V
1936–1936 Edward VIII
1936–1952 George VI
1952– Elizabeth II

Prime ministers
1902–1905 Arthur James Balfour
1905–1908 Henry Campbell-Bannerman
1908–1916 H.H. Asquith
1916–1922 David Lloyd George
1922–1923 Bonar Law
1923–1924 Stanley Baldwin
1924–1924 Ramsay MacDonald
1924–1929 Stanley Baldwin
1929–1935 Ramsay MacDonald
1935–1937 Stanley Baldwin
1937–1940 Neville Chamberlain
1940–1945 Winston Churchill
1945–1951 Clement Attlee
1951–1955 Winston Churchill
1955–1957 Anthony Eden
1957–1963 Harold Macmillan
1963–1964 Alec Douglas-Home
1964–1970 Harold Wilson
1970–1974 Edward Heath
1974–1976 Harold Wilson
1976–1979 James Callaghan
1979–1990 Margaret Thatcher
1990–1997 John Major
1997– Tony Blair

Northern Ireland

Prime ministers
1921–1940 James Craig
1940–1943 John Miller Andrews
1943–1963 Basil Stanlake Brooke
1963–1969 Terence O'Neill
1969–1971 James Chichester-Clark
1971–1972 Brian Faulkner

Chief executive
1974–1974 Brian Faulkner

First minister
1998– David Trimble

United States of America

Presidents
1789–1797 George Washington
1797–1801 John Adams
1801–1809 Thomas Jefferson
1809–1817 James Madison
1817–1825 James Monroe
1825–1829 John Quincy Adams
1829–1837 Andrew Jackson
1837–1841 Martin Van Buren
1841–1841 William Henry Harrison
1841–1845 John Tyler
1845–1849 James K. Polk
1849–1850 Zachary Taylor
1850–1853 Millard Fillmore
1853–1857 Franklin Pierce
1857–1861 James Buchanan
1861–1865 Abraham Lincoln
1865–1869 Andrew Johnson
1869–1877 Ulysses S. Grant
1877–1881 Rutherford B. Hayes
1881–1881 James A. Garfield
1881–1885 Chester A. Arthur
1885–1889 Grover Cleveland
1889–1893 Benjamin Harrison
1893–1897 Grover Cleveland
1897–1901 William McKinley
1901–1909 Theodore Roosevelt
1909–1913 William Howard Taft
1913–1921 Woodrow Wilson
1921–1923 Warren G. Harding
1923–1929 Calvin Coolidge
1929–1933 Herbert Hoover
1933–1945 Franklin D. Roosevelt
1945–1953 Harry S. Truman
1953–1961 Dwight D. Eisenhower
1961–1963 John F. Kennedy
1963–1969 Lyndon B. Johnson
1969–1974 Richard M. Nixon
1974–1977 Gerald R. Ford
1977–1981 Jimmy Carter
1981–1989 Ronald Reagan
1989–1993 George Bush
1993– Bill Clinton

Venezuela

Supreme Executive Power
1811–1812 First triumvirate
1812–1812 Second triumvirate

Generals-in-Chief
1812–1812 Francisco de Miranda
1813–1813 Simón Bolívar

Liberator
1813–1814 Simón Bolívar

Supreme Chief
1816–1819 Simón Bolívar

Presidents
1819–1819 Simón Bolívar
1830–1835 José Antonio Páez
1835–1835 José María Vargas
1835–1835 Pedro Briceño
1835–1835 Santiago Mariño
1835–1835 José María Carreño
1835–1836 José María Vargas
1836–1836 Andrés Narvarte
1837–1839 Carlos Soublette
1839–1843 José Antonio Páez
1843–1847 Carlos Soublette
1847–1851 José Tadeo Monagas
1851–1855 José Gregorio Monagas
1855–1858 José Tadeo Monagas
1858–1858 Pedro Gual
1858–1859 Julián Castro
1859–1859 Juan Crisóstomo Falcón
1859–1861 Manuel Felipe de Tovar
1861–1863 José Antonio Páez
1863–1865 Juan Crisóstomo Falcón
1865–1868 Juan Crisóstomo Falcón
1868–1869 Guillermo Tell Villegas
1870–1877 Antonio Guzmán Blanco
1877–1878 Francisco Linares Alcántara
1879–1879 Gregorio Cedeño
1879–1879 Antonio Guzmán Blanco
1879–1884 Antonio Guzmán Blanco
1884–1886 Joaquín Crespo
1886–1888 Antonio Guzmán Blanco
1888–1890 Juan Pablo Rojas Paúl
1890–1892 Raimundo Andueza Palacio
1892–1894 Joaquín Crespo
1894–1898 Joaquín Crespo
1898–1899 Ignacio Andrade
1899–1909 Cipriano Castro
1909–1910 Juan Vicente Gómez
1910–1914 Juan Vicente Gómez
1914–1922 Victorino Márquez Bustillos
1922–1929 Juan Vicente Gómez
1929–1931 Juan Bautista Pérez
1931–1935 Juan Vicente Gómez
1935–1936 Eleazar López Contreras
1936–1941 Eleazar López Contreras
1941–1945 Isaías Medina Angarita
1945–1948 Rómulo Betancourt
1948–1948 Rómulo Gallegos
1948–1952 Military junta
1952–1958 Marcos Pérez Jiménez
1958–1958 Wolfgang Larrazábal
1958–1959 Edgar Sanabria Arcia
1959–1964 Rómulo Betancourt
1964–1969 Raúl Leoni
1969–1974 Rafael Caldera
1974–1979 Carlos Andrés Pérez
1979–1984 Luis Herrera Campins
1984–1989 Jaime Lusinchi
1989–1993 Carlos Andrés Pérez
1994–1999 Rafael Caldera
1999– Hugo Chávez

Vietnam

Emperors (era names)
1889–1907 Thanh Tai
1907–1916 Duy Tan
1916–1925 Khai Dinh
1926–1945 Bao Dai

Democratic Republic of Vietnam

Presidents
1945–1969 Ho Chi Minh
1969–1976 Ton Duc Thang

Prime ministers
1945–1955 Ho Chi Minh
1955–1976 Pham Van Dong

Associated State of Vietnam

Chiefs of state
1949–1955 Bao Dai
1955–1955 Ngo Dinh Diem

Prime ministers
1949–1950 Bao Dai
1950–1950 Nguyen Van Long
1950–1952 Tran Van Huu
1952–1953 Nguyen Van Tam
1954–1954 Buu Loc
1954–1955 Ngo Dinh Diem

Republic of Vietnam

Presidents
1955–1963 Ngo Dinh Diem
1963–1964 Duong Van Minh
1964–1964 Nguyen Khanh
1964–1964 Duong Van Minh
1964–1965 Phan Khac Suu
1965–1975 Nguyen Van Thieu
1975–1975 Tran Van Huong
1975–1975 Duong Van Minh

Republic of South Vietnam

President
1975–1976 Huynh Tan Phat

Prime minister
1975–1976 Nguyen Huu Tho

Socialist Republic of Vietnam

General secretaries of the Communist Party
1976–1986 Le Duan
1986–1986 Truong Chinh
1986–1991 Nguyen Van Linh
1991–1997 Do Muoi
1997– Le Kha Phieu

Presidents
1976–1980 Ton Duc Thang

Chairmen of the State Council
1981–1987 Truong Chinh
1987–1992 Vo Chi Cong

Presidents
1992–1997 Le Duc Anh
1997– Tran Duc Luong

Yugoslavia

Serbia

Monarchs
1882–1889 Milan I Obrenovic
1889–1903 Aleksandar I Obrenovic
1903–1918 Petar I Karadjordjevic

Prime ministers
1880–1883 Milan Pirocanac
1883–1884 Nikola Hristic
1884–1887 Milutin Garasanin
1887–1888 Jovan Ristic
1888–1888 Sava Grujic
1888–1889 Nikola Hristic
1889–1889 Kosta Protic
1889–1891 Sava Grujic
1891–1892 Nikola Pasic
1892–1893 Jovan Avakumovic
1893–1893 Lazar Dokic
1893–1894 Sava Grujic
1894–1894 Doka Simic
1894–1894 Svetomir Nikolajevic
1894–1895 Nikola Hristic
1895–1896 Stojan Novakovic
1896–1897 Doka Simic
1897–1900 Vladan Dordevic
1900–1901 Aleksa Jovanovic
1901–1902 Mihajlo Vujic
1902–1902 Petar Velimirovic
1902–1903 Dimitrije Cincar-Markovic
1903–1903 Jovan Avakumovic
1903–1904 Sava Grujic
1904–1905 Nikola Pasic
1905–1906 Ljubomir Stojanovic
1906–1906 Sava Grujic
1906–1908 Nikola Pasic
1908–1909 Petar Velimirovic
1909–1909 Stojan Novakovic
1909–1911 Nikola Pasic
1911–1912 Milovan Milovanovic
1912–1912 Marko Trifkovic
1912–1918 Nikola Pasic

Montenegro

Prince
1860–1910 Nikola I Petrovic Njegos

King
1910–1918 Nikola I Petrovic Njegos

Prime ministers
1907–1912 Lazar Tomanovic
1912–1913 Mitar Martinovic
1913–1915 Janko Vukotic
1915–1916 Milo Matanovic
1916–1916 Lazar Mijuskovic
1916–1917 Andrija Radovic
1917–1917 Milo Matanovic
1917–1918 Eugen Popovic

Yugoslavia

Secretary-general of the Communist Party
1940–1963 Josip Broz Tito

Presidents of the Presidium of the League of
Communists
1963–1980 Josip Broz Tito
1979–1980 Stevan Doronjski
1980–1981 Lazar Mojsov
1981–1982 Dusan Dragosavac
1982–1983 Mitja Ribicic
1983–1984 Dragoslav Markovic
1984–1985 Ali Sukrija
1985–1986 Vidoje Zarkovic
1986–1987 Milanko Renovica
1987–1988 Bosko Krunic
1988–1989 Stipe Suvar
1989–1990 Milan Pancevski

Kings
1918–1921 Petar I Karadjordjevic
1921–1934 Aleksandar I Karadjordjevic
1934–1941 Petar II Karadjordjevic
1943–1945 Petar II Karadjordjevic

Chairman of the Presidium of the Provisional
People's Assembly
1943–1945 Ivan Ribar

Chairman of the Presidium of the National
Assembly
1945–1953 Ivan Ribar

President
1953–1980 Josip Broz Tito

Presidents of the Collective Presidency
1980–1980 Lazar Kolisevski
1980–1981 Cvijetin Mijatovic
1981–1982 Sergej Kraigher
1982–1983 Petar Stambolic
1983–1984 Mika Spiljak
1984–1985 Veselin Djuranovic
1985–1986 Radovan Vlajkovic
1986–1987 Sinan Hasani
1987–1988 Lazar Mojsov
1988–1989 Raif Dizdarevic
1989–1990 Janez Drnovsek
1990–1991 Borisav Jovic
1991–1991 Stipe Mesic

Presidents
1992–1993 Dobrica Cosic
1993–1997 Zoran Lilic
1997–   Slobodan Milosevic

Zimbabwe

Prime minister
1965–1979 Ian D. Smith

Zimbabwe Rhodesia

President
1979–1979 Josiah Zion Gumede

Governor
1979–1980 Arthur Christopher John, Baron
Soames

Prime minister
1979–1979 Abel T. Muzorewa

Zimbabwe

Presidents
1980–1987 Canaan Banana
1987–   Robert Mugabe

Prime minister
1980–1987 Robert Mugabe

Time Line

800 Charlemagne crowned head of Holy Roman Empire

814 Death of Charlemagne

843 Charlemagne's empire splits into three parts: France, Germany, and a narrow strip from the North Sea to central Italy

960 Sung dynasty established in northern China

975 Sung kingdom defeats southern Chinese Tang kingdom and unites China

987 Hugh Capet elected king of France

1054 Eastern churches refuse to recognize papal supremacy: separation of western (Catholic) and eastern (Orthodox) Christian churches

1065 Seljuk Turks invade Asia Minor

1076 Seljuk Turks capture Jerusalem and Damascus

1088 First university in Europe founded, at Bologna, Italy

1115 Bernard of Clairvaux becomes first abbot of the new monastery of Clairvaux. Peter Abelard becomes lecturer at the Cathedral school of Notre Dame in Paris.

1126 Juchen capture Sung Chinese capital

1141 Southern Sung make peace with Juchen

1158 Italian theologian Peter Lombard completes *Four Books of the Sentences*—selections from church fathers and medieval scholars

1176 Seljuk Turks defeat Byzantine emperor

1185 Kamakura shogunate begins in Japan

1206 Genghis Khan proclaims himself supreme leader of all Mongols. Muslim rule established over northern India.

1209 Pope Innocent III recognizes the Franciscan order of friars

1213 Genghis Khan invades China

1215 King John of England forced to sign the Magna Carta, giving rights and privileges to the nobles

1218 Genghis Khan invades central Asia

1223 First Mongol invasion of Russia

1226 Teutonic Knights invited to conquer and convert Prussia

1235 Mongols establish rule over northern China

1238 Mongols capture Moscow

1241 Commercial agreement between Lübeck and Hamburg marks beginning of future Hanseatic League

1243 Battle of Köse Dagh: Mongols reduce Seljuk Turks to vassal state

1255 Death of Sundiata, ruler of Mali

1260 Kublai Khan becomes Mongol leader

1266 Catholic scholar Thomas Aquinas begins his *Summa Theologiae*

1271 Marco Polo sets out on overland journey to China

1275 Marco Polo enters service of Kublai Khan

1279 Kublai Khan establishes rule over all of China and founds the Yuan dynasty

1281 Typhoon ends attempted Mongol invasion of Japan

1288 Turkoman amir Osman founds Ottoman dynasty

1295 Marco Polo returns to Venice

1297 Italian painter and architect Giotto paints frescoes in the Church of St. Francis in Assisi

1298 Marco Polo publishes his *Travels*

1303 Pope Boniface VIII claims supreme political authority for the papacy; the French king imprisons him and he dies

1307 Accession of Mansa Musa, ruler of Mali

c. 1314 Italian poet Dante Alighieri begins writing *The Divine Comedy*

1324 Mansa Musa makes pilgrimage to Mecca

1336 Kamakura shogunate in Japan overthrown, Ashikaga shogunate established

1337 Beginning of Hundred Years' War between England and France

1346 Battle of Crécy: English longbow defeats French cavalry

1348 Black Death (outbreak of bubonic plague) spreads across Europe. Foundation of University of Prague in Bohemia.

1354 Ottoman Turks establish military base at Gallipoli

1361 Ottoman Turks capture Adrianople

1364 Foundation of University of Cracow in Poland

1368 Ming dynasty established in China

1370 Teutonic Knights defeat Lithuanians at Rudau

1375 First European map of West Africa shows kingdom of Mali

1378 Beginning of the "Great Schism": two rival popes claim authority over the Catholic church. English writer John Wycliffe attacks the role of pope and priests in the Catholic church.

1380 John Wycliffe publishes his translation of the Bible into English. Mongols defeated by Dmitri Donskoi, prince of Moscow.

1386 Poland and Lithuania united under the Jagiellon dynasty

c. 1387 English poet Geoffrey Chaucer begins writing *The Canterbury Tales*

1389 Battle of Kosovo: Ottoman Turks defeat Serbians and allies

1393 Tamerlane takes Baghdad

1397 Union of Colmar links Denmark, Norway, and Sweden

c. 1400 Beginnings of the Renaissance. Port of Malacca established on the Malay Peninsula. By this date many Native American peoples have adopted farming as well as hunting.

1402 Battle of Ankara: Tamerlane defeats and captures Ottoman sultan Bayezid I

1405 Chinese naval expeditions commanded by Cheng Ho begin to explore west toward Africa and Arabia. Death of Tamerlane; his empire disintegrates.

1410 Battle of Tannenberg (Grünwald): Ladislaus II of Poland defeats Teutonic Knights. Ptolemy's *Geographia* published in Constantinople.

1415 Bohemian writer and preacher Jan Hus executed for heresy at Constance, Germany

1417 End of the "Great Schism": papacy reunited in Rome

1419 Followers of Jan Hus revolt against Holy Roman Emperor. Henry, prince of Portugal ("Henry the Navigator"), establishes an academy of navigation at Sagres in Portugal.

c. 1420 German mystic Thomas à Kempis writes *The Imitation of Christ*

c. 1426 Italian artist Tommaso Masaccio makes first attempts at perspective in painting

1433 Chinese naval exploration ends. The Great Withdrawal: Ming China ceases overseas exploration.

1434 Portuguese voyage down the west coast of Africa rounds Cape Bojador. Cosimo de' Medici becomes ruler of Florence.

1439 Ottoman Turks reconquer Serbia

1441 Portuguese voyage to West Africa reaches Cape Blanco

1444 First major shipment of African slaves reaches Portugal

1445 Portuguese voyage to West Africa reaches Cape Verde

1446 Portuguese naval expedition reaches the Cape Verde islands

1448 Portuguese build warehouse for slave trade near Cape Blanco

c. 1450 Invention of printing press

1453 End of Hundred Years' War. Ottoman Turks capture Constantinople (modern Istanbul).

1454 Outbreak of Thirteen Years' War between Poland and Teutonic Knights

1455 Johannes Gutenberg publishes the first printed edition of the Bible

1462 Accession of Ivan III as grand duke of Muscovy

1466 Peace of Thorn: Poland regains West Prussia and becomes feudal overlord of Teutonic Knights in East Prussia

1469 Marriage of Ferdinand of Aragon and Isabella of Castile

1470 Posthumous publication of the lyric poems of Petrarch

1472 Ivan III, grand duke of Moscow, proclaims himself czar of Russia

1476 Swiss defeat Charles the Bold, last Duke of Burgundy

1477 French defeat and kill Charles the Bold. Burgundian lands pass to France and the Austrian Habsburgs.

1478 Lorenzo de' Medici becomes sole ruler of Florence. Ivan III gains control of Novgorod.

1479 Completion of Cathedral of the Assumption in the Kremlin, Moscow

1480 Ivan III rejects Tatar overlordship

1481 Ferdinand and Isabella attack Grenada, the last Moorish kingdom in Spain

1482 Diogo Cão reaches the mouth of the River Congo in West Africa

1484 Ottoman empire in Europe reaches Danube River

1485 Posthumous publication of *De re Aedificatoria* by Italian architect Leon Batista Alberti. End of Wars of Roses in England.

1486 Provence becomes part of France

1487 Bartolomeu Dias rounds the Cape of Good Hope, the southern tip of Africa

1492 Italian artist and inventor Leonardo da Vinci draws plans for a flying machine. Ferdinand and Isabella of Spain capture Grenada. Christopher Columbus sails the Atlantic and reaches the Americas.

1493 Horse reintroduced to America by Colombus

1494 Luca Pacioli, Italian developer of double-entry bookkeeping, publishes *Summa de Arithmetica*. Treaty of Tordesillas divides newly discovered lands between Spain and Portugal.

1497 Vasco da Gama leaves Portugal to try to sail to Asia via the Cape of Good Hope. John Cabot reaches America via the North Atlantic. Italian artist Leonardo da Vinci paints *The Last Supper.*

1498 German artist Albrecht Dürer publishes his first great series of woodcuts, illustrating the Apocalypse. Vasco da Gama reaches Calicut in southern India. Italian monk Savonarola executed for heresy in Florence, Italy.

c. 1498 Italian artist Michelangelo completes the sculpture *Pietà*

c. 1500 Beginning of inflation in Europe

1500 Pedro Alvarez Cabral reaches the coast of Brazil

1502 Safavid dynasty founded in Iran

1503 Michelangelo completes the sculpture *David*

c. 1504 Leonardo da Vinci paints the *Mona Lisa*

1506 Construction begins on St. Peter's Basilica, Rome

1507 German geographer Martin Waldseemüller names the New World "America" in honor of the explorer Amerigo Vespucci

1509 Dutch humanist Desiderius Erasmus publishes *The Praise of Folly*

1510 Portuguese establish trading post at Goa, on the west coast of India

1511 Raphael paints *The School of Athens*

1512 Spain outlaws use of Indians as slaves in its colonies

1513 Portuguese reach the Moluccas, the Spice Islands. Italian philosopher Niccoló Machiavelli writes *The Prince*.

1514 Battle of Chaldiran: Ottoman Turks defeat Iranian army.

European explorers arrive at Chinese court.

1515 German theologian Johann Eck defends charging of interest on loans

1516 Ottoman Turks defeat Egyptian Mamluks and conquer Syria and Arabia. English humanist Thomas More publishes *Utopia*.

1517 German monk Martin Luther nails his Ninety-five Theses to the door of Wittenberg Castle Church to protest against practices of the Roman Catholic Church. Portuguese reach China.

1518 Hernán Cortés embarks on his invasion of Mexico. First smallpox epidemic in the Americas, on the island of Hispaniola.

1519 Ferdinand Magellan sails from Spain, attempting to reach the Spice Islands by sailing west

1520 Accession of Ottoman emperor Süleyman

1520s Scandinavia adopts Lutheranism

1521 Luther refuses to recant and receives backing from German princes: the Protestant Reformation begins. Cortés captures the Aztec capital (now Mexico City). Magellan's expedition crosses the Pacific and reaches the Moluccas.

1522 Magellan's expedition returns to Spain having circumnavigated the globe

c. 1522 Venetian artist Titian paints *Bacchus and Ariadne*

1523 Spain sets up the Council of the Indies to supervise the Spanish colonies in Latin America. Giovanni da Verrazano's expedition follows the coastline of North America from Cape Fear to Newfoundland.

1524 Twelve Franciscan friars arrive in Mexico

1525 Peasant revolt in Germany

1526 Turkish warrior Babur invades northern India and becomes first Mogul ruler. Battle of Mohács: Ottoman Turks defeat and kill Louis II of Hungary and Bohemia. Crown of Hungary and Bohemia passes to Habsburgs.

1528 Italian diplomat Baldassarre Castiglione publishes *The Courtier*

1529 Ottoman Turks of Süleyman the Magnificent besiege Vienna

1533 German painter Hans Holbein the Younger paints *The Ambassadors*. Marriage of Catherine de' Medici to Henry II of France. Francisco Pizarro conquers the Inca kingdom of Peru.

1534 Henry VIII makes himself supreme head of the Church in England, in place of the pope

1535 Jacques Cartier sails up the St. Lawrence River as far as present-day Montreal

1538 Last Venetian possessions in Aegean fall to Ottoman Turks

1539 Humayun, son of Babur, defeated by Afghans and driven into exile in Iran; Afghans sack Delhi. Potato brought to Europe from Peru.

1542 Portuguese ship makes accidental landfall in Japan. Spain bans the encomienda system in its colonies.

1545 Michelangelo completes tomb for Pope Julius II. Spanish discover silver deposits at Potosí in Bolivia.

1547 Accession of Ivan IV of Russia (Ivan the Terrible)

1549 Jesuit missionary Francis Xavier arrives in Japan

1550 Italian painter and architect Giorgio Vasari publishes *The Lives of the Artists*. Ivan IV of Russia reforms local government to limit powers of local nobles.

1550s Calvinism becomes popular in Netherlands

1554 Humayun reconquers northern India. Italian composer Palestrina publishes his first book of masses.

1556 Death of Humayun, accession of his son Akbar as Mogul emperor. Moguls capture Punjab from Afghans. Beginning of Eighty Years' War: Dutch revolt against Spanish rule.

1568 Mercator uses for the first time the map projection later named after him

1569 Poland and Lithuania form Commonwealth of the Two Nations

1570 Italian architect Andrea Palladio publishes *Treatise on Architecture*

1571 Ottoman Turks conquer Tunis and Cyprus. Battle of Lepanto: European coalition destroys Ottoman fleet, but Ottomans soon regain control of eastern Mediterranean.

1575 Powhatan, father of Pocahantas, begins to extend control over neighboring tribes

1576 French political philosopher Jean Bodin publishes *Les Six Livres de la République*

1580 Portuguese crown passes to the Spanish king Philip II

1585 Walter Raleigh's first expedition to Roanoke Island

1587 Italian composer Claudio Monteverdi composes his first book of madrigals

1588 Shah Abbas I ascends throne in Iran. Dutch Republic established. English defeat Spanish Armada, an expedition to invade England.

1589 Italian political theorist Giovanni Botero publishes *On the Reason of State*

1590 Raleigh finds Roanoke settlement abandoned

1594 Willem Barents sails along the north coast of Russia as far as Novaya Zemlya in search of a Northeast Passage from Europe to the Pacific

1598 Edict of Nantes gives religious and political freedoms to French Protestants. Election of Boris Gudonov as czar of Russia.

c. 1600 League of the Iroquois established

1600 British East India Company founded. Battle of Sekigehara in Japan: Tokugawa clan defeat Toyotomi clan.

1602 Dutch East India Company founded

1603 Japanese emperor appoints Tokugawa Ieyasu shogun

1604 Samuel de Champlain founds a colony on Nova Scotia

1607 Jamestown colony established in Virginia. Dutch East India Company establishes post on Java. Claudio Monteverdi writes opera *Orfeo*.

1608 Champlain founds Quebec (Quebec City)

1609 Henry Hudson discovers Hudson Bay and the Hudson River. First Exchange Bank opens in Amsterdam.

1610 Polish army occupies Moscow; son of Polish king becomes czar

1612 Russians recapture Moscow. Michael Romanov elected czar, founding the Romanov dynasty. Tokugawa Ieyasu begins persecution of Japanese Christians. Tobacco cultivation begins in the southern North American colonies.

1613 Michael Romanov becomes czar of Russia, founding the Romanov dynasty

1615 Tokugawa Ieyasu arranges murder of Toyotomi Hideyori

1618 Protestant nobles in Bohemia revolt against Holy Roman Emperor Ferdinand II, setting off the Thirty Years' War. Manchu establish kingdom in northeastern China.

1619 Domestic turkey introduced to Europe from America

1620 *Mayflower* voyagers establish Plymouth Colony

1621 Nurhaci, king of the Manchus, invades Chinese territory. Islanders on Great Banda try to revolt against the Dutch.

1622 British East India Company destroys Portuguese fort at Hormuz, on the Persian Gulf

1623 Dutch massacre English traders at Amboina in the Spice Islands (Moluccas)

1624 Dutch establish a town on Manhattan Island

1626 Death of Nurhaci; succeeded by Hong Taiji

1628 Siege of La Rochelle

1629 Peace of Alais: French Protestants lose political freedoms

1630 Cardinal Richelieu becomes first minister of France. Beginning of the "Great Migration" of Puritans from England to Massachusetts Bay. Hanseatic League dissolved.

1632 Death of King Gustav Adolph of Sweden. Maryland colony founded on Chesapeake Bay.

1635 Shogun Iemitsu requires Japanese feudal lords to spend every second year in Edo (Tokyo). France enters Thirty Years' War.

1637 Russian explorers in Siberia reach Pacific Ocean. Pequot War between Native Americans and New England settlers.

1638 Sweden tries to found a colony on the Delaware River

1639 Shogun Iemitsu establishes policy of Japanese seclusion

1642 The Dutch largely abandon attempts to trade with China. Death of Cardinal Richelieu; Cardinal Mazarin succeeds him as first minister of France. English Civil War begins. Monteverdi writes opera *The Coronation of Poppea*.

1643 Death of Louis XIII. Louis XIV becomes king of France. Portuguese revolt against Spanish rule. Death of Hong, king of the Manchus, after conquering the Korean peninsula.

1644 Manchus end Ming dynasty in China and establish their own succession as the Ching dynasty. Last Ming emperor of China commits suicide.

1645 Death of Michael Romanov. Succession of his son Alexis as czar of Russia.

1646 English Civil War ends

1648 Peace of Westphalia ends Thirty Years' War. Paris parlement rebels against Cardinal Mazarin's tax proposals: first Fronde uprising.

1649 Execution of Charles I; England becomes a parliamentary republic ("Commonwealth"). Russia imposes strict laws on serfs.

1651 England passes First Navigation Act. English political philosopher Thomas Hobbes publishes *Leviathan*.

1652 Defeat of second Fronde confirms royal absolutism in France. Dutch settlers arrive in southern Africa.

1653 French artist Nicholas Poussin paints *The Holy Family*. Oliver Cromwell dismisses Parliament and becomes Lord Protector of England.

1655 Northern War begins between Sweden and Denmark

1659 Defense of Copenhagen

1660 End of Northern War: Sweden gains southern Swedish provinces from Denmark. Commonwealth ends in England; Charles II returns as king. French Catholic missionaries arrive in Siam (Thailand). In Prussia, the Hohenzollerns overthrow the Prussian parliament and become absolute rulers.

1661 Death of Cardinal Mazarin in France; Colbert becomes chief minister. Death of Shunzhi, first Ching emperor of China; succeeded by K'ang-hsi.

1662 Dutch lose control of island of Taiwan to supporters of Chinese Ming dynasty

1663 England passes Second Navigation Act

1664 Peter Stuyvesant surrenders New Netherland to England. French Company of the East Indies founded.

1667 Russia and Poland-Lithuania agree to divide Ukraine along Dnieper River

1669 First performance of comedy *Tartuffe*, by French playwright Jean-Baptiste Molière

1672 France invades Dutch Republic (United Provinces)

1675 King Philip's War: the Wampanoag chief Metacomet leads native resistance to colonial expansion

1678 End of King Philip's War

1679 End of Dutch War: southern Swedish provinces returned to Denmark

1681 Louis XIV occupies Strasbourg. William Penn founds Pennsylvania as a refuge for Quakers.

1682 René Robert Cavalier La Salle travels down the Mississippi

to its mouth, claiming the interior of North America for France. William Penn makes treaty with Delaware tribe and founds Philadelphia. Accession of Peter the Great of Russia.

1683 Admiral Shi Lang captures Taiwan for Ching dynasty. Ottoman Turks besiege Vienna.

1685 Louis XIV revokes Edict of Nantes: French Protestants lose freedom of worship

1686 League of Augsburg formed by the Holy Roman Empire against France

1688 "Glorious Revolution" in England: William of Orange invited to replace James II. French expelled from Siam. Death of Frederick William, elector of Brandenburg; succeeded by his son Frederick.

1689 James II abdicates as king of England; William and Mary ascend throne. English Parliament passes Bill of Rights to limit powers of sovereign. Battle of Killiecrankie: Scottish supporters of James II defeated. European alliance against France triggers Nine Years' War. China and Russia agree borders. Outbreak of King William's War between French and English in North America.

1690 English philosopher John Locke publishes *Second Treatise of Government*. With French help, James II raises an army in Ireland but is defeated by William at the Battle of Boyne.

1691 Final defeat of James II's supporters in Ireland

1692 Chinese emperor K'ang-hsi gives Jesuits permission to make converts in China, providing they do not interfere with traditional ancestor worship. Witch trials at Salem, Massachusetts.

1694 Bank of England founded

1696 K'ang-hsi defeats Mongols

1697 End of King William's War. Charles XII becomes king of Sweden. Peter the Great of Russia visits western Europe.

1698 Nine Years' War ends with defeat of France

1700 Swedish East India Company founded. Outbreak of Great Northern War.

1701 Outbreak of War of Spanish Succession. Frederick of Brandenburg becomes first king of the new state of Prussia. English agriculturalist Jethro Tull invents horse-drawn drill for planting seeds.

1702 Death of William of Orange. Queen Anne ascends thrones of England and Scotland. Outbreak of Queen Anne's War in North America: English against French and Spanish. East and West Jersey united to form New Jersey.

1704 Delaware separates from Pennsylvania. British capture Gibraltar. Grand Alliance defeats French at Battle of Blenheim.

1706 French defeated in Italy

1707 Act of Union: England and Scotland become Great Britain. British capture Minorca.

1709 Alliance defeats French at Battle of Malplaquet, but at great cost. Swedish forces defeated in Russia at Battle of Poltava.

1711 Death of the Holy Roman Emperor, Joseph I; Archduke Charles succeeds him. English attempts to take Quebec and Montreal fail.

1713 Treaty of Utrecht ends war between France, England, and the Dutch Republic and Queen Anne's War in North America

1714 Death of Queen Anne. Crowns of England and Scotland pass to the Hanoverian dynasty: Georg Ludwig, elector of Hanover, becomes George I of England and Scotland. Treaties of Rastadt and Baden end War of Spanish Succession: Emperor Charles forced to give up claims to Spanish throne.

1715 Death of Louis XIV of France; Louis XV succeeds him

1718 Death of Charles XII of Sweden

1719 English writer Daniel Defoe publishes *Robinson Crusoe*

1720 Last major outbreak of plague in western Europe, in Marseilles, France. New Swedish constitution increases power of Riksdag (parliament). Tuscarora tribe joins the League of the Iroquois. Japanese shogun Yoshimune lifts ban on foreign books.

1721 Robert Walpole becomes first minister of England. German composer Johann Sebastian Bach completes his *Brandenburg Concertos*.

1722 Isfahan, the capital of Iran, falls to Afghan warriors

1726 Anglo-Irish writer Jonathan Swift publishes *Gulliver's Travels*

1727 Members of Moravian religious sect begin to arrive in America

1728 Treaty between Russia and China

1729 Carolina divides into North and South Carolina

1732 Swedish naturalist Carolus Linnaeus (Carl von Linné) publishes *Genera Plantarum*. Georgia established. Benjamin Franklin begins to publish *Poor Richard's Almanac*.

1733 Outbreak of War of Polish Succession

1734 French philosopher Voltaire publishes *Philosophical Letters on the English*. English poet Alexander Pope completes publication of his *Essay on Man*.

1735 English artist William Hogarth completes his series of paintings *A Rake's Progress*

1736 Nadir Shah reunites Iran and becomes ruler in place of the Safavids

1739 Iranians sack Delhi and capture the Peacock Throne. Scottish philosopher David Hume publishes *Treatise of Human Nature*. The "Great Awakening" religious revival begins in America.

1740 Accession of Frederick II of Prussia (Frederick the Great). Death of Habsburg Emperor Charles VI; Maria Theresa succeeds. Prussia invades Silesia; war of Austrian Succession begins. English writer Samuel Richardson publishes *Pamela*.

1741–43 Sweden fights unsuccessful war against Russia

1745 French fort of Louisbourg on Cape Breton Island falls to British

1746 Benjamin Franklin begins his researches into electricity. France and Britain begin to fight for control of India.

1747 French invade Netherlands; William IV becomes Dutch king. Nadir Shah murdered.

1749 Ohio Company given charter

c. 1749 English artist Thomas Gainsborough paints *Portrait of Mr. and Mrs. Andrews*

1751 French writer and editor Denis Diderot publishes the first volume of his *Encyclopedia*. Italian artist Giovanni Tiepolo paints ceiling frescoes for palace of Würzburg.

1753 Porcelain factory built at Sèvres in France. French build new fortifications in Ohio Valley. Benjamin Franklin becomes deputy postmaster general for the American colonies.

1754 Outbreak of French and Indian War. French defeat George Washington at Battle of Fort Necessity.

1755 Lisbon earthquake. Sankey Canal built in England.

1756 Prussia invades Saxony. Seven Years' War begins.

1757 French destroy Fort William Henry. British defeat the nabob of Bengal at the Battle of Plassey. Sweden begins unsuccessful war against Prussia.

1758 French artist François Boucher paints *Madame de Pompadour*. British capture Louisbourg.

1759 British capture Quebec

1760 Chinese restrict foreign trade to the port of Canton. British capture Montreal. British victory at the Battle of Wandiwash ends the French challenge for control of India.

1761 French philosopher Jean-Jacques Rousseau publishes *The New Heloise*

1762 Death of Russian czarina Elizabeth I; her son, Peter III, suc-

ceeds, but is murdered. Peter's wife becomes czarina as Catherine II (Catherine the Great). Rousseau publishes *Treatise on Education* and *The Social Contract*.

1763 Death of Augustus III of Poland-Lithuania. Catherine II of Russia sends troops to place her own nominee on the throne. Treaty of Paris ends French and Indian War: French lose almost all North American possessions. Ottawa chief Pontiac forms confederation to drive settlers back across the Appalachians. Royal Proclamation bans settlement west of the Appalachians. British gain Canada.

1764 French writer Voltaire publishes *The Philosophical Dictionary*. German archaeologist Johann Joachim Winckelmann publishes *History of the Art of Antiquity*. British Sugar Act taxes importation of molasses from West Indies to the American colonies.

1765 British Stamp Act imposes further taxes on American colonies. Joseph II becomes coregent of Austria with Maria Theresa. Karim Khan takes power in Iran.

1766 French artist Jean Fragonard paints *The Swing*. Stamp Act repealed.

1767 New British taxes on American colonies. English artist George Stubbs publishes *Anatomy of the Horse*.

1768 Royal Academy of Arts founded in London with Sir Joshua Reynolds as president. Russia at war with Turkey. Rebellion against Russia in Poland-Lithuania.

1769 New taxes in American colonies repealed

1770 The Boston Massacre. Economic depression begins in France. Captain James Cook lands in Australia and New Zealand. Rousseau publishes *Confessions*.

1772 First partition of Poland-Lithuania by Russia, Austria, and Prussia. Swedish king Gustav III curbs powers of Riksdag.

1773 Revolt for serfs' rights in Russia. British government grants to East India Company monopoly on tea imports into the American colonies: Boston Tea Party results.

1774 The Intolerable Acts: measures designed to restore British authority in Massachusetts. German writer Johann Wolfgang von Goethe publishes *The Sorrows of Young Werther*. Quebec Act recognizes rights of French-Canadian Catholics and extends boundary of Canada to Ohio River. First Continental Congress.

1775 Outbreak of American Revolution. Second Continental Congress authorizes formation of Continental Army.

1776 Tom Paine publishes *Common Sense*. American Declaration of Independence. Scottish economist Adam Smith publishes *Wealth of Nations*.

1777 Burgoyne surrenders at Santiago

1778–79 War of Bavarian Succession (the "Potato War")

1780 Death of Maria Theresa of Austria; Joseph II becomes sole ruler

1781 Articles of Confederation ratified. Cornwallis surrenders at Yorktown. German philosopher Immanuel Kant publishes *Critique of Pure Reason*.

1783 Treaty of Paris: Britain recognizes independence of the United States of America

1784 British East India Company brought under government control. Immanuel Kant publishes *What is Enlightenment?* First performance of comedy *The Marriage of Figaro* by French playwright Pierre de Beaumarchais.

1785 Englishman Edmund Cartwright invents power loom. French artist Jacques-Louis David paints *Oath of the Horatii*.

1786 French state close to financial collapse

1787 Constitutional Convention: U.S. Constitution drawn up. Prussia intervenes in Netherlands to support the house of Orange. First performance of opera *Don Giovanni* by Austrian composer Wolfgang Amadeus Mozart.

1788 Depression in France peaks after bad harvest. British establish penal colony in Australia. U.S. Constitution ratified.

1788–90 Sweden fights unsuccessful war against Russia

1789 George Washington sworn in as first president of the United States of America. French Revolution begins. Uprising in Austrian Netherlands establishes Union of Belgian States.

1790 French Constituent Assembly makes all church offices elective and sells church lands

1790s Toussaint-Louverture leads slave revolt against French in Haiti

1791 Austrian Habsburgs regain control of Austrian Netherlands. French Constituent Assembly replaced by Legislative Assembly. Sejm of Poland-Lithuania establishes written constitution. Constitutional Act divides Quebec into Upper and Lower Canada.

1792 France declares war on Austria and Prussia. Paris crowd storms Tuileries Palace and kills prisoners in Paris jails. French Legislative Assembly replaced by Constitutional Convention. French Republic declared. Gustav III of Sweden assassinated. English writer Mary Wollstonecraft publishes *A Vindication of the Rights of Woman*.

1793 French king Louis XVI executed. Britain joins coalition against France. American Eli Whitney invents cotton gin. Second partition of Poland-Lithuania. Alexander Mackenzie crosses Canada to the Pacific.

1794 French revolutionary leader Robespierre executed. First turnpike in United States opened. National uprising in Poland-Lithuania.

1795 Third partition of Poland-Lithuania: last remaining territory absorbed by Russia, Austria, and Prussia. French Directory established. Collapse of Dutch Republic.

1796 English doctor Edward Jenner proves that vaccination with cowpox gives immunity against smallpox. Napoleon defeats Austrians: Treaty of Campo Formio gives Austrian Netherlands to France and makes Lombardy independent. Death of Catherine the Great of Russia.

1798 Battle of the Pyramids: Napoleon defeats Egyptian Mamluks. Battle of the Nile: British admiral Horatio Nelson destroys French fleet at Aboukir Bay. English poets William Wordsworth and Samuel Taylor Coleridge publish *Lyrical Ballads*.

1799 Directory overthrown in France: Napoleon becomes one of three consuls. First recorded ascent of Mont Blanc in the Alps.

1800 New French constitution makes Napoleon first consul and effective ruler. Battle of Marengo: Napoleon defeats Austrians. Italian physicist Alessandro Volta builds first electrical battery.

1801 Papacy recognizes French republic; readmittance of Catholicism to France. Alexander I becomes czar of Russia. Thomas Jefferson becomes third U.S. president.

1802 Napoleon becomes consul for life. British theologian William Paley publishes *Natural Theology*.

1803 Britain declares war on France. First circumnavigation of Australia. United States buys Louisiana Territory from France.

1804 Haiti gains independence from France. Napoleon proclaims himself emperor of France. Napoleonic Code of law established in France. Rising in Serbia against Ottoman rule. German composer Ludwig van Beethoven writes *Heroic* Symphony, originally dedicated to Napoleon.

1805 Battle of Austerlitz: Napoleon defeats Austrian and Russian armies. Battle of Trafalgar: British defeat French and Spanish fleets. Lewis and Clark expedition crosses North America to Pacific. Egyptians rebel against Ottoman rule and install Muhammad Ali as leader. Scottish explorer Mungo Park explores course of the Niger River. English chemist John Dalton develops atomic theory.

1806 English conquer Cape Town, previously a Dutch colony. Napoleon abolishes Holy Roman Empire, defeats Prussians at battles of Jena and Auerstädt, establishes the Confederation of the Rhine, makes his brothers kings of Holland and Naples, and initiates continental system against British goods. Napoleon commissions Arc de Triomphe in Paris. Russia invades Ottoman territory in Balkans. Venezuelan patriot Francisco de Miranda leads unsuccessful rebellion against Spanish rule.

1807 Napoleon invades Spain and Portugal, defeats the Russians at the battle of Friedland, and meets Czar Alexander I at Tilsit. Portugese royal family flee to Brazil. Britain bans slave trade. U.S. president Jefferson embargoes trade with Britain and France. English chemist Humphrey Davy discovers sodium and potassium. Ottoman sultan Selim III overthrown by Janissaries.

1808 United States bans slave trade. Napoleon makes his brother Joseph king of Spain.

1809 Napoleon occupies Vienna. Battle of Wagram: Napoleon defeats Austrian army. Russia gains Finland from Sweden.

1810 Spanish viceroy in Argentina overthrown. Catholic priest Miguel Hidalgo begins peasant uprising in Mexico. Bernardo O'Higgins leads attempted rebellion in Chile. Miranda leads second rebellion in Venezuela and becomes dictator.

1811 Mexican peasant uprising defeated; Hidalgo executed

1812 Spanish regain power in Venezuela; Simón Bolívar replaces Miranda as leader of independence movement. Napoleon invades Russia. Spanish assembly proclaims a liberal constitution. War between United States and Britain.

1813 Battle of the Nations at Leipzig: Napoleon is defeated and exiled to Elba. Welsh social reformer Robert Owen publishes *A New View of Society*. British East India Company loses monopoly of Indian trade. Gas streetlighting introduced in London. Bolívar's soldiers enter Caracas, Venezuela.

1814 Spanish troops recapture Caracas; Bolívar flees to Jamaica. Congress of Vienna begins. Treaty of Ghent ends war between United States and Britain. Sweden gains Norway from Denmark. Netherlands bans slave trade.

1815 Napoleon returns to France; defeated at battle of Waterloo; exiled to St. Helena. Congress of Vienna creates kingdom of Holland. Portuguese heir Dom Jão gives Brazil equal status with Portugal.

1816 Dom Jão becomes king of Portugal and Brazil

1817 French anatomist Georges Cuvier publishes *The Animal Kingdom Arranged According to its Organization*. Bolívar returns to Venezuela. Argentinian patriot José de San Martín captures capital of Chile from Spanish.

1818 O'Higgins becomes first independent ruler of Chile. Shaka Zulu becomes king of the Zulus. Border between United States and Canada established. English novelist Jane Austen publishes *Northanger Abbey*. English writer Mary Wollstonecraft Shelley publishes *Frankenstein*.

1819 Carlsbad Decrees. Bank panic in United States. "Peterloo massacre" in England: soldiers kill eleven at reform meeting. Bolívar captures Bogotà, capital of Colombia.

1820 Missouri Compromise sets out rules on slavery in new states in United States. Mutiny in Spanish army in Cadiz weakens Spanish control of South America. San Martín attacks Peru from the sea. Scottish novelist Walter Scott publishes *Ivanhoe*. English poet Percy Bysshe Shelley publishes *Prometheus Bound*.

1821 Mexico gains independence from Spain. Bolívar becomes president of Gran Colombia and conquers rest of Venezuela. Dom Pedro becomes regent of Brazil. Greeks revolt against Ottoman rule. English scientist Michael Faraday invents electric motor.

1822 Dom Pedro proclaimed emperor of Brazil. Bolívar's forces conquer Ecuador.

1823 Liberal uprising in Spain. Federation of Central American republics formed. Mexico becomes a republic. O'Higgins resigns in Chile. U.S. president James Monroe proclaims Monroe Doctrine.

1824 Bolívar's forces defeat Spanish in Peru. Royal Society for the Prevention of Cruelty to Animals founded in Britain. Saudis rebel against Ottoman rule and establish an Arabian kingdom.

1825 Portugal acknowledges Brazil's independence. Erie Canal completed, linking Great Lakes and Hudson River. Death of czar Alexander I; Decembrist revolt in Russia. Ban on trade unions lifted in Britain.

1826 British conquer Assam in India. Ottoman sultan Mahmud II announces plans for European-style army. Swedish chemist Jacob Berzelius publishes atomic weights for many compounds.

1827 Battle of Navarino: ships of Russia, France, and Britain destroy Ottoman navy

1828 Steam road carriage service in England between London and Bath. German chemist Friedrich Wöhler synthesizes an organic compound from inorganic elements. Ottoman sultan Mahmud II orders adoption of fez in place of turban.

1829 George Stephenson's *Rocket* chosen for Liverpool-Manchester Railway in Britain. Abolition of suttee in British India. Colony of Western Australia established. Roman Catholics allowed to sit in British Parliament for first time since English Civil War. Ottomans defeated by Russians and forced to surrender territory in Balkans and Anatolia. Antonio López de Santa Anna defeats Spanish attempt to reconquer Mexico. Argentinian landowner Juan Manuel Rosas seizes governorship of Buenos Aires.

1830 Venezuela and Ecuador secede from United States of Gran Colombia; Bolívar resigns and dies. Indian Removal Act passed in the United States. Joseph Smith founds Church of Jesus Christ of Latter Day Saints (Mormons). Ottomans recognize autonomy of Serbia. July Revolution in France replaces King Charles X with Louis Philippe. First performances of Polish composer Frédéric Chopin's first and second piano concertos. First performance of French composer Hector Berlioz's *Symphonie fantastique*. French force occupies Algiers.

1831 Italian nationalist Giuseppe Mazzini founds Young Italy organization. Brazilian emperor Pedro I abdicates; his five-year-old son succeeds as Pedro II. French foreign legion founded. Egyptians under Muhammad Ali invade Syria.

1832 Algerian tribes launch jihad against French invaders. Juan Manuel Rosas begins campaign against Indians in Argentina. Reform Bill in Britain. Poland becomes Russian province. Goethe completes publication of *Faust*.

1833 First effective Factory Act in Britain: inspectors appointed to check factory conditions. Scottish geologist Charles Lyell completes publication of *Principles of Geology*. New constitution in Chile.

1834 Completion of German Zollverein customs union. British Poor Laws enacted. Michael Faraday publishes basic laws of electrolysis.

1835 Invention of electric telegraph. Rosas extends rule over most of Argentina. Uprising in Texas against Mexican rule. Boer Great Trek begins. Japanese artist Katsushika Hokusai publishes *A Hundred Views of Mount Fuji*.

1836 Louis Napoleon fails in bid to claim French throne. Colony of South Australia established. Siege of the Alamo: Santa Anna defeats Texan garrison. Battle of San Jacinto: Texans achieve independence.

1837 Bank panic in United States

1838 U.S. government orders eviction of many eastern Native American tribes: death of 4,000 Native Americans on the Trail of Tears. Santa Anna expels French from Veracruz.

1839 Ottoman Edict of Gulhane proclaims equality of all subjects. Boers proclaim republic of Natal. Start of First Opium War between Britain and China. Britain bans slavery. First photographic processes announced.

1840 National postal service established in Britain. Louis Napoleon fails in second bid to claim French throne.

1841 Upper and Lower Canada reunited as United Province of Canada. Ottomans proclaim Muhammad Ali's family as hereditary rulers of Egypt.

1842 Britain defeats China in Opium War, ended by the Treaty of Nanking. First performance of opera *Nabucco*, a first major success for Italian composer Giuseppe Verdi.

1843 British annex Indian provinces of Sind and Natal. First Christmas card printed in Britain. Danish philosopher Søren Kierkegaard publishes *Either-Or.*

1844 United States gains trade access to China. English artist Joseph Turner paints *Rain, Steam and Speed*. French artist Gustave Courbet begins exhibiting realistic paintings of peasant life.

1845 Potato crop fails in Europe; famine in several countries

1846 Further poor potato harvest; peak of Irish famine. Britain allowed to establish Christian mission in Okinawa. United States declares war on Mexico and acquires Texas, California, New Mexico, and part of Oregon.

1847 United States defeats Santa Anna and occupies Mexico City. English novelist Emily Brontë publishes *Wuthering Heights*. Credit crisis in Europe. Swiss government breaks up Sonderbund league of Catholic cantons. Brigham Young leads emigration of Mormons to Great Salt Lake area.

1848 Revolutions for liberal reform in Europe, especially in Habsburg territories and Prussia. French king Louis Philippe abdicates; Louis Napoleon is elected president. Mexico cedes all land north of the Rio Grande to the United States. First public health act in Britain. Canada becomes self-governing. Karl Marx and Friedrich Engels publish *The Communist Manifesto*.

1849 British Columbia established as British colony. California Gold Rush. British annex Punjab in India.

1850 Hung Hsiu-ch'uan begins Taiping Rebellion. English artist Dante Gabriel Rossetti forms the Pre-Raphaelite Brotherhood.

1851 Gold discovered in Australia. Great Exhibition in London. First performance of Verdi's opera *Rigoletto*.

1852 English writer Charles Dickens publishes *Hard Times*. Louis Napoleon proclaims himself French emperor. Rosas overthrown in Argentina. Boers proclaim republic of Transvaal.

1853 Gadsden Purchase transfers a strip of land from Mexico to United States. Squadron of U.S. ships arrives in Japan. German composer Richard Wagner begins *The Ring of the Nibelung*. Taiping capital established in Nanking. U.S. flotilla arrives in Japan seeking a trade treaty.

1854 Outbreak of Crimean War: Britain and France declare war on Russia. Clash between miners and troops in Australia; reforms result. Japan signs treaty opening two ports to U.S. trade. Boers proclaim republic of Orange Free State. Henry David Thoreau publishes *Walden; or, Life in the Woods*. French artist Eugène Delacroix paints *The Tiger Hunt*.

1855 Scottish explorer David Livingstone reaches the Victoria Falls

1856 New Zealand achieves effective self-rule. Start of Second Opium War between Britain and China. End of Crimean War: Russia defeated. German-English scientist William Siemens invents new type of gas-fired furnace, leading to the open-hearth process for steel-making.

1857 A new Mexican constitution reduces power of army and church. Indian Mutiny against British rule. French novelist Gustave Flaubert publishes *Madame Bovary*. French poet Charles Baudelaire publishes *Les Fleurs du Mal*.

1858 The "Great Stink": pollution of the Thames River forces Parliament to move out of London. French chemist Louis Pasteur begins study of bacteria. "Unequal Treaties" allow European traders into Japan. British East India Company abolished: rule of India passes to British crown.

1859 Italian nationalists defeat Austrians at Battle of Solferino and Bourbon rulers of Naples at Battle of Calatafami. English naturalist Charles Darwin publishes *The Origin of Species*.

1860 British and French defeat Taiping rebels at Shanghai. End of Second Opium War. Oxford debate on evolution in Britain. Abraham Lincoln elected U.S. president. Italian nationalist Giuseppe Garibaldi conquers Sicily and Naples. Liberals win Mexican civil war. Bessemer process for making iron into steel patented. Pony Express inaugurated in United States.

1861 Italy unified under King Victor Emmanuel. Emancipation of serfs in Russia. Outbreak of American Civil War. Electric telegraph replaces Pony Express. Benito Juárez elected first civilian president of Mexico.

1862 Otto von Bismarck becomes chief minister of Prussia. Lincoln makes Emancipation Proclamation. Homestead Act passed in United States. Napoleon III invades Mexico.

1863 Battle of Gettysburg: decisive defeat of Confederate forces. Polish revolt against Russian rule. Japanese shogun abolishes restrictions on daimyo. English novelist Charles Kingsley publishes *The Waterbabies*.

1864 Prussia and Austria defeat Denmark. European nations sign Geneva Convention. William Sherman leads Union forces through Georgia. "First International" formed: international trade union conference. French artist Édouard Manet paints *Olympia*. Habsburg archduke Maximilian becomes emperor of Mexico.

1865 Confederate capital Richmond falls. Civil war ends in United States. U.S. president Abraham Lincoln assassinated. Slavery banned (13th Amendment) and Freedmen's Bureau set up. Ku Klux Klan founded. World's first department store opens in Paris. Kiangnan arsenal opened in Shanghai.

1866 Prussia defeats Austria at Battle of Sadowa; Italy gains Venetia from Austria. First western-style shipyard opened in China. In Japan, four daimyo families ally against the shogunate. Russian novelist Fyodor Dostoyevsky publishes *Crime and Punishment*. Napoleon III withdraws French troops from Mexico. In the United States, rioters in Memphis and New Orleans kill African Americans.

1867 North German Confederation formed. Self-government for Hungarians in Dual Monarchy of Austria and Hungary. Execution of Maximilian in Mexico; Benito Juárez re-elected president. Reconstruction Act in United States. Dominion of Canada formed. Paris Exhibition.

1868 Fourteenth Amendment gives equality before law to all U.S. citizens. First African American elected to U.S. Congress. U.S. president Andrew Johnson impeached by Congress. British transportation of convicts to Australia ends. Meiji Restoration ends Tokugawa shogun era in Japan. Russian chemist Dmitri Mendeleyev produces first modern periodic table.

1869 Suez Canal opened. Ku Klux Klan goes underground. First U.S. transcontinental railway line completed. American author Louisa M. Alcott publishes *Little Women*. Russian novelist Leo Tolstoy completes publication of *War and Peace*.

1870 Canadian province of Manitoba created. Outbreak of Franco-Prussian War. Italians seize Papal States. In the United States, the Fifteenth Amendment gives former slaves the right to vote.

1871 Prussia occupies Paris. William I of Prussia declared German emperor. Treaty of Frankfurt ends Franco-Prussian War. Revolutionary Paris Commune put down by French government.

World's first elevated steam railway built in New York. American artist Thomas Eakins paints *Max Schmitt in a Single Scull*. Chicago fire. Japanese nobles surrender to emperor, ending feudal system. British Columbia becomes province of Canada.

1872 Russian anarchist Mikhail Bakunin expelled from First International. Death of Benito Juárez, president of Mexico.

1873 Scottish physicist James Clerk Maxwell publishes *Treatise on Electricity and Magnetism*. French poet Arthur Rimbaud publishes *A Season in Hell*.

1874 French artist Claude Monet paints *Impression: Sunrise*, the first Impressionist painting. First collection of Impressionist work shown at Salon des Réfusés in Paris. Wagner completes *The Ring of the Nibelung*. Introduction of barbed wire fencing onto Great Plains.

1875 Railway completed between Tokyo and Yokohama in Japan.

1876 Battle of Little Big Horn: Sioux and Cheyenne wipe out a U.S. cavalry detachment. Election of Rutherford B. Hayes as U.S. president marks end of Reconstruction. Central Park opened in New York. Porfirio Díaz becomes president of Mexico. First International dissolved. Britain and France establish joint protectorate over Egypt. New Ottoman constitution. King Leopold of Belgium founds International Association of the Congo. First train service in China. Leo Tolstoy completes *Anna Karenina*. German composer Johannes Brahms completes his first symphony. French artist Edgar Degas paints *The Dance Class*.

1877 Russia renews war against Ottoman empire. Samurai rising in Japan. Pittsburgh railroad strike. American inventor Thomas Edison patents the phonograph. English author Anna Sewell publishes *Black Beauty*.

1878 Foundation of the Salvation Army. Treaty of Berlin tries to bring stability to Balkans. Edison develops first practical light bulb. Taiping rebellion crushed in China.

1879 Zulus defeat British at Ishandhlwana

1880 Start of First Boer War. Fyodor Dostoyevsky completes publication of *The Brothers Karamazov*. American author Joel Chandler Harris publishes *Uncle Remus*.

1881 Assassination of Russian czar Alexander II. End of First Boer War: British accept independence of Transvaal. French establish protectorate over Tunisia. Foundation of American Federation of Labor.

1882 Russian laws restrict rights of Jews. British take control of Egypt.

1883 Brooklyn Bridge completed. End of War of the Pacific: Chile gains nitrate fields from Peru.

1885 French novelist Émile Zola publishes *Germinal*. Formation of Indian National Congress. Canadian Pacific Railway connects east and west coasts. Berlin Conference divides overseas spheres of European influence. German philosopher Friedrich Nietzsche completes *Thus Spake Zarathustra*. French protectorate over Annam recognized by China. Mahdi drives British from Sudan.

1886 South African gold rush

1888 Dutch-born artist Vincent van Gogh paints *Sunflowers*; French artist Paul Cézanne anticipates cubist principles. German physicist Heinrich Hertz discovers radio waves. Pasteur Institute established. Brazil becomes the last South American country to ban slavery. Apache chief Geronimo captured. Kodak makes first box camera.

1889 Second International formed. Eiffel Tower constructed in Paris. Brazilian emperor Pedro II deposed; Brazil becomes republic. Parliamentary constitution in Japan.

1890 Sherman Antitrust Act passed in United States. Ghost Dance movement among Native Americans. Sioux massacred at Battle of Wounded Knee. American writer Jacob Riis publishes *How the Other Half Lives*.

1891 English novelist Arthur Conan Doyle begins publication of *The Adventures of Sherlock Holmes*. French artist Paul Gauguin goes to Tahiti to paint.

1892 Cholera epidemic in Hamburg. Art nouveau movement begins in Belgium. Populist, or People's, Party formed in United States.

1893 Independent Labour Party formed in Britain. Norwegian artist Edvard Munch paints *The Scream*. Financial crash in United States.

1894 Nicholas II becomes czar of Russia. South Australia gives vote to women. Pullman Strike by railway workers in United States. Turks begin repression of Armenians. Japan sends troops to Korea; outbreak of Sino-Japanese War. French composer Claude Debussy writes *Prélude à l'après-midi d'un faune*.

1895 Treaty of Shimonoseki ends Sino-Japanese War, but Western powers limit Japanese gains. Jameson Raid in southern Africa. Revolt in Cuba. World's first electric-powered elevated railway built in Chicago. First production of *The Importance of Being Earnest* by British writer Oscar Wilde. World's first movie theater opens in Paris.

1896 *Daily Mail* mass-circulation newspaper founded in Britain. Liberal Party wins Canadian elections. Klondike Gold Rush. Battle of Adowa: Ethiopians defeat Italian army.

1897 First performance of *A Doll's House* by Norwegian dramatist Henrik Ibsen.

1898 French writer Émile Zola publishes "J'accuse" on the Dreyfus affair. Spanish-American War: United States defeats Spain. "Hundred Days of Reform" in China; defeated by conservative empress. Battle of Omdurman: British defeat Mahdi in Sudan. Fashoda incident between British and French forces in Africa. Viennese artists form the Secession movement.

1899 Boxer Rebellion begins in China. Boers invade Natal: outbreak of Second Boer War. Last European cholera epidemic. Austrian doctor Sigmund Freud publishes *The Interpretation of Dreams*.

1900 Boxer rebellion in China; Russians occupy Manchuria. International force sacks Beijing. William McKinley becomes Republican U.S. president.

1901 McKinley assassinated. Theodore Roosevelt becomes U.S. president. Mass production of cars begins in Detroit. Death of British Queen Victoria. End of Boxer Rebellion in China. Thomas Mann publishes *Buddenbrooks*.

1902 Coal strike in Pennsylvania. Russian revolutionary Vladimir Lenin publishes *What Is To Be Done?* Britain signs treaty with Japan. Second Boer War ends in British victory. Military treaty between Britain and Japan.

1903 Wright brothers make first powered flight. Panama gains independence from Colombia. Entente cordiale between Britain and France.

1904 British annex Tibet. Outbreak of Russo-Japanese War when Japan attacks Port Arthur.

1905 Japanese defeat Russians in Russo-Japanese War. British partition of Bengal: Hindu boycott of British goods. Norway achieves independence from Sweden. Attempted revolution in Russia leads to creation of duma (parliament). Algeciras Conference on Morocco crisis between Germany and France.

1906 San Francisco earthquake. Indian National Congress calls for Indian self-rule. Launch of HMS *Dreadnought*, first of new class of British battleships, triggers naval arms race in Europe.

1907 Hague Peace Conference. Entente between Britain and Russia. Sinn Féin League formed in Ireland. Deaths of dowager empress of China and emperor Tzu-hsi. In Southwest Africa, the Herero people rebel against German rule. Spanish artist Pablo Picasso paints *Les Demoiselles d'Avignon*, the first important cubist painting.

1321

1908 Young Turk revolt; Ottoman sultan Abdülhamid forced to restore constitution. Austria formally annexes Bosnia-Herzegovina. Austrian composer Arnold Schoenberg starts experimenting with atonal music. French novelist Marcel Proust begins to write *À la recherche du temps perdu*.

1909 Young Turks depose Ottoman sultan. Ballet Russe arrives in Paris.

1910 Mexican Revolution begins. Japan formally annexes Korea. Union of South Africa formed. Russian artist Wassily Kandinsky experiments with abstract painting.

1911 Sarekat Islam (Islamic Association) founded in Indonesia. Rebellion against French in Morocco; Germany sends gunboat to demand transfer of French Congo to Germany. Last Chinese emperor abdicates; Sun Yat-sen becomes provisional president of Chinese republic. Porfirio Díaz forced to quit presidency of Mexico; Francisco Madero elected. British move Indian capital to Delhi.

1912 French artist Georges Braques completes painting *Man with a Guitar*. Theodore Roosevelt forms Progressive Party. South African Native National Congress formed. Serbia, Bulgaria, Montenegro, and Greece form Balkan League. First Balkan War: Turkey loses almost all lands in Europe. Albania declares independence. New Mexico and Arizona are admitted to the Union. U.S. troops sent to Nicaragua to support conservative government. Woodrow Wilson becomes U.S. president. Chinese warlord Yuan Shikai becomes president of China. Indonesian Indies Party calls for independence from Netherlands.

1913 Armory Show of modernist painting in New York City. In Mexico, Victoriano Huerta declares himself president. Second Balkan War. First performance of Igor Stravinsky's ballet *The Rite of Spring*.

1914 Assassination of Archduke Franz Ferdinand of Austria by Serbian nationalists. Austria declares war on Serbia, leading to start of World War I. U.S. troops occupy Mexican port of Veracruz; Venustiano Carranza declares himself president of Mexico. Panama Canal opens. Further antitrust acts passed in United States.

1915 German submarine blockade of Britain begins. First use of chlorine gas in battle. Allied landings at Gallipoli. Liner *Lusitania* sunk. Italy enters war on side of Allies. Japan issues Twenty-One Demands, aimed at making China a vassal state. D. W. Griffith's film *The Birth of a Nation* opens.

1916 Lawrence of Arabia leads Arab revolt against Turks. Germans attack French defenses at Verdun. Easter Rising in Dublin, Ireland, against British rule. Battles of Jutland and the Somme. First use of tanks in battle. Lloyd George becomes British prime minister. Russian monk Rasputin murdered by Russian nobles. U.S. president Woodrow Wilson sets up Council for National Defense to oversee war preparations. Pancho Villa kills U.S. citizens in New Mexico.

1917 Germany starts to sink neutral shipping bound for Britain. Mutinies in French army; Georges Clemenceau becomes prime minister of France. Battle of Passchendaele. First use of tanks in large numbers at Battle of Cambrai. United States enters World War I. New constitution in Mexico. South African Native National Congress becomes African National Congress. British India Office announces policy of involving more Indians in government. Balfour Declaration: British prime minister supports

idea of Jewish state in Palestine. February and October Revolutions in Russia; Bolsheviks seize power.

1918 End of World War I. Start of Russian Civil War; Allies support White counterrevolutionary forces. Takashi Hara becomes first nonaristocratic prime minister of Japan. Dutch establish Volksraad (People's Council) in Indonesia. Food rationing in Britain. Treaty of Brest-Litovsk between Germany and Russia. German Kaiser abdicates. Beginning of civil war in Germany. In eastern Europe, Finland, Estonia, Latvia, Lithuania, Poland, Ukraine, and Czechoslovakia become independent countries. President Woodrow Wilson outlines his Fourteen Points in speech on U.S. war aims.

1919 Paris Peace Conference: Treaty of Versailles imposes severe peace terms on Germany. League of Nations founded. Britain receives mandate to govern Palestine. Germany's African colonies awarded to Britain and South Africa. Irish uprising against British rule. U.S. president Woodrow Wilson suffers stroke. Italian nationalist Gabriele D'Annunzio and followers occupy port of Fiume. Benito Mussolini founds Italian Fascist Party. Start of Polish-Soviet War; Polish and White Russian forces advance to within 100 miles of Moscow. Greek troops land at Smyrna in Turkey. Demonstration in Beijing triggers May Fourth Movement in China. Death of Mexican peasant leader Emiliano Zapata. Amritsar massacre in India. Government of India Act introduces limited democratic reforms. Mahatma Gandhi calls for boycott of British goods and institutions.

1920 Russian Civil War ends in Bolshevik victory. Alvaro Obregón comes to power in Mexico. Government of Ireland Act proposes separate home rule for northern and southern Ireland. Russian Communist invasion of Poland defeated; peace treaty partitions Ukraine and Belorussia between Russia and Poland. In the United States, Congress votes against Treaty of Versailles and U.S. membership in League of Nations. The Eighteenth Amendment enforces Prohibition; the Nineteenth Amendment gives women the vote. U.S. attorney general Mitchell Palmer jails and deports political dissidents.

1921 Warren G. Harding becomes U.S. president. Financier Andrew Mellon becomes U.S. secretary of the treasury. Federal Highway Act passed. Washington Treaty involves United States in international cooperation in the Pacific. Five million die in famine in Russia, where Lenin introduces New Economic Policy. Economic slump in Britain. Southern Ireland becomes Irish Free State, Northern Ireland remains part of United Kingdom. Chinese Communist Party founded. Assassination of Japanese prime minister Takashi Hara.

1922 British arrest Mahatma Gandhi. Benito Mussolini comes to power in Italy. First congress of Chinese Communist Party. British proclaim mandate in Palestine. Turkish republic replaces Ottoman sultanate. Formation of Union of Soviet Socialist Republics (USSR). Economic conference at Genoa; Rapallo alliance between USSR and Germany. Lenin suffers a stroke; Josef Stalin becomes general secretary of Communist Party of USSR. Michael Collins becomes president of the Irish Free State but is killed by Republicans. F. Scott Fitzgerald publishes *Tales of the Jazz Age*.

1923 Calvin Coolidge becomes U.S. president. France and Belgium occupy German Ruhr. Hyperinflation makes German currency worthless. Adolf Hitler fails to overthrow the Bavarian government in the Munich Putsch. Turks drive Greek forces from Asia Minor. USSR agrees to supply Chinese nationalist Guomindang.

1924 Death of Lenin; Stalin succeeds to leadership of USSR. Election of first Labour government in Britain. Johnson-Reed Act effectively ends Asian immigration to the United States. Army-led revolution in Chile. In Mexico, Peruvian exiles form American Popular Revolutionary Alliance (Aprista). Mahatma Gandhi released from jail in India.

1925 Locarno Treaty guarantees borders of France and Belgium with Germany. Mussolini assumes dictatorial powers in Italy. The "Monkey Trial" in Tennessee opposes Darwinists and Creationists in a legal test of the theory of evolution. Charleston dance craze sweeps New York City. Adolf Hitler publishes first volume of *Mein Kampf.* Widespread strikes in China. Death of Sun Yat-sen leads to succession of Chiang Kai-shek as Guomindang leader.

1926 Chiang Kai-shek launches campaign to win control of southern China. General strike in Britain. Mussolini dissolves all opposition political parties in Italy. Syrians revolt against French rule. Germany joins League of Nations. Hirohito becomes emperor of Japan. Communist rising against Dutch in Java. John Logie Baird demonstrates a working television in London. Death of Italian American film star Rudolph Valentino.

1927 Communist insurrection in Sumatra. Sukarno becomes leader of Indonesian Nationalist Party. Execution in United States of Italian anarchists Nicola Sacco and Bartolomeo Vanzetti. Charles Lindbergh makes first solo nonstop flight across the Atlantic. First "talkie" appears: *The Jazz Singer*, with Al Jolson. U.S. baseball player Babe Ruth hits record sixty home runs. Stalin expels Leon Trotsky from Communist Party of the USSR. Chiang Kai-shek captures Shanghai and begins suppression of China's communists.

1928 Chiang captures Beijing and becomes president of China. Stalin starts first Five-Year Plan in USSR. Women in Britain gain equal voting rights with men (women over 30 had received vote in 1918). End of postwar construction boom in United States. Walt Disney makes *Steamboat Willie*, the first Mickey Mouse cartoon. Kellogg-Briand Pact: sixty-five nations pledge to go to war only in self-defense.

1929 Iraq and Iran sign treaty of friendship. India becomes a dominion. Jawaharlal Nehru becomes leader of Indian Congress. Herbert Hoover becomes U.S. president. St. Valentine's Day Massacre: gangster killings in Chicago. Wall Street Crash. Stalin exiles Trotsky and begins forced collectivization of agriculture. The Young Plan revises terms of German reparations payments.

1930 U.S. Congress passes public works plan to create jobs. Argentine president Hipólito Irigoyen overthrown by army. Mahatma Gandhi leads civil disobedience against British rule by staging a salt march. Start of Great Depression.

1931 First trans-Africa railroad completed. King of Spain abdicates. Japanese troops occupy Manchuria and parts of Mongolia. Round Table talks in London discuss future government of India. Al Capone arrested. Empire State Building completed in New York City. Elections in Argentina mark nominal return to democracy. Getúlio Vargas becomes president of Brazil.

1932 Lausanne Conference abandons demands for German payment of reparations. Nazis become biggest party in German Reichstag (parliament). Geneva Disarmament Conference discusses peaceful solution of international problems. Famines kills many thousands in USSR. U.S. Reconstruction Finance Corporation founded. Bonus army marches in Washington. Start of Chaco War between Bolivia and Paraguay. Japanese prime minister assassinated; Japanese troops advance into China. British propose new Indian constitution. Attempted army coup in Spain fails.

1933 Nazi Party successful in German elections: Adolf Hitler becomes chancellor. Reichstag fire results in suspension of civil liberties in Germany. Hitler assumes dictatorial powers and introduces official persecution of the Jews. First concentration camp opens at Dachau. Germany leaves League of Nations. Franklin D. Roosevelt becomes U.S. president and begins New Deal. Prohibition ends. Second Five-Year Plan begins in USSR. Marx Brothers' film *Duck Soup* appears.

1934 Night of the Long Knives in Germany: SA leaders shot. A plebiscite approves Hitler's dictatorship. In Russia, assassination of Sergey Kirov, a leading Communist. The USSR withdraws from the League of Nations. Greece, Turkey, Romania, and Yugoslavia form Balkan Entente to resist the great powers. Italy, Hungary, and Austria form a pact. Drought in U.S. midwest. Chinese Communists begin Long March to escape nationalist forces. Mahatma Gandhi withdraws from Indian National Congress. Strikes and violent clashes in Spain.

1935 Italy invades Abyssinia (modern Ethiopia) and makes it a colony. Japanese troops advance on Beijing. Government of India Act attempts to make India a federation of the Raj and the princely states. Conflict between Franklin D. Roosevelt and U.S. Supreme Court. Second New Deal, including Works Progress Administration and Social Security Act. Congress of Industrial Organizations founded. National Labor Relations Act grants workers' right to join a union. Rural Electrification Administration begins constructing rural electricity networks. End of Chaco War in South America. Nuremberg Laws attack civil rights of German Jews. Germany introduces conscription. France signs mutual assistance pact with USSR.

1936 Stalin begins show trials and terror campaign in USSR. Germany reoccupies Rhineland and forms Rome-Berlin Axis with Italy. Left-wing Popular Front wins elections in Spain. Army mutiny led by Francisco Franco leads to the Spanish Civil War. Roosevelt reelected as U.S. president. U.S. writer John Steinbeck publishes *In Dubious Battle*; John Dos Passos completes publication of his *U.S.A.* trilogy. Military rule established in Paraguay and Bolivia. Charlie Chaplin stars in *Modern Times*. Military rebels seize control of Japanese government. Dutch reject self-government for Indonesia. British end protectorate over Egypt, apart from the Suez Canal Zone.

1937 Germany signs Anticomintern Pact with Japan against spread of communism; Italy joins later. Japan invades China and captures Shanghai and Beijing. The capture of Nanking leads to the deaths of about 250,000 Chinese. Indian elections: Congress wins landslide victory. Roosevelt cuts U.S. government spending to avoid inflation. Sit-down strikes succeed against General Motors and U.S. Steel Corporation. Novelist John Steinbeck publishes *Of Mice and Men*. Brazilian president Vargas introduces New State reforms to reorganize government on fascist principles. In Spanish Civil War, German Condor Legion bombs the city of Guernica. In the USSR, Stalin purges army generals. New Irish Constitution: Irish Free State becomes Eire.

1938 Germany annexes Austria, then claims Sudetenland in Czechoslovakia. Munich agreement: Hitler receives Sudetenland

and promises to make no more territorial demands. Kristallnacht (Night of Broken Glass): Jewish shops and synagogues in Germany destroyed. Mussolini introduces anti-Jewish laws in Italy. Third Five-Year Plan begins in USSR. Mexican oil fields nationalized under the National Petroleum Corporation. Death of Turkish leader Kemal Atatürk.

1939 Franco wins Spanish Civil War. Molotov-Ribbentrop nonaggression pact between Germany and the Soviet Union. Germany annexes the remainder of Czechoslovakia, then invades Poland, beginning World War II in Europe. Italy annexes Albania. British Parliament approves plan for creation of independent Palestine. Japanese establish puppet Chinese ruler in Nanking. John Steinbeck publishes *The Grapes of Wrath*. American photographer Dorothea Lange publishes *An American Exodus: A Record of Human Erosion*. Film version of *Gone with the Wind* appears, one of the most successful movies ever made.

1940 British defeat Italians in Libya; German Eighth Army reconquers Libya. British and native troops defeat Italians and declare independence for Ethiopia. Germany invades France, Belgium, and the Netherlands. France surrenders. Battle of Britain between German and British air forces. Germans bomb London and other British cities. U.S. president Roosevelt gives Britain fifty destroyers in exchange for naval bases. Roosevelt elected president for third time. Japan announces Greater East Asia Co-Prosperity Sphere. In India, the Muslim League calls for a independent Muslim state.

1941 The "lend-lease" act allows Britain and other allies to order U.S. war materials on credit. Germany invades Yugoslavia, Greece, and Russia. Japan invades Indochina and attacks Pearl Harbor. After Pearl Harbor, Germany declares war on the United States.

1942 U.S. bombers join Allied war in Europe. British defeat Germans in North Africa at Battle of El Alamein. Allied invasion of northwest Africa. Japanese capture the Philippines, Malaya, Indonesia, Burma, and U.S. Pacific islands. Sea battles of Coral Sea and Midway. Indian Congress demands British leave India.

1943 In the Pacific, U.S. troops capture Japanese-held islands. Famine in Bengal kills about 1,500,000 Indians. German and Italian forces in Africa surrender. German Sixth Army surrenders at Stalingrad. Allies invade Italy; Mussolini's government falls. U.S. government introduces witholding tax.

1944 In Italy, Allies liberate Rome. D-Day: Allied forces invade Normandy and go on to liberate France. G.I. Bill of Rights passed to aid U.S. veterans. Japanese invasion of India defeated; first U.S. air raids on Japan, recapture of Marianas and New Guinea from Japanese, and beginning of recapture of Philippines with battle of Leyte Gulf.

1945 Allied bombing of German cities culminates in attack on Dresden. Yalta Conference: Roosevelt, Churchill, and Stalin discuss future of Europe. Allied forces cross the Rhine and advance into Germany as Russians advance from the east. Hitler commits suicide. The war in Europe ends and the Allies divide Germany at the Potsdam Conference. In the Pacific, the U.S. advance toward Japan culminates in the dropping of atomic bombs on Hiroshima and Nagasaki. The Japanese surrender ends the war. Elections in India confirm Muslim strength in north. Indonesian leaders proclaim independence from Dutch rule. Ho Chi Minh announces Democratic Republic of Vietnam.

United Nations founded. Death of Franklin D. Roosevelt; Harry Truman becomes U.S. president. Election in Britain brings Labour Party to power. Fifth Pan-African Congress demands independence for black Africa.

1946 Juan Perón becomes president of Argentina. British prime minister Winston Churchill speaks of a future "United States of Europe" but describes a communist "iron curtain" falling across Europe. France allows delegates from French African colonies to sit in the French national assembly. Nuremburg war crime trials order the execution of eleven leading Nazis. The United States grants independence to Philippines. Violence breaks out in India between Hindus and Muslims. France signs treaty with Ho Chi Minh, recognizing Vietnam as self-governing but not independent, but fighting breaks out between French and Vietnamese.

1947 India gains independence; Muslim areas become a separate country, Pakistan. Dutch try to reconquer Indonesia. U.S. proposes Marshall Aid plan for economic recovery of Europe. Communist members of French and Italian governments ousted. Communists seize power in Hungary. USSR forms Cominform to coordinate economies of Eastern Europe. Taft-Hartley Act limits union rights in the United States. Britain passes responsibility for Palestine to the United Nations, which proposes a division between Jews and Arabs. Transistor invented at Bell Telephone Laboratories.

1948 Organization of American States (OAS) founded. South African National Party formalizes policy of apartheid. Syngman Rhee comes to power in South Korea. The state of Israel is established and immediately attacked by neighboring Arab countries. Communists seize power in Czechoslovakia. Marshall Aid begins. Western powers propose new federal German state. Soviet forces blockade Berlin, which is relieved by an Allied air lift. Truman orders desegregation of U.S. armed forces. Mahatma Gandhi assassinated by Hindu fanatic. Britain grants independence to Burma (now Myanmar) and Ceylon (now Sri Lanka). Indonesian independence leader Sukarno defeats communist groups. World Health Organization (WHO) set up to fight disease in developing countries.

1949 Communists win control of China. France recognizes Vietnamese independence but install Bao Dai as emperor; the communist Viet Minh reject this. North Atlantic Treaty Organization (NATO) founded. Ten European countries form Council of Europe. Berlin air lift ends. Russia explodes its first atomic bomb. Arab-Israeli War ends. Communists take power in mainland China; Guomindang establishes Nationalist republican government on Taiwan. Women gain right to vote in Argentina.

1950 Joseph McCarthy begins "witch-hunts" for communists in United States. Korean War begins. Pass laws established in South Africa. Mao Tse-tung visits Moscow: treaty of friendship signed between China and USSR. Egypt bars Israeli vessels from using Suez Canal. European Convention for the Protection of Human Rights.

1951 Marshall Aid ends. Six countries, led by France and Germany, form European Steel and Coal Community. Conservative Party wins British general election. Jacobo Arbenz elected president of Guatemala with communist support.

1952 Populist revolution in Bolivia. Death of Eva Perón in Argentina. U.S. occupation of Japan ends. General Dwight D. Eisenhower elected U.S. president. Abdul Nasser becomes pres-

ident of Egypt. Nationalist Mau Mau movement begins killing white settlers in Kenya.

1953 Death of Joseph Stalin; Nikita Khrushchev becomes the new leader of USSR. Ethel and Julius Rosenberg are executed as spies in the United States. Korean War ends. Chinese begin first Five-Year Plan. Francis Crick, James Watson, and Rosalind Franklin discover structure of DNA.

1954 Japanese economy recovers to prewar level. U.S. Central Intelligence Agency destabilization of Guatemala; elected president replaced by military government. IBM develops FORTRAN, the first international computer language. French withdraw from Vietnam after defeat by communists. International conference leaves country split in two, with commitment to elections to reunite it. U.S. Supreme Court rules racially segregated schools unconstitutional. Algerian War of Independence begins.

1955 Formation of the Warsaw Pact provides a unified military command for communist countries of Eastern Europe. Martin Luther King leads boycott of segregated buses in Montgomery, Alabama. James Dean appears in the movie *Rebel Without a Cause*.

1956 USSR crushes popular uprising in Hungary and installs Josef Kádár as Hungarian leader. Rift between China and USSR after Khrushchev denounces Stalin. Freedom of speech officially encouraged in China. Sudan gains independence; guerrilla war begins in south. Outbreak of mercury poisoning from marine pollution in Minamata, Japan. Pakistan becomes a republic. Eisenhower reelected U.S. president. French grant independence to Tunisia and Morocco. Egypt nationalizes Suez Canal. Britain and France conspire with Israel to seize it back, but are forced to give way to a UN peace force.

1957 Malaysia and Ghana (formerly the Gold Coast) gain independence from Britain. Soviet Union launches Sputnik, the first artificial satellite in space. U.S. troops enforce desegregation of school in Little Rock, Arkansas. Clampdown on freedom of speech in China. Vietnam War begins between South Vietnamese army and Viet Cong guerrillas. Treaty of Rome establishes European Economic Community (EEC). First black march on Washington; Martin Luther King calls for end to voting restrictions. U.S. author Jack Kerouac publishes *On the Road*.

1958 Charles de Gaulle becomes president of France. In China, Mao Tse-tung announces Great Leap Forward. French colonies offered choice of autonomous status in French Community or full independence. U.S. researchers develop integrated circuit.

1959 Revolution in Cuba, led by Fidel Castro, establishes communist government. Singapore gains independence from Britain. Mao resigns as chairman of Chinese central government council.

1960 Cuban missile crisis. Russians shoot down U.S. spy plane and put the pilot on trial in Moscow. Police kill rioters against pass laws at Sharpeville in South Africa. Mass protests force resignation of South Korean ruler Syngman Rhee. New city of Brasília becomes capital of Brazil. U.S. Congress passes laws to protect black voters. John F. Kennedy becomes U.S. president. U.S. Navy introduces Polaris submarine for launching ballistic missiles. France grants independence to fourteen African colonies. Kwame Nkrumah declares himself president-for-life of Ghana. Congo gains independence from Belgium; Katanga and South Kasai provinces try to break away. Nigeria gains independence from Britain. Contraceptive pill licensed for sale in the United States.

1961 Tanzania (formerly Tanganyika) gains independence from Britain. Bay of Pigs: failed CIA-backed invasion of Cuba by anticommunist Cubans. East Germany erects Berlin Wall. Increasing U.S. involvement in Vietnam. Park Chung Hee comes to power in South Korea. Soviet cosmonaut Yuri Gagarin makes first space orbit of Earth. Britain applies for membership of the EEC.

1962 Mao Tse-tung comes out of retirement to launch a new "socialist education movement" in China. Border war between India and China. Nelson Mandela imprisoned in South Africa. Sandinista National Liberation Front formed in Nicaragua. U.S. biologist Rachel Carson publishes *The Silent Spring*. Dutch relinquish control of last Indonesian territory, West Irian (now Irian Jaya). The Cuban missile crisis is resolved when Khrushchev agrees to withdraw the missiles. Algeria gains independence from France and Uganda from Britain.

1963 Kenya gains independence from Britain. John F. Kennedy visits Berlin. Kennedy is assassinated and succeeded as president by Lyndon B. Johnson. North Vietnamese gunboats allegedly fire on a U.S. warship; U.S. military intervention in Vietnam increases. Martin Luther King makes the speech "I Have a Dream." U.S. author Betty Friedan publishes *The Feminine Mystique*. Organization for African Unity (OAU) founded. Iranian authorities suppress antigovernment demonstrations. Charles de Gaulle vetoes British membership of the EEC.

1964 China explodes its first atomic bomb. Ayatollah Khomenei leaves Iran to go into exile in Europe. Lyndon Johnson launches "Great Society" program. U.S. Congress passes Civil Rights Bill. Bob Dylan records "The Times They are A-changin'." Death of Nehru in India. U.S. intervention in Vietnam becomes full-scale war. Khrushchev deposed as leader of USSR; Leonid Brezhnev succeeds him. Palestine resistance movements form Palestine Liberation Organization (PLO). Zambia (formerly Northern Rhodesia) and Malawi (formerly Nyasaland) gain independence from Britain.

1965 White government of Southern Rhodesia makes unilateral declaration of independence. Race riots in Los Angeles. U.S. Congress ends many restrictions on black Americans' right to vote. U.S. Immigration Reform Act passed. U.S. Marines intervene in Dominican Republic to suppress a popular reformist rebellion. Massacres of Chinese population in Indonesia. Singapore secedes from Malaysian Federation. Military coups in Nigeria and Burundi; General Mobutu takes power in Congo (renamed Zaire). Nicolae Ceausescu becomes ruler of Romania.

1966 Unmanned Soviet space mission lands on moon. Mao Tse-tung launches the Great Proletarian Cultural Revolution in China. Nkrumah overthrown by military coup in Ghana. Military coups in Central African Republic, Upper Volta (later renamed Burkina Faso), and in Nigeria, where the coup sparks a massacre of Ibos in north. Former movie star Ronald Reagan elected governor of California. National Organization for Women (NOW) founded in United States. Botswana and Lesotho gain independence from Britain. Nehru's daughter, Indira Gandhi, becomes prime minister of India. Attempted communist coup in Indonesia.

1967 Nasser orders UN peace force to leave Egypt. Israel attacks and defeats Egypt, Syria, and Jordan in Six-Day War; Israeli troops occupy east Jerusalem, the West Bank, the Gaza Strip, Sinai, and the Golan Heights. Public opinion in United States begins to turn against Vietnam War. Race riots in Newark, New Jersey, and Detroit. In China, Mao calls out army to take back control from Red Guards. Sukarno displaced as leader of Indonesia. Katangan revolt in Zaire ends. Nigerian civil war begins when Biafra claims independence. Christiaan Barnard performs world's first heart transplant. British Labour government legalizes abortion and decriminalizes homosexuality. President de Gaulle repeats his veto of British membership of the EEC.

1968 French students and sympathizers demonstrate against de Gaulle's government; police suppression results in a wave of strikes. "Prague Spring," a movement to liberalize communist rule in Czechoslovakia, suppressed by Soviet army. Hungarian communist government proposes to adopt a mixed economy. Liu Shao-chi falls from position of power in China. Communist Tet offensive in Vietnam. Lyndon B. Johnson announces scaling down of U.S. involvement in Vietnam. Democratic Convention in Chicago: antiwar protests result in fighting between demonstrators and police. Martin Luther King and Robert Kennedy assassinated. General Velasco Alvarado seizes power in Peru. Swaziland gains independence from Britain. Sukarno replaced by General Suharto in Indonesia.

1969 U.S. withdrawal from Vietnam continues, but U.S. air forces bomb Laos and Cambodia. Yasir Arafat becomes leader of the PLO. Richard Nixon replaces Johnson as U.S. president. United States and USSR begin talks in Helsinki on limiting international nuclear weapons. U.S. astronauts land on the moon. Woodstock rock festival. Homosexuals in the United States begin to campaign against discrimination. Cultural Revolution in China officially declared over. Mu'ammar Gadhafi comes to power in Libya. De Gaulle falls from power in France. British government makes divorce easier and abolishes capital punishment.

1970 Anwar Sadat becomes president of Egypt, replacing Nasser. Surrender of Biafra ends Nigerian civil war. Four U.S. students killed when National Guardsmen open fire on anti–Vietnam War protestors at Kent State University. Marxist Salvador Allende elected president of Chile. Palestinian terrorist activity increases with the hijack of airliners.

1971 Indo-Pakistan War. East Pakistan seeks independence from West Pakistan. Greenpeace founded in Canada. Lin Biao killed in China. U.S. president Richard Nixon allows China to join United Nations. Idi Amin seizes power in Uganda. Britain reapplies for membership of the EEC.

1972 Referendum in Norway rejects membership of the EEC. U.S. president Nixon visits China; many trade and travel restrictions between United States and China lifted. Ebola virus appears in Sudan, Africa. Hutus massacred by Tutsi government in Burundi. East Pakistan becomes independent country of Bangladesh. Palestinian Black September group murders Israeli athletes at Olympic Games. United States and USSR agree on first part of Strategic Arms Limitation Treaty (SALT). Watergate break-in occurs in Washington, D.C. Intel develops world's first microprocessor. U.S. government bans use of DDT.

1973 U.S. Supreme Court ruling gives women the right to abortion. CIA backs right-wing uprising in Chile. United States and North Vietnamese agree to ceasefire in Vietnam. Rapid rise in world oil prices begins. Major famine in Ethiopia. Britain, Denmark, and Ireland join the EEC.

1974 Inflation and mass unemployment in Western world. Strikes in Britain bring down Conservative government. Coup in Portugal brings left-wing army officers to power. Emperor Haile Selassie of Ethiopia overthrown, replaced by left-wing military junta. Riots against apartheid in Soweto township in South Africa. Guinea-Bissau gains independence from Portugal. Resignation of U.S. president Richard Nixon. Augusto Pinochet becomes military dictator of Chile.

1975 Angola, Mozambique, and Cape Verde gain independence from Portugal; civil war begins in Angola. South Vietnam falls to communists, as do Laos and Cambodia. Vietnam War ends. Civil war begins in Lebanon, with Muslims and PLO fighting Christians. Referendum in Britain confirms membership of the EEC.

1976 Concorde, the world's first supersonic airliner, goes into service. Death of Mao Tse-tung. Ebola outbreak in Sudan. Vietnam reunited as Socialist Republic of Vietnam. Israeli commandos assassinate three Palestinian leaders. Egypt and Syria attack Israel in Yom Kippur War. Communist-backed forces gain control in Angola. Milton Friedman wins Nobel Prize for Economics.

1977 United States resumes capital punishment. Egyptian leader Anwar Sadat becomes first Arab leader to visit Israel. Eritrea and Ogaden begin fight for independence from Ethiopia. Human rights group Charter 77 formed in Czechoslovakia.

1978 Deng Xiaoping emerges as leader of China. Religious students in Iran killed by police during antigovernment protest. Vietnamese forces invade Cambodia and overthrow Pol Pot, whose regime has killed two million Cambodians.

1979 Soviet troops invade Afghanistan to support communist regime. Egypt and Israel sign Camp David peace accord. Socialist Sandanista movement deposes Nicaraguan dictator Anastasio Somoza. Revolution in Iran: Ayatollah Khomenei takes power and imposes fundamentalist regime. Militants storm U.S. embassy in Tehran and take 52 hostages. Shiite extremists occupy the Great Mosque in Mecca. Saddam Hussein becomes president of Iraq. In China, Deng Xiaoping gives approval to democracy wall movement. Assassination of General Park Chung Hee, leader of South Korea. USSR sends troops to Afghanistan to support communist government against Islamic mountain tribes. Tanzanian invasion force ends Idi Amin's rule in Uganda. White government of Rhodesia forced to accept democratic elections. Margaret Thatcher becomes British prime minister. Solidarity trade union emerges in Poland. Nuclear incident at Three Mile Island, Pennsylvania.

1980 Death of Marshal Tito, leader of Yugoslavia. Deng Xiaoping clamps down on democracy wall movement in China. U.S. attempt to rescue hostages in Iran fails. Iraq invades Iran, setting off Iran-Iraq War. Rhodesia becomes Zimbabwe with Robert Mugabe as head of government. Smallpox eradicated worldwide. Labor union Solidarity presses for democratic reforms in Poland.

1981 Ronald Reagan becomes U.S. president. United States launches first reusable space shuttle. Militant Muslims assassinate Egyptian leader Anwar Sadat. Solidarity leads strikes in

Poland; martial law is declared and Solidarity declared illegal. Iran frees U.S. hostages. Greece joins the EEC.

1982 Israeli invasion of Lebanon against PLO. Strategic Arms Reduction Talks (START) begin between the United States and the USSR. Death of Leonid Brezhnev; Yuri Andropov becomes president of the USSR.

1983 Ronald Reagan proposes Strategic Defence Initiative (SDI): "Star Wars." START negotiations resume. Death of Andropov; Konstantin Chernenko succeeds as leader of USSR. U.S. troops enter Lebanon as part of multinational force (MNF); suicide bomb attack on MNF barracks kills 239 U.S. and 58 French personnel; U.S. embassy also destroyed by a bomb; MNF withdraws from Lebanon. Lech Walesa, leader of Polish Solidarity trade union, wins Nobel Peace Prize. U.S. invasion of Grenada. Argentina returns to civilian government.

1984 China designates Shanghai an open city to encourage foreign investment. Leak of toxic chemicals in Bhopal, India. Indira Gandhi assassinated; her son Rajiv Gandhi becomes prime minister of India.

1985 Economic sanctions imposed on South Africa by United States and Britain. Mikhail Gorbachev becomes leader of the USSR and announces an end to Soviet interference in Eastern Europe. Jacques Delors becomes president of the European Commission.

1986 Libya blamed for terrorist bomb explosion in a West Berlin discotheque; U.S. air strikes on Libya. Nuclear reactor explodes at Chernobyl in Ukraine. Demonstrations against Soviet rule in Latvia, Estonia, Lithuania, and Belarus. Portugal and Spain join the EEC; EEC countries agree to create a single European market by 1992. South Africa abolishes pass laws. Challenger disaster: space shuttle explodes on takeoff. Irangate/Contragate scandal in United States.

1987 Costa Rican president Oscar Arias wins Nobel Peace Prize for establishing a peace plan for Central America. USSR forces begin to withdraw from Afghanistan. Japanese economy becomes second-largest in world. Robert Mugabe turns Zimbabwe into a one-party socialist state. Slobodan Milosevic becomes leader of Serbia. Palestinians in West Bank and Gaza Strip begin uprising (intifada) against Israeli rule.

1988 Yasser Arafat acknowledges Israel's right to exist. Strikes in Poland against government economic policies. Hungarian Communist Party replaces Kádár as leader. Terrorist bomb kills 270 people on PanAm flight over Lockerbie, Scotland; Libyan agents believed responsible. Ceasefire ends Iran-Iraq War.

1989 Chinese government suppresses prodemocracy demonstrations in Tiananmen Square, Beijing. USSR completes withdrawal of troops from Afghanistan. Communist one-party rule ends in Poland. Latvia, Estonia, and Lithuania seek autonomy from Soviet rule. Hungary declares itself a democracy. Anticommunist demonstrations in East Germany; border with West Germany reopened. Police suppress student demonstration in Czechoslovakia. Czech opposition forms Civic Forum and strikes force resignation of communist government; Václav Havel elected president. In Romania, the Ceausescu regime falls. Vietnamese forces leave Cambodia. Congress Party loses power in Indian elections. Exxon *Valdez* oil spill off Alaskan coast. U.S. troops land in Panama and capture General Manuel Noriega.

1990 End of Pinochet's dictatorship in Chile. Sandinistas voted out of power in Nicaragua; Violeta Chamorro becomes first female head of state in Latin America. U.S. launches Hubble Space Telescope. Reunification of East and West Germany. Elections in Hungary: communists lose power. Communist Party loses monopoly of political power in USSR; Boris Yeltsin elected president of Russian Federation on anti-Soviet program. Margaret Thatcher loses leadership of British Conservative Party. Lech Walesa elected president of Poland. F. W. de Klerk becomes president of South Africa; Nelson Mandela released, ban on ANC lifted, and racial segregation laws begin to be dismantled.

1991 Iraqi forces invade Kuwait but are expelled by the United States and its allies in Gulf War. Famine in Sudan. Military junta overthrown in Ethiopia. Somali president Siyad Barre overthrown by warlords. Slovenia and Croatia declare independence from Yugoslavia; Serbia attacks Croatia. Unsuccessful coup against Mikhail Gorbachev by hardline Soviet communists; Communist Party outlawed; Russia, Ukraine, and Belarus form Commonwealth of Independent States; USSR abolished. Anticommunist revolution in Albania. Chechnya declares independence from Russia. USSR dissolved; Warsaw Pact disbanded. Cutbacks in U.S. Strategic Defense Initiative.

1992 Coup in Venezuela fails to overthrow government. Abimael Guzmán, leader of Shining Path guerrilla movement, captured in Peru. First "earth summit," in Rio de Janeiro, Brazil. Maastricht Treaty agrees on plan for European monetary union. Boris Yeltsin elected leader of Russia. Truce between Serbia and Croatia; Bosnia-Herzegovina declares independence from Serbia. Last Beirut hostages set free. United Nations forces intervene in Somalia.

1993 Israeli prime minister Yitzhak Rabin and PLO leader Yasir Arafat agree on limited Palestinian self-rule. Military government in Algeria blocks election victory by Islamic fundamentalist party; widespread killings begin. Eritrea gains independence from Ethiopia. Continued famine in Sudan. Democratic civilian government established in South Korea. Czechoslovakia divides into the Czech Republic and Slovakia. In Russia, political opponents impeach Boris Yeltsin. World Trade Center in New York bombed by Muslim group. North American Free Trade Agreement (NAFTA) creates free trade in North America.

1994 Zapatista guerrilla group becomes active in Mexico. Palestinian self-rule begins in Gaza Strip and West Bank. Socialist Party wins power in Hungary. Russian troops enter Chechnya to suppress independence movement. Channel Tunnel opens for rail travel between Britain and the European mainland. Democratic elections result in first multiracial government in South Africa, led by Nelson Mandela. In Rwanda, government militia begin to exterminate some 500,000 Tutsis and government opponents.

1995 Israeli prime minister Yitzhak Rabin assassinated by Jewish extremist. Benjamin Netanyahu becomes prime minister and promotes Jewish settlements in Palestinian territory. Ebola outbreak in western Zaire. Austria, Finland, and Sweden join the European Union (EU). BJP Hindu Nationalist Party becomes biggest party in Indian parliament on anti-Muslim platform. Peruvian Shining Path guerrilla movement ceases operations. Federal building in Oklahoma City bombed by antigovernment Americans.

1996 Civil war in Guatemala ends. Truth and Reconciliation Commission set up in South Africa. Armed Muslim fundamentalist group, the Taleban, establish regime in Afghanistan.

1997 Britain returns Hong Kong to China. Second "earth summit" in Kyoto, Japan. Petronas Towers, the world's tallest building, completed in Kuala Lumpur, Malaysia. Currency collapse in Thailand, Malaysia, and Indonesia. British scientists successfully clone a sheep, Dolly. Britain hands back Hong Kong to China.

1998 India and Pakistan test nuclear weapons. Five former Soviet bloc countries and Cyprus begin negotiations for future membership of EU. President Suharto of Indonesia forced to resign. Two U.S. embassies in Africa bombed by Muslim extremist group.

1999 The euro becomes official EU currency. Poland, Hungary, and the Czech Republic join NATO. Serbia begins campaign of ethnic cleansing against Albanians in Kosovo; NATO air strikes force Serbian troops to withdraw from Kosovo. Benjamin Netanyahu defeated in Israeli elections. Former Warsaw Pact states Poland, Hungary, and the Czech Republic join NATO. Global economic crisis spreads to Latin America.

Glossary

absolution In the Catholic Church, the forgiveness of sins, made by a priest on behalf of Christ.

absolutism a system of government in which the ruler has unrestricted power and is responsible to no one. Absolutism developed as the feudal system collapsed and monarchs grew in power.

agitprop Lenin's term to describe the combination of propaganda and political agitation used to win political support. He defined propaganda as the use of reasoned arguments and agitation as the use of slogans and emotionalism.

alchemy a form of chemistry that originated in Alexandria about 100 B.C.E. and was still practiced in the Middle Ages. Alchemy aimed to find the elixir of life—a medicinal preparation that would prolong life—and a way of turning metals into gold.

anarchism a political philosophy that argues against all forms of government in favor of free cooperation between members of society. Modern anarchist theories developed in the nineteenth century, when some of their supporters argued that violence was necessary to overthrow the existing order and establish anarchist society.

ancien regime a French phrase meaning the "old order." The term refers to the monarchical and aristocratic society that ruled France before the revolution of 1789.

Anticomintern Pact a treaty signed between Germany and Japan in 1937, by which they agreed to act together to fight the spread of communism.

anti-Semitism a prejudice against Jewish, or Semitic, people. Anti-Semitism is an old phenomenon but its modern resurgence began in the nineteenth century, when Jews in Russia and Poland were killed in pogroms. In the twentieth century, Nazi anti-Semitism culminated in the murder of about six million Jews in the Holocaust. *See also:* pogrom.

apartheid an Afrikaans word for "apartness," used to describe the policy of formal racial segregation imposed by the white government of South Africa between 1948 and 1991. The policy classified people into four groups—white, black, Colored (mixed race), and Asian—and limited the civil rights and work and residential opportunities of non-whites.

appeasement the name given to the policy of trying to preserve peace in Europe by giving in to Adolf Hitler's territorial demands in the late 1930s. The policy, which influenced British and French dealings with Hitler, ultimately failed.

apprentice somebody legally bound for a number of years to a master craftsman in order to learn a trade. The apprentice system originated in the fourteenth century and was the accepted way of training new recruits into the craft guilds.

aristocracy the hereditary nobility of a state whose titles, status, and privilege may or may not bring them special political power.

armada a Spanish word meaning "an armed force." In particular, armada was the name given to the fleet of 130 warships sent by Philip II of Spain to invade England in 1588. The Spanish ships were attacked by the English navy and put to flight.

arms race a period when hostile countries compete to develop armaments to gain military supremacy, as in the nuclear arms race between the United States and the Soviet Union during the Cold War.

art nouveau an ornate style of art and architecture that originated in Belgium in 1892 and featured long, flowing lines and stylized patterns of flowers and leaves. Art nouveau influenced the design of furniture, vases, glassware, jewelry, interior decoration, and poster and book illustration.

Aryan a term that originally referred to a group of Indo-European peoples but in later usage came to refer to the peoples of northern Europe, typified by blond hair, blue eyes, and pale complexions. Nazi ideology depicted such Aryans as superior to other races.

assembly line a method of mass production, introduced in the early twentieth century, in which an item being made passes through a sequence of workers and machines, each of which performs one stage of the process.

astrolabe a navigational aid used for measuring the altitude of the sun or stars. It was widely used by mariners in the fifteenth and sixteenth centuries until superseded by the sextant.

atom bomb the earliest type of nuclear bomb, which utilized energy released by fission, or splitting the nuclei of plutonium or uranium atoms. The bomb was developed by the U.S. Manhattan Project during World War II.

autocracy a system of government by a single ruler with no restraints on his or her behavior.

auto-da-fé a Spanish term meaning "act of faith." Auto-da-fé referred to the ceremony of the passing of judgment by a court of the Inquisition and the carrying out of the sentence. Those found guilty of heresy were generally burnt at the stake.

avant-garde a French term meaning vanguard, used to refer to people who experiment with new intellectual approaches, especially in the arts. The concept was important in the early twentieth century, when movements in art, literature, and music sought to break with the past.

Aztecs a Native American people who ruled an empire in Mexico for about a century before 1521, when it was destroyed by Spanish conquistadores.

bakufu the government of the Japanese shogun.

balance of power in international relations, a situation in which no one nation or alliance can dominate others because power is evenly distributed between them. Maintaining the balance of power was a priority of European diplomacy in the nineteenth and early twentieth centuries.

Balfour Declaration a statement, issued by the British foreign secretary Arthur Balfour in 1917, saying that the British government favored the establishment in Palestine of a national home for the Jewish people. The League of Nations endorsed the Declaration in 1922.

Baluchi a nomadic Asia people who now live in Pakistan.

banana republic a derogatory term for a small, usually tropical, country often dependent on one product and run

1329

by a despot. The term first applied to Honduras at the beginning of the twentieth century, when U.S. fruit companies made banana-growing the dominant economic activity.

baroque a style of art and architecture that evolved in Europe in the seventeenth century. It was characterized by rich colors and ornate, flowing lines.

bill of exchange a signed instruction to pay a sum of money to a specified person that emerged in the sixteenth century as a vital means of trade.

black codes various laws passed in former Confederate states after the U.S. Civil War to restrict the rights of African Americans, who might be banned from owning land, put in jail if unemployed, or punished for infringements by whipping. Congress countered the black codes by passing the Fourteenth Amendment, guaranteeing equality before the law, and the Reconstruction Act, which placed the South under military control.

Black Death an epidemic of bubonic plague that killed up to 40 percent of the population of Europe between 1348 and 1377.

blitzkrieg a German word meaning "lightning war.". The term describes the highly mobile form of warfare the Germans adopted, using air power to support rapid advances by tanks and motorized infantry.

body politic a traditional concept of social organization in which each person had an allotted role to perform. The idea of the body politic began to break down in the fifteenth century.

Bolsheviks one of the two factions of the Social Democratic Party formed in Russia in 1898. The name, which means "greater" in Russian, was adopted by the Bolshevik leader Lenin after the faction won a crucial vote over party membership in 1903. Lenin labeled the opposing faction *Mensheviks*, meaning "lesser." *See also* Mensheviks.

bootlegger someone who made or smuggled illicit alcohol in the United States during Prohibition. The word came from the smugglers' habit of concealing bottles of alcohol in their boots. *See also* Prohibition

bourgeoisie in Karl Marx's analysis of capitalist society, the class that owns and manages the means of production and distribution, such as factories and other businesses. The word is sometimes used as an equivalent for "middle class," particularly with reference to nineteenth-century society. *See also* class.

Buddhism a major world religion founded in India by Siddhartha Gautama in the sixth century B.C.E. Buddhists aim to reach nirvana, or enlightenment, which brings release from desires and the cycle of life, death, and rebirth. Therevada Buddhism, which is common in Sri Lanka, Myanmar, and Thailand, emphasizes individual effort and monastic life. Mahayana Buddhism, which is common in Tibet, China, Korea, and Japan, believes that holy beings can help ordinary people achieve enlightenment.

bureaucracy a form of government characterized by specialized administrators and hierarchies of officials.

Byzantine Empire the Greek, Christian empire that ruled from Byzantium (Constantinople) from the fourth century. It survived until the Ottoman Turks captured Constantinople in 1453.

Calvinism a branch of Protestantism preached by followers of the French theologian John Calvin (1509–1564). Calvinism taught that people could achieve salvation only through God's grace not their own efforts and that God predestined history. Calvinism influenced Presbyterians, Puritans, and French Huguenots.

camera obscura a Latin term meaning dark room that described a device artists used to project an image. The camera obscura was a lightproof box with a small hole in one side. An image of an outside scene or object was projected through the hole onto the opposite wall of the box, enabling artists to see perspective in a scene or to trace an image.

capitalism an economic system whose roots lay in the early modern period but which developed fully during the Industrial Revolution. In a capitalist economy, private individuals and companies control the production and distribution of goods and services, making profit in return for the investment of money, or capital.

caravan a group of people and pack animals traveling together.

cardinal a high-ranking priest in the Catholic Church. A cardinal ranks immediately below the pope, who appoints a college of cardinals to assist him. There are about seventy cardinals at any one time, and it is they who elect a new pope.

carpetbaggers a Southern name for Northerners who moved in the Southern states in the Reconstruction era after the U.S. Civil War. The name referred to the bags in which they supposedly carried their belongings. *See also* Scalawags.

caste system the traditional division of Hindu society in India into hereditary classes, or castes, which were split into four main divisions. Brahmans, the highest caste, were originally religious leaders and scholars; Kshatriyas were rulers, aristocrats, and warriors; Vaisyas included farmers and merchants; Sudras included craftsmen, laborers, and servants. At the bottom of the system were the outcastes, called "untouchables," who performed many of the most lowly occupations.

Catholicism. *See* Roman Catholicism

caudillo a Spanish word used to refer to Latin American dictators who gained political power through personal charisma, often after military command during wartime.

Central Intelligence Agency (CIA) a U.S. government agency, established in 1947 to collect political, economic, and military intelligence about foreign countries. The agency is also responsible for protecting national security. Its methods include spying, counterintelligence, and covert operations abroad.

Central Powers in World War I, Germany and Austria-Hungary, with Bulgaria and Turkey. They were opposed by the Allies, led by Britain, France, Russia, and, later, the United States.

Chartism a working-class movement that agitated for political and social reform in Britain in the mid–nineteenth century.

chiaroscuro a Latin term meaning "light and dark" that describes a technique used in baroque painting of using intense contrasts between light areas and shade to increase dramatic effect.

Christendom a term used in the late Middle Ages to refer to the Christian part of the world; it corresponded to the area we now call western Europe.

Church of England the reformed church established in England during the sixteenth century with the English monarch as its head.

civil rights the name given to the rights of an individual, particularly the right to personal liberty, freedom from injustice, and equality of treatment. Civil rights movements became prominent in the United States in the 1960s, when they opposed segregation and other forms of discrimination against black people. Other civil rights campaigns have campaigned to end discrimination against women and gay people.

class a division of society whose members have in common similar degrees of wealth and status, and often share similar occupations. In industrial society, the most universal divisions are the upper class, the middle class, and the lower or working class. Class divisions were traditionally based on birth and heredity, but today more commonly reflect education, wealth, and occupation.

classicism a style of art inspired by the architecture and sculpture of ancient Greece and Rome. Classicism avoided the use of unnecessary ornamentation and emphasized harmony, balance, and formality.

closed shop a workplace where all the workforce has to belong to a labor union.

Cold War the name given to the period of hostile confrontation (1945– 1989) between the Soviet Union and its communist allies on one hand and the United States and its allies on the other.

collaborator the name given to a person who voluntarily assists an enemy of their own country during wartime, particularly if their homeland is under occupation by enemy forces, such as French people who worked with the Nazis in World War II.

collectivization in the Soviet Union, the policy of replacing privately owned farms by state-controlled villages in which land was held in common. Forced collectivization was begun by Stalin in 1929. *See also* kulaks.

colony a settlement or collection of settlements established in a new region but which retains ties with the parent country of the settlers.

commonwealth a type of government in which power is exercised for the good of all a state's people. England was declared a commonwealth after the execution of Charles I in 1649.

commune the smallest administrative district of many countries. In communist Russia and China, the term refers to a rural settlement organized around collective ownership of land rather than private enterprise. In Russia, such communes were also called collectives.

communism a political doctrine, based on the writings of the German political philosopher Karl Marx (1818–1883), that shares with socialism the aim of creating a classless society. In Marxist theory, communism can be achieved only by the violent overthrow of capitalism and the establishment of working-class or proletarian rule. After the 1917 Russian Revolution, communism became the official ideology of the Soviet Union and directly or indirectly dominated much of the globe.

concentration camp a camp built to detain people, especially ethnic groups and political prisoners. The word was first used to describe camps in South Africa in which the British confined Boer families during the Second Boer War (1899–1902). In the twentieth century, Stalin confined criminals and political prisoners in labor camps in the Soviet Union. The Nazis in Germany confined and killed millions of Jews and other victims in concentration camps.

Concert of Europe the name given to the tacit agreement by which Britain, Russia, Austria, and France worked to preserve traditional political systems and the European balance of power in the first half of the nineteenth century.

Confucianism a Chinese philosophy based on the teachings of Confucius (K'ung Fu-tse, c. 551–c.479 B.C.E.). It advocated an orderly life of public service and respect for tradition and authority.

conquistadores Spanish soldiers and adventurers who conquered much of central and South America in the early 1500s.

Constitutional Convention the meeting of delegates from the North American colonies at Philadelphia in 1787 that drew up the Constitution of the United States, which went into effect in July 1788.

constitutional monarchy a monarchy in which the ruler's powers are limited by law and the monarch is responsible to a parliament or other elected body.

consumerism a preoccupation with and inclination toward the buying of consumer goods, sometimes allied with a theory that the increased consumption of such goods is economically desirable. Consumerism emerged during the 1950s, when growing prosperity allowed ordinary people to buy consumer goods such as cars, vacuum cleaners, televisions, and fashionable clothes. The word consumerism is also used for the movement that grew up to protect the interests of consumers.

Continental Army the American army established in 1775 to fight against the British.

Continental Congress two assemblies of delegates from the American colonies in Philadelphia. The First Continental Congress (September 1774) drew up a Declaration of Rights. The Second Continental Congress (1775–1781) established the Continental Army, adopted the Declaration of Independence, and initiated the Articles of Confederation.

continental system the blockade system established by Napoleon in 1806 to try to undermine the British economy by halting all trade between Britain and those parts of continental Europe under direct or indirect French control.

contrabands the name used by Union supporters during the U.S. Civil War for African American slaves who escaped to the North or were freed by Union forces.

Cossack a member of a mainly Slav people from what is now Ukraine. Cossacks were also joined by escaped serfs, criminals, army deserters, and other outlaws from Russian authority. The Cossacks were noted horsemen and warriors.

counterculture a culture that emerged in the late 1960s in the United States, mainly among young people who consciously rejected the values of estab-

lished society with regard to matters of appearance and behavior. Members of the counterculture also distrust government and business, reject traditional relationships between men and women, and encourage an awareness of non-Christian paths to spiritual growth.

counterrevolution the fight to preserve the established order against a revolution, often led by those members of the nobility, clergy, or social elite who have the most to lose from any upheaval in government.

creoles people of Spanish descent born in Spain's American colonies. They are sometimes also called criollos.

crossbow a common weapon from the fourteenth century, comprising a horizontal bow fixed on a wooden stock. It was easier to use than a longbow and its short arrows, called bolts, could pierce armor.

crusades medieval military expeditions by European Christians to capture Palestine, or the Holy Land, from the Muslims.

Cultural Revolution a movement launched in 1966 in China by Mao Tse-tung that aimed to revive radical fervor in Chinese communism. Many leading officials were replaced and a youth organization called the Red Guards was formed to promote the teachings of Mao. The Guards' activities disrupted society and industry so much that the Cultural Revolution was abandoned and Chinese society began to get back to normal after 1969.

czar the title used by the emperors of Russia; the empress was called czarina.

daimyo Japanese feudal lords. *See also* fudai and tozama.

dead reckoning a method of estimating a ship's position at sea from its speed and direction.

decolonization the process of freeing colonies from imperial control to become independent countries.

deforestation the loss of woodland, mainly due to human activity such as the clearance of woodland for agriculture or the felling of trees for fuel and timber. Large-scale deforestation contributes to climatic change because forests convert atmospheric carbon dioxide into oxygen.

democracy a system of government based on the wishes of a majority of a nation's people. Citizens elect representatives such as members of Congress or members of Parliament to represent them in the decision-making process.

democracy wall movement a movement that developed in China in 1979, when Chinese who wanted political reform began using a wall in Beijing to put up posters outlining their views. Similar walls developed in other cities but in 1980 the goverment banned all forms of prodemocracy agitation, including democracy walls.

depression a serious decline in an economy, characterized by falling sales, reduced investment, and rising unemployment. Many depressions also involve falling prices and wages, though the prices of scarce necessities such as food may rise.

diet a council or legislative body, most often the council or assembly of the constituent estates of the Holy Roman Empire. Diets are named for the towns or cities where they were held.

Diggers a radical group that appeared in England after the Civil War. They demanded the abolition of private property and the distribution of land to the people so that they could grow crops.

dirty war the name given to the state terrorism carried out by the military regime in Argentina between 1976 and 1983, during which thousands of the regime's opponents were imprisoned without trial, tortured, or killed.

dissolution the name given to the destruction of monasteries and other religious foundations during the Reformation. In particular, the term refers to Henry VIII's seizure of the land and wealth of England's religious foundations between 1536 and 1540.

divine right the theory that a monarch's right to rule derives from God and thus cannot be challenged.

Dominicans members of a Christian order of friars founded by St. Dominic of Spain in 1216. The order emphasized mental rather than physical labor, and Dominicans were important as teachers, preachers, and missionaries.

dominion a name given in the early twentieth century to self-governing nations that were also part of the British Empire. The dominions included Canada, Australia, New Zealand, South Africa, and India.

domino theory the influential theory that, if a country became communist, its neighbors were likely to become communist as well. During the Cold War, the theory influenced U.S. military involvement in various parts of the world.

draft a system of military conscription, or compulsory military service for men of fighting age.

Dreyfus Affair a scandal that split French society in the 1890s and revealed deep-seated anti-Semitism. A Jewish army officer, Alfred Dreyfus, was wrongly jailed as a spy. Dreyfus's case became a popular cause for left-wing activists and liberals. He was declared innocent in 1906.

duma an elected national assembly set up in Russia after the attempted revolution of 1905. The fourth duma, elected in 1912, helped force the czar's abdication in 1917.

dynasty a succession of rulers who all come from the same family. Prominent dynasties in early modern Europe included the Habsburgs of Austria and Spain, the Valois of France, and the Tudors of England.

earth summit the name given to two meetings of world political leaders to discuss environmental problems. The first was in Rio de Janeiro, Brazil, in 1992, and the second in Kyoto, Japan, in 1997.

East India companies private companies formed in various European countries to import products such as spices from India and the islands of Southeast Asia.

El Niño a Spanish phrase for "the Christ child," used to describe a regular disruption in the weather systems of the Pacific. Among the effects of the disruption is a warm ocean current that appears off the west coast of South America, usually soon after Christmas, from which the phenomenon derives its name. El Niño can have consequences all around the world, including extreme weather, ecological disasters, and serious crop failures.

empirical a term describing knowledge gained by experience or observation, particularly from a scientific process of experiment, observation, and deduction. Empirical knowledge was a foundation of the scientific revolution of the sixteenth and seventeenth centuries.

enclosure the process of fencing off fields and common land for private use. Sixteenth-century European landowners enclosed land in order to keep sheep. The process often deprived villagers of land they used to raise crops or graze animals.

encomienda system a system of landholding used by the Spanish to attract settlers to their American empire. Colonists received generous tracts of land to farm and the right to the slave labor of the Native Americans living on them.

Enlightenment an eighteenth-century movement in European thought whose followers sought to look critically at beliefs and institutions, replace superstition with reason, and attack injustice and tyranny.

Entente Cordiale a French term for "cordial understanding" that refers particularly to the 1904 agreement between Britain and France that ended their traditional enmity.

episcopalian a word describing a type of church organization in which authority rests in a formal network of bishops. The word applies particularly to Anglican churches outside England, as in Scotland and the United States.

estates the traditional divisions or classes of feudal society, used in particular to refer to French society before the 1789 revolution. There were three main estates: the nobility, the clergy, and everyone else. In France, all three were represented in a political assembly, the Estates General.

ethnic cleansing a policy of removing an ethnic group from an area by violence, intimidation, or extermination, so that another ethnic group can occupy it. The term originated in the wars in the former Yugoslavia in the early 1990s.

European Community a political and economic grouping of European states, originally called the European Economic Community, created by the Treaty of Rome in 1957. In 1992, the Maastricht Treaty turned the European Community into the European Union and created closer links between the twelve member states.

evolution the process by which living things have changed over time to create more highly adapted descendants. The theory of evolution was formulated in the mid–nineteenth century by English naturalist Charles Darwin (1809–1882), who argued that evolution was the result of "natural selection," a process in which random mutations favor the survival of certain members of a species or of certain species over others.

excommunication expulsion from the Roman Catholic Church, usually as a punishment for heresy.

factory a European trading post in Asia, Africa, and early North America. The agent in charge was called a "factor."

Fair Deal the name given to a program of social, welfare, and labor legislation proposed by U.S. president Harry S. Truman in his second term (1949–1953). The effects of the program were diluted by political opposition.

family planning the use of contraception and sex education to limit the size of families.

fascism a political ideology based on aggressive nationalism, the priority of the state over the individual, centralized authoritarian rule, and the suppression of opposition and minority groups. The term derives from the Latin *fascis*, a bundle of wooden rods surrounding an ax. This ancient Roman symbol of political authority was adopted by Italian fascist leader Benito Mussolini in the 1920s. Fascism is sometimes used to describe any extreme right-wing political movement.

feminism a belief that women are entitled to equal civil, legal, and individual rights as men.

feudal system a form of social organization, common in medieval Europe, that divided society into three estates: the nobility, the clergy, and everyone else. The estates were bound by a system of mutual duties and obligations. Lords provided protection for the peasants on their estates, for example; in return, peasants were tied to laboring in the service of the lord. The feudal system began to collapse in much of Europe in the early modern period.

five-year plan a five-year program for an intensive increase in a nation's economic development. The first was launched in the Soviet Union under Stalin, but the idea was later used in many other countries, such as India and China.

Franciscans members of various Christian orders of friars based on the teachings of Saint Francis of Assisi (c. 1181–1226). The first Franciscan order was founded by Saint Francis in 1209.

freemasonry a brotherhood or organization based on ancient labor guilds whose members meet in lodges. Masonic lodges were an important forum for the dissemination of Enlightenment thought. Freemasons are encouraged to help each other, promote morality, and fund charitable work.

free trade *See* laissez-faire.

Freedmen's Bureau a welfare agency set up to help ex-slaves in the aftermath of the U.S. Civil War. The bureau provided food, shelter, and educational opportunities, protected civil rights, and supervised work contracts.

friar a member of certain Roman Catholic religious orders, including the Dominicans, Franciscans, Carmelites, and Augustinians. Unlike monks, friars preached and did missionary and social work. They often supported themselves by begging.

fudai Japanese nobles descended from lords who supported the Tokugawa clan in 1600 and were rewarded with land.

fundamentalism an approach to religion that emphasises adherence to basic beliefs and literal interpretations of scripture.

gauchos South American cowboys, traditionally found on the plains or pampas of Argentina and Uruguay.

geisha a young Japanese woman trained from childhood to entertain men with dance, music, and conversation.

Genoese belonging to Genoa, an Italian city-state that was an important maritime power in the Mediterranean from about 1100 to 1400.

Ghost Dance a mystical Native American religious movement of the late nineteenth century that promised a restoration of traditional ways of life and the end of Euro-American domination. The movement became associated with Sioux resistance to U.S. control, which was crushed in 1890 at the Battle of Wounded Knee.

glasnost a Russian word for "publicity," used to describe the increased freedom of political discussion introduced to the Soviet Union by Mikhail Gorbachev.

globalization the process by which all parts of the world become increasingly interconnected economically and culturally, regardless of national boundaries.

global warming a process that many scientists believe is gradually increasing the average temperature of the earth's atmosphere, largely due to the increase in the atmosphere of gases that trap the sun's heat close to the planet. The theory is challenged by scientists who argue that warm periods occur naturally.

Golden Horde a part of the Mongol empire, established in 1241, and occupying what is now southern Russia and the Ukraine.

gold standard an economic mechanism, common until the 1930s, that used gold as the measure of a nation's currency, so that one unit of the currency always bought a fixed amount of gold. This stabilized currency exchange rates and helped check inflation and government spending.

Good Neighbor Policy a U.S. policy formulated in 1933 that aimed at treating Latin American countries with respect rather than interfering in their affairs. It contrasted with the Monroe Doctrine, which provided a pretext for U.S. interference. *See also* Monroe Doctrine.

Gothic a word describing a style of art and architecture, dominant in the later Middle Ages in Europe, that was characterized by pointed arches and other features in great cathedrals. The style was revived in nineteenth-century neo-Gothic churches and public buildings. So-called gothic novels thrilled readers with mysterious or supernatural stories, often in medieval settings.

grand tour an extensive trip through Europe undertaken by young nobles of the seventeenth and eighteenth centuries as part of their education. The most important part of the tour was normally a visit to Italy.

grand vizier the highest government official in the Ottoman Empire and in some other Islamic countries. Grand viziers exercised great power as the Ottoman sultans withdrew from everyday government.

Great Awakening a religious revival that occurred in the North American colonies in the mid–eighteenth century and established the evangelical style of Christianity as a major feature of American life.

Great Leap Forward a policy launched in China by Mao Tse-tung in 1958 to speed up economic development by a reorganization of industry and the creation of farming communes. Within three years, the policy produced a slump in industrial output and food production; in the resulting famine, some 30 million people died.

Great Society the term used by U.S. president Lyndon B. Johnson to describe the goal of his social legislation from 1964 on.

green revolution the name given to the introduction of new farming methods in the developing world encouraged by the United Nations in the 1960s and 1970s. Although agricultural production rose in numerous countries, the new methods were often expensive and thus unsuited to the long-term needs of developing countries.

greenhouse gases gases such as carbon dioxide and many pollutants that accumulate in the earth's atmosphere and prevent heat escaping into space, thus possibly causing the atmospheric temperature to build up. *See also* global warming.

gross national product (GNP) an economic measure that judges the total annual value of the goods and services that a country produces.

guerrilla warfare a style of warfare adopted by small mobile groups of fighters who avoid direct confrontation with a more powerful enemy and rely instead on hit-and-run tactics, ambushes, and sabotage.

guild a medieval craft association formed to protect its members, maintain standards, and regulate the training of apprentices. From around the twelfth century, guilds grew to be very powerful in many European towns.

gunboat diplomacy in the nineteenth and early twentieth centuries, the use of a show of naval force by a major power to intimidate a weaker country.

hacienda a Spanish word for a ranch, plantation, or farm with a dwelling house.

Hamas a militant Palestinian organization that uses terrorist tactics to attack the state of Israel.

Hanseatic League a group of chiefly German cities that gained control of sea trade in the Baltic and North Sea in the fouteenth century but declined in the fifteenth.

heliocentric placing the sun rather than the Earth at the center of the universe. A heliocentric view of the solar system was proposed by Copernicus in the sixteenth century in opposition to the teaching of the Catholic Church.

herbal a book that cataloged plants according to their medicinal properties.

heresy an opinion or belief that is contrary to the accepted doctrine, in particular of the Roman Catholic Church. In the fifteenth and sixteenth centuries, heresy was a serious crime and those found guilty of it were dealt with severely.

heretic someone, particularly a baptized Catholic, who held a view that was not acceptable to the Catholic Church.

Hinduism a major world religion that is particularly important in India. Hinduism developed over several thousand years and worships many gods, including Brahma, Shiva, and Vishnu. Hindus believe in reincarnation.

the Holocaust the name given to the mass killing of Jews and other victims of the German Nazis during World War II. Many were murdered in gas chambers in extermination camps. By 1945, about six million people had been killed, most of them Jews.

Holy Roman Empire a central European empire of mainly Germanic

states. The empire was ruled by an emperor elected by the most powerful German princes and had the pope as its spiritual head.

Huguenot the name given to French Protestants who mainly followed the Calvinist faith. The name Huguenot may have derived from an old German word for confederate or comrade.

humanism a tradition of thought that emphasizes the needs and abilities of humankind. Modern humanism contrasted with medieval European ideas, which saw humanity as essentially sinful and earthly life as something to be despised.

hyperinflation an economic phenomenon in which prices increase very rapidly, causing money to lose its value and savings and wages to become worthless.

icon a religious image, usually painted on wood, of God, Jesus, a saint, or the Virgin Mary. Icons form an important sacred tradition in Eastern Orthodox Christianity.

illuminated manuscripts medieval manuscripts containing bright-colored, painted ornamentation and decoration. Monks produced the earliest illuminated manuscripts, but from the 1200s on urban craftworkers took over their production.

imperialism the policy or practice of nations obtaining and exploiting dependent territories, such as the nineteenth-century accumulation of African and Asian empires by many European powers. In "economic imperialism," powerful countries exploit weaker ones economically without claiming formal jurisdiction over them.

impressionism an influential artistic style that originated in painting in France in the 1860s. Impressionist painters tried to convey a faithful impression of a scene as perceived by the artist's eye rather than an image shaped by pre-formed assumptions or artistic tradition.

Incas a Native American people who ruled a large empire on the west coast of South America, centered on southern Peru. The empire lasted for about 100 years before 1532, when it was overcome by Spanish conquistadores.

Indian National Congress a Hindu-dominated political organization that led the campaign for Indian self-rule and, after independence, became the country's biggest political party. The Congress Party formed all Indian governments until 1989. Its first prime minister, Jawaharlal Nehru, was succeeded by his daughter Indira Gandhi, and then by her son Rajiv.

indulgence in the Catholic Church, relief from all or part of the penance necessary to atone for sins. Indulgences were sometimes sold by the Roman Catholic Church to raise funds, a practice that led to vigorous objections by Martin Luther and other religious reformers.

industrialization the development and concentration of industry as a major source of a region's wealth. After the Industrial Revolution of the nineteenth century, industry replaced agriculture and traditional crafts as the main economic activity in many parts of Europe and North America.

inflation a general rise in prices in a country's economy, such that the same goods and services cost more than they did before.

inquisition the name for several different Catholic ecclesiastical courts set up to find and punish heretics. The chief inquisitions were the Roman Inquisition and the Spanish Inquisition.

integration the opening of facilities such as schools to everyone, regardless of their racial origin. *See also* segregation.

intercontinental ballistic missile (ICBM) a missile capable of traveling from one continent to another, up to a maximum of over 9,000 miles, which is powered and steered for the first part of its flight.

international debt the debts owned by countries to other countries, either because of direct financial loans or because of an imbalance in trade. The term is especially applied to the large sums owed by developing countries to the developed world as a result of loans made in the Cold War period. Many debtor nations now find it difficult even to pay the interest on the loans.

International Monetary Fund an agency of the United Nations that uses its large financial reserves to help individual countries with problems caused by economic growth, unemployment, balance of payments, and debt.

Internet a worldwide electronic communications network that links computers and computer systems. The Internet has many commercial, academic, and recreational uses.

iron curtain a phrase coined by British prime minister Winston Churchill to describe the separation of western Europe from the Soviet bloc to the east.

Iroquois one of the main Native American language groups of northeastern America. The name also applies to a confederation of Iroquois-speaking tribes in the region.

Islam a major world religion, founded in the sixth and seventh centuries by the prophet Muhammad (c. 570–632). The followers of Islam, called Muslims, worship one god, Allah. Islam is split into two branches. Shia Islam is popular in Iran. Sunni Islam dominates the rest of the Islamic world.

isolationism a political policy of remaining separate from international affairs and the concerns of other nations. Isolationism has been a recurrent force in U.S. political history.

Jacobites supporters of the exiled Stuart kings of Britain who lost the throne in 1688. Jacobites took their name from the Latin for James, the name of both the exiled king and his son.

Jainism a minority South Asian religion that rejects Hindu ideas of caste and teaches total nonviolence.

Janissaries an elite military corps in the Ottoman Empire, recruited mainly from young Christians taken as tribute from their parents. Established in the 1300s, they were noted for their discipline but later became a threat to the sultan's authority and were outlawed in 1826.

Jazz Age a name coined by U.S. writer F. Scott Fitzgerald (1896–1940) to refer to the 1920s in the United States.

Jesuits members of a Roman Catholic religious order, the Society of Jesus. The Jesuits were notable for their missionary activities around the world and for their emphasis on education.

1335

jihad an Arabic word meaning "holy war" that refers to Islamic teachings about religious warfare against non-Muslims.

junta a Spanish word for a committee, usually applied to a small group, often of military officers, that seizes power in a country. Numerous Latin American countries were governed by juntas in the 1970s and 1980s.

kibbutz a communal farm or settlement in Israel.

Koran the holy book of Islam, containing the revelations of Allah to Muhammad.

kowtow in China, the act of kneeling and knocking one's head against the ground in a gesture of obedience to the emperor.

kremlin a Russian word for "fortress." The kremlin in Moscow dates from the late fifteenth century and includes several cathedrals and palaces.

Ku Klux Klan a secret society, founded in 1865 by former Confederate soldiers, that aimed to preserve white supremacy by violence. Forced underground in the 1870s, the Klan re-emerged in the early twentieth century. Its current membership is probably about 6,000.

kulak a Russian term for a farmer who owned land privately. In 1928, Stalin denounced kulaks as enemies of the revolution and launched a program of forced collectivization and violent persecution.

labor union a formal association of workers who combine to protect their own interests in matters such as pay and work conditions. Unions' strength lies in their collective power, as when a union calls a strike in which all its members stop work.

laissez-faire an influential economic theory developed by Adam Smith (1723–1790). Smith opposed tariffs and other government restraints on trade and argued that markets should be regulated by the forces of supply and demand, which would encourage efficiency and progress. Laissez-faire shaped orthodox economic thinking in the eighteenth and nineteenth centuries.

lateen sail a triangular sail used on Arab dhows and later on European caravels. It hangs from a sloping spar attached to the mast and allows great maneuverability.

Latin America the parts of the western hemisphere where Spanish or Portuguese is the official language, including South America, Central America, Mexico, and parts of the Caribbean.

latitude how far north or south a place is, measured from the equator.

League of Nations an international organization founded in 1919 to preserve peace. The league was weakened by the refusal of the United States to join and became discredited by its lack of authority. After World War II, it was replaced by the United Nations.

Lebensraum a German word, meaning "living space," used in the 1930s by Adolf Hitler to describe the territory he demanded from Germany's neighbors to provide space for German population growth and economic expansion.

lend-lease an arrangement adopted by the U.S. Congress in March, 1941, that allowed Britain, and later the USSR and China, to order war materials and food from the United States without having to pay for them until the end of the war.

Levellers a political group that arose in England during the Civil War. The Levellers wanted to declare a republic with equal rights for all citizens and religious tolerance.

liberalism a political philosophy valuing individual and economic freedom and equality that emerged in the eighteenth century in reaction to traditional privilege and oppressive government. Liberal thought was influential in establishing constitutional governments in Europe and America.

liberation theology a form of Catholicism that developed in Latin America in the 1970s and argued that priests should actively promote the welfare and political rights of the poor despite the church's traditional allies among landowners and conservative elements in society.

liberty bonds U.S. government bonds issued during World War I to help raise money to pay for the cost of the war.

longbow a large bow that is held vertically and shoots a long arrow. It was the main weapon of English armies in the fourteenth and fifteenth centuries. It had great range but required skill and practice to use.

longhouse a type of dwelling used by some Native American peoples. Longhouses were large, rectangular, and made of wood.

longitude how far east or west a place is, measured from an imaginary line around the earth that passes through Greenwich, England.

Lutheranism a major branch of Protestantism, based on the teachings of German theologian Martin Luther (1483–1546). Luther's protests against the Catholic Church triggered the Reformation. His chief doctrines concerned the authority of the Bible and salvation through faith, rather than through one's own moral efforts or good works.

Mahayana Buddhism *See* Buddhism.

Mamluks a group that emerged in the twelfth century as bodyguards to the sultans of Egypt. In 1250 they seized power. Rival Mamluk groups ruled Egypt until the Ottoman invasion in 1517 but retained great power until the nineteenth century.

mandates former colonies of Germany and the Ottoman Empire which, at the end of World War I, were placed under the mandate, or administration, of one of the Allies, under League of Nations supervision, with the goal of preparing them for self-government.

Manhattan Project the U.S. program that developed the atomic bomb during World War II. The project was led by U.S. physicist J. Robert Oppenheimer, and employed many European scientists who had fled from the Nazis. The project began in 1939 and culminated in the test of the first atom bomb at Alamogordo in New Mexico in July 1945.

manifest destiny the nineteenth-century belief that the United States had both a right and a duty to govern all of North America. Manifest destiny was an important spur for U.S. expansion across the continent to the Pacific coast.

Marxism a political theory based on the writings of Karl Marx and Friedrich Engels. Marxism analyses history and politics as a sequence of struggles between different classes to control the economic means of production. *See also* communism.

mendicant a member of a religious order of friars or monks that forbids ownership of any kind of property. Mendicants had to exist on alms and begging.

Mensheviks with the Bolsheviks, one of the two factions of the Russian Social Democratic Party. The Mensheviks wanted the party to be broad and open; they welcomed support from socialists of all kinds. *See also* Bolsheviks.

mercantilism an economic policy followed by many European countries in the sixteenth to eighteenth centuries that aimed to increase a nation's wealth by governmental economic regulation. Mercantile governments placed high tariffs on foreign imports, helped home industries, encouraged population growth to enlarge the labor force and the market for products, and tried to win colonies abroad as sources of raw materials and markets for exports. In the late eighteenth century, mercantilism gave way to laissez-faire policies.

mestizo/mestiza a Latin American man or woman of mixed European and Native American parentage.

Mfecane a Zulu word for "crushing" that refers to a period of violence and upheaval among the peoples of southern Africa between 1819 and 1838, caused by the expansion of the Zulu and their displacement of other peoples over a large area.

middle class *See* class, bourgeoisie.

militarism in politics, a belief that military interests should dominate government policies and national ideals, as in Japan in the period before World War II.

mixed economy a term that describes either an economy that includes both private and state-owned businesses or one that is partially subject to government planning and partly left to the free market forces of supply and demand. In practical usage, a mixed economy is one in which state and private ownership, government planning, and market forces all play a major role.

modernism an artistic and literary movement that flourished in the Western world from about 1910 to about 1950. In prose, poetry, painting, and music, modernism rejected traditional techniques and rules in favor of abstraction and disjunction.

monastery a building occupied by a community of monks who withdraw from the world to live according to rules of poverty and chastity, accompanied by regular praying and fasting.

Mongols a nomadic Asiatic people whose homeland is the area of modern Mongolia, to the north of China. In the thirteenth century, Genghis Khan united the Mongol tribes to conquer the largest land empire in history, stretching from far eastern Asia to eastern Europe.

Monroe Doctrine the principle, asserted in 1823 by U.S. president James Monroe, that the United States would oppose new European colonial ventures in the Americas and would not tolerate European interference in the affairs of independent American countries. The doctrine effectively proclaimed U.S. primacy in the Americas and is still used as a justification for U.S. activity elsewhere in the hemisphere.

monsoon a regular seasonal wind that brings heavy rains to India and southeast Asia. The reliability of the monsoon was a great aid to early navigators in the Indian Ocean.

Moors a name once given to Arabic-speaking Muslims of northwest Africa—modern Morocco, Algeria, Tunisia, and Mauretania. Moors and Arabs conquered Spain from 711 to 718 and created a Moorish kingdom noted for its architecture and culture.

Moral Majority a largely Baptist religious organization that emerged in the southern United States in the late 1970s to promote the moral regeneration of society through Christian fundamentalism and right-wing politics. The Moral Majority opposed abortion, feminism, and homosexual rights, and campaigned against pornography, crime, prostitution, and drug taking.

mosque a Muslim place of worship.

Muslim a follower of Islam.

multinational corporation a company that has operations in a number of countries around the world, often to take advantage of cheap labor, materials, or transport costs. Motor vehicle manufacturers, drug companies, and oil companies are typical examples. Multinationals often have a major impact on the economies of developing countries in which they operate.

mutual assured destruction (MAD) a term used to describe the nuclear stalemate between the United States and the USSR during the Cold War. Each power had so many strategic nuclear weapons that, if either attacked, the other would counterattack and both would be destroyed.

nabob a provincial governor in the Mogul empire in India.

Napoleonic Code the name of a collection of civil laws established in France in 1804, called in French the Code Civil. The code combined revolutionary ideals of liberty and equality with traditional principles such as property rights and had a major influence on legal systems in Europe and parts of North and South America.

nationalism a political belief in the right of a people bound by language, history, and culture to rule itself in its own nation or state. Nationalism was a major force in European and South American politics in the nineteenth century and in Asia and Africa in the twentieth.

nationalization the taking of an industry into state ownership, usually as part of a program to ensure that a country's major economic activities, such as railroads and utilities, are run for the benefit of the majority rather than for private profit.

nation-state the main political entity of the post-medieval world, replacing the earlier feudal system. A nation state is a country with clearly defined borders, a central government more powerful than any local or regional authorities, and a population that gives primary allegiance to the nation rather than to anything inside or outside it.

naturalism in art, a tradition that aims to reproduce as faithful a representation of the visible world as possible.

natural theology an eighteenth- and nineteenth-century approach to theology that sought to gather evidence for the existence of God from reason and

the study of nature, rather than from supernatural revelation.

neoclassicism a style of art popular in late-eighteenth-century Europe that adopted the subject matter and style of ancient Greece and Rome by imitating classical sculptures and other artefacts and stressing the perceived values of classical cultures.

neocolonialism a situation in which a country continues to dominate a former colony, usually for economic or geopolitical reasons, as in continued European economic influence in Africa and Asia after decolonization.

New Deal the name given to the program of reforms introduced by U.S. president Franklin D. Roosevelt to counter the effects of the Great Depression of the 1930s. The program represented an unprecedented level of government involvement in the American economy.

New World a name given to the Americas by sixteenth-century Europeans.

no-man's-land in the fixed trench warfare of World War I, the ground between the opposing trenches.

Northeast Passage a sea route that Europeans imagined must lie north of Russia, allowing them to reach the Indies without sailing around Africa.

Northwest Passage a much sought-after sea route that explorers imagined would lead from Europe to the Indies around the north of Canada.

oligarchy a form of government by a limited ruling elite based on wealth, hereditary status, ability, or membership of a group such as a civil service.

one-party state a country in which only one political party is allowed by law. Such countries include communist and fascist totalitarian states, but also some newly independent countries in Africa and Asia.

Order of the Golden Fleece an order of knighthood established by Philip the Good, duke of Burgundy, in 1429. It was revived in 1713 by Charles VI of Austria for use in Austria and Spain.

Orthodox Christianity the main form of Christianity in Greece, Russia, and other parts of eastern Europe and west-ern Asia. The Orthodox Church separated from Roman Catholicism because of longstanding differences in doctrine, especially concerning the authority of the pope.

Ottoman Empire a Muslim empire centered in Turkey that lasted from around 1300 to 1922. It was founded by the Ottoman Turks, nomads from central Asia.

outrigger a framework fixed to the side of a boat—also called an outrigger—to act as a stabilizer and prevent it from turning over. Outriggers are traditionally used in the southern Pacific and Indian Oceans.

Pacific Rim a geographic term for countries bordering on or located in the Pacific Ocean, used particularly in relation to the rapidly developing economies of Asia.

pagoda a multi-storied tower characteristic of east and southeast Asia, where they are usually associated with the Buddhist religion. Each storey has a roof that curves upwards at the edges.

pampas the plains of southern South America, especially in Argentina.

parish a district with its own church and priest, in the Catholic church and some Protestant churches. In some countries, such as England, it also acts as the smallest unit of local government.

parliament a representative assembly of a nation's people that comes together to advise the ruler or to act as a law-making body. In early modern countries, the parliament was dominated by the traditional nobility.

parliamentary democracy a democracy in which the legislature is a parliament elected by the general population and the government, or executive, is made up of members of parliament.

peninsulares Spaniards living in Spanish America but born in Spain.

peon a Native American agricultural laborer in the Spanish empire in America. Peons had no land of their own and were tied by debt to working for their master.

perestroika a Russian word meaning "restructuring" that refers to the program of political and economic reforms launched in the USSR by Mikhail Gorbachev after he became Soviet leader in 1985.

philosophes the French name given to a group of mainly French eighteenth-century thinkers, including Voltaire and Diderot, who espoused progress over tradition. The philosophes attempted to reevaluate old beliefs and practices through the tests of reason, experience, and usefulness.

plague a fatal disease that appeared on numerous occasions in early modern Europe, killing great numbers of people. The disease, which was carried by fleas, caused fever, headache, sores, and enlarged glands in the groin and armpit. The Black Death, a particularly severe plague epidemic, killed between one-third and one-half of Europe's population in the fourteenth century.

plantation a large agricultural estate, usually in the Americas or Asia, on which European planters used native or slave labor to grow crops such as sugar cane or tobacco. The word plantation was also sometimes used to mean a new settlement in a colony, as in Plymouth Plantation.

plantation economy a term referring to an economic system in which estates grow produce such as sugar cane or tobacco for large-scale export, using part of the profits to import staple produce such as wheat that the plantations do not grow.

pogrom a Yiddish word used to refer to an organized massacre, particularly massacres of Jews in Russia and Poland in the late nineteenth and early twentieth centuries.

Presbyterianism a Protestant movement in which churches are governed by a group of elders rather than by a minister or bishop.

privy council a body of close advisers appointed to help a monarch govern the country.

Prohibition the banning of alcohol in the United States from 1920 to 1933.

proletariat in Karl Marx's theory of communism, the lowest class of capitalist society, the industrial workers who have nothing to sell but their labor. Marx believed that the proletariat, driven by intolerable living conditions, would lead the revolution to overthrow capitalism.

protectionism an economic policy in which governments impose restrictions such as high duties on imported goods in order to protect their own industries or agriculture from foreign competition. Protectionism is fundamentally opposed to doctrines of laissez-faire and free trade.

protector a term often used to describe a person put in charge of a kingdom if the legitimate monarch was a child. The title Lord Protector was also given to Oliver Cromwell during the time of the English Commonwealth.

Protestantism a major form of Christianity founded in western Europe in the sixteenth century, when many Christians separated from Catholicism.

psychoanalysis an influential method of understanding the mind developed by the Austrian doctor Sigmund Freud (1856–1939). Freud emphasized the importance of the unconscious mind, which represses the early experiences that shape adult behavior.

pueblo a Spanish word for the flat-roofed, many-roomed dwellings built of stone or dried mud by some Native American groups in what is now the southwest of the United States. The word *pueblo* also refers to a village of such structures.

Puritanism a Protestant movement that emphasized Bible reading, preaching, and prayer, and rejected elaborate ceremonial. Puritanism was highly important in the New England colonies of North America.

Quakers a pacifist Protestant group, officially called the Society of Friends, which was founded in England in about 1650. The Quakers' refusal to acknowledge any political authority except the will of God earned them persecution from established governments and churches. The colony of Pennsylvania was founded as a Quaker refuge.

racism a system of treating people as inferior or undesirable because of their ethnic background and most often because of their different skin color. Racism may take the form of verbal abuse or physical violence or of discrimination in education, housing, work opportunities, and political and social rights.

radicalism any political philosophy that stresses the need for basic and immediate change in order to solve social issues, in contrast to moderate approaches that emphasize gradual reform.

raj the Hindu word for "reign," applied to the period of British imperial rule in India from 1858 to 1947.

realpolitik a German word describing a political approach, particularly in international affairs, that is based on realistic goals and immediate self-interest rather than ideology or idealism.

reconquista the Spanish word for "reconquest". It is the name given to the campaign against the Moors of Granada begun in 1481 by the Spanish rulers Ferdinand and Isabella. Granada was the last surviving Islamic kingdom on the Iberian peninsula, and it was finally overthrown in 1492.

red scare an occasion when a government in a noncommunist country, particularly the United States, tries to increase popular support by playing on fears of socialist plots.

reduktion the seventeenth-century recovery by the Swedish crown of land that had passed to the nobility.

referendum an often national vote on a single political issue, particulary those involving major constitutional change.

Reformation the religious movement in Europe in the sixteenth century that began as a reform movement within Roman Catholicism but led to the formation of separate Protestant churches.

Renaissance the name given to the flowering of European culture and thought in the fifteenth and sixteenth centuries. Taken from the French for "rebirth," the word *Renaissance* reflected contemporaries' belief that they were renewing the intellectual achievements of the classical Greeks and Romans.

reparations payments for war damage, usually inflicted on defeated powers by the victors, as in the fines imposed on Germany after World War I.

representative government a system in which government is carried on by representatives elected by a majority of voters.

republicanism the principle of having an elected or nominated head of state, rather than a hereditary ruler.

resistance movements underground organizations in occupied or nearly occupied countries that wage secret campaigns of sabotage or guerrilla warfare against the occupation forces and their collaborators.

revolution the usually violent overthrow of a political system by its own subjects, as in the French Revolution of 1789 and the Russian Revolution of 1917. Not all violent political changes are revolutions, however: rulers may be replaced without the political system changing. Historians sometimes use the word *revolution* to refer to great social or cultural changes, such as the Industrial Revolution.

rights politics a term describing a political approach that emphasizes the fight for civil and human rights for groups that suffer discrimination, such as black people, women, gay people, and others. More generally, much of the developing world has seen long battles for human rights against authoritarian or colonial regimes.

Risorgimento an Italian word for "resurgence." The risorgimento was the name given to the nineteenth-century movement for Italian unification and independence. It was also the title of a journal edited by Camillo di Cavour, one of the movement's leaders.

rococo a style of art and architecture popular in Europe from about 1700 to 1780. Drawing on the baroque tradition, the rococo was characterized by lavish ornamentation.

Roman Catholicism a major world religion and the form of Christianity with the largest number of followers. The Roman Catholic Church, which is led by the pope from Rome, was western Europe's only form of Christianity until the Reformation of the early sixteenth century.

romanticism an early-nineteenth-century artistic and literary movement that emphasized emotion, imagination, and freedom over the reason and order of the classical tradition. Romanticism also placed new emphasis on the appreciation of nature.

Rus a state centered in Kiev, in what is now Ukraine. It developed in the ninth

century, when adventurers from Scandinavia known as Varangians set up trading bases on rivers between the Baltic and the Black Sea, and established their rule over the local Slavs. In 980 Kiev Rus was conquered by Vladimir I, ruler of the city of Novgorod. He converted to Christianity and made Rus a significant European power. In 1240 Mongol tribes conquered much of Rus. Northern areas later fell to Lithuania and Poland.

Safavid the Shia Muslim dynasty that ruled Iran from 1501 to 1722.

salon a French term for a social gathering, often hosted by wealthy aristocrats, where a variety of talented people met to discuss art, literature, and ideas, to read, dine, listen to music, and play games.

salvation in the Roman Catholic Church, the deliverance from the consequences of sin and the attainment of eternal bliss after death.

samurai the name of a hereditary caste of Japanese feudal warriors who were bound to their lords by the code of bushido, which emphasized courage, honor, and loyalty.

sanitation the provision for the disposal of sewage and solid waste. The lack of sanitation in the fifteenth and sixteenth centuries was a serious health risk.

Sanskrit an ancient South Asian language that is the original language of many Hindu classical and religious works.

scalawags a derogatory Southern term for local whites who cooperated with Northerners and African Americans in the Reconstruction era after the U.S. Civil War to bring social reform and pass civil rights legislation. *See also* carpetbaggers.

schism a split or division into two opposed parties. The Great Schism in the Catholic Church occurred in 1378, when two opposing popes both claimed to be the spiritual head of the church: Urban VI in Rome and Clement VII in Avignon. The division remained until 1417 when Martin V was elected as sole pope.

Schmalkaldic League a league of eight German princes and eleven German cities formed in 1531 for the purpose of defending the Lutheran faith. The league was a response to the decree made by the Diet of Augsburg in 1530 that all Lutherans should recognize the supremacy of the pope.

scholasticism the system of thought that dominated Christian theology in the later Middle Ages, reaching its peak in the 13th century. It was partly a response to new translations of the ancient Greek philosopher, Aristotle.

scourging lashing or whipping as a punishment. Scourging, sometimes self inflicted, was a common punishment or penance in the Roman Catholic Church

scurvy a disease that used to be common among sailors. It was caused by a lack of vitamin C in the diet on long sea voyages.

secular belonging to the civil rather than the church authorities.

secularization the process of reducing the role of religion in politics and national life, either through the adoption of formal legislation but more often through a gradual and general decline in the influence of religion in daily life and the political establishment.

segregation a government or administrative policy of separating people from different ethnic backgrounds, especially in the provision of work, education, and public facilities such as transport and restrooms. The facilities provided for one ethnic group are seldom as good as those for another. Many states in the South were segregated until the civil rights campaigns of the 1960s.

sejm the parliament of Poland-Lithuania, which elected the king and and kept a close check on his actions. Members of the sejm were chosen by the nobility at local assemblies called *selmiki*.

self-determination the government of a territory by its own people rather than an outside power. *See also* nationalism.

serf in the feudal system, a peasant whose status lay between that of a free person and a slave. A serf could not leave his or her lord's land and had to work for and make payments to the lord. Serfs also possessed some rights, however, and held some land for their own use.

shah the title used by kings of Iran.

sharecropping a system of agricultural landholding in which tenant farmers give their landlords a share of the crops they grow rather than pay rent.

Shia a branch of Islam that is dominant in Iran. Shia separated from the Sunni majority over the question of the succession of political and religious authority following Muhammad's death in 632.

shogun in feudal times Japan's supreme military commander, the shogun had become by the fourteenth century the country's real ruler, rather than the emperor. The position was hereditary and passed through the Minamoto and Ashikaga families to the Tokugawa, who ruled from 1603 to 1867.

show trial one of numerous trials staged in the USSR from 1936 to 1938 in which potential opponents of Stalin were condemned for crimes they did not commit.

Slavs a group of peoples who spread through eastern and southeastern Europe between 200 and 600 C.E. In the tenth century, the Slavs split into three groups. The east Slavs became modern Russians, Byelorussians, and Ukrainians. The west Slavs became modern Poles, Czechs, and Slovaks. The south Slavs of the Balkan Peninsula became modern Croats, Serbs, Bulgarians, and Slovenes.

smallpox a highly contagious disease that spread to America with the early European explorers. Smallpox killed millions of Native Americans who had no natural resistance to the disease.

social contract a concept developed by the English political philosopher Thomas Hobbes who argued that human society was made possible by a social contract according to which individuals gave up a certain amount of freedom in exchange for the benefits of living in groups with other people. The idea was influential in the later evolution of the argument that government must be acceptable to the governed.

Social Darwinism an analysis of society and politics based on Charles Darwin's theory of evolution, which argues that natural selection creates superior and inferior individuals, races, or nations. The theory was used

to justify policies such as Europe's colonization of Africa in the late nineteenth century.

social democracy a political movement that seeks a gradual achievement of socialist goals through democratic processes. *See also* socialism.

socialism a political doctrine that aims to create a classless society by removing factories and businesses from private ownership for the good of all. Some socialists advocate state ownership, some local ownership, and some ownership by associations of workers. Although most socialists believe that the transition to socialism can be achieved through democratic processes, others argue that capitalism can only be ended by violent revolution.

sovereignty a country's formal political control over its own affairs and freedom from outside interference.

soviet a Russian word for a local council of workers, soldiers, sailors and other communists, championed by Lenin as a revolutionary alternative to parliamentary government. Later the word was also used for higher bodies elected by local soviets.

space race the name given to the intense competition between the United States and the Soviet Union to achieve breakthroughs in space exploration. The space race was given political urgency by the Cold War. The USSR took an early lead by launching the world's first artificial satellite in 1957 and putting Yuri Gagarin into orbit above the earth in 1959, but the United States achieved the goal of landing the first man on the moon in 1969.

Spice Islands a group of islands in Indonesia, now called the Moluccas. They were famous from medieval times as the source of spices, such as cloves and nutmeg, that were highly valued in Europe.

spice trade the importation into Europe of spices such as cloves and nutmeg. The most important source was the Spice Islands, the Moluccas of modern Indonesia.

square rigger a ship with rectangular sails that hang from horizontal spars attached to the masts.

stadtholder the military governor of a province of the Dutch Republic; in the

hands of the Orange family, the office of stadtholder became similar to that of a monarch.

Stamp Act an act passed by the British Parliament in March 1765 that aimed to raise money in the North American colonies by imposing a flat-rate tax on all legal documents and contracts as well as other printed materials. Opposition to the act, which the British repealed in 1766, led to an American declaration that no taxes could be imposed without consent and contributed to the outbreak of the American Revolutionary War.

star wars the term popularized by the media for the Strategic Defense Initiative (SDI) proposed by U.S. president Ronald Reagan in 1983. The program aimed to develop space-based weapons, such as lasers, to shoot down intercontinental ballistic missiles, thus undermining the nuclear stalemate that existed between the United States and the Soviet Union. SDI never came to fruition, largely because of its vast cost.

stock market the financial mechanism by which people buy shares in companies or government bonds as an investment, on the expectation that they will rise in value. The name also sometimes refers to the place where such transactions occur, also called the stock exchange, which in New York is in Wall Street.

strappado an instrument of torture by which a victim was bound and repeatedly raised above the ground and allowed to fall, wrenching his or her arms from their sockets. The strappado was used during the Inquisition.

Strategic Arms Limitation Treaty (SALT) a treaty signed between the United States and the USSR in 1972 that marked the first step toward reducing the nuclear arms race. The treaty limited each country to two defensive missile sites—later reduced to one site—with fewer than 100 antiballistic missiles at each. A further agreement limited the distribution of intercontinental nuclear weapons for five years. SALT II (1979) limited each side's long-range bombers and missiles, though it was never ratified by the U.S. Senate.

suffragettes women who campaigned in the early 1900s, particularly in Britain and the United States, for women's right to vote.

Sunni the majority branch of Islam, numbering about 85 percent of all Muslims.

sustainable growth a form of economic development that does not exhaust natural resources but instead is based on the exploitation of renewable resources.

swaraj the Hindu word for "self-government," used to describe the goal of independence from British rule adopted by the Indian National Congress in 1906. *See also* Indian National Congress.

symbolism a late-nineteenth-century literary movement promoted by French poets as a reaction against realism. Symbolism tried to convey emotions and ideas indirectly by the use of unexplained images.

Tamil a South Asian language that is spoken mainly in Tamil Nadu, a state in southeastern India, and on the island of Sri Lanka.

Taoism a Chinese philosophy founded in the sixth century B.C.E. that values simplicity, spontaneity, meditation, and closeness to nature.

Tatars a mainly Muslim people living in central and southern Russia and in neighboring areas such as Kazakhstan and Uzbekistan, as well as Romania, Turkey, and China. Originally Turkic-speaking nomads, the Tatars formed part of the Mongol invasions of the thirteenth century.

temperance movement a social movement popular in the late nineteenth century that advocated complete abstinence from alcohol. Temperance organizations encouraged adherents to take pledges to abstain from alcohol.

Terra Australis a Latin name meaning "southern land" that European explorers gave to an imaginary continent they thought might be discovered in the southern Pacific.

the Terror the name given to the most violent period of the French Revolution, in 1793 and 1794, when thousands of people were executed, usually by guillotine, for their perceived counterrevolutionary activities. Many victims of the Terror were themselves members of the original revolutionaries of 1789.

terrorism the use of often indiscriminate violence or the threat of violence to obtain political or religious ends through acts such as bombings, killings, kidnaps, and hijacks.

Teutonic Knights a group that developed in the twelfth century to organize German knights for the crusades. Later they set out to convert pagan areas of Europe to Christianity and conquered areas of what are now Poland, Lithuania, Latvia, and Estonia. They lost most of their power in the fourteenth century but controlled Latvia and Estonia for another 200 years.

Theravada Buddhism *See* Buddhism.

Third Reich German for "Third Empire," used by the Nazis to refer to Germany from 1933 to 1945. The two previous German empires were the Holy Roman Empire (800–1806) and the Hohenzollern empire (1871–1919).

tithes a donation or tax of a tenth on land or labor paid to a local church. In medieval times, tithes were the main source of income for Christian priests and their churches.

totalitarianism a system of government in which the state controls every aspect of life and suppresses all political opposition.

tozama Japanese nobles from families that opposed the Tokugawa clan in 1600 and were forced to accept lands in peripheral areas during the Tokugawa shogunate.

transcendentalism a philosophical movement that originated from the work of German philosopher Immanuel Kant (1724-1804), who argued that reality is not found through nature alone but through the workings of the mind. Later, the New England transcendentalists, such as Ralph Waldo Emerson (1803–1882), argued that the divine lies within nature and the human soul, and emphasized individual inspiration and self-reliance.

trusts alliances formed between businesses to force prices up and bring costs down. Several U.S. industries, such as oil and steel, formed such anticompetitive associations to avoid laws against trade monopolies. Trusts were outlawed by the Sherman Antitrust Act of 1890.

United Nations an international organization set up in 1945 to replace the League of Nations as a means of resolving international disputes and avoiding military conflict. The UN consists of a General Assembly of representatives of all member nations; a Security Council, which includes six elected and five permanent members (the United States, the United Kingdom, Russia, France, and China); and a Secretariat, which administers the organization and is headed by a secretary general. The UN includes the International Court of Justice and numerous agencies, including the World Bank, the International Monetary Fund, the World Health Organization, and UNESCO (the United Nations Educational, Scientific, and Cultural Organization).

urbanization the growth and development of towns and cities, and the movement of population to them from rural areas. In the developed world, urbanization has long been associated with industrialization and commerce.

usury nowadays this means charging interest on loans of money at a very high rate, but in medieval Christian theology any charging of interest on loans of money was defined as usury, and, therefore, sinful.

utopianism a belief that an ideal human society can be achieved in which everyone is happy, all needs are met, and all talents are given full play. The word comes from the title of Thomas More's 1516 book *Utopia*, which imagined such a place.

Uzbeks a group of nomadic Turkish tribes from central Asia.

vassal in the feudal system, a vassal was anyone who received something from a superior in return for service and loyalty. Peasants were vassals to their local lord, but lords were also vassals to greater lords, greater lords to their king, and even some kings to more powerful kings.

venality a willingness to be bribed or otherwise corrupted. Religious reformers often accused the Catholic clergy of venality.

Venetian belonging to Venice, an Italian city-state that was an important maritime power in the eastern Mediterranean, especially in the fourteenth and fifteenth centuries.

viceroy an official who rules a colony or region on behalf of a king.

viceroyalty a colony or region ruled by a viceroy on behalf of a king or queen.

villein a peasant in the feudal system who was partly a slave and partly free. A villein was tied to his or her lord but in other respects he or she had the rights of a free person.

welfare state a domestic policy by which a nation's central government takes responsibility for keeping its citizens healthy and free from poverty. Typical welfare state provisions include free health care, insurance against illness and unemployment, pensions for the old and those with families, housing schemes for those on low incomes, and free state education. The welfare state originated in Germany in the 1880s and 1890s and became common in western Europe after World War II.

witch trial the trial of someone accused of being a witch. The accused at witch trials were usually women whose alleged crimes included black magic and worshiping the devil.

women's rights a loose collection of civic rights aimed at overcoming the restrictions historically placed on women's involvement in education, work, and politics. The movement for women's rights emerged in the United States as part of the Christian revival of the 1830s and 1840s. The first women's rights convention was organized in 1848 by Lucretia Coffin Mott and Elizabeth Cady Stanton.

woodcut a picture or design printed from a block of wood (also the block itself). Sections of wood are cut away by the artist and what is left is coated with ink to produce the printed picture. Woodcuts began to be used as an artform in the 1400s. The woodcuts of Albrecht Dürer (1471–1528) are masterpieces of Western art.

workhouse a mainly nineteenth-century institution where the destitute performed menial or manual labor in return for food and lodging. Also known as poorhouses, workhouses provided the main form of poor relief in many countries. Conditions were frequently made harsh in order to discourage claimants.

working class the lowest class in industrial society. Members of this class work for wages and do some of the least prestigious jobs, such as manual work in industry or agriculture, operating checkouts in stores, or working in fast-food restaurants. *See also* proletariat.

Young Turks a group of nationalist Turkish officers that emerged in the 1890s and later deposed the Ottoman sultan.

zemsky sobor the "land assembly," a form of parliament in Russia made up of nobles and merchants. It usually had little power, however, in 1598 and 1613 it elected czars when there was no male heir. The 1613 election of Michael Romanov as czar founded the Romanov dynasty.

zemstvo one of a network of elected provincial assemblies created in czarist Russia after the 1861 emancipation of the serfs. Zemstvos were usually dominated by nobles whose attempts to improve local conditions often led to conflict with the central government.

Further Resources

General Works

Barraclough, G., et al (eds). *Times Atlas of World History*. Hammond, 1993.

Beckett, W. *Sister Wendy's Story of Painting*. London: DK Publishing, 1994.

Boorstin, D. J. *The Discoverers: A History of Man's Search to Know His World and Himself*. New York: Random House, 1985.

————. *The Creators: A History of Heroes of the Imagination*. New York: Vintage Books, 1993.

————. *The Seekers: The Story of Man's Continuing Quest to Understand His World*. New York: Random House, 1998.

Braudel, F. *A History of Civilizations*. New York: Penguin USA, 1995.

Brogan, H. *The Penguin History of the United States of America*. New York, Viking Press, 1991.

Colton, J., and Palmer, R. R. *A History of the Modern World*. New York: Knopf, 1995.

Davies, N. *Europe: A History*. New York: Oxford University Press, 1996.

Gombrich, E. *The Story of Art*. London: Phaidon Press Inc.

Grun, B. *The Timetables of History: A Horizontal Linkage of People and Events*. New York: Touchstone Books, 1991.

Keegan, J. *A History of Warfare*. New York: Vintage Books, 1994.

————. *The Face of Battle*. New York: Viking Press, 1995.

Kennedy, P. M. *The Rise and Fall of the Great Empires: Economic Change and Military Conflict from 1500 to 2000*. New York: Vintage Books, 1989.

Reader, J. *Africa: A Biography of a Continent*. New York: Knopf, 1998.

Roberts, J. M. M. *The Penguin History of the World*. New York: Penguin USA, 1995.

————. *A History of Europe*. London: Allen Lane, 1997.

Zeldin, T. *An Intimate History of Humanity*. New York: HarperPerennial Library, 1996.

Volume 1 Origins of the Modern World

Continuity and Change

Chambers, M., et al. *The Western Experience. Volume 1: To the Eighteenth Century*. New York: McGraw-Hill, 1995.

Detwiler, D. S. *Germany: A Short History*. Carbondale, IL: Southern Illinois University Press, 1976.

History of the Ancient and Medieval World, 12 vols. Tarrytown, NY: Marshall Cavendish Corporation, 1996.

Hollister, C. W. *Medieval Europe: A Short History*. New York: McGraw-Hill, 1998.

Jacobs, J., ed. *The Horizon Book of Great Cathedrals*. New York: American Heritage Publishing Co., 1968.

MacDonald, F. *The World in the Time of Leonardo Da Vinci*. Parsippany, NJ: Silver Burdett Press, 1998.

Palmer, R. R., and Colton, J. *A History of the Modern World to 1815*. New York: McGraw-Hill, 1995.

Pinkney, D. H., and De Sauvigny, G. B. *History of France*. Centreport, NY: The Forum Press, 1983.

Rice, E. F., and Grafton, A. *The Foundations of Early Modern Europe, 1460–1559*. New York: W. W. Norton & Co., 1994.

The World of Christendom

Collins, J. B. *The State in Early Modern France*. New York: Cambridge University Press, 1995.

Doran, S. *England and Europe in the Sixteenth Century*. New York: St. Martin's Press, 1999.

Eltis, D. *The Military Revolution of Sixteenth-Century Europe*. London: IB Tauris & Co., 1995.

Merrick, J. *Early Modern European History: Renaissance to 1789*. New York: Markus Wiener Publishing, 1988.

Smith, A. G. R. *The Emergence of a Nation State: The Commonwealth of England, 1529–1660*. Reading, MA: Addison Wesley Publishing Company, 1997.

Strayer, J. R. *On the Medieval Origins of the Modern State*. Princeton, NJ: Princeton University Press, 1973.

Population and Agriculture

Gunst, P. *Agrarian Development and Social Change in Eastern Europe*. Brookfield, VT: Variorum, 1996.

Herlihy, D. *The Black Death and the Transformation of Europe*. Cambridge, MA: Harvard University Press, 1997.

Platt, C. *King Death: The Black Death and its Aftermath in Late Medieval England*. Toronto, Ontario: University of Toronto Press, 1996.

Schmal, H. *Patterns of European Urbanisation Since 1500*. London: Routledge Kegan & Paul, 1981.

Sweeney, D., ed. *Agriculture in the Middle Ages: Technology, Practice, and Representation*. Philadelphia, PA: University of Pennsylvania Press, 1995.

Ziegler, P. *The Black Death*. New York: HarperCollins, 1971.

Trade and Wealth

Braudel, F. *Capitalism and Material Life, 1400–1800*. Fontana 1974.

————. *Civilization and Capitalism, 15th–18th Century. Vol 1: The Structures of Everyday Life*. Berkeley, CA: University of California Press, 1992.

————. *Civilization and Capitalism, 15th–18th Century. Vol 2: The Wheels of Commerce*. Berkeley, CA: University of California Press, 1992.

————. *Civilization and Capitalism, 15th–18th Century. Vol 3: The Perspective of the World*. Berkeley, CA: University of California Press, 1992.

Jardine, L. *Worldly Goods: A New History of the Renaissance*. London: Papermac, 1996.

Kamen, H. *European Society, 1500–1700*. New York: Unwin Hyman, 1984.

Scholasticism and the Universities

Giuberti, F. *Materials for a Study on Twelfth Century Scholasticism*. Amherst, NY: Prometheus Books, 1982.

Langholm, O. I. *The Legacy of Scholasticism in Economic Thought: Antecedents of Choice and Power*. New York: Cambridge University Press, 1998.

Pedersen, O. *The First Universities: Studium Generale and the Origins of University Education in Europe*. New York: Cambridge University Press, 1998.

Plott, J. *Global History of Philosophy: The Period of Scholasticism*. South Asia Books, 1990.

Southern, R. W. *Scholastic Humanism and the Unification of Europe: Foundations*. Malden, MA: Blackwell Publishing, 1995.

Humanism and the Spread of Knowledge

Cassirer, E., ed. *Renaissance Philosophy of Man*. Chicago, IL: University of Chicago Press, 1956.

Demolen, R., ed. *Erasmus of Rotterdam: A Quincentennial Symposium*. New York: Irvington Publishing, 1971.

Gilmore, M. P. *The World of Humanism, 1453–1517*. Westport, CT: Greenwood Publishing Group, 1983.

Hale, J. *Machiavelli and Renaissance Italy*. New York: Macmillan Inc., 1960.

Kristeller, P. O. *Renaissance Thought and the Arts: Collected Essays*. Princeton, NJ: Princeton University Press, 1990.

Olin, J., ed. *Christian Humanism and the Reformation: Selected Writings of Erasmus*. New York: Fordham University Press, 1987.

Social Structures

Black, M. *Feudal Society: Social Classes and Political Organization*. Chicago, IL: University of Chicago Press, 1982.

Duby, G. *The Knight, the Lady, and the Priest: The Making of Modern Marriage in Medieval France*. Chicago, IL: University of Chicago Press, 1994.

Gies, F. *Marriage and the Family in the Middle Ages*. New York: HarperCollins, 1989.

Stone, L. *Family, Sex, and Marriage in England, 1500–1800*. New York: HarperCollins, 1986.

Van Os, H. *The Art of Devotion in the Late Middle Ages in Europe*. Princeton, NJ: Princeton University Press, 1995.

Vauchez, A. *The Laity in the Middle Ages: Religious Beliefs and Devotional Practices*. Notre Dame, IN: University of Notre Dame Press, 1997.

The Renaissance and the Arts

Burckhardt, J. *The Civilization of the Renaissance in Italy*. New York: Penguin U.S.A., 1990.

Kerrigan, W., and Brach, G. *The Idea of the Renaissance*. Baltimore MD: John Hopkins University Press, 1991.

Hartt, F., ed. *History of Italian Renaissance Art*, 4th ed. New York: Harry N. Abrams Publishing, 1994.

Murray, L. L. *The High Renaissance and Mannerism: Italy, the North, and Spain, 1500–1600*. New York: Thames and Hudson, 1985.

Murray, P. *The Architecture of the Italian Renaissance*. New York: Schocken Books, 1997.

Murray, P., and Murray, L. L. *Art of the Renaissance*. New York: Thames and Hudson, 1985.

Pope-Hennessy, J. *Italian Renaissance Sculpture, Vol 1*. New York: Random House, 1986.

The Margins of Europe

Crummey, R. O. *The Formation of Muscovy, 1304–1613*. Reading, MA: Addison Wesley Publishing Company, 1987.

Davis, N. *Heart of Europe: A Short History of Poland*. New York: Oxford University Press, 1986.

Dmytryshyn, B., ed. *Medieval Russia: A Source Book, 850–1700*. Austin, TX: Holt Rinehart & Winston, 1997.

Martin, J. *Medieval Russia, 980–1584*. New York: Cambridge University Press, 1996.

Rowell, S. C. *Lithuania Ascending: A Pagan Empire Within East-Central Europe, 1295–1345*. New York: Cambridge University Press, 1994.

The Ottoman Turks

Goodwin, J. *Lords of the Horizon: A History of the Ottoman Empire*. New York: Henry Holt & Co., 1999.

Inalck, H., ed. *An Economic and Social History of the Ottoman Empire, 1300–1914*. New York: Cambridge University Press, 1995.

Itzkowitz, N. *Ottoman Empire and Islamic Tradition*. Chicago, IL: University of Chicago Press, 1980.

Lord Kinross. *Ottoman Centuries: The Rise and Fall of the Turkish Empire*. New York: William Morrow & Co., 1988.

Lewis, B. *Istanbul and the Civilization of the Ottoman Empire*. Norman, OK: University of Oklahoma Press, 1989.

Kafador, C. *Between Two Worlds: The Construction of the Ottoman State*. Berkeley, CA: University of California Press, 1995.

Woodhead, C., ed. *Süleyman the Magnificent and His Age: The Ottoman Empire in the Early Modern World*. Reading, MA: Addison Wesley Publishing Company, 1995.

Developments in Africa

Diamond, J. *Guns, Germs, and Steel: The Fates of Human Societies*. New York: W. W. Norton & Co., 1998.

Diop, C. A. *Precolonial Black Africa: A Comparative Study of the Political and Social Systems of Europe and Black Africa*. Lawrenceville, NJ: Red Sea Press, 1990.

Isichei, E. *Africa Before 1800*. London: Longman Group UK, 1984.

Kostow, P., and King, M. L., Jr. *Centuries of Greatness: The West African Kingdoms, 750–1900*. Broomall, PA: Chelsea House Publishing, 1995.

Niame, D. T., ed. *Africa from the Twelfth to the Sixteenth Century*. Berkeley, CA: University of California Press, 1986.

Vogel, J. and Vogel, J. O. *Encyclopaedia of Precolonial Africa: Archaeology, History, Languages, Cultures and Environments*. London: Altamira Press, 1997.

Developments in Asia

Hansen, V. *Changing Gods in Medieval China*. Princeton, NJ: Princeton University Press, 1990.

Hymes, R. P., ed. *Ordering the World: Approaches to State and Society in Sung Dynasty China*. Berkeley, CA: University of California Press, 1993.

Martell, H. *Imperial China, 221 B.C. to A.D. 1294*. Austin, TX: Raintree/Steck Vaughn, 1998.

Shiba, Y. *Commerce and Society in Sung China*. Ann Arbor, Michigan: Center for Chinese Studies, 1970.

Volume 2 Religion and Change in Europe

Religious Protest

Bainton, R. H. *The Reformation of the Sixteenth Century*. Boston, MA: Beacon Press, 1985.

———. *Age of the Reformation*. Melbourne, FL: Krieger Publishing Company, 1983.

Hillebrand, H., ed. *Protestant Reformation*. New York: HarperCollins, 1984.

Kittelson, J. M. *Luther the Reformer*. Minneapolis, MN: Augsburg Fortress Publications, 1987.

Lohse, B. *Martin Luther: An Introduction to his Life and Work*. Minneapolis, MN: Fortress Press, 1986.

Pettegree, A., ed. *The Early Reformation in Europe*. New York: Cambridge University Press, 1993.

Catholic Reform

Bossy, J. *Peace in the Post-Reformation*. New York: Cambridge University Press, 1998.

DeMolen, R. L., ed. *Religious Orders of the Catholic Reformation: In Honor of John C. Olin on His Seventy-Fifth Birthday*. New York: Fordham University Press, 1994.

Hsia, R. *The World of Catholic Renewal, 1540–1770*. New York: Cambridge University Press, 1998.

Jones, M. *The Counter Reformation: Religion and Society in Early Modern Europe*. New York: Cambridge University Press, 1996.

Kidd, B. *The Counter Reformation, 1550–1600*. Westport, CT: Greenwood Publishing Group, 1980.

Lindberg, C. *The European Reformations*. Malden, MA: Blackwell Publishing, 1996.

Mullett, M. *Counter Reformation*. New York: Routledge, 1984.

Olin, J., ed. *The Catholic Reformation: Savonarola to Ignatius Loyola*. New York: Fordham University Press, 1993.

O'Malley, J. *The First Jesuits*. Cambridge, MA: Harvard University Press, 1993.

Outram Evennett, H. *The Spirit of the Counter-Reformation*. Notre Dame, IN: University of Notre Dame Press, 1986.

Dissent and Control

Hansen, C. *Witchcraft at Salem*. New York: George Braziller, 1985.

Kamen, H. A. F. *The Spanish Inquisition: A Historical Revision*. New Haven, CT: Yale University Press, 1998.

Peters, E. *Inquisition*. Berkeley, CA: University of Calilfornia Press, 1989.

———. *Torture*. Philadelphia, PA: University of Pennsylvania Press, 1996.

Roth, C. *Spanish Inquisition*. London: W.W. Norton & Co., 1996.

Sharpe, J. *Instruments of Darkness: Witchcraft in Early Modern England*. Philadelphia, PA: University of Pennsylvania Press, 1997.

Spain and the Habsburg Empire

Berenger, J., and Simpson, C. A. *History of the Habsburg Empire, 1273–1700*. Reading, MA: Addison Wesley Publishing Company, 1994.

Ingrao, C. W. *The Habsburg Monarchy, 1618–1815*. New York: Cambridge University Press, 1994.

———. *State and Society in Early Modern Austria*. West Lafayette, IN: Purdue University Press, 1994.

Kann, R. A. *A History of the Habsburg Empire, 1526–1918*. Berkeley, CA: University of California Press, 1980.

Lovett, A. W. *Early Habsburg Spain, 1517–1598*. New York: Oxford University Press, 1986.

Mamatey, V. S. *Rise of the Habsburg Empire, 1526–1815*. Melbourne, FL: Krieger Publishing Company, 1978.

The Wars of Religion

Hale, J. R. *War and Society in Renaissance Europe, 1450–1620*. Montreal: McGill Queens University Press, 1998.

Holt, M. P. *The French Wars of Religion, 1562–1629*. New York: Cambridge University Press, 1996.

Knecht, J. R. and Segun, M. *The French Wars of Religion, 1559–1598*. Reading, MA: Addison Wesley Publishing Company, 1996.

Sproxton, J. *Violence and Religion: Attitudes Towards Militancy in the French Civil Wars and the English Revolution*. New York: Routledge, 1995.

Wood, J. B. *The King's Army: Warfare, Soldiers, and Society During the Wars of Religion in France, 1562–1576*. New York: Cambridge University Press, 1996.

Tudor England

Doran, S. *England and Europe in the Sixteenth Century*. New York: St. Martin's Press, 1999.

Elton, G. R. *England Under the Tudors*. New York: Routledge, 1991.

Harrison, W. *The Description of England: The Classic Contemporary Account of Tudor Social Life*. Mineola, NY: Dover Publications, 1995.

Palliser, D. M. *The Age of Elizabeth: England Under the Later Tudors, 1547–1603*. Reading, MA: Addison Wesley Publishing Company, 1992.

Weir, A. *Life of Elizabeth I*. New York: Ballantine Books, 1998.

Williams, P. *The Later Tudors: England, 1547–1603 (New Oxford History of England)* Oxford: Clarendon Press, 1995.

The Revolt of the Netherlands

Duke, A. *Reformation and Revolt in the Low Countries*. Rio Grande, OH: Hambledon Press, 1990.

Limm, P. *The Dutch Revolt, 1559–1648*. Reading, MA: Addison Wesley Publishing Company, 1995.

Schama, S. *The Embarrassment of Riches: An Interpretation of Dutch Culture in the Golden Age*. New York: Knopf, 1987.

Van Gelderen, M. *The Political Thought of the Dutch Revolt, 1555–1590*. New York: Cambridge University Press, 1993.

The Thirty Years' War

Asch, R. G. *The Thirty Years' War: The Holy Roman Empire and Europe, 1618–48*. New York: St. Martin's Press, 1997.

Limm, P. *The Thirty Years' War*. Reading, MA: Addison Wesley Publishing Company, 1984.

Parker, G. *The Military Revolution*. New York: Cambridge University Press, 1996.

Parker, G., & Adams, S., eds. *The Thirty Years' War*. London: Routledge Kegan & Paul, 1997.

Rabb, T. *The Thirty Years' War*. Lanham, MD: University Press of America, 1982.

England's Civil War

Ashley, M. P. *The English Civil War*. New York: St. Martin's Press, 1997.

Bennett, M. *The Civil Wars in Britain and Ireland, 1638–1651*. Malden, MA: Blackwell Publishing, 1996.

Carlin, N. *The Causes of the English Civil War*. Malden, MA: Blackwell Publishing, 1998.

Emberton, W., and Adair, J. *The English Civil War Day by Day*. Stroud, UK: Sutton Publishing, 1997.

Gaunt, P. *The British Wars, 1637–1651*. New York: Routledge, 1997.

Hill, C. *World Turned Upside Down: Radical Ideas During the English Revolution*. New York: Viking Press, 1991.

Hughes, A. *The Causes of the English Civil War*. New York: St. Martin's Press, 1999.

Kenyon, J. P., ed. *The Civil Wars: A Military History of England, Scotland & Ireland, 1638–1660*. New York: Oxford University Press, 1998.

Everyday Life in Europe

Burt, R. *Enclosure Acts: Sexuality, Property, and Culture in Early Modern England*. Ithaca, NY: Cornell University Press, 1994.

Davis, N. Z. *Women on the Margins: Three Seventeenth Century Lives*. Stanford, CA: Stanford University Press, 1977.

Hill, C. *Liberty Against the Law: Some Seventeenth Century Controversies*. London: Allen Lane, 1996.

Mingay, G. *Parliamentary Enclosure in England: An Introduction to Its Causes, Incidence, and Impact, 1750–1850*. Reading, MA: Addison Wesley Publishing Company, 1998.

Neeson, J. M. *Commoners: Common Right, Enclosure, and Social Change in England, 1700–1820*. New York: Cambridge University Press, 1996.

Slater, M. *Family Life in the Seventeenth Century: The Veneys of Claydon House.* New York: Routledge, Kegan & Paul, 1984.

The Baroque World

Baroque Painting. Hauppauge, NY: Barron's Educational Series, 1998.

Collaway, S. *Baroque Baroque: The Culture of Excess.* London: Phaidon Press Inc., 1994.

Finaldi, G., and Kitson, M. *Discovering the Italian Baroque: The Denis Mahon Collection.* New Haven, CT: Yale University Press, 1997.

Gruber, A., ed. *Classicism and the Baroque in Europe.* New York: Abbeville Press, 1996.

Sadie, J. A. *Companion to Baroque Music.* Berkeley, CA: University of California Press, 1998.

Summerson, J. N. *The Architecture of the Eighteenth Century.* New York: Thames and Hudson, 1986.

Toman, R., ed. *The Baroque.* Konemann, 1998.

The Scientific Revolution

Boorstin, D. J. *The Discoverers.* New York: Random House, 1983.

Fantoli, A. *Galileo: For Copernicanism and for the Church.* Notre Dame, IN: University of Notre Dame Press, 1996.

Koyre, A. *Astronomical Revolution: Copernicus–Kepler–Barelli.* Mineola, NY: Dover Publications, 1992.

Kuhn, T. S. *The Structure of Scientific Revolutions.* Chicago, IL: University of Chicago Press, 1996.

Newhouse, E. L., ed. *Inventors and Discoverers: Changing Our World.* Washington, D.C.: National Geographic Society, 1994.

Wright, R. *Scientific Romance.* London: Picador, 1999.

Volume 3 Old and New Worlds

Europe Looks Outward

Corn, C. *The Scents of Eden: A Narrative of the Spice Trade.* New York: Kodansha, 1998.

Doran, S. *England and Europe in the Sixteenth Century.* New York: St. Martin's Press, 1999.

Koenigsberger, H., et al. *Europe in the Sixteenth Century.* London: Longman Group U.K., 1990.

Mackenney, R. *Sixteenth Century Europe: Expansion and Conflict.* New York: St. Martin's Press, 1993.

Morris, T. A. *Europe and England in the Sixteenth Century.* New York: Routledge, 1998.

Mosse, G. L. *Europe in the Sixteenth Century.* Reading, MA: Addison Wesley Publishing Co. 1989.

Voyages and Encounters

Clendennen, I. *Ambivalent Conquests, Maya and Spaniard in Yucatan, 1515–70.* New York: Cambridge University Press, 1989.

Morison, S. E. *Admiral of the Ocean Sea: A Life of Christopher Columbus.* Boston, MA: Little, Brown & Co., 1991.

———. *The European Discovery of America: The Southern Voyages, 1492–1616.* New York: Oxford University Press, 1974.

Stefoff, R. *Ferdinand Magellan and the Discovery of the World Ocean.* Broomall, PA: Chelsea House Publishing, 1990.

Williams, G. *The Great South Sea: English Voyages and Encounters, 1570–1750.* New Haven, CT: Yale University Press, 1998.

Southeast Asia

A Past Regained. Alexandria, VA: Time-Life Books, 1995.

Chandler, D. P. *A History of Cambodia.* Boulder, CO: Westview Press, 1996.

Miksic, J. N., et al. *Indonesian Heritage.* Vol. 1. Singapore: Didier Millet, 1996.

———. *Indonesian Heritage.* Vol. 6. Singapore: Didier Millet, 1998.

Reat, R. *Buddhism: A History.* Freemont, CA: Jain Publishing Company, 1996.

Zephir, T. *Khmer: The Lost Empire of Cambodia.* New York: Harry N. Abrams, 1998.

Europe in Asia

Daum, P. *Ups and Downs of Life in the Indies.* Amherst, MA: University of Massachusetts Press, 1987.

de Figueroa, M. *Spaniard in the Portuguese Indies: The Narrative of Martin Fernandez de Figueroa.* Cambridge, MA: Harvard University Press, 1967.

Lach, D. *Asia in the Making of Europe: A Century of Advance.* Chicago, IL: University of Chicago Press, 1998.

Vlekke, B. H. M. *The Story of the Dutch East Indies.* New York: AMS Press, 1973.

The North American World

Hoxie, F. E. *Encyclopedia of North American Indians.* Boston, MA: Houghton Mifflin Co., 1996.

Josephy, A. M., ed. *America in 1492: The World of the Indian Peoples Before the Arrival of Columbus.* New York: Vintage Books, 1993.

———. *500 Nations: An Illustrated History of North American Indians.* New York: Knopf, 1998.

Nabokov, P., and Easton, R. *Native American Architecture.* New York: Oxford University Press, 1989.

Trigger, B. G., and Washburn, W.E. *The Cambridge History of the Native Peoples of the Americas.* New York: Cambridge University Press, 1996.

Waldman, C., and Braun, M. *Atlas of the North American Indian.* New York: Facts on File, Inc., 1995.

Spanish America

Del Castillo, B. D. *The Discovery and Conquest of Mexico, 1517–1521.* New York: Da Capo Press, 1996.

Helps, Arthur. *The Spanish Conquest in America.* New York: AMS Press, 1972.

Leonard, I. A. *Books of the Brave: Being an Account of Books and of Men in the Spanish Conquest and Settlement of the Sixteenth Century New World.* Berkeley, CA: University of California Press, 1992.

Lockhart, J., and Schwartz, S. B. *Early Latin America: A History of Colonial Spanish America and Brazil.* New York: Cambridge University Press, 1983.

Taylor, W. B., ed. *Colonial Spanish America: A Documentary History.* Wilmington, DE: Scholarly Resources, 1998.

Thomas, H. *Conquest: Montezuma, Cortés, and the Fall of Old Mexico.* New York: Touchstone Books, 1995.

Settling North America

Brachen, J. M. *Life in the American Colonies: Daily Lifestyles of the Early Settlers.* Carlisle, MA: Discovery Enterprises Ltd., 1997.

Friedenberg, P. M. *Life, Liberty and the Pursuit of Land: The Plunder of Early America.* Amherst, NY: Prometheus Books, 1992.

Hawke, D. F. *Everyday Life in Early America.* New York: HarperCollins Juvenile Books, 1989.

Starr-Lebeau, G. D., ed. *American Eras: Early American Civilizations and Exploration to 1600*. Detroit, MI: Gale Research, 1998.

The Immigrant Experience
Breen, T. H. *Puritans and Adventurers: Change and Persistence in Early America*. New York: Oxford University Press, 1982.
Doherty, K. *Puritans, Pilgrims, and Merchants: Founders of the Northeastern Colonies*. Minneapolis, MN: Oliver Press, 1998.
Nash, G. B. *Red, White and Black: The Peoples of Early North America*. New York: Prentice Hall, 1991.
Vaughan, A. T., ed. *The Puritan Tradition in America, 1620–1730*. Hanover, NE: University Press of New England, 1997.
Waller, G. M. *Puritanism in Early America*. D.C. Heath & Co., 1973.

Slavery in the New World
Blackburn, R. *The Making of New World Slavery: From the Baroque to the Modern, 1492–1800*. New York: Verso Books, 1997.
Bourne, G. *Picture of Slavery in the United States of America*. St. Claire Shores, MI: Scholarly Press, 1972.
Davis, D. B. *The Problem of Slavery in Western Culture*. New York: Oxford University Press, 1988.
Koslow, P. *Building a New World: Africans in America, 1500–1900*. Broomall, PA: Chelsea House Publishing, 1997.
Piersen, W. D. *From Africa to America: African American History from the Colonial Era to the Early Republic, 1526-1790*. New York: Twayne Publishing, 1996.
Thomas, H. *The Slave Trade: The Story of the Atlantic Slave Trade, 1440-1870*. New York: Touchstone Books, 1999.

The Safavid Empire
Melville, C. P., ed. *Safavid Persia: The History and Politics of an Islamic Society*. London: IB Tauris & Co., 1996.
Jackson, P., ed. *The Cambridge History of Iran: The Timurid and Safavid Periods*. New York: Cambridge University Press, 1993.
Ghougassian, V. S. *The Emergence of the Armenian Diocese of New Julfa in the Seventeenth Century*. Atlanta: Scholars Press, 1998.
Matthee, R. P. *The Politics of Trade in Safavid Iran: Silk for Silver*. New York: Cambridge University Press, 1999.
Melville, C., ed. *Safavid Persia: The History and Politics of an Islamic Society*. London: IB Tauris & Co., 1996.

Mogul India
Berinstain, V. *India and the Mughal Dynasty*. New York: Harry N. Abrams, 1998.
Edwardes, H. L. *Mughal Rule in India*. New York: AMS Press, 1930.
Ganeri, A. *India Under the Mughal Empire*. Austin, TX: Raintree/Steck Vaughn, 1998.
Hintze, A. *The Mughal Empire and Its Decline: An Interpretation of the Sources of Social Power*. Brookfield, VT: Variorum, 1998.
Richards, J. F. *The Mughal Empire (The New Cambridge History of India)*. New York: Cambridge University Press, 1993.
———. *Power, Administration and Finance in Mughal India*. Brookfield, VT: Ashgate Publishing Company, 1993.
Spear, T. G. P. *Twighlight of the Mughals*. New York: Oxford University Press, 1982.

Volume 4 The Age of the Enlightenment

Protestant Northern Europe
Bowen, M. *For God and the King*. Inheritance Publications, 1995.
Derry, T. K. *A History of Scandinavia: Norway, Sweden, Denmark, Finland, and Iceland*. Minneapolis, MN: University of Minnesota Press, 1980.
Hempton, D. *Religion and Political Culture in Britain and Ireland: From the Glorious Revolution to the Decline of Empire*. New York: Cambridge University Press, 1996.
Jacob, M. C., ed. *The Dutch Republic in the Eighteenth Century: Decline, Enlightenment and Revolution*. Ithaca, NY: Cornell University Press, 1992.
Miller, J. *The Glorious Revolution*. Reading, MA: Addison Wesley Publishing Co., 1998.
Szechi, D. *The Jacobites, Britain and Europe, 1688–1788*. Manchester: Manchester University Press, 1994.

Absolutism
Barnes, T. *Renaissance, Reformation and Absolutism, 1400–1660*. Lanham, MD: University Press of America, 1979.
Beik, W. *Absolutism and Society in Seventeenth Century France: State Power and Provincial Aristocracy in Languedoc*. New York: Cambridge University Press, 1989.
Birce, Y. M. *The Birth of Absolutism: A History of France, 1598–1661*. New York: St. Martin's Press, 1996.
Birn, R. *Crisis, Absolutism, Revolution: Europe, 1648–1789*. HBH College & School Div., 1997.
Henshall, N. *The Myth of Absolutism: Change and Continuity in Early Modern European Monarchy*. Reading, MA: Addison Wesley Publishing Co., 1992.
Miller, J. *Absolutism in Seventeenth Century Europe*. New York: St. Martin's Press, 1990.

Europe's Dynastic Wars
Anderson, M. S. *The War of the Austrian Succession, 1740–1748*. Reading, MA: Addison Wesley Publishing Company, 1995.
Boles, L. H., Jr. *The Hugenots, the Protestant Interest and the War of the Spanish Succession, 1702–1714*. Peter Lang Publishing, 1997.
Browning, R. *The War of the Austrian Succession*. New York: St. Martin's Press, 1995.
Chandler, D., ed. *Military Memoirs of Marlborough's Campaigns, 1702–1712*. Mechanicsburg, PA: Stackpole Books, 1998.
Parker, G. *The Military Revolution*. New York: Cambridge University Press, 1996.

The Enlightenment
Berlin, I., ed. *Age of Enlightenment: The Eighteenth Century Philosophers*. New American Library, 1993.
Gay, P. *The Enlightenment: An Interpretation: The Science of Freedom*. London: W. W. Norton & Co., 1996.
———. *The Enlightenment: The Rise of Modern Paganism*. London: W. W. Norton & Co., 1995.
Hampson, N. *The Enlightenment*. London: Penguin Books, 1990.
Outram, D. *The Enlightenment*. New York: Cambridge University Press, 1995.
Reill, P. H., and Wilson, E. J. *Encyclopedia of the Enlightenment*. New York: Facts on File, 1996.
Saisselin, R. G. *The Enlightenment Against the Baroque: Economics and Aesthetics in the Eighteenth Century*. Berkeley, CA: University of California Press, 1992.

Yolton, J. W., Stafford, B. M. and Rogers, P,. eds. *The Blackwell Companion to the Enlightenment.* Malden, MA: Blackwell Publishing, 1995.

Central and Eastern Europe
De Madariaga, I. *Politics and Culture in Eighteenth Century Russia.* Reading, MA: Addison Wesley Publishing Co., 1998.
Gawthrop, R. L. *Pietism and the Making of Eighteenth Century Prussia.* New York: Cambridge University Press, 1993.
Kahan, A., et al. *The Plow, the Hammer, and the Knout: An Economic History of Eighteenth Century Russia.* Chicago, IL: University of Chicago Press, 1985.
Komlos, J. *Nutrition and Economic Development in the Eighteenth Century Habsburg Monarchy.* Princeton, NJ: Princeton University Press, 1990.
Marczali, H. *Hungary in the Eighteenth Century.* North Stratford, NH: Ayer Publishing Company, 1970.
Scott, H. M., ed. *The European Nobilities in the Seventeenth and Eighteenth Centuries: Northern, Central, and Eastern Europe.* Reading, MA: Addison Wesley Publishing Co., 1995.

The Rococo and Classical World
Bazin, G. *Baroque and Rococo.* New York: Thames & Hudson, 1985.
Levey, M. *Rococo to Revolution: Major Trends in Eighteenth Century Painting.* New York: Thames & Hudson, 1985.
Millon, H. A. *Baroque and Rococo Architecture.* New York: George Braziller, 1961.
Pouget, J. H. P. *550 Authentic Rococo Designs and Motifs for Artists and Craftspeople.* Mineola, NY: Dover Publications, 1994.
Woods, M. *Visions of Arcadia: European Gardens from Renaissance to Rococo.* London: Aurum Press, 1996.

Life in Eighteenth-Century Europe
Black, J. *Eighteenth-Century Europe, 1700–1789.* New York: Macmillan Press, 1990.
Becker, M. B. *The Emergence of Civil Society in the Eighteenth Century: A Privileged Moment in the History of England, Scotland, and France.* Bloomington, IN: Indiana University Press, 1994.
De Vries, J. *European Urbanization, 1500–1800.* Cambridge, MA: Harvard University Press, 1984.
Fubini, E. *Music and Culture in Eighteenth-Century Europe: A Source Book.* Chicago, IL: University of Chicago Press, 1994.
Rude, G. *Europe in the Eighteenth Century: Aristocracy and the Bourgeois Challenge.* Cambridge, MA: Harvard University Press, 1985.
Woloch, I. *Eighteenth-Century Europe: Tradition and Progress, 1715–1789.* London: W. W. Norton & Co., 1986.

Manchu China
Dennerline, J. *Chia Ting Loyalists: Confucian Leadership and Social Change in Seventeenth-Century China.* New Haven, CT: Yale University Press, 1981.
Naquin, S. *Chinese Society in the Eighteenth Century.* New Haven, CT: Yale University Press, 1987.
Wakeman, F. *The Great Enterprise: The Manchu Reconstruction of the Imperial Order in Seventeenth-Century China.* Berkeley, CA: University of California Press, 1986.
Will, P. E. *Bureacracy and Famine in Eighteenth-Century China.* Stanford, CA: Stanford University Press, 1990.

Tokugawa Japan
Bellah, R. N. *Tokugawa Religion: The Cultural Roots of Modern Japan.* New York: Free Press, 1985.

Haley, S. B. *Everyday Things in Premodern Japan: The Hidden Legacy of Material Culture.* Berkeley, CA: University of California Press, 1997.
Jansen, M. B. *China in the Tokugawa World.* Cambridge, MA: Harvard University Press, 1992.
Nakone, C. *Tokugawa Japan: The Social and Economic Antecedents of Modern Japan.* Tokyo: University of Tokyo Press, 1992.
Robertson, J. R. *Japan Meets the World: Birth of a Superpower.* Brookfield, CT: Millbrook Press, 1998.
Smitka, M., ed. *The Japanese Economy in the Tokugawa Era, 1600–1868.* New York: Garland Publishing, 1998.
Vlastos, S. *Peasant Protests and Uprisings in Tokugawa Japan.* Berkeley, CA: University of California Press, 1990.

Colonial America
Baseler, M. C. *Asylum for Mankind: America, 1607-1800.* Ithaca, NY: Cornell University Press, 1998.
Greene, J. P. *Colonial British America: Essays in the New History of the Early Modern Era.* Baltimore, MD: John Hopkins University Press, 1984.
Hofstadter, R. *America at 1750: A Social Portrait.* New York: Random House, 1973.
Middleton, R. *Colonial America: A History, 1585–1776.* Malden, MA: Blackwell Publishing, 1996.
Reich, J. R. *Colonial America.* New York: Prentice Hall, 1997.
Reiss, O. *Blacks in Colonial America.* Jefferson, NC: McFarland & Co., 1997.
Ward, H. M. *Colonial America, 1607–1763.* New York: Prentice Hall, 1991.

The American Revolutionary War
Fleming, T. J. *1776: Year of Illusions.* Edison, NJ: Book Sales, 1996.
Foner, E., ed. *The American Revolution.* New York: Hill & Wang Publishing, 1985.
Greene, J. P., and Pole, J.R., eds. *The Blackwell Encyclopedia of the American Revolution.* Malden, MA: Blackwell Publishing, 1991.
Kross, J., ed. *American Eras: The Revolutionary Era, 1754–1783.* Detroit, MI: Gale Research, 1998.
Morgan, E. S., and Boorstin, D. J. *The Birth of the Republic, 1763–89 (The Chicago History of American Civilization).* Chicago, IL: University of Chicago Press, 1993.
Tuchman, B. *The First Salute.* New York: Ballantine Books, 1989.
Wardo, P., ed. *The American Revolution.* San Diego, CA: Greenhaven Press, 1998,

Volume 5 Revolution and Change

The French Revolution
Blanning, T. C. W. *The French Revolution: Class War or Culture Clash?* New York: St. Martin's Press, 1998.
Hunt, J. *The French Revolution.* New York: Routledge, 1998.
Kennedy, E. *A Cultural History of the French Revolution.* New Haven, CT: Yale University Press, 1988.
Lefebvre, G. *Coming of the French Revolution.* Princeton, NJ: Princeton University Press, 1988.
Schama, S. *Citizens: A Chronicle of the French Revolution.* New York: Random House, 1990.
Nardo, D. *The French Revolution.* Turning Points in World History Series. San Diego, CA: Greenhaven Press, 1999.

Napoleon's Europe

Durant, W. J. *The Age of Napoleon: A History of European Civilization from 1789 to 1815*. New York: Fine Communications, 1997.

Ellis, G. *The Napoleonic Empire*. New York: Macmillan Publishing, 1991.

Gance, A. *Napoleon*. Winchester, MA: Faber & Faber, 1990.

Herold, J. C. *The Age of Napoleon*. American Heritage Publishing Co., 1986.

Muir, R. *Tactics and the Experience of Battle in the Age of Napoleon*. New Haven, CT: Yale University Press, 1998.

The Age of Metternich

Broers, M. *Europe After Napoleon: Revolution, Reaction and Romanticism, 1814–1848*. Manchester, UK: Manchester University Press, 1996.

Gilbert, F. *Age of Revolution and Reaction, 1789–1850*. London: W. W. Norton & Co., 1980.

Pilbeam, P. M. *Themes in Modern European History, 1780–1830*. New York: Routledge, 1995.

Schroeder, P. W. *The Transformation of European Politics, 1763–1848*. Oxford, UK: Clarendon Press, 1994.

The Industrial Revolution

Dudley, W., ed. *The Industrial Revolution: Opposing Viewpoints*. San Diego, CA: Greenhaven Press, 1997.

Fisher, D. *The Industrial Revolution: A Macroeconomic Viewpoint*. New York: St. Martin's Press, 1994.

Hobsbawm, E. J. *The Age of Revolution, 1789–1848*. New York: Vintage Books, 1996.

Stearns, P. N., ed. *ABC-Clio World History Companion to the Industrial Revolution*. Santa Barbara, CA: ABC-Clio, 1996.

Wilkinson, P., and Pollard, M. *The Industrial Revolution*. Broomall, PA: Chelsea House Publishing, 1995.

Industrial Society

Elster, J. *Nuts and Bolts for the Social Sciences*. New York: Cambridge University Press, 1989.

Garner, J. S., ed. *The Company Town: Architecture and Society in the Early Industrial Age*. New York: Oxford University Press, 1992.

Kirk, N. *Change, Continuity, and Class: Labour in British Society, 1850–1920*. Manchester, UK: Manchester University Press, 1998.

Montgomery, D. *Citizen Worker: The Experience of Workers in the United States with Democracy and the Free Market During the Nineteenth Century*. New York: Cambridge University Press, 1994.

More, C. *The Industrial Age: Economy and Society in Britain, 1750–1995*. Reading, MA: Addison Wesley Publishing Company, 1997.

Romanticism

Curran, S., ed. *The Cambridge Companion to British Romanticism*. New York: Cambridge University Press, 1993.

Gilmore, M. T. *America, Romanticism, and the Marketplace*. Chicago, IL: University of Chicago Press, 1988.

Honour, H. *Romanticism*. New York: HarperCollins, 1979.

Reardon, B. J. *Religion in the Age of Romanticism: Studies in Early Nineteenth Century Thought*. New York: Cambridge University Press, 1985.

Wu, D., ed. *A Companion to Romanticism*. Malden, MA: Blackwell Publishing, 1997.

The New United States

Ambrose, S. E. *Undaunted Courage: Meriwether Lewis, Thomas Jefferson, and the Opening of the American West*. New York: Touchstone Books, 1997.

Ellis, J. J. *After the Revolution: Profiles of Early American Culture*. London: W. W. Norton & Co., 1981.

Hutchins, C. E., ed. *Everyday Life in the Early Republic*. Winterthur, DE: Winterthur Museum, 1997.

Lubin, D. M. *Picturing a Nation: Art and Social Change in Nineteenth-Century America*. New Haven, CT: Yale University Press, 1994.

Saxton, A. *The Rise and Fall of the White Republic: Class, Politics, and Mass Culture in Nineteenth-Century America*. New York: Verso Books, 1997.

Sharp, J. R. *American Politics in the Early Republic: The New Nation in Crisis*. New Haven, CT: Yale University Press, 1995.

Taylor, A. *William Cooper's Town: Power and Persuasion on the Frontier of the Early American Republic*. New York: Vintage Books, 1996.

Wood, G. S. *The Creation of the American Republic, 1776–1787*. Chapel Hill, NC: University of North Carolina, 1998.

Nationalism in Europe

Breuilly, J. *The Formation of the First German Nation State, 1800–1871*. New York: St. Martin's Press, 1996.

Cunsulo, R. S. *Italian Nationalism: From Its Origins to World War Two*. Melbourne, FL: Krieger Publishing Company, 1990.

Kramer, L. *Nationalism: Political Cultures in Europe and America, 1775–1865*. New York: Twayne Publishing, 1998.

Shulze, H. *The Course of German Nationalism from Frederick the Great to Bismark, 1763–1867*. New York: Cambridge University Press, 1991.

Exploration and Empire

Bayly, C. A. *Indian Society and the Making of the British Empire*. New York: Cambridge University Press, 1990.

Cohen, W. B., ed. *European Empire Building: Nineteenth-Century Imperialism*. Centreport, NY: The Forum Press, 1980.

Headrick, D. R. *The Tools of Empire: Technology and European Imperialism in the Nineteenth Century*. New York: Oxford University Press, 1981.

Hughes, R. *The Fatal Shore: The Epic of Australia's Founding*. New York: Vintage Books, 1986.

James, L. *The Rise and Fall of the British Empire*. New York: St. Martin's Press, 1996.

———. *The Making and Unmaking of British India*. New York: St. Martin's Press, 1999.

Judd, D. *Empire: The British Imperial Experience from 1765 to the Present*. New York: Basic Books, 1997.

Kitchen, M. *The British Empire and Commonwealth: A Short History*. New York: St. Martin's Press, 1996.

The American Civil War

Catton, B. *America Goes to War: The Civil War and Its Meaning in American Culture*. Middletown, CT: Wesleyan University Press, 1992.

Catton, B., et al. *American Heritage New History of the Civil War*. New York: Viking Press, 1996.

Donovan, T. H., ed. *The American Civil War*. Wayne, NJ: Avery Publishing Group, 1987.

Foote, S. *The Civil War: A Narrative*. 3 vols. New York: Vintage Books, 1986.

Garrison, W. *The Amazing Civil War*. Nashville, TN: Rutledge Hill Press, 1998.

Hood, J. B. *Advance and Retreat: Personal Experiences in the United States and Confederate States Armies*. New York: Da Capo Press, 1993.

McPherson, J. M. *Battle Cry of Freedom: The Civil War Era*. New York: Ballatine Books, 1988.

Stevens, J. E. *1863: The Rebirth of a Nation*. New York: Bantam Doubleday, 1999.

Russia in the Nineteenth Century

Jelavich, B. *Russia's Balkan Entanglements, 1806–1914*. New York: Cambridge University Press, 1991.

Mackenzie, D. *Imperial Dreams, Harsh Realities: Tsarist Russia's Foreign Policy, 1815–1917*. HBJ College & School Division, 1997.

Mosse, W. E. P. *An Economic History of Russia, 1856–1914*. London: IB Tauris & Co., 1996.

Vucinich, W. S., ed. *The Peasant in Nineteenth-Century Russia*. Stanford, CA: Stanford University Press, 1968.

Waldron, P. *The End of Imperial Russia, 1855–1917*. New York: St. Martin's Press, 1997.

Westwood, J. N. *Endurance and Endeavour: Russian History, 1812–1992*. New York: Oxford University Press, 1993.

Science and Religion in the Nineteenth Century

Buell, J. *Darwinism: Science or Philosophy?* Foundation for Thought and Ethics, 1994.

Conkin, P. K. *When All the Gods Trembled: Darwinism, Scopes, and American Intellectuals*. Lanham, MD: Rowman & Littlefield, 1998.

Jobson, P. E. *Defeating Darwinism by Opening Minds*. Downers Grove, IL: Intervarsity Press, 1997.

Numbers, R. L. *Darwinism Comes to America*. Cambridge, MA: Harvard University Press, 1998.

———. *The Creationists*. Berkeley, CA: University of California Press, 1993.

Roberts, J. H. *Darwinism and the Divine in America: Protestant Intellectuals and Organic Evolution, 1859–1900*. Madison, WI: University of Wisconsin Press, 1988.

Volume 6 The Changing Balance of Power

The Shrinking Ottoman World

Brown, L. Carl. *Imperial Legacy: The Ottoman Imprint on the Balkans and the Middle East*. New York: Columbia University Press, 1997.

Godwin, J. *Lords of the Horizons: A History of the Ottoman Empire*. New York: Henry Holt & Co., 1999.

Gondicas, D., and Issawi, C., eds. *Ottoman Greeks in the Age of Nationalism: Politics, Economy, and Society in the Nineteenth Century*. Pennington, NJ: Darwin Press, 1998.

Kasaba, R. *The Ottoman Empire and the World Economy: The Nineteenth Century*. State University of New York Press, 1989.

Kent, M., ed. *The Great Powers and the End of the Ottoman Empire*. Ilford: Frank Cass & Co, 1995.

Palmer, A. W. *The Decline and Fall of the Ottoman Empire*. M. E. Evans and Co., 1994.

Revolution in Mexico

Eisenhower, J. S. D. *Intervention! The United States and the Mexican Revolution, 1913–1917*. London: W. W. Norton & Co., 1995.

Katz, F. *The Life and Times of Pancho Villa*. Stanford, CA: Stanford University Press, 1998.

Knight, A. *The Mexican Revolution: Porfirians, Liberals, and Peasants*. Lincoln, NE: University of Nebraska Press, 1990.

Tinkle, L. *13 Days to Glory: The Seige of the Alamo*. Texas A&M University Press, 1996.

Tutino, J. *From Insurrection to Revolution in Mexico: Social Bases of Agrarian Violence, 1750–1940*. Princeton, NJ: Princeton University Press, 1989.

Revolution in South America

Bethell, L., ed. *The Cambridge History of Latin America: Colonial Latin America, Vol. 2*. New York: Cambridge University Press, 1985.

Costeloe, M. P. *Response to Revolution: Imperial Spain and the Spanish American Revolutions, 1810–1840*. New York: Cambridge University Press, 1986.

Hooker, T. *The Armies of Bolívar and San Martín*. New York: Osprey Publishing Co., 1991.

Lynch, J. *The Spanish American Revolution, 1808–26*. London: W. W. Norton & Co., 1986.

Lynch, J., ed. *Latin American Revolutions, 1808–26: Old and New World Origins*. Norman, OK: University of Oklahoma Press, 1996.

South America After Independence

Bethell, L. *The Cambridge History of Latin America: From Independence to 1870*. New York: Cambridge University Press, 1985.

Bushnell, D. *The Emergence of Latin America in the Nineteenth Century*. New York: Oxford University Press, 1995.

Graham, R. *Independence in Latin America: A Comparative Approach*. New York: McGraw Hill Text, 1994.

Kingsbruner, J. *Independence in Spanish America: Civil Wars, Revolutions, and Underdevelopment*. Albuquerque, NM: University of New Mexico Press, 1994.

Rodriguez, J. E. *The Independence of Spanish America*. New York: Cambridge University Press, 1998.

China in the Nineteenth Century

Fay, P. W. *The Opium War, 1840–42: Barbarians in the Celestial Empire in the Early Part of the Nineteenth Century*. Chapel Hill, NC: University of North Carolina Press, 1998.

Paludan, A. *Chronicle of the Chinese Emperors: The Reign-by-Reign Record of the Rulers of Imperial China*. New York: Thames and Hudson, 1998.

Prazniak, R. *Of Camel Kings and Other Things: Rural Rebels Against Modernity in Late Imperial China*. Lanham, MD: Rowman and Littlefield, 1999.

Schrecker, C. *Reform in Nineteenth Century China*. Cambridge, MA: Harvard University Press, 1976.

Spence, J. D. *God's Chinese Son: The Taiping Heavenly Kingdom of Hong Xinquan*. London: W. W. Norton & Co., 1996.

Nineteenth-Century Japan

Iriye, A. *Japan and the Wider World: From the Mid–Nineteenth Century to the Present*. Reading, MA: Addison Wesley Publishing Co., 1997.

Jansen, M. B., ed. *The Cambridge History of Japan: The Nineteenth Century*. New York: Cambridge University Press, 1989.

Kelly, W. W. *Deference and Defiance in Nineteenth-Century Japan*. Princeton, NJ: Princeton University Press, 1985.

Kornicki, P. F. *The Book in Japan: A Cultural History from the Beginnings to the Nineteenth Century*. Boston, MA: Brill Academic Publishers, 1997.

Mehl, M. *History and the State in Nineteenth-Century Japan*. New York: St. Martin's Press, 1998.

The Second Wave of Industrialization

Bradley, J. *Guns for the Tsar: American Technology and the Small Arms Industry in Nineteenth-Century Russia*. De Kalb, IL: Northern Illinois University Press, 1990.

Briggs, A. *Victorian Things*. Chicago: University of Chicago Press, 1989.

McCullogh, D. *The Great Bridge: The Epic Story of the Building of the Brooklyn Bridge*. New York: Simon and Schuster, 1983.

Morus, I. R. *Frankenstein's Children: Electricity, Exhibition, and Experiment in Early Nineteenth-Century London*. Princeton, NJ: Princeton University Press, 1998.

Late-Nineteenth-Century Society in the West

Barth, G. *City People: The Rise of Modern City Culture in Nineteenth-Century America*. New York: Oxford University Press, 1982.

Dale, P. A. *In Pursuit of a Scientific Culture: Science, Art, and Society in the Victorian Age*. Madison, WI: University of Wisconsin Press, 1990.

Kocka, J. *Bourgeois Society in Nineteenth-Century Europe*. Indianapolis, IN: Berg Publishing Ltd., 1994.

Marcus, S. *Apartment Stories: City and Home in Nineteenth-Century Paris and London*. Berkeley, CA: University of California Press, 1999.

Sante, L. *Low Life: Lures and Snares of Old New York*. New York: Vintage Books, 1992.

Schlereth, T. *Victorian America: Transformations in Everyday Life, 1876–1915*. New York: HarperCollins, 1991.

The Rise of Socialism

Brandt, W. *German Essays on Socialism in the Nineteenth Century*. New York: Continuum Publishing Groups, 1990.

Charlton, J. *The Chartists: The First National Workers Movement*. Oxford, UK: Pluto Press, 1997.

Docherty, J. C. *Historical Dictionary of Socialism*. Lanham, MD: Scarecrow Press, 1997.

Feurbach, L. *German Socialist Philosophy*. New York: Continuum Publishing Group, 1996.

Messer-Kruse, T. *The Yankee International: Marxism and the American Reform Tradition, 1848–1876*. Chapel Hill, NC: University of North Carolina Press, 1998.

Proudhon, P-J. *The General Idea of the Revolution in the Nineteenth Century*. Oxford, UK: Pluto Press, 1989.

The Scramble for Africa

Chamberlain, M. E. *The Scramble for Africa*. Reading, MA: Addison Wesley Publishing Co., 1974.

Curtin, P. D. *Disease and Empire: The Health of European Troops in the Conquest of Africa*. New York: Cambridge University Press, 1998.

Nutting, A. *Scramble for Africa: The Great Trek to the Boer War*. London: Constable and Co., 1994.

Oliver, O., and Atmore, A. *Africa Since 1800*. New York: Cambridge University Press, 1994.

Pakenham, T. *The Scramble for Africa: White Man's Conquest of the Dark Continent from 1876 to 1912*. New York: Random House, 1991.

Sagay, J. O. *Africa: A Modern History, 1800–1975*. New York: Holmes and Maier Publishing, 1981.

The Triumph of the Dollar

Allison, R. J., ed. *America Eras: Development of the Industrial United States*. Detroit, MI: Gale Research, 1997.

Ambrose, S. E. *Crazy Horse and Custer: The Parallel Lives of Two American Warriors*. Anchor, 1996.

Foner, E. *America's Reconstruction: People and Politics After the Civil War*. Baton Rouge, LA: Louisiana State University Press, 1997.

Franklin, J. H. *Reconstruction After the Civil War*. Chicago, IL: University of Chicago Press, 1995.

Litwak, L. F. *Trouble in Mind: Black Southerners in the Age of Jim Crow*. New York: Knopf, 1998.

McCullogh, D. *Path Between the Seas: The Creation of the Panama Canal, 1870–1914*. New York: Simon and Schuster, 1978.

Morris, E. *The Rise of Theodore Roosevelt*. New York: Ballantine Books, 1988.

Traxel, D. *1898: The Birth of the American Century*. New York: Knopf, 1998.

Ward, G. C., et al. *The West: An Illustrated History*. New York: Little Brown and Co., 1996.

The Arts in the Late Nineteenth Century

Barnhill, G. B. *The Cultivation of Artists in Nineteenth-Century America*. New Castle, DE: Oak Knoll Press, 1997.

Bowe, N. G. *Art and the National Dream: The Search for Vernacular Expression in Turn of the Century Design*. Dublin: Irish Academic Press, 1993.

Canady, J. E. *Mainstreams of Modern Art*. Austin, TX: Holt, Rinehart & Winston, 1981.

Garb, T. *Sisters of the Brush: Women's Artistic Culture in Late-Nineteenth-Century Paris*. New Haven, CT: Yale University Press, 1994.

Herbert, R. L. *Impressionism: Art, Leisure, and Parisian Society*. New Haven, CT: Yale University Press, 1988.

Schwartz, V. R. *Spectacular Realities: Early Mass Culture in Fin-de-Siecle Paris*. Berkeley, CA: University of California Press, 1998.

Sternau, S. A. *Art Nouveau: The Spirit of the Belle Epoque*. Todtri Productions Ltd., 1998.

Thomson, B. *The Post-Impressionists*. London: Phaidon Press, 1995.

Volume 7 World War I and Its Consequences

The Road to War

Hayne, M. B. *The French Foreign Office and the Origins of the First World War, 1898–1914*. Oxford: Clarendon Press, 1993.

Herrman, D. G. *The Arming of Europe and the Making of the First World War*. Princeton, NJ: Princeton University Press, 1997.

Joll, J. *The Origins of the First World War*. Reading, MA: Addison Wesley Publishing Co., 1992.

Martel, G. *The Origins of the First World War*. Reading, MA: Addison Wesley Publishing Co., 1996.

Massie, R. K. *Dreadnought: Britain, Germany, and the Coming of the Great War*. New York: Ballantine Books, 1992.

Miller, S. E., ed. *Military Strategy and the Origins of the First World War*. Princeton, NJ: Princeton University Press, 1991.

Stevenson, D. *Armaments and the Coming of War: Europe, 1904–14*. Oxford: Clarendon Press, 1996.

Tuchman, B. W. *The Guns of August*. New York: Ballantine Books, 1994.

World War I

Drury, I. *German Stormtrooper, 1914–18*. New York: Osprey Publishing Company, 1995.

Fergusson, N. *The Pity of War*. New York: Basic Books, 1999.

Gilbert, M. *The First World War: A Complete History*. New York: Henry Holt & Co., 1996.

Herwig, H. H. *Germany and Austria-Hungary, 1914-18.* London: Edward Arnold, 1997.

Keegan, J. *The First World War.* New York: Knopf, 1999.

Pegler, M. M. *British Tommy, 1914–18.* New York: Osprey Publishing Company, 1998.

Strachan, H., ed. *World War I: A History.* New York: Oxford University Press, 1998.

Winter, D. *Death's Men: Soldiers of the Great War.* New York: Penguin USA, 1993.

The Effects of the War

Bessel, R. *Germany After the First World War.* Oxford: Clarendon Press, 1995.

Brooman, J. *World Re-Made: The Results of the First World War.* Longman Group United Kingdom, 1985.

Gallagher, J. *The World War Through the Female Gaze.* Carbondale, IL: Southern Illinois University Press, 1999.

Harries, M., and Harries, S. *The Last Days of Innocence: America at War, 1917–1918.* New York: Random House, 1997.

Higonnet, M. P. *Behind the Lines: Gender and the Two World Wars.* New Haven, CT: Yale University Press, 1989.

Kennedy, D. M. *Over Here: The First World War and American Society.* New York: Oxford University Press, 1986.

Winter, J. *Sites of Memory, Sites of Mourning: The Great War in European Cultural History.* New York: Cambridge University Press, 1998.

The Russian Revolution

Acton, E., ed. *Critical Companion to the Russian Revolution, 1914–21.* Bloomington, IN: Indiana University Press, 1997.

Brovkin, V. N. *The Bolsheviks in Russian Society: The Revolution and the Civil Wars.* New Haven, CT: Yale University Press, 1997.

Figes, O. *A People's Tragedy: The Russian Revolution, 1891–1924.* New York: Penguin USA, 1998.

Read, C. *From Tsar to Soviets: The Russian People and Their Revolution, 1917–21.* New York: Oxford University Press, 1996.

Sherrow, V. *Life During the Russian Revolution.* San Diego, CA: Lucent Books, 1998.

Shukman, H. *The Blackwell Encyclopedia of the Russian Revolution.* Malden, MA: Blackwell Publishing, 1994.

Lenin and Stalin

Conquest, R. *The Great Terror: A Reassessment.* New York: Oxford University Press, 1991.

Fitzpatrick, S. *Stalin's Peasants: Resistance and Survival in the Russian Village After Collectivization.* New York: Oxford University Press, 1996.

———. *Everyday Stalinism: Ordinary Life in Extraordinary Times: Soviet Russia in the 1930s.* New York: Oxford University Press, 1999.

McDermott, K. *The Comintern: A History of International Communism from Lenin to Stalin.* New York: St. Martin's Press, 1996.

Pomper, P. *Lenin, Trotsky, and Stalin: The Intelligentsia and Power.* New York: Columbia University Press, 1990.

Rosenberg, W. G. *Social and Cultural History of the Soviet Union: The Lenin and Stalin Years.* New York: Garland Publishing, 1992.

Serge, V. *From Lenin to Stalin.* New York: Pathfinder Press, 1973.

Smart, D. *Russia Under Lenin and Stalin.* Stanley Thomas Publishing Ltd., 1998.

Volkogonov, D. *Autopsy of An Empire: The Seven Leaders Who Built the Soviet Regime.* New York: Simon and Schuster, 1998.

Revolution in China

Becker, J. *Hungry Ghosts: Mao's Secret Famine.* New York: Henry Holt & Co., 1998.

Fairbank, J. K. *The Cambridge History of China: Republican China, 1912–49.* New York: Cambridge University Press, 1983.

Jiang, J-L. *Red Scarf Girl: A Memoir of the Cultural Revolution.* New York: HarperCollins Juvenile Books, 1997.

Porter, R. *Industrial Reformers in Republican China.* Armonk, NY: M. E. Sharpe, 1997.

Sheridan, J. E. *China in Disintegration: The Republican Era in Chinese History, 1912–49.* New York: Free Press, 1977.

Spence, J. D. *The Gate of Heavenly Peace: The Chinese and Their Revolution, 1895–1980.* New York: Viking Press, 1982.

Postwar America and Europe

Boemeke, M. F., ed. *The Treaty of Versailles: A Reassessment After Seventy-five Years.* New York: Cambridge University Press, 1998.

Kent, B. *The Spoils of War: The Politics, Economics and Diplomacy of Reparations, 1918–32.* Oxford, UK: Clarendon Press, 1992.

Kleine-Ahlbrandt, W. L. *The Burden of Victory: France, Britain and the Enforcement of the Versailles Peace, 1919–25.* Lanham, MD: University Press of America, 1995.

Knock, T. J. *To End All Wars: Woodrow Wilson and the Quest for A New World Order.* Princeton, NJ: Princeton University Press, 1995.

Orde, A. *British Policy and European Reconstruction After the First World War.* New York: Cambridge University Press, 1990.

Ostrower, G. B. *The League of Nations: 1919–29.* Wayne, NJ: Avery Publishing Group, 1996.

Sharp, A. *Versailles Settlement Peacemaking in Paris, 1919.* New York: St. Martin's Press, 1991.

Stirk, P. M. R., ed. *European Unity in Context: The Interwar Period.* London: Pinter Publishing Ltd., 1989.

The Great Depression

Bordo, M. D., ed. *The Defining Moment: The Great Depression and the American Economy in the Twentieth Century.* Chicago, IL: University of Chicago Press, 1998.

Feinstein, C. H., ed. *Banking, Currency, and Finance in Europe Between the Wars.* New York: Oxford University Press, 1995.

Galbraith, J. K. *The Great Crash, 1929.* Boston, MA: Houghton Mifflin Co., 1997.

Hall, T. E., and Ferguson, J. D. *The Great Depression: An International Disaster of Perverse Economic Policies.* Ann Arbor, MI: University of Michigan Press, 1998.

McElvaine, R. S. *The Great Depression: America, 1929–1941.* New York: Times Books, 1994.

Pells, R. H. *Radical Visions and American Dreams: Culture and Social Thought in the Depression Years.* Illinois University Press, 1998.

Watkins, T. H. *The Great Depression: America in the 1930s.* Boston, MA: Little, Brown & Co., 1993.

Wicker, E. *The Banking Panics of the Great Depression.* New York: Cambridge University Press, 1996.

Latin America Between the Wars

Beezley, W. H., and Ewell, J., eds. *The Human Tradition in Latin America: The Twentieth Century.* Wilmington, DE: Scholarly Resources, 1987.

Bethell, L. *Latin America Since 1930: Ideas, Culture, and Society.* Cambridge History of Latin America, vol. 9. New York: Cambridge University Press, 1999.

Calvert, P. *Latin America in the Twentieth Century*. New York: St. Martin's Press, 1993.

Farcau, B. W. *The Chaco War*. Praeger Publishing, 1996.

Henderson, J. D. *Conservative Thought in Twentieth Century Latin America: The Ideas of Laureano Gomez*. Athens, OH: Ohio University Center for International Studies, 1988.

Thorp, R. *Progress, Poverty, and Exclusion: An Economic History of Latin America in the Twentieth Century*. Washington, D.C.: Inter-American Development Bank, 1998.

Wiarda, H. J. *The Democratic Revolution in Latin America: History, Politics, and U.S. Policy*. New York: Holmes & Maier Publishing, 1990.

Hitler and Mussolini

Brooker, P. *Twentieth-Century Dictatorships: The Ideological One-Party States*. New York University Press, 1995.

Bullock, A. *Hitler and Stalin: Parallel Lives*. New York: Vintage Books, 1993.

Carsten, F. L. *The Rise of Fascism*. Berkeley, CA: University of California Press, 1982.

Ceplair, L. *Under the Shadow of War: Fascism, Anti-Fascism, and Marxists, 1918–39*. New York: Columbia University Press, 1987.

Goldhagen, D. J. *Hitler's Willing Executioners: Ordinary Germans and the Holocaust*. New York: Knopf, 1996.

Hoyt, E. P. *Mussolini's Empire: The Rise and Fall of the Fascist Vision*. New York: John Wiley & Sons, 1994.

Kershaw, I. *Hitler: 1889–1936: Hubris*. New York: W. W. Norton & Co., 1999.

Ludwig, E. *Three Portraits: Hitler, Mussolini, Stalin*. New York: AMS Press, 1982.

Pauley, B. F. *Hitler, Stalin, and Mussolini: Totalitarianism in the Twentieth Century*. Wheeling, IL: Harlan Davidson, 1997.

Ridley, J. *Mussolini*. New York: St. Martin's Press, 1998.

Shirer, W. *Rise and Fall of the Third Reich: A History of Nazi Germany*. New York: Simon & Schuster, 1990.

Volume 8 World War II and the Cold War

Asia Between the Wars

Brown, I. *Economic Change in Southeast Asia, 1830–1980*. New York: Oxford University Press, 1997.

Christie, C. J., ed. *Southeast Asia in the Twentieth Century: A Reader*. London: IB Tauris & Co., 1998.

Lindblad, J. T. *Foreign Investment in Southeast Asia in the Twentieth Century*. New York: St. Martin's Press, 1998.

Myers, R. H., and Peattie, M. R., eds. *Japanese Colonial Empire, 1895–1945*. Princeton, NJ: Princeton University Press, 1987.

Young, L. *Japan's Total Empire: Manchuria and the Culture of Wartime Imperialism*. Berkeley, CA: University of California Press, 1998.

The Road to War

Bell, P. M. H. *The Origins of the Second World War in Europe*. Reading, MA: Addison Wesley Publishing Company, 1997.

Boyce, R., ed. *Paths to War: New Essays on the Origins of the Second World War*. New York: St. Martin's Press, 1989.

Iriye, A. *Origins of the Second World War in Asia and the Pacific*. Reading, MA: Addison Wesley Publishing Company, 1987.

Offner, A. A. *The Origins of the Second World War: American Foreign Policy and World Politics*. Melbourne, FL: Krieger Publishing Company, 1986.

Roberts, G. K. *The Soviet Union and the Origins of the Second World War, 1933–1941*. New York: St. Martin's Press, 1995.

Taylor, A. J. P. *Origins of the Second World War*. New York: Scribner, 1996.

World War II: Europe and North Africa

Ambrose, S. E. *Citizen Soldiers: The U.S. Army from the Normandy Beaches to the Bulge to the Surrender of Germany, June 7, 1944–May 7, 1945*. New York: Simon & Schuster, 1997.

Beevor, A. *Stalingrad*. New York: Viking Press, 1998.

Boog, H. *Germany and the Second World War: The Attack on the Soviet Union*. Oxford, UK: Clarendon Press, 1998.

Griess, T. E., ed. *The Second World War: Europe and the Mediterranean*. Wayne, NJ: Avery Publishing Group, 1995.

Keegan, J. *The Second World War*. New York: Penguin USA, 1990.

Stegemann, B., et al. *Germany and the Second World War: The Mediterranean, South-East Europe, and North Africa 1939–41*. Oxford, UK: Clarendon Press, 1995.

Zulzberger, C. I., et al. *American Heritage New History of World War II*. New York: Viking Press, 1997.

World War II: The Pacific Theater

Bergerud, E. *Touched with Fire: The Land War in the South Pacific*. New York: Penguin USA, 1997.

Chang, I. *The Rape of Nanking: The Forgotten Holocaust of World War II*. New York: Basic Books, 1997.

Cook, H. T., and Cook, T. F. *Japan at War: An Oral History*. New Press, 1993.

Dockrill, S., ed. *From Pearl Harbor to Hiroshima: The Second World War in Asia and the Pacific, 1941–45*. New York: St. Martin's Press, 1994.

Dunnigan, J. F. *Victory at Sea: World War Two in the Pacific*. New York: Quill, 1996.

Dunnigan, J. F., and Nofi, A. A. *The Pacific War Encyclopedia*. New York: Facts on File, 1998.

Greiss, T. E., ed. *The Second World War: Asia and the Pacific*. Wayne, NJ: Avery Publishing Group, 1985.

Hersey, J. *Hiroshima*. New York: Vintage Books, 1989.

Spector, R. H. *Eagle Against the Sun: The American War with Japan*. New York: Random House, 1985.

Total War

Aron, R. *The Century of Total War*. Westport, CT: Greenwood Publishing Group, 1981.

Baker Wise, N. *A Mouthful of Rivets: Women at Work in World War II*. San Francisco, CA: Jossey-Bass Publishers, 1994.

Buckley, J. *Air Power in the Age of Total War*. Bloomington, IN: Indiana University Press, 1999.

Doughty, R. *World War Two: Total Warfare Around the Globe*. Boston, MA: D. C. Heath & Co., 1996.

Markusen, E. *The Holocaust and Strategic Bombing: Genocide and Total War in the Twentieth Century*. Boulder, CO: Westview Press, 1995.

Terkel, S. *The Good War: An Oral History of World War Two*. New York: New Press, 1997.

Wright, G. *The Ordeal of Total War, 1939–1945*. Prospect Heights, IL: Waveland Press, 1997.

The West After the War

Barr, N. *The Economics of the Welfare State*. Stanford, CA: Stanford University Press, 1999.

Calvocoressi, P. *Fall Out: World War Two and the Shaping of Postwar Europe*. Reading, MA: Addison Wesley Publishing Company, 1997.

Ellwood, D. W. *Rebuilding Europe: Western Europe, America, and Postwar Reconstruction*. White Plains, NY: Longman Publishing Group, 1992.

Stirk, P. M. R. *Shaping Postwar Europe: European Unity and Disunity, 1945–57*. New York: St. Martin's Press, 1991.

The Cold War: 1945–1960

Cohen, W. I. *The Cambridge History of American Foreign Relations: America in the Age of Soviet Power, 1945–91*. New York: Cambridge University Press, 1995.

Hogan, M. J. *A Cross of Iron: Harry S. Truman and the Origins of the National Security State, 1945–54*. New York: Cambridge University Press, 1998.

Isaacs, J. *Cold War: An Illustrated History, 1945–1991*. Boston, MA: Little Brown & Co., 1998.

Leffler, M. P. *The Specter of Communism: The United States and the Origins of the Cold War, 1917–53*. New York: Hill & Wang Publishing, 1994.

May, E. E. *American Cold War Strategy: Interpreting NSC 68*. New York: St. Martin's Press, 1993.

Parrish, T. *Berlin in the Balance: The Blockade, the Airlift, the First Major Battle of the Cold War*. Reading, MA: Perseus Press, 1998.

Pierpaoli, P. G., Jr. *Truman and Korea: The Political Culture of the Early Cold War*. Columbia, MO: University of Missouri Press, 1999.

Zubok, V., and Pleshakov, C. *Inside the Kremlin's Cold War: From Stalin to Khrushchev*. Cambridge, MA: Harvard University Press, 1997.

The Cold War: 1961–1989

Gaddis, J. L. *We Now Know: Rethinking Cold War History*. New York: Oxford University Press, 1998.

Garthoff, R. L. *Reflections on the Cuban Missile Crisis*. Washington, DC: Brookings Institute, 1989.

Karnow, S. *Vietnam: A History*. New York: Penguin USA, 1997.

McCauley, M. *Russia, America and the Cold War, 1949–91*. White Plains, NY: Longman Publishing Group, 1998.

Van Oudmaren, J. *Detente in Europe: The Soviet Union and the West Since 1953*. Durham, NC: Duke University Press, 1991.

Woods, R. B. *J. William Fulbright, Vietnam, and the Search for a Cold War Foreign Policy*. New York: Cambridge University Press, 1998.

The Partition of India

Adams, J., et al. *The Dynasty: The Nehru-Gandhi Story*. TV Books Inc., 1998.

Chadha, Y. *Gandhi: A Life*. New York: John Wiley and Sons, 1998.

Chatterji, J. *Bengal Divided: Hindu Communalism and Partition, 1932–47*. New York: Cambridge University Press, 1995.

French, P. *Liberty or Death: India's Journey to Independence and Division*. North Pomfret, VT: Trafalgar Square, 1999.

Harrison, S. S., ed. *India and Pakistan: The First Fifty Years*. New York: Cambridge University Press, 1998.

Hassan, M., ed. *India's Partition: Process, Strategy and Mobilization*. New York: Oxford University Press, 1994.

Merion, R., and Bhasin, K. *Borders and Boundaries: Women in India's Partition*. Piscataway, NJ: Rutgers University Press, 1998.

Singh, A. I. *The Origins of the Partition of India, 1936–47*. New York: Oxford University Press, 1991.

Decolonization

Betts, R. F. *Decolonization*. New York: Routledge, 1998.

Birmingham, D. *The Decolonization of Africa*. Athens, OH: Ohio University Press, 1996.

Chamberlain, M. E. *The Longman Companion to Decolonization in the Twentieth Century*. Reading, MA: Addison Wesley Publishing Company, 1998.

Christie, C. J. *A Modern History of Southeast Asia: Decolonization, Nationalism, and Separatism*. New York: St. Martins Press, 1998.

Clayton, A. *The Wars of French Decolonization*. Reading, MA: Addison Wesley Publishing Company, 1994.

Hargreaves, J. D. *Decolonization in Africa*. Reading, MA: Addison Wesley Publishing Company, 1996.

McIntyre, W. D. *British Decolonization, 1946–97: When, Why, and How Did the British Empire Fall?* New York: St. Martin's Press, 1999.

Van Dinh, T. *Independence, Liberation, Revolution: An Approach to the Understanding of the Third World*. Greenwich, CT: Ablex Publishing Corporation, 1987,

Israel and the Middle East

Bailey, S. D. *Four Arab-Israeli Wars and the Peace Process*. New York: St. Martin's Press, 1990.

Goldberg, D. J. *To the Promised Land: A History of Zionist Thought from Its Origins to the Modern State of Israel*. New York: Penguin USA, 1997.

Hadawi, S. *Bitter Harvest: A Modern History of Palestine*. New York: Interlink Publishing Group, 1998.

Rouhana, N. N. *Palestinians in an Ethnic Jewish State: Identities in Conflict*. New Haven, CT: Yale University Press, 1997.

Rubin, B. *Great Powers in the Middle East, 1941–47: The Road to the Cold War*. Ilford, UK: Frank Cass & Co., 1980.

Sayigh, Y. *The Cold War and the Middle East*. Oxford, UK: Clarendon Press, 1997.

Vatikiotis, P. J. *The Middle East: From the End of Empire to the End of the Cold War*. New York: Routledge, 1997.

Volume 9 The World Today

The Political Debate 1960–1999

Brinkley, A. *Liberalism and Its Discontents*. Cambridge, MA: Harvard University Press, 1998.

Dutton, D. *British Politics Since 1945: The Rise, Fall and Rebirth of Consensus*. Malden, MA: Blackwell Publishing, 1997.

Padgett, S. *A History of Soviet Democracy in Postwar Europe*. White Plains, NY: Longman Publishing Group, 1991.

Karvonen, L., and Sundberg, J. *Social Democracy in Transition: Northern, Southern and Eastern Europe*. Aldershot, UK: Dartmouth Publishing Company, 1991.

Milner, H. *Social Democracy and Rational Choice: The Scandinavian Experience and Beyond*. New York: Routledge, 1995.

Varson, A., ed. *Europe 1945–1990: The End of an Era?* New York: St. Martin's Press, 1994.

Life in the Nuclear Age

Branch, T. *Parting the Waters: America in the King Years, 1954–63*. New York: Touchstone Books, 1989.

———. *Pillar of Fire: America in the King Years, 1963–65*. New York: Simon & Schuster, 1998.

Bundy, William P. *Tangled Web: The Making of Foreign Policy in the Nixon Presidency*. New York: Hill & Wang Publishing, 1998.

Evans, H., et al. *The American Century*. New York: Knopf, 1998.

Francese, C. *From Tupela to Woodstock: Youth, Race and Rock-and-Roll in America 1954–69*. Dubuque, IA: Kendall/Hunt Publishing Company, 1995.

Wexler, S. *The Civil Rights Movement*. New York: Facts on File, 1993.

China 1949–1999

Hunt, M. H. *The Genesis of Chinese Communist Foreign Policy.* New York: Columbia University Press, 1996.

Lawrence, A. *China Under Communism.* New York: Routledge, 1998.

Lieberthal, K. *Governing China: From Revolution Through Reform.* London: W. W. Norton & Co., 1995.

MacFarquhar, R., ed. *The Politics of China: The Eras of Mao and Deng.* New York: Cambridge University Press, 1997.

Zhang, Y. *China in International Society Since 1949: Alienation and Beyond.* New York: St. Martin's Press, 1998.

Toward a United Europe

Dawson, A. H. *A Geography of European Integration.* New York: John Wiley and Sons, 1993.

Lubbers, R. *Europe: A Continent of Traditions.* New York: Cambridge University Press, 1994.

Nicoll, W. *Understanding the New European Community.* New York: Harvester Wheatsheaf, 1994.

Salmon, T. C., ed. *Building European Union: A Documentary History and Analysis.* Manchester, UK: Manchester University Press, 1997.

Urwin, D. W. *The Community of Europe: A History of European Integration Since 1945.* Reading, MA: Addison Wesley Publishing Company, 1995.

Wood, D. M. *The Emerging European Union.* Reading, MA: Addison Wesley Publishing Company, 1995.

Latin America Since 1945

Cottam, M. L. *Images and Intervention: U.S. Policies in Latin America.* University of Pittsburgh Press, 1994.

Dominguez, J. I., ed. *Economic Strategies and Policies in Latin America.* New York: Garland Publishing, 1994.

Feitlowitz, M. *A Lexicon of Terror: Argentina and the Legacies of Torture.* New York: Oxford University Press, 1998.

Fraser, N. *Evita: The Real Life of Eva Perón.* London: W. W. Norton & Co., 1996.

Randall, L., ed. *The Political Economy of Latin America in the Postwar Period.* Arlington, TX: University of Texas Press, 1997.

Ward, J. *Latin America: Development and Conflict Since 1945.* New York: Routledge, 1997.

Economies of the Pacific Rim

Collinwood, D. W. *Japan and the Pacific Rim.* Guilford, CT: Dushkin Publishing Group, 1997.

Cotterall, A. *East Asia: From Chinese Predominance to the Rise of the Pacific Rim.* New York: Oxford University Press, 1995.

Frost, L. *Coming Full Circle: An Economic History of the Pacific Rim.* Boulder, CO: Westview Press, 1993.

Morley, J. W., ed. *Driven by Growth: Political Change in the Asia Pacific Region.* Armonk, NY: ME Sharpe, 1999.

Simone, V. *The Asian Pacific: Political and Economic Development in a Global Context.* Reading, MA: Addison Wesley Publishing Company, 1994.

Postcolonial Africa

Ayittey, G. *Africa Betrayed.* New York: St. Martin's Press, 1993.

———. *Africa in Chaos.* New York: St. Martin's Press, 1998.

Davidson, B. *The Black Man's Burden: Africa and the Curse of the Nation-State.* Times Books, 1993.

Gourevitch, P. *We Wish to Inform You That Tomorrow We Will Be Killed with Our Families: Stories from Rwanda.* New York: Farrar, Straus & Giroux, 1998.

Maier, K. *Into the House of the Ancestors: Inside the New Africa.* New York: John Wiley & Sons, 1997.

Waldmeir, P. *Anatomy of a Miracle: The End of Apartheid and the Birth of the New South Africa.* London: W. W. Norton & Co., 1997.

Welliver, T. K. *African Nationalism and Independence.* New York: Garland Publishing, 1993.

Islamic Ferment

Al-Ashmawy, M. S. *Against Islamic Extremism.* Gainesville, FL: University Press of Florida, 1998.

Huband, M. *Warriors of the Prophet: The Struggle for Islam.* Boulder, CO: Westview Press, 1998.

Jansen, J. J. G. *The Dual Nature of Islamic Fundamentalism.* Ithaca, NY: Cornell University Press, 1997.

Naipaul, V. S. *Among the Believers: An Islamic Journey.* New York: Random House, 1982.

Sayyid, B. S. *A Fundamental Fear: Eurocentrism and the Emergence of Islamism.* London: Zed Books, 1997.

Tibi, B. *The Challenge of Fundamentalism: Political Islam and the New World Disorder.* Berkeley, CA: University of California Press, 1998.

Viorst, M. *In the Shadow of the Prophet: The Struggle for the Soul of Islam.* New York: Anchor Books, 1998.

The Postcommunist World

Boettke, P. J. *Why Perestroika Failed: The Politics and Economics of Socialist Transformation.* New York: Routledge, 1993.

Dobbs, M. *Down with Big Brother: The Fall of the Soviet Empire.* New York: Vintage Books, 1998.

Maier, C. S. *Dissolution: The Crisis of Communism and the End of East Germany.* Princeton, NJ: Princeton University Press, 1997.

Remnick, D. *Lenin's Tomb: The Last Days of the Soviet Empire.* New York: Vintage Books, 1994.

———. *Resurrection: The Struggle for a New Russia.* New York: Vintage Books, 1998.

Rosenberg, T. *The Haunted Land: Facing Europe's Ghosts After Communism.* New York: Vintage Books, 1996.

The World of Technology

Beniger, J. R. *The Control Revolution: Technological and Economic Origins of the Information Society.* Cambridge, MA: Harvard University Press, 1989,

Levinson, P. *The Soft Edge: A Natural History and Future of the Information Revolution.* New York: Routledge, 1997.

Pineira, R. J. *Breakthrough.* New York: Tor Books, 1999.

Schefter, J. L. *The Race: The Uncensored Story of How America Beat Russia to the Moon.* New York: Doubleday, 1999.

The Natural World

Carson, R. *Silent Spring.* Boston, MA: Houghton Mifflin Company, 1994.

Daly, H. E. *Beyond Growth: The Limits of Sustainable Development.* Boston, MA: Beacon Press, 1997.

Karliner, J. *The Corporate Planet: Ecology and Politics in the Age of Globalization.* San Francisco, CA: Sierra Club Books, 1997.

Ponting, C. *A Green History of the World: The Environment and the Collapse of Great Civilizations.* New York: Penguin USA, 1993.

Tokar, B. *Earth for Sale: Reclaiming Ecology in the Age of Corporate Greenwash.* Cambridge, MA: South End Press, 1997.

Problems for the Twenty-first Century

Castells, M. *End of Millennium*. Malden, MA: Blackwell Publishing, 1998.

Dobkowsk, M. N., ed. *The Coming Age of Scarcity: Preventing Mass Death and Genocide in the Twenty-first Century*. Syracuse, NY: Syracuse University Press, 1998.

Eldredge, N. *Life in the Balance: Humanity and the Biodiversity Crisis*. Princeton, NJ: Princeton University Press, 1998.

Jameson, F., and Miyoshi, M., eds. *The Cultures of Globalization*. Durham, NC: Duke University Press, 1998.

Robertson, D. S. *The New Renaissance: Computers and the Next Level of Civilization*. New York: Oxford University Press, 1998.

Schell, J. *The Fate of the Earth and the Abolition*. Stanford, CA: Stanford University Press, 1999.

Stephen, J. C. *Dragon Within the Gates: The Once and Future AIDS Epidemic*. New York: Carroll & Graf, 1993.

Utgoff, V. A., ed. *The Coming Crisis: Nuclear Proliferation, U.S. Interests, and World Order*. Cambridge, MA: MIT Press, 1999.

Web Sites

African Studies
http://www.sas.upenn.edu/African_Studies/AS.html

American Historial Association
http://www/theaha.org

American History
http://falcon.jmu.edu/~ramseyil.amhist.htm

American Memory: Historical Collections for the National Digital Library
http://lcweb2.loc.gov/ammem/amhome.html

Asian Studies WWW Virtual Library
http://www.coombs.anu.edu.au/WWWVL-AsianStudies.html

BBC News
http://news.bbc.co.uk/

Canadiana: The Canadian Resource Page
http://www.cs.cmu.edu/Unofficial/Canadiana/

CIA World Factbook
http://www.odci.gov/CIA/publications/nsolo/factbook

EuroDocs: Primary Historical Documents from Western Europe
http://library.byu.edu/~rdh/eurodocs/

From Revolution to Reconstruction
http://odur.let.rug.nl/~usa/

Archiving Early America
http://earlyamerica.com/earlyamerica/index.html

The Historical Text Archive
http://www.msstate.edu/Archives/History/index.html

The History Index
http://history.cc.ukans.edu/history/index/html

The History Online Project
http://www.jacksonesd.k12.or.us/k12projects/jimperry/history/html

The History Place
http://www.historyplace.com/

Library of Congress: Country Studies
http://lcweb2.loc.gov/frd/cs/cshome.html

Library of Congress HLAS Online: Handbook of Latin American Studies
http://lcweb2.loc.gov/hlas/

Schomburg Center for Research in Black Culture
http://web.nypl.org/research/sc/sc.html

Smithsonian National Museum of American History
http://www.si.edu/nmah

Sophia Smith Collection
http://www.smith.edu/libraries/ssc

The United States Constitution
http://www.law.ou.edu/hist.constitution/

The United States Historical Documents Page
http://www.ukans.edu/carrie.docs/amdocs.index/html

United States Holocaust Memorial Museum
http://www.ushmm.org.index.html

Virtual Library Museum Pages
http://palimpsest.stanford.edu/vlmp
or
http://www.comlab.ox.ac.uk/archive/other/museums/html

Video Resources

American History
Liberty! – The American Revolution (1998)
(3 tapes). ASIN: 0780620135

Native Americans (1994)
(6 tapes). ASIN: 6303359981

Lewis and Clark: The Journey of the Corps of Discovery (1997)
(2 tapes). ASIN0780618831

The West (1996)
(9 tapes). ASIN: 6304209908

Eyes on the Prize (1986)
(7 tapes). ASIN: 6303674992

World History
Leonardo da Vinci: Renaissance Man (1997)
(1 tape). ASIN: 6304425511

Campaigns of Napoleon (1999)
(3 tapes). ASIN: 156127562X

World War I Collection (1996)
(5 tapes). ASIN: 0783585705

World War II: War Chronicles (1998)
(7 tapes). ASIN: 6303422861

Hitler: The Whole Story (1989)
(3 tapes). ASIN 6304880685

Africa (1997)
(5 tapes). ASIN: 6304400039

China Rising: The Epic History of 20th-Century China (1992)
(3 tapes). ASIN: 6304263139

Thematic Indexes

ARTS and CULTURE

À la Recherche du Temps Perdu (Marcel Proust)
6: 848
Abbey in the Oak Forest (Caspar David Friedrich)
5: *635*
Abelard, Peter **1:** 51
Académie des Sciences (Paris) **2:** 274
academies/academicians **4:** 496–497
    French **2:** 262, 274 **4:** 500
    Royal Academy (London) **4:** 496
Academy Awards **7:** 951
*Across the Continent: Westward the Course of
    Empire Takes Its Way* (Fanny Palmer) **6:** *829*
Adam, Robert and James **4:** 497
Age of Reason **2:** 273
    the Enlightenment **4:** 471–480
    and science **5:** 697–698
Agee, James **7:** 968
Alberti, Leon Battista **1:** *80*
alchemy **1:** 56
Alcott, Louisa May **6:** 804
Alembert, Jean Le Rond d' **4:** 477
Almagest (Ptolemy) **1:** 53
almanacs **4:** 522
Altar of Saint Teresa (Gian Bernini) **2:** 259
Ambassadors, The (Hans Holbein the Younger)
    1: *88*
"American dream, the" **9:** 1169, 1170–1171, 1173
Amory Show (1913) **6:** 850
Ampère, André-Marie **5:** 704–705
anatomy **1:** 56
Angkor Wat **3:** *318*, 321
Anxiety (Edvard Munch) **6:** 850
Apollo Belvedere **4:** *495*, 497
Arabs, preserving ancient Greek knowledge
    1: 52–53
Archimedes **1:** 52
architecture
    Renaissance **1:** 88
    Saint Peter's in Rome **2:** *172*
    Tudor **2:** *213*
    Baroque **2:** 255–256, 257 **4:** *465*
    premodern Iranian **3:** *401*
    Mogul **3:** *407*, *411*, 412–413
    rococo **4:** 492–493
    classical style **4:** 495, 498, *499*
    Palladian **4:** 495, *498*
    the Eiffel Tower **6:** *841*, 846
    art nouveau **6:** 846–847
    National Congress Building (Brasilia) **9:** *1201*
Aristotle **1:** 57, 64, 73 **2:** 266
    and slavery **3:** 376
armillary spheres **2:** *266*
Arnolfini Marriage (Jan van Eyck) **2:** *251*
art nouveau **6:** 846–847
Art of Painting, The (Jan Vermeer) **2:** *261*
arts
    vogue for exotic art in Europe **6:** 784–785, 799,
        824
    in the late 1800s **6:** 841–850
    See also paintings; under various types of arts,
        e.g., music
astrolabes **2:** *267* **3:** *302*, *311* **4:** *529*
astrology **1:** 56
astronomy
    Ptolemaic view of **2:** *265*, 266, 268, 269
    Ptolemy's views challenged **2:** 267–270
atomic weights **5:** 703–704
atonal music **6:** 847, 850
Austen, Jane **5:** 636, 642
Averroës (Ibn Rushd) **1:** 57

Bacchus and Ariadne (Titian) **1:** *84*
Bach, Johann Sebastian **4:** 500
Bacon, Sir Francis **2:** 270–271
Baker, Josephine **7:** 951, *955*
Ballet Russe **6:** 850
ballets de cour **4:** *457*

Balzac, Honoré de **6:** 806, 846
Baroque **2:** 255–264 **4:** *465*, 491
Bartolommeo, Fra, painting by **1:** *58*
battery, discovery **5:** 704
Battle Between Carnival and Lent, The (Pieter
    Breughel the Elder) **1:** *11*
Baudelaire, Charles **6:** *842*
Bauhaus, and Hitler **7:** 991
Beaumarchais, Pierre Augustin Caron de **4:** 497
Beethoven, Ludwig van **5:** 598, 638, 639, 644
Berlioz, Hector **5:** 644
Bellini, Gentile, portrait by **1:** *104*
Bernini, Gianlorenzo **2:** 259, 263 **4:** *449*
Berry, Chuck **9:** 1171
Berzelius, Jakob **5:** 703–704
Bessarion, Cardinal **1:** 53, 64
bestiaries **4:** 506
Birth of a Nation, The (D. W. Griffith) **7:** 951
Black Beauty (Anna Sewell) **6:** 805
Blake, William **4:** *501* **5:** *615*, 637
Blenheim Palace **4:** *465*
Bodleian Library (Oxford) **1:** *53*
Bond, James (fictional character) **8:** *1097*
Bonnie and Clyde **7:** 969
Book of Hours, French **1:** *35* **2:** *195*
Book of Martyrs (John Foxe) **2:** 211
books **1:** 80
    and theology **1:** 56–57
    printed by Gutenberg **1:** 60–61
    and languages **1:** 61–62
    spread and impact of **1:** 61, 66
    censorship of **1:** 62
    in the 1700s **4:** 472–473, *474*, 521–522
    See also libraries; printing
Borromini, Francesco **2:** 257
Bosch, Hieronymus, painting by **1:** *34*
Botticelli, Sandro, painting by **1:** *87*
Boucher, François, painting by **4:** *493*
Boyle, Robert **5:** 697–698
Brady, Mathew **6:** 843
Brahe, Tycho **2:** *268*, 269–270
Brahms, Johannes **6:** 847
Bramante, Donato **1:** 84
Braque, Georges **6:** 850
Breughel the Elder, painting by **1:** *11*
Brontë sisters **5:** 642
    Emily Brontë **5:** 636
Brown, "Capability" **4:** 499
Brueghel, Pieter, the Elder, paintings by **2:** *216*,
    245
Brunel, Isambard Kingdom **5:** *706*
Brunelleschi, Filippo **1:** *79*, 81
Buddenbrooks (Thomas Mann) **6:** 850
Buffon, Georges-Louis Leclerc, Comte de **5:** 698
Bunyan, John **2:** 241, *243*
Byron, Lord **5:** *611*, 638

Cajuns **3:** 374
calculus **2:** 272
camera obscura **2:** 264
Camp Life in the Thirty Years' War (lithograph)
    2: *234*
Canaletto **4:** 496
Canova, Antonio **4:** 497
Canterbury Tales, The (Geoffrey Chaucer) **1:** 50
Caravaggio (Michelangelo da Merisi) **2:** 257–259
    painting by **2:** *256*, 259
Carpaccio, Vittore, painting by **3:** *298*
carpets
    Persian **3:** *399*
    Indian **3:** 413
Carracci, Annibale **2:** 255 **4:** 494–495
Carson, Rachel **9:** 1265
Cassatt, Mary, painting by **6:** *843*
Castagno, Andrea del, painting by **1:** *63*
Castiglione, Baldassare **1:** 9
Catholic Church
    Baroque art and architecture **2:** 257–259
    rococo architecture **4:** 492–493

Cervantes, Miguel de, *Don Quixote* **2:** *194*
Cézanne, Paul **6:** 843–844
Cham people **3:** 314, *318*, 321
chapels, Renaissance **1:** 80
Charleston (dance) **7:** *945*
Chaucer, Geoffrey **1:** 50
chemistry **5:** 703–704
Chopin, Frédéric **5:** *643*, 644
Chrysler Building **6:** 846
Church, Frederic **5:** 641
Cicero **1:** 63
classical style **4:** 494–496, 498, 499 **5:** *611*
    neoclassicism **4:** 497 **5:** 621, 636 **6:** *801*
    reaction against **5:** 635
classification, of the living world **4:** 507
Claude Lorrain (pseudonym of Claude Gellée)
    4: *494*, 495, 498
clavichords **1:** 86 **4:** *516*
coffee, and European social life **4:** *473*
Cole, Thomas **5:** 641, 643
Coleridge, Samuel Taylor **5:** 636, 639
Collins, Wilkie **6:** 805
commedia dell'arte **4:** 492
Common Sense (Tom Paine) **4:** 557
Comte, Auguste **5:** 703
Confessions (Jean-Jacques Rousseau) **5:** 637
Confucius (K'ung Ch'iu) **1:** 124 **4:** 530
Constable, John **5:** *637*, 643
Copernicus, Nicolaus **2:** 267–268
    and his heliocentric theory **2:** 170, 268–269
Copley, John Singleton **4:** 497
Cornfields with Flight of Birds (Vincent Van
    Gogh) **6:** 844
Coronation of Poppea, The (Claudio Monteverdi)
    1: 84
Cosby Show, The (TV show) **9:** *1178*
Courbet, Gustave **6:** 841–842
Courtier, The (Baldassare Castiglione) **1:** 9
Cranach, Lucas, "the Elder" **2:** 255
    paintings by **2:** *152*, *157*, *159*
Critique of Pure Reason (Immanuel Kant) **4:** *479*
crown
    of Rudolf II **1:** *69*
    of Charles V **2:** *155*
    of George I **4:** *444*
Crucifix in the Pine Forest (Caspar David
    Friedrich) **5:** *641*
cubism **6:** 850
Cuvier, Georges **5:** 698

Daguerre, Louis Jacques **6:** 842
Dalton, John **5:** 703
Dante Alighieri **1:** 50
Darrow, Clarence **5:** 700
Darwin, Charles **4:** 507 **5:** *697*, 698–699, *706*
    6: 812
David, Jacques-Louis **4:** 497
Davy, Humphry **5:** *701*, 703, 704
Dean, James **9:** 1171
Death of General Wolfe (Benjamin West) **4:** 497
Debussy, Claude **6:** 844
Defoe, Daniel **4:** 500
Degas, Edgar **6:** 842, 843
Delacroix, Eugène, paintings by **5:** *605*, *643*, 644
    6: *824*
Deposition, The or *Descent from the Cross*
    (Rubens) **2:** 257, 261
Depression Breadline, The (George Segal) **7:** *959*
Descartes, René **2:** 264, 271, 272
Dickens, Charles **5:** 626 **6:** 804, 806, 845
    Oliver Twist **5:** 632
    The Old Curiosity Shop **6:** 804
    Hard Times **6:** 845
    Martin Chuzzlewit **6:** 845
Diderot, Denis **4:** 476, 492
    Encyclopedia **4:** 476, 477, *502*, 510, *514*
dissection, human **1:** 56
Divine Comedy, The (Dante) **1:** 50
Doll's House, A (Henrik Ibsen) **6:** 850

Volume numbers appear in **boldface type**. Page numbers in *italic type* refer to illustrations and captions.

Volume numbers appear in **boldface type**. Page numbers in *italic type* refer to illustrations and captions.

Lorrain, Claude **4:** *494, 495,* 498
Louis XIV, king of France, and arts and culture **2:** 262–263 **4:** 458, 491, 492, 496, 497, 500
Lumière brothers **6:** 850
Lyell, Charles **5:** 698
Lyrical Ballads (Samuel Taylor Coleridge) **5:** 639

macaronies **4:** 496
Machiavelli, Niccolò **1:** 17, 65, 67, 68
Madame Bovary (Gustave Flaubert) **6:** 845
Maderna, Carlo **2:** *172*
madrigals **1:** 86
Mahler, Gustav **6:** 847
Mallarmé, Stéphane **6:** 844
Manet, Edouard **6:** 842
Mann, Thomas **6:** 850
Manon Lescaut (Prévost) **4:** 517
Mantegna, Andrea, painting by **1:** *72*
Manutius, Aldus **1:** 61, 63
Marcuse, Herbert **9:** 1165
Marriage of Figaro, The (Beaumarchais) **4:** 497
Marriage of Isaac and Rebecca (Claude Lorrain) **4:** *494*
Martin Chuzzlewit (Charles Dickens) **6:** 845
Marx Brothers **7:** *963*
Masaccio, Tommaso **1:** 81
   painting by **1:** *80*
Masolino **1:** 81
Massys, Quentin, painting by **1:** *39*
Maxwell, James Clerk **5:** *702,* 705
Mein Kampf (Adolf Hitler) **7:** 988 **8:** 1034, 1066–1067
melodrama **6:** 805, 845
Mendel, Gregor **5:** 699
Mendeleyev, Dmitri **5:** *701,* 704
Mengs, Anton **4:** 497
Mercator (Gerhard Kremer), maps **2:** *217* **3:** 301
Merchant of Venice, The (Shakespeare) **7:** 990
metric system, development **4:** *480*
Michelangelo **1:** 87
   sculptures by **1:** 81–82
   Sistine Chapel ceiling **1:** *83,* 84
microscopes **2:** 273–274
Milton, John **2:** 241
minarets, Persian **3:** *403*
Miracles of Ignatius of Loyola, The (Rubens) **2:** *171*
Mississippian culture **3:** 332–333, *338*
modernism **6:** 850
Modigliani, Amedeo **6:** 784, 824
Mogul empire, culture and architecture **3:** *407, 411,* 412–413, *416*
Molière **4:** 458, 460, *471,* 497
Mona Lisa (Leonardo da Vinci) **1:** 84, *85*
Monet, Claude **6:** 843
   paintings by **6:** *790,* 843, *845*
Montesquieu, Charles de Secondat, baron de **4:** *476*
Monteverdi, Claudio **1:** 84, 86
Moonstone, The (Wilkie Collins) **6:** 805
Moral Majority **9:** 1177–1178
More, Sir Thomas
   and humanism **1:** 67–68
   Utopia **1:** 67–68 **3:** 376
Moreau, Gustave **6:** 844
Mother and Her Child (Mary Cassatt) **6:** 843
movies **6:** 850 **9:** 1171
   spy **8:** *1097*
   See also film industry
Mozart, Wolfgang Amadeus **4:** 500, 521
Munch, Edvard, paintings by **6:** 850
music
   Renaissance **1:** 84, 85–86
   and Protestant worship **2:** *159*
   and the Dutch Reformed Church **2:** 224
   classical **4:** 500
   in eighteenth century homes **4:** *516*
   Romantic **5:** *638, 639, 643,* 644
   impressionism in **6:** 844
   atonal **6:** 847, 850
   and Vienna **6:** 847
   rock and roll **9:** 1171
   See also operas
musical instruments, Renaissance **1:** 85–86
Muybridge, Eadweard **6:** 842

Nash, Paul, sketches by **7:** *883*
natural selection, theory of **5:** 699
nature, and Romanticism **5:** 636, 637, 639, 640–641
Navajo (Native Americans) **3:** *342*
neoclassicism **4:** 497 **5:** *621,* 636 **6:** *801*
New Heloise, The (Jean-Jacques Rousseau) **4:** 478
Newton, Sir Isaac **2:** 224, 271–273, *274*
Niemeyer, Oscar **9:** 1201
Nietzsche, Friedrich **6:** 850
Night Watch, The (Rembrandt) **2:** 224
Nijinsky, Vaslav **6:** *850*
Northanger Abbey (Jane Austen) **5:** 636
novels
   in the 1700s **4:** 500, 517, 521
   on the effects of industrialization **5:** 626
   Romantic **5:** 638, *639,* 642
   sentimental **6:** 804
   melodramatic **6:** 805
   thriller **6:** 805
   spy **8:** *1097*

Oath of the Horatii (Jacques-Louis David) **4:** 497
Old Curiosity Shop, The (Charles Dickens) **6:** 804
Old Shepherd's Chief Mourner, The (Edwin Landseer) **6:** 805
Oliver Twist (Charles Dickens) **5:** 632
Olsen, Tillie **7:** 968
Olympia (Édouard Manet) **6:** 842
On the Chisholm Trail (Frederic Remington) **6:** *838*
On the Road (Jack Kerouac) **9:** 1171
One-Dimensional Man (Herbert Marcuse) **9:** 1165
opera houses **6:** 802, *803*
operas **4:** 500, 521 **6:** 848
   of Claudio Monteverdi **1:** 84
Orfeo (Monteverdi) **1:** 84
Origin of Species, The (Charles Darwin) **5:** 699, 700
Oscars (Academy Awards) **7:** 951

Paganini, Nicolò **5:** 644
Paine, Tom, *Common Sense* **4:** 557
paintings
   Renaissance **1:** *80, 81, 82, 84, 85*
   perspective **1:** 81
   landscape **1:** 121 **2:** *262* **5:** *637, 641,* 643
   Dutch (1600s) **2:** 223–224
   Baroque **2:** 256, *257–259,* 261–264
   still life **2:** 261–262
   Romantic **5:** 641
   portrait **6:** 842
   abstract **6:** 850
   cubist **6:** 850
Palestrina **1:** 86
Paley, William **5:** 698
Palladio, Andrea **4:** 495
Palmer, Fanny, painting by **6:** *829*
Pamela, or Virtue Rewarded (Samuel Richardson) **4:** 500, *513*
Paradise Lost (John Milton) **2:** 241
Paris Exhibition (1867) **6:** 794
Pasteur, Louis **5:** *704,* 705
Peacock Throne **3:** *406, 417*
Peasant Wedding, The (Pieter Brueghel the Elder) **2:** *245*
Pennsylvania Gazette (newspaper) **4:** 551
periodic table **5:** *701,* 704
perspective, in paintings **1:** 81
Petrarca, Francesco *See* Petrarch
Petrarch **1:** *63,* 64
Philosophical Dictionary, The (Voltaire) **4:** 476
philosophy, and Descartes **2:** 271, *272*
photography **6:** *788, 789,* 842–843, *844*
   color **5:** *702*
Picasso, Pablo **6:** 824, 850
Pietà (Michelangelo) **1:** 81
Pilgrim's Progress (John Bunyan) **2:** 241, *243*
Pisano, Andrea **1:** *31*
Pissarro, Camille **6:** 843
Plato **1:** 64–65
   and slavery **3:** 376
plays
   Romantic **5:** 638
   melodrama **6:** 805

Poe, Edgar Allan **6:** 790
poetry
   in the 1700s **4:** 500
   Romantic **5:** 636, *637,* 638–639, 640
   of Charles Baudelaire **6:** *842*
   symbolism in **6:** 844
Politics (Aristotle) **1:** 73
polyphony **1:** 86 **4:** 500
Poor Richard's Almanac (Benjamin Franklin) **4:** 551
Pope, Alexander **4:** 500
porcelain, Ming **1:** 127
Portrait of a Young Man with a Medal (Botticelli) **1:** *87*
portraits **6:** 842
Post-Impressionists **6:** 843–844
posters
   World War I **7:** *902, 903,* 918
   and the Russian Revolution **7:** 918, *921*
   and the Russian Civil War **7:** *920*
   American fashion (1920s) **7:** *952*
   film **7:** *963, 970* **8:** *1097*
   Work Projects Administration **7:** *967*
   and the Great Depression **7:** *968*
   and the Spanish Civil War **8:** *1032, 1033*
   World War II **8:** *1041, 1042, 1058, 1061, 1068*
   Marshall Plan **8:** *1088*
   Vietnamese nationalist **8:** *1117*
potlatch ceremonies **3:** 341
pottery
   Chinese **1:** 121
   Wedgwood **4:** *473,* 496
Pottier, Eugène **6:** 815
Poussin, Nicolas **4:** 454, 495
   painting by **2:** *262* **4:** *491*
Pre-Raphaelites **6:** 842
Presley, Elvis **9:** 1171
Prévost, Antoine-François **4:** 517
Prince, The (Niccolò Machiavelli) **1:** 65, 67
printing **1:** *66,* 94 **2:** 267
   Gutenberg's printing press **1:** *59,* 60–61 **2:** 254
   in China **1:** 60, 121
   and the spread of Protestantism **1:** 62 **2:** 158
   in the 1700s **4:** 521
   mechanized **5:** 642
Prodigal Son, The (Hieronymus Bosch) **1:** *34*
Prometheus Bound (Percy Bysshe Shelley) **5:** 638
Protestantism
   and art **2:** 255
   and Baroque **2:** *260,* 261
Proust, Marcel **6:** 848
psychoanalysis **6:** 849
Ptolemy
   Almagest **1:** 53
   and astronomy **1:** 53 **2:** *265,* 266, 268, 269
   Geographia **1:** 65 **3:** 300
   and the world **3:** 300–301, 304

Racine, Jean **4:** 497
radio waves, discovery **5:** 705
Rain, Steam, and Speed (J. M. W. Turner) **5:** *642*
Raphael **1:** 82
Reason, Age of, *See* Enlightenment, the
Rebel Without a Cause (movie) **9:** 1171
Record of Human Erosion, A (Dorothea Lange) **7:** *968*
Rembrandt, paintings by **2:** 224, 264
Remington, Frederic, painting by **6:** *838*
Renaissance **1:** 21, 39, 79–88 **2:** 255, 257, 267
   northern **1:** 85, 88, 94
   French **1:** 88
   and religion **1:** 95–96 **2:** 152
   and geography **3:** 300–301
Renoir, Auguste **6:** 843
Repton, Humphrey **4:** 498–499
Requiem (Giuseppe Verdi) **5:** *658*
Reynolds, Sir Joshua **4:** 496
Reza Abbasi **3:** *402, 403, 406*
Richardson, Samuel, *Pamela, or Virtue Rewarded* (novel) **4:** 500, *513*
rights, human, and Enlightenment thought **4:** 475, 480
Rimbaud, Arthur **6:** 844
Ring of the Nibelung, The (Richard Wagner) **6:** 848

Volume numbers appear in **boldface type**. Page numbers in *italic type* refer to illustrations and captions.

Rite of Spring, The (Igor Stravinsky) **6:** *850*
Rivera, Diego **7:** *976*
Robinson Crusoe (Daniel Defoe) **4:** 500
rock and roll **9:** 1171
rococo style **4:** 491, *492–493*
Romanticism **4:** 500, 510, 517 **5:** 635–644 **6:** 841
Rome, ancient
   and humanism **1:** 63
   influence on classicism **4:** 494–496
Rossetti, Dante Gabriel **6:** 842
Rousseau, Jean-Jacques **2:** 233 **4:** 476–478, 498,
   510, 512, 513 **5:** 637 **6:** 811
Royal Academy (London) **4:** 496
Royal Academy of Painting and Sculpture
   (France) **2:** 262
Royal Society (London) **2:** 274
Rubens, Peter Paul **2:** 260–261
   paintings by **2:** *171, 257, 260–261*
Ruth, Babe **7:** *950*, 951
Ruysch, Rachel **2:** 262

Safavid empire, and the arts **3:** 400–402, *406*
Saint Peter's, Rome **1:** 11–12, 84 **2:** *172*
   Michelangelo's *Pietà* **1:** *81*
Saint-Simon, Henri **5:** 703
salons **4:** 472, 521
Sargent, John Singer **6:** 842
Schoenberg, Arnold **6:** 847, 850
School of Athens, The (Raphael) **1:** 82
Schoolmen **1:** 57, 58
schools **2:** *250*, 252
   cathedral **1:** 54
   grammar schools **1:** 54
   in the 1700s **4:** 518
Schubert, Franz **5:** 644
Schumann, Robert (musician) **5:** 644
science **1:** 56
   in the 1800s **5:** 697–706
   developments (1900s) **9:** 1253–1262
scientific revolution (1600s) **2:** 256, 265–274
   5: 697–698
   and art **2:** 264
   and the Enlightenment **4:** 471–472
Scopes, John **5:** 700
Scott, Sir Walter **5:** 636, 642
Scream, The (Edvard Munch) **6:** 850
sculpture
   Renaissance **1:** 81–82
   African **1:** *112*, 113
   Baroque **2:** 256, 259, 263
   Soviet **7:** *928*
Secession movement **6:** 847
Second Treatise of Government (John Locke)
   4: 475
Segal, George, sculpture by **7:** *959*
Sèvres, porcelain from **4:** 492
Sewell, Anna **6:** 805
Shahn, Ben **7:** *968*
Shakespeare, William **2:** 209
   The Merchant of Venice **7:** 990
Shelley, Mary Wollstonecraft **5:** 638, *639*
Shelley, Percy Bysshe **5:** 638
Shilling, David, mother's hat **9:** *1194*
Silent Spring (Rachel Carson) **9:** 1265
Sinan **1:** *107*
Sisley, Alfred **6:** 843
Sistine Chapel, ceiling **1:** *83*, 84
slaves/slavery, culture **3:** 385–386
Smith, Adam **4:** *479*, 480
Social Contract, The (Jean-Jacques Rousseau)
   4: 478–479 **5:** 637
Son of the Sheik (film) **7:** *950*
sonatas **4:** 500
songs, Renaissance **1:** 86
Songs of Innocence (William Blake) **5:** *637*
Sontag, Susan **9:** 1164
Sorrows of Young Werther (Johann Wolfgang von
   Goethe) **5:** 638
Spain, and Catholic Baroque **2:** 260
Spenser, Edmund **2:** 209
Spinoza, Baruch **2:** 224
Steinbeck, John **7:** *965*, 968
Steno, Nicholaus **5:** 698
Stephenson, George **5:** 620, *706*
Stephenson, Robert **5:** *706*

Stevin, Simon **2:** 224
still life paintings **2:** 261–262
Stravinsky, Igor **6:** 850
Stubbs, George **4:** 496
Sturm und Drang movement **5:** 638
Supper at Emmaus (Caravaggio) **2:** 256, 259
Swift, Jonathan **4:** 500
Swing, The (Jean Honoré Fragonard) **4:** *494*
symbolist movement **6:** 844
symphonies **4:** 500

Taj Mahal **3:** 412, *417*
Talbot, William Henry Fox **6:** 842, *844*
Tartuffe (Molière) **4:** 458, 460
Tax Collector, The (Quentin Massys) **1:** *39*
telescopes **2:** 270, *273*
television **9:** 1170–1171, 1178, 1261
tepees **3:** 333, 335, *337*
theaters **6:** *803*, 806
   commedia dell'arte **4:** *492*
   Kabuki **4:** 540
theosophy **6:** 850
Thirty Three Arches, Bridge of the **3:** *401*
Thoreau, Henry David **5:** 637, 640–641 **9:** 1263
three wise monkeys **4:** *535*
Tiepolo, Giovanni Battista **4:** 493
Tiger Hunt, The (Eugène Delacroix) **5:** *643*
Tin Pan Alley **7:** 950
Tintoretto **1:** 84
Titian **1:** 84
Toledo, Juan de **2:** 191
Tolstoy, Leo **1:** 106 **5:** 696 **6:** 845–846
tombs, Renaissance **1:** 82
Toscanelli, Paolo **1:** 65
total artwork **6:** 847–848
totems **3:** *331, 340*
Toulouse-Lautrec, Henri **6:** 784
tribes, Native American **3:** 331, 333, 335
Trinity College (Cambridge) **1:** *53*
Trollope, Anthony **6:** 806
Trouble I've Seen, The (Martha Gellhorn) **7:** 968
Turner, J. M. W., paintings by **5:** *642*, 643
Tyson, Edward **5:** 699

Uccello, Paolo, painting by **1:** *73*
Uncle Remus (Joel Chandler Harris) **6:** 804
universities
   European **1:** 40, 50–52, *53*, 58, 66
   North American **3:** 367
U.S.A. (John Dos Passos) **7:** 968
Ussher, James **5:** 698
Usurers, The (Van Reymersae) **2:** *216*
Utopia (Thomas More) **1:** 67–68 **3:** 376

Valentino, Rudolph **7:** *950*
Van Gogh, Vincent *See* Gogh, Vincent Van
Vasari, Giorgio **1:** 87
vases
   delftware **2:** *221*
   Iranian **3:** *404*
   Greek-style **5:** *611*
Velásquez, Diego de **2:** 260
   paintings by **2:** *259*, 260
Venice, paintings of **4:** 496
Verdi, Giuseppe **5:** *658* **6:** 848
Verlaine, Paul **6:** 844
Vermeer, Jan **2:** 224, 264
   paintings by **2:** *222, 253, 261, 264*
Veronese **1:** 84
Verrochio, Andrea del, statue by **1:** *82*
Versailles, Palace of **1:** 38 **2:** 263 **4:** 458, *459,*
   460, 472, 491
   gardens **4:** 454, 498, 499 **5:** 635
   court of Louis XIV **4:** 458–459
   convention of the Estates General (1789) **5:** *584*
   Petit Trianon **5:** *585*
Vesalius **2:** 267
View of Delft (Jan Vermeer) **2:** *222*
Vindication of the Rights of Woman, A (Mary
   Wollstonecraft) **4:** 480
viols **1:** 85
Volta, Alessandro **5:** 704
Voltaire, François Marie Arouet de **4:** 475–476,
   544

Wagner, Richard **6:** *843*, 847–848
Walden, or Life in the Woods (Henry David
   Thoreau) **5:** 641 **9:** 1263
Walpole, Hugh **4:** 496
Water Carrier of Seville (Diego Velásquez) **2:** *259*,
   260
Waterbabies, The (Charles Kingsley) **6:** 804, *809*
Watteau, Antoine **4:** 492
Wealth of Nations, The (Adam Smith) **4:** 480
Wedgwood, Josiah, pottery **4:** *473*, 496
Werther (Johann Wolfgang von Goethe) **4:** 500
West, Benjamin **4:** 497
What is Enlightenment? (Immanuel Kant) **4:** 479
wigwams **3:** 333, 335, 340
Wilberforce, Samuel **5:** 705–706
Wilde, Oscar **6:** 848
Winckelmann, Johann Joachim **4:** 497
Wöhler, Friedrich **5:** 704
Wollstonecraft, Mary **4:** 480, 512
women, and Enlightenment thought **4:** 480
woodcuts, Japanese **4:** 540, *542*
Woodstock rock festival **9:** *1176*
Wordsworth, William **5:** 636, 639, 640, 641
Worth, Charles Frederick **6:** 846
Wren, Sir Christopher **2:** *244*
Wright, Frank Lloyd **6:** 784
writing, Chinese **4:** *526*
Wuthering Heights (Emily Brontë) **5:** 636

Yung-lo ta-tien (encyclopedia) **1:** 66
yuppies **9:** 1178

Zola, Émile **5:** 626 **6:** 806, 844, 846, *847*

Volume numbers appear in **boldface type**. Page numbers in *italic type* refer to illustrations and captions.

CUSTOMS and EVERYDAY LIFE

abortion **9:** 1166, 1177
affirmative action **9:** 1168, 1178
African-Americans
  and World War I **7:** 898–899
  and affirmative action **9:** 1168, 1178
agricultural revolution **4:** 501–502
agriculture *See* farming
AIDS **9:** 1272, *1276*
  in Africa **9:** 1223
aircraft
  stunts on **7:** *947*, 951
  first trans-Atlantic flight **7:** 951
  passenger flights (1920s) **7:** *952*
  development (1900s) **9:** 1260
alcohol
  and Native Americans **3:** 391–393
  temperance **6:** 801
  Prohibition in the United States **7:** 948
almanacs **4:** 522
alms **1:** *36*
American Civil War (1861–1865), social effects
  5: 684
"American dream, the" **9:** 1169, 1170–1171, 1173
Anasazi people **3:** 332
anesthetics **5:** 705 **6:** 801
animals
  selection and breeding **4:** 503
  and sentimentality **6:** 804–805
antiseptics **5:** 705 **6:** 801
apprentices/apprenticeships **2:** 252 **4:** 518
armor **1:** 15 **4:** *454*
Arnolfini Marriage (Jan van Eyck) **2:** *251*
Ascot race meetings **9:** *1194*
astrology **1:** 56
automobile industry **6:** 793 **7:** 949
automobiles **7:** *960* **9:** *1170*

babies, in the 1700s **4:** 512–513
baby boom **9:** 1162
barbed wire **6:** 839
Barnard, Christiaan **9:** 1262
baseball **7:** *950*, 951
Battle Between Carnival and Lent, The (Pieter
  Breughel the Elder) **1:** *11*
beds **6:** *801*
beer **2:** 249
bees, introduced to the Americas **3:** 395, *396*
bestiaries **4:** 506
bicycles **6:** 793
birth control **6:** 799
Black Death **1:** 8–9, 30, *31*, 43–44 **2:** 165, 245
  and central Europe **1:** 93
boats, building **3:** 302
bookbinding **1:** *33*
books **1:** 80
  and theology **1:** 56–57
  printed by Gutenberg **1:** 60–61
  and languages **1:** 61–62
  spread and impact of **1:** 61, 66
  censorship of **1:** 62
  in the Middle Ages **2:** 254
  See also libraries; printing
bootleggers **7:** 948
bovine spongiform encephalopathy (BSE) **9:** 1275
boxing **4:** *519*
bread **4:** 522
buffalo **3:** 341–342, 395 **6:** 839

cafés *See* coffeehouses
cameras **6:** *788*, 789, 842, *844*
  See also photography
candles **2:** 247
canoes, Pacific island **3:** *314*
Carlyle, Thomas **6:** 800–801
carnivals **4:** 521
carpetbaggers **6:** 831
carpets
  Persian **3:** *399*
  Indian **3:** 413
carriages, steam **5:** *621*
caste system
  in the Spanish colonies **3:** 351–354
  in India **8:** 1109, 1111

cattle, and colonial America **3:** 394
cereals **1:** 33
chapbooks **4:** 522
Charleston (dance) **7:** *945*
children
  in the late Middle Ages **1:** 10
  in the 1700s **4:** 512, 514–519
  and industrialization (1800s/1900s) **5:** *617*, 629,
    631–634 **6:** *811*, 815, *840*
  deaths **5:** *633* **6:** 804, *805*
  in the late 1800s **6:** 799–800, 804
chimney sweeps **5:** *633*
Chisholm Trail **6:** *838*
cholera **5:** 701, 705 **6:** 790, 801, 802
Christmas, Victorian **6:** 797, 805
Chrysler Building **7:** 948
cities and towns
  in early modern Europe **1:** 16, 77 **2:** 252–253
  and vagrancy **1:** 36
  fortifications **1:** 73
  shops **1:** *73*, 77, 78
  industrial (1800s) **5:** 612, 625–626 **6:** 802–803
  redesigned (late 1800s) **5:** 655
  suburbs **6:** 802 **9:** 1170
  See also urbanization
class/rank, social
  and the feudal system **1:** 8, 13–14
  in early modern Europe **1:** 75–76
  in the 1700s **4:** 512, 516
  under the Japanese Tokugawa clan **4:** 534
  and industrialization **5:** 628, 630
  in the late 1800s **6:** 797
  Karl Marx's view of **6:** 812
clothing **2:** 251 **4:** *519*
  fashion in France (1600s) **4:** *458*
  early 1800s **5:** *607*, 642
  fashion in France (1800s) **6:** *846*
  during World War I **7:** 893, *894*
  American fashion (1920s) **7:** *952*
  Nazi uniforms **8:** *1028*
coal **4:** 510
  mining **4:** *509*, 510 **5:** 619, *701* **6:** *811*
Coca-Cola **7:** *960* **9:** 1274, 1277
cod, in colonial America **3:** 366, 388–389, *390*
coffeehouses (cafés) **4:** *473*, 521, 522
community ties (1500s/1600s) **2:** 251–252
compasses, magnetic **3:** 301, 302
computers **9:** 1258–1259, *1262*
  and the Internet **9:** 1259–1260, 1277
Concorde (aircraft) **9:** 1260, *1261*
Conestoga wagons **3:** *369*
contraband (slaves) **5:** 684
contraception **6:** 799 **9:** 1172, 1176
cookbooks **6:** *800*
corn **3:** 350, *371*, 389, 392, *393* **4:** 504
corregidors **1:** 71–72
cowboys **6:** 838, 839
craftsmen, master **4:** 518
Creutzfeldt-Jakob disease (CJD) **9:** 1275
Crick, Francis **9:** 1262
crime, in western Europe (1500s) **1:** 36
crops
  in sub-Saharan Africa **1:** 110–111, 117
  and the agricultural revolution **4:** 501–502
  Latin American **7:** *972*
  See also farming
currency, paper **1:** 121
cutlery **2:** *249*
cycling **6:** *792*, 793

dancing
  Charleston **7:** *945*
  marathon **7:** 951
DDT **9:** 1265
death rate, in Europe (1700s) **4:** 522
department stores, first **5:** 657
disease
  in the 1500s/1600s **2:** 247–248, 249
  discovery of microorganisms **2:** 274
  brought to the Americas from Europe **3:** 346,
    387, 390–391 **4:** 544
  in Africa **3:** 393
  brought to Europe from the Americas **3:** 393
  in Europe (c. 1700s) **4:** 510, 522
  and scientific discovery **4:** *522* **5:** 705

and industrialization **5:** 626, *629*
  in the 1800s **6:** 801
  combating (1900s) **9:** 1271–1272
  See also plague
divorce **9:** 1172
DNA **9:** 1262
doctors **2:** 247–248
domestic service, employment in **6:** *800*
ducking stools, and witches **2:** *182*

Ebola virus **9:** 1272
education **2:** 254
  the spread of learning in Europe **1:** 49–58,
    59–62, 78
  and the rise of humanism **1:** 59–68, 80
  in the 1700s **4:** 472, 515–518
  and segregation in the United states **8:** 1082
  See also schools; universities
electrical appliances, domestic **6:** 790
electricity, development of streetlamps **6:** *788*, 790
employment, for women (late 1800s) **6:** 799–800
enclosure **1:** 34–35, 36 **2:** 246, *247*, 252
engines, steam **4:** *509*, 510 **5:** *619*
environmental concerns (1900s) **9:** 1263–1272,
  1274, 1282
environmental movements **9:** 1165–1166, 1271
Estates General **4:** 450, 451, 452
  dissolved by Louis XIII **4:** 453
Europe
  everyday life (1300s–1500s) **1:** 7–9
  everyday life (1500s/1600s) **1:** 8 **2:** 245–254
  everyday life (1700s) **4:** 511–522
Eurostar train **9:** *1196*

factories, in the 1700s **4:** 510
families
  early modern European **1:** 76
  in the 1700s **4:** 512–513, 514–515
  middle-class (late 1800s) **6:** 798–799
  working-class (late 1800s) **6:** 799–800
famines **9:** 1275
  in early modern Europe **1:** 8, 30, 32–33 **2:** 248
  potato famine (1845) **5:** 612, 650
  in Bengal (1943) **8:** 1062, 1113
  in Sudan (1990s) **9:** 1224
  in North Korea (late 1990s) **9:** 1276
farming
  in early modern Europe **1:** 16, *18*, 29–30,
    32–35 **2:** 247
  and trade **1:** 40
  during the reign of Henry VII **2:** 206–207
  Native American **3:** 333–334, 340
  colonies in America **3:** 349–350, *365* **4:** 505
  and the agricultural revolution **4:** 501–502, 503
  in France (1700s) **4:** 520
  nationalization under Stalin **7:** 927–928
  collective farms in China (1960s) **9:** *1181*,
    1182, *1183*
  adverse side effects of (1900s) **9:** 1264
  green revolution **9:** 1264–1265
  and pesticides **9:** 1265
  slash-and-burn **9:** *1266*, 1267
  See also famines
fashion *See* clothing
feet, binding **7:** *938*, 939
feminism **9:** 1166
feudal system **1:** 8–9, 13–14, 41
  and raising armies **1:** 27, 72
  decline **1:** 34, 35, *38*
  and the king **1:** 70
fiber-optics **9:** *1261*
fin de siècle **6:** 848, 850
fish, dried **1:** 114–115
fisheries
  Atlantic **2:** 210, 248 **3:** 355, 388, 389, *390*
  Southeast Asian **3:** 316
  in colonial America **3:** 366, 388–389, *390*
  and El Niño **9:** 1268
  overfishing **9:** 1269
flappers **7:** *945*, 950
flight *See* aircraft
flyboats **1:** 42, *44*
food
  in Europe (1500s/1600s) **2:** 248–249, *250*
    3: 389

food (continued)
   in colonial America **3:** 350, *371*, 395
   brought to Europe from the Americas **3:** 389, 392, *394*, 395–396
   and the Mogul empire **3:** 414–415
   in Europe (1700s) **4:** 522
   rationing during World War II **8:** 1068–1069
forks, cutlery **2:** *249*
fortifications, town **1:** 73
Franklin, Rosalind **9:** 1262
Freemasonry **4:** *472*
furniture **2:** 250–251
   in the 1700s **4:** 516–517
   in colonial America **4:** *552*
   in the late 1800s **6:** 798–799

Galen (Roman physician) **2:** 247–248
galleons **3:** 302
gaslighting, domestic **6:** 790
gauchos **6:** *760* **7:** *973*
gay rights **9:** *1165*, 1166
geishas **4:** 538, *541*
gender, in the 1700s **4:** 512, 518
gentlemen **1:** 75
girls, education **1:** 54
glassmaking, in Mogul India **3:** 413
grain, storage **4:** *504*, 508
Great Fire of London **2:** 242–243, *244*
Great Plague **2:** 242–243, 247
Great Stink (1848) **5:** *629*, 705 **6:** 802
green revolution **9:** 1264–1265
guilds **1:** 16, 43, *44* **4:** 518
Gutenberg, Johannes, printing press **1:** *59*, 60–61 **2:** 254

haciendas **3:** *349*, 350 **6:** 742
Haida people **3:** *331*
harnesses **1:** 16, *18*
helicopters, military **9:** *1254*, 1255
herbals **4:** 506
Hine, Lewis Wickes **6:** 815, *840*
HIV (human immunodeficiency virus) **9:** 1272
homes, middle-class (late 1800s) **6:** 798–799
honey **3:** 390, 395, *396*
honeybees, introduced to the Americas **3:** 395, *396*
horses
   and colonial America **3:** 342, 387, 394–395
   in Europe (1700s) **4:** *518*, 520
hospitals **6:** 801
   charitable **2:** *249*
houses
   European (1600s) **2:** 250
   in colonial America **3:** *367*
   European (1700s) **4:** 516, 517
   in industrial London (1800s) **5:** *625*
hovercraft **9:** 1260
How the Other Half Lives (Jacob Riis) **5:** 626
human immunodeficiency virus (HIV) **9:** 1272
humors, bodily **2:** 248

Indians
   North American *See* Native Americans
   Latin American **6:** *762, 764, 765*
Industrial Revolution, effects on women and children **5:** *617, 629*, 631–634
Industrial Revolution, "Third" **9:** 1254
influenza, post-World War I pandemic **7:** 883
ink **1:** 60
Internet **9:** 1259–1260, 1277
iron
   ironworking in Africa **1:** 113, 117
   production **4:** 510
   iron foundry in Kiel **7:** *873*

Jenner, Edward **4:** *522*
journeymen **4:** 518
justices of the peace **1:** 72

Khmer people **3:** *319*
kivas **3:** 342
knights **1:** *38*
knives, cutlery **2:** *249*
kulaks **7:** 927–930

landfill sites **9:** *1263*

language
   Latin and the vernacular **1:** 49–50, 59–60, 61
   and books **1:** 61–62
"la Peur" **4:** 450
Latin **1:** 49–50, 52, 59–60
libraries **1:** 80 **4:** 521
life expectancy
   in the Middle Ages **1:** 10
   in early modern Europe **1:** 31–32
lighting
   street **6:** *788*, 790
   domestic **6:** 790
Lindbergh, Charles **7:** 951
log cabins **3:** 363
Long Drive **6:** 838
longhouses, Native American **3:** 335, 340, *341*

mad cow disease **9:** 1275
maglev trains **9:** 1260
malaria **3:** 396 **9:** 1271–1272
manioc **3:** 396
maps
   Flanders (1540) **2:** *217*
   Vienna **3:** *297*
   portolan charts **3:** *300*, 301
   world **3:** *300*, 301, *312*
Mardi Gras **4:** 521
marriages
   in early modern Europe **1:** 30, 32, 77 **2:** *245*, 251
   in Europe (1700s) **4:** *515*, 520
   in Japanese society **4:** 538
Masonic lodges **4:** 472
master craftsmen **4:** 518
Mayan empire **3:** 332, 392
Medicaid **9:** 1160
Medicare **9:** 1160
medicine **1:** *31* **2:** 247–248 **6:** 801
   and technology **9:** 1262
melons **4:** *520*
mestizos **3:** 351–354
   post-independence **6:** 758–759
metalworking, in Africa **1:** 113
middle class **5:** 628, 630
   in the late 1800s **6:** 797, 798–799
midwives **2:** 248
millet **1:** *117*
mining
   in Europe **1:** *32, 33*
   silver **1:** *32* **3:** 348, 388
   salt **3:** 348
   copper **9:** *1223*
   See also coal
Mogul empire, lives of the poor **3:** 415
money
   begins to supercede barter **1:** 34
   hyperinflation in Germany (1923) **7:** 953–954, 988
Moral Majority **9:** 1177–1178
Morse, Samuel **6:** 840
motherhood, in the 1700s **4:** 512–513, *515*
motor transport, after World War I **7:** *946*, 949
movies **6:** 850
mulattos **3:** 351–354, 386
music, in eighteenth-century homes **4:** *516*
music halls **6:** 806

National Organization for Women (NOW) **9:** 1166
national parks (American) **5:** 641 **6:** 840
Native Americans **6:** 839
   daily life **3:** 333–338, 340–342
   and colonists **3:** 350, 354, 358, 359, 368, 373–374 **4:** 543
   as slaves **3:** 350, 380–381
   conflicts with colonists **3:** 368 **4:** 543–546
   and alcohol **3:** 391–393
   and European diseases **3:** 393 **4:** 544
   and horses **3:** 395
   view of the natural world **3:** 396
   wars against the U.S. army (1862–1890) **6:** *835*, 839
   and the Ghost Dance **6:** 839
natural world
   viewed by Native Americans **3:** 396
   viewed in the 1700s **4:** *476*, 498, 501–510, 510, 512

industrial development (1700s) **4:** 508–510
   See also rural life
navigation **3:** 301–302
newspapers **6:** 806
   in Europe (1700s) **4:** 522
North America
   colonial life in **3:** 365–374
   frontier life **3:** 367–368
   resources and colonial exploitation **3:** 387–396
nuts, from the Americas **3:** 396

optical fibers **9:** *1261*
organ grinders **5:** *628*
organs, transplants **9:** 1262
Owen, Robert **5:** 703 **6:** *809*, 811

paper currency **1:** 121
papermaking **1:** 33, 60 **2:** 254
parchment **1:** *33*
pasteurization **5:** 705
peaches **3:** *395*
peanuts **3:** 396
Peasant Wedding, The (Pieter Brueghel the Elder) **2:** *245*
peasants
   European (post-Black Death) **1:** 9, 30
   European (1500s) **1:** 35–36
   revolt in Germany (early 1500s) **1:** 35–36 **2:** 156
   repressed in central Europe (the second serfdom) **1:** 94
   revolt in Russia (1600s) **1:** 98
   European (1700s) **4:** 504, 517, 519–520
   in Prussia and the Habsburg empire **4:** 505
   Japanese **4:** 534–536 **6:** 778–779
   European (early 1800s) **5:** 609
   in Russia (1800s) **5:** 687, 691, 693, 694
   and the Spanish Civil War **8:** 1032
   See also serfs
penicillin **9:** 1262
Pennsylvania Gazette (newspaper) **4:** 551
periodicals, in Europe (1700s) **4:** 522
pesticides **9:** 1265, 1275
Philadelphia Centennial Exposition (1876) **6:** *801*
photography **6:** *788*, 789, 842–843
   color **5:** *702*
   of child laborers **6:** 815, *840*
pigs **4:** *503*
   in colonial America **3:** 394
plague **4:** 522
   Black Death (1347) **1:** 8–9, 30, *31*, 43–44 **2:** 165, 245
   Great Plague (1665) **2:** 242–243, 247
plankhouses, Native American **3:** 335, 341
plantations **3:** 349, 387
   tea **4:** *531*
   cotton **5:** 647, *654*, 677
plants, European plants colonizing the Americas **3:** 394
plows **1:** 16, *18* **4:** *502*
police **2:** 251
pollution **9:** 1267, 1270, *1272*
   and global warming **9:** 1267–1268
   oil spills **9:** 1268–1269
   atmospheric **9:** 1269, *1274*
   burning oil wells **9:** *1273*
Pony Express **6:** 840
poorhouses **5:** 632
population(s)
   in early modern Europe **1:** 29, 30–31
   in France (1400s–1500s) **2:** 196
   in Europe (1600s) **2:** 234, 245–246
   shifting **2:** 254
   of colonial America **3:** 365–366 **4:** 549
   in Europe (1700s) **4:** 505–508, 511
   in postcolonial Africa **9:** 1222
   world growth (1800s–1900s) **9:** 1264, 1275
portolan charts **3:** *300*, 301
postal services **5:** 624 **6:** 793
potatoes **3:** 350, 389, 392, *394* **4:** 504, 508
potato famine (1845) **5:** 612, 650
potlatch ceremonies **3:** 341
printing **1:** *66*, 94 **2:** 267
   Gutenberg's printing press **1:** *59*, 60–61 **2:** 254
   in China **1:** 60, 121

Volume numbers appear in **boldface type**. Page numbers in *italic type* refer to illustrations and captions.

and the spread of Protestantism **1:** 62 **2:** 158
  in the 1700s **4:** 521
  mechanized **5:** 642
Prohibition, in the United States **7:** 948
propaganda
  during World War I **7:** 901–902, 918
  during the Russian Revolution **7:** 918
  under Stalin's dictatorship **7:** 926
  during World War II **8:** *1042, 1043, 1053,* 1060, 1066–1067
  Vietnamese nationalist **8:** *1117*
prostitution **6:** 800
public houses **4:** 521
Pueblo Bonito **3:** 332
pueblos **3:** 332, 335, *339*

quadrants **3:** 301–302
quinine **3:** 396

rabies **5:** *704,* 705
radio
  in 1920s America **7:** 950, 951
  and World War II **8:** 1067–1068
  Japanese-manufactured **9:** *1211*
railroads **4:** 509 **5:** *649*
  and the Industrial Revolution **5:** 619–620, 622, *623*
  timetables **5:** 620
  tunnels **5:** *621*
  United States **5:** 622, *623, 649* **6:** *832,* 838, 840
  Canadian transcontinental **5:** 675
  Russian **5:** *693,* 694–695
  Mexican **6:** *737,* 741–743, 746
  South American **6:** 764, *765*
  European **6:** 790, 791
  underground and elevated **6:** *791,* 792
  Chinese **7:** *941*
  Indonesian **8:** *1020*
rank, social *See* class/rank, social
rationing, food, during World War II
  8: 1068–1069
rats, black **1:** 30, *31*
recycling **9:** *1271*
refrigeration **6:** 793 **7:** *967*
refuse **9:** *1263*
rice, cultivation **1:** 121 **3:** 316–317 **4:** 524, *530*
Riis, Jacob **5:** 626
Rosie the Riveter (fictional character) **8:** *1061*
Royal Society for the Prevention of Cruelty to Animals **6:** 804
rubber **3:** 395 **6:** 794 **9:** 1265–1266
rural life
  in Europe **1:** 16 **2:** 247
  in France (1400s) **1:** *35* **2:** *195*
  in France (1700) **4:** *520*

sago palm **3:** 316
Salem (Massachusetts), witch trials **2:** 182 **3:** 370, *373*
salt, mining **3:** 348
sanitation **2:** 249–250 **6:** 801–802
  See also sewage systems
Santa Fe Trail **6:** *839*
scalawags **6:** 831
schools **2:** *250,* 252
  cathedral **1:** 54
  grammar schools **1:** 54
  in the 1700s **4:** 518
scribes **1:** *49,* 60
seaside, vacations at **6:** 806
seed drills **4:** *502,* 503
segregation, in the United states **6:** 831
sensibility, cult of **4:** 517
sentimentality, in the late 1800s **6:** 804–805
serfdom, "the second" **1:** 94
serfs
  in Europe **1:** 34, 35 **4:** 481–482, 483, 504–505 **5:** 602
  in Russia **4:** 481, 482, 504–505 **5:** 689–690, 691, 692–693 **6:** 809 **7:** 909
servants
  indentured **3:** 367
  in Europe (1700s) **4:** 513–514, 516, 520
sewage systems **5:** *629* **6:** 802, *803*
sex *See* gender

sexual freedom, (post-1960s) **9:** 1165
shamans, Native American **3:** *335*
sharecropping **6:** 831
sheep
  shearing **1:** *33* **2:** *246, 247*
  and enclosure **1:** 34, 35 **2:** 246
  Thomas More quoted on **2:** 208
shellfish **4:** *505*
ships **3:** 302
  slave **3:** *375,* 380–*381*
  built in the American colonies **4:** 549
  steamships **6:** 792–793
shoes **2:** 251
shops, early modern European **1:** *73,* 77, *78*
Skimmington parties **2:** 251
skyscrapers **6:** *787,* 789 **7:** *947, 948,* 960
slaves/slavery
  Ottoman **1:** 104
  Tatar **1:** 104
  daily life in the new World **3:** 384–385
smallpox
  brought to the New World from Europe **3:** 346, 390–391, 393 **4:** 544
  vaccination against **4:** *522*
  eradication **9:** 1271, 1280
soap **2:** 249–250
social status *See* class/rank, social
society
  divided into three estates (Middle Ages) **1:** 8
  divided into three estates (France) **5:** 583
  Western society in the late 1800s **6:** 797–806
sodbusters **9:** 1264
soil, improvement **4:** 503
sorghum **1:** *117*
Spectator (periodical) **4:** 522
steam engines *See* engines, steam
steamboats **5:** *622, 648,* 649
steamships **6:** 792–793
stocks **2:** 254
streetlamps, electric **6:** *788,* 790
students, protests by western students (1960s) **9:** 1162, 1163–1164, 1165
suburbs **6:** 802 **9:** 1170
suffragettes **7:** 898, 948
sugar **3:** 390, *391*
superstition, in Europe (1700s) **4:** 520–521
suttee **5:** 668
swaddling **4:** 512, *513*
syphilis **3:** 393

Tatler (periodical) **4:** 522
taverns **4:** 521
tea **4:** 522
teahouses, Japanese **4:** *540*
telecommunications **9:** 1261–1262
telegrapy **5:** 624 **6:** 832, 840
telephones, mobile phones **9:** *1260,* 1262
television **9:** 1170–1171, 1178, 1261
  satellite **9:** 1277
temperance **6:** 801
temples, Southeast Asian **3:** 317–318, 320, 321, *322*
tepees **3:** 333, 335, *337*
textiles, African **1:** 114
Thanksgiving **3:** 359, *371*
thuggee **5:** 668
Times (newspaper) **4:** 522
Tin Pan Alley **7:** 950
tobacco **3:** 334, 358, 390 **4:** 543–544, *545*
toilets **6:** 801
tomatoes **3:** 396
towns *See* cities and towns
Townshend, Charles **4:** 503
trade associations **4:** 518
trains
  Eurostar **9:** *1196*
  magnetic levitation (maglev) **9:** 1260
transplants, organ **9:** 1262
transport, in early modern Europe **1:** 42
tribes, Native American **3:** 331, 333, 335
tricycles **6:** *792*
tsetse flies **1:** 110
tuberculosis **5:** 705
Tull, Jethro **4:** 503
turkeys **3:** 396

turnips **4:** 503
turnpikes **4:** 509
typhoid **6:** 802

universities
  European **1:** 40, 50–52, *53,* 58, 66, 94
  semesters **1:** 40
  North American **3:** 367
untouchables **8:** 1111
urbanization
  in early modern Europe **1:** 16, 33, 36, 37–38, 40, 44, *73, 78*
  in the 1800s **5:** 625–628 **6:** 802–803
  and urban replanning (1800s) **6:** 789–790
  See also cities and towns

vacations **6:** 806
vaccinations **5:** 705
  smallpox **4:** *522*
valentines **6:** *804*
vellum **1:** 60 **2:** 254
villages, early modern European **1:** 77, 78

wagons, Conestoga **3:** *369*
water closets **6:** 801
water filters **9:** 1257
water sellers **2:** 249
weddings *See* marriages
wet-nursing **4:** 512–513
wheat **1:** 33 **3:** 350
wigs **5:** 642
wigwams **3:** 333, 335, 340
wine **2:** 249
wire, barbed **6:** 839
witches **2:** 173, *179* **3:** 366
witch trials **2:** 181–182, 274 **3:** 370 **4:** 521
women
  in early modern Europe **1:** 9, 76–77
  in Europe (1700s) **4:** 512–513
  in Japanese society **4:** 538, *540*
  and the French Revolution **5:** *588*
  and industrialization **5:** 631–634
  middle-class (late 1800s) **6:** 798, 799
  working-class (late 1800s) **6:** 799–800
  and World War I **7:** 897–898, *899,* 945
  and the vote **7:** 898, 948
  flappers **7:** *945,* 950
  post–World War I **7:** 945
  and World War II **8:** 1064
  women's movement/rights (1960s/1970s) **9:** 1166, 1172–1174, 1177
  role in American society (1950s) **9:** 1170
  in Latin American society (late 1900s) **9:** 1208
wood, gathering **1:** *35*
workhouses **5:** 632, *633*
working class **5:** 628
World Wide Web (www) **9:** 1259

GEOGRAPHICAL LOCATIONS

AFRICA

Abyssinia *See* Ethiopia
Accra, Independence Arch **8**: *1127*
Adowa **6**: 826
Africa
  empires **1**: 109–118
  North Africa **1**: 109–110 **6**: 820
  Sub-Saharan **1**: 109, 110–111 **6**: 818
  geography **1**: *110*, 111
  rivers **1**: *111*
  slaves from **1**: *111* **3**: 348, 350, 354, 356, 367, 375–386, *377* **5**: 616
  trade **1**: *111*, 112, 113, 114–115 **6**: 817–818, 819
  languages **1**: 116
  European exploration (1500s) **3**: *295*, 300, 305–306, 307
  Dutch settlement **3**: 328–329
  diseases **3**: 393
  scramble for Africa: European colonization (1800s) **5**: 676 **6**: 817–828 **7**: 873–874 **9**: 1221
  missionaries in **6**: *817*, 820
  European exploration (1800s) **6**: 819–820, *821*, 824
  German colonies taken during World War I **7**: 885–886
  World War II in North Africa **8**: 1045–1046
  colonies independent from Europe **8**: 1124–1128 **9**: 1221, *1224*
  postcolonial **9**: 1221–1230
  droughts **9**: 1222, 1224, *1225*, 1268, 1275, 1276
  international debts **9**: 1278
  See also Southern Africa
Agadir **7**: 874
Algeria **1**: *111*
  and the French **6**: 732, 820
  nationalism and independence **8**: 1099, 1126–1127
  civil strife (1992) **9**: 1230
  Islamic fundamentalism (1990s) **9**: 1241–1242
Algiers **6**: 820 **8**: *1126*
Angola **6**: 823, 828
  independence and civil war (1975–1991) **8**: 1099–1102 **9**: 1227–1229
Belgian Congo **6**: 822–823 **7**: 873 **9**: 1225–1226
Benin **1**: *112*, 113 **6**: 818
  and the Portuguese **3**: *295*, *301*
Biafra **9**: 1226
Blanco, Cape **3**: 305
Bojador, Cape **3**: 305
Botswana, independence **8**: 1128
Burundi, massacre of Hutus (1972) **9**: 1230
Cairo **6**: 818
Cameroon
  Bantu language **1**: 117
  and World War I **7**: 885–887
Canary Islands, and the Spanish Civil War **8**: 1032
Cape Colony **6**: 818, 820–821, 828
Cape Town **3**: 328–329
Cape Verde Islands **3**: 305
Ceuta **3**: 303
Congo, Democratic Republic of (*formerly* Zaire)
  copper **1**: 114 **9**: *1223*
  Belgian Congo **6**: 822–823 **7**: 873 **9**: 1225–1226
  communist state **8**: 1099 **9**: *1160*
  independence **8**: 1099, 1128
Congo, Republic of the, French Congo **7**: 875
Congo River **3**: 306
Egypt
  Mamluks **1**: 105–107 **6**: 732
  Napoleon in **5**: 596 **6**: 730, 732, 820
  independence from the Ottomans **6**: 732–733, *735*
  Suez Canal **6**: 821, *823*, 825 **7**: 887
  British control of **6**: 825
  end of the British protectorate **8**: 1024
  relationship with the Soviets (1950s) **8**: 1099, 1135

Suez Crisis (1956) **8**: 1127, 1133, 1135
  and the creation of Israel **8**: 1132
  war against Israel (1973) **8**: 1136–1137
  Camp David peace accords **8**: 1137 **9**: 1236, *1237*
  westernization **9**: 1232, 1235–1236
  Islamic fundamentalism (from 1980s) **9**: 1235–1236
Eritrea **9**: 1226
Ethiopia (*formerly* Abyssinia) **1**: 118
  crops **1**: *117*
  invasion by Mussolini (1936) **6**: 824 **7**: 987 **8**: 1030
  not a European colony **6**: 826
  droughts and famines (1970s/1980s) **9**: 1224, 1268
  military regime and independence movements (1970s) **9**: 1226
  Selassie overthrown in military coup (1974) **9**: 1226
Fashoda **6**: 825
German East Africa **7**: 887
Ghana (*formerly* Gold Coast) **1**: 112, 115
  decolonization **8**: 1124–1125, 1127
  military coup (1966) **9**: 1225
Gold Coast *See* Ghana
Good Hope, Cape of, rounding **3**: 305–306, *307*
Great Zimbabwe **1**: 115
Guinea **3**: 303
  independence **8**: 1127
Ishandhlwana **6**: 826
Jenne **1**: 118
Kaba Kangaba **1**: *114*
Kanem-Bornu **1**: 112
Katanga **9**: *1223*, 1226
Kenya
  a British colony **8**: 1124
  Mau Mau **8**: 1125
  independence **8**: 1128 **9**: *1221*, 1225
  tribal groups **9**: 1225
Kilwa **1**: 113
Kimberley **6**: 826
Kinshasa, population rise **9**: 1222
Ladysmith **6**: 826
Lagos (Nigeria), postcolonial **9**: 1222, *1223*
Lesotho, independence **8**: 1128
Libya, and terrorism **9**: 1236–1237
Madagascar **1**: 117 **3**: 323, 328, 330
  peoples **1**: 110, 111, 116 **3**: 315
  language **1**: 116
Mafeking **6**: 826
Maghreb **1**: 110
Malawi (*formerly* Nyasaland), independence **8**: 1128
Mali **1**: 16, 18, *109*, *114*, 115–118
  neocolonialism **9**: 1222
Malindi **3**: 307
Mauritania, drought **9**: *1222*
Mauritius **3**: 328
Mogadishu **1**: 113
Mombasa **1**: 113
Mopti **1**: *118*
Morocco
  and the lead-up to World War I **7**: 874
  and the Spanish Civil War **8**: 1032
  independence **8**: 1126
Mozambique **6**: 823, 828
Namibia **7**: 887
Natal **6**: 819, 821
Niger River **1**: *111*, 118
Nigeria
  Bantu language **1**: 117
  decolonization **8**: 1124–1125, 1128
  military coup (1966); Ibos massacred **9**: 1226
  the secession and return of Biafara **9**: 1226
North Africa, and World War II **8**: 1045–1046
Northern Rhodesia (*later* Zambia), independence **8**: 1128
Nyasaland, independence **8**: 1128
Rhodesia *See* Zimbabwe
Rwanda, civil war (1994) **9**: 1230, 1278
Sahara Desert **1**: *111*, 112
Senegal **6**: 819 **9**: 1222
Sharpville, riots (1960) **9**: *1228*, 1229
Sierra Leone **3**: 305 **6**: 819

Sinai **8**: 1133, 1134, 1135, 1136
Sofala **3**: 306–307
Somalia
  food aid hijacked by warlords (1992) **9**: *1229*, 1230
  famine (1992) **9**: *1276*
Songhai **1**: 115–118
South Africa
  dominion status (1926) **5**: 676
  self-government **5**: 676
  and black Africans **6**: 828
  and independence **8**: 1127–1128
  Western support for the racist regime **9**: 1222
  subversive campaigns in Angola and Mozambique **9**: 1227–1229
  apartheid **9**: 1228, 1229–1230
  Sharpville riots (1960) **9**: *1228*, 1229
  end of apartheid for black Africans **9**: 1229, 1230, 1281
southern Africa
  and the Dutch **3**: 328–329 **6**: 820–821
  and the Boers **6**: 826–827 **7**: 874
  and the Cold War **9**: 1226–1227
Southern Rhodesia (*later* Zimbabwe), decolonization **8**: 1124, *1125*, 1128
Southwest Africa **6**: 827
Soweto **9**: 1229
Spanish Sahara **6**: 823
Sudan **6**: *824* **9**: 1282
  conversion to Islam in **1**: 112
  Egyptian invasion **6**: 732
  and the French **6**: 823–825
  an Anglo-Egyptian protectorate **6**: 825
  Britain subdues Mahdi revolt **6**: 825–826
  droughts and famines (1990s) **9**: 1224, *1225*, *1280*
  guerrilla warfare (from 1956) **9**: 1226
  Ebola virus **9**: 1272
  Tangiers **7**: 874
Swaziland, independence **8**: 1128
Tanzania (*formerly* Tanganyika)
  Khoisan speakers **1**: 116
  German East Africa **7**: 887
  independence **8**: 1128
Timbuktu **1**: 118
Togoland **7**: 885
Transvaal **6**: 821, 826
Tunisia
  and the French **6**: 732, 820
  independence **8**: 1126
Uganda
  independence **8**: 1128
  Idi Amin's rule after independence **9**: 1225
"United States of Africa" **9**: 1221
Verde, Cape **3**: 305
Victoria Falls **6**: *821*
Yoruba **1**: 113
Zaire *See* Congo, Democratic Republic of
Zambesi River **6**: *821*
Zambia (*formerly* Northern Rhodesia)
  Zulu migration to **6**: 819
  independence **8**: 1128
  copper **9**: 1224
Zanzibar **1**: *113*
Zimbabwe (*formerly* Southern Rhodesia)
  site of Great Zimbabwe **1**: 115
  and Cecil Rhodes **6**: 826
  decolonization **8**: 1124, *1125*, 1128
  independence (1980) **9**: *1227*, 1229

EUROPE

Aachen **1:** *21*, 50
Aargau **2:** 183
Abingdon, workhouse **5:** *633*
Adrianople **1:** 100
Aigues-Mortes **2:** 190
Albania
    independence **7:** 879
    collapse of communism **9:** 1247
    and globalization **9:** *1274*
Albazin **4:** 530
Albi, cathedral **2:** *175*
Alsace-Lorraine
    gained by Germany **7:** 871
    lost by Germany (post–World War I) **8:** 1026
Amiens **7:** *955*
Amsterdam
    rise in importance **1:** 44 **2:** 222 **3:** 325
    banks **1:** 48
    a cultural center **2:** 223
    population **2:** 252
    Baroque architecture **2:** *260*, 261
    stock exchange **4:** *441*
Anatolia **1:** 101
Angers **2:** 200
Ankara **1:** 101
Antwerp
    a trading port **1:** 40, 42, 44 **2:** *215*, 216, 222
    refugees from **1:** 44–45
    "Fury of" **2:** 219
    and Catholic Baroque **2:** 260–261
Aquitaine **1:** *13*
Aragon **1:** 23–24 **2:** 179
    and the War of the Spanish Succession **4:** 465
Ardennes **8:** 1048
Armenia **9:** 1248
Arras **7:** *885*
Asturias **8:** 1032
Austria
    Catholicism **2:** 172
    and the Habsburg dynasty **2:** 187 **4:** 460 **5:** 655
    and the War of the Spanish Succession **4:** 464, 465
    reform (1700s) **4:** 489
    a powerful force in Europe **4:** 490
    and the French Revolutionary Wars **5:** 595–596
    liberalism **5:** 610
    and the 1848 revolutions **5:** 613–614
    Seven Weeks' War (1866) **5:** 661
    nationalism (1800s) **5:** 664–665
    May Day **6:** *811*
    post–World War I **7:** 907
    annexed by Hitler (1938) **7:** 993 **8:** *1028*, 1031
Austria-Hungary (1867–1918)
    Dual Monarchy **5:** 665
    and the lead-up to World War I **7:** 877–880
    and World War I **7:** 884, 895
Austrian Netherlands
    revolt (1789) **5:** 590–592
    Union of Belgian States **5:** 590–592
    and the French Revolutionary War **5:** 592, 596
Auvillar, market hall **1:** *40*
Avignon, anti-pope established at **1:** 20 **2:** 164, *165*
Azerbaijan **5:** 691 **9:** 1248
Azores **3:** 304–305
Baku **5:** 691, *694*, 695 **7:** *931*
Balearics, and the Spanish Civil War **8:** 1032
Balkans
    and the Ottomans **6:** 733–734 **7:** 877
    and the lead-up to World War I **6:** 736 **7:** 876–880
    First Balkan War (1912) **7:** *876*, 879
    Second Balkan War (1913) **7:** 879
    and World War II **8:** 1069–1070
Baltic States *See* Estonia; Latvia; Lithuania; Livonia
Barcelona
    and the Spanish Civil War **4:** *462*
    and the War of the Spanish Succession **4:** 467
Basque country **8:** 1032
Bavaria
    Catholicism **2:** 172
    rococo style **4:** 493

Bayreuth **6:** *843*
Beauvais, cathedral roof **1:** 7, 18
Belarus **9:** 1248
Belgian States, Union of **5:** 590
Belgium
    desire for independence **5:** 608
    and World War I **7:** 881, 882, 890, 895
    occupation of the Ruhr (1923) **7:** 953
    and World War II **8:** 1038
    post–World War II **8:** 1075–1076
    colonies lost in Africa **8:** 1128
    See also Austrian Netherlands; Flanders; Low Countries; Spanish Netherlands
Bergen **1:** *16*
Berlin
    post–World War I **7:** 952, *953*
    and the end of World War II in Europe **8:** 1048, 1084
    blockade **8:** 1089–1090
    postwar split **8:** 1089, 1095–1096
Berlin Wall **8:** 1095–1096, *1097*, 1106 **9:** 1248
Bessarabia **7:** 907
Bithynia, and the Ottomans **1:** 99
Black Sea **1:** *108* **6:** 730
Blois **2:** 200
Bohemia
    and the Jagiello dynasty **1:** 93
    anti-Catholicism of Jan Hus **1:** 94, *95* **2:** 164
    markets **1:** *94*
    and the Thirty Years' War **1:** 95 **2:** 225, 226, 227, 229
    Catholicism **2:** 172
Bologna, university **1:** 50, 51, *52*, *56*
Bosnia-Herzegovina
    and the Ottomans **6:** 734
    and the lead-up to World War I **7:** 877, 878, 879–880
    independence **9:** 1252
    invasion by Serb forces **9:** 1252, 1278
Bosporus channel **6:** *731*
Brielle **2:** 219
Bristol, and the slave trade **3:** *379*, 382
Brittany **1:** 23 **2:** 203
Brussels **1:** 16 **2:** 215, 220
Budapest
    parliament **5:** *666*
    and the Hungarian Uprising (1956) **8:** 1094
Bukovina **7:** 907
Bulgaria
    and the Ottomans **1:** 101 **6:** 734 **7:** 877
    and World War I **7:** 890
    collapse of communism **9:** 1247
Burgundy **1:** 23, 25–28 **2:** 189, 190, 203
Byzantine empire **3:** 297
    Orthodox Christianity **1:** 10
    and the Ottomans **1:** 16–18, 19, 100–101, 103 **3:** 298
    and ancient Greek texts **1:** 64
    legacy to Russia **1:** 92
Calais **1:** 23 **2:** 211
Cambridge, university **1:** 52, *53*
Cassino **8:** *1046*
Castile **1:** 23, 24 **2:** 179, 180
    and social discipline **1:** 71–72
    revolt (1520) **2:** 187
    and the monarchy (1600s) **4:** 463
Catalonia, and the Spanish Civil War **8:** 1032, 1033
Champagne, fairs **1:** 40
Chartres, cathedral **1:** 7
Chechnya, invaded by Russian troops (1992) **9:** 1251
Chernobyl, nuclear accident **9:** 1244, 1249, 1269–1270
Chicago **5:** 625–626
China
    encyclopedia (11,000 volumes) **1:** 66
    gunpowder **1:** 66, 121
Cluny **1:** 11
Cologne **1:** *37*
Commonwealth of Independent States (CIS) **9:** 1249
Copenhagen
    Christianborg Palace **4:** *445*
    and the Northern War **4:** 446

Cracow, university **1:** 94
Crimea **4:** 485
Croatia, attacked by Serbia (1991–1992) **9:** 1252
Cyprus
    and the Ottomans **1:** 108 **2:** 194 **6:** *733*
    taken by the British **6:** *733*, 734
Czech Republic **9:** 1246
    acid rain **9:** *1270*
Czechoslovakia
    Bohemian Charter **5:** 614
    an independent state (1918) **7:** *904*, 906, 956
    Sudetenland annexed by Germany **7:** 993 **8:** 1034–1035, 1036
    totally annexed by Germany **8:** 1036
    communists seize power (1948) **8:** 1089
    collapse of communism **8:** 1106 **9:** 1246
Dalmatia **5:** 599
    division (1992) **9:** 1246
Danzig *See* Gdansk
Delft **2:** 222, 223, *253*
Denmark
    and the Union of Colmar **1:** 24
    and the Thirty Years' War **2:** 227–228
    religion **4:** 440
    trade (1600s) **4:** 445–446
    monarchy and national assembly (1600s) **4:** 446
    power struggle with Sweden over the Baltic (1600s) **4:** 446
    Norway secedes from **5:** 666
    and European union **9:** 1194, 1197
Djerba **2:** 193
Dresden **5:** 625
    elector of Saxony's court **4:** 500
    and World War II **8:** 1063
Drogheda, storming of **2:** 241
Dublin **2:** 213
Dunkirk, evacuation from **8:** 1038, *1039*
Düsseldorf, French occupation of **7:** *956*
Dutch Republic (United Provinces of the Netherlands) **2:** 220 **4:** 440–441
    See also Netherlands
Edirne **1:** 100
    mosque **1:** *107*
Eire, dominion status (1926) **5:** 676
Elba **5:** 604
Elbe River **1:** 42
England
    growth of a centralized monarchy **1:** 23
    enclosures **1:** 34–35
    migration of vagrants to towns (1500s) **1:** 36
    Protestantism and the monarchy **1:** 70–71
    common law **1:** 72
    justices of the peace **1:** 72
    Parliament **1:** 72
    Spanish Armada sails against **2:** 194, 213–214, 221
    Tudor England **2:** 205–214
    Stuart dynasty **2:** 214, 235–244
    Civil War **2:** 235–244
    Glorious Revolution **2:** *243*, 244 **4:** 442–444, 472, 502
    settlers in South America **3:** 348
    colonies in North America **3:** 356–360, 370–371 **4:** 544–552
    the Bill of Rights and the monarchy **4:** 444
    paintings (1600s/1700s) **4:** 493–494
    See also Great Britain
Estonia **4:** 446
    independence **7:** 906
    nationalism **9:** 1248, 1249
Europe
    everyday life (1300s–1500s) **1:** 7–9
    transition from the medieval to the modern world **1:** 7–18, 69–78
    and the Black Death **1:** 8–9, 30, *31*, 43–44 **2:** 165, 245
    everyday life (1500s/1600s) **1:** 8 **2:** 245–254
    religion in the Middle Ages **1:** 10–12 **3:** 297–298
    rise of the monarchy **1:** 12–14, 69, 70
    trade and wealth in early modern Europe **1:** 15, 39–48
    political shape (1400s) **1:** 19–28
    map of (1400s) **1:** *20*, 22
    rise of the idea of **1:** 21–22

Volume numbers appear in **boldface type**. Page numbers in *italic type* refer to illustrations and captions.

Europe (continued)
  nation-states **1:** 22–23, 70 **4:** 460
  population and agriculture **1:** 29–38
  inflation (1500s) **1:** 36, 48
  customs barriers **1:** 42
  bills of exchange **1:** 48
  scholasticism and universities **1:** 49–58, 94
  colonies in Africa (1800s) **1:** 118 **6:** 817–828
    7: 873–874
  world exploration (1400s/1500s) **3:** 295–302,
    303–312
  trade with the East **3:** 298, 417 **4:** 524–525, 532
  Protestant northern Europe **4:** 439–448
  dynastic wars (1700s) **4:** 461–470
  the Enlightenment **4:** 471–480
  religion and superstition (1700s) **4:** 476,
    520–521
  central and eastern (1600s/1700s) **4:** 481–490
  cities (1700s) **4:** 508, 511–512
  everyday life (1700s) **4:** 511–522
  colonial conflicts in North America **4:** 544–549
  and Napoleon **5:** 595–604
  revolution and reform **5:** 605–614, 629–630
  spread of industrialization (1800s) **5:** 623
  immigration to the United States **5:** 650 **6:** 806,
    833, *834*, 837
  vogue for exotic art (1800s) **6:** 784–785, 799,
    824
  railroads **6:** 790, 791
  transport improvements (1800s) **6:** 790,
    791–793
  emigration from (1800s) **6:** 806
  colonies after World War I **7:** 905
  post–World War I **7:** 905, 945, 951–958,
    960–961
  Latin American imports (1870s–1914)
    7: 971–972
  World War II in Europe **8:** 1037–1048
  post–World War II recovery **8:** 1071–1077,
    1078–1079, 1088–1089
  welfare states **8:** 1077 **9:** 1160
  iron curtain **8:** *1084, 1086*, 1087, 1096
  and NATO **8:** *1084*, 1090, 1102, 1106 **9:** 1245
  and the Warsaw Pact **8:** *1084*, 1093–1094, 1102
    9: 1243
  colonies gain independence **8:** 1117–1128
  western Europe: experiments with government
    (1960–1999) **9:** 1159–1168
  toward a united Europe **9:** 1189–1198
  single currency **9:** 1196, 1197
  fall of communism; revival of nationalism
    9: 1243–1252
Finland **4:** 446
  struggle for independence from Russia **5:** 666
  under Russian control **5:** 688
  post–World War II **8:** 1075
Fiume **7:** 984
Flanders **1:** 23 **2:** 220, 221, 252
  part of the Habsburg Empire **1:** 25
  agriculture **1:** *33*
  urbanization **1:** 40
  and the Renaissance **1:** 85
  Mercator's map of **2:** *217*
  food imports **3:** 389
  Battle of Malplaquet (1709) **4:** *461*
Florence
  moral renewal preached by Savonarola **1:** *10*, 11
  and the Renaissance **1:** 28, *79*, 80, 87
  humanists **1:** 64–65, 80
  churches **1:** *79, 80*
Flushing **2:** 219
Fontainbleu, palace at **1:** 88 **2:** 200
France
  rise of the monarchy **1:** 12–13
  as a nation-state **1:** 22–23
  Wars of Religion (1562–1598) **1:** 31 **2:** 161,
    172, 195–204
  monarchy and religion **1:** 70
  population increase (1400s/1500s) **2:** 196
  Grand Siècle (Great Century; 1600s) **2:** 204
  and the Thirty Years' War **2:** 232, 233 **4:** 453,
    455
  Baroque style **2:** 262–263
  trade with Asia **3:** 330
  piracy **3:** 348

colonies in North America (New France)
  3: *355*, 360, 373–374 **4:** 545–549
  parts of North America claimed for France
    3: 355–356
  bases in India **3:** 418
  French Revolution **4:** 453, 497, 511, 521
    5: 583–594 **6:** 748
  and the War of the Spanish Succession **4:** *461*,
    464, 465
  and the Enlightenment (1700s) **4:** 472, 492
  cultural dominance (1700s) **4:** 491–492
  slow development of agricultural innovation
    (1700s) **4:** 503
  economic depression (1700s) **5:** 584–585
  republic declared **5:** 592
  and Napoleon **5:** 595–604
  July Revolution (1830) **5:** 605, 608, *610*, 655
    6: 820
  Charles X replaced **5:** 608
  liberalism **5:** 610
  nationalism (1800s) **5:** 611, 655–657
  banquet campaigns **5:** 612–613, 656
  and industrialization (1800s) **5:** 623
  Second Empire **5:** 657
  Franco-Prussian War (1870–1871) **5:** 662–663,
    664 **6:** 794 **7:** 871, 892 **8:** 1026
  colonies in Africa **6:** 732, 820, *822*
  involvement in Mexico (1860's) **6:** 740–741
  railroads **6:** 791
  schooling (1800s) **6:** 800
  city homes (late 1800s) **6:** 802–803
  voting rights (1830s) **6:** 809
  the Dreyfus affair **6:** 846 **7:** 990
  and fashion **6:** 846
  and the lead-up to World War I **7:** 871, 874
  loses Alsace-Lorraine **7:** 871
  and World War I **7:** 881, 882, 884, 890, 895,
    896, 903
  occupation of the Ruhr (1923) **7:** 953, *956*
  postwar recovery (1920s) **7:** 954–956
  and World War II **8:** 1037, 1038, *1039*, 1048,
    1067, 1068, 1071
  post–World War II **8:** 1075–1076, 1077
  decolonization of Indochina **8:** 1100, *1117*,
    1122, 1123
  French-Vietnamese War (1946–1954) **8:** 1122
  colonies lost in Africa **8:** 1125–1127, 1128
  and the Algerian War of Independence
    (1954–1962) **8:** 1126–1127
  and the Suez Crisis (1956) **8:** 1127, 1133, 1135
  labor union and student protests (1968) **9:** *1164*,
    1165
  and European union **9:** 1193–1194, 1197
Fredrikshamn **4:** *446*
Gallipoli **1:** 100
Galve, Lake **1:** *91*
Gdansk (*formerly* Danzig) **1:** 16, 93 **4:** 482
  8: 1106
Geneva
  infant mortality **1:** 10
  religion **2:** 160, *161*, 197
Genoa **1:** 15, 22, 28, 41, 106 **2:** 188–189
Georgia (Caucasus) **5:** 691
  independence **9:** *1247*, 1249
Germany
  Luther and the birth of Protestantism **1:** 10, 12
    2: 151–160, 162
  Hanseatic League **1:** 15, *16*, 24, 41, *42* **3:** 298
  Fugger dynasty **1:** 46–47 **2:** *185*, 187
  part of the Holy Roman Empire **1:** 71 **2:** 184,
    190, 191–192, 225
  peasant revolts (early 1500s) **2:** 156
  and the Thirty Years' War **2:** 225–234
  immigrants to North America (c. 1700s) **3:** 371,
    372
  canals **4:** 509
  nationalism **5:** 602, 611, *656*, 659–664
  liberalism **5:** 610, 611
  and the 1848 revolutions **5:** *613*, 614, 629
  industrialization (1800s) **5:** 623 **6:** 794–796
  Social Democratic Party **5:** 628
  immigration to the United States **5:** 650
  unification (1871) **5:** 664 **7:** 871
  railroads **6:** 791
  African colonies **6:** 796, 825

  gains Alsace-Lorraine **7:** 871
  and the lead-up to World War I **7:** 871–876
  and World War I **7:** 880–882, 884–896
  and the postwar Treaty of Versailles
    7: 903–905, 908, 952, 953, 987, 988, 993
    8: 1026–1028, 1030–1031
  civil war after World War I **7:** 952
  Weimar Republic **7:** 952–953, 987 **8:** 1029
  alliance with the Soviet Union (1922) **7:** 953
  France occupies the Ruhr (1923) **7:** 953, *956*
  hyperinflation (1923) **7:** 953–954, 988
  and the rise of Hitler **7:** 987–994
  and the road to World War II **8:** 1025–1036
  and the Spanish Civil War **8:** 1031, 1032, 1038
  and World War II **8:** 1037–1048, 1062–1063,
    1066–1068
  post–World War II **8:** *1072, 1073, 1074, 1075*,
    1089–1090
  reunification (1990) **8:** *1105* **9:** 1196,
    1247–1248
Germany, East (GDR), and the Berlin Wall
  8: *1095*, 1096, *1097*, 1106 **9:** 1248
Germany, West
  Social Democratic Party **9:** 1166–1167
  and European union **9:** 1194
Gibraltar **2:** 253
  and the War of the Spanish Succession **4:** *464*,
    465, 467
Granada **1:** 24
Great Britain
  and the War of the Spanish Succession **4:** 464,
    465, 466, 467
  and the Enlightenment **4:** 472, 473–475,
    479–480
  agricultural revolution **4:** 502, 503
  society (1700s) **4:** 502
  enclosures **4:** 503–504
  trade with China **4:** 532
  and the North American colonies **4:** 544–552,
    550–552, 553–562
  wars against France in North America
    4: 545–548, 553
  and Napoleon **5:** 598, *599*, 600
  liberal advances and reform **5:** 608
  Chartist movement **5:** 612
  the Industrial Revolution **5:** 615–624
  industrial society (1800s) **5:** 625–634
  urbanization (1800s) **5:** 625 **6:** 803
  Empire **5:** 667–676
  Commonwealth **5:** 676 **8:** 1120 **9:** 1190
  decline in economic performance (1800s)
    6: 789
  the rise of socialism **6:** 807–811
  trade unions **6:** *807*, 809 **7:** *957*, 958
  Parliamentary democracy **6:** 809
  abolition of slavery and the slave trade **6:** 819
  and the lead-up to World War I **7:** 872, 873,
    874, 875–876, 882
  and World War I **7:** 888, 890, 894, 896, 901,
    902, 903
  general strike (1926) **7:** *957*, 958
  post–World War I **7:** 957–958
  and the road to World War II **8:** *1035*, 1036
  and World War II in Europe **8:** 1037–1042,
    1045–1048
  and World War II in North Africa **8:** 1045, 1046
  and World War II in the Pacific **8:** 1050, 1051
  and World War II **8:** 1064, 1067–1068, 1069
  post–World War II **8:** 1076–1077, *1078*
  and the welfare state **8:** 1077
  and the postwar treatment of Germany
    8: 1084–1086
  and independence and partition in India
    8: 1107–1114
  economic depression and India **8:** 1109
  loss of the African colonies **8:** 1124–1125,
    1127–1128
  and the Suez Crisis (1956) **8:** 1127, 1133, 1135
  and Jewish immigration to Palestine **8:** 1130
  "rights politics" (1960s) **9:** 1166
  swing to the political right (1980s)
    9: 1167–1168
  turn to the political left (1970s) **9:** 1167
  and a united Europe **9:** 1190, 1194, 1197
  CJD and mad cow disease **9:** 1275

Volume numbers appear in **boldface type**. Page numbers in *italic type* refer to illustrations and captions.

Greece
    rebellion against Ottoman rule **5:** 607, *611*
      6: 731–732
    War of Independence **5:** *611*
    and World War II **8:** 1043
    EEC membership **9:** 1195
Greece, ancient
    and humanism **1:** 17, 62, 63–64
    and learning **1:** 52–53
    influence on classicism **4:** 494–495
Grenada (Spain) **2:** 180
Haarlem **2:** 223 **4:** *439*
Hague, the **2:** 220
Hamburg **2:** 188
    and industrialization **1:** 16 **5:** 612
    cholera **6:** 790
Hanover **2:** 188
Heidelberg **8:** *1031*
Herculaneum **4:** 495
Hesse-Kassel **5:** 660
Holland **5:** 608
Holstein **5:** 661
Hungary
    and the Habsburg Empire **1:** 93 **4:** 485–486
    and the Jagiello dynasty **1:** 93
    and the Ottomans **1:** 93, 107 **6:** 729
    nomad invasion **3:** 297
    struggle for independence from Austria
      5: 613–614
    Dual Monarchy with Austria **5:** 665
    uprising (1956) **8:** 1094
    and communism **8:** 1106
    collapse of communism; rise of nationalism
      9: 1245–1246
Ingria **4:** 446
Innsbruck **2:** 192
Ireland
    Tudor **2:** 213
    Protestants massacred (1641) **2:** 239
    and Oliver Cromwell **2:** 241
    immigrants to North America (c. 1700s) **3:** 371
    and the potato **3:** 392 **4:** 508
    Catholic-Protestant hostilities and the Battle of
      the Boyne (1690) **4:** 444–445
    potato famine **5:** 612, 650
    immigration to the United States (1800s) **5:** 650
    Easter Rising (1916) **7:** 905
    post–World War I **7:** 905–908, 957–958
    southern counties independent as the Irish Free
      State (1922) **7:** 957–958
    and EEC membership **9:** 1194
Ireland, Northern, terrorists/terrorism **9:** 1238,
    1279, 1280
Irish Free State **7:** 958
Italy
    wars between city-states (1300s/1400s) **1:** 14,
      26, 28
    part of the Holy Roman Empire **2:** 188–189
    Spanish power in (1700s) **4:** 468
    and the grand tour **4:** 495–496
    opera **4:** 500
    Napoleon Bonaparte invades **5:** 596
    nationalism (1800s) **5:** 602, 657–659
    invasion of Abyssinia **6:** 824 **7:** 987 **8:** 1030
    African colonies **6:** 825
    D'Annunzio's private army takes Fiume **7:** 984
    Mussolini's fascist dictatorship **7:** 984–987
      8: *1029*
    and World War I **7:** 984
    and the road to World War II **8:** *1029*, 1030,
      1031
    and the Spanish Civil War **8:** 1031, 1032
    and World War II **8:** 1046
    post–World War II **8:** 1075–1076
Kazakhstan **9:** 1248, 1249
Kiel **7:** *873*, 952
Kiev **1:** 89, 92 **7:** 920
Kiev Rus empire **1:** 89, 90, 92
Kosovo **9:** 1252, 1278
Lagos (Portugal) **3:** *308*, 376
Lake District (England), and Romanticism **5:** 640,
    641
Languedoc **2:** 203
La Rochelle **2:** 201, 202
    siege of (1627–1628) **4:** 453

Latvia **7:** 906 **9:** 1248, 1249
Leiden **3:** 358
Leipzig **9:** 1248
Leningrad *See* Saint Petersburg
Liège, cloth guild **1:** 43
Lisbon **3:** 324, 325 **4:** 460
    slavery in **3:** 377
    and Napoleon **5:** 600
Lithuania
    Poland-Lithuania **1:** 13, 25, 91–93, 98
      4: 483–484, 485
    and the Teutonic Knights **1:** 91
    and the Jagiello dynasty **1:** 93
    Union of Lublin (1569) **1:** 98
    independence **7:** 906
    nationalism **9:** 1248, 1249
Liverpool, and the slave trade **3:** 382
Livonia **1:** 97 **4:** 446
Lockerbie, air disaster over **9:** 1237, *1238*, *1240*
Lombardy **5:** 657, 658, 659
London
    population **1:** 33 **2:** 252
    beggars (1500s) **1:** 36
    in the 1700s **4:** 508, 511–512
    industrialization and houses **5:** 625
    Great Stink (1848) **5:** *629*, 705 **6:** 802
    and World War II **8:** 1063
    Telecom Tower **9:** *1168*
Lorraine **2:** 192 **4:** 468
Low Countries
    center of commerce **1:** 15
    the Eighty Years' War **1:** 44 **2:** 215–224
Lübeck **1:** 16, *42*
Luxembourg, European Parliament **9:** *1197*
Lyons, poverty (1500s) **1:** 36, **2:** 200
Macedonia, taken by the Ottomans **1:** 101
Madeira **3:** 304
Madrid **2:** 253
    monastery and palace of El Escorial **2:** *191*, 194
    in the 1700s **4:** *462*
    and the Spanish Civil War **8:** 1032, 1033
Magdeburg, destruction of **2:** 230
Mainz, books censored **1:** 62
Majorca **1:** 23
Malta **5:** 598
Manchester, and industrialization **5:** 612, 625, 626
Manresa **2:** *170*
Mantua **1:** *49*, 72 **5:** 596
Marseilles **2:** 189
    plague **4:** 522
Mediterranean islands, part of Europe **1:** 21
Messina, Arab control of **1:** *101*
Metz **2:** 192, 193
Milan **2:** 190, 193
    and mercenary soldiers **1:** 26
    city-state **1:** 28
    struggle between Habsburg and Valois
      monarchs **2:** 188–189
    taken by Napoleon **5:** 596
Minorca **1:** 23
    and the War of the Spanish Succession **4:** 466,
      467
Minsk **9:** 1248
Moldova **9:** 1249
Monaco **1:** 28
Monastir **6:** 736
Montagnana **1:** *28*
Montenegro **6:** 734
Montepulciano **1:** *64*
Moscow
    grand principality of *See* Muscovy
    and the Orthodox faith **1:** 24, 92
    churches and cathedrals **1:** 92 **4:** *481*
    Kremlin **1:** 92, *96*
    Napoleon's retreat from **5:** *603*, 604, 688
    Russian capital **7:** 919
    buildings and architecture under Stalin **7:** 926
    Kremlin Palace **7:** 932
    May Day parades **8:** *1093*
    Red Square **9:** *1160*
Munich **7:** 952
    terrorist attack at the Olympic Games (1972)
      8: 1136
Muscovy **1:** 24, 92, 96 **4:** 483
Nagorno-Karabakh **9:** 1248

Nancy **4:** 456
Nantes **4:** *377*, 382
Naples **5:** 658
    Spanish kingdom of **1:** 24, 28 **2:** 189
    besieged by the French (1528) **2:** 190
Navarre **2:** *186*
Nea Paphos **1:** *108*
Netherlands
    colonies *See* Indonesia; New Netherland
    part of the Habsburg Empire **1:** 25
    flyboats **1:** 42, *44*
    refugees from Antwerp **1:** 44
    Revolt of the (Eighty Years' War) **1:** 44 **2:** 172,
      215–224 **4:** 440
    villages **1:** *77*
    United Provinces of the **2:** 220
    a thriving culture (1600s) **2:** 222–224, 261
      4: *442*
    and the Thirty Years' War **2:** 227–228, 233
    trade and empire in Asia **3:** *323*, 324–330
    Dutch settlements in Africa **3:** 328–329
    piracy **3:** 348
    religion **4:** 440
    republicanism **4:** 440–441, 442
    invasion by the French (1670s; Franco-Dutch
      War) **4:** 441, 457, 462
    decline (late 1600s) **4:** 442
    invasion by the French (1747) **4:** 442
    and the War of the Spanish Succession **4:** 464,
      465, 466
    abolition of the slave trade **6:** 819
    immigration to the United States **6:** *837*
    and World War II in Europe **8:** 1038
    and World War II in the Pacific **8:** 1050
Netherlands, Austrian *See* Austrian Netherlands
Netherlands, Spanish *See* Spanish Netherlands
New Amsterdam **2:** 244
Newcastle upon Tyne **2:** 238
New Lanark, model society at **6:** *809*, 811
Nice **2:** 190 **5:** 659
Nicosia **6:** *733*
Nile Valley **1:** 109–110
Nordhausen **8:** *1062*
Normandy
    weddings (1700s) **4:** *515*
    D-Day landings in **8:** *1047*, 1048
Norway
    and the Union of Colmar **1:** 24
    nationalism and independence **5:** 666
Nottingham **2:** 239
Novaya Zemlya **3:** 326
Novgorod **1:** 89, 96
Nuremberg **1:** 28
    war trials **8:** 1070
Old Sarum, cathedral **1:** 7
Orléans **2:** 200
Osnabruck **1:** 31
Oxford, university **1:** 40, 51, 52, *53*
Palatinate, Spanish invasion of **2:** 227
Papal States **5:** 658, 659
Paris **2:** 253
    controlled by the British and Burgundians **1:** 23
    pre-Versaille growth **1:** 38
    University of **1:** *51*
    shops **1:** *78*
    in 1590 **2:** *198*
    and the Wars of Religion **2:** 203, 204
    Halles trading district **4:** *450*
    in the 1700s **4:** 511–512
    and the French Revolution **5:** 590–591, 592
    Arc de Triomphe **5:** 602
    redesigned (late 1800s) **5:** 655
    June Days (1848) **5:** 656
    besieged by the Germans (1871) **5:** 664, *665*
    declared a self-governing commune (1871)
      5: 664
    urban replanning **6:** 789–790
    sewers **6:** *803*
    Eiffel Tower **6:** *841*, 846
    a fashion center **6:** 846
    and World War I **7:** 884, *888*
    post–World War I **7:** 951–952
    student demonstrations **9:** *1164*
Petrograd *See* Saint Petersburg
Pisa **1:** 28

1369

Volume numbers appear in **boldface type**. Page numbers in *italic type* refer to illustrations and captions.

Poissy **2:** 199
Poland
    Poland-Lithuania **1:** 13, 25, 91–93, 98
        4: 483–484, 485, 490
    nobility **1:** 76
    and the Teutonic Knights **1:** 90–91
    and the Jagiello dynasty **1:** 91, 93
    prosperity (1400s) **1:** 93–94
    and the Reformation **1:** 95
    Union of Lublin (1569) **1:** 98
    Catholicism **2:** 172
    nomad invasion **3:** 297
    hostilities with Sweden (1600s) **4:** 446
    War of the Polish Succession **4:** 468
    and Napoleon **5:** 600, 691
    part of the Russian empire **5:** 691–692, 696
    independence (1918) **7:** 906, 956
    Polish-Soviet War (1919–1920) **7:** 920
    German invasion of (1939) **8:** 1025–1026,
        1036, 1037–1038
    post–World War I **8:** 1026
    population lost in World War II **8:** 1071
    Solidarity labor union **8:** 1105–1106 **9:** 1244,
        1245
    collapse of communism **9:** 1244–1245
Poltava **4:** 447
Pompeii **4:** 495
Portugal
    colonies and trade in Asia **1:** 41 **3:** 323–324,
        325, 326, 399
    world exploration by **3:** *295,* 302, 303–307
    slaves/slave trade **3:** 305, *308,* 376–377, 381,
        383
    New World divided for **3:** 310–311
    colonies in the New World **3:** 347–348, 354,
        383
    absolute monarchies **4:** 460
    and the War of the Spanish Succession **4:** 464,
        465
    trade with Japan **4:** 538
    Napoleon's invasion of (1807) **6:** 749, 755
    independence for Brazil **6:** 755–756
    African colonies **6:** 828 **8:** 1128
    African colonies lost **8:** 1128
    military coup (1974) **9:** 1166
    EEC membership **9:** 1195
Prague, university **1:** 94
Provence **1:** 23
Prussia **4:** 442
    and the Teutonic Knights **1:** 90
    Hohenzollern family **4:** 460
    under Frederick the Great **4:** *466,* 469, 470,
        488–489
    and European dynastic wars **4:** 469, 488, 489
    partition of Poland-Lithuania **4:** *484,* 490
    formation of the state of **4:** 488
    a powerful force in Europe **4:** 490
    peasants **4:** 505
    and the French Revolutionary Wars **5:** 592,
        595–596
    and German nationalism **5:** 602, *656,* 659–664
    Seven Weeks' War (1866) **5:** 661
    Franco-Prussian War (1870–1871) **5:** 662–663,
        664 **6:** 794 **7:** 871, 892 **8:** 1026
    railroads **6:** 791
    lands lost (post–World War I) **8:** 1026
Pyrenees mountain chain **2:** *186*
Rhineland
    post–World War I **8:** 1026
    reoccupied by Germany (1936) **8:** 1030, *1031*
Riga **1:** 16, *78* **7:** *911,* 952
    siege of **4:** *447*
Romania
    independence **6:** 734 **7:** 877
    and the lead-up to World War I **7:** 877
    and World War I **7:** 895
    post–World War I **7:** 907
    collapse of communism **9:** 1246–1247
Rome
    Saint Peter's basilica **1:** 11–12, 84 **2:** *172*
    violence **1:** 80
    rebuilt (1400s/1500s) **1:** 84
    sacked by the Habsburg army (1527) **2:** 189
    streets **2:** 253
    and the Baroque **2:** 257, 259

Mussolini marches on **7:** 985–986
    and World War II **8:** 1046
Rome, ancient
    and humanism **1:** 63
    influence on classicism **4:** 494–496
Ruhr Basin, French occupation of (1923) **7:** 953,
    956
Rus **1:** 89, 90
Russia
    and the Orthodox religion **1:** 24, 92
    Kiev Rus empire **1:** 89, 90, 92
    feuds of the boyars (1500s) **1:** 96
    from the grand duchy of Moscow **1:** 96
    Ivan the Terrible **1:** 96–97 **4:** *481*
    power of the czar **1:** 96
    Time of Troubles (1598–1613) **1:** 97–98 **4:** 482
    expansion (1600s) **1:** 98
    Romanov dynasty **1:** 98 **4:** 460, 482–483
    wars against Sweden (1700s) **4:** 447, 448
    serfs **4:** 481, 482, 504–505 **5:** 689–690,
        692–693 **6:** 809 **7:** 909
    nobles **4:** 482, 489–490
    ethnic groups **4:** *483*
    partition of Poland-Lithuania **4:** *484,* 490
    under Peter the Great **4:** 486–488
    a powerful force in Europe **4:** 490
    border with China **4:** 530
    Napoleon's invasion **5:** *603,* 604, 688
    tradition and modernization (1800s) **5:** 623,
        687–696
    Decembrist revolt (1825) **5:** *688,* 689, 690
    and the Crimean War **5:** *689,* 692
    and Poland **5:** 691–692, 696
    and Ottoman Turkey **5:** 692 **6:** 728, 730, 732,
        733–734
    railroads **5:** *693,* 694–695
    Russian Revolution (1917) **5:** 694 **7:** 909–919
        8: 1083–1084
    intelligentsia **5:** 695–696
    Russian-Japanese War (1904–1905) **5:** *695,* 696
        6: 782–783, *786* **8:** 1015
    elected assembly (Duma) **5:** 696 **7:** 910,
        913–914
    Russian Revolution (1905) **5:** 696 **7:** 909
    and industrialization (1800s) **6:** 796
    and the lead-up to World War I **7:** 872,
        877–879, 880, 881, 882
    and the Balkans **7:** 877
    and World War I **7:** 880, 881, 882, 884, 890,
        894–895, *911*
    Civil War (1918–1920) **7:** 919–920, 921
        8: 1084, 1085
    Polish-Soviet War (1919–1920) **7:** 920
    and nationalistic uprisings in the USSR
        9: 1248–1249
    See also Russian Federation *(from 1991);*
    Soviet Union *(from 1922)*
Russian Federation
    and nuclear weapons **8:** 1106
    economic failure (1990s) **9:** 1250, 1251
    Chechnya invaded by Russian troops (1994)
        9: 1251
Ruthenia **4:** 483
Saarland **8:** 1026
Sagres **3:** 304, *307*
Saint Helena **5:** *603,* 604
Saint Petersburg *(or Leningrad or Petrograd)*
    5: 688
    and Peter the Great **4:** 487
    and the Russian Revolution (1905) **5:** 696
    Winter Palace **5:** 696 **7:** *909, 915,* 916
    and the Russian Revolution (1917) **7:** *909,* 913,
        916, *917*
    and World War II **8:** 1044
    after collapse of the Soviet Union **9:** *1251*
Saint Vincent, Cape of (Portugal) **3:** *306*
San Marino **1:** 28
Sardinia **1:** 24 **4:** 467
Sardinia-Piedmont **5:** 658
Savoy **5:** 659
    and the War of the Spanish Succession **4:** 464,
        465
Saxony **2:** 188
    invasion by Prussia **4:** 469
Scandinavia, Union of Colmar **1:** 24

Scheldt River **2:** 222
Schleswig **5:** 661
Scotland
    Tudor **2:** 214
    and Charles I's religious reforms **2:** 238, *239*
    immigrants to North America (c. 1700s) **3:** 371
    with England as the United Kingdom **4:** 444
Segovia **1:** *24* **2:** *189*
Seine River **2:** *198* **4:** *451*
Serbia
    taken by the Ottomans **1:** 101
    revolution (1804) **6:** 730
    autonomous from the Ottomans **6:** 732, 734
        7: 877
    and the lead-up to World War I **7:** 877, 878,
        879, 880
    and World War I **7:** 890
    attack on Albanians in Kosovo (1999) **9:** 1252,
        1278
    attack on Bosnia-Herzegovina **9:** 1252, 1278
    attack on Croatia (1991–1992) **9:** 1252
Sèvres, porcelain from **4:** 492
Siberia, gulags (labor camps) **7:** 927, 928
Sicily **1:** 24 **5:** 658
    scholarship in **1:** 53
    and World War II **8:** 1046
Silesia, invasion by Prussia **4:** 469, 488, 489
Slovakia **9:** 1246
Soviet Union (USSR)
    under Lenin **7:** 921–924, *925*
    under Stalin **7:** 923–932, 936
    and China (1920s) **7:** 936
    liberates Manchuria for China (1945) **7:** 943
        8: 1060
    alliance with Germany (1922) **7:** 953
    and the Spanish Civil War **8:** 1032, 1033
    nonaggression pact with Germany (Molotov-
        Ribbentrop Pact; 1939) **8:** *1035,* 1036
    and World War II **8:** *1037, 1042,* 1043–1045,
        1048, 1061, 1062, *1067,* 1070, 1071
    invasion of Poland (1939) **8:** 1038
    rejection of post–World War II Marshall Aid
        8: 1072, *1076,* 1089
    and the Cold War (1945–1960) **8:** 1083–1094
    and the Hungarian Uprising (1956) **8:** 1094
    space race **8:** 1094 **9:** 1256
    and the Cold War (1960–1989) **8:** 1095–*1098,*
        1102–1106
    and the Cuban missile crisis **8:** 1096–1097
    and war in Afghanistan (1979–1989)
        8: 1102–1104 **9:** 1167, 1241
    dissolution **8:** 1106 **9:** 1196, 1198
    communism (post-1960) **9:** 1161
    insignia **9:** *1161*
    and China (1950s) **9:** 1180, *1182,* 1186
    and Ethiopia **9:** 1226
    domination of Soviet-bloc countries **9:** 1243
    reforms under Gorbachev **9:** 1243–1244
    breakup **9:** 1248–1250
    See also Russia; Russian Federation
Spain
    kingdoms of Aragon and Castile **1:** 23–24
    Moorish occupation of **1:** *23,* 24
    and discovery of the New World **1:** 41
        3: 309–311
    scholarship in **1:** 53
    monarchy and religion **1:** 70
    nobility **1:** 76
    reform of the Catholic Church **2:** 165–166
    eradicating Islam from (1400s) **2:** *166*
    and Catholicism **2:** 172
    part of the Holy Roman Empire **2:** 187–188,
        192–193, 226
    under Philip II **2:** 193–194
    Armada sails against England (1588) **2:** 194,
        213–214, 221
    and the Thirty Years' War **2:** 227, 231
    and Catholic Baroque **2:** 260
    New World divided for **3:** 310–311
    American colonies **3:** 343–354, 356, 374, 380
    racial purity **3:** 351, 354
    Bourbon dynasty **4:** 460 **5:** 600 **6:** 747–748
    War of the Spanish Succession **4:** *461,* 463–470
    in decline (1600s) **4:** 463
    dynastic struggles **5:** 665–666

1370

Volume numbers appear in **boldface type**. Page numbers in *italic type* refer to illustrations and captions.

South American colonies gain independence **6:** 747–756
Napoleon's invasion of (1808) **6:** 749
Spanish Civil War (1936–1939) **8:** 1031, 1032–1033
EEC membership **9:** 1195
Spanish Netherlands
rebellion against Spain (Eighty Years' War) **1:** 44 **2:** 213, 215–224 **4:** 440
and the Inquisition **2:** 180
and art **2:** *257*
Stalingrad, and World War II **8:** 1044–1045
Strasbourg
invasion by France (1681) **4:** 462
and the Franco-Prussian War **5:** *662*
court of human rights **8:** 1074
meeting of foreign ministers (1949) **9:** *1191*
Sudetenland **7:** 993 **8:** 1034–1035, 1036
Sweden
and the Union of Colmar **1:** 24
trade and coinage **1:** 42
and the Thirty Years' War **2:** *225, 228,* 230–231, 232, 233
trade with Asia (1700s) **3:** 330
colonies in North America **3:** 360, 362–363
religion **4:** 440
trade (1600s) **4:** 445–446
power of the nobles (1600s) **4:** 446–447
power struggle in the Baltic (1600s/1700s) **4:** 446, 447 448
reduktion policy (1600s) **4:** 447
the crown versus parliament (1700s) **4:** 448
everyday life (1700s) **4:** *511*
welfare state **9:** 1160
Switzerland
Everlasting League **1:** 26
liberal constitutions **5:** 608
Sonderbund league **5:** 612
Tajikistan **9:** 1249, 1250
Tbilisi **9:** *1247,* 1249
Telc **1:** *89*
Thames, River, and the Great Stink (1848) **5:** *629,* 705 **6:** 802
Thrace **1:** 100
Toul **2:** 192, 193
Tournai **2:** 189
Tours **2:** 200
Trakai **1:** *91*
Transylvania **1:** 93 **6:** 729 **7:** 907
Trent **2:** *169*
Tripoli **2:** 193
Turin, Stupinigi Palace **4:** *493*
Turkmenistan **9:** 1249
Tuscany **4:** 460
Ukraine **4:** 484–485
post–World War I **7:** 907
and the Russian Civil War **7:** 920
and nationalism in the USSR **9:** 1248–1249
pollution **9:** *1274*
Ulster
Protestants massacred in (1600s) **2:** 239
post–World War I **7:** 908
United Kingdom, formation **4:** 444
United Provinces of the Netherlands **2:** 220
See also Netherlands
USSR *See* Soviet Union
Uzbekistan **9:** 1249
Valencia **8:** 1032
Vassy, Huguenots massacred at **2:** 199
Venetia **5:** 599, 658, 659
Venice **2:** 188–189, *252*
and trade **1:** 15, 18, 22, 41, *104,* 106 **3:** 298
city-state **1:** 28
and music **1:** 84
and the Renaissance **1:** 84
and the Ottomans **1:** 101–102 **6:** 727–728, 729
paintings of **4:** 496
Verdun **2:** 192, 193 **7:** 894
Vienna
besieged by the Turks (1529) **1:** 93, 107 **2:** 188 **3:** *297,* 298
map **3:** *297*
besieged by the Turks (1683) **4:** 485 **6:** 729
in the 1700s **4:** *488*
and Napoleon **5:** 599

the Ringstrasse **5:** *655*
Vienna State Opera House **6:** *803*
and European music **6:** 847
Vitebsk **5:** *693*
Volga River **1:** 21–22
Volgograd (*formerly* Stalingrad), and World War II **8:** *1044,* 1045
Warsaw **4:** *485,* 490
Grand Duchy created **5:** 600, 691
Wittenberg **1:** 28 **2:** 153, 155
Württemberg, duchy of **2:** 234
Yugoslavia
post–World War I **7:** 906
D'Annunzio of Italy takes the port of Fiume **7:** 984
and World War II **8:** 1043, *1069,* 1070 **9:** 1252
inter-republic tensions **8:** 1106 **9:** 1251–1252
dissolution (1990s) **9:** 1198
See also Bosnia-Herzegovina; Croatia; Macedonia; Montenegro; Serbia
Zaragoza **8:** 1032
Zurich **2:** 160

FAR EAST

Agra **3:** *412*
Taj Mahal **3:** 412, *417*
Amchitka Island **9:** 1271
Amritsar
massacre at (1919) **8:** 1108
Golden Temple **8:** *1109,* 1115
Amur Valley **6:** 772
Angkor **3:** 320, 321, 322
Annam **1:** 127 **3:** 317
See also Vietnam
Arabia, and World War I **7:** 890
Asia
European trade with **1:** *41* **3:** 323–330, 417
European view of **1:** 119–120
between the world wars **8:** 1015–1024
independent nation states post-World War II **8:** *1118*
post–World War II economies in the Pacific Rim **9:** 1209–1220
Asia, East *See* China; Hong Kong; Japan; Korea; Mongolia; Taiwan
Asia, South *See* Bangladesh; India; Pakistan; Sri Lanka
Asia, Southeast
during the 1500s **3:** 313–322
geography **3:** 313–314, 315–316
early peoples **3:** 314–315
trading empire **3:** 319–321
nationalist movements and decolonization **8:** 1118–1124
post–World War II economic development **9:** 1217–1218
financial depression (1990s) **9:** 1220
See also Borneo; Cambodia; Indonesia; Laos; Malaysia; Myanmar; Philippines; Singapore; Thailand; Vietnam
Australia
James Cook lands in **5:** *667*
part of the British Empire **5:** 671–674
dominion status (1926) **5:** 676
and World War II **8:** 1052, 1054
Asian influences on the economy **9:** 1218–1219
Bali **8:** 1020
Ballarat **5:** 673
Banda islands **3:** 328
Bangalore **8:** 1116
Bangkok, and the Vietnam War **9:** 1217
Bangladesh **8:** 1115, 1116
and global warming **9:** 1268
Bathurst **5:** 673
Beijing
and Marco Polo **1:** 119
Yuan dynasty **1:** 123
Forbidden City **1:** *128* **4:** *525* **6:** *775*
Manchu take over **1:** 128–129 **4:** 526
Monument to the People's Heroes **6:** *771* **7:** *933*
and the Boxer Rebellion **6:** *774,* 775
Gate of Heavenly Peace **7:** *940*
Tiananmen Square **9:** *1182, 1187,* 1188
Bengal **3:** 418 **5:** 667
partition of **5:** 670, 671 **8:** 1114, 1115
famine (1943) **8:** 1062, 1113
Bhopal, chemical accident **9:** 1270
Bikini Atoll, atomic tests **8:** 1087
Bokhara **1:** 123
Bombay **3:** 330, 418 **5:** *669* **8:** 1108, *1112*
Borneo **3:** *315,* 316 **7:** *873* **8:** 1020
Indian influences **3:** 317
nationalism post–World War II **8:** *1118*
Bougainville **8:** *1056*
Boven Digul **8:** 1022
Brisbane **9:** *1219*
Burma *See* Myanmar
Calcutta **3:** 418 **5:** 667, 671 **6:** *792*
Calicut **3:** 307, 323–324, *325,* 329
Cambodia
religion **3:** 314
kingdom of Angkor **3:** 320, 321, 322
and Pol Pot **8:** 1099 **9:** 1281
and the Vietnam War **8:** 1101
Japanese occupation of **8:** 1119, 1122
Marxist regime (1970s) **9:** 1167
Canton **4:** *531,* 532

1371

Carnatic **3:** 418
Cathay **1:** 119
Ceylon *See* Sri Lanka
China
    Ming dynasty **1:** 16, 18, *120*, 127–128
        4: 523–525, 526
    Confucianism **1:** 18, 40, 66, 124, 127–128
    trade **1:** 18, 113 **3:** *302*, 319–321, 327, 330
        4: 523, 524–525, 528, 532 **6:** 767, 773
    Sung dynasty **1:** 120–123
    Yuan dynasty **1:** 123–125, 127
    isolationism (Great Withdrawal) **1:** 127–128
        6: 768
    Manchu (Ching) dynasty **1:** 128–129
        4: 523–532 **6:** 768–776
    and world exploration **3:** 302, 323
    influence on Southeast Asia **3:** 317, 322
    jewelry **3:** *321*
    European impact on (1500s–1600s) **4:** 523–525
    rice cultivation **4:** 524, *530* **6:** *770*
    tributary system **4:** 527–530
    anti-Western Boxer Rebellion (1900) **5:** 696
        6: 774–775, 776
    and western influences (1800s) **6:** 767–776
    opium and the Opium Wars **6:** 769–771
    population (1850) **6:** 769
    Taiping Rebellion (1850s and 1860s)
        6: 771–772, 784
    Sino-Japanese War (1894–1895) **6:** 772, 782
    Hundred Days of Reform **6:** 773
    becomes a republic **6:** 776 **7:** 933
    dictatorship of Yuan Shikai **6:** 776 **7:** 933–934
    Japanese ultimatums to (Twenty-One Demands;
        1915) **6:** 783–786 **7:** 934 **8:** 1016
    and the post–World War I treaties **7:** 908,
        934–936
    communism triumphs over nationalism
        7: 933–944
    communists in power (1949–1999) **7:** 933
        9: 1179–1188
    Long March **7:** *934*, *940*, 941
    and World War I **7:** 934
    May Fourth Movement (1919) **7:** 935
    Sun Yat-sen president of nationalist government
        7: 936
    united front with Mao **7:** 936–937
    Northern Expedition **7:** 938–939
    Japanese invasion of Manchuria (1931)
        7: 941–942 **8:** *1015*, 1018, 1019, 1031
    Japan renews invasion of China (1937–1938)
        7: 942–943 **8:** 1025, 1034
    Sino-Japanese War (1937–1945) **7:** 942–943
        8: 1019, 1025, 1034
    Soviet Union liberates Manchuria (1945) **7:** 943
    and World War II **7:** 943
    Civil War (1945–1949) **7:** 944
    and the Cold War **8:** 1092–1093, 1097
    and the Korean War (1950–1953) **8:** *1092*, 1093
        9: 1181–1182
    Nixon's visit to (1972) **8:** 1102
    Britain returns Hong Kong to **8:** 1128 **9:** 1188,
        1216, 1220
    and the Soviet Union (1950s) **9:** 1180, *1182*,
        1186
    Great Leap Forward **9:** 1182–1183
    Cultural Revolution **9:** 1184, 1185
    nuclear arms **9:** 1186
    reform under Deng Xiaoping **9:** 1186–1188
    prodemocracy movement **9:** *1187*, 1188, 1216
    family planning measures **9:** 1275
Delhi
    and the Moguls **1:** 130 **3:** *407*, *415*
    and Muslim India **1:** 130
    sacked by the Iranians (1739) **3:** 406, 416–417
    and the Indian Mutiny **5:** 669
    British capital moved to **5:** 671
    and independence **8:** *1110*, *1113*
Diu **3:** *325*
Dutch East Indies *See* Indonesia
East Indies
    and the spice trade **2:** 222
    and World War II **8:** 1050, 1052
    See also Indonesia; Philippines; Spice Islands
Edo (*later* Tokyo) **4:** 537, *538*, 540 **6:** 777, 778
Formosa *See* Taiwan

Fuji, Mount **6:** *777*
Funan **3:** 319
Gilbert Islands, Battle of Tarawa (1943) **8:** 1054,
    1055
Goa
    Portuguese colony **3:** *308*, 324, *399*
    Jesuit missionaries from **3:** *411*, 412
Great Banda **3:** 328
Guadalcanal, battles for (1942) **8:** 1053–1054
Guam, and World War II **8:** 1052, *1054*
Guangzhou **7:** 938
Haiphong **8:** *1122*
Hangzhou **1:** 119
Hanoi **8:** 1123
Hiroshima **8:** 1059, 1086 **9:** 1255
Ho Chi Minh City (*formerly* Saigon) **8:** 1099
    9: *1217*
Hong Kong
    ceded to Britain **6:** 771 **9:** 1216
    returned to China (1997) **8:** 1128 **9:** 1188,
        1216, 1220
    economic growth **9:** 1214–1217
Hyogo, Himeji Castle **1:** *126*
Imphal **8:** 1058
India
    Mogul **1:** *120*, 130 **3:** 402, 406, 407–418 **5:** 667
    rise of Muslim India **1:** 129–130
    Roman ports **3:** 298
    Portuguese discover a sea route to **3:** 307, 323
    influence on Southeast Asia **3:** 317
    and international trade **3:** 321, 324, *325*, 330
    the English in (1600s) **3:** 330
    European trade with **3:** 417
    part of the British Empire **5:** 667–671 **7:** 873
    partition **8:** 1015
    independence and partition **8:** 1107–1116
    and World War I **8:** 1107
    massacre at Amritsar **8:** 1108
    caste system **8:** 1109, 1111
    and World War II **8:** 1112–1114
    flag **8:** *1113*
    nuclear weapons **8:** 1116
    and state socialism **9:** 1161
    war with China (1962) **9:** 1186
    green revolution in farming **9:** 1265
    chemical accident at Bhopal **9:** 1270
    population (1999) **9:** 1275
Indian Ocean, Portuguese control of **3:** 307
Indochina
    and France **6:** 772 **8:** 1050
    Japanese occupation (1941) **8:** 1050, 1119
    and communism (1950s) **8:** 1093
    post–World War II economic development
        9: 1217
    See also Cambodia; Laos; Vietnam
Indonesia (*formerly* Dutch East Indies)
    peoples **3:** 315
    fishing **3:** *316*
    Buddhism **3:** 320
    and the Dutch **3:** 327, *328* **7:** 873 **8:** 1020,
        1120–1121
    nationalism and independence **8:** 1015,
        1020–1023, 1120–1121
    Japanese occupation (1942–1945) **8:** 1023, §
        1119, 1120
    and World War II **8:** 1023, 1050
    communist coup **8:** 1121–1122
    post–World War II economy **9:** 1217, 1218
    economic crisis (1990s) **9:** 1220
    prodemocracy demonstrations **9:** 1280
Iran, arms sold to Iran by the U.S. **9:** 1205
Irian Jaya **8:** 1022, 1121
Jakarta **3:** 327 **9:** *1218*
Jamma **8:** *1115*
Japan
    first (Kamakura) shogunate **1:** 125–126
    and the Mongols **1:** 125
    and Chinese culture **1:** 126–127
    Ashikaga shogunate **1:** 127
    samurai warriors **1:** 127 **4:** 533–537 **6:** 777,
        778, 780
    and world exploration **3:** 323
    Catholic missionaries **3:** *324*
    trade with Europe **3:** *324*, *327* **4:** 538, 541
        6: 779–780

    trade with China **4:** 528 **6:** 773
    daimyo (landowning princes) **4:** 533–537, 539,
        540 **6:** 777–778, *779*
    Tokugawa clan **4:** 533–542 **6:** 777–780
    class structure **4:** 534–538
    peasants **4:** 534–536 **6:** 778–779
    merchant class **4:** 536 **6:** 778
    economic and military rise (1800s) **4:** 540
        6: 777–786
    Russian-Japanese War (1904–1905) **5:** *695*, 696
        6: 782–783, *786* **8:** 1015
    Sino-Japanese War (1894–1895) **6:** 772, 782
    Meiji Restoration **6:** 780
    Western influences (1800s) **6:** 780, 784, 785
    ultimatums to China (Twenty-One Demands;
        1915) **6:** 783–786 **7:** 934 **8:** 1016
    and the lead-up to World War I **7:** 873
    and World War I **7:** 887
    and post–World War I treaties **7:** 908, 934–935
    invasion of Manchuria (1931) **7:** 941–942
        8: *1015*, 1018, 1019, 1031
    renews invasion of China (1937–1938)
        7: 942–943 **8:** 1025, 1034
    Sino-Japanese War (1937–1945) **7:** 942–943
        8: 1019, 1025, 1034
    and the United States (1920s) **7:** 948
    in the early 1900s **8:** 1015–1016
    militarism **8:** 1015–1016, 1019–1020
    between the world wars **8:** 1016–1020
    Western influences (early 1900s) **8:** 1016, *1017*
    and the Depression **8:** 1017–1018
    flag **8:** *1018*
    nationalism (1930s) **8:** 1018
    and World War II (1939–1945) **8:** 1025, 1042,
        1049–1060, 1062, 1070, 1113, 1119–1120
    anti-communism pact with Germany (1937)
        8: 1031–1034
    and nationalism in European colonies
        8: 1119–1120
    economic success (late 1900s) **9:** 1209–1212,
        1214, 1217
    economic recession (late 1990s) **9:** 1277
Java **3:** *313*, 314
    religion and temples **3:** 317–318, 320
    Majapahit kingdom **3:** 321
    and the Dutch **3:** 327 **8:** 1020, 1022
    communist insurrection (1926) **8:** 1022
    nationalism **8:** *1120*
Jhansi **5:** *669*
Jiangxi **7:** 940
Jiaozhou **7:** 934, 935
Jinzhou **4:** 526
Kaifeng **1:** 122
K'aip'ing **6:** 772
Kaohsiung **9:** *1215*
Karakorum **1:** *124*
Kashmir **8:** 1114 **9:** 1278
Kohima **8:** 1058
Korea
    and the Sino-Japanese War (1894–1895) **6:** 772,
        782
    annexed by Japan (1910) **6:** 783
    divided into North and South **9:** 1212
Korea, North
    and the Korean War **8:** 1093 **9:** 1212
    famine (late 1990s) **9:** 1276
Korea, South
    and the Korean War **8:** 1093 **9:** 1212
    postwar poverty followed by economic growth
        9: 1212–1213
    financial depression (1990s) **9:** 1220
Kuala Lumpur, Petronas Towers **9:** 1218
Kyoto **1:** 127 **4:** 540
    earth summit **9:** 1271
Laos **3:** 314 **8:** 1099, 1101
    Japanese occupation of **8:** 1119, 1122
Leyte **8:** 1056
Liao, Qidan people **1:** 120, 122
Liaodong **1:** 128
Liaotung Peninsula, and the Sino-Japanese War
    6: 772, 782
Liaoyang **4:** 525
Luzon **8:** 1051, 1057
Macao **3:** 324, 327 **4:** 524 **6:** 772
Madras **3:** 330, 418 **5:** 667

Majapahit kingdom **3:** 321
Malacca **3:** 322, 327 **8:** *1119*
Malaya
  and World War II **8:** 1050, 1051, 1119
  and communism (1950s) **8:** 1093
  independence **8:** 1120
Malaysia
  Indian influences **3:** 317
  independence **8:** *1119*
  arrested economic development (1950s/1960s)
    9: 1217
  economy (1990s) **9:** 1218
  financial depression (1990s) **9:** 1220
  rubber production **9:** *1266*
  deforestation **9:** 1274
Maldives **9:** 1268
Manchukuo **7:** 941–942 **8:** 1049
Manchuria **4:** 525
  Russians enter **5:** 696
  Japanese occupation of (late 1800s) **6:** 772, 783
  Japanese occupation of (by 1914) **7:** 934
  Japanese occupation of (1931) **7:** 941–942
    8: *1015*, 1018, 1019, 1031, 1049
  liberated by the Soviets for China (1945) **7:** 943
  See also Mukden
Manila **8:** 1057
Mariana Islands **3:** 312 **8:** 1055, 1056
Marshall Islands, atomic tests at Bikini Atoll
  8: 1087
Masulipatam **3:** 330
Mecca, and the Ottomans **1:** 107
Melbourne **5:** 674
Minamata, mercury poisoning **9:** 1268
Moluccas **3:** 315, 316, 324, *329*
  and the Dutch **3:** 327
  See also Spice Islands
Mongolia, Karakorum **1:** *124*
Mukden *See* Shenyang
Myanmar (*formerly* Burma) **3:** 314 **6:** 772
  peoples **3:** 321–322
  and World War II **8:** 1050, 1052, 1054, 1058,
    1113, 1119
  independence **8:** 1120
Nagasaki **4:** 540 **6:** 779 **8:** 1060, 1086 **9:** 1255
Nanjing (Nanking) **6:** 771
  Japanese invasion of **7:** 943 **8:** 1034
New Britain **8:** 1054
New Delhi **8:** *1114, 1116*
  and Gandhi **8:** *1110*
New Guinea, and World War II **8:** 1052, 1053,
  1054, 1056
New Zealand
  peoples **3:** 315 **5:** *673*, 674
  part of the British Empire **5:** *673*, 674
  dominion status (1926) **5:** 676
  Asian influences on the economy **9:** 1218–1219
North Korea *See* Korea, North
Okinawa **6:** 779 **8:** 1060
Osaka **4:** 536, 540 **6:** *782*
  siege of Osaka Castle **4:** *535*
Pagan (kingdom) **3:** 321, *322*
Pakistan **8:** 1116
  creation **8:** 1112, 1114–1115
Palembang **8:** *1021*
Panjipat **1:** 130
Philippines
  Magellan sails to **3:** 312
  peoples **3:** 315
  and World War II **8:** 1050, 1051, *1052*, 1054,
    1056–1057, *1058*, 1119
  independence **8:** 1120
  and the Vietnam War **9:** 1217
  green revolution in farming **9:** 1265
Polynesia **3:** 315
Port Arthur, and the Sino-Japanese War **6:** 782
Punjab **8:** 1114, 1115
Qingdao **7:** 887, 935
Saigon *See* Ho Chi Minh City
Saipan **8:** 1055
Sakhalin Island **8:** 1017
Samarkand **1:** 123, 130
Samoa **3:** 315
Sarawak **3:** *315*, 316 **8:** *1118*
Seoul **9:** 1213
Shaanxi **7:** 941

Shahjahanabad **3:** 414
Shandong **7:** 935 **8:** 1016, 1017
Shanghai **9:** *1188*
  industrialization **6:** 772, *773*
  and the May Fourth Movement **7:** 935
  strikes (1925) **7:** 938
  Chiang Kai-shek enters (1927) **7:** 939
Shenyang (*formerly* Mukden) **1:** 128 **4:** 525
  7: 944 **8:** 1019
Shimabara **4:** 539
Siam *See* Thailand
Sikandara **3:** *413*
Singapore
  and World War II **8:** 1051, 1113, 1119
  independence **8:** 1120 **9:** 1218
  economic boom **9:** 1218, 1220
Solomon Islands, and World War II **8:** 1052,
  1053–1054
South Korea *See* Korea, South
Spice Islands
  search for a sea route to **1:** 41 **3:** 308–312, 316,
    324
  See also East Indies; Moluccas
Sri Lanka (*formerly* Ceylon) **3:** 327 **9:** 1282
  independence **8:** 1120
Sukhothai **3:** 322
Sumatra
  Islam **3:** 322
  and the Dutch **3:** 327 **8:** 1020, *1021*, 1022
  communist insurrection (1926) **8:** 1022
  deforestation **9:** *1277*
Sydney **5:** 674
Syria, castle of Krak des Chevaliers **1:** *101*
Tahiti **3:** 315
Taipei **9:** *1209, 1215*
Taiwan (*formerly* Formosa) **3:** 315 **4:** 527
  becomes part of China **4:** 527
  and the Sino-Japanese War **6:** 772, 782
  Chiang Kai-shek's nationalist government in
    7: 944 **9:** 1180, 1214
  economic success (late 1900s) **9:** *1209*, 1214,
    1215–1217
Thailand (*formerly* Siam) **1:** 127 **3:** 314
  religion **3:** *317, 320*
  Mon people **3:** 321–322
  French missionaries (1660–1688) **3:** 330
  and the Vietnam War **9:** 1217
  economy (1990s) **9:** 1218, 1220
Tibet **4:** 527 **5:** 670
Tinian **8:** 1055
Tokyo
  formerly Edo **4:** 537, *538*, 540 **6:** 777, 778
  railroad to Yokohama **6:** *784*
  and World War II **8:** 1052, 1055–1056, *1057*
  Stock Exchange **9:** *1220*
Tonga **3:** 315
Tonkin, Gulf of **8:** 1100
Turkestan **1:** 123
Vietnam **3:** 314
  and the Mongols **1:** 125
  Cham people **3:** 314, *318*, 321
  art styles **3:** 317
  Indian influences **3:** 317, *318*
  part of China **3:** 317, 321
  and the Cold War **8:** 1083
  decolonization and French withdrawl from
    8: 1099, 1100, *1117*, 1122–1123
  split into North and South **8:** 1099, 1100, 1123
  Vietnam War (1959–1975) **8:** 1099, 1100–1101
    9: 1217
  reunited (1976) **8:** 1101
  Japanese occupation of **8:** 1119, 1122–1123
  French-Vietnamese War (1946–1954) **8:** 1123
  Marxist regime (1970s) **9:** 1167
  See also Annam
Wake **8:** 1052
Xia **1:** 120

MIDDLE EAST

Acre **8:** 1133
Afghanistan
  civil war and Islamic fundamentalism (1990s)
    9: *1240*, 1241
  war aided by the Soviets (1979–1989)
    8: 1102–1104 **9:** 1167, 1241
Anatolia **7:** 907
Aqaba, Gulf of **8:** 1133, 1135
Arabia
  Wahhabi people **6:** 732
  post–World War I **7:** 905 **8:** 1023–1024
Asia Minor, post–World War I **7:** 908
Ayvalik **8:** *1023*
Azerbaijan **8:** 1086–1087
Baghdad **9:** *1235*
Bandar Abbas **3:** 403
Beersheba **8:** 1133
Beirut
  westerners kidnapped (1980s) **9:** 1238–1239,
    1241
  U.S. embassy bombed (1983) **9:** *1239*
Byzantine empire **3:** 297
  Orthodox Christianity **1:** 10
  and the Ottomans **1:** 16–18, 19, 100–101, 103
    3: 298
  and ancient Greek texts **1:** 64
  legacy to Russia **1:** 92
  Constantinople *See* Istanbul
Deir Yasin, massacre **8:** 1132
Elath **8:** 1133
Gaza Strip **8:** 1132, 1133, 1137, 1138 **9:** 1242
Golan Heights **8:** 1133, 1134, 1136
Haifa **8:** *1129*, 1130, *1136*
Hormuz, Portuguese expelled from **3:** 330, 403
Iran
  the Safavid empire **1:** 105 **3:** 397–406 **6:** 728,
    729
  Soviet intention to occupy Azerbaijan
    8: 1086–1087
  revolution (1970s) **9:** 1231, 1232–1235
  modernization under the shah (1950s–1970s)
    9: 1232–1233
  return of Ayatollah Khomeini **9:** *1233*, 1234
  U.S. embassy hostages (1979) **9:** 1234
  Iran-Iraq War (1980–1988) **9:** 1235
  and terrorism **9:** 1236
  Ayatollah Khatami elected **9:** 1242
Iraq
  post–World War I **7:** 905 **8:** 1023
  and the creation of Israel **8:** 1132
  Iran-Iraq War (1980–1988) **9:** 1235
  post-Gulf War sanctions against **9:** *1241*
Isfahan **3:** *398, 401*, 403, 405
Israel
  post–World War I **7:** 905, 907
  creation of **8:** 1024, 1129–1132 **9:** 1232
  conflicts with its neighbors **8:** 1129–1138
    9: 1240
  Six-Day War (1967) **8:** 1133–1134, *1136*
    9: 1279
  kibbutzim **8:** *1136*
  Camp David peace accords **8:** 1137 **9:** 1236,
    1237
Istanbul (*formerly* Constantinople) **6:** *731, 732*
  captured by the Ottomans (1453) **1:** 16–18, 19,
    26, 41, 52, 92, 99, 102, *103*, 104
  Topkapi Palace **1:** *105*
  Hagia Sophia **3:** *296*
  and the Byzantine Empire **3:** 297
  and the Russians **5:** 692 **6:** 733
  and the lead-up to World War I **7:** 877–878
  British troops in **8:** 1023
Izmir (*formerly* Smyrna) **8:** *1022*
Jaffa **8:** 1130, 1133
Jerusalem
  Seljuk invasion of **1:** 99
  and the Ottomans **1:** *106*
  tomb of Theodore Herzl **8:** *1131*
  and Israel **8:** 1133, *1134*
Jordan, and the creation of Israel **8:** 1132
Kabul **9:** 1241
  and Babur **1:** *129, 130*
Kerbala **3:** 399

1373

Kerman **3**: 405
Khorasan **3**: 399, 402
Kuwait, Gulf War and burning oil wells **9**: *1273*
Lebanon
    post–World War I **7**: 905 **8**: 1023
    and the creation of Israel **8**: 1132
    Israeli invasion of (1982) **8**: 1137–1138 **9**: 1240
    and Islamic fundamentalism **9**: 1237–1241
    Palestinian refugee camps **9**: 1237–1240
    civil war (1975) **9**: 1240
    Shiite terrorists (Hezbollah) **9**: 1240, 1241, 1242
Levant, and the Ottomans **1**: 106 **3**: 298
Libya, and the Lockerbie bombing **9**: 1237, *1238*,
    1240
Mashhad **3**: 405, 406
Mecca
    Mansa Musa's pilgrimage to **1**: 118
    Wahhabi occupation of **6**: 732
    Great Mosque occupied by Shiites (1979)
      9: 1234
Mesopotamia
    and World War I **7**: 887, 890
    See also Iraq
Middle East **1**: 106
    post–World War I **7**: 905 **8**: 1023–1024
    Israeli conflicts **8**: 1129–1138
Najaf **3**: 399
New Julfa **3**: 403, 405
Ottoman Empire **1**: 99–108 **3**: 298
    attacking the Byzantine Empire **1**: 16–18, 19,
      100–101 **3**: 298
    capture of Constantinople (1453) **1**: 16–18, 19,
      26, 41, 52, 92, 99, 102, *103*, 104
    and trade **1**: 40, 104, *108* **3**: 298
    besieging Vienna (1529) **1**: 93, 107 **2**: 188
      3: *297*, 298
    Süleyman the Magnificent **1**: *100*, 107–108
      2: *190* **3**: *297*
    a meritocracy of slaves **1**: 104
    sultans **1**: 104
    encroaching on Europe (c. 1559) **2**: 193–194
    conflict with the Safavid empire **3**: 399–400,
      405, 406 **6**: 729
    besieging Vienna (1683) **4**: 485 **6**: 729
    Greek rebellion against **5**: 607, *611* **6**: 731–732
    and Russia **5**: 692 **6**: 728, 730, 732, 733–734
    decline of the Turkish Empire **6**: 727–736
    Western influences on **6**: 729–730
    and Turkish nationalism **6**: 735–736
    and lead-up to World War I **7**: *877*, 878
    and World War I **7**: *885*, 887
    post–World War I colonies **7**: 905
    post–World War I **7**: 907
    Israel part of **8**: 1129
Palestine
    and World War I **7**: 890, 905 **8**: 1023
    a British mandate **7**: 905 **8**: 1130, 1131
    and the creation of Israel within **8**: 1024,
      1129–1134 **9**: 1232
Persia *See* Iran
Qazvin **3**: 400
Qom **9**: 1233, 1234
Riyadh **6**: 732
Shiraz **3**: 406
Smyrna **7**: 908 **8**: *1022*
Syria
    Egyptian invasion (1831) **6**: 732
    post–World War I **7**: 905 **8**: 1023, 1024
    and the creation of Israel **8**: 1132
    war against Israel (1973) **8**: 1136–1137
Tabriz **3**: 398
Tel Aviv **8**: *1133*
Tehran, U.S. embassy hostages (1979) **9**: 1234
Transjordan, post–World War I **7**: 905
Turkey
    nationalism under Ottomans **6**: 735–736 **7**: 878
    and World War I **7**: *885*, 887, 890
    Turks drive Greeks from Asia Minor (1920s)
      7: 908 **8**: 1022
    under Kemal Atatürk **8**: *1022*, 1023
    lands lost after World War I **8**: 1023
    See also Ottoman Empire
Zayandeh River **3**: *401*
West Bank **8**: 1132, 1133, 1134, 1136, 1138
    9: 1242

NORTH AMERICA

Abilene **6**: 838
Abraham, Heights of **4**: *549*
Acadia **3**: 374 **4**: 467, 545
Alamogordo **8**: 1059, 1060
Alaska
    Native Americans **3**: 341
    Exxon *Valdez* oil spill **9**: 1268–1269
Alberta **5**: 676
Alexandria (Virginia) **5**: *678*
Annapolis **3**: *370*
Annapolis Royal (*formerly* Port Royal) **3**: 360
    4: 546
Antigua, slavery **3**: *378*
Antilles **3**: 348, *384*
Arizona, Native Americans **3**: *333*
Arlington **8**: *1049*
Atlantic City **7**: *951*
Bahamas, discovery by Columbus **3**: 309, *310*
Bethlehem (Pennsylvania) **3**: 372
Birmingham (Alabama) **9**: 1175
Bodie **6**: *837*
Boston **3**: *367*
    immigration **5**: 650
British Columbia **5**: 675
    Native Americans **3**: 340–341
Cahokia **3**: 332
California
    Native Americans **3**: 342
    Catholic missions **3**: 352
    gold rush **5**: *651*, 654 **6**: 837–840
    and slavery **5**: 654
    Bodie State Historic Park **7**: *946*
    Asian influences on the economy (1990s)
      9: 1219
Canada
    Native Americans **3**: 341
    Cartier lands in **3**: *355*, 356
    and British rule **5**: 674–676
    immigration from Europe **5**: 674
    Lower and Upper **5**: 674, 675
    border with the United States **5**: 675
    Dominion of **5**: 675
    transcontinental railroad **5**: 675
    United Province of **5**: 675
    dominion status (1926) **5**: 676
    Sikhs prevented from entering **8**: 1108
    Asian influences on the economy **9**: 1219
Cape Fear **3**: 356
Caribbean islands
    Columbus's voyages to **3**: 301, 309, 310
    Spanish colonies **3**: 343, 346, 348
    slavery on **3**: 348, 350–351, 377–380
    plantations **3**: 349, 387, 389–390
    post–World War I **7**: 971
Carolina **3**: 361
Charleston **3**: *370* **4**: 546
    and the American Revolutionary War
      4: 559–561
Chesapeake Bay colony **3**: 360, 390
Chiapas **9**: 1206, 1277
Chicago **5**: 625–626 **6**: 832
    fire (1871) **5**: *630*
Cincinnati **5**: 650
Connecticut **3**: 369
Costa Rica, post–World War I **7**: 971
Cuba
    visited by Columbus **3**: 309
    and the Spanish-American War (1898) **6**: 766,
      835
    sugar trade **7**: 973
    Bay of Pigs invasion (1961) **8**: 1096 **9**: 1173,
      1203
    missile crisis (1962) **8**: 1096, *1098* **9**: 1203
    and the Soviet Union **9**: *1201*, 1204
    Batista overthrown; Castro president (1958)
      9: 1203
Cuernavaca **6**: *742*
Deerfield
    massacre at (1704) **3**: 368
    attacked by Native Americans (1675) **4**: *543*
Detroit **7**: 949
    car industry **7**: 949 **8**: *1081*
Dodge City **6**: 838, *839*

Dominican Republic
    and Columbus **3**: 309, *310*
    U.S. suppression of reformist rebellion (1965)
      9: 1204
El Salvador
    post-independence **6**: 764
    internal conflict **9**: 1204, 1206
Ellis Island **6**: *834*
Florida **3**: 356
    Native Americans **3**: *334*
Fort Christina **3**: 362
Fort Duquesne **4**: 548
Fort Garry **5**: *674*
Fort Niagara **4**: 548
Fulton, Winston Churchill at **8**: *1086*, 1087
Georgia (North America) **3**: 364 **5**: *654*
Great Plains (North American) **3**: 341–342, 395
    9: 1264
Grenada (West Indies), U.S. invasion (1983)
    9: *1205*, 1206
Guam **6**: 835
Guanahani **3**: 309
Guatemala
    land reform program (from 1951) **9**: 1201
    U.S. backed destabilization of government
      9: 1201–1202
    internal conflict **9**: 1204, 1206
    overuse of pesticides **9**: 1275
Haiti
    and Columbus **3**: 309, *310*
    slave revolt **3**: 386
    independence **6**: 748
Harlem **7**: 950
Havana **8**: *1098*
Hawaii, Pearl Harbor attacked **8**: 1025, 1042,
    1049, 1050–1051, 1053, 1067
Hispaniola
    and Columbus **3**: 309, *310*
    slave revolt **3**: 386
    smallpox **3**: 390, 393
    See also Dominican Republic; Haiti
Hollywood **7**: 951, *963*
Homestead **6**: *795*
Honduras, bananas **6**: *761*, 763 **7**: 973
Jamestown, colony at **3**: 357–358, 359, *371*
    4: 543–544
Labrador **3**: 355
Little Rock **8**: 1082
Long Island **3**: 362
Los Angeles **8**: 1082
    Hollywood **7**: 951, *963*
    smog **9**: *1269*
Louisbourg, and colonial America **4**: 547–548
Louisiana
    Cajuns **3**: 374
    and Napoleon **5**: 600–601, 646
Manhattan Island **3**: *360*, 362, *363* **7**: 947
Manitoba **5**: 675
Maryland, colonial **3**: *359*, 373
Massachusetts
    Salem witch trials **2**: 182 **3**: 370, *373*
    Plymouth colony **3**: 358–359
Massachusetts Bay Colony **3**: 359–360
Mexico
    under Spanish rule **3**: 346, 348, 349–350 **6**: 737
    introduction of European plants to **3**: 394
    French involvement in (1860's) **5**: 657
      6: 740–741
    and independence from Spain **5**: 665
      6: 737–738
    Mexican Revolution (1910–1920) **6**: *737*, 742,
      743–746
    Indians (1800's) **6**: 738–739, 742
    Texan independence from **6**: 738, 739
    lands lost to the United States **6**: 739–740
    war with the United States **6**: 739
    Reform (La Reforma) **6**: 740
    Constitution of 1857 **6**: 742
    Diaz's rule (Pax Porfiriana) **6**: 743–744
    Constitution of 1917 **6**: 746
    post-independence **6**: 763, 764
    period between the World Wars **7**: 971, 973,
      979, 980
    major companies nationalized **7**: 980
    post–World War II **9**: 1199, 1206

economic crisis (1990s) **9:** 1206–1207
international debt **9:** 1278
Mexico City **3:** *343*
and the Aztecs **3:** 344
and the Spanish colonies **3:** 347
uprising (1811) **6:** 737
captured by U.S. forces (1847) **6:** 739
and the Mexican Revolution **6:** 745
Aprista movement **7:** 974
Minnesota, immigrants **6:** *837*
Mississippi River, exploration **3:** 360
Montana, range wars (1880s) **6:** 839
Montgomery (Alabama), bus boycott **8:** 1082
9: *1171*
Monticello, home of Thomas Jefferson **4:** 495
Montreal
and Cartier **3:** 356
British assault on (1711) **4:** 546
British assault on (1760) **4:** 549
and the American Revolutionary War **4:** 556
New Amsterdam **3:** 362
New Brunswick **5:** 674, 675
Morelos **6:** *742, 744*
Nairobi **9:** *1221*
Newark (New Jersey), race riots (1967) **9:** *1174,*
1175
New England **3:** 359, 369 **4:** 552
See also North America, colonial
Newfoundland **3:** 355 **4:** 467, 546
fisheries **3:** 388, *390*
New France **3:** *355,* 360, 373–374
conflicts with other colonial powers **4:** 545–549
New Harmony **6:** 811
New Haven **3:** 360
New Jersey **3:** 361–364
New Mexico
pueblos **3:** 332, *339*
Catholic missions **3:** *352*
New Netherland **3:** 360, 361–364
New Orleans **5:** *648*
and the Civil War **5:** 682
New Spain **3:** 346, 374, 380
New Sweden **3:** 360
New York
iron works **6:** *795*
suburban development **9:** 1170
New York City **2:** 244 **3:** 366
formerly New Amsterdam **3:** 362, *363*
Wall Street **3:** 381 **7:** *962*
and the American Revolutionary War
4: 556–557, 559
and immigration **5:** 650 **6:** *834*
railroads **6:** *791*
Brooklyn Bridge **6:** *796*
tenements **6:** 803
Central Park **6:** 806 **9:** *1162*
Triangle Shirtwaist Company fire **6:** *814,* 815
Chrysler Building **6:** 846
skyscrapers **7:** 947, *948*
Harlem **7:** 950
Fifth Avenue (1921) **7:** *960*
and the Great Depression **7:** *962, 964*
anti–Vietnam War demonstrations **9:** *1162*
rich-poor divide **9:** *1178*
World Trade Center bombed **9:** 1242, 1282
Nicaragua
bananas **6:** *761, 763* **7:** 973
U.S. marines stationed in (1920s) **7:** 973
U.S. intervention in (1980s) **8:** 1104
Sandinista government and Contra rebels
9: *1199,* 1205
female president ousts Sandinistas **9:** 1208
North America
Native Americans **3:** 331–342
railroads **5:** 622, *623, 649* **6:** 790–791, 792
transport improvements (1800s) **6:** 790–793
experiments with government (1960–1999)
9: 1159–1168
See also Canada; Mexico; North America,
colonial; United States
North America, colonial
and Native Americans **3:** 350, 354, 358, 359,
368, 373–374 **4:** 543
European settlement of the eastern seaboard
3: 355–364

life in **3:** 365–374
population **3:** 365–366 **4:** 549
frontier life **3:** 367–368
conflicts with Native Americans **3:** 368
4: 543–544, 545–546
resources and colonial exploitation **3:** 387–396
wars and conflicts **4:** 543–552, 553–562
religious revival (Great Awakening) **4:** 549–550
trade with Britain **4:** 550–552
American Revolutionary War **4:** 553–562
independence from Britain **4:** *554,* 557, *558,*
559, 561–562
and taxes **4:** 554–555
North Carolina **3:** 361, 371
Nova Scotia **4:** 546 **5:** 674, 675
Acadia **3:** 374 **4:** 467, 545
Ohio, earth mounds **3:** *338*
Ohio Valley **3:** 368 **4:** *546,* 548, 553
Oklahoma, Native Americans resettled in **5:** *653*
Oklahoma City, bombing (1995) **9:** 1282
Oregon, Native Americans **3:** 340–341
Panama
independence **6:** 766, 835
Panama Canal **6:** 766, 835 **9:** 1200
U.S. invasion (1989) **9:** 1206
Pearl Harbor, Japanese attack on **8:** 1025, 1042,
1049, 1050–1051, 1053, 1067
Pennsylvania, colony **3:** *361,* 364, *369, 370*
Philadelphia **3:** 364, 366, 367
Liberty Bell **4:** *562*
Philippines **6:** 835
Pittsburgh **5:** 631 **6:** 832
formerly Fort Duquesne **4:** 548
Plymouth colony **3:** 358–359
Plymouth Rock **3:** 358
Port Royal **3:** 360 **4:** 546
Puerto Rico **6:** 835
Quebec (province) **5:** 674
Quebec City
a French colonial settlement **3:** 360, 366, 373
British assault on (1711) **4:** 546
British capture (1759) **4:** 549
and the American Revolutionary War **4:** 556
Rhode Island, colonial **3:** 360, 369, 373
Richmond (Virginia), and the Civil War **5:** 678,
679, 680, 681, 682, 685, 686
Roanoke Island, colony **3:** 356–357
Salem (Massachusetts) **3:** *361*
Salem (North Carolina) **3:** 372
Saint Augustine (Florida) **4:** 546, 547
Saint Lawrence River **3:** 356 **4:** 546, *549*
Saint Louis **5:** 650
Saint Paul (Minnesota) **9:** *1170*
San Francisco
and the 1849 gold rush **5:** *651*
anti–Vietnam War demonstrations **8:** *1101*
San Salvador (Bahamas), and Columbus **3:** 309,
310
Saskatchewan **5:** 676
South Carolina **3:** 361
Savannah, cotton exchange **5:** *647*
Tenochtitlán **3:** 344, 345
Texas, independence from Mexico **6:** 738, 739
Three Mile Island **9:** 1269
Tlaxcala **3:** 345
United States
Monroe Doctrine (1823) **5:** 607, 647 **6:** 741,
766, 835 **7:** 973
cotton production **5:** 616, *622,* 647, *648, 654,*
678
slavery **5:** 616, 647, 654, *678*
and industrialization (1800s) **5:** 622–623,
630–631, 647–649 **6:** 832–833
railroads **5:** 622, *623,* 649 **6:** *832,* 838
labor movement **5:** 631 **6:** *814,* 833 **7:** 970
Romanticism **5:** 640–641, 643
national parks **5:** 641 **6:** 840
expansion (1800–1850) **5:** 645–654
and the War of 1812 **5:** 646–647
American Civil War **5:** 647, 677–686 **6:** 794
intervention in Latin America **5:** 647 **6:** 741,
766, 835 **9:** 1200–1204, 1205–1206
transportation revolution **5:** 649–650
westward expansion **5:** 649, 652–654, 677
6: 829, 836–840

Democratic Party **5:** 650 **6:** 814
immigration (1800–1850) **5:** 650
abolition of slavery **5:** 651–652, 654, 682, *683*
6: 819, 830, 831
Manifest Destiny **5:** 654 **6:** 739, 836–837
border with Canada **5:** 675
Confederate States of America **5:** 677
evolution and the Monkey Trial **5:** 700, 706
lands gained from Mexico **6:** 739–740, 741
Gadsden Purchase **6:** 740
and the Mexican Revolution **6:** 744, 745
and the Panama Canal **6:** 766, 835 **9:** 1200
Spanish-American War (1898) **6:** 766, 835
Theodore Roosevelt's presidency **6:** 766,
835–836
Farmers' Alliances **6:** 811–814, 833–834
Jacksonian democracy **6:** 811
populism **6:** 811–814
antitrust laws **6:** *814*
progressivism **6:** 814
workers' rights **6:** 814–815
socialism **6:** *815,* 816
abolition of the slave trade **6:** 819
Reconstruction after the Civil War **6:** 829–831
post–Civil War industrialization **6:** 832–833
trusts **6:** 832, 836
immigration (post-1860) **6:** 833, 834, *837*
politics at the turn of the century **6:** 834–835
dollar diplomacy **6:** 835
Progressive Party **6:** 836
World War I **7:** *894,* 895–896, 899, 900,
902–903
and the Civil War in China **7:** 944
and the Korean War (1950–1953) **7:** 944
post–World War I **7:** 945–951, 959–960
Red Scare (1920) **7:** 946
consumer boom (1920s) **7:** 948–949
immigration from Asia (1920s) **7:** 948
prohibition of alcohol **7:** 948
financial aid to Germany (1920s) **7:** 954
Great Depression **7:** 954, 958, 959–970
stock market crash (1929) **7:** 958
and Roosevelt's New Deal **7:** 959, 966–970
8: 1079
Wall Street Crash (1929) **7:** 961–963
Dust Bowl **7:** *968,* 969, 970 **9:** 1264
economic interest in Latin America
(1920s/1930s) **7:** 972–973, 975–976
Good Neighbor Policy **7:** 973, 980 **9:** 1200
and the road to World War II **8:** 1034
and lend-lease **8:** 1038–1041
World War II **8:** 1038–1041, 1042–1043, 1045,
1062, 1063–1066, 1068, 1071
World War II in the Atlantic **8:** 1042
World War II in Africa **8:** 1046
World War II in the Pacific **8:** 1049–1060
postwar aid to Europe (Marshall Plan)
8: 1072–1073, 1074, *1076,* 1088–1089
post–World War II recovery **8:** 1077–1082
and desegregation **8:** 1081, 1082
civil rights **8:** 1082 **9:** 1162–1163, 1166, 1171,
1174, 1175
and the Cold War (1945–1960) **8:** 1083–1094
anticommunist paranoia **8:** *1091,* 1092, 1095
9: 1169
and the Cold War (1960–1989) **8:** 1095–1106
and the Cuban missile crisis **8:** 1096–1097
and the Vietnam War **8:** 1099, 1100–1101
9: *1162,* 1163, 1164, 1172, 1177, 1217
and China (1960s/1970s) **8:** 1102 **9:** 1186, *1187*
and post–World War II colonialism **8:** 1119
experiments with government (1960–1999)
9: 1159–1168
social programs under Johnson **9:** 1160, 1175
swing to the political right (1980s)
9: 1167–1168
changes in society (1950s–1980s) **9:** 1169–1178
Watergate affair **9:** 1176–1177
Moral Majority **9:** 1177–1178
Iran-Contra Affair (Irangate) **9:** 1205–1206,
1241
and postwar Japan **9:** 1209–1210
Asian influences on the economy **9:** 1219
and Iran **9:** 1233, 1234
air strikes on Libya **9:** 1237

1375

Volume numbers appear in **boldface type**. Page numbers in *italic type* refer to illustrations and captions.

United States (continued)
  and Afghanistan **9:** 1241
  two embassies in Africa bombed (1998) **9:** 1242
  space race **9:** 1256–1257
Valley Forge **4:** 559, *560*
Vancouver **9:** 1219
Veracruz **3:** 344
  attacked (1838) **6:** 738
  seized by the United States (1914) **6:** 745
Virginia (North America)
  colonial **3:** 356, 357–358, 373 **4:** *545*, 549
  colonial conflicts in **4:** *545*
Washington, Native Americans **3:** 340–341
Washington, D.C.
  Franklin D. Roosevelt Memorial **7:** *959*
  bonus marchers (1932) **7:** *964*, 965
  Korean War Memorial **8:** *1092*
  and Martin Luther King **9:** *1172*
Wilmington (*formerly* Fort Christina) **3:** 362–363
Winnipeg **5:** *674*
Yucatán, Maya revolt **6:** 738–739

SOUTH AMERICA

Amazonia **9:** 1265, 1266, 1267, 1274
Andes **6:** 752, *754*
Angostura **6:** 752
Argentina
  and the Spanish colonies **3:** 349–350
  horses **3:** *387*
  post-independence **6:** 760–761, 763, 764
  Paraguayan War (War of the Triple Alliance) **6:** 764
  period between the World Wars **7:** 971, 977, 979, 980
  military coup ushers in conservative governments (1930) **7:** 977
  rise of the military (1920s) **7:** 977
  Juan Domingo and Eva Péron **9:** 1200, 1202
  "dirty war" **9:** 1204, *1207*, 1208, 1280
  military rulers (from 1970s) **9:** 1205
  civilian government (1983) **9:** 1206
Arica **7:** 978
Bogotá **6:** 749, *753*
Bolivia
  a Spanish colony **3:** 348, 388
  period between the World Wars **7:** 971, 973, 974, 978–979
  war against Paraguay (Chaco War 1932–1935) **7:** 978–979
  fascists seize power (1943) **7:** 979, 982
  Marxists seize power (1946) **7:** 979, 982
  military rule (1936) **7:** 979
  revolution (1952) **9:** 1201
  producing cocaine **9:** 1208, 1278
Brasilia **9:** *1201*
Brazil
  a Portuguese colony **3:** 311, 347–348, 349, 350, 354
  sugar **3:** 349
  slavery in **3:** 350, *383*, 384, *385*, 386 **6:** 758, *759*
  route to independence **6:** 755–756
  becomes a republic **6:** 756
  post-independence **6:** 756, 757, 760, 763, 764
  abolition of slavery **6:** 819
  period between the World Wars **7:** 971, 977, 979, 980–982
  wheat fields **7:** *972*
  dictator Vargas in power (1930) **7:** 977, 980–982
  rise of the military (1920s) **7:** 977
  post–World War II **9:** 1199
  currency devalued (1999) **9:** 1207
  deforestation **9:** 1267
  Rio Earth Summit (1992) **9:** 1271, *1272*
  international debt **9:** 1278
Buenos Aires **6:** 749 **9:** *1207*, 1208, 1280
Caracas **6:** 749, 750, 751
Chile
  and the Spanish colonies **3:** 346, 349–350
  fight for independence **6:** *748*, 753–754
  post-independence **6:** 761, 762, 763–764, 764
  period between the World Wars **7:** 971, 973, 974, 977, 979, 980
  and the United States (1920s) **7:** 973
  rise of the military (1920s) **7:** 977
  and the Catholic Church **7:** 980
  post–World War II **9:** 1199
  dictatorship under Pinochet **9:** *1203*, 1204
  social reform under Marxist president Allende **9:** 1204
  fishing and El Niño **9:** 1268
Colombia
  post-independence **6:** 760
  post–World War I **7:** 971
  Tolima people **7:** *976*
  post–World War II **9:** 1199
  U.S. aid to **9:** 1204
  drug barons **9:** 1208
Cuzco **6:** 754
Ecuador **4:** *507*
  and Simon Bolívar **6:** 753
  post-independence **6:** 760
  post–World War I **7:** 971, *977*
  producing cocaine **9:** 1208
Eldorado (mythical country) **3:** 387–388

Gran Chaco **7:** 979
Gran Colombia **6:** 752–753, 755, 758
Guayaquil **6:** 754, *755*
Junín **6:** 754
Latin America
  U.S. intervention in **5:** 647 **6:** 741, 766, 835 **9:** 1200–1204, 1205–1206
  between the World Wars **7:** 971–982
  fight for self-determination (from 1945) **9:** 1199–1208
Lima (Peru)
  and the Spanish colonies **3:** 347 **6:** 747
  and independence from Spain **6:** 754
Magellan, Strait of **3:** 312
Maracaibo, Lake **7:** *971*
Montevideo **5:** *641* **7:** 979
New Grenada **6:** 747–748
  Bolívar's attack on **6:** 752
Paraguay
  post-independence **6:** 760
  post–World War I **7:** 971
  war against Bolivia (Chaco War 1932–1935) **7:** 978–979
  rule after the Chaco War **7:** 979
Peru
  Incas **3:** 332, 343, *389*, *391*
  ancient death mask **3:** *345*
  a Spanish colony **3:** 349–350
  moves toward independence **6:** 754–755
  post-independence **6:** 760, *765*
  Central Railroad **6:** *765*
  post–World War I **7:** 971, 973, 974
  Aprista movement **7:** 974
  avoids military conflict (1930s) **7:** 978
  inflation (1980s) **9:** 1199
  Alvarado seizes power (1968) **9:** 1204
  Shining Path guerrilla movement **9:** 1206
  producing cocaine **9:** 1208
  fishing and El Niño **9:** 1268
Pisco **6:** 754
Plate, River **3:** *347*
Potosí **3:** 348–349, 388, 392
Rio de Janeiro **6:** *756* **7:** *981*
  Earth Summit (1992) **9:** 1271, *1272*
Rio Grande do Sol **7:** 981
San Salvador (Brazil)
  Portuguese settlement **3:** *347*
  Jesuits murdered **9:** *1207*
Santiago **6:** 749, 754
Sao Paulo **9:** 1199
South America
  named **3:** 311
  Spanish colonies in **3:** 346–354
  breaking colonial rule **6:** 747–756
  officer corps **6:** 748–749
  after independence **6:** 757–766
  Latin America between the World Wars **7:** 971–982
  and World War I **7:** 971
  rise of the military (1920s/1930s) **7:** 976–977, *978*
  emergence of democratic rule (1980s) **9:** 1168
  See also America; Latin America
Uruguay
  post-independence **6:** 760, 763
  period between the World Wars **7:** 971, 979
  gauchos **7:** *973*
  miltary dictatorship (1933–1942) **7:** 975
  post–World War II **9:** 1199
Venezuela
  salt mines **3:** 348
  and independence **6:** 747, 749, 750–752
  post-independence **6:** 760, 764
  European immigration **6:** *766*
  post-World War I **7:** 971
  failed military coup (1992) **9:** 1206

Volume numbers appear in **boldface type**. Page numbers in *italic type* refer to illustrations and captions.

GOVERNMENT and POLITICS

Abbas I, Safavid shah of Persia **3:** *401*, 402–404
Abbas II, Safavid shah of Persia **3:** 404
Abdülaziz, Ottoman sultan **6:** 733
Abdülhamid II, Ottoman sultan **6:** 734–735, 736
Abdülmecid I, Ottoman sultan **6:** 733
abolition, slavery **6:** 808–809, 819
  in the United States **5:** 651–652, 654, 682, *683*
    6: 819, 830, 831
absolutism **4:** 439, 449–460
  and Louis XIV of France **4:** 449–450, 455–460
  and Louis XIII of France **4:** 452–455
  in Europe other than France (1700s) **4:** 460
  and Louis XV of France **4:** 460
Accession, Treaty of (1973) **9:** 1194
Acheson, Dean **8:** 1073, 1088
Action Committee for the United States of Europe
  9: 1193
Action Française **7:** 955
Adams, John **4:** *562*
Adams, Samuel **4:** 555
Adenauer, Konrad **9:** 1192, *1193*
Adham Khan **3:** 410, 411
Adil Shah, shah of Iran **3:** 406
African National Congress (ANC) **6:** 828 **9:** 1228,
  1229
African Unity, Organization for (OAU) **9:** 1221
Aga Muhammed, shah of Iran **3:** 406
agitation, and Lenin **7:** 918
agitprop **7:** 918
Agriculture Adjustment Act (1933) **7:** 967
Akbar, Mogul emperor **1:** 130 **3:** 408–414
Alais, Peace of (1629) **4:** 453
Alamgir, Mogul emperor **3:** 415–416
Albert, prince consort to Queen Victoria **6:** 804,
  805 **7:** 871
Albrecht, duke of Bavaria **1:** 85
Alexander, grand duke of Lithuania **1:** 93
Alexander I, czar of Russia **5:** 600, 603–604,
  687–689
Alexander II, czar of Russia
  Russia under **5:** 692–694
  assassination **7:** *910*
Alexander III, czar of Russia, Russia under
  5: 694–696
Alexandrina, czarina of Russia **7:** 912, *913*
Alexis, czar of Russia **4:** 482, 485
Alfonso XIII, king of Spain **5:** 666
All-India Congress Committee **8:** 1113
All-India Muslim League **8:** 1107
Allende, Salvador **9:** 1204
Alliance for Progress **9:** 1204
Alva, Ferdinand, duke of **2:** 217, 218, 219
Alvarado, Velasco **9:** 1204
American Civil War (1861–1865), Reconstruction
  after **6:** 829–831
Amin, Idi **9:** 1225, 1236
anarchists **6:** 815, 816
ANC (African National Congress) **6:** 828 **9:** 1228,
  1229
Andropov, Yuri **8:** 1106
Anne, queen of Great Britain and Ireland **4:** 445
Anne of Austria **4:** 455
Anne of Cleves **2:** 209
Anne of Savoy **2:** 189
Anti-Comitern Pact (1937) **8:** 1031–1034
apartheid **6:** 821 **9:** 1228, 1229–1230
Aprista movement **7:** 974–975
Arafat, Yasir **8:** 1136, 1137, 1138 **9:** 1242
Arbenz, Jacobo **9:** 1201, 1203
Arias, Oscar, Central American peace plan
  9: 1206
Armas, Castillo **9:** 1203
arms race
  East-West **8:** 1091–1092, 1096, 1102
  between India and Pakistan **8:** *1116*
Arras, Union of (1578) **2:** 219
ASEAN (Association of South-East Asian
  Nations) **9:** 1217
Ashikaga shogunate **1:** 127
Association of South-East Asian Nations
  (ASEAN) **9:** 1217
Atatürk, Kemal (Mustafa Kemal) **6:** *736* **7:** 907
  8: *1022*, 1023

attainder, powers of **2:** 206
Attlee, Clement **8:** *1077*, 1085–1086
Augsburg, League of **4:** 462
Augsburg Interim **2:** 191
Augustus II, the Strong, king of Poland-Lithuania
  4: 490
Augustus III, king of Poland-Lithuania **4:** 490
Aurangzebe, Mogul emperor **3:** 415–416
autocracy **4:** 460 **7:** 910

Babur, Mogul emperor **1:** *129*, 130 **3:** 407–408
Bahadur Shah II, emperor of India **5:** 668, 669
bakufu system **4:** 534, 536, 540
  decline **4:** 540–542
Bakunin, Mikhail **6:** 815, 816
Baldomir, Alfredo **7:** 975
Baldwin, Stanley **7:** 958
Balfour, Arthur **8:** 1024, 1130
Balfour Declaration (1917) **8:** 1024, 1130
Balkan League **7:** 879
banquet campaigns **5:** 612–613, 656
Bao Dai (Vietnamese emperor) **8:** 1123
Barcelona, Treaty of (1529) **2:** 190
Barre, Siyad **9:** 1230
Basil (IV) Shuisky, czar of Russia **1:** 97
Batista, Fulgencio **9:** 1203
Bayezid I, sultan of the Ottoman empire **1:** 101
beer-hall putsch **7:** 988
Begin, Menachem **8:** 1137 **9:** *1237*
Belgrade, Treaty of (1739) **6:** 729
Ben-Gurion, David **8:** 1131–1132
Benelux countries **9:** 1192, 1193
Berisla, Sali **9:** 1247
Berlin Conference (1885) **6:** 822–823
Beveridge, Sir William **8:** 1077
Beza, Theodore **2:** 202
Bhutto, Benazir **8:** *1116*
Bill of Rights (1689) **4:** 444
Bismarck, Otto von **5:** 660–661, 662, 664, *665*
  7: 871, 872
  and the Berlin Conference (1885) **6:** 822, 823
BJP Hindu Nationalist Party **8:** 1116
black codes **6:** 830
Black Hand Gang **7:** 879, 880
Blackshirts **7:** 985–986
Blood, Council of **2:** 217–218
Blood, League of **8:** 1018
Bloody Sunday **7:** 912
Bohemian Charter **5:** 614
Bokassa, Jean **9:** 1225
Boleyn, Anne **2:** 207, 209
Bolívar, Simón **5:** 665 **6:** 749–753, 754–755, 758
Bolsheviks **7:** 911, 914–915, 916, 918, 919
  and the Russian Civil War **7:** 919–920
Bonaparte, Joseph **6:** 749
Bonaparte, Louis-Napoleon *See* Napoleon III
Bonaparte, Napoleon *See* Napoleon I
bonus army **7:** *964*, 965
Booth, John Wilkes **5:** 686 **6:** 829
Borgia, Cesare **1:** 85
Bose, Subhas Chandra **8:** 1110
Boston Tea Party **4:** 555
Botero, Giovanni **1:** 70
Bourbon dynasty **2:** 203 **4:** 460, 470
  and Napoleon **5:** 600, 604
  reforms in the Latin American colonies
    6: 747–748
Boxer Rebellion (1900) **5:** 696 **6:** 774–775, 776
boyars (Russian nobles) **1:** 96, 97, 98
Brain Trust **7:** 965, 966
Brezhnez, Leonid **8:** *1103*, 1106 **9:** *1201*
Briand, Aristide **7:** 956
British North America Act (1867) **5:** *675*
Broz, Josip (Marshal Tito) **8:** *1069*, 1070
Burr, Aaron **5:** 646
Bush, George **9:** *1245*, 1246

Calhoun, John C. **5:** 646, 647, 654
Calonne, Charles-Alexandre de **5:** 585, 586
Cambrai, Treaty of (1529) **2:** 190
Camp David peace accords **8:** 1137 **9:** 1236, *1237*
Capet, Hugh, king of France **1:** 12
capitalism
  versus communism *See* Cold War
  link with the Reformation **2:** 159

emergence in Britain **5:** 618–619
  triumph (1980s) **9:** 1168
Caps, and the Hats **4:** 448
Carlists **5:** 666
Carlos, Don **5:** 666
Carlsbad Decrees (1819) **5:** 607
Carranza, Venustiano **6:** 745–746
Carter, Jimmy **8:** 1137 **9:** 1205, *1237*
Casimir IV, king of Poland **1:** 91–93
Castlereagh, Robert Stewart, Viscount **5:** 606
Castro, Fidel **8:** 1095, 1096, *1098* **9:** *1201*, 1203,
  1205
catalogs of complaint **5:** *584*
Cateau-Cambresis, Treaty of (1559) **2:** 193
Catherine II, the Great, empress of Russia **4:** 480,
  489–490 **5:** 592, 688
Catherine of Aragon **2:** 207
Catholic Church, Roman Catholics in the British
  Parliament **6:** 808
caudillos/caudillisimo **6:** 759–760, 761 **7:** 976,
  977–978
Cavour, Camillo Benso, conte di **5:** 658–659
Ceausescu, Nicolae **8:** 1106 **9:** 1246
Cecil, Sir Robert **2:** 235–236
Central American Republics, Federation of **6:** 760
Chamberlain, Neville **8:** *1035*, 1036
Chambord, Treaty of (1552) **2:** 191–192
Chamorro, Violeta **9:** 1208
Charlemagne **1:** 12, 20, *21*, 50
Charles I, king of Great Britain and Ireland
  (1600–1649) **2:** 235, 237–241
Charles I, king of Spain *See* Charles V, Holy
  Roman emperor
Charles II, king of England and Scotland
  (1630–1685) **2:** 241, 242–244
  and the North American colonies **3:** 361, 364
Charles II, king of Spain **4:** 463
Charles IV, king of Spain **6:** 749
Charles V, Holy Roman emperor **2:** 183, *184*,
  187–193
  and the Schmalkaldic League **1:** 47 **2:** 156, 188,
    190
  crown/crowning **2:** *155*, 190
  and Luther **2:** 155
  succeeding to the title **2:** *185*, 186–187
  Habsburg empire during reign of **2:** *186*
  and Spanish America **3:** *344*, 348
Charles VI, Holy Roman emperor (and Charles
  III, archduke of Austria and king of
  Hungary) **4:** 466, 467, 468, 488
Charles IX, king of France (1550–1574) **2:** 198,
  199, 201, 202, 219
Charles X, king of France **5:** 608 **6:** 820
Charles XI, king of Sweden **4:** 447
Charles XII, king of Sweden **4:** 447
Charles, duke of Mayenne **2:** *198*, 199
Charles the Bold, duke of Burgundy **1:** 25, 26
Charles Edward Stuart, the Young Pretender
  (Bonnie Prince Charlie) **4:** *443*
Charlotte, empress of Mexico **6:** 740, 741
Chartists **5:** 612, 628–629 **6:** 811
Cheka **7:** 919, 920
Chernenko, Konstantin **8:** 1106
Chernomyrdin, Viktor **9:** 1250, *1252*
Chiang Kai-shek **7:** 935, 936, 938–944 **8:** 1034,
  1049
  nationalist government in Taiwan **7:** 944
    9: 1180, 1181, 1214
Chicago Democratic Convention (1968) **9:** 1165
chiefs, Native American **3:** 337–339
Ch'ien-lung, emperor of China **4:** 531 **6:** 767
Ching dynasty *See* Manchu (Ching) dynasty
Chou En-lai **9:** 1184
Christian IV, king of Denmark (1577–1684)
  2: 228
Christian of Anhalt (1568–1630) **2:** 226, 227
Chun Doo-Hwan **9:** 1213–1214
Churchill, Winston **8:** *1086*
  and the road to World War II **8:** 1036
  and World War II **8:** 1038, 1045–1046, 1063
  and postwar Europe **8:** 1084–1085, *1086*, 1087
    9: 1189
  quoted on European union **9:** 1190
civil rights **8:** 1082 **9:** 1162–1163, 1166, 1171,
  1174, 1175

Volume numbers appear in **boldface type**. Page numbers in *italic type* refer to illustrations and captions.

Civil Rights Act (1964) **9:** *1174*, 1175
Clay, Henry **5:** 646, 647, 651, 654
Clemenceau, Georges **7:** 903, *904*
Clément, Jacques **2:** 203
Clement VII, Pope **2:** 189
Clinton, Sir Henry **4:** 559
Cognac, League of **2:** 189
Colbert, Jean-Baptiste **2:** 263 **4:** 454, 456–457, 460
Cold War **8:** 1044, 1083 **9:** 1190, 1255
    (1945–1960) **8:** 1083–1094, 1135
    and NATO **8:** *1084*, 1090, 1095, 1102, 1106
    and the Warsaw Pact **8:** *1084*, 1090, 1093–1094, 1095, 1102
    (1960–1989) **8:** 1095–1106
    and European colonies **8:** 1119
    and China **9:** 1181
    and Latin America **9:** 1200–1201
    and independent African countries **9:** 1222, 1226–1227
    and Iran **9:** 1233
Coligny, Gaspard II de **2:** 199, *200*, 201–202
Collins, Michael **7:** 958
Colmar, Union of **1:** 24
Cominform (Communist Information Bureau) **8:** 1089
common law **1:** 72
Common Market, European **9:** 1190, 1194
Common Sense (Tom Paine) **4:** 557
Communards **5:** 664
Commune of Paris **5:** 591, 592, 593, 594
communism **7:** 921
    and industrialization **5:** 629–630
    birth of **6:** 812–813
    under Lenin and Stalin **7:** 921–932
    triumphs over nationalism in China **7:** 933–944
    in Japan (early 1900s) **8:** 1016
    Hitler's hatred of **8:** 1043
    post–World War II **8:** 1075–1076
    communists exposed in the United States **8:** *1091*, 1092
    in Central America **8:** 1104
    crumbling in Europe **8:** 1106
    and the European colonies **8:** 1119 **9:** *1160*
    Soviet communism (post-1960) **9:** 1161
    Eurocommunism (1970s) **9:** 1166
    collapse in eastern Europe (1980s) **9:** 1168
    in China (1949–1999) **9:** 1179–1188
    collapse of communism in Europe **9:** 1243–1252
    See also Cold War; Communist Party
Communist Information Bureau (Cominform) **8:** 1089
Communist Manifesto, The (Marx and Engels) **5:** *626*, 629–630 **6:** 811, 812–813 **7:** 921
Communist Party
    Soviet **7:** 919, 921
    Chinese **7:** 936
    French **7:** 955 **8:** *1089*
    Indonesian **8:** 1121
Concert of Europe **5:** 606, 607–608
Confederate States of America **5:** 677
Confederation, Articles of (1781) **4:** 561–562
Confederation of the Rhine **5:** 601
Confucianism, and government **1:** 124
Congo, International Association of the **6:** 822
Congress of Europe **8:** 1073
Congress Party **8:** 1115
Constantine XI, Byzantine emperor **1:** 102
Constituent Assembly (France) **5:** 586, 588–589
Constitution of the United States **1:** 51 **4:** 562
    Amendments **6:** 830–831 **7:** 948
Constitutional Act of Canada (1791) **5:** 674
Constitutional Convention (1787; United States) **4:** 562
Constitutional Convention (France) **5:** 592, 593–594
Continental Congress, First (1774) **4:** 556
Continental Congress, Second (1775) **4:** 556, 561
Contra rebels **8:** 1104
Contragate (Iran-Contra Affair) **9:** 1205–1206, 1241
Coolidge, Calvin **7:** 946, 948, *961*
Corday, Charlotte **5:** *594*
corregidors **1:** 71–72

Corvinus, Matthias *See* Matthias I Corvinus
Cosimo I (Cosimo de' Medici; 1519–1574) **1:** 83, 87
Council of Europe **8:** 1073–1074
Counter-Reformation, secular **2:** 170–172
counterrevolution, French
    in France **5:** 589–590
    outside France **5:** 590–592
Creoles *See* criollos
Crespy, Truce of (1544) **2:** 190
criollos (Creoles) **3:** 347
    in Mexico **6:** 737, 738
    in the officer corps **6:** 748–749
    and independence in Latin America **6:** 749
    post-independence **6:** 757–758
Cripps, Stafford **8:** 1113
Cromwell, Oliver **2:** 240, 241–242 **4:** 444
Cromwell, Thomas **1:** 30–31 **2:** 208
Cuba, missile crisis (1962) **8:** 1096, *1098*
cujus regio, ejus religio **2:** 226
Cultural Revolution, in China **9:** 1184, 1185
Curzon, Lord **5:** 670
Czech League **7:** 920

daimyo (landowning princes) **4:** 533–557, 539, 540 **6:** 777–778, *779*
D'Annunzio, Gabriele **7:** 984
Das Kapital (Karl Marx) **6:** 812
Davis, Jefferson **5:** 677
Dawes, Charles **7:** 954
Dawes Plan (1924) **7:** 954
Debs, Eugene V. **6:** *815*, 816
Decembrist revolt (1825) **5:** 688, 689, 690
Declaration of Independence (1776) **4:** 480, 557, *558*, *562*
Declaration of the Rights of Man and Citizen (document) **5:** 588
decolonization **8:** 1117–1128
de Klerk, F. W. **9:** 1228, 1229
Delors, Jacques **9:** 1196
democracy
    "participatory" **9:** 1164
    liberal **9:** 1168, 1190
    triumph (1900s) **9:** 1273–1274
Democracy Wall, in China **9:** 1188
Democratic Party (U.S.) **5:** 650–651, 654
Deng Xiaoping **9:** 1184, 1185, 1186–1188
détente **8:** 1102 **9:** 1166
Diaz, Porfirio **6:** 742, 743
    and the Mexican Revolution **6:** 743–744
dictators **7:** 983
    in western Europe (1900s) *See* Hitler, Adolf; Mussolini, Benito; Stalin, Joseph
    Latin American (from 1970s) **9:** 1204–1205
Diggers (political movement) **2:** 247
diplomatic revolution **4:** 469
Directory, the (French government) **5:** 594, 595, 596
Division of the North **6:** 745
Dmitry, False **1:** 97
dollar diplomacy **6:** 835
domino theory **8:** 1097–1098
Dorgon, prince of the Manchu people **4:** 526
Douglass, Frederick **5:** 652 **6:** 830
Dreyfus, Alfred **6:** 846, *847*
Dreyfus affair **6:** 846 **7:** 990
Dudley, John, earl of Warwick and duke of Northumberland **2:** 210, 211
Dudley, Robert **2:** 220, 221
Dulles, John Foster **8:** 1100 **9:** 1209–1210
Duma **5:** 696 **7:** 910, 913–914
Dutschke, Rudi **9:** *1162*, 1164
Dzerzhinski, Feliks **7:** 930

Easter Rising **7:** 905
ECSC (European Coal and Steel Community) **9:** 1191–1193
Edward IV, king of England **2:** 205
Edward VI, king of England **2:** 210
Edward VII, king of Great Britain **6:** *793*, *798*
Edward VIII, king of Great Britain **6:** 798
EEC (European Economic Community) **9:** *1192*, 1193–1196
Eighteenth Amendment, to the U.S. Constitution **7:** 948

Eisenhower, Dwight D. **8:** *1080*, 1081–1082, 1098
Elizabeth I, czarina of Russia **4:** 489
Elizabeth I, queen of England **2:** 209–214, 220, 235 **3:** 356
Elizabeth of York **1:** *23*
Emancipation Proclamation **5:** 682
Enclosure Acts (late 1700s) **4:** 503–504
Engels, Friedrich **5:** *626* **6:** 812
    The Communist Manifesto (Marx and Engels) **5:** 629–630 **6:** 811, 812–813
"enlightened despots" **4:** 489–490
Enlightenment, the, and monarchy **4:** 460, 476, 489
Entente Cordiale **7:** 872
Estates General **5:** *584*, 586
EU *See* European Union
Eurocommunism **9:** 1166
Europe
    Habsburg Empire **2:** 183–194, 225
    Protestant northern Europe **4:** 439–448
Europe, Congress of **8:** 1073
Europe, Council of **8:** 1073–1074 **9:** 1190
European Coal and Steel Community (ECSC) **9:** 1191–1193
European Economic Community (EEC) **9:** *1192*, 1193–1196
European Union (EU) **9:** 1197–1198
European Union Treaty (1991) **9:** 1196–1197
exclusion crisis **2:** 243–244
Executive Order 9981 **8:** 1081

Factory Acts (from the 1830s) **5:** 634
Fair Deal **8:** 1080
Farmers' Alliances **6:** 811–814, 833–834
Farnese, Alessandro, duke of Parma **2:** 220, 221
Farnese, Elizabeth **4:** 468
Fawkes, Guy **2:** 236, *237*
Febrerista revolt **7:** 979
February Revolution **7:** 914
Federal Highway Act (1921) **7:** 950
Ferdinand I, Holy Roman emperor **2:** 192
    before accession to the title **1:** 93 **2:** *184*, 187, 188
Ferdinand II, Holy Roman emperor **1:** 95 **2:** 229, *230*
    as Archduke Ferdinand **2:** 226, 227
Ferdinand III, Holy Roman emperor **2:** 229
    before accession to the title **2:** 231
Ferdinand V and Isabella I, king and queen of Spain **1:** 24
    and the Moors of Grenada **1:** 24
    and the Spanish Inquisition **1:** 24 **2:** 179, 180
    marriage **2:** 179
    and Columbus's voyages **3:** 309
Ferdinand VII, king of Spain **6:** 749, 751
Fifteenth Amendment, to the U.S. Constitution **6:** 830–831
First International **6:** 813, 815–816
Five-Year Plans, of Stalin **7:** 926–927, *928*
FLN (Front de Libération National) **8:** 1126
FNLA (National Front for the Liberation of Angola) **8:** 1099–1102 **9:** 1227
Food Administration **7:** 900
forfeiture, powers of **2:** 206
Founders, of the American Constitution **1:** 51
Fourteen Points **7:** 902–903, 906 **8:** 1024
    and China **7:** 934–935
    and India **8:** 1108
Fourteenth Amendment, to the U.S. Constitution **6:** 830
Francis, duke of Anjou **2:** 203
Francis I, Holy Roman emperor, bust of **4:** *497*
Francis I, king of France **1:** *13* **2:** 187
    and the arts **1:** 88
    and Protestantism **2:** 161, 170–172, 197
    and the Habsburg Empire **2:** 188–189, 190–191
    marriage **2:** 190
    and explorers **3:** 355
Francis II, king of France **2:** 198, 199
Francis Joseph I, emperor of Austria **5:** 665
Franco, Francisco, and the Spanish Civil War **8:** 1031, 1032, 1033
Franklin, Benjamin **4:** *562*
Franz Ferdinand, archduke of Austria **7:** *878*, 879–880

Frederick II, the Great, king of Prussia **4:** *466,* 469, 470, 488–489, 500, 509
  and Enlightenment thought **4:** 480
Frederick II, king of Sicily and Holy Roman emperor **1:** 53
Frederick II, the Wise, elector of Saxony **2:** 154–155, 156, 187, 188
Frederick III, Holy Roman emperor **2:** 183, 184–185
Frederick III, king of Denmark **4:** 446
Frederick IV of the Palatinate **2:** 226
Frederick V of the Palatinate **2:** 227, 231
Frederick William, elector of Brandenburg **4:** 488
Frederick William I, king of Prussia **4:** 488
  army **4:** *467,* 488
Frederick William IV, king of Prussia **5:** *612,* 614, 659–660
Freedman's Bureau **6:** 830
Freikorps **7:** 952, 987
French Community **9:** 1222
French Republic, declared **5:** 592
French Revolution **4:** 453, 511 **5:** 583–594 **6:** 748
  heroic style **4:** 497
  and free speech **4:** 521
  legacy **5:** 594, 656
Front de Libération National (FLN) **8:** 1126
Frontenac, Louis de Baude, Comte de **4:** 546
FSA (Farm Security Administration) **7:** 968
FSLN *See* Sandinista movement
Fugger dynasty **1:** 45, 46–47 **2:** *185,* 187
Fyodor (Theodore) I, czar of Russia **1:** 97
  lands acquired under **1:** *90*

Gadhafi, Mu'ammar **9:** 1236, 1237, *1240*
Gadsden Purchase **6:** 740
Gandhi, Indira **8:** *1114,* 1115
Gandhi, Mohandas (*known as* Mahatma) **6:** 828 **8:** *1107,* 1108–1109, 1111, 1112–1113 **9:** 1175
  assassination of **8:** 1115
Gandhi, Rajiv **8:** 1115
Garibaldi, Giuseppe **5:** 659, *660*
Garrison, William Lloyd **5:** 652
Gaulle, Charles de
  and the Algerian War of Independence **8:** 1127
  and France's African colonies **8:** 1127
  and European union **9:** 1193–1194
Genghis Khan **1:** 123, *124*
George I, king of Britain and Ireland **4:** *444,* 445
George III, king of Great Britain, and the American colonies **4:** 556, 557
George V, king of Great Britain **6:** *798* **7:** *872*
  and India **5:** *669*
German Confederation **5:** 660
German Workers' Party **7:** 987
Gettysburg Address **5:** 685
Ghent, Treaty of (1814) **5:** 646
GI Bill of Rights (1944; Serviceman's Readjustment Act) **8:** 1081
Girondins **5:** 592, 593, 594
glasnost **8:** 1106 **9:** 1244, 1248
Glorious Revolution (accession of William and Mary) **2:** 243, 244 **4:** 442–444, 472, 502
Godunov, Boris **1:** 97
  lands acquired under **1:** *90*
Goebbels, Joseph **7:** *983,* 991 **8:** 1067
Gonzaga, Ludovico **1:** *72*
Good Neighbor Policy **7:** 973, 980 **9:** 1200
Gorbachev, Mikhail Sergeyevich **8:** 1104, 1105, 1106 **9:** 1168, 1243–1244, *1245,* 1248, 1249, 1250
Gore, Al **9:** *1272*
Gosplan **7:** 926
Government of India Act (1919) **8:** 1108
Government of India Act (1935) **8:** 1112
Government of Ireland Act (1920) **7:** 957–958
governments
  and trade **1:** 45
  role post–World War II **8:** 1078–1079
  in the West (1960–1999) **9:** 1159–1168
Gowon, Yakubu **9:** 1226
Grand Alliance
  and the War of the Spanish Succession **4:** *461,* 464–465
  and the War of the Austrian Succession **4:** 469

grand viziers **6:** 728
Grant, Ulysses S., U.S. president **6:** 830
Great Leap Forward **9:** 1182–1183
Great Reform Act (1832) **6:** 809, 810
Greater Serbia **8:** 878
green parties **9:** 1271
Grey, Edward **7:** *882*
Grey, Lady Jane **2:** 210
Group Areas Act (1950) **9:** 1228
Guatemalan National Revolutionary Unity (UNRG) **9:** 1203
Guevara, Ernesto "Che" **9:** *1163,* 1164, 1203
Guise brothers **2:** *198,* 199, 200, 201
Guizot, François **5:** 612
Gulhane, Edict of (1839) **6:** 733
Guomindang (Nationalist Party) **7:** *934, 935,* 936
  joins forces with the communists **7:** 936–938
Gustav III, king of Sweden **4:** *446,* 448
Gustav Adolph (Gustavus Adolphus), king of Sweden **2:** *225,* 228, 230, 231 **4:** 446
Guzmán, Abimael **9:** 1206

Habsburg Empire **1:** 20 **2:** 183–194, 225 **4:** 485–486 **5:** *606*
  the Low Countries **1:** 25 **2:** 215–216 **5:** 590
  and Poland-Lithuania **1:** 25 **4:** *484,* 490
  and the Fugger dynasty **1:** 47
  and Hungary **1:** 93 **4:** 485–486
  and the Jagiello rulers **1:** 93
  and the Reformation **1:** 94–95
  and the Ottomans **1:** 107, 108
  in Austria **1:** 187 **4:** 460 **5:** 655
  line of succession **2:** *187*
  and wealth from the Americas **3:** 348
  absolutism **4:** 460
  peasants **4:** 505
  suppressing uprisings (1848) **5:** 613–614
Hague, Coalition of the **2:** 228
Hamas **8:** 1138 **9:** 1242
Hamilton, Alexander **5:** 650
Hampden, John **2:** 238
Hampton Court Conference (1604) **2:** 236
Hancock, John **4:** 555
Hanford, Ben **6:** *815*
Hanoverians **4:** *444,* 445
Hara, Takashi **8:** 1016, 1017
Harding, Warren G. **7:** 946–947
Hats, and the Caps **4:** 448
Havel, Václav **9:** 1246
Hayes, Rutherford B. **6:** 831
Heath, Edward **9:** 1194
Hedvig, queen of Poland **1:** 91
Henry I of Lorraine, duke of Guise **2:** *198,* 199, 203
Henry II, king of France (1519–1559) **1:** *9* **2:** 191–192, 199
Henry III, king of France **2:** 198, 202, 203, 220
Henry IV, king of France, known as Henry of Navarre (1553–1610) **2:** 201, 202, 203–204 **4:** 453
Henry VII, (Henry Tudor), king of England **1:** 23, 71, 72 **2:** 205, 206, 214 **3:** 355
Henry VIII, king of England **1:** 71 **2:** 207–209
  court painter **1:** 88
  and the Habsburg Empire **2:** 189, 190–191
  invasion of France (1544) **2:** 190
Herder, Johann Gottfried von **5:** 611
Herzl, Theodore **8:** 1129, *1131*
Hidalgo, Miguel **6:** 737, *738*
Hideyoshi **4:** 533, 539
Hindenburg, Paul von **7:** 989
Hinduism/Hindus
  and independence in India **8:** 1110–1112
  and partition in India **8:** 1114
  fundamentalism in India **8:** 1116
Hirohito, emperor of Japan **8:** 1017, 1019, *1031, 1060*
Hitler, Adolf **7:** 908, 958, 983, 987–994 **8:** *1025, 1027*
  and the Jews **7:** 988, 990, 991, 993–994
  and the road to World War II **8:** *1025*–1036
  annnexation of Austria (1938) **8:** *1028*
  and Mussolini **8:** *1029*
  and the Spanish Civil War **8:** 1032
  Mein Kampf **8:** 1034, 1066–1067

and World War II **8:** 1037, 1048
Hitler Youth **7:** 992, *993* **8:** 1048
Ho Chi Minh **8:** 1099, 1100, 1123 **9:** 1165
Hohenzollern dynasty **4:** 460, 488 **5:** 661
Holocaust **7:** 991 **8:** 1129
Holy Alliance **5:** 608
Holy Roman emperors **1:** 20, 28, 71 **2:** 154, 225
  See also Habsburg Empire
Holy Roman Empire **1:** 28 **2:** 154, 183–184 **4:** 485
  and the Reformation **1:** 71
  Germany part of **2:** 184, 190, 191–192, 225
  and the Thirty Years' War **2:** 225–234
Homestead Act (1862) **6:** 837
Honeker, Erich **8:** *1105* **9:** 1248
Hong Taiji **4:** 526
Hoover, Herbert **7:** 900, 946, *961–965* **8:** *1073*
House of Representatives **4:** 562
House Unamerican Activities Committee (HUAC) **8:** 1092
Howard, Catherine **2:** 209
HUAC (House Unamerican Activities Committee) **8:** 1092
Huerta, Victoriano **6:** 745
Humayun, Mogul emperor **1:** 130 **3:** *407*
Hundred Days of Reform **6:** 773
Hunt, Henry **6:** 807
Husák, Gustáv **9:** 1246
Husayn, Safavid shah of Iran **3:** 404–405
Hussein, Saddam **9:** 1235

Iemitsu, shogun of Japan **4:** 537, 539
Ieyasu, shogun of Japan **4:** 533–534, *535,* 539
Iguala, Plan of **6:** 738
Illiescu, Ion **9:** 1246–1247
Immigration Reform Act (1965) **9:** 1178
Independence, Declaration of (1776) **4:** 480, 557, *558, 562*
Independent Labour Party **6:** 816
India Office **8:** 1107–1108
Indian National Congress **5:** 670, 671 **8:** 1107
Indian Removal Act (1830) **6:** 839
Indies, Council of **3:** 347
Indies Party **8:** 1020–1021
Institutional Revolutionary Party (PRI) **9:** 1206
intendant system, in France **4:** 453–455
International Brigades **8:** 1032
Internationals, the **6:** *811,* 813, 815–816
Intolerable Acts (1774) **4:** 555, 556, 557
Iran-Contra Affair (Irangate) **9:** 1205–1206, 1241
Irigoyen, Hipólito **7:** 977
iron curtain **8:** *1084, 1086,* 1087, 1096 **9:** 1190
Isabella I *See* Ferdinand V and Isabella I
Islamic Association **8:** 1020
Isma'il, shah of Iran **3:** 398–399, 400
Iturbide, Agustín de **6:** 738
Ivan III, czar of Russia, known as "Ivan the Great" **1:** 24, 92, 96, 98
  lands acquired under **1:** *90*
Ivan IV, czar of Russia, known as "Ivan the Terrible" **1:** 96–97 **4:** *481*
  lands acquired under **1:** *90*

Jackson, Andrew **5:** 647, 650–651 **6:** 811
Jackson, Jesse **9:** 1175
Jadwiga, queen of Poland **1:** 91
Jagiello dynasty **1:** 13, 25, 91–93, 98
  and the Habsburgs **1:** 93
Jahan, Shah *See* Shah Jahan, Mogul emperor
Jahangir, Mogul emperor **3:** *412,* 413, 414
James II, king of England *See* James VII, king of Scotland
James V, king of Scotland **2:** 214
James VI, king of Scotland and James I of England **2:** 214, 228, 235–237
James VII, king of Scotland and James II of England **2:** 244 **4:** 441–442, 444, 462
  as Duke of York **2:** 243
  invasion and defeat in Ireland **4:** 444–445
Jaruzelski, Wojciech **8:** 1106 **9:** 1244, *1245*
Jaurès, Jean **6:** 816 **7:** 884
Jayavarman IV, king of Angkor **3:** 320
Jayavarman VII, king of Angkor **3:** 320
Jefferson, Thomas **4:** 557 **5:** 601, 645–646, 650
  home at Monticello **4:** 495

Volume numbers appear in **boldface type**. Page numbers in *italic type* refer to illustrations and captions.

Jim Crow laws **6:** 831
Jinnah, Mohammed Ali **8:** 1112, 1113, 1114
Joan (Juana), wife of Philip I **2:** 185–186
João, Dom (John VI) **6:** 755, 756
John, surnamed Lackland, king of England **1:** 13
    and the Magna Carta **1:** *14*
John I Albert, king of Poland **1:** 93
John II, king of Portugal **3:** 305–306, 308
John III Sobieski, king of Poland-Lithuania **4:** 485
John VI (Dom João), prince regent then king of
    Portugal **6:** 755, 756
John of Austria, known as Don **2:** 219
Johnson, Andrew **6:** 829, 830
Johnson, Lyndon B. **8:** 1099, 1100, 1101 **9:** 1160,
    1173, *1174*, *1177*
Johnson-Reed Act (1924) **7:** 948
Joseph, king of Naples **5:** 600
Joseph I, Holy Roman emperor **4:** 466
Joseph II, Holy Roman emperor **4:** 489 **5:** 590
Joseph Ferdinand, prince of Bavaria **4:** 463
Juárez, Benito **6:** 740, 741–743
July Revolution (1830) **5:** *605*, 608, *610*, 655
    6: 820
justices of the peace **1:** 72

Kádár, János **9:** 1245
Kamakura shogunate **1:** 125–126, 127
Kamenev, Lev **7:** 931
K'ang-hsi, emperor of China **4:** 527, 529,
    530–531
Karim Khan, first Zand ruler of Iran **3:** 406
Karmal, Babbrak **8:** 1103
Kaunda, Kenneth **9:** 1225
Keiki, shogun of Japan **4:** 542
Kellogg-Briand Pact **8:** 1029
Kennedy, Edward **9:** *1173*
Kennedy, Jacqueline Bouvier **9:** 1173
Kennedy, John F. **8:** 1082, 1096 **9:** 1172
    and the Cuban missile crisis **8:** 1096–1097
    and the Vietnam War **8:** 1100
    Alliance for Progress **9:** 1204
Kennedy, Robert F. **9:** 1173, 1176
Kenyatta, Jomo **8:** 1124, 1125 **9:** *1221*, 1225
Kerensky, Aleksandr **7:** 916
KGB **7:** 930
Khatami, Ayatollah Seyyed Mohammad **9:** 1242
Khmer Rouge **8:** 1099 **9:** 1281
Khomeini, Ayatollah Ruhollah **9:** 1233, 1234,
    1235, 1241, 1242
Khrushchev, Nikita **8:** 1093, 1094, *1098* **9:** 1161
    and the Cuban missile crisis **8:** 1096–1097
    and China **9:** 1186
Kim Il Sung **9:** *1205*
King, Martin Luther **8:** 1082 **9:** 1162, *1172*, 1175,
    1176
kings *See* monarchy
Kirov, Sergey **7:** 930, *931*
Kissinger, Henry **8:** 1102, 1137
Kohl, Helmut **9:** 1196
Kossuth, Lajos **5:** 613–614
Koxinga **4:** 527
Kristallnacht **7:** 994
Kruger, Paul **6:** 826
Ku Klux Klan **6:** 831 **7:** 948
Kuang-hsü, emperor of the Ching dynasty **6:** 773,
    776
Kublai Khan, Mongol emperor **1:** 119, 123–124,
    125

labor legislation **6:** 814
laissez-faire **6:** 808
Lamartine, Alphonse de **5:** 613
Land and Freedom party **5:** 693–694
Laud, William **2:** 238, 239
Laurier, Wilfrid **5:** 675, 676
Lausanne Conference (1932) **7:** 954
League of Nations *See* Nations, League of
Lee Kuan Yew **9:** 1218
legitimacy, principle of **5:** 606, 607
Leicester, Robert Dudley, earl of **2:** 220, 221
Lenin, Vladimir Ilyich **7:** 930, 945 **9:** *1160*, *1161*
    pre-1917 **5:** 696 **7:** 911, *913*, 918
    and the Russian Revolution (1917) **7:** 914–915,
        916, 917, 918, 919
    and the Polish-Soviet War **7:** 920

post-1917 **7:** 921–924, *925*
    and the kulaks **7:** 928
    and China **7:** 936
Leopold I, king of Belgium **6:** 820, 822, 823
    7: 873
Lesczinski, Stanislas **4:** 468
Le Tellier, Michel, marquis de Louvois **4:** 454,
    456, 462
Letter from Jamaica (Simón Bolívar) **6:** 751
Letter of Majesty **2:** 226
Levellers (political movement) **2:** 247, 254
liberal democracy **9:** 1168, 1190
Liberal Democratic Party (LDP), of japan **9:** 1211
liberalism **5:** 609, 610–611
Liberals (Russian) **7:** 911
Liberator, The (journal) **5:** 652
Liebknecht, Karl **7:** 952
Lin Bao **9:** 1184
Lincoln, Abraham **5:** 677, 679, *685*, 686 **6:** 829
Little Red Book (Mao Tse-tung) **9:** *1184*, 1185
Liu Shao-chi **9:** 1183, 1185
Lloyd George, David **7:** 903, *904*, 957
Locarno Treaty (1925) **7:** 956, 958 **8:** 1029
London Men's Working Association **6:** 811
Long, Huey P. **7:** 967
Long March **7:** *934*, *940*, 941
Louis, cardinal of Lorraine **2:** *198*, 199
Louis, prince of Condé **2:** 199, 200, 201
Louis II, king of Bohemia and Hungary **1:** 93
    2: *184*, 188
Louis IX, king of France **1:** 12–13
Louis XIII, king of France **4:** *451*, 452–453
    and Cardinal Richelieu **4:** 453–455
Louis XIV, king of France
    and arts and culture **2:** 262–263 **4:** 458, 491,
        492, 496, 497, 500
    and colonies in America **3:** 360 **4:** 545, 546
    war with the Netherlands (1670s; Franco-Dutch
        War) **4:** 441, 457, 462
    and the rise of absolute monarchy **4:** 449–460
    army **4:** 454, 456
    as the Sun King **4:** *457*, 458, *460*
    and the War of the Spanish Succession **4:** *463*,
        464, 466, 467
Louis XV, king of France **4:** 460, 491
Louis XVI, king of France, and the French
    Revolution **5:** 585, 586, *589*
Louis XVIII, king of France **5:** 604
Louis-Napoleon *See* Napoleon III
Louis-Philippe, king of the French **5:** 608, *609*,
    612, 613, 655, 656
Louvois, Michel Le Tellier, marquis de **4:** 454,
    456, 462
Lowell, James Russell **5:** 652
Lübeck, Treaty of (1628) **2:** 229
Lublin, Union of (1569) **1:** 98
Ludendorff, Erich **7:** 987
Lumumba, Patrice **9:** 1225–1226
Luxemburg, Rosa **7:** 952
Lvov, Georgi Evenievich **7:** 912, 913–914,
    915–916

Maastricht Treaty (1992) **9:** *1196*, 1197
MacArthur, Douglas **7:** *964*, 965
Macartney, George, 1st earl **6:** 767–768
McCarthy, Joseph **8:** *1091*, 1092 **9:** 1169
Macdonald, Ramsay **7:** *956*, 957
McKinley, William **6:** 816, 835
Macmillan, Harold **8:** 1128 **9:** 1194
Madero, Francisco **6:** 743–745
Madison, James **5:** 645, 646
Madrid, Treaty of (1526) **2:** 189, 190
Magna Carta **1:** *14*
magnates **1:** 70
Mahmud (Afghan ruler) **3:** *397*, 405
Mahmut II, Ottoman sultan **6:** 730–732
Malcolm X **9:** 1175
Manchu (Ching) dynasty **1:** 128–129 **4:** 523–532
    6: 768–776
    and the Boxer Rebellion **6:** 774
Mandela, Nelson **9:** 1228, 1229, 1281
Manifest Destiny **5:** 654 **6:** 739, 836–837
Mao Tse-Tung (Mao Zedong) **6:** 785 **7:** 933,
    936–944 **8:** 1049, 1093 **9:** 1165, 1179–1185
Marat, Jean-Paul **5:** *594*

Marathas **3:** 416
Margaret, queen of Denmark **1:** 24
Marguerite de Valois **2:** 201
Maria Luisa of Savoy **4:** 465, 466
Maria Theresa, Holy Roman empress **4:** 468–469,
    488, 489
Marie Antoinette **4:** 497, 499 **5:** 593
market socialism, in China **9:** 1186–1187
Marshall, George C. **8:** 1072–1073, 1088–1089
Marshall, John **5:** 646
Marshall Aid **8:** 1072–1073, 1074,
    Marshall Plan/Marshall Aid **8:** 1072–1073, 1074,
    1076, 1088–1089
Marx, Karl **6:** 812, 813 **7:** 921
    and liberalism **5:** 611
    The Communist Manifesto (Marx and Engels)
        5: 629–630 **6:** 811, 812–813 **7:** 921
    Das Kapital **6:** 812
    and revolution **6:** 812 **7:** 911 **9:** 1179
    and the international movement **6:** 815
Marxist Party of the Revolutionary Left (PIR)
    7: 979
Marxist People's Movement for the Liberation of
    Angola (MPLA) **8:** 1099 **9:** 1227
Mary, queen of Scots **2:** 214, 221, 236
Mary I, Tudor, queen of England **2:** 169, 207, 209,
    210–211
    marriage **2:** *190*, 192, 211
Mary of Burgundy **1:** 25 **2:** *184*
Matthias I Corvinus, king of Hungary **1:** 94
Mau Mau **8:** 1125
Maurice, elector of Saxony **2:** 191, 192
Maurice, prince of Nassau **2:** 220–221
Maximilian, duke of Bavaria **2:** 226
Maximilian I, Holy Roman emperor **2:** *184*, 185,
    186
    wife **1:** 25 **2:** *184*
    army **1:** *27*
    election **1:** 46
    and the Fugger dynasty **1:** 46, 47
    education **1:** *71*
Maximilian, Ferdinand-Joseph, emperor of
    Mexico **5:** 657 **6:** 740–741
May Fourth Movement (1919) **7:** 935
Mayflower Compact **3:** 358–359
Mazarin, Jules (*originally* Giulio Mazarini)
    4: 455, *456*
Mazzini, Giuseppe **5:** 658
Medici, Catherine de' **1:** *9* **2:** 198–199, 200–201,
    202
Medici, Lorenzo de' **1:** *22*, 67, 83
Mehmed (Mehmet or Mohammed) II, Ottoman
    sultan (1432–1481) **1:** 16, 101, 102, 104, *105*
Meiji, emperor of Japan **4:** 542 **6:** 780
Meiji Restoration **6:** 780
Mein Kampf (Adolf Hitler) **7:** 988 **8:** 1034,
    1066–1067
Mellon, Andrew **7:** 947, 948
Menelik II, emperor of Ethiopia **6:** 826
Mensheviks **7:** 911, 915
Metternich, Klemens von **5:** 605–610, 614
Miller, Arthur **8:** 1092
Milosevic, Slobodan **9:** 1252
Minamoto, house (clan) of **1:** 125, 127
Minamoto Yorimoto **1:** *124*, 125–126, 127
Ming dynasty **1:** 16, 18, 127–128 **4:** 523–525, 526
    map of Ming China (late 1500s) **1:** *120*
Miranda, Francisco de **6:** 749, 750
Missouri Compromise **5:** 654
Mitterand, François **9:** 1196
Mobutu, Sese Seko **9:** 1226
Mogul empire **1:** 16, 130 **3:** 402, 406, 407–418
    5: 667
    insularity **1:** 18
    map of (late 1500s) **1:** *120*
Mohammed VI, sultan of Turkey **8:** 1023
Molotov-Ribbentrop Pact (1939) **8:** *1035*, 1036
monarchy
    rise in early modern Europe **1:** 12–14, 69–73
    and warfare **1:** 27
    encouraging trade **1:** 45
    and the feudal political system **1:** 70
    absolutism **4:** 439, 449–460 **5:** 583
    autocracy **4:** 460 **7:** 910
    and the Enlightenment **4:** 460, 476, 489
    and the French Revolution **5:** 583

1380

Monmouth, James, duke of **2**: 244
Monnet, Jean **8**: 1073 **9**: 1190–1192, 1193
Monroe, James **5**: 645, 646, 647 **6**: 741
Monroe Doctrine (1823) **5**: 607, 647 **6**: 741, 766, 835 **7**: 973
Montagnards/Mountain **5**: 592, 593
Moors, occupation of Spain **1**: *23*, 24
More, Sir Thomas **2**: 246
Mountain/Montagnards **5**: 592, 593
Mountbatten, Louis **8**: 1114
Mubarak, Hosni **9**: 1236, *1240*
Mugabe, Robert **9**: *1227*
Muhammad Ali, viceroy and pasha of Egypt **6**: 732, 820
Munich Conference and Munich Agreement (1938) **8**: *1034, 1035*, 1036
Murad II, Ottoman emperor **1**: 101–102
Musa, emperor (mansa) of Mali **1**: *109*, 115–118
Muslim Brotherhood **9**: 1232
Muslim League **8**: 1114
Muslims
    and independence in India **8**: 1110–1112, 1113
    and the partition of India **8**: 1114–1115
    fundamentalism in India **8**: 1116
Mussolini, Benito **7**: 983, *984*–987 **8**: 1030
    and the invasion of Abyssinia **6**: 824 **7**: 987
        8: 1030
    and World War II **8**: *1025*, 1038
    and Hitler **8**: *1029*
    and the Spanish Civil War **8**: 1032
Mustafa Kemal (Kemal Atatürk) **6**: *736* **7**: 907
        8: *1022*, 1023

nabobs **3**: 417
Nadir Shah (Iranian ruler) **3**: 405–406
Napoleon I, emperor of France **5**: 595–604, 655
    and the French Revolution **5**: 591, 594, 595
    declared emperor **5**: 594, *595*, 598, 638
    and Egypt **5**: 596 **6**: 730, 732, 820
    and Beethoven **5**: 598, *638*, 639
    and India **5**: 600, 667
    and Louisiana **5**: 600–601, 646
    invasion of Portugal **6**: 749, 755
    invasion of Spain **6**: 749
Napoleon III, Louis-Napoleon Bonaparte, emperor of France **5**: 604, 614, 655–657, 659, 661, 664, *665*
    and Mexico **5**: 657 **6**: 740–741
    and Paris **6**: 789
Napoleonic Code **5**: 597–598
Naseby, Battle of (1645) **2**: 240
Nasser, Gamal Abdel **8**: 1099, 1133, 1135
        9: 1235–1236
nation-states **1**: 22–23, 70 **4**: 460
National Assembly, French **5**: *583*
National Front for the Liberation of Angola (FNLA) **8**: 1099–1102 **9**: 1227
National Industrial Recovery Act (NIRA) **7**: 967
National Purity Society **8**: 1018
National Security Council (NSC) **9**: 1205
National Socialist German Workers' Party **7**: 987
National Socialist Party *See* Nazis
National Union for the Total Independence of Angola (UNITA) **8**: 1102 **9**: 1227–1228
nationalism **9**: 1278
    in Europe **5**: 594, 602, 609, 610–611, 655–666
        6: 730, 822 **9**: 1189–1190, 1198
    in Japan (1930s) **8**: 1018
Nationalist Party, of China *See* Guomindang
Nationalist Revolutionary Movement (MNR) **7**: 979
Nations, League of **7**: 903, 908, 956 **8**: 1026, *1027*, 1028
    and post–World War I mandates **7**: 905 **8**: 1023, 1024
    and the United States **7**: 945–946 **8**: *1027*
    Germany leaves **8**: 1030
    Japan leaves **8**: 1031
Native Americans, leadership **3**: 337–340
Navigation Acts **4**: 552
Nazi-Soviet Pact (1939) **9**: 1249
Nazis **7**: 958, *983*, 989–992 **8**: 1084
    and the Holocaust **7**: 991
    uniforms **8**: *1028*
Necker, Jacques **5**: 585–586

Nehru, Jawaharlal **8**: 1112–1113, 1115
Nemours, Treaty of (1585) **2**: 203
neocolonialism, in Africa **9**: 1222
Netanyahu, Benjamin **8**: 1138 **9**: 1242
Netherlands, republicanism **4**: 440–441
Neuilly, Treaty of (1919) **7**: 903
New Deal **7**: 959, 966–970 **8**: 1079 **9**: 1160
    Second **7**: 967–970
New Economic Policy (NEP), Russia's **7**: 922–923
Ngo Dinh Diem **8**: 1123
Nicholas I, czar of Russia, Russia under **5**: *688*, 689–692
Nicholas II, czar of Russia **5**: 696 **7**: 909
    and World War I **7**: 871, *872*, 880
    and the Russian Revolution (1917) **7**: 910–911, 913, 919
Night of Broken Glass **7**: 994
Night of the Long Knives **7**: 992
NIRA (National Industrial Recovery Act) **7**: 967
Nixon, Richard **8**: *1103* **9**: 1177
    and the Vietnam War **8**: 1099, 1101
    visit to China **8**: 1102 **9**: 1186, *1187*
Nkrumah, Kwame **8**: 1124 **9**: 1221, 1225
NKVD **7**: 930
NMR (Nationalist Revolutionary Movement) **7**: 979
nobles
    and the monarchy in early modern Europe **1**: 13–14, 25, 70
    a new nobility in early modern Europe **1**: 75–76, 77–78
    in central Europe **1**: 93–94
    Russian **1**: 96, 97, 98 **4**: 482, 489–490
    Ottoman (notables) **1**: 102 **6**: 728, 729
    Swedish (1600s) **4**: 446–447
Noriega, Manuel **9**: 1206
North German Confederation **5**: 661–664
North, Oliver **9**: 1205
Northern Expedition **7**: 938–939
Northumberland, John Dudley, duke of and earl of Warwick **2**: 210, 211
notables (Turkish nobles) **1**: 102 **6**: 728, 729
Nuremberg Laws **7**: 993–994
Nurhaci, king of the Manchu **4**: 525–526
Nyerere, Julius **9**: 1225

OAS (Organization of American States) **9**: 1200
Oates, Titus **2**: 243
Obregon, Alvaro **6**: 746
October Revolution (1917) **7**: *909*, *915*, 917
Oglethorpe, James **4**: 547
O'Higgins, Bernardo **6**: *748*, 753, 754, 761
Ojukwu, Chukumeka **9**: 1226
Oldenbarnevelt, Johan van **2**: 220
On the Reason of State (G. Botero) **1**: 70
On the Right of Magistrates over their Subjects (Theodore Beza) **2**: 202
Orangists **4**: 441
Organization of American States (OAS) **9**: 1200
Orhan, sultan of Turkey **1**: 100
Orlando, Vittorio **7**: *904*
Ortega, Daniel **9**: *1208*
Osman I, Ottoman sultan **1**: 99–100
Oswald, Lee Harvey **9**: 1173

Pahlavi, Reza Shah **9**: 1232–1233, 1234
Paine, Tom, *Common Sense* **4**: 557
Palestinian Liberation Organization (PLO) **8**: 1134–1136, 1137, 1138 **9**: 1240
Pan-African Congress (1945) **8**: 1124
Pan-Islamic movement **6**: 732–733
Paris, Treaty of (1763) **4**: 549, 553
Paris, Treaty of (1783) **4**: 562
Paris, Treaty of (1951) **9**: 1192
Paris Peace Conference **7**: 903–905
Park Chung Hee **9**: 1212
Parlement **1**: 13
Parliament **1**: 72
    development in England **1**: 23
    Long **2**: 238, 242
    Short **2**: 238
    Catholics in **6**: 808
Parma, Alessandro Farnese, duke of **2**: 220, 221
Parr, Catherine **2**: 209

Patriotic Front **9**: *1227*
Patriots, Dutch **4**: 442
Patton, George **7**: *964*
Paul, emperor of Russia **5**: 687
Pax Porfiriana **6**: 743
Pedro I (*formerly* Dom Pedro), emperor of Brazil **6**: 755–756
Pedro II, emperor of Brazil **6**: 756, 760, 763
peninsulares **3**: 347 **6**: 748
    in Mexico **6**: 737, 738
Penn, William **4**: 544
People's Action Party, of Singapore **9**: 1218
People's Party **6**: 834
perestroika **9**: 1244
Perón, Juan **7**: 977, 982 **9**: 1200, 1202
Perón, Maria Eva "Evita" **9**: 1200, 1202
Péronne, Declaration of (1585) **2**: 203
Pershing, John Joseph **6**: 746
personalismo **6**: 759
Peter I, the Great, czar of Russia **4**: 486–488
Peter III, czar of Russia **4**: 489
Peterloo massacre **6**: 808
Petition of Right **2**: 237
Petrograd Workers' and Soldiers' Soviet **7**: 914
Philip I, "the Handsome," king of Castile **2**: *184*, 185–186
Philip II, king of Spain **2**: *191*, 192–194
    before accession to the title **2**: 190
    marriage **2**: *190*
    and the Armada **2**: 213
    and the Spanish Netherlands **2**: 215, 216–217, 218, 220
    and Portugal **3**: 324
    and Spanish America **3**: 348
Philip IV, king of France **1**: 13
Philip IV, king of Spain **4**: 463
Philip V, duke of Anjou and first Bourbon king of Spain **4**: *462*–467, 470, 500
PIR (Marxist Party of the Revolutionary Left) **7**: 979
PLO (Palestinian Liberation Organization) **8**: 1134–1136, 1137, 1138 **9**: 1240
Poincaré, Raymond **7**: 955–956
Pol Pot **8**: 1099
politiques (moderate French Catholics) **2**: 204
Polk, James Knox **5**: 653–654
Pombal, Sebastien **4**: 460
Poniatowski, Stanislaw **4**: 490
Poor Laws (1834) **5**: *633* **6**: 811
Popular Front **8**: 1032
Population Registration Act (1950) **9**: 1228
populism, in the United States **6**: 811–814, 834
Porfirio's Peace **6**: 743
Potsdam Conference (1945) **8**: 1085–1086, 1089
Powhatan (Native American chief) **3**: 339, 358
Prague, Defenestration of **2**: 226–227
Prague, Peace of (1635) **2**: 231
Prester John **3**: 297–298, 299–300, 303
PRI (Institutional Revolutionary Party) **9**: 1206
Proclamation of 1763 **4**: 553, 555
Progressive Party (U.S.) **6**: 836
progressivism **6**: 814
Protestant Union **2**: 226
Public Safety, committee for **5**: 593
Puritans **4**: 440
    English **2**: 236–237, 238, 241 **4**: 440
    and Oliver Cromwell's rule **2**: 241
    colonies in North America **3**: 358–359, 360, 370
Purna Swaraj resolution **8**: 1112
Puyi, emperor of China **7**: 941
Pym, John **2**: 238–239

Qidan people **1**: 120, 122
Qizilbash tribal groups **3**: 398, 399, 400, 402
Quebec Act (1774) **4**: 555 **5**: 674
Quit India resolution **8**: *1112*, 1113

Rabin, Yitzhak **8**: 1138 **9**: 1242
Raj, age of the **5**: 669–671 **8**: 1107
Raleigh, Sir Walter **2**: 209, *214*, 236
    and North America **3**: 356
Rapallo, Treaty of (1922) **7**: 953
Rasputin **7**: 912, *913*

1381

Volume numbers appear in **boldface type**. Page numbers in *italic type* refer to illustrations and captions.

Reagan, Ronald **9:** *1159*, 1166, 1167, 1168, 1177, *1245*
  and Central America **8:** 1104 **9:** 1205
  and Libya **9:** 1237
  Star Wars program **9:** 1255
realpolitik **5:** 661
"reason of state" **2:** 234
Reconstruction Act (1866) **6:** 830
Red Guards **7:** *909*, *917*, 919
Red Scare (1920) **7:** 946
Red Shirts (Italy) **5:** 659, *660*
reduktion policy, Swedish **4:** 447
Reform Act (1832) **5:** 608 **6:** 809, 811
Reichstag **5:** 661–664
  and Hitler **7:** 989
Representatives, House of **4:** 562
Republicans, Dutch **4:** 441, 442
Reza Shah Pahlavi, shah of Iran **9:** 1232–1233, 1234
Rhee, Syngman **9:** 1212
Rhine, Confederation of the **5:** 601
Richard III, king of England **1:** 23 **2:** 205
Richelieu, Armand Jean du Plessis, cardinal, duc de **4:** 453–455
Right, Petition of **2:** 237
Rights, Bill of (1689) **4:** 444
"rights politics" **9:** 1166
Riksdag (Swedish parliament) **4:** 448
Robespierre, Maximilien **5:** 592, 593, 594
Roger II, king of Sicily **1:** 53
Roh Tae Woo **9:** *1213*, 1214
Röhm, Ernst **7:** 992
Romanov, Alexei **1:** *92*
Romanov, Michael **1:** *92*, 98 **4:** 482
  lands acquired under **1:** *90*
Romanov dynasty **1:** 98 **4:** 460, 482–483 **7:** 909
Rome, Treaty of (1957) **9:** *1192*, 1193
Rome-Berlin Axis **8:** *1029*, 1031, 1034
Romero, Oscar **9:** 1206
Roosevelt, Franklin D.
  and the Great Depression **7:** 959, 965–970
  New Deal **7:** 959, 966–970 **8:** 1079
  Good Neighbor Policy **7:** 973 **9:** 1200
  and the road to World War II **8:** 1034
  and World War II **8:** 1039–1040, 1046, 1049, 1077
  and postwar Europe **8:** 1084, 1085, 1087
  and the British in India **8:** 1113–1114
Roosevelt, Theodore **6:** 766, 835–836, 840
Rosas, Juan Manuel **6:** *759*, 760–761
Rosenberg, Ethel and Julius **8:** 1091
Rudolf II, Holy Roman emperor **1:** *69*, 95
Russian Revolution (1917) **5:** 694 **7:** 909–919 **8:** 1083–1084
  October Revolution **7:** *909*, *915*, 917
  February Revolution **7:** 914
  and Indonesian politics **8:** 1021
  and Indian politics **8:** 1108
Russian War (1812)
  Napoleon's retreat from Moscow **5:** *603*, 604, 688
  Battle of Borodino (1812) **5:** 604
  and the Poles **5:** 691
russification **5:** 696

Sacco, Nicola **7:** 946, *949*
Sadat, Anwar **8:** 1137 **9:** 1236, *1237*
Safavid empire **1:** 105, 108 **3:** 397–406 **6:** 728
  conflict with the Ottomans **1:** 105 **3:** 399–400, 405, 406 **6:** 729
Safi, shah of Persia **3:** 404
Safi al-Din **3:** 398
Saint Germain, Treaty of (1919) **7:** 903
SALT (Strategic Arms Limitation Treaty) **8:** 1102, *1103*
San Martin, José de **5:** 665 **6:** 749, 750, 753–754, *755*
Sandinista movement **8:** 1104 **9:** 1205, 1206, 1208
sansculottes **5:** *591*, 592
Santa Anna, Antonio López de **6:** 738, 739
Sarekat Islam **8:** 1020
satyagraha movement **8:** 1109, 1110
Saudi dynasty **6:** 732
Savimbi, Jonas **9:** 1227–1229
Savonarola, Girolamo **1:** *10*, 11, 65

Schuman, Robert **8:** 1073
SDI *See* Strategic Defense Initiative
Second Empire (France) **5:** 657
Second International **6:** *811*, 816
Second New Deal **7:** 967–970
Sef dynasty **1:** 112
segregation, in the United States **6:** 831 **8:** 1082 **9:** 1171
sejm **1:** 13, 25, 93 **4:** 484, 485, 490
sejmiki **4:** 484
Selassie, Haile, emperor of Ethiopia **8:** 1030 **9:** 1226
Selective Service Act (1940) **8:** 1040, 1063
Selim I, Ottoman sultan **1:** 105–107
  Ottoman acquisitions under **1:** *100*
Selim III, Ottoman sultan **6:** *729*, 730
Seljuks **1:** 99, 103
Senate **4:** 562
Senghor, Léopold **9:** 1225
Serviceman's Readjustment Act (1944; GI Bill of Rights) **8:** 1081
Sèvres, Treaty of (1920) **7:** 903, 908 **8:** 1023
Seymour, Edward, 1st duke of Somerset **2:** 210
Seymour, Jane **2:** 209
Sforza, Francesco, statue of **1:** 82
Sforza, Lodovico **1:** 84
Sforza family **1:** 28
Shah Jahan, Mogul emperor **3:** 414–415, 417
Shaka, Zulu leader **6:** 819
Shidehara Kijuro, Danshaku **8:** 1019
Shirley, William **4:** 547
Shiusky, Basil **1:** 97
Shivaji Bosle **3:** 416
shoguns **4:** 533 **6:** 777
Shunzhi, Manchu emperor of China **4:** 526, 527, 528
Sieyès, Emmanuel **5:** 596
Sigismund, Holy Roman emperor **1:** 94
Sigismund II Augustus, king of Poland **1:** 98
Sigismund III, king of Poland **1:** 97–98
Sikhs **3:** 416 **8:** 1108, *1109*, 1114, 1115
Silva Xavier, Joaquim José da (*pseudonym* Tiradentes) **6:** 755, *756*
Single European Act (1986) **9:** 1196
slaves/slavery
  in Brazil **3:** 350, *383*, 384, *385*, 386 **6:** 758, *759*
  abolition in the United States **5:** 651–652, 654, 682, *683* **6:** 819, 830, 831
  slave or free states (U.S.) **5:** 654
  and the American Civil War **5:** 677, 682
  post-abolition freedmen (U.S.) **6:** 830–831
Slavophiles **5:** 690–691
Smith, Ian **9:** 1229
Sobieski *See* John III Sobieski
Social Democratic Party, German **5:** 628
Social Democratic Party, Russian **7:** 911, 919, 921
Social Revolutionaries, Russian **7:** 911
Social Security Act (1935) **7:** 970
socialism
  rise of (1800s–1900s) **6:** 807–816
  post–World War II **8:** 1075–1080
Socialist Party, U.S. **6:** *815*
Solidarity labor union **8:** 1105–1106 **9:** 1244, 1245
Somerset, 1st duke of **2:** 210
Somoza, Anastasio **8:** 1104
Somoza family **9:** 1205
Sonderbund **5:** 612
Sons of Liberty **4:** 555
South African Indian Congress **6:** 828
South African Native National Congress **6:** 828
soviets **7:** 914
Spartacists **7:** 952
Springtime of the Peoples **5:** 614
Srivijaya **3:** 319
stadtholders **4:** 441
Stalin, Joseph **7:** 923–932, 936, 945, 983 **8:** 1084, 1093 **9:** *1249*
  nonaggression pact with Germany **8:** *1035*
  and the Soviet war with Japan (1945) **8:** 1060
  and the postwar treatment of Germany **8:** 1084, 1085–1086
  intention to occupy Azerbaijan **8:** 1086–1087
  and the British in India **8:** 1114
  and China **9:** 1180

Stamp Act (1765) **4:** 555
Star Wars *See* Strategic Defense Initiative
START (Strategic Arms Reduction Talks) **8:** 1104, 1105
state, role post–World War II **8:** 1078–1079
States General **2:** 216, 218, 220 **3:** *360* **4:** 440
Stevenson, Adlai **8:** 1082
Strafford, Thomas Wentworth, 1st earl of **2:** 238, 239
Strategic Arms Limitation Treaty (SALT) **8:** 1102, *1103*
Strategic Arms Reduction Talks (START) **8:** 1104, 1105
Strategic Defense Initiative (SDI; Star Wars) **8:** 1104 **9:** 1255
Stuart dynasty **2:** 214, 235–244
  Charles Edward, the Young Pretender **4:** *443*
Suez Crisis (1956) **8:** 1127, 1133, 1135
Sugar Act (1764) **4:** 554
Suharto, Thojib N. J. **8:** 1121–1122 **9:** 1220, 1280
Sukarno, Achmad **8:** *1021*, 1022–1023, 1120–1121, 1122 **9:** 1217
Sulayman, Safavid shah of Iran **3:** 404–405
Süleyman I, "the Magnificent" **1:** 107–108 **2:** 190 **3:** *297*
  Ottoman acquisitions under **1:** *100*
sultans, Ottoman **1:** 104
Sun King, the *See* Louis XIV, king of France
Sun Yat-sen **6:** 776 **7:** 933, 936, *937*
Sundiata **1:** *114*, 115
Sung dynasty **1:** 120–123
Supreme Court (United States) **4:** 562 **5:** 646
Suryavarman II, Khmer ruler **3:** *318*
Sweden, *reduktion* policy (1600s) **4:** 447
Sworn Confederates, Society of **6:** 776

Tadakuni, Mizuno **4:** 541
Taft, William Howard **6:** 836
Taft-Hartley Act (1947) **8:** 1080–1081
Tahmasp I, Safavid shah of Iran **3:** 400–403
Tahmasp II, Safavid shah of Iran **3:** 405
T'ai Tsu, emperor of China **1:** 120
Taira, house of (clan) of **1:** 125
Talleyrand, Charles Maurice de **5:** 606
Tamerlane *See* Timur
Tanzimat (Ottoman reform movement) **6:** 733, 734
Taraki, Nur Mohammed **8:** 1103
Taylor, Zachary **6:** 739
Tennis Court Oath **5:** *585*, 586
Terra, Gabriel **7:** 975
Terror, the **5:** *592*, 593, 594
Thatcher, Margaret **9:** 1167, 1196
theocracy **6:** 728
Theodore (Fyodor) I, czar of Russia **1:** 97
  lands acquired under **1:** *90*
third estate **5:** 586, *590*
Third International **7:** *931*
Third Reich **7:** 988
Thirteenth Amendment, of the U.S. Constitution **6:** 830
Thousand, the (Red Shirts) **5:** 659, *660*
Tilly, Johann t'Serclaes, baron **2:** 228–229, 231
Timur (Tamerlane) **1:** 101
Tipu, sultan of Mysore **5:** 667
Tiradentes **6:** 755, *756*
Tito (Josip Broz) **8:** *1069*, 1070 **9:** 1251, 1278
Tjokroaminoto, Omar Said **8:** 1020
Tojo, Hideki **8:** *1025*
Tokugawa clan **4:** 533–542 **6:** 777–780
Tories, and Whigs **4:** 444, 445
totalitarianism, in Europe (1900s) *See* Hitler, Adolf; Mussolini, Benito; Stalin, Joseph
Toyotomi clan **4:** 533
tozama **4:** 534
Trianon, Treaty of (1920) **7:** 903
tribalism, in Africa **9:** 1224–1225
Triple Alliance **7:** 872–873, 875, 887
Triple Entente **7:** 872–873, 875, 887
Trotsky, Leon **7:** 930
  and the Russian Revolution **7:** 916, 917, *919*
  and the Russian Civil war **7:** 920
  and Stalin **7:** 924, 925–926
Troubles, Council of **2:** 217
Troubles, Time of (1598–1613) **1:** 97–98 **4:** 482

Volume numbers appear in **boldface type**. Page numbers in *italic type* refer to illustrations and captions.

Trujillo, Rafael **9:** 1204
Truman Doctrine **8:** 1087–1088
Truman, Harry S. **8:** *1071*
    and the atomic bomb **8:** 1059, 1060
    and post–World War II America **8:** 1073,
      1077–1081
    and post–World War II Europe **8:** 1086, 1087,
      1088
t'Serclaes, Johan, baron Tilly **2:** 228–229, 231
Tsunayoshi, shogun of Japan **4:** 540, *541*
Tudor England **2:** 205–214
Twenty-One Demands **6:** 783–786 **7:** 934 **8:** 1016
Two Nations, Commonwealth of the **1:** 98
Tzu-hsi, dowager empress of China **6:** 773–776

Ulászló II, king of Bohemia and Hungary **1:** 93
Ulyanov, Vladimir Ilyich *See* Lenin, Vladimir
    Ilyich
Union, Act of (1707) **4:** 444
Union and Progress, Committee of **6:** 736
United Kingdom, formation **4:** 444
United Nations **8:** 1070 **9:** 1198, 1280
    Relief and Rehabilitation Administration
      (UNRRA) **8:** 1071–1072, 1073
    and the Korean War **8:** 1093
    and Israel **8:** 1129, 1131, 1133, *1134*
    and the Suez Crisis **8:** 1133, 1135
    and China **9:** 1186
    and the Congo **9:** 1226
    and Somalia **9:** *1229*, 1230
Utrecht, Union of (1579) **2:** 219

Valois dynasty **1:** 23 **2:** 156, 196, *197*
    and the struggle for Milan **2:** 188–189
Van Buren, Martin **5:** 647
Vanzetti, Bartolomeo **7:** 946, *949*
Vargas, Getúlio **7:** 977, 980–982
Vasily III, czar of Russia **1:** 96
    lands acquired under **1:** *90*
Versailles, Treaty of (1919) **7:** 903–905, *906*, *907*,
    908, 934–935, 956, 987, 988, 993
    8: 1026–1027
    and the League of Nations **7:** 903, 945–946
      8: 1028
    "war guilt" clause **8:** 1027
    German contradiction of **8:** 1030–1031
Victor Emmanuel III, king of Italy **7:** 986
Victor Emmanuel, king of Sardinia **5:** 659
Victoria, queen of Great Britain **6:** 798
    technology during reign of **5:** *706*
    in mourning **6:** 804
    German relatives **7:** 871
Vienna, Congress of (1815) **5:** 605–607, 608, 609,
    691
Viet Minh **8:** 1100, 1123
Villa, Francisco "Pancho" **6:** 742, 744, 745, 746
Villaroel, Gualberto **7:** 979
Villiers, George **2:** 236
viziers **1:** 104
Volksraad **8:** 1022
voting rights **6:** 816
    in Britain **6:** 809
    in France **6:** 809
    of freed slaves in the United States **6:** 830–831
Vytautas, grand duke of Lithuania **1:** 91

Walesa, Lech **8:** 1106 **9:** 1244, 1245
Wallenstein (Albrecht of Valstejn) **2:** *225*, 229,
    231
Walpole, Robert **4:** 445
War Powers Act (1941) **8:** 1063
Warren Commission (1964) **9:** 1173
Warwick, John Dudley, earl of and duke of
    Northumberland **2:** 210, 211
Washington, George, president **4:** 562
Washington Naval Conference **7:** 948
Watergate affair **9:** 1176–1177
Webster, Daniel **5:** 647, 651, 654
Weimar Republic **7:** 952–953, 987 **8:** 1029
welfare states **8:** 1077 **9:** 1160
Wentworth, Thomas (earl of Strafford) **2:** 238, 239
West European Union **9:** 1190
Westernizers **5:** 690, 691
Whigs (England), and Tories **4:** 444, 445
Whigs (U.S.) **5:** 651, 654

White Army, and the Russian Civil War **7:** *912*,
    919, 920, 921 **8:** 1084
White Terror **5:** 594
Wilhelm II, emperor (kaiser) of Germany and king
    of Prussia **7:** 871, *872*, 874, 880, 952, 987
William I, first German emperor and king of
    Prussia **5:** 660, 664
William I, prince of Orange (William the Silent;
    1533–1584) **2:** 213, 218, 219, 220
William II, emperor of Germany and king of
    Prussia *See* Wilhelm II
William III and Mary II, king and queen of Britain
    and Ireland (William of Orange) **2:** *243*, 244
    4: 441–444, 545
    defeat of James Stuart in Ireland **4:** 445
William IV, stadtholder of the Netherlands **4:** 442
Willkie, Wendell **8:** 1040
Wilmot Proviso **5:** 654
Wilson, Woodrow **6:** 745, 746, 836 **7:** 946
    and World War I **7:** 896, 902–903, *904*, 952
    and the League of Nations **7:** 908, 945–946
    8: 1028
Wladyslaw II Jagiello, grand duke of Lithuania
    and king of Poland **1:** 91
Wladyslaw IV Vasa, czar of Russia **1:** 97
Wolsey, Thomas **2:** 207, 208

Yalta Conference (1945) **8:** 1084–1085
Yeltsin, Boris **9:** *1248*, 1249, 1250, 1251
Yeshov, Nikolai **7:** 932
Yongzheng, emperor of China **4:** 530
Yorimoto *See* Minamoto Yorimoto
Yoshimune, shogun of Japan **4:** 536, 540
Young, Owen D. **7:** 954
Young Plan (1929) **7:** 954
Young Turks **6:** 735, 736 **7:** 878, 887
Yuan dynasty **1:** 123–125, 127
Yuan Shih-k'ai **6:** 776 **7:** 933–934, 936

Zand dynasty **3:** 406
Zapata, Emiliano **6:** 742, 744, 745, 746
Zapatistas **9:** 1206
zemsky sobor (or land assembly) **4:** 482–483
zemstvos **5:** 692–693, 694, *695* **7:** 910
Zhikov, Todor **9:** 1247
Zinovyev, Grigory **7:** 931
Zionist World Congress, first **8:** 1129
Zionists **8:** 1129, 1130, 1132
Zola, Emile, and the Dreyfus affair **6:** 846
Zulu Inkhata movement **9:** 1228

RELIGION

Albigensian Crusade **2:** *175*
Alexander VI, Pope **1:** 11
Amish **2:** 162 **3:** 372
Anabaptists **1:** 17 **2:** 162, 216 **3:** 372
Anglicans/Anglicanism **4:** 440
    prayer book **2:** 210, 238
    See also Church of England
Aquinas, Thomas **1:** 57, *58*
Arminians (religious sect) **2:** 246
Augustine of Hippo, St. **1:** 56–57 **2:** 152
autos-da-fé (executions) **2:** 179
Avignon, anti-pope established at **1:** 20 **2:** 164,
    165

Bakker, Jim **9:** 1178
Baptists **6:** 808
Barnabites **2:** 166
Benedict XIII, Pope **2:** *165*
Bernard of Claivaux **1:** 11
Bessarion, Cardinal **1:** 53, 64
Beza, Theodore **2:** 202
Bible
    Gutenberg/Mainz Bible **1:** 60, *61*
    and Martin Luther **1:** 62 **2:** 155
    in the vernacular **1:** 62
    Erasmus's Latin edition **2:** *165*
    Vulgate translation **2:** 169
    first French Protestant **2:** 175
    King James Version **2:** 236
blood libel **7:** 990
Boleyn, Anne **2:** 207, 209
Book of Martyrs (John Foxe) **2:** 211
books, and theology **1:** 56–57
Booth, William **5:** *626*, 632
Bora, Catherine von **2:** 155, *157*
Borgia, Alexander **2:** 151
Brethren of the Common Life **1:** 54
brotherhoods, Catholic **2:** 165
Buddhism
    Zen **1:** *125*, 127
    temple gardens **1:** *126*
    in Southeast Asia **3:** 317, 318, 320, 322
    in Japan **6:** 781
    in China **7:** *936*
Bunyan, John **2:** 241, *243*

cabala **1:** 66
Calvin, John **2:** 160–161, 170, 197
    and infant mortality **1:** 10
Calvinism **1:** 95 **2:** 172, 175
    in France **2:** 197–198
    in the Low Countries **2:** 216, 217, 220, 223
    4: 440
    See also Huguenots
Capuchin order **2:** 166
Carmelites, reformed by Teresa of Avila **2:** 166,
    168
Castiglione, Giuseppe **4:** *528*, 531
Cathari **2:** 174, *175*
cathedrals
    schools **1:** 54
    and humanism **1:** 65
Catherine of Aragon **2:** 160
Catholic Church
    and the spread of literacy *49*
    pre-Reformation **1:** 10–11 **2:** 151–152, 163–167
    Great/Western Schism (papal schism;
      1378–1417) **1:** 11, 20 **2:** 151, 164, *165*
    religious festivals **1:** 11
    sale of indulgences **1:** 11–12, 46 **2:** 152, 153
    reform in the late Middle Ages **1:** *17*
    and usury **1:** 44, 73
    and education **1:** 52, 56–57, 78
    and universities **1:** 52, 58
    and intellectual inquiry **1:** 56
    and humanism **1:** 68
    Counter-Reformation **2:** 163–172
    Baroque art and architecture **2:** 257–259
    in the Spanish American colonies **3:** *351*,
      352–353
    and New England **3:** *359*
    and abstinence from meat **3:** 388–389
    rococo architecture **4:** 492–493

1383

Catholic Church (continued)
  science and traditionalism (1800s) **5:** 702
  in Mexico (1800s) **6:** 738, *742*
  in post-independence Latin America **6:** 762, 764
  Roman Catholics in the British Parliament **6:** 808
  influence in Latin America between the World Wars **7:** *979*, 980
  liberation theology in Latin America **9:** 1208
  See also Inquisition; missionaries; popes/papacy; Reformation
Catholic League
  formed by Henry, duke of Guise **2:** 203
  formed by Maximilian, duke of Bavaria **2:** 226, 228–229
chapels, Renaissance **1:** 80
Charles V, Holy Roman emperor
  and Luther **2:** 155, 156
  and the Council of Trent **2:** 168
Charles, duke of Mayenne **2:** *198*, 199
Christendom, decline **1:** 20–21, 68
Christianity
  and age of the Earth **5:** 698
  and the theory of evolution **5:** 699
  revival (late 1800s) **5:** 702
Church of England
  founded by Henry VIII **2:** 160, 208
  Anglican prayer book **2:** 210, 238
  and Elizabeth I **2:** 212
  See also Anglicans/Anglicanism
Church of Jesus Christ of Latter-day Saints **5:** 702
churches, and humanism **1:** *64*, 65
Clement VII, Pope **2:** 189, 207
Clement VIII, Pope **4:** 485
Clement XI, Pope **4:** 529
Clément, Jacques **2:** 203
clergy, educated **1:** 49, 50, 78
Coligny, Gaspard II de **2:** 199, *200*, 201–202
Confucianism
  and trade **1:** 18, 40
  and modernization **1:** 66
  and government **1:** 124
  and the Great Withdrawal **1:** 127–128
  and the Cultural Revolution **9:** 1185
Congregational church **4:** 550
Constance, Council of (1414–1418) **1:** 94 **2:** 164–165
Coronaro Chapel, Rome **2:** *259*
Counter-Reformation, Catholic **2:** 163–172
Cranmer, Thomas **2:** 210, 211
Cromwell, Thomas **2:** 208
crucifixes **2:** *166*
Crusades **1:** 16, 90, *101*, 102 **2:** 174 **3:** 297
cujus regio, ejus religio **2:** 226
Curia **2:** 163, 165, 167

Dalai Lama **4:** 527
deism **5:** 698
Din Ilahi (Divine Faith) **3:** 412, 414
Divine Faith **3:** 412, 414
Dominicans **1:** 11, 50 **2:** 176
dualist heresy **2:** 180
Dutch Reformed Church **2:** 224

Eastern Orthodox Church/Christianity **1:** 10 **3:** 297
  split with the Roman Catholic Church **1:** 90
  Russian Orthodox Church **1:** 92 **4:** *481*, 530 **5:** *691* **7:** 990
  and the Uniate Church **4:** 485
Eck, Johann **1:** 44
Enlightenment, the, and religion **4:** 476
Episcopalian church **4:** 550
Erasmus, Desiderius **1:** 54, 57–58, 65–68 **2:** 152, 165
Europe
  religious unity in the Middle Ages **3:** 297–298
  Protestant northern Europe **4:** 439–448
  religion and superstition (1700s) **4:** 476, 520–521
evangelical churches, in Latin America **9:** 1208

Farnese, Cardinal **2:** 203
fatwas **6:** 729
Fountains Abbey, Yorkshire **2:** *209*

Four Books of the Sentences (Peter Lombard) **1:** 56–57
Foxe, John **2:** 211
Francis I, king of France
  and Protestantism **2:** 161, 170–172
  and the Council of Trent **2:** 168
Franciscans **1:** 11, 50, *54* **2:** 166
  missionaries in Mexico **3:** 352–353
fundamentalism **9:** 1273, 1279
  Islamic **9:** 1231–1242, 1279
  Christian **9:** 1279

Geneva, religion **2:** 160, *161*, 197
Germany, Luther and the birth of Protestantism **1:** 10 **2:** 151–160, 162
Ghost Dance **6:** 839
Graham, Billy **9:** *1177*, 1178
Great Awakening **4:** 549–550
  Second **5:** 652
Great Migration **3:** 359
Great/Western Schism (papal schism; 1378–1417) **1:** 11, 20 **2:** 151, 164, *165*
Gregory IX, Pope **2:** 174
Gregory XIII, Pope **2:** 202, 270
Guadalupe, Virgin of **3:** 353
Guevara, Fernando Niño de **2:** *178*
Gui, Bernard **2:** 176, 179
Guise brothers **2:** *198*, 199, 200, 201

Hamas **8:** 1138 **9:** 1242
Henry I of Lorraine, duke of Guise **2:** *198*, 199, 203
Henry VIII, king of England **2:** 160
heresy
  punishing *See* Inquisition
  dualist **2:** 180
Hezbollah **9:** 1240, 1241, 1242
Hildegard, abbess of Bingen **1:** 11
Hinduism/Hindus
  in Southeast Asia **3:** 317–318, 320, 322
  under the Moguls **3:** 410–411, 412, 414
  caste system in India **8:** 1109, 1111
  and independence in India **8:** 1110–1112, 1113
  and partition in India **8:** 1114
  fundamentalism in India **8:** 1116
Holy Union (Sainte-Union) **2:** 203
Huguenots
  and the Wars of Religion **2:** 161, 172, 195–204
  churches **2:** *196*
  in South Africa **3:** 329
  after the Wars of Religion **4:** 451, 453
  and Louis XIV **4:** 459, 462
humanism/humanists **1:** 9, 17 **2:** 152, 160
  and ancient Greece and Rome **1:** 17, 62–64
  a reaction to Scholasticism **1:** 57–58
  and the spread of knowledge **1:** 59–68, 80
  in Florence **1:** 64–65, 80
  and wealth **1:** 73
  and nobility **1:** 75
  and the Bible **2:** 165
  and Latin **2:** 252
  See also Erasmus, Desiderius
Hus, Jan **1:** 11, 94, *95* **2:** 152, 164, 165
Hussites **1:** 94, 95 **2:** 152
hymnbooks, Protestant **2:** *159*

Ignatius of Loyola, St. **2:** 170, *171*, 257
Imitation of Christ, The (Thomas à Kempis) **1:** 11 **2:** 165
Index of Prohibited Books **2:** 169
indulgences, sale of **1:** 11–12, 46, 47 **2:** 152, 153
Innocent III, Pope **1:** *54* **2:** 175
Innocent X, Pope **2:** 260
Inquisition **2:** 174–180
  Spanish **1:** 24 **2:** 172, *175*, 179, 216–217
  Roman **2:** 167, 175, 180
  established (1231) **2:** 174
  Supreme Council of the **2:** 179
  and witches **2:** 180
  and Galileo **2:** 270
  in India **3:** 324
Institutes of the Christian Religion (Calvin) **2:** 161
Islam
  Crusades against **1:** 16, 90, *101*, 102 **2:** 174 **3:** 297

and ancient Greek culture **1:** 64
Islamic scholarship **1:** 66
in North Africa **1:** 110
in East Africa **1:** 112–113
in Mali (West Africa) **1:** 115
ridding Spain of (1400s) **2:** *166*
and Prester John **3:** 297–298, 299–300
introduced in Southeast Asia **3:** 322
in Mogul India **3:** 410–412, 414
Muslims and independence in India **8:** 1110–1112, 1113
rise of militant fundamentalism **9:** 1231–1242, 1279
and education **9:** *1235*
jihad **9:** 1238, 1279
See also Muslims; Shiism; Sunni Islam
Islamic Salvation Party **9:** 1230

Jansenists, and Louis XIV **4:** 459
Jesuits (Society of Jesus) **2:** 166, 170–171, 172
  in Japan **3:** *324* **4:** 538–539
  in Siam **3:** *330*
  in Spanish Latin America **3:** 352
  in India **3:** *411*, 412
  in China **4:** 524, 528–529 **6:** 768
Jews **3:** 297
  and humanism **1:** 66
  immigration to central Europe **1:** 93
  persecuted in Europe (1500s) **1:** 97
  persecuted in the German states (1493) **2:** *173*
  persecuted in Spain **2:** 180 **3:** 297
  Sephardic **2:** 223
  British **3:** 297 **6:** 808
  persecuted in Russia **5:** 694, 696 **7:** 990
  and Hitler's (Nazi) Germany **7:** 988, 990, 991, 993–994 **8:** 1062, 1066, 1070, 1131
  and the creation of Israel **8:** 1024, 1129–1132
  diaspora **8:** 1129
  Zionists **8:** 1129, 1130, 1132
  jihad **9:** 1238, 1279
Joachim of Fiore **1:** 17
John Paul II, Pope **9:** *1245*
Joseph, Chief **6:** 839
Julius II, Pope **1:** 11, 84
  tomb **1:** *82*, 84

Kempis, Thomas à **1:** 11 **2:** 165
Khomeini, Ayatollah Ruhollah **9:** 1233, 1234, 1235, 1241, 1242
Kierkegaard, Soren **5:** 702
Knox, John **2:** 161, 214
Koran **1:** *99*
Kramer, Heinrich **2:** 180

Las Casas, Bartolomé de **3:** 353
Lateran Council, Fifth **2:** 165
Laud, William **2:** 238, 239
Leo X, Pope **1:** 11–12 **2:** 153
Life of the Mother Teresa of Jesus (Saint Teresa of Avila) **2:** 259
Livingstone, David **6:** 820, *821*, 824
Lollards **2:** 152
Lombard, Peter **1:** 56–57
Louis, cardinal of Lorraine **2:** *198*, 199
Louis, prince of Condé **2:** 199, 200, 201
Luther, Martin **1:** 10, 21 **2:** 151–156, *157*, *159*, 163, 168, 170, 188
  and the sale of indulgences **1:** 12, 47 **2:** 153
  and the social order **1:** 17
  and the importance of education **1:** 55
  German translation of the Bible **1:** 62 **2:** 155
Lutheranism **1:** 12, 95 **2:** 157–160, 172 **4:** 440

Machiavelli, Niccolò **1:** 17, 65, 67, 68
Malleus Maleficarum (book about witches) **2:** 180
Marranos **2:** 180
Martin V, Pope **1:** 84
Mary I, Tudor, queen of England **2:** 169, 207, 210–211
Medici, Catherine de' **1:** *9* **2:** 198–199, 200–201, 202
Mennonites **2:** 162 **3:** 372
Merici, Angela **2:** 167
Methodists **5:** 702

millenarian groups **2:** 241
Milton, John **2:** 241
minarets, Persian **3:** *403*
missionaries
    in Asia **3:** 324, 330, *411*, 412 **4:** 524, 528–529, 532
    in the Spanish American colonies **3:** 352–353
    in New France **3:** 360, 374
    in China **4:** 524, 528–529, 532 **6:** 768, 771, 774, 784
    in India **5:** 668
    in Africa **6:** *817*, 820, 828
    See also Franciscans; Jesuits
Mogul empire, and Akbar's syncretism **3:** 410–412
monasteries
    dissolution under Henry VIII **1:** 38 **2:** 208, *209*
    education in **1:** 50, 54, *55*
Moors, persecuted in Spain **2:** 180
Moral Majority **9:** 1177–1178
Moravians **3:** 372
Mormons **5:** 702
mosques, Ottoman **1:** *107* **6:** *727, 733*
music
    and Protestant worship **2:** *159*
    and the Dutch Reformed Church **2:** 224
Muslim Brotherhood **9:** 1232
Muslims
    and independence in India **8:** 1110–1112, 1113
    and the partition of India **8:** 1114–1115
    fundamentalism in India **8:** 1116
    fundamentalism in the Middle East **9:** 1231–1242
    See also Islam

Native Americans
    religion **3:** *334, 335*, 336–337
    and the Ghost Dance **6:** 839
natural theology **5:** 698
Nemours, Treaty of (1585) **2:** 203

On the Right of Magistrates over their Subjects (Theodore Beza) **2:** 202
Oratory of Divine Love **2:** 165
Orthodox Church *See* Eastern Orthodox Church/Christianity

Pan-Islamic movement **6:** 732–733
pantheism, and Romanticism **5:** 636, 637
Paradise Lost (John Milton) **2:** 241
Paul III, Pope **2:** 167–168
Paul VI, Pope **2:** 180
"Pennsylvania Dutch" **3:** 372
Péronne, Declaration of (1585) **2:** 203
Pietists **5:** 702
Pilgrim's Progress (John Bunyan) **2:** 241, *243*
Pius V, Pope **2:** 194
Pius VII, Pope **5:** 597
Pius IX, Pope **5:** 702
pogroms **7:** 990
popes/papacy
    two simultaneous *See* Great/Western Schism
    and the Holy Roman Empire **1:** 20
    and Europe's secular rulers **1:** 51
    and the Renaissance **1:** 83–84
    in late Medieval (pre-Reformation) times **2:** 152
possession, demonic **2:** *180*
Praise of Folly, The (Erasmus) **1:** 58, 67–68 **2:** 165
prayer book
    Anglican **2:** 210, 238
    for Scotland (1637) **2:** 238, *239*
predestination **2:** 161
Presbyterian Church/Presbyterianism **2:** 161, 214 **4:** 550
    Scottish **2:** 238, *239* **3:** 371
Prester John **3:** 297–298, *299*–300, 303
printing, and the spread of Protestantism **1:** 62 **2:** 158
processions, religious **1:** *75*
Protestant Union **2:** 226
Protestantism **1:** 21 **2:** 167
    birth of **1:** 10 **2:** 151–162
    and the monarchy **1:** 70–71
    and the Renaissance **1:** 95–96

name **2:** 156
    development in England (1500s) **2:** 208–209, 210
    and art **2:** 255
    Protestant northern Europe **4:** 439–448
    See also Huguenots; Reformation
Protocols of the Learned Elders of Zion **7:** 990
Puritans **4:** 440
    English **2:** 236–237, 238, 241 **4:** 440
    and Oliver Cromwell's rule **2:** 241
    colonies in North America **3:** 358–359, 360, 370

Quakers **2:** 241 **4:** 550
    and Pennsylvania **3:** *361*, 364, *370*
    and New Jersey **3:** 364

Ranters (religious sect) **2:** 241
Reformation **1:** 12, 21, 28 **2:** 151–162, 163, 182, 246 **4:** 440
    and education **1:** 55, 78
    effect on the monarchy **1:** 70–71
    in central Europe **1:** 94–96
    in France **2:** 197
    "Henrician" **2:** 208–209
    and the scientific revolution **2:** 267
Reformed Church, Dutch **2:** 224
religion
    and humanism **1:** *64*, 65
    and age of the Earth **5:** 698
    and the theory of evolution **5:** 699
Religion, Wars of (1562–1598) **2:** 161, 172, 195–204 **4:** 450
    and Philip II **2:** 194
Restitution, Edict of (1629) **2:** 229, 231, 233
Ricci, Matteo **4:** 524, 528
Roman Catholics *See* Catholic Church
Russian Orthodox Church **1:** 92 **4:** *481*, 530 **5:** *691*

Saint Bartholemew's Day Massacre **2:** *199, 200*, 201–202, 219
Saint Peter's basilica, Rome **1:** 11–12, 84 **2:** *172*
    Michelangelo's *Pietà* **1:** *81*
Saint-Germain, Edict of **2:** 199
Saint-Germain, Treaty of (1570) **2:** 201
Salem (Massachusetts), witch trials **2:** 182 **3:** 370, *373*
Salvation Army **5:** *626*, 632, 702
Salvation Front **9:** 1241–1242
Savonarola, Girolamo **1:** *10*, 11, 65
Schall von Bell, Johann Adam **4:** 528–529
Schmalkaldic League **1:** 47 **2:** 156, 188, 190
Scholasticism **1:** 57
Schoolmen **1:** 57, 58
Second Great Awakening **5:** 652
Seekers (religious sect) **2:** 241
Separatists **3:** 358
Seymour, Edward, 1st duke of Somerset **2:** 210
Shiism
    in Iran **3:** 398, 400, 406 **9:** 1233, 1234, 1237
    Lebanese Shiite terrorists (Hezbollah) **9:** 1240, 1241, 1242
Shinto religion **6:** 781, 782, *783*
Shiva **3:** *318*
Sikhs **3:** 416 **8:** 1108, *1109*, 1114, 1115
Sixtus IV, Pope **2:** 179
Smith, Joseph **5:** 702
Society of Jesus *See* Jesuits
Somerset, 1st duke of **2:** 210
Southern Baptist Church **9:** 1178
Spain
    reform of the Catholic Church **2:** 165–166
    and Catholicism **2:** 172
    Eighty Years' War (war with the Netherlands) **2:** 172, 215–224 **4:** 440
Spanish Inquisition *See* Inquisition, Spanish
Spiritual Exercises (Ignatius of Loyola) **2:** 170, *171*
Sprenger, Jacob **2:** 180
strappado (instrument of torture) **2:** *176*, 177
Summa Theologiae (Thomas Aquinas) **1:** 57
Sunni Islam
    and the Safavid empire **3:** 399
    in Iran **9:** 1234

Supremacy, Act of (1534) **2:** 208
Syllabus of Errors (Pius IX) **5:** 702

Taleban **9:** 1241
Talmud **1:** 66
temples, Southeast Asian **3:** 317–318, 320, 321, *322*
Teresa of Avila, Saint **2:** 166, *168*, 259
Tetzel, Johann **2:** 153, *154*
Teutonic Knights **1:** 90–91
Theatines **2:** 166
theocracy **6:** 728
theology **1:** 56–57, 58
Torquemada, Tomás de **2:** 179–180
torture, and the Inquisition **2:** *176*, 177
transcendentalists **5:** 640–641
Trent, Council of (1545–1563) **2:** *163*, 167–169

ulema **6:** 729, 730, 731
Uniate Church **4:** 485
Unitarians **6:** 808
Ursulines **1:** 54 **2:** 166–167, 169
usury **1:** 44, 73

Verbiest, Ferdinand **4:** *529*
Vishnu **3:** 317

Waldenses **2:** 174–175
Waldo, Peter **2:** 175
Wartburg Castle, Luther's cell **2:** *157*
Western Schism *See* Great/Western Schism
Whitefield, George **4:** 550
Wilberforce, Samuel **5:** 700
witches **2:** 173, *179* **3:** 366
    witch trials **2:** 181–182, 274 **3:** 370
Wolsey, Thomas **2:** 208
Worms, Diet/council of (1521) **2:** 155, *156*, 188
Wovoka **6:** 839
Wycliffe, John **1:** 11 **2:** 164

Xavier, Francis **2:** 170, *171* **4:** 538–539

Young, Brigham **5:** 702

Zen Buddhism **1:** *125*, 127
Zinzendorf, Nikolaus Ludwig von **3:** 372
Zwingli, Huldrych **2:** 160–162

Volume numbers appear in **boldface type**. Page numbers in *italic type* refer to illustrations and captions.

TRADE and ECONOMY

accounting systems, and Luca Pacioli **1:** 45, 48
Agriculture Adjustment Act (1933) **7:** 967
American Federation of Labor **5:** *631*
American Railroad Union **6:** *814*
apprentices/apprenticeships **2:** 252 **4:** 518
arms industry
    in Europe (1600s) **4:** *454*
    in Britain (1800s) **5:** *618*
    and industrial development **6:** 794
Ascensius, Iodocus **1:** *66*
ASEAN (Association of South-East Asian
    Nations) **9:** 1217
Asia, Southeast, trading empire **3:** 319–321
asiento **4:** 467
Association of South-East Asian Nations
    (ASEAN) **9:** 1217
automobile industry **6:** 793 **7:** 949
    under Hitler **7:** *994*
    Korean **9:** *1213*

Baltimore and Ohio Railroad **5:** *649*
bananas, Central American **6:** *761*, 763 **7:** 973
Bank of England **4:** 444
banks **1:** 44, 48
    Fugger banking dynasty **1:** 46–47
Bessemer, Henry **6:** 788
Bessemer process **6:** *787*
bills of exchange **1:** 48
Blackbeard (pirate) **4:** *547*
bookbinding **1:** *33*
bookkeeping **1:** 45
Boston Tea Party **4:** 555
Boulder Dam **7:** 967
Bridgewater Canal **4:** *508*, 509

canals **4:** 508–509
CAP (Common Agricultural Policy) **9:** 1194, 1198
capitalism
    link with the Reformation **2:** 159
    emergence in Britain **5:** 618–619
    triumph (1980s) **9:** 1168
Carnegie, Andrew **5:** *631* **6:** *833*, 834
carpets, Persian **3:** *399*
carriages, steam **5:** *621*
Cartwright, Edmund **5:** 616
catalogs, shopping **6:** 789
chemical industry **6:** 794
chocolate **6:** *820*
Chrysler Corporation **7:** 949
CIO (Congress of Industrial Organizations) **7:** 970
cities and towns
    and development of European trade **1:** 16
    industrial (1800s) **5:** 612, 625–626
    redesigned (late 1800s) **5:** *655*
Civil Works Administration (CWA) **7:** 966–967
Civilian Conservation Corps **7:** 966
cloth
    trade in **1:** 114
    markets **2:** *253*
cloves **3:** 315, 316, 328, *329*
coal
    mining **4:** *509*, 510 **5:** 619, *701* **6:** *811*
    industry **5:** 619 **6:** 788
Coca-Cola **7:** *960* **9:** *1274*, 1277
cocaine **9:** 1208
cocoa **6:** *820*
cod, in colonial America **3:** *366*, 388–389, *390*
coffee **3:** 327, *391*
    Brazilian **6:** *757*
coins **1:** 42, 45, *73* **3:** *350*
collective rights **5:** 628
Comecon **9:** 1243, 1249
Common Agricultural Policy (CAP) **9:** 1194, 1198
Common Market, European **9:** 1190, 1194
Confucianism
    and trade **1:** 18, 40
    and modernization **1:** 66
Congress of Europe **8:** 1073
Congress of Industrial Organizations (CIO) **7:** 970
copper, African **1:** 114
corn **3:** 350
cotton **3:** 298
    mills **4:** *501* **5:** *618* **6:** *840*

gins **5:** *616*, 647
    and the Industrial Revolution **5:** 616, *617*, 619,
        622
    plantations **5:** 647, *654*, 677
    after slavery abolition (U.S.) **6:** 831
Council of Europe **8:** 1073–1074
coureurs de bois **3:** 360
Crystal Palace **5:** 615, 624, 634
customs barriers **1:** 42
CWA (Civil Works Administration) **7:** 966–967

Daewoo **9:** *1213*
Dawes, Charles **7:** 954
Dawes Plan (1924) **7:** 954
debt, international **9:** 1278
Denmark, trade (1600s) **4:** 445–446
department stores **6:** 789
Depression *See* Great Depression
dollar diplomacy **6:** 835
dyes, chemical **6:** 794

East India Company, British **3:** 330, 403, 418
    and the American colonies **4:** 555
    and India **5:** 667, 668, 669
East India Company, Dutch **3:** 326–327, 329–330,
        362, 403 **6:** 821
East India Company, French **3:** 330
East India Company, Swedish **3:** 330
East Indies, and the spice trade **2:** 222
economics, classical political **5:** 621
economy, Pacific Rim **9:** 1209–1220
ECSC (European Coal and Steel Community)
    9: 1191–1193
EEC (European Economic Community)
    9: *1192*, 1193–1196
encomienda system **3:** 350
Engineers, Amalgamated Society of **6:** *807*
engines, steam **4:** 509, 510 **5:** *619*
Erie Canal **5:** 649
EU *See* European Union
EURATOM (European Atomic Energy
    Community) **9:** *1192*, 1193
Europe, Congress of **8:** 1073
Europe, Council of **8:** 1073–1074
European Atomic Energy Community
    (EURATOM) **9:** *1192*, 1193
European Coal and Steel Community (ECSC)
    9: 1191–1193
European Economic Community (EEC) **9:** *1192*,
    1193–1196
European Space Agency **9:** *1192*
European Steel and Coal Community **8:** 1073
European Union (EU) **9:** 1197–1198
    flag **9:** *1189*
euro (currency) **9:** 1197

factories **5:** 616–617, 631
factors, for slave procurement **3:** 382
fairs, trading **1:** 40–41
Farm Security Administration (FSA) **7:** 968
Federal Emergency Relief Administration (FERA)
    7: 967
fertilizers
    from Chile **6:** 763–764
    chemical **6:** 794
film industry, in the 1920s **7:** *950*, 951
fisheries
    in colonial America **3:** *366*, 388–389
    EU quotas **9:** 1197–1198
Ford, Henry **7:** 949, 991
France, trade with Asia **3:** 330
French Company of the East Indies **3:** 330
Frick, Henry Clay **5:** *631*
Friedman, Milton **9:** 1167
Fugger dynasty **1:** 45, 46–47 **2:** *185*, 187
fur trade, in colonial America **3:** 360, 371, 374

Galbraith, J. K. **9:** 1159
Gates, Bill **9:** 1252
GATT (General Agreement on Tariffs and Trade)
    9: 1198
General Agreement on Tariffs and Trade (GATT)
    9: 1198
General Motors **7:** 949 **8:** *1081*
General Strike (1926) **7:** 958

Germany, peasant revolts (early 1500s) **2:** 156,
    246
globalization **9:** 1219, 1276–1277, 1282
gold
    African **1:** 115 **6:** 826
    European trade with West African gold **3:** 303,
        305
    from the Americas **3:** 348, *389*
    California gold rush **5:** *651*, 654 **6:** 837–840
    discovered in Australia **5:** 673
    Klondike Gold Rush **5:** 675
gold standard **7:** 965, 972–973
Great Depression **7:** 954, 958, 959–970 **8:** *1079*
    9: 1159
    and Latin America **7:** 974–975
    and Japan **8:** 1017–1018
Great Exhibition (1851) **5:** 615, 622, 624, 634
Great Reform Act (1832) **6:** 809, 810
Grimaldi family of Genoa **1:** 46
group rights **5:** 628
guilds **1:** 16, 43, *44* **4:** 518

halles **1:** 40
Hanseatic League **1:** 15, *16*, 24, 41, *42* **3:** 298
Heeren Seventeen **3:** *326*
Honda **9:** 1210
Hoover Dam **7:** 967
horses, in Africa **1:** 114
Hudson Bay Company **5:** 675
hyperinflation, German (1923) **7:** 953–954, 988

IMF (International Monetary Fund) **9:** 1220
incense **3:** 298, 315, *316*
India, European trade with **3:** 417
Industrial Revolution **5:** 609–612, 615–624
    laying the basis for **4:** 501, 510
    effects on women and children **5:** *617*, 629,
        631–634
    and India **5:** 668
industrialization
    after 1500 **1:** 33
    after the Industrial Revolution **5:** 625–634
    and Romanticism **5:** 637
    second wave of **6:** 787–796
    in Stalin's Soviet Union **7:** 926–927, 928, *929*,
        930
    in China **7:** 941
    effects on the natural world **9:** 1263
industries, nationalized post–World War II
    8: 1077, 1078, 1079 **9:** 1160
inflation, European (1500s) **1:** 36, 48
insurance, marine **1:** 73
International Monetary Fund (IMF) **9:** 1220
iron
    and the Industrial Revolution **5:** *618*, 619, 620
    and industrialization **6:** 788, *795*

Keynes, John Maynard **7:** 905, 953
kibbutzim **8:** *1136*
Klondike Gold Rush **5:** 675

laissez-faire **5:** 621, 628
lathes **5:** 618
Levitt, Bill **9:** 1170
loans, system of **1:** 45
looms, power looms **5:** 616, 618

market socialism, in China **9:** 1186–1187
markets **1:** 40, *94* **2:** *253*
Marshall, George C. **8:** 1072–1073, 1088–1089
Marshall Plan/Marshall Aid **8:** 1072–1073, 1074,
    1076, 1088–1089
mercantilism **4:** 550–552
merchant bankers **1:** 44
merchants **1:** 41, 44, 45, 73, *74*, 75
    Japanese **4:** 536 **6:** 778
    See also trade
Messerschmitt Company **8:** *1074*
Middle Passage **3:** 380–*381*
mills, cotton **4:** *501* **5:** *618*
mining
    in Europe **1:** *32*, 33
    silver **1:** *32* **3:** 348, 388
    salt **3:** 348
    See also coal

Volume numbers appear in **boldface type**. Page numbers in *italic type* refer to illustrations and captions.

Mitsubishi **6:** 781
molasses, British taxes on **4:** 554
Moluccas **3:** 315, 316, 324
  and the Dutch **3:** 327
  See also Spice Islands
Monnet, Jean **8:** 1073 **9:** 1190–1192
motorcycles, manufacture **9:** *1210*
Mutual Economic Assistance, Council for
  (Comecon) **9:** 1243, 1249

NAFTA (North American Free Trade Agreement)
  9: 1198
National Industrial Recovery Act (NIRA) **7:** 967
National Recovery Administration (NRA) **7:** *966,*
  967, 970
nationalization
  farming nationalized under Stalin **7:** 927–928
  post–World War II **8:** 1077, 1078, 1079 **9:** 1160
Netherlands, trade and empire in Asia **3:** *323,*
  324–330
New Deal **7:** 959, 966–970 **8:** 1079 **9:** 1160
  Second **7:** 967–970
New Economic Mechanism **9:** 1245
NIRA (National Industrial Recovery Act) **7:** 967
"no taxation without representation" **4:** 555
North America, colonial, trade with Britain
  4: 550–552
North American Free Trade Agreement (NAFTA)
  9: 1198
NRA (National Recovery Administration) **7:** *966,*
  967, 970
numerals, Arabic **1:** 48
nutmeg **3:** 316
nuts, from the Americas **3:** 396

open-hearth process **6:** 788
opium, trade in **4:** 532 **6:** 769–771
Organization for European Economic Cooperation
  (OEEC) **8:** 1073 **9:** 1190
Ottoman Turks, and trade **1:** 40, 104, *108* **3:** 298
Owen, Robert **5:** 619

Pacioli, Luca **1:** 45–48
paddle steamers **5:** *622*
papermaking **1:** 33, 60 **2:** 254
parchment **1:** *33*
peanuts **3:** 396
peons/peonage **3:** 350 **6:** 761–762 **7:** 972
pepper **3:** 298, 316
perestroika **8:** 1106
piracy **3:** 348 **4:** *547*
plantations **3:** 349, 387
  tea **4:** *531*
  cotton **5:** 647, *654,* 677
Portugal, trade with Japan **4:** 538
postal services **5:** 624 **6:** 793
power looms **5:** 616, 618
Public Works Administration (PWA) **7:** 967
Pullman Strike (U.S.) **6:** *814*
putting-out system **1:** 37, 77
PWA (Public Works Administration) **7:** 967

railroads
  and the Industrial Revolution **5:** 619–620, 622,
    623
  timetables **5:** 620
  tunnels **5:** *621*
  United States **5:** 622, *623, 649* **6:** *832,* 838
  Canadian transcontinental **5:** 675
  Russian **5:** *693,* 694–695
  Mexican **6:** 741–743
  South American **6:** 764, *765*
  European **6:** 790, 791
  Chinese **7:** *941*
Rapallo, Treaty of (1922) **7:** 953
REA (Rural Electrification Administration) **7:** 967
Reclamation, Bureau of **7:** 967
Reconstruction Finance Corporation **7:** 963–964
Reform Act (1832) **6:** 809, 810
Resettlement Administration **7:** 968
Rhodes, Cecil **6:** 826
rhubarb **3:** 298
robber barons **6:** 832, 834
Rockefeller, John D. **6:** 834
Rocket (steam locomotive) **5:** 620

Romans, traders in India **3:** 315
Rome, Treaty of (1957) **9:** *1192*
Royal African Company of London **3:** 381, 382
rubber **3:** 395
Rural Electrification Administration (REA) **7:** 967

Safavid empire, and trade **3:** 399, 403–404
salt
  trade in **1:** 112 **3:** 298, *299*
  cellars **3:** *301*
  mining **3:** 348
Sankey Canal **4:** 509
Schuman Plan **9:** *1191,* 1192
sea trade, Dutch (1500s/1600s) **2:** 222
Second New Deal **7:** 967–970
sharecropping **6:** 831
shells, cowrie **1:** 113
ships
  slave **3:** *375, 380–381*
  See also sea trade
shops, early modern European **1:** *73,* 77, *78*
Siemens, William **6:** 788
silk **3:** 298
  Iranian silk trade **3:** 403–404
  and the Depression in Japan **8:** 1017–1018
Silk Road **1:** 106
silver
  mining in Europe **1:** *32*
  from the Americas **3:** 348, *350,* 388
  European silver in China **4:** 524–525
Sketches of British Wealth (paintings) **5:** *617*
slave trade **5:** *678*
  Arab slave traders **3:** 375, *376* **6:** 818
  the triangular trade **3:** *379* **5:** 616
  across the Atlantic **3:** 380–384 **5:** 616
    6: 817–818
  contraband slaves **5:** 684
  banned **6:** 819
slaves/slavery
  early European slavery (1400s/1500s) **3:** 305,
    308, 376–377
  for the Dutch in Asia **3:** 327, 328 **6:** 818
  in the American colonies **3:** 348–349, 350–351,
    354, 356, 373, 377–386
  in the New World **3:** 375–386, 384–385
  roots **3:** 376
  in the United States **5:** 647, 654, *678*
  abolition in the United States **5:** 651–652, 654,
    682, *683* **6:** 830, 831
  and the American Civil War **5:** 677, 682
Smith, Adam **5:** 621–624
soda ash **6:** 794
Sons of Liberty **4:** 555
Sony **9:** 1210, *1211, 1212, 1217*
Spice Islands **3:** 316, *329*
  search for a sea route to **1:** 41 **3:** 308–312, 316,
    324
  See also spice trade
spice trade **2:** 222 **3:** 298, *299,* 316
  and Portugal **1:** 41 **3:** 324
  and world exploration **3:** 303–304
  and the Dutch **3:** 327
  See also Spice Islands
spinning **1:** 76
  mechanized **5:** *617,* 618
Srivijaya, trading empire **3:** 319–321
Stamp Act (1765) **4:** 555
Standard Oil Company **6:** 832
steam engines *See* engines, steam
steamboats **5:** 622, *648,* 649
steel
  exported to the East **3:** 298
  and industrialization **6:** 787, 788, *795, 796*
  "factories" in China (1950s) **9:** 1183
Stourbridge Lion (locomotive) **5:** *623*
strike(s)
  right to **6:** 809
  Pullman Strike (U.S.) **6:** *814*
Suez Canal **6:** 821, 825
  opening of **5:** 670 **6:** *823*
  and World War I **7:** 887
sugar **3:** 349, 390
  and the slave trade **3:** 377, *378*
Sugar Act (1764) **4:** 554
Sweden, trade with Asia (1700s) **3:** 330

taxes
  in early modern Europe **1:** *39*
  imposed on the American colonies by Britain
    4: 554–555
  on salt in India **8:** 1110
tea **3:** 330 **4:** 522
  plantation in China **4:** *531*
  taxes imposed on American colonies by Britain
    4: 554
  plantation in Sri Lanka **5:** *670*
Tennessee Valley Authority (TVA) **7:** 967
tolls **1:** 42
towns *See* cities and towns
Toyota **9:** 1211
trade
  Dutch (1500s/1600s) **1:** 15 **2:** 222–223
  in early modern Europe **1:** 15, 39–48, 73
  European trade with the East **1:** 15 **3:** 298, 417
    4: 524–525, 532
  and the spread of Protestantism **2:** 159–160
  during the reign of Henry II **2:** 206
  triangular **3:** *379* **5:** 616
  free trade and Enlightenment thought **4:** *479,*
    480
  mercantilism and the American colonies
    4: 550–552
  Latin American trade after World War I
    7: 971–973
  See also fairs; Hanseatic League; markets;
    merchants
trade associations **4:** 518
Trades Union Council **7:** 958
tramways **6:** 791
triangular trade **3:** *379* **5:** 616
trusts, in the United States **6:** 832, 836
tunnels **5:** *621*
TVA (Tennessee Valley Authority) **7:** 967
Tweed, William Marcy "Boss" **6:** 836

Unequal Treaties (1858) **4:** 541–542
unions, labor
  after the Industrial Revolution **5:** 628, 631, 634
  in the United States **5:** 631 **6:** *814,* 833 **7:** 970
  and the rise of socialism **6:** 807, 809, *814*
  and the British general strike **7:** *957,* 958
  Solidarity in Poland **8:** 1105–1106 **9:** 1244,
    1245
United Fruit Company **7:** 973 **9:** 1201
United States Steel Corporation **6:** 832

Walesa, Lech **8:** 1106 **9:** 1244, 1245
Wall Street Crash (1929) **7:** 961–963
War Mobilization, Office of **8:** 1064
War Production Board **8:** 1064
Watt, James **5:** *619*
Wealth of Nations, The (Adam Smith) **5:** 621–624
weaving **1:** 76, 77
  mechanized **5:** 616
Wedgwood, Josiah **5:** 620–621
Westerners, the **6:** 772, 776
wheat **3:** 350
Whitney, Eli **5:** 647
wool
  woolen industry **1:** 35, *76* **2:** 206
  trade **1:** 40
  and the putting-out system **1:** 77
Works Progress Administration (*also* Works
  Projects Administration; 1935) **7:** *967,* 970
World Bank, and African economies **9:** 1230
World Trade Organization (WTO) **9:** 1198
World War II, postwar recovery in the West
  8: 1071–1082
WTO (World Trade Organization) **9:** 1198

Yamaha **9:** 1210
Young, Owen D. **7:** 954
Young Plan (1929) **7:** 954

zaibatsu **6:** 781

Volume numbers appear in **boldface type**. Page numbers in *italic type* refer to illustrations and captions.

WARS and BATTLES

Aboukir, Battle of (1799) **5:** 596
Acre, Battle of (1796) **5:** 596
Afghan War (1978–1992), and the Soviets
  8: 1102–1104 **9:** 1241
African-Americans
  and World War II **8:** 1064–1066
  and desegregation of the U.S. armed forces
    8: 1081
aircraft
  World War I **7:** 890, 891
  World War II **8:** 1047, 1048, 1055
  development (1900s) **9:** *1192*, 1254–1255
  European fighter **9:** *1192*
airships, World War I **7:** 891, 893
Alamo, Battle of the (1836) **6:** 738
Algerian War of Independence (1954–1962)
  8: 1126–1127
Allerheim, Battle of (1645) **2:** 233
Allied Intervention, War of *See* Russian Civil War
  (1918–1920)
Allies, in World War I **7:** 887
Amasya, Treaty of (1555) **3:** 400
American Civil War (1861–1865) **5:** 647, 677–686
  6: 794
  Reconstruction after **6:** 829–831
  photography in **6:** 843
American Revolutionary War **4:** 553–562 **5:** 674
  6: 748
  and the Dutch **4:** 442, 558
Anderson, Robert **5:** 678
Antietam, Battle of (1862) **5:** 681–682
Antwerp, "Fury of" **2:** 219
Appomattox Courthouse **5:** 686
Armada, Spanish, sails against England (1588)
  2: 194, 213–214, 221
arms race
  East–West **8:** 1091–1092, 1096, 1102
  between India and Pakistan **8:** *1116*
Army of the Republic of Vietnam (ARVN)
  8: 1100
army/armies
  early modern European **1:** 26–27, 72–73, 76
  and the feudal system **1:** 27, 72
  under Louis XIV of France **4:** 454, 456
  European armies (1690s) **4:** 461
  of the American Revolutionary War **4:** 556–557,
    560
  See also mercenaries; warfare
arquebus **1:** 26, *27*
artillery
  growth in the use of (1400s) **1:** 26
  and industrialization **6:** 794
  World War I **7:** *886*, 888–889, 892, 893
ARVN (Army of the Republic of Vietnam)
  8: 1100
Atlantic, Battle of the **8:** 1041–1042
Augsburg, Peace of (1555) **2:** 156, 192, *193*, 225,
  229
Austerlitz, Battle of (1805) **5:** 599
Austrian Succession, War of the (1740–1748)
  4: 469, 488, 547
  American phase *See* King George's War
Ayacucho, Battle of (1824) **6:** *754*, 755

B-2 stealth bombers **9:** *1255*
Bairam Khan **3:** 410
Barbarossa, Operation (1941) **8:** 1043–1044
Bastille, storming of the (1789) **5:** *587*, 588
battleships, dreadnought class **7:** *871*, 875, 876,
  893
Bavarian Succession, War of the (1778–1779)
  4: 469
Bay of Pigs invasion (1961) **8:** 1096 **9:** 1173,
  1203
bayonets **4:** 461
Berlin, Treaty of (1878) **6:** 734
Blenheim, Battle of (1704) **4:** 465
blitzkrieg **8:** 1038
Boer Wars **5:** 701
  Second Boer War (1899–1902) **5:** 676
  6: 826–827 **7:** 874
bombs
  incendiary **8:** 1055–1056, *1057*

World War II **8:** 1055–1056, *1057*, 1059, 1060,
  1062–1063, 1086
  atomic/fission **8:** 1059, 1060, 1086, *1089*, 1091
    9: 1186, 1253, 1255
  nuclear tests at Bikini Atoll **8:** 1087
  hydrogen/fusion bombs **8:** 1091 **9:** 1255
bonus army **7:** *964*, 965
Borodino, Battle of (1812) **5:** 604
Boston Massacre (1770) **4:** *554*, 555
Bosworth Field, Battle of (1485) **1:** 23 **2:** 205
Boxer Rebellion (1900) **5:** 696 **6:** 774–775
Boyne, Battle of the (1690) **2:** 244 **4:** 445
Braddock, Edward **4:** 548
Brady, Mathew **6:** 843
Brandywine Creek, Battle of (1777) **4:** 558
Breitenfeld, Battle of (1631) **2:** 231
Breitenfeld, Battle of (1642) **2:** 233
Brest-Litovsk, Treaty of (1918) **7:** 919
Britain, Battle of (1940–1941) **8:** 1038, *1040*,
  1047 **9:** 1255
Broz, Josip (Marshal Tito) **8:** *1069*, 1070
Brusilov Offensive **7:** 895
Buena Vista, Battle of (1847) **6:** 739
Bulge, Battle of the (1944–1945) **8:** 1048
Bull Run, Second Battle of (1862) **5:** 681, *682*
Bunker Hill, Battle of (1775) **4:** 556
Burgoyne, Sir John **4:** 558, *559*

Çesme, Battle of (1770) **6:** 730
Calatafami, Battle of (1859) **5:** *660*
Cambrai, Battle of (1917) **7:** 893
Camden, Battle of (1780) **4:** 561
Camp Life in the Thirty Years' War (lithograph)
  2: *234*
Campo Formio, Treaty of (1797) **5:** 596
cavalry **4:** *466*
Central Powers, in World War I **7:** 887
Chaco War (1932–1935) **7:** 978–979
Chaldiran, Battle of (1514) **1:** 105 **3:** 399
Chancellorsville, Battle of (1863) **5:** 683
Charles, duke of Mayenne **2:** *198*, 199
Chausa, Battle of (1539) **1:** 130
Chinese Civil War (1945–1949) **7:** 944
Churchill, John, duke of Marlborough **4:** 465
Civil War, American *See* American Civil War
Civil War, English *See* English Civil War
Civil War, Russian *See* Russian Civil War
Civil War, Spanish *See* Spanish Civil War
clothing, during World War I **7:** 893, *894*
Cold War **8:** 1044, 1083 **9:** 1190, 1255
  (1945–1960) **8:** 1083–1094, 1135
  and NATO **8:** *1084*, 1090, 1095, 1102, 1106
  and the Warsaw Pact **8:** *1084*, 1090, 1093–1094,
    1095, 1102
  (1960–1989) **8:** 1095–1106
  and European colonies **8:** 1119
  and China **9:** 1181
  and Latin America **9:** 1200–1201
  and independent African countries **9:** 1222,
    1226–1227
  and Iran **9:** 1233
Common Sense (Tom Paine) **4:** 557
concentration camps **8:** *1062*, 1067
Concord, Battle of *See* Lexington and Concord,
  Battle of
Condor Legion **8:** 1032, 1033
condottiere **1:** 26
Continental Army **4:** 556–557, *560*
Coral Sea, Battle of the (1942) **8:** 1052–1053
Cornwallis, Charles **4:** 561
Cowpens, Battle of (1781) **4:** 561
Crécy, Battle of (1346) **1:** 15
Crespy, Truce of (1544) **2:** 190
Crimean War (1853–1856) **5:** 657, *662*, 689, 692
  6: 733 **7:** 871
Cromwell, Oliver **2:** 240, 241–242
Cromwell, Richard **2:** 242
crossbows **1:** 15, 26
Crusades **1:** 16, 90, *101*, 102 **2:** 174 **3:** 297
Culloden, Battle of (1746) **4:** *443*
Custer, George **6:** *835*, 839

D-Day landings (1944) **8:** *1047*, 1048
Davout, Marshal **5:** 600
Deerfield, massacre at (1704) **3:** 368

Desert Campaign (1879–1880) **6:** 764
Desert Rats **8:** *1045*
détente **8:** 1102 **9:** 1166
Dien Bien Phu, Battle of (1954) **8:** *1122*, 1123
Downs, Battle of the (1639) **2:** *232*, 233
Dreadnought (ship) **7:** *875*, 876
dreadnought battleships **7:** *871*, 875, 876, 893
Drogheda, storming of **2:** 241
Dual Alliance **7:** 881
Dundee, John Graham of Claverhouse, 1st
  Viscount **4:** 444
Dunkirk, evacuation from **8:** 1038, *1039*
Dutch Revolt (Revolt of the Netherlands) *See*
  Eighty Years' War
Dutch War (1672–1679) **4:** 447

Easter Rising **7:** 905
Eighty Years' War (Revolt of the Netherlands;
  1568–1648) **1:** 44 **2:** 172, 215–224 **4:** 440
Eisenhower, Dwight D., and World War II **8:** *1047*
El Alamein, Battle of (1942) **8:** 1045
England, Hundred Years' War (1338–1453) **1:** 8,
  13, 14–15
English Civil War (1642–1649) **2:** 235–244
  and the Enlightenment **4:** 472
Enola Gay (aircraft) **8:** 1059
Eugene, prince of Savoy **4:** 465

Fairfax, Thomas **2:** 240
Falkenhayn, Erich von **7:** 894
Falklands War (1982) **9:** 1206
Farnese, Cardinal **2:** 203
Fifth Coalition, War of the (1809) **5:** 601
firearms
  arquebus **1:** 26, *27*
  flintlock muskets **4:** 461, *466*
  pistols **4:** *462*
First Balkan War (1912) **7:** 876, 879
First Indochina War (1946–1954; French-
  Vietnamese War) **8:** 1123
First World War *See* World War I
Flodden, Battle of (1513) **2:** 214
FNLA (National Front for the Liberation of
  Angola) **8:** 1099–1102 **9:** 1227
Fort Duquesne **4:** 548
Fort Necessity, Battle of (1754) **4:** 548
Fort Sumter, Battle of (1861) **5:** 677–678
Fort William Henry, Battle of (1757) **4:** 548
Fourteen Points **7:** 902–903, 906 **8:** 1024
  and China **7:** 934–935
  and India **8:** 1108
Fourth Coalition, War of the (1806–1807)
  Battle of Friedland **5:** 600
  Battle of Jena and Auerstädt **5:** 600
Franco-Dutch War (1672–1679) **4:** 441, 457, 462
Franco-Prussian War (1870–1871) **5:** 662–663,
  664 **6:** 794 **7:** 871, 892 **8:** 1026
Fredericksburg, Battle of (1862) **5:** 682
French, Sir John **7:** 888
French-Vietnamese War (1946–1954) **8:** 1123
French and Indian War (1754–1763) **3:** 368, 373,
  374 **4:** *546*, 548–549, 552 **5:** 674
French Revolutionary Wars (1792–1802) **5:** 592,
  595–596
Friedland, Battle of (1807) **5:** 600
Fronde, the **4:** 455, *456*

Gage, Thomas **4:** 556
Gallipoli campaign (1916) **7:** *885*, 890
gas, poison **7:** 888
gas masks **7:** 888
Gates, Horatio **4:** 558
gazis **1:** 99–100
Geneva Convention (1864) **5:** 663
Germantown, Battle of (1777) **4:** 558
Geronimo **6:** 839
Gettysburg, Battle of (1863) **5:** 683, *686*
Ghent, Pacification of (1576) **2:** 219
ghulams **3:** 403
Goeben (ship) **7:** 875
Gordon, Charles G. **6:** 824, 825
Grand Armée of Napoleon **5:** 598–599, *603*, 604
Grant, Ulysses S. **5:** *681*, 682, 685–*686*
Gravelines, Battle of (1558) **2:** 212
Graves, Robert **7:** 895

Volume numbers appear in **boldface type**. Page numbers in *italic type* refer to illustrations and captions.

Great Fear **5:** 588
Great Northern War (1700–1721) **4:** 447
Great War, as a name for World War I **7:** 873, 883
Greene, Nathanael **4:** 561
Grünwald, Battle of (1410) **1:** 91
Guadalcanal, battles for (1942) **8:** 1053–1054
Guildford Court House, Battle of (1781) **4:** 561
Guise brothers **2:** *198*, 199, 200, 201
Gulf War (1991) **9:** *1279*
  helicopters **9:** 1255
  burning oil wells **9:** *1273*
gunboat diplomacy **7:** 875
gunpowder **1:** 15, 26, 66 **4:** *470*
Gustav Adolph (Gustavus Adolphus), king of
  Sweden **2:** *225*, 228, 230, 231

Haarlem, siege of (1573) **2:** 219
Haig, Douglas **7:** 894
Hamburg, Treaty of (1641) **2:** 233
"Haw-Haw, Lord" (William Joyce) **8:** 1068
helicopters, military **9:** *1254*, 1255
Henry I of Lorraine, duke of Guise **2:** *198*
Hessians **4:** 558
Holy League **1:** 108
Homer, Winslow **6:** 842–843
Howe, William **4:** 556–557, 558
Hundred Years' War (1338–1453) **1:** 8, *13*, 14–15,
  23
Hung Hsiu-ch'uan **6:** 771, 772
hussars **4:** *466*

Independence, War of (Greek) **5:** *611*
Indian Mutiny **5:** 668–669
Indo-Pakistan wars **8:** 1114
Indochina War
  Second *See* Vietnam War
  First (1946–1954; French-Vietnamese War)
    8: 1123
Iran-Iraq War (1980–1988) **9:** 1235
Iron Cross **8:** *1066*
Iwo Jima, Battle of (1945) **8:** *1049*, 1055, *1057*,
  1060

Jackson, Thomas "Stonewall" **5:** 680, *681*
Jacobins **5:** 590–592
Jankov, Battle of (1645) **2:** 233
Japanese-Americans, and World War II **8:** *1065*,
  1066
Jarnac, Battle of (1569) **2:** 201
Jena-Auerstädt, Battle of (1806) **5:** 600
Jenkins's Ear, War of **4:** 469
Joyce, William ("Lord Haw-Haw") **8:** 1068
June Days (1848) **5:** 656
Jutland, Battle of (1916) **7:** 876, *891*

kamikaze attacks **8:** *1058*–1060
Khmelnytsky, Bohdan **4:** 485
Khmer Rouge **8:** 1099 **9:** 1281
Killiekrankie, Battle of (1689) **4:** 444
King George's War (1744–1748) **4:** 546–548
King Philip's War (1675) **3:** *368* **4:** *543*, 544
King William's War (1689–1697) **4:** 545–546
King's Mountain, Battle of (1780) **4:** 561
Kitchener, Horatio, 1st earl Kitchener **6:** 826
Korean War (1950–1953) **7:** 944 **8:** 1081, *1092*,
  1093 **9:** 1171, 1181–1182, 1209, 1212
Köse Dagh, Battle of (1243) **1:** 99
Kosovo, Battle of (1389) **1:** 101
Krueger, Walter **8:** 1056
Küçük-Kainardji, Treaty of (1774) **6:** 730, 733
Kursk, Battle of (1943) **8:** 1045

Lafayette, marquis de **4:** *560*, 561
Lawrence, T. E. (Lawrence of Arabia) **7:** 890
Lee, Robert E. **5:** 681, 682–683, 686
Leiden, siege of (1574) **2:** 219
Leipzig, Battle of (1813) **5:** 604
lend-lease, and the United States **8:** 1038–1041
Lepanto, Battle of (1571) **1:** 108 **2:** 194
Lexington, USS **8:** *1053*
Lexington and Concord, Battle of (1775) **4:** 556,
  557
  and Paul Revere **4:** *554*
Leyte Gulf, Battle of (1944) **8:** 1057, 1058–1060
Liberty ships **8:** *1064*

Little Bighorn, Battle of (1876) **6:** *835*, 839
London, Treaty of (1839) **7:** 882
longbows **1:** 15, 26
Louis, cardinal of Lorraine **2:** *198*, 199
Louisbourg, Battle of (1745) **4:** 547–548
Lübeck, Treaty of (1628) **2:** 229
Luftwaffe **8:** 1038, 1048
Lusitania (ship) **7:** 894, 895
Lützen, Battle of (1632) **2:** *225*, 228, 231

MacArthur, Douglas **8:** 1051, 1054
McClellan, George **5:** 681
machine guns **7:** 892
  Maxim **7:** *886*
Magdeburg, destruction of **2:** 230
Mahdi **6:** 825, 826
Mahmud (Afghan ruler) **3:** *397*, 405
Malplaquet, Battle of (1709) **4:** *461*, 466
Manhattan Project **8:** 1059 **9:** 1255
maps
  major battles of the Thirty Years' War **2:** *227*
  England in the Civil War **2:** *240*
Marengo, Battle of (1800) **5:** 596
Marlborough, John Churchill, 1st duke of **4:** 465
Marne, Battle of the (1914) **7:** 884
Marston Moor, Battle of (1644) **2:** *240*
Marxist People's Movement for the Liberation of
  Angola (MPLA) **8:** 1099 **9:** 1227
Maxim machine guns **7:** *886*
mercenaries **1:** 14, 72 **4:** *467*, 470
  condottiere **1:** 26
Mexican Revolution (1910–1920) **6:** 742, 743–746
  and the railroads **6:** *737*
Midway, Battle of (1942) **8:** 1052, 1053
Minutemen **4:** 556, *557*
missiles
  and the Cold War **8:** *1083*, 1094, 1096, *1102*
  intercontinental ballistic **8:** 1094
Missouri, USS **8:** *1060*
Mobile Bay, Battle of (1864) **5:** 685
Mohács, Battle of (1526) **1:** 93, 107
Molotov-Ribbentrop Pact (1939) **8:** *1035*, 1036
Moltke, Helmuth von **5:** 661, 663 **6:** 731, 791
  7: 880
Mongols, defeated by the Chinese (1696) **4:** 527
Monmouth, James, duke of **2:** 244
Montcalm, Louis Joseph, marquis de **4:** 548–549
Montcontour, Battle of (1569) **2:** 201
MPLA (Marxist People's Movement for the
  Liberation of Angola) **8:** 1099 **9:** 1227
Mühlberg, Battle of (1547) **2:** 156, 190
mujahideen **8:** 1103 **9:** *1231*, 1241
Mukden, Battle of (1905) **5:** 696 **6:** 783
Münster, Treaty of (1648) **2:** *233*
Murrow, Edward **8:** 1068
Murten, Battle of (1476) **1:** 26
muskets, flintlock **4:** *461*, *466*

Nanking, Treaty of (1842) **6:** 771
Nantes, Edict of (1598) **2:** *196*, 204 **4:** 451
  revoked by Louis XIV (1685) **4:** 459
Napoleonic Wars **5:** 599, 600, 601, 604, 646
  6: 794
  and Russia **5:** 604, 688
  relative peace following **7:** 871
National Front for the Liberation of Angola
  (FNLA) **8:** 1099–1102 **9:** 1227
National Union for the Total Independence of
  Angola (UNITA) **8:** 1102 **9:** 1227–1228
Nations, Battle of the (1813) **5:** 604
NATO **8:** *1084*, 1090, 1095, 1102
  former Warsaw Pact countries in **8:** 1106
  9: 1245
Navarino, Battle of (1827) **6:** 732
Nelson, Horatio **5:** 596, *599*
Neuilly, Treaty of (1919) **7:** 903
New Mexico, USS **8:** *1054*
New Model Army **2:** 240, 241
Nijmegen, Battle of (1585) **2:** *221*
Nimitz, Chester **8:** 1054, 1056
Nine Years' War (1689–1698) **4:** 457
Nördlingen, Battle of (1634) **2:** 231
North America, colonial, wars and conflicts
  4: 543–552, 553–562
Northern War (1655–1660) **4:** 446

nuclear weapons, tests **8:** 1087 **9:** *1253*, 1271
Nuremberg, war trials **8:** 1070

OAS (Organisation Armée Secrète) **8:** 1127
Omdurman, Battle of (1898) **6:** 825–826
O'Neill, Hugh **2:** 214
Opium Wars (1839–1842; 1856–60) **4:** 541
Oquendo, Antonio de **2:** *232*
Organisation Armée Secrète (OAS) **8:** 1127
Ottoman Turks
  besieging Vienna (1529) **1:** 93, 107 **2:** 188
    3: *297*, 298
  conflict with the Safavid empire **1:** 105
    3: 399–400, 405, 406 **6:** 729
  encroaching on Europe (c. 1559) **2:** 193–194
  besieging Vienna (1683) **4:** 485 **6:** 729
Oxenstierna, Axel **2:** 231

Paine, Tom, *Common Sense* **4:** 557
Paraguayan War (1865–1870) **6:** 764
Paris gun **7:** *893*
Paris, siege of (1590) **2:** 204
Paris, Treaty of (1763) **4:** 549, 553
Paris Peace Conference **7:** 903–905
Pasha, Mehmed **7:** *877*
Passchendaele campaign (1917; Battle of Ypres)
  7: *883*, 895
Pavia, Battle of (1524) **2:** 189
Pequot War (1637) **4:** 544
Pétain, Henri **7:** 895
Petersburgh, Battle of (1864–1865) **5:** 685–686
Philippine Sea, Battle of (1944) **8:** 1056
Phips, Sir William **4:** 546
pikes **1:** 26
Pilsudski, Józef **7:** 920
Plassey, Battle of (1757) **3:** 418 **5:** 667
Polaris (missile) **8:** 1096
Polish Succession, War of the (1733-1738) **4:** 468
Polish-Soviet War (1919–1920) **7:** 920
Pondicherry, Battle of (1761) **3:** 418 **5:** 667
Pontiac (North American chief) **4:** 553
Port Arthur, Battle of (1904; Russian–Japanese
  War) **5:** *695*, 696 **6:** 783, *786*
"Potato War" **4:** 469
Potsdam Conference (1945) **8:** 1085–1086, 1089
Powers, Gary **8:** 1095, *1096*
propaganda
  during World War I **7:** 901–902, 918
  during World War II **8:** *1042*, *1043*, *1053*, 1060,
    1066–1067
Pyramids, Battle of the (1798) **5:** 596

Queen Anne's War (1702–1713) **4:** 546

Race to the Sea (World War I) **7:** 884
Rastadt, Treaty of (1714) **4:** 467
Red Army (Chinese) **9:** *1179*
Red Army (Soviet)
  and the Russian Civil War **7:** *912*, 919, 920, 921
    8: 1084
  and World War II **8:** 1044, 1045, 1060
Red Baron **7:** 891
Redoubtable (ship) **5:** 599
Religion, Wars of (1562–1598) **1:** 31 **2:** 161, 172,
  195–204 **4:** 450
  and Philip II **2:** 194
  ended with the Edict of Nantes **2:** *196*, 204
    4: 451
resistance fighters, World War II **8:** *1068*, 1069
Revere, Paul **4:** *554*
Revolt of the Netherlands *See* Eighty Years' War
Richmond, Battle of (1865) **5:** *685*, 686
Richthofen, Manfred von **7:** 891
Roses, Wars of the (1455–1485) **1:** 23 **2:** 205
Russian Civil War (1918–1920) **7:** 919–920
  8: 1084, 1085
Russian-Japanese War (1904–1905) **5:** *695*, 696
  6: 782–783, *786* **7:** 888 **8:** 1015
Russo-Swedish War (1788–1790) **4:** 446, 448

Sadowa, Battle of (1866) **5:** 661, 662
St. Bartholemew's Day Massacre **2:** *199*, *200*,
  201–202, 219
Saint Germain, Treaty of (1570) **2:** 201
Saint Germain, Treaty of (1919) **7:** 903

Volume numbers appear in **boldface type**. Page numbers in *italic type* refer to illustrations and captions.

SALT (Strategic Arms Limitation Treaty) **8:** 1102, *1103*
San Jacinto, Battle of (1836) **6:** 738
Saratoga, Battle of (1777) **4:** 558, *559*
Savannah, Battle of (1778) **4:** 559
Savannah, Battle of (1864) **5:** 685
Schlieffen, Alfred von **7:** 881
Schlieffen Plan **7:** 880–882, 884
Schmalkaldic League **1:** 47 **2:** 156, 188, 190
Scott, Winfield **6:** *739*
Second Balkan War (1913) **7:** 879
Second Coalition, War of the (1798–1800) **5:** 596
Second Indochina War *See* Vietnam War
Second World War *See* World War II
Sedan, Battle of (1870) **5:** 664, *665*
Sekigehara, Battle of (1600) **4:** 533
Selective Service Act (1940) **8:** 1040, 1063
sepoys **5:** 668–669
Sevastopol, Battle of (1854–1855; Crimean War) **5:** *689*
Seven Days' Battles (1862) **5:** 681
Seven Weeks' War (1866) **5:** 661
Seven Years' War (1756–1763) **4:** 469, 489, 548
    American involvement *See* French and Indian War in India **3:** 418
Sèvres, Treaty of (1920) **7:** 903, 908 **8:** 1023
shell shock **7:** 889
Sherman, William T. **5:** *681*, 685
Shiloh, Battle of (1862) **5:** 682
Shimonoseki, Treaty of (1895) **6:** 772, 782
Sino-Japanese War (1894–1895) **6:** 772, 782
Sino-Japanese War (1937–1945) **7:** 942–943 **8:** 1019, 1025, 1034
Six-Day War (1967) **8:** 1133–1134, *1136* **9:** 1279
Sixth Coalition, War of the (1813-1815) **5:** 604
Slim, William **8:** 1058
soldiers, mercenaries **1:** 14 **4:** *467*, 470
Solferino, Battle of (1859) **5:** 659, 663
Somme, Battle of the (1916) **7:** *891*, 894
Spanish Civil War (1936–1939) **8:** 1032–1033
    and Germany/Italy **8:** 1031, 1032
Spanish Succession, War of the (1701–1714) **4:** *461*, 463–470
    in North America *See* Queen Anne's War
Spanish-American War (1898) **6:** 766, 835
Spotsylvania, Battle of (1864) **5:** 685
stealth bombers **9:** *1255*
Steuben, Friedrich von **4:** 559
Stilwell, Joseph **8:** 1058
Strategic Arms Limitation Treaty (SALT) **8:** 1102, *1103*
submarines
    World War I U-boats **7:** 890, 893, *894*, 895
    World War II **8:** 1054–1055
    and the Cold War **8:** 1096
    and nuclear missiles **9:** *1254*
Sucre, Antonio José de **6:** 752–753, 754–755
Süleyman I, "the Magnificent" **2:** 190 **3:** 297
Swiss Guards **1:** 26
swords **4:** *470*

Taiping Rebellion (1850s and 1860s) **6:** 771–772, 784
tanks
    World War I **7:** 888, *892*, 893
    World War II **8:** *1043*
    Soviet **8:** *1103*
Tannenberg, Battle of (1410) **1:** 91
Tannenberg, Battle of (1914) **7:** 884
Tarawa, Battle of (1943) **8:** 1054, *1055*
Tennessee, USS **8:** *1051*
Tet offensive **8:** 1100–1101
Teutonic Knights **1:** 90–91
Third Coalition, War of the (1805) **5:** 599
    Battle of Trafalgar **5:** 598, *599*
Thirteen Years' War (1454–1466) **1:** 91
Thirty Years' War (1618–1648) **1:** 95, 98 **2:** 172, 193, 225–234 **4:** 452, 461
    end *See* Westphalia, Peace of (1648)
    and France **2:** 232, 233 **4:** 453, 455
    and potatoes **3:** 392
    and Sweden **4:** 446
Three Henries, War of the (1585–1589) **2:** 203
Tilly, Johann t'Serclaes, baron **2:** 228–229, 231
Tilsit, Treaty of (1807) **5:** 600, 601

Tito (Josip Broz) **8:** *1069*, 1070
"Tokyo Rose" **8:** 1068
Toussaint-Louverture, Pierre Dominique **3:** 386
Trafalgar, Battle of (1805) **5:** 598, *599*
trench warfare, in World War I **7:** 888, 889–890
Trenton, Battle of (1776) **4:** *553*, 558
Trianon, Treaty of (1920) **7:** 903
Triple Alliance, War of the (1865–1870) **6:** 764
Tromp, Maarten **2:** *232*
t'Serclaes, Johan, baron Tilly **2:** 228–229, 231
Tsushima, Battle of (1905) **6:** 783
Turks, Ottoman *See* Ottoman Turks

U-boats
    World War I **7:** 890, 893, *894*, 895
    World War II **8:** *1040*, 1041
UNITA (National Union for the Total Independence of Angola) **8:** 1102 **9:** 1227–1228
United Nations **8:** 1070 **9:** 1198, 1280
    Relief and Rehabilitation Administration (UNRRA) **8:** 1071–1072, 1073
    and the Korean War **8:** 1093
    and the Suez Crisis **8:** 1133, 1135
    and China **9:** 1186
UNRRA (United Nations Relief and Rehabilitation Administration) **8:** 1071–1072, 1073
Utrecht, Treaty of (1713) **4:** 467, 546

V-2 rockets **8:** 1063 **9:** *1255*
Valmy, Battle of **5:** 592
Varna, Battle of (1444) **1:** 102
Versailles, Treaty of (1919) **7:** 903–905, *906*, *907*, 908, 934–935, 952, 953, 988, 993 **8:** 1026–1027
    and the League of Nations **7:** 903, 945–946 **8:** 1028
    "war guilt" clause **8:** 1027
    German contradiction of **8:** 1030–1031
Vicksburg, Battle of (1863) **5:** 683
Victory (ship) **5:** *599*
Victory in Europe (VE) **8:** 1084
Viet Cong movement **8:** 1099, 1100, 1123–1124
Vietnam War (1962–1975) **8:** 1099, 1100–1101, 1124 **9:** *1162*, 1163, 1172, 1177
    televised **9:** 1171
    U.S. bases in Southeast Asia **9:** 1217
    helicopters **9:** 1255

Wallenstein (Albrecht of Valstejn) **2:** *225*, 229, 231
Wandiwash, Battle of (1760) **3:** 418
war bonds **8:** 1068
War Mobilization, Office of **8:** 1064
War of 1812 **5:** 646
    and the United States **5:** 646–647
War Powers Act (1941) **8:** 1063
War Production Board **8:** 1064
warfare
    European (1400s/1500s) **1:** 26–27
    See also army/armies; artillery; firearms
Warsaw Pact **8:** *1084*, 1090, 1093–1094, 1095, 1102 **9:** 1243
    dissolution **8:** 1106
Washington, George
    and the French and Indian War **4:** 548
    and the American Revolutionary War **4:** *553*, 556, 557–558, *560*
Waterloo, Battle of (1815) **5:** 604
Welles, Gideon **5:** 679
Wellesley, Arthur *See* Wellington, Arthur Wellesley, duke of
Wellington, Arthur Wellesley, duke of **5:** 602, *604*
West Virginia, USS **8:** *1051*
Westphalia, Peace of (1648) **2:** 172, 233–234
White Mountain, Battle of the (1620) **2:** *226*, 227
Wolfe, James **4:** 549
Women's Land Army **8:** 1064
World War I **7:** 883–896, 983
    events leading to **6:** 734, 736 **7:** 871–882
    and Latin America **6:** 766
    and socialism **6:** 816
    Battle of Jutland (1916) **7:** 876, *891*

Schlieffen Plan **7:** 880–882, 884
Battle of Ypres (1917; Passchendaele campaign) **7:** *883*, 895
Battle of the Marne (1914) **7:** 884
Battle of Tannenberg (1914) **7:** 884
Gallipoli campaign (1916) **7:** *885*, 890
weapons **7:** *886*, 888–889, 892–893
trench warfare **7:** 888, 889–890
Battle of the Somme **7:** *891*, 894
Battle of Cambrai (1917) **7:** 893
social and political aftermath **7:** 897–908
postwar treaties **7:** 903–905, 906–907, 908, 934–935, 945, 987, 988, 993 **8:** 1026–1028
and the Russian Revolution (1917) **7:** 912
and China **7:** 934
postwar America and Europe **7:** 945–958
veterans demonstrate in the United States **7:** *964*, 965
and Japan **8:** 1016
German lands lost after **8:** 1026
German resentment after **8:** 1026
and India **8:** 1107
World War II
    and Latin America **7:** *981* **9:** 1199
    German invasion of Poland (1939) **8:** 1025–1026, 1036, 1037–1038
    the road to **8:** 1025–1036
    in Europe **8:** 1037–1048
    and France **8:** 1037, 1038, *1039*, 1048
    and the Soviet Union **8:** *1037*, *1042*, 1043–1045, 1048
    Battle of Britain (1940–1941) **8:** 1038, *1040*, 1047 **9:** 1255
    Dunkirk evacuation **8:** 1038, *1039*
    United States and lend-lease **8:** 1038–1041
    Battle of the Atlantic **8:** 1041–1042
    Operation Barbarossa **8:** 1043–1044
    war in the eastern Europe **8:** 1043
    Battle of El Alamein (1942) **8:** 1045
    in North Africa **8:** 1045, 1046
    liberation of Italy **8:** 1046
    D-Day landings (1944) **8:** *1047*, 1048
    Allied bombing campaign in Europe **8:** 1047–1048
    Japanese attack on Pearl Harbor **8:** 1049, 1050–1051, 1053, 1067
    in the Pacific **8:** 1049–1060
    and Burma **8:** 1050, 1052, 1054, 1058
    and the Philippines **8:** 1050, 1051, *1052*, 1054, 1056–1057, *1058*
    Battle of the Coral Sea (1942) **8:** 1052–1053
    victims **8:** 1055–1056, *1057*, 1059, 1060, 1062–1063, 1071, 1131
    Battle of Leyte Gulf (1944) **8:** 1057, 1058–1060
    and the atomic bomb **8:** 1059, 1060, 1086 **9:** 1255
    total war **8:** 1061–1070
    concentration camps **8:** *1062*, 1067
    information control in **8:** 1066–1068
    resistance fighters **8:** *1068*, 1069
    postwar trials **8:** 1070
    and the United Nations **8:** 1070
    postwar recovery in the West **8:** 1071–1082
    and India **8:** 1112–1114
    and decolonization **8:** 1117–1119
    the postwar return of Jews to Palestine **8:** 1131
    and technology **9:** 1253
Wounded Knee, Battle of (1890) **6:** 839

Yalta Conference (1945) **8:** 1084–1085
Yamamoto, Isoroku **8:** 1050, *1051*
Yorktown, Battle of (1781) **4:** 561
Ypres, Battle of (1917; Passchendaele campaign) **7:** *883*, 895

zeppelins **7:** 891, 893

Volume numbers appear in **boldface type**. Page numbers in *italic type* refer to illustrations and captions.

Index

À la Recherche du Temps Perdu (Proust) **6:** 848
Aachen **1:** *21*, 50
Aargau **2:** 183
Abbas I, Safavid shah of Persia **3:** *401*, 402–404
Abbas II, Safavid shah of Persia **3:** 404
Abbey in the Oak Forest (C. D. Friedrich) **5:** *635*
Abdülaziz, Ottoman sultan **6:** 733
Abdülhamid II, Ottoman sultan **6:** 734–735, 736
Abdülmecid I, Ottoman sultan **6:** 733
Abelard, Peter **1:** 51
Abenakis (Native Americans) **3:** 368
Abilene **6:** 838
Abingdon, workhouse **5:** *633*
abolition, slavery **6:** 808–809, 819
    in the United States **5:** 651–652, 654, 682, *683*
    6: 819, 830, 831
aborigines **5:** 671–672, *671*, 672–673
abortion **9:** 1166, 1177
Aboukir, Battle of (1799) **5:** 596
Abraham, Heights of **4:** *549*
absolutism **4:** 439, 449–460
    and Louis XIV of France **4:** 449–450, 455–460
    and Louis XIII of France **4:** 452–455
    in Europe other than France (1700s) **4:** 460
    and Louis XV of France **4:** 460
Abyssinia *See* Ethiopia
Académie des Sciences (Paris) **2:** 274
academies/academicians **4:** 496–497
    French **2:** 262, 274 **4:** 500
    Royal Academy (London) **4:** 496
Academy Awards **7:** 951
Acadia **3:** 374 **4:** 467, 545
Accession, Treaty of (1973) **9:** 1194
accounting systems, and Luca Pacioli **1:** 45, 48
Accra, Independence Arch **8:** *1127*
Acheson, Dean **8:** 1073, 1088
acid rain **9:** 1269, *1270*
Acre **8:** 1133
Acre, Battle of (1796) **5:** 596
Across the Continent: Westward the Course of
    Empire Takes Its Way (F. Palmer) **6:** *829*
Action Committee for the United States of Europe
    9: 1193
Action Française **7:** 955
Adam, Robert and James **4:** 497
Adams, John **4:** *562*
Adams, Samuel **4:** 555
Adenauer, Konrad **9:** 1192, *1193*
Adham Khan **3:** 410, 411
Adil Shah, shah of Iran **3:** 406
Adowa **6:** 826
Adrian of Utrecht **2:** 187
Adrianople **1:** 100
affirmative action **9:** 1168, 1178
Afghan War (1978–1992), and the Soviets
    8: 1102–1104 **9:** 1241
Afghanistan
    war aided by the Soviets (1979–1989)
        8: 1102–1104 **9:** 1167, 1241
    civil war and Islamic fundamentalism (1990s)
        9: *1240*, 1241
Afghans, invasion of Iran (1722) **3:** 405
Africa
    rounding the tip *See* Good Hope, Cape of
    empires **1:** 109–118
    North Africa **1:** 109–110 **6:** 820
    Sub-Saharan **1:** 109, 110–111 **6:** 818
    geography **1:** *110*, 111
    rivers **1:** *111*
    slaves from **1:** *111* **3:** 348, 350, 354, 356, 367,
        375–386, 377 **5:** 616
    trade **1:** *111*, 112, 113, 114–115 **6:** 817–818, 819
    languages **1:** 116
    European exploration (1500s) **3:** *295*, 300,
        305–306, 307
    Dutch settlement **3:** 328–329
    diseases **3:** 393
    scramble for Africa: European colonization
        (1800s) **5:** 676 **6:** 817–828 **7:** 873–874
        9: 1221

missionaries in **6:** *817*, 820
European exploration (1800s) **6:** 819–820, *821*,
    824
German colonies taken during World War I
    7: 885–886
World War II in North Africa **8:** 1045–1046
colonies independent from Europe **8:** 1124–1128
    9: 1221, *1224*
postcolonial **9:** 1221–1230
droughts **9:** 1222, 1224, *1225*, 1268, 1275, 1276
international debts **9:** 1278
See also Southern Africa
African National Congress (ANC) **6:** 828 **9:** 1228,
    1229
African Unity, Organization for (OAU) **9:** 1221
African-Americans
    and World War I **7:** 898–899
    and World War II **8:** 1064–1066
    and desegregation of U.S. armed forces **8:** 1081
    and affirmative action **9:** 1168, 1178
    See also civil rights
Afrikaans language **3:** 329
Aga Muhammed, shah of Iran **3:** 406
Agadir **7:** 874
Age of Reason **2:** 273
    the Enlightenment **4:** 471–480
    and science **5:** 697–698
Agee, James **7:** 968
agitprop **7:** 918
agitation, and Lenin **7:** 918
Agra **3:** *412*
    Taj Mahal **3:** 412, *417*
agricultural revolution **4:** 501–502
Agriculture Adjustment Act (1933) **7:** 967
agriculture *See* farming
AIDS **9:** 1272, *1276*
    in Africa **9:** 1223
air-cushion vehicles (ACVs) **9:** 1260
aircraft
    World War I **7:** 890, 891
    stunts on **7:** *947*, 951
    first trans-Atlantic flight **7:** 951
    passenger flights (1920s) **7:** *952*
    World War II **8:** 1047, 1048, 1055
    development (1900s) **9:** *1192*, 1254–1255, 1260
    European fighter **9:** *1192*
airships, World War I **7:** 891, 893
Aka people **1:** 116–117
Akbar, Mogul emperor **1:** 130 **3:** 408–414
Akuta **1:** 122
Alais, Peace of (1629) **4:** 453
Alamgir, Mogul emperor **3:** 415–416
Alamo, Battle of the (1836) **6:** 738
Alamogordo **8:** 1059, 1060
Alaska
    Native Americans **3:** 341
    Exxon *Valdez* oil spill **9:** 1268–1269
Albania
    independence **7:** 879
    collapse of communism **9:** 1247
    and globalization **9:** *1274*
Albazin **4:** 530
Albert, prince consort **6:** 804, 805 **7:** 871
Alberta **5:** 676
Alberti, Leon Battista **1:** *80*
Albi, cathedral **2:** 175
Albigensian Crusade **2:** *175*
Albrecht, duke of Bavaria **1:** 85
Alcázar **1:** *24*
alchemy **1:** 56
alcohol
    and Native Americans **3:** 391–393
    temperance **6:** 801
    Prohibition in the United States **7:** 948
Alcott, Louisa May **6:** 804
Aldrin, Edwin "Buzz" **9:** 1256
Alembert, Jean Le Rond d' **4:** 477
Aleuts **3:** 341
Alexander, grand duke of Lithuania **1:** 93
Alexander I, czar of Russia **5:** 600, 603–604,
    687–689
Alexander II, czar of Russia
    Russia under **5:** 692–694
    assassination **7:** *910*
Alexander III, czar of Russia, Russia under
    5: 694–696

Alexander VI, Pope **1:** 11
Alexandria (Virginia) **5:** *678*
Alexandrina, czarina of Russia **7:** 912, *913*
Alexis (son of Peter the Great) **4:** 487
Alexis, czar of Russia **4:** 482, 485
Alfonso XIII, king of Spain **5:** 666
Algeria **1:** *111*
    and the French **6:** 732, 820
    nationalism and independence **8:** 1099,
        1126–1127
    civil strife (1992) **9:** 1230
    Islamic fundamentalism (1990s) **9:** 1241–1242
Algerian War of Independence (1954–1962)
    8: 1126–1127
Algiers **6:** 820 **8:** *1126*
Algonquian tribes (Native Americans) **3:** 358, 368
All-India Congress Committee **8:** 1113
All-India Muslim League **8:** 1107
Allende, Salvador **9:** 1204
Allerheim, Battle of (1645) **2:** 233
Alliance for Progress **9:** 1204
Allied Intervention, War of *See* Russian Civil War
    (1918–1920)
Allies, in World War I **7:** 887
Almagest (Ptolemy) **1:** 53
almanacs **4:** 522
Almoravids **1:** 112, 115
alms **1:** *36*
Alsace-Lorraine
    gained by Germany **7:** 871
    lost by Germany (post-World War I) **8:** 1026
Altar of St. Teresa (Bernini) **2:** 259
Alva, Ferdinand, duke of **2:** 217, 218, 219
Alvarado, Velasco **9:** 1204
Amasya, Treaty of (1555) **3:** 400
Amazonia **9:** 1265, 1266, 1267, 1274
Ambassadors, The (H. Holbein the Younger) **1:** *88*
Amchitka Island **9:** 1271
America
    named **3:** 311
    Spanish colonies **3:** 343–354
    See also North America; South America
American Civil War (1861–1865) **5:** 647, 677–686
    6: 794
    social effects **5:** 684
    Reconstruction after **6:** 829–831
    photography in **6:** 843
"American dream, the" **9:** 1169, 1170–1171, 1173
American Federation of Labor **5:** *631*
American Railroad Union **6:** *814*
American Revolutionary War **4:** 553–562 **5:** 674
    6: 748
    and the Dutch **4:** 442, 558
Amiens **7:** *955*
Amin, Idi **9:** 1225, 1236
Amish **2:** 162 **3:** 372
Amory Show (1913) **6:** 850
Ampère, André-Marie **5:** 704–705
Amritsar
    massacre at (1919) **8:** 1108
    Golden Temple **8:** *1109*, 1115
Amsterdam
    rise in importance **1:** 44 **2:** 222 **3:** 325
    banks **1:** 48
    a cultural center **2:** 223
    population **2:** 252
    Baroque architecture **2:** *260*, 261
    stock exchange **4:** *441*
Amur Valley **6:** 772
Anabaptists **1:** 17 **2:** 162, 216 **3:** 372
Anancy **3:** 386
anarchists **6:** 815, 816
Anasazi people **3:** 332
Anatolia **1:** 101 **7:** 907
anatomy **1:** 56
ANC (African National Congress) **6:** 828 **9:** 1228,
    1229
Anderson, Robert **5:** 678
Andes **6:** 752, *754*
Andropov, Yuri **8:** 1106
anesthetics **5:** 705 **6:** 801
Angers **2:** 200
Angkor **3:** 320, 321, 322
Angkor Wat **3:** *318*, 321

Volume numbers appear in **boldface type.** Page numbers in *italic type* refer to illustrations and captions.

Anglicans/Anglicanism **4:** 440
  prayer book **2:** 210, 238
  See also Church of England
Angola **6:** 823, 828
  independence and civil war (1975–1991)
    8: 1099–1102 **9:** 1227–1229
Angostura **6:** 752
animals
  selection and breeding **4:** 503
  and sentimentality **6:** 804–805
Ankara **1:** 101
Annam **1:** 127 **3:** 317
  See also Vietnam
Annapolis **3:** *370*
Annapolis Royal (*formerly* Port Royal) **3:** 360
  4: 546
Anne, queen of Great Britain and Ireland **4:** 445
Anne of Austria **4:** 455
Anne of Cleves **2:** 209
Anne of Savoy **2:** 189
Antarctica, Scott's expedition **5:** *676*
anthrax **5:** 705
Anti-Comitern Pact (1937) **8:** 1031–1034
antiauthoritarianism **9:** 1165
Antietam, Battle of (1862) **5:** 681–682
Antigua, slavery **3:** *378*
Antilles **3:** 348, *384*
antiseptics **5:** 705 **6:** 801
Antwerp
  a trading port **1:** 40, 42, 44 **2:** *215*, 216, 222
  refugees from **1:** 44–45
  "Fury of" **2:** 219
  and Catholic Baroque **2:** 260–261
Anxiety (Munch) **6:** 850
apartheid **6:** 821 **9:** 1228, 1229–1230
apes **4:** *507*
Apollo Belvedere **4:** *495*, 497
Apollo space program **9:** 1256
Apple Mac computers **9:** 1259
Appomatox Courthouse **5:** 686
apprentices/apprenticeships **2:** 252 **4:** 518
Aprista movement **7:** 974–975
Aqaba, Gulf of **8:** 1133, 1135
Aquinas, Thomas **1:** 57, *58*
Aquitaine **1:** *13*
Aquitania (ship) **7:** *874*
Arabia
  Wahhabi people **6:** 732
  and World War I **7:** 890
  post–World War I **7:** 905 **8:** 1023–1024
Arabs, preserving ancient Greek knowledge
  1: 52–53
Arafat, Yasir **8:** 1136, 1137, 1138 **9:** 1242
Aragon **1:** 23–24 **2:** 179
  and the War of the Spanish Succession **4:** 465
Arbenz, Jacobo **9:** 1201, 1203
Arc de Triomphe **5:** *602*
Archimedes **1:** 52
architecture
  Renaissance **1:** 88
  St. Peter's in Rome **2:** *172*
  Tudor **2:** *213*
  Baroque **2:** 255–256, 257 **4:** *465*
  premodern Iranian **3:** *401*
  Mogul **3:** *407*, *411*, *412–413*
  rococo **4:** 492–493
  classical style **4:** *495*, *498*, *499*
  Palladian **4:** *495*, *498*
  the Eiffel Tower **6:** *841*, 846
  art nouveau **6:** 846–847
  National Congress Building (Brasilia) **9:** *1201*
Ardennes **8:** 1048
Argentina
  and the Spanish colonies **3:** 349–350
  horses **3:** *387*
  post-independence **6:** 760–761, 763, 764
  Paraguayan War (War of the Triple Alliance)
    6: 764
  period between the World Wars **7:** 971, 977, 979,
    980
  military coup ushers in conservative
    governments (1930) **7:** 977
  rise of the military (1920s) **7:** 977
  Juan Domingo and Eva Péron **9:** 1200, 1202
  military's anti-left campaign ("dirty war")
    9: 1204, *1207*, 1208, 1280

military rulers (from 1970s) **9:** 1205
  civilian government (1983) **9:** 1206
Arguin Island **3:** 305
Arias, Oscar, Central American peace plan **9:** 1206
Arica **7:** 978
Aristotle **1:** 57, 64, 73 **2:** 266
  and slavery **3:** 376
Arizona, Native Americans **3:** *333*
Arlington **8:** *1049*
Armada, Spanish, sails against England (1588)
  2: 194, 213–214, 221
Armas, Castillo **9:** 1203
Armenia **9:** 1248
armillary spheres **2:** 266
Arminians (religious sect) **2:** 246
armor **1:** 15 **4:** *454*
arms industry
  in Europe (1600s) **4:** *454*
  in Britain (1800s) **5:** 618
  and industrial development **6:** 794
arms race
  East–West **8:** 1091–1092, 1096, 1102
  between India and Pakistan **8:** *1116*
Armstrong, Neil **9:** 1256
Army of the Republic of Vietnam (ARVN) **8:** 1100
army/armies
  early modern European **1:** 26–27, 72–73, 76
  and the feudal system **1:** 27, 72
  under Louis XIV of France **4:** 454, 456
  European armies (1690s) **4:** 461
  of the American Revolutionary War **4:** 556–557,
    560
  See also mercenaries; warfare
Arnolfini Marriage (Jan van Eyck) **2:** *251*
arquebus **1:** 26, *27*
Arras **7:** *885*
Arras, Union of (1578) **2:** 219
Arrhenius, Svante **9:** 1268
art nouveau **6:** 846–847
Art of Painting, The (Jan Vermeer) **2:** *261*
artillery
  growth in the use of (1400s) **1:** 26
  and industrialization **6:** 794
  World War I **7:** *886*, 888–889, 892, 893
arts
  vogue for exotic art in Europe **6:** 784–785, 799,
    824
  in the late 1800s **6:** 841–850
  See also paintings; under various types of arts,
    e.g., music
ARVN (Army of the Republic of Vietnam) **8:** 1100
Ascensius, Iodocus **1:** 66
Ascot race meetings **9:** *1194*
ASEAN (Association of South-East Asian Nations)
  9: 1217
Ashanti people **6:** 827
Ashikaga shogunate **1:** 127
Asia
  European trade with **1:** *41* **3:** 323–330, 417
  European view of **1:** 119–120
  between the world wars **8:** 1015–1024
  independent nation states post–World War II
    8: *1118*
  post–World War II economies in the Pacific Rim
    9: 1209–1220
Asia, East *See* China; Hong Kong; Japan; Korea;
  Mongolia; Taiwan
Asia, South *See* Bangladesh; India; Pakistan; Sri
  Lanka
Asia, Southeast
  during the 1500s **3:** 313–322
  geography **3:** 313–314, 315–316
  early peoples **3:** 314–315
  trading empire **3:** 319–321
  -nationalist movements and decolonization
    8: 1118–1124
  post–World War II economic development
    9: 1217–1218
  financial depression (1990s) **9:** 1220
  See also Borneo; Cambodia; Indonesia; Laos;
    Malaysia; Myanmar; Philippines; Singapore;
    Thailand; Vietnam
Asia Minor, post–World War I **7:** 908
asiento **4:** 467
Association of South-East Asian Nations (ASEAN)
  9: 1217

astrolabes **2:** *267* **3:** 302, *311* **4:** *529*
astrology **1:** 56
astronomy
  Ptolemaic view of **2:** *265*, 266, 268, 269
  Ptolemy's views challenged **2:** 267–270
Asturias **8:** 1032
Atatürk, Kemal (Mustafa Kemal) **6:** *736* **7:** 907
  8: *1022*, 1023
Atlantic, Battle of the **8:** 1041–1042
Atlantic City **7:** *951*
Atlantis (space shuttle) **9:** *1257*
atlases **3:** 301
atomic weights **5:** 703–704
atonal music **6:** 847, 850
attainder, powers of **2:** 206
Attlee, Clement **8:** *1077*, 1085–1086
Augsburg, League of **4:** 462
Augsburg, Peace of (1555) **2:** 156, 192, *193*, 225,
  229
Augsburg Interim **2:** 191
Augustine of Hippo, St. **1:** 56–57 **2:** 152
Augustus II, the Strong, king of Poland-Lithuania
  4: 490
Augustus III, king of Poland-Lithuania **4:** 490
Aurangzebe, Mogul emperor **3:** 415–416
Aurora (ship) **7:** *915*
Austen, Jane **5:** 636, 642
Austerlitz, Battle of (1805) **5:** 599
Australia
  James Cook lands in **5:** 667
  part of the British Empire **5:** 671–674
  dominion status (1926) **5:** 676
  and World War II **8:** 1052, 1054
  Asian influences on the economy **9:** 1218–1219
Austria
  Catholicism **2:** 172
  and the Habsburg dynasty **2:** 187 **4:** 460 **5:** 655
  and the War of the Spanish Succession **4:** 464,
    465
  reform (1700s) **4:** 489
  a powerful force in Europe **4:** 490
  and the French Revolutionary Wars **5:** 595–596
  liberalism **5:** 610
  and the 1848 revolutions **5:** 613–614
  Seven Weeks' War (1866) **5:** 661
  nationalism (1800s) **5:** 664–665
  May Day **6:** *811*
  post–World War I **7:** 907
  annexed by Hitler (1938) **7:** 993 **8:** *1028*, 1031
Austria-Hungary (1867–1918)
  Dual Monarchy **5:** 665
  and the lead-up to World War I **7:** 877–880
  and World War I **7:** 884, 895
Austrian Netherlands
  revolt (1789) **5:** 590–592
  Union of Belgian States **5:** 590–592
  and the French Revolutionary War **5:** 592, 596
Austrian Succession, War of the (1740–1748)
  4: 469, 488, 547
  American phase *See* King George's War
autocracy **4:** 460 **7:** 910
automobile industry **6:** 793 **7:** 949
  under Hitler **7:** 994
  Korean **9:** *1213*
automobiles **7:** *960* **9:** *1170*
autos-da-fé (executions) **2:** 179
Auvillar, market hall **1:** *40*
Averroës (Ibn Rushd) **1:** 57
Avignon, anti-pope established at **1:** 20 **2:** 164, *165*
Ayacucho, Battle of (1824) **6:** *754*, 755
Ayvalik **8:** *1023*
Azerbaijan **5:** 691 **8:** 1086–1087 **9:** 1248
Azores **3:** 304–305
Aztec empire **3:** 332
  Spanish conquest **3:** 344–346, 391, 394–395
  food **3:** 392

B-2 stealth bombers **9:** *1255*
Baader-Meinhof Gang **9:** 1165, 1238
babies, in the 1700s **4:** 512–513
Babur, Mogul emperor **1:** *129*, 130 **3:** 407–408
baby boom **9:** 1162
Bacchus and Ariadne (Titian) **1:** *84*
Bach, Johann Sebastian **4:** 500
Bacon, Francis **2:** 270–271
Bacon's Rebellion (1676) **4:** 545

Baghdad **9:** *1235*
Bahadur Shah II, emperor of India **5:** 668, 669
Bahamas, discovery by Columbus **3:** 309, *310*
Bairam Khan **3:** *409*, 410
Baker, Josephine **7:** 951, *955*
Bakker, Jim **9:** 1178
Baku **5:** 691, *694*, 695 **7:** *931*
bakufu system **4:** 534, 536, 540
   decline **4:** 540–542
Bakunin, Mikhail **6:** 815, 816
Baldomir, Alfredo **7:** 975
Baldwin, Stanley **7:** 958
Balearic Islands, and the Spanish Civil War **8:** 1032
Balfour, Arthur **8:** 1024, 1130
Balfour Declaration (1917) **8:** 1024, 1130
Bali **8:** 1020
Balkan League **7:** 879
Balkans
   and the Ottomans **6:** 733–734 **7:** 877
   and the lead-up to World War I **6:** 736
     7: 876–880
   First Balkan War (1912) **7:** *876*, 879
   Second Balkan War (1913) **7:** 879
   and World War II **8:** 1069–1070
Ballarat **5:** 673
Ballet Russe **6:** 850
ballets de cour **4:** *457*
Baltic States *See* Estonia; Latvia; Lithuania;
   Livonia
Baltimore, George Calvert, Lord **3:** 360
Baltimore and Ohio Railroad **5:** *649*
Balzac, Honoré de **6:** 806, 846
bananas, Central American **6:** *761*, 763 **7:** 973
Banda islands **3:** 328
Bandar Abbas **3:** 403
Banerjea, Surendranath **5:** 670
Bangalore **8:** 1116
Bangladesh **8:** 1115, 1116
   and global warming **9:** 1268
Bank of England **4:** 444
Bankey, Vilma **7:** *950*
Bankok, and the Vietnam War **9:** 1217
banks **1:** 44, 48
   Fugger banking dynasty **1:** 46–47
banquet campaigns **5:** 612–613, 656
Bantu **1:** 111, 116–117 **6:** 818–819
Bao Dai (Vietnamese emperor) **8:** 1123
Baptists **6:** 808
Barbarossa, Operation (1941) **8:** 1043–1044
barbed wire **6:** 839
Barcelona
   and the Spanish Civil War **4:** *462*
   and the War of the Spanish Succession **4:** 467
Barcelona, Treaty of (1529) **2:** 190
Barents, Willem **3:** 326
Barnabites **2:** 166
Barnard, Christiaan **9:** 1262
Baroque **2:** 255–264 **4:** *465*, 491
Barre, Siyad **9:** 1230
Bartolommeo, Fra, painting by **1:** *58*
baseball **7:** *950*, 951
Basil (IV) Shuisky, czar of Russia **1:** 97
Basque country **8:** 1032
Basque people **5:** 666
Bastille, storming of the (1789) **5:** *587*, 588
Bathurst **5:** 673
Batista, Fulgencio **9:** 1203
battery, discovery **5:** 704
Battle Between Carnival and Lent, The
   (Breughel the Elder) **1:** *11*
battleships, dreadnought class **7:** *871*, *875*, 876, 893
Baudelaire, Charles **6:** *842*
Bauhaus, and Hitler **7:** 991
Bavaria
   Catholicism **2:** 172
   rococo style **4:** 493
Bavarian Succession, War of the (1778–1779)
   4: 469
Bay of Pigs invasion (1961) **8:** 1096 **9:** 1173, 1203
Bayezid I, sultan of the Ottoman empire **1:** 101
bayonets **4:** 461
Bayreuth **6:** *843*
Beauharnais, Joséphine **5:** *597*
Beaumarchais, Pierre Augustin Caron de **4:** 497
Beauvais, cathedral roof **1:** *7*, 18

beds **6:** *801*
beer **2:** 249
beer-hall putsch **7:** 988
Beersheba **8:** 1133
bees, introduced to the Americas **3:** 395, *396*
Beethoven, Ludwig van **5:** 598, 638, 639, 644
Begin, Menachem **8:** 1137 **9:** *1237*
Beijing
   and Marco Polo **1:** 119
   Yuan dynasty **1:** 123
   Forbidden City **1:** *128* **4:** *525* **6:** *775*
   Manchu take over **1:** 128–129 **4:** 526
   Monument to the People's Heroes **6:** *771* **7:** *933*
   and the Boxer Rebellion **6:** *774*, 775
   Gate of Heavenly Peace **7:** *940*
   Tiananmen Square **9:** *1182*, *1187*, 1188
Beirut
   westerners kidnapped (1980s) **9:** 1238–1239,
     1241
   U.S. embassy bombed (1983) **9:** *1239*
Belarus **9:** 1248
Belgian Congo **6:** 822–823 **7:** 873 **9:** 1225–1226
Belgian States, Union of **5:** 590
Belgium
   desire for independence **5:** 608
   and World War I **7:** 881, 882, 890, 895
   occupation of the Ruhr (1923) **7:** 953
   and World War II **8:** 1038
   post–World War II **8:** 1075–1076
   colonies lost in Africa **8:** 1128
   See also Austrian Netherlands; Flanders; Low
     Countries; Spanish Netherlands
Belgrade, Treaty of (1739) **6:** 729
Bellini, Gentile, portrait by **1:** *104*
Ben-Gurion, David **8:** 1131–1132
Benedict XIII, Pope **2:** 165
Benelux countries **9:** 1192, 1193
Bengal **3:** 418 **5:** 667
   partition of **5:** 670, 671 **8:** 1114, 1115
   famine (1943) **8:** 1062, 1113
Benin **1:** *112*, 113 **6:** 818
   and the Portuguese **3:** *295*, *301*
Benz **6:** 793
Berber people **1:** 110, 112
Bergen **1:** *16*
Berisla, Sali **9:** 1247
Berkley, John **3:** 364
Berlin
   post–World War I **7:** 952, *953*
   and the end of World War II in Europe **8:** 1048,
     1084
   blockade **8:** 1089–1090
   postwar split **8:** 1089, 1095–1096
   Berlin Wall **8:** 1095–1096, *1097*, 1106 **9:** 1248
Berlin, Treaty of (1878) **6:** 734
Berlin Conference (1885) **6:** 822–823
Berlioz, Hector **5:** 644
Berners-Lee, Timothy **9:** 1259
Bernini, Gianlorenzo **2:** 259, 263 **4:** *449*
Berry, Chuck **9:** 1171
Berzelius, Jakob **5:** 703–704
Bessarabia **7:** 907
Bessarion, Cardinal **1:** 53, 64
Bessemer, Henry **6:** 788
Bessemer process **6:** *787*
bestiaries **4:** 506
Bethlehem (Pennsylvania) **3:** 372
Beveridge, Sir William **8:** 1077
Beynac Castle **1:** *13*
Beza, Theodore **2:** 202
Bhopal, chemical accident **9:** 1270
Bhutto, Benazir **8:** *1116*
Biafra **9:** 1226
Bible
   Gutenberg/Mainz Bible **1:** 60, *61*
   and Martin Luther **1:** 62 **2:** 155
   in the vernacular **1:** 62
   Erasmus's Latin edition **2:** 165
   Vulgate translation **2:** 169
   first French Protestant **2:** 175
   King James Version **2:** 236
bicycles **6:** 793
Bikini Atoll, atomic tests **8:** 1087
Bill of Rights (1689) **4:** 444
bills of exchange **1:** 48

biology, molecular **9:** 1262
Birmingham (Alabama) **9:** 1175
birth control **6:** 799
Birth of a Nation, The (Griffith, D. W.) **7:** 951
Bismarck, Otto von **5:** 660–661, 662, 664, *665*
   7: 871, 872
   and the Berlin Conference (1885) **6:** 822, 823
Bithynia, and the Ottomans **1:** 99
BJP Hindu Nationalist Party **8:** 1116
Black Beauty (Anna Sewell) **6:** 805
black codes **6:** 830
Black Death **1:** 8–9, 30, *31*, 43–44 **2:** 165, 245
   and central Europe **1:** 93
Black and Decker **9:** 1257
Black Hand Gang **7:** 879, 880
Black Sea **1:** *108* **6:** 730
Black September (terrorist organization) **8:** 1136
Blackbeard (pirate) **4:** 547
Blackfeet (Native Americans) **3:** 340
Blackshirts **7:** 985–986
Blake, William **4:** *501* **5:** *615*, 637
Blanco, Cape **3:** 305
Blenheim, Battle of (1704) **4:** 465
Blenheim Palace **4:** *465*
blitzkrieg **8:** 1038
Blois **2:** 200
Blood, Council of **2:** 217–218
Blood, League of **8:** 1018
blood libel **7:** 990
Bloody Sunday **7:** 912
Bloomer, Amelia **6:** 793
boats, building **3:** 302
Bodie **6:** *837*
Bodie State Historic Park **7:** *946*
Bodleian Library (Oxford) **1:** *53*
body politic **2:** 246
Boer Wars **5:** 701
   Second Boer War (1899–1902) **5:** 676
     6: 826–827 **7:** 874
Boers **3:** 329 **5:** 676 **6:** 820–821
Bogotá **6:** 749, *753*
Bohemia
   and the Jagiello dynasty **1:** 93
   anti-Catholicism of Jan Hus **1:** 94, 95 **2:** 164
   markets **1:** *94*
   and the Thirty Years' War **1:** 95 **2:** 225, 226, 227,
     229
   Catholicism **2:** 172
Bohemian Charter **5:** 614
Bojador, Cape **3:** 305
Bokassa, Jean **9:** 1225
Bokhara **1:** 123
Boleyn, Anne **2:** 207, 209
Bolívar, Simón **5:** 665 **6:** 749–753, 754–755, 758
Bolivia
   a Spanish colony **3:** 348, 388
   period between the World Wars **7:** 971, 973, 974,
     978–979
   war against Paraguay (Chaco War 1932–1935)
     7: 978–979
   fascists seize power (1943) **7:** 979, *982*
   Marxists seize power (1946) **7:** 979, *982*
   military rule (1936) **7:** 979
   revolution (1952) **9:** 1201
   producing cocaine **9:** 1208, 1278
Bologna, university **1:** 50, 51, *52*, 56
Bolsheviks **7:** 911, 914–915, 916, 918, 919
   and the Russian Civil War **7:** 919–920
Bombay **3:** 330, 418 **5:** *669* **8:** 1108, *1112*
bombs
   incendiary **8:** 1055–1056, *1057*
   World War II **8:** 1055–1056, *1057*, 1059, 1060,
     1062–1063, 1086
   atomic/fission **8:** 1059, 1060, 1086, *1089*, 1091
     9: 1186, 1253, 1255
   nuclear tests at Bikini Atoll **8:** 1087
   hydrogen/fusion bombs **8:** 1091 **9:** 1255
Bonaparte, Joseph **6:** 749
Bonaparte, Louis-Napoleon *See* Napoleon III
Bonaparte, Napoleon *See* Napoleon I
Bond, James (fictional character) **8:** *1097*
Bonnie and Clyde **7:** 969
bonus army **7:** *964*, 965
Book of Hours, French **1:** *35* **2:** *195*
Book of Martyrs (J. Foxe) **2:** 211
bookbinding **1:** *33*

Volume numbers appear in **boldface type**. Page numbers in *italic type* refer to illustrations and captions.

bookkeeping **1:** 45
books **1:** 80
    and theology **1:** 56–57
    printed by Gutenberg **1:** 60–61
    and languages **1:** 61–62
    spread and impact of **1:** 61, 66
    censorship of **1:** 62
    in the Middle Ages **2:** 254
    in the 1700s **4:** 472–473, *474*, 521–522
    See also libraries; printing
Booth, John Wilkes **5:** 686 **6:** 829
Booth, William **5:** *626*, 632
bootleggers **7:** 948
Bora, Catherine von **2:** 155, *157*
Borgia, Alexander **2:** 151
Borgia, Cesare **1:** *85*
Borneo **3:** *315*, 316 **7:** 873 **8:** 1020
    Indian influences **3:** 317
    nationalism post–World War II **8:** *1118*
Borodino, Battle of (1812) **5:** 604
Borromini, Francesco **2:** 257
Bosch, Hieronymus, painting by **1:** *34*
Bose, Subhas Chandra **8:** 1110
Bosnia-Herzegovina
    and the Ottomans **6:** 734
    and the lead-up to World War I **7:** 877, 878,
      879–880
    independence **9:** 1252
    invasion by Serb forces **9:** 1252, 1278
Bosporus channel **6:** *731*
Boston **3:** *367*
    immigration **5:** 650
Boston Massacre (1770) **4:** *554*, 555
Boston Tea Party **4:** 555
Bosworth Field, Battle of (1485) **1:** 23 **2:** 205
Botero, Giovanni **1:** 70
Botswana, independence **8:** 1128
Botticelli, Sandro, painting by **1:** *87*
Boucher, François, painting by **4:** *493*
Bougainville **8:** *1056*
Boulder Dam **7:** 967
Bourbon dynasty **2:** 203 **4:** 460, 470
    and Napoleon **5:** 600, 604
    reforms in the Latin American colonies
      6: 747–748
bourgeoisie **5:** 628
Bourneville **6:** *810*
Boven Digul **8:** 1022
bovine spongiform encephalopathy (BSE) **9:** 1275
Bowood, gardens **4:** *499*
Boxer Rebellion (1900) **5:** 696 **6:** 774–775, 776
boxing **4:** *519*
boyars (Russian nobles) **1:** 96, 97, 98
Boyer, Lillian **7:** *947*
Boyle, Robert **5:** 697–698
Boyne, Battle of the (1690) **2:** 244 **4:** 445
Braddock, Edward **4:** 548
Brady, Mathew **6:** 843
Brahe, Tycho **2:** *268*, 269–270
Brahms, Johannes **6:** 847
Brain Trust **7:** 965, 966
Bramante, Donato **1:** 84
Brandywine Creek, Battle of (1777) **4:** 558
Braque, Georges **6:** 850
Brasilia **9:** *1201*
Brazil
    a Portuguese colony **3:** 311, 347–348, 349, 350,
      354
    sugar **3:** 349
    slavery in **3:** 350, *383*, 384, *385*, 386 **6:** 758, *759*
    route to independence **6:** 755–756
    becomes a republic **6:** 756
    post-independence **6:** 756, 757, 760, 763, 764
    abolition of slavery **6:** 819
    period between the World Wars **7:** 971, 977, 979,
      980–982
    wheat fields **7:** *972*
    dictator Vargas in power (1930) **7:** 977, 980–982
    rise of the military (1920s) **7:** 977
    post–World War II **9:** 1199
    currency devalued (1999) **9:** 1207
    deforestation **9:** 1267
    Rio Earth Summit (1992) **9:** 1271, *1272*
    international debt **9:** 1278
Brazza, Pierre Savorgnan de **6:** 824
bread **4:** 522

Breitenfeld, Battle of (1631) **2:** 231
Breitenfeld, Battle of (1642) **2:** 233
Brest-Litovsk, Treaty of (1918) **7:** 919
Bretheren of the Common Life **1:** 54
Brezhnez, Leonid **8:** *1103*, 1106 **9:** *1201*
Briand, Aristide **7:** 956
Bridgewater Canal **4:** *508*, 509
Brielle **2:** 219
Brisbane **9:** *1219*
Bristol, and the slave trade **3:** *379*, 382
Britain, Battle of (1940–1941) **8:** 1038, *1040*, 1047
    9: 1255
British Columbia **5:** 675
    Native Americans **3:** 340–341
British North America Act (1867) **5:** *675*
Brittany **1:** 23 **2:** 203
Brontë sisters **5:** 642
    Emily Brontë **5:** 636
Brooklyn Bridge **6:** *796*
brotherhoods, Catholic **2:** 165
Brouwer, Adriaen **2:** 261
Brown, "Capability" **4:** 499
Broz, Josip (Marshal Tito) **8:** *1069*, 1070
Brueghel, Pieter, the Elder, paintings by **1:** *11*
    2: *216*, *245*
Brunel, Isambard Kingdom **5:** *706*
Brunelleschi, Filippo **1:** *79*, 81
Brusilov Offensive **7:** 895
Brussels **1:** 16 **2:** 215, 220
Bryan, William Jennings **5:** 700
BSE (bovine spongiform encephalopathy) **9:** 1275
Budapest
    parliament **5:** *666*
    and the Hungarian Uprising (1956) **8:** 1094
Buddenbrooks (Thomas Mann) **6:** 850
Buddhism
    Zen **1:** *125*, 127
    temple gardens **1:** *126*
    in Southeast Asia **3:** 317, 318, 320, 322
    in Japan **6:** 781
    in China **7:** *936*
Buena Vista, Battle of (1847) **6:** 739
Buenos Aires **6:** 749 **9:** *1207*, 1208, 1280
buffalo **3:** 341–342, 395 **6:** 839
Buffon, Georges-Louis Leclerc, Comte de **5:** 698
Bukovina **7:** 907
Bulgaria
    and the Ottomans **1:** 101 **6:** 734 **7:** 877
    and World War I **7:** 890
    collapse of communism **9:** 1247
Bulge, Battle of the (1944–1945) **8:** 1048
Bull Run, Second Battle of (1862) **5:** 681, *682*
Bunker Hill, Battle of (1775) **4:** 556
Bunyan, John **2:** 241, *243*
Burgoyne, Sir John **4:** 558, *559*
Burgundy **1:** 23, 25–28 **2:** 189, 190, 203
Buridan, Jean **1:** 56
Burke, Robert O'Hara **5:** 673
Burma *See* Myanmar
Burr, Aaron **5:** 646
Burundi, Hutus massacred by Tutsis (1972) **9:** 1230
Bush, George **9:** *1245*, 1246
bushido **4:** 536
Byron, Lord **5:** *611*, 638
Byzantine empire **3:** 297
    Orthodox Christianity **1:** 10
    and the Ottomans **1:** 16–18, 19, 100–101, 103
      3: 298
    and ancient Greek texts **1:** 64
    legacy to Russia **1:** 92

cabala **1:** 66
Cabot, John **3:** 355, *356*
Cabral, Pedro Alvarez **3:** 311
cafés *See* coffeehouses
Cahokia **3:** 332
Cairo **6:** 818
Cajuns **3:** 374
Calais **1:** 23 **2:** 211
Calatafami, Battle of (1859) **5:** *660*
calculus **2:** 272
Calcutta **3:** 418 **5:** 667, 671 **6:** *792*
Calhoun, John C. **5:** 646, 647, 654
Calicut **3:** 307, 323–324, *325*, 329
California
    Native Americans **3:** 342

Catholic missions **3:** 352
    gold rush **5:** *651*, 654 **6:** 837–840
    and slavery **5:** 654
    Bodie State Historic Park **7:** *946*
    Asian influences on the economy (1990s)
      9: 1219
Calonne, Charles-Alexandre de **5:** 585, 586
Calvert, George, Lord Baltimore **3:** 360
Calvin, John **2:** 160–161, 170, 197
    and infant mortality **1:** 10
Calvinism **1:** 95 **2:** *172*, 175
    in France **2:** 197–198
    in the Low Countries **2:** 216, 217, 220, 223
      4: 440
    See also Huguenots
Cambodia
    religion **3:** 314
    kingdom of Angkor **3:** 320, 321, 322
    and Pol Pot **8:** 1099 **9:** 1281
    and the Vietnam War **8:** 1101
    Japanese occupation of **8:** 1119, 1122
    Marxist regime (1970s) **9:** 1167
Cambrai, Battle of (1917) **7:** 893
Cambrai, Treaty of (1529) **2:** 190
Cambridge, university **1:** 52, *53*
Camden, Battle of (1780) **4:** 561
camera obscura **2:** 264
cameras **6:** *788*, *789*, 842, *844*
    See also photography
Cameroon
    Bantu language **1:** 117
    and World War I **7:** 885–887
Camp David peace accords **8:** 1137 **9:** 1236, *1237*
Camp Life in the Thirty Years' War (lithograph)
    2: *234*
Campo Formio, Treaty of (1797) **5:** 596
Canada
    Native Americans **3:** 341
    Cartier lands in **3:** *355*, 356
    and British rule **5:** 674–676
    immigration from Europe **5:** 674
    Lower and Upper **5:** 674, 675
    border with the United States **5:** 675
    Dominion of **5:** 675
    transcontinental railroad **5:** 675
    United Province of **5:** 675
    dominion status (1926) **5:** 676
    Sikhs prevented from entering **8:** 1108
    Asian influences on the economy **9:** 1219
Canaletto **4:** 496
canals **4:** 508–509
Canary Islands, and the Spanish Civil War **8:** 1032
candles **2:** 247
cannon foundries **4:** *454*
canoes, Pacific island **3:** *314*
Canova, Antonio **4:** 497
Canterbury Tales, The (Geoffrey Chaucer) **1:** 50
Canton **4:** *531*, 532
Cão, Diogo **3:** 306
CAP (Common Agricultural Policy) **9:** 1194, 1198
Cape Colony **6:** 818, 820–821, 828
Cape Fear **3:** 356
Cape Town **3:** 328–329
Cape Verde Islands **3:** 305
Capet, Hugh, king of France **1:** 12
capitalism
    versus communism *See* Cold War
    link with the Reformation **2:** 159
    emergence in Britain **5:** 618–619
    triumph (1980s) **9:** 1168
Capone, Al **7:** *949*
Caps, and the Hats **4:** 448
Capuchin order **2:** 166
Caracas **6:** 749, 750, 751
Caravaggio (Michelangelo da Merisi) **2:** 257–259
    painting by **2:** *256*, 259
caravels **3:** 302
carbon dioxide, and global warming **9:** 1266,
    1267–1268, 1274–1275
Carbonari **5:** 658
Caribbean islands
    Columbus's voyages to **3:** 301, 309, 310
    Spanish colonies **3:** 343, 346, 348
    slavery on **3:** 348, 350–351, 377–380
    plantations **3:** 349, 387, 389–390
    post–World War I **7:** 971

1394

Volume numbers appear in **boldface type.** Page numbers in *italic type* refer to illustrations and captions.

Carlists **5:** 666
Carlos, Don **5:** 666
Carlsbad Decrees (1819) **5:** 607
Carlyle, Thomas **6:** 800–801
Carmelites, reformed by Teresa of Avila **2:** 166, *168*
Carnatic **3:** 418
Carnegie, Andrew **5:** *631* **6:** *833*, 834
carnivals **4:** 521
Carolina **3:** 361
carousels **4:** *455*
Carpaccio, Vittore, painting by **3:** *298*
carpetbaggers **6:** 831
carpets
    Persian **3:** *399*
    Indian **3:** 413
Carr, Robert **2:** 236
Carracci, Annibale **2:** *255* **4:** 494–495
Carranza, Venustiano **6:** 745–746
carriages, steam **5:** *621*
Carson, Rachel **9:** 1265
Carter, Jimmy **8:** 1137 **9:** 1205, *1237*
Carteret, Sir George **3:** 364
Cartier, Jacques **3:** *355*, 356
Cartwright, Edmund **5:** 616
Casimir IV, king of Poland **1:** 91–93
Cassatt, Mary, painting by **6:** *843*
Cassino **8:** *1046*
Castagno, Andrea del, painting by **1:** *63*
caste system
    in the Spanish colonies **3:** 351–354
    in India **8:** 1109, 1111
Castiglione, Baldassare **1:** 9
Castiglione, Giuseppe **4:** *528*, 531
Castile **1:** 23, 24 **2:** 179, 180
    and social discipline **1:** 71–72
    revolt (1520) **2:** 187
    and the monarchy (1600s) **4:** 463
Castlereagh, Robert Stewart, Viscount **5:** 606
Castro, Fidel **8:** 1095, 1096, *1098* **9:** *1201*, 1203, *1205*
Catalan people **5:** 666
catalogs, shopping **6:** 789
catalogs of complaint **5:** *584*
Catalonia, and the Spanish Civil War **8:** 1032, 1033
Cateau-Cambrésis, Treaty of (1559) **2:** 193
Cathari **2:** 174, *175*
Cathay **1:** 119
cathedrals
    schools **1:** 54
    and humanism **1:** 65
Catherine II, the Great, empress of Russia **4:** 480, 489–490 **5:** 592, 688
Catherine of Aragon **2:** 160, 207
Catholic Church
    and the spread of literacy *49*
    pre-Reformation **1:** 10–11 **2:** 151–152, 163–167
    Great/Western Schism (papal schism; 1378–1417) **1:** 11, 20 **2:** 151, 164, *165*
    religious festivals **1:** 11
    sale of indulgences **1:** 11–12, 46 **2:** 152, 153
    reform in the late Middle Ages **1:** *17*
    and usury **1:** 44, 73
    and education **1:** 52, 56–57, 78
    and universities **1:** 52, 58
    and intellectual inquiry **1:** 56
    and humanism **1:** 68
    Counter-Reformation **2:** 163–172
    Baroque art and architecture **2:** 257–259
    in Spanish America **3:** *351*, 352–353
    and New England **3:** 359
    and abstinence from meat **3:** 388–389
    rococo architecture **4:** 492–493
    science and traditionalism (1800s) **5:** 702
    in Mexico (1800s) **6:** 738, *742*
    in post-independence Latin America **6:** 762, 764
    Roman Catholics in the British Parliament **6:** 808
    influence in Latin America between the World Wars **7:** *979*, 980
    liberation theology in Latin America **9:** 1208
    See also Inquisition; missionaries; popes/papacy; Reformation
Catholic League
    formed by Henry, duke of Guise **2:** 203
    formed by Maximilian, duke of Bavaria **2:** 226, 228–229

cattle, and colonial America **3:** 394
caudillos/caudillísimo **6:** 759–760, 761 **7:** 976, 977–978
cavalry **4:** *466*
Cavour, Camillo Benso, conte di **5:** 658–659
Ceausescu, Nicolae **8:** 1106 **9:** 1246
Cecil, Sir Robert **2:** 235–236
Central American Republics, Federation of **6:** 760
Central Intelligence Agency (CIA) **8:** 1069, 1095, 1103
    and Guatemala **9:** 1201–1203
Central Powers, in World War I **7:** 887
cereals **1:** 33
Cervantes, Miguel de, *Don Quixote* **2:** *194*
Çesme, Battle of (1770) **6:** 730
Ceuta **3:** 303
Ceylon *See* Sri Lanka
Cézanne, Paul **6:** 843–844
CFCs (chlorofluorocarbons) **9:** 1269, 1270
Chaco War (1932–1935) **7:** 978–979
Chaldiran, Battle of (1514) **1:** 105 **3:** 399
Cham people **3:** 314, *318*, 321
Chamberlain, Neville **8:** *1035*, 1036
Chambord, Treaty of (1552) **2:** 191–192
Chamorro, Violeta **9:** 1208
Champagne, fairs **1:** 40
Champlain, Samuel de **3:** 360
Chancellorsville, Battle of (1863) **5:** 683
Channel Tunnel **9:** *1196*
Chao Kou **1:** 122
chapbooks **4:** 522
chapels, Renaissance **1:** 80
Charlemagne **1:** 12, 20, *21*, 50
Charles I, king of Great Britain and Ireland (1600–1649) **2:** 235, 237–241
Charles I, king of Spain *See* Charles V, Holy Roman emperor
Charles II, king of England and Scotland (1630–1685) **2:** 241, 242–244
    and the North American colonies **3:** 361, 364
Charles II, king of Spain **4:** 463
Charles IV, king of Spain **6:** 749
Charles V, Holy Roman emperor **2:** 183, *184*, 187–193
    and the Schmalkaldic League **1:** 47 **2:** 156, 188, 190
    crown/crowning **2:** *155*, 190
    and Luther **2:** 155, 156
    and the Council of Trent **2:** 168
    succeeding to the title **2:** *185*, 186–187
    Habsburg empire during reign of **2:** *186*
    and Spanish America **3:** *344*, 348
Charles VI, Holy Roman emperor (and, as Charles III, archduke of Austria and king of Hungary) **4:** 466, 467, 468, 488
Charles IX, king of France (1550–1574) **2:** 198, 199, 201, 202, 219
Charles X, king of France **5:** 608 **6:** 820
Charles XI, king of Sweden **4:** 447
Charles XII, king of Sweden **4:** 447
Charles, duke of Mayenne **2:** *198*, 199
Charles the Bold, duke of Burgundy **1:** 25, 26
Charles Edward Stuart, the Young Pretender (Bonnie Prince Charlie) **4:** *443*
Charleston **3:** 370 **4:** 546
    and the American Revolutionary War **4:** 559–561
Charleston (dance) **7:** *945*
Charlotte, empress of Mexico **6:** 740, 741
Charter 77 group **9:** 1244, 1246
Chartists **5:** 612, 628–629 **6:** 811
Chartres, cathedral **1:** *7*
Chaucer, Geoffrey **1:** 50
Chausa, Battle of (1539) **1:** 130
Chechnya, invaded by Russian troops (1992) **9:** 1251
Cheka **7:** 919, 920
chemical industry **6:** 794
chemistry **5:** 703–704
Cheng Ho (Chinese admiral) **3:** 302, 322
Chernenko, Konstantin **8:** 1106
Chernobyl, nuclear accident **9:** 1244, 1249, 1269–1270
Chernomyrdin, Viktor **9:** 1250, *1252*
Cherokee (Native Americans) **5:** *653*, 654 **6:** 839
Chesapeake Bay colony **3:** 360, 390
Cheyenne (Native Americans) **3:** *337* **6:** 839

Chiang Kai-shek **7:** *935*, 936, 938–944 **8:** 1034, 1049
    nationalist government in Taiwan **7:** 944 **9:** 1180, 1181, 1214
Chiapas **9:** 1206, 1277
Chicago **5:** 625–626 **6:** 832
    fire (1871) **5:** *630*
Chicago Democratic Convention (1968) **9:** 1165
chiefs, Native American **3:** 337–339
Ch'ien-lung, emperor of China **4:** 531 **6:** 767
children
    in the late Middle Ages **1:** 10
    in the 1700s **4:** 512, 514–519
    and industrialization (1800s/1900s) **5:** *617*, *629*, 631–634 **6:** *811*, 815, *840*
    deaths **5:** *633* **6:** 804, *805*
    in the late 1800s **6:** 799–800, 804
Chile
    and the Spanish colonies **3:** 346, 349–350
    fight for independence **6:** 748, 753–754
    post-independence **6:** 761, *762*, 763–764, 764
    period between the World Wars **7:** 971, 973, 974, 977, 979, 980
    and the United States (1920s) **7:** 973
    rise of the military (1920s) **7:** 977
    and the Catholic Church **7:** 980
    post–World War II **9:** 1199
    dictatorship under Pinochet **9:** *1203*, 1204
    social reform under Marxist president Allende **9:** 1204
    fishing and El Niño **9:** 1268
chimney sweeps **5:** *633*
China
    Ming dynasty **1:** 16, 18, *120*, 127–128 **4:** 523–525, 526
    Confucianism **1:** 18, 40, 66, 124, 127–128
    trade **1:** 18, 113 **3:** *302*, 319–321, 327, 330 **4:** 523, 524–525, 528, 532 **6:** 767, 773
    encyclopedia (11,000 volumes) **1:** 66
    gunpowder **1:** 66, 121
    Sung dynasty **1:** 120–123
    Yuan dynasty **1:** 123–125, 127
    isolationism (Great Withdrawl) **1:** 127–128 **6:** 768
    Manchu (Ching) dynasty **1:** 128–129 **4:** 523–532 **6:** 768–776
    and world exploration **3:** 302, 323
    influence on Southeast Asia **3:** 317, 322
    jewelry **3:** *321*
    European impact on (1500s-1600s) **4:** 523–525
    rice cultivation **4:** 524, *530* **6:** *770*
    tributary system **4:** 527–530
    anti-Western Boxer Rebellion (1900) **5:** 696 **6:** 774–775, 776
    and western influences (1800s) **6:** 767–776
    opium and the Opium Wars **6:** 769–771
    population (1850) **6:** 769
    Taiping Rebellion (1850s and 1860s) **6:** 771–772, 784
    Sino-Japanese War (1894–1895) **6:** 772, 782
    Hundred Days of Reform **6:** 773
    becomes a republic **6:** 776 **7:** 933
    dictatorship of Yuan Shikai **6:** 776 **7:** 933–934
    Japanese ultimatums to (Twenty-One Demands; 1915) **6:** 783–786 **7:** 934 **8:** 1016
    and the post–World War I treaties **7:** 908, 934–936
    communism triumphs over nationalism **7:** 933–944
    communists in power (1949–1999) **7:** 933 **9:** 1179–1188
    Long March **7:** *934*, *940*, 941
    and World War I **7:** 934
    May Fourth Movement (1919) **7:** 935
    Sun Yat-sen president of nationalist government **7:** 936
    united front with Mao **7:** 936–937
    Northern Expedition **7:** 938–939
    Japanese invasion of Manchuria (1931) **7:** 941–942 **8:** *1015*, 1018, 1019, 1031
    Japan renews invasion of China (1937–1938) **7:** 942–943 **8:** 1025, 1034
    Sino-Japanese War (1937–1945) **7:** 942–943 **8:** 1019, 1025, 1034
    Soviet Union liberates Manchuria (1945) **7:** 943
    and World War II **7:** 943
    Civil War (1945–1949) **7:** 944

1395

Volume numbers appear in **boldface type**. Page numbers in *italic type* refer to illustrations and captions.

China (continued)
  and the Cold War **8:** 1092–1093, 1097
  and the Korean War (1950–1953) **8:** *1092*, 1093
    9: 1181–1182
  Nixon's visit to (1972) **8:** 1102
  Britain returns Hong Kong to **8:** 1128 **9:** 1188,
    1216, 1220
  and the Soviet Union **9:** 1180, *1182*, 1186
  Great Leap Forward **9:** 1182–1183
  Cultural Revolution **9:** 1184, 1185
  nuclear arms **9:** 1186
  reform under Deng Xiaoping **9:** 1186–1188
  prodemocracy movement **9:** *1187*, 1188, 1216
  family planning measures **9:** 1275
Chinese Civil War (1945–1949) **7:** 944
Ching dynasty *See* Manchu (Ching) dynasty
chips, silicon **9:** 1258
Chiricahua (Native Americans) **6:** 839
Chisholm Trail **6:** *838*
chlorofluorocarbons (CFCs) **9:** 1269, 1270
chocolate **6:** *820*
cholera **5:** 701, 705 **6:** 790, 801, 802
Chopin, Frédéric **5:** *643*, 644
Chou En-lai **9:** 1184
Christendom, decline **1:** 20–21, 68
Christian IV, king of Denmark (1577–1684) **2:** 228
Christian, prince of Anhalt (1568–1630) **2:** 226,
  227
Christianity
  and age of the Earth **5:** 698
  and the theory of evolution **5:** 699
  revival (late 1800s) **5:** 702
Christmas, Victorian **6:** *797*, 805
Chrysler Building **6:** 846 **7:** 948
Chrysler Corporation **7:** 949
Chun Doo-Hwan **9:** 1213–1214
Church, Frederic **5:** 641
Church of England
  founded by Henry VIII **2:** 160, 208
  Anglican prayer book **2:** 210, 238
  and Elizabeth I **2:** 212
  See also Anglicans/Anglicanism
Church of Jesus Christ of Latter-day Saints **5:** 702
churches, and humanism **1:** *64*, 65
Churchill, John, duke of Marlborough **4:** 465
Churchill, Winston **8:** *1086*
  and the road to World War II **8:** 1036
  and World War II **8:** 1038, 1045–1046, 1063
  and postwar Europe **8:** 1084–1085, *1086*, 1087
    9: 1189
  quoted on European union **9:** 1190
CIA *See* Central Intelligence Agency
Cicero **1:** 63
Cincinnati **5:** 650
CIO (Congress of Industrial Organizations) **7:** 970
circumnavigation of the world, by Magellan
  3: 311–312
cities and towns
  and development of European trade **1:** 16
  in early modern Europe **1:** 16, 77 **2:** 252–253
  and vagrancy **1:** 36
  fortifications **1:** 73
  shops **1:** 73, 77, *78*
  industrial (1800s) **5:** 612, 625–626 **6:** 802–803
  redesigned (late 1800s) **5:** *655*
  suburbs **6:** 802 **9:** 1170
  See also urbanization
civil rights **8:** 1082 **9:** 1162–1163, 1166, 1171,
  1174, 1175
Civil Rights Act (1964) **9:** *1174*, 1175
Civil War, American *See* American Civil War
Civil War, English *See* English Civil War
Civil War, Russian *See* Russian Civil War
Civil War, Spanish *See* Spanish Civil War
Civil Works Administration (CWA) **7:** 966–967
Civilian Conservation Corps **7:** 966
CJD (Creutzfeldt-Jakob disease) **9:** 1275
Clark, William **5:** 646
class/rank, social
  and the feudal system **1:** 8, 13–14
  in early modern Europe **1:** 75–76
  in the 1700s **4:** 512, 516
  under the Japanese Tokugawa clan **4:** 534
  and industrialization **5:** 628, 630
  in the late 1800s **6:** 797
  Marx's view of **6:** 812

classical style **4:** 494–496, *498*, *499* **5:** *611*
  neoclassicism **4:** 497 **5:** 621, 636 **6:** *801*
  reaction against **5:** 635
classification, of the living world **4:** 507
Claude Lorrain (*pseudonym of* Claude Gellée)
  4: *494*, 495, 498
clavichords **1:** 86 **4:** *516*
Clay, Henry **5:** 646, 647, 651, 654
Clemenceau, Georges **7:** 903, *904*
Clément, Jacques **2:** 203
Clement VII, Pope **2:** 189, 207
Clement VIII, Pope **4:** 485
Clement XI, Pope **4:** 529
clergy, educated **1:** 49, 50, 78
climate
  global warming **9:** 1266, 1267–1268
  and El Niño **9:** 1268
Clinton, Sir Henry **4:** 559
Clive, Robert **5:** 667
cloning **9:** 1262
cloth
  trade in **1:** 114
  markets **2:** *253*
clothing **2:** 251 **4:** *519*
  fashion in France (1600s) **4:** *458*
  early 1800s **5:** *607*, 642
  fashion in France (1800s) **6:** 846
  during World War I **7:** 893, *894*
  American fashion (1920s) **7:** *952*
  Nazi uniforms **8:** *1028*
clover **3:** 394
cloves **3:** 315, 316, 328, *329*
Cluny **1:** 11
coal **4:** 510
  mining **4:** *509*, 510 **5:** 619, *701* **6:** *811*
  industry **5:** 619 **6:** 788
coats of arms **1:** *71*
Coca-Cola **7:** *960* **9:** *1274*, 1277
cocaine **9:** 1178, 1208, 1278
cocoa **6:** *820*
cod, in colonial America **3:** *366*, 388–389, *390*
Coen, Jan Pieterszoon **3:** 327
coffee **3:** 327, *391*
  and European social life **4:** *473*
  Brazilian **6:** *757*
coffeehouses (cafés) **4:** *473*, *521*, 522
coffeepots **4:** *473*
Cognac, League of **2:** 189
coins **1:** 42, 45, *73* **3:** *350*
Colbert, Jean-Baptiste **2:** 263 **4:** 454, 456–457, 460
Cold War **8:** 1044, 1083 **9:** 1190, 1255
  (1945–1960) **8:** 1083–1094, 1135
  and NATO **8:** *1084*, 1090, 1095, 1102, 1106
  and the Warsaw Pact **8:** *1084*, 1090, 1093–1094,
    1095, 1102
  (1960–1989) **8:** 1095–1106
  and European colonies **8:** 1119
  and China **9:** 1181
  and Latin America **9:** 1200–1201
  and independent African countries **9:** 1222,
    1226–1227
  and Iran **9:** 1233
Cole, Thomas **5:** 641, 643
Coleridge, Samuel Taylor **5:** 636, 639
Coligny, Gaspard II de **2:** 199, *200*, 201–202
collective rights **5:** 628
collèges **4:** 518
Colleoni, Bartolomeo **1:** *82*
Collins, Michael **7:** 958
Collins, Wilkie **6:** 805
Colmar, Union of **1:** 24
Cologne **1:** 37
Colombia
  post-independence **6:** 760
  post–World War I **7:** 971
  Tolima people **7:** 976
  post–World War II **9:** 1199
  U.S. aid to **9:** 1204
  drug barons **9:** 1208
Columbus, Christopher **1:** 24, 65 **3:** 301, *305*,
  307–310, 316, 343, 392
Comecon **9:** 1243, 1249
Cominform (Communist Information Bureau)
  8: 1089
commedia dell'arte **4:** *492*
Common Agricultural Policy (CAP) **9:** 1194, 1198

common law **1:** 72
Common Market, European **9:** 1190, 1194
Common Sense (Tom Paine) **4:** 557
Commonwealth, British **5:** 676 **8:** 1120 **9:** 1190
Commonwealth of Independent States (CIS)
  9: 1249
Communards **5:** 664
Commune of Paris **5:** 591, 592, 593, 594
communism **7:** 921
  and industrialization **5:** 629–630
  birth of **6:** 812–813
  under Lenin and Stalin **7:** 921–932
  triumphs over nationalism in China **7:** 933–944
  in Japan (early 1900s) **8:** 1016
  Hitler's hatred of **8:** 1043
  post–World War II **8:** 1075–1076
  communists exposed in the United States
    8: *1091*, 1092
  in Central America **8:** 1104
  crumbling in Europe **8:** 1106
  and the European colonies **8:** 1119 **9:** *1160*
  Soviet communism (post-1960) **9:** 1161
  Eurocommunism (1970s) **9:** 1166
  collapse in eastern Europe (1980s) **9:** 1168
  in China (1949–1999) **9:** 1179–1188
  collapse of communism in Europe **9:** 1243–1252
  See also Cold War; Communist Party
Communist Information Bureau (Cominform)
  8: 1089
Communist Manifesto, The (Marx and Engels)
  5: *626*, 629–630 **6:** 811, 812–813 **7:** 921
Communist Party
  Soviet **7:** 919, 921
  Chinese **7:** 936
  French **7:** 955 **8:** *1089*
  Indonesian **8:** 1121
community ties (1500s/1600s) **2:** 251–252
compasses, magnetic **3:** 301, 302
computers **9:** 1258–1259, *1262*
  and the Internet **9:** 1259–1260, 1277
Comte, Auguste **5:** 703
comuneros **2:** 187
concentration camps **8:** *1062*, 1067
Concert of Europe **5:** 606, 607–608
Concord, Battle of *See* Lexington and Concord,
  Battle of
Concorde (aircraft) **9:** 1260, *1261*
Condor Legion **8:** 1032, 1033
condottiere **1:** 26
Conestoga wagons **3:** *369*
Confederate States of America **5:** 677
Confederation, Articles of (1781) **4:** 561–562
Confederation of the Rhine **5:** 601
Confessions (Rousseau) **5:** 637
Confucianism
  and trade **1:** 18, 40
  and modernization **1:** 66
  and government **1:** 124
  and the Great Withdrawl **1:** 127–128
  and the Cultural Revolution **9:** 1185
Confucius (K'ung Ch'iu) **1:** 124 **4:** 530
  See also Confucianism
Congo, Democratic Republic of (*formerly* Zaire)
  copper **1:** 114 **9:** *1223*
  Belgian Congo **6:** 822–823 **7:** 873 **9:** 1225–1226
  communist state **8:** 1099 **9:** *1160*
  independence **8:** 1099, 1128
Congo, International Association of the **6:** 822
Congo, Republic of the, French Congo **7:** 875
Congo River **3:** 306
Congregational church **4:** 550
Congress of Europe **8:** 1073
Congress of Industrial Organizations (CIO) **7:** 970
Congress Party **8:** 1115
conquistadores **1:** 18
  See also Cortés, Hernán; Pizarro, Francisco
Constable, John **5:** *637*, 643
Constance, Council of (1414–1418) **1:** 94
  2: 164–165
Constantine XI Palaeologus Dragases, last
  Byzantine emperor **1:** 102
Constantinople *See* Istanbul
Constituent Assembly (France) **5:** 586, 588–589
Constitution of the United States **1:** 51 **4:** 562
  Amendments **6:** 830–831 **7:** 948

Volume numbers appear in **boldface type.** Page numbers in *italic type* refer to illustrations and captions.

Constitutional Act of Canada (1791) **5:** 674
Constitutional Convention (1787; United States) **4:** 562
Constitutional Convention (France) **5:** 592, 593–594
Continental Army **4:** 556–557, *560*
Continental Congress, First (1774) **4:** 556
Continental Congress, Second (1775) **4:** 556, 561
Contra rebels **8:** 1104
contraband (slaves) **5:** 684
contraception **6:** 799 **9:** 1172, 1176
Contragate (Iran-Contra Affair) **9:** 1205–1206, 1241
Cook, James **5:** 667, *672, 673*
cookbooks **6:** *800*
Coolidge, Calvin **7:** 946, 948, *961*
Copenhagen
    Christianborg Palace **4:** *445*
    and the Northern War **4:** 446
Copernicus, Nicolaus **2:** 267–268
    and his heliocentric theory **2:** 170, 268–269
Copley, John Singleton **4:** 497
copper, African **1:** 114
Coral Sea, Battle of the (1942) **8:** 1052–1053
Corday, Charlotte **5:** *594*
corn **3:** 350, *371,* 389, 392, *393* **4:** 504
Cornfields with Flight of Birds (Van Gogh) **6:** 844
Cornwallis, Charles **4:** 561
Coronaro Chapel, Rome **2:** *259*
Coronation of Poppea, The (Monteverdi) **1:** 84
corregidors **1:** 71–72
Cortés, Hernán **3:** 343–346, 349, 395
Corvinus, Matthias *See* Matthias I Corvinus
Cosby Show, The (TV show) **9:** *1178*
Cosimo I (Cosimo de' Medici; 1519–1574) **1:** 83, 87
Cossacks **4:** 482, *483,* 484, 485
Costa Rica, post–World War I **7:** 971
cotton **3:** 298
    mills **4:** *501* **5:** 618 **6:** *840*
    gins **5:** *616,* 647
    and the Industrial Revolution **5:** 616, *617,* 619, *622*
    plantations **5:** 647, *654,* 677
    after slavery abolition (U.S.) **6:** 831
Council of Europe **8:** 1073–1074
Counter-Reformation
    Catholic **2:** 163–172
    secular **2:** 170–172
counterrevolution, French
    in France **5:** 589–590
    outside France **5:** 590–592
Courbet, Gustave **6:** 841–842
coureurs de bois **3:** 360
Courtier, The (B. Castiglione) **1:** 9
Covilha, Pêro da **3:** 306–307
cowboys **6:** 838, 839
Cowpens, Battle of (1781) **4:** 561
Cracow, university **1:** 94
craftsmen, master **4:** 518
Cranach, Lucas, "the Elder" **2:** 255
    paintings by **2:** *152, 157, 159*
Cranmer, Thomas **2:** 210, 211
Crécy, Battle of (1346) **1:** 15
Creoles *See* criollos
Crespy, Truce of (1544) **2:** 190
Creutzfeldt-Jakob disease (CJD) **9:** 1275
Crick, Francis **9:** 1262
crime, in western Europe (1500s) **1:** 36
Crimea **4:** 485
Crimean War (1853–1856) **5:** 657, *662, 689,* 692 **6:** 733 **7:** 871
criollos (Creoles) **3:** 347
    in Mexico **6:** 737, 738
    in the officer corps **6:** 748–749
    and independence in South America **6:** 749
    post-independence **6:** 757–758
Cripps, Sir Stafford **8:** 1113
Critique of Pure Reason (Kant) **4:** *479*
Croatia, attacked by Serbia (1991–1992) **9:** 1252
Cromwell, Oliver **2:** 240, 241–242 **4:** 444
Cromwell, Richard **2:** 242
Cromwell, Thomas **1:** 30–31 **2:** 208
crops
    in sub-Saharan Africa **1:** 110–111, 117
    and the agricultural revolution **4:** 501–502

Latin American **7:** *972*
    See also farming
crossbows **1:** 15, 26
crown
    of Rudolf II **1:** *69*
    of Charles V **2:** *155*
    of George I **4:** *444*
Crucifix in the Pine Forest (Caspar David Friedrich) **5:** *641*
crucifixes **2:** *166*
Crusades **1:** 16, 90, *101,* 102 **2:** 174 **3:** 297
Crystal Palace **5:** 615, 624, 634
Cuba
    visited by Columbus **3:** 309
    and the Spanish-American War (1898) **6:** 766, 835
    sugar trade **7:** 973
    Bay of Pigs invasion (1961) **8:** 1096 **9:** 1173, 1203
    missile crisis (1962) **8:** 1096, *1098* **9:** 1203
    Che Guevara **9:** *1163,* 1164
    and the Soviet Union **9:** *1201,* 1204
    Batista overthrown; Castro president (1958) **9:** 1203
cubism **6:** 850
Cuernavaca **6:** *742*
cujus regio, ejus religio **2:** 226
Culloden, Battle of (1746) **4:** 443
Cultural Revolution, in China **9:** 1184, 1185
Cumberland (National) Road **5:** 649
Curia **2:** 163, 165, 167
currency, paper **1:** 121
Curzon, Lord **5:** 670
Cusa, Nicholas de **1:** 79–80
Custer, George **6:** *835,* 839
customs barriers **1:** 42
cutlery **2:** *249*
Cuvier, Georges **5:** 698
Cuzco **6:** 754
CWA (Civil Works Administration) **7:** 966–967
cycling **6:** *792,* 793
Cyprus
    and the Ottomans **1:** 108 **2:** 194 **6:** *733*
    taken by the British **6:** *733,* 734
czars **1:** 96
Czech League **7:** 920
Czech Republic **9:** 1246
    acid rain **9:** *1270*
Czechoslovakia
    Bohemian Charter **5:** 614
    an independent state (1918) **7:** *904,* 906, 956
    Sudetenland annexed by Germany **7:** 993 **8:** *1034–1035,* 1036
    totally annexed by Germany **8:** 1036
    communists seize power (1948) **8:** 1089
    collapse of communism **8:** 1106 **9:** 1246
    division (1992) **9:** 1246

D-Day landings (1944) **8:** *1047,* 1048
Daewoo **9:** *1213*
Daguerre, Louis Jacques **6:** 842
Daimler **6:** 793
daimyo (landowning princes) **4:** 533–557, *539, 540* **6:** 777–778, *779*
Dalai Lama **4:** 527
Dalmatia **5:** 599
Dalton, John **5:** 703
dancing
    Charleston **7:** *945*
    marathon **7:** 951
D'Annunzio, Gabriele **7:** 984
Danzig *See* Gdansk
Dark Ages **1:** 53
Darkest England (William Booth) **5:** 632
Darrow, Clarence **5:** 700
Darwin, Charles **4:** 507 **5:** *697,* 698–699, *706* **6:** 812
    See also Social Darwinism
Das Kapital (Karl Marx) **6:** 812
David, Jacques-Louis **4:** 497
    paintings by **5:** *585, 595*
Davis, Jefferson **5:** 677
Davout, Marshal **5:** 600
Davy, Humphry **5:** *701,* 703, 704
Davy lamps **5:** 701

Dawes, Charles **7:** 954
Dawes Plan (1924) **7:** 954
DDT **9:** 1265
Dean, James **9:** 1171
Death of General Wolfe (Benjamin West) **4:** 497
death rate, in Europe (1700s) **4:** 522
Debs, Eugene V. **6:** *815,* 816
debt, international **9:** 1278
Debussy, Claude **6:** 844
Decembrist revolt (1825) **5:** *688,* 689, 690
Decker, Eduard Douwes **3:** 328
Declaration of Independence (1776) **4:** 480, 557, *558, 562*
Declaration of the Rights of Man and Citizen (document) **5:** 588
decolonization **8:** 1117–1128
Deerfield
    massacre at (1704) **3:** 368
    attacked by Native Americans (1675) **4:** *543*
Defoe, Daniel **4:** 500
deforestation **9:** 1266–1267, 1274, *1277*
Degas, Edgar **6:** 842, 843
Deir Yasin, massacre **8:** 1132
deism **5:** 698
de Klerk, F. W. **9:** 1228, 1229
Delacroix, Eugène, paintings by **5:** *605, 643,* 644 **6:** *824*
De Lancey, James **3:** 367
Delaware confederacy (Native Americans) **4:** 544
Delft **2:** 222, 223, *253*
Delhi
    and the Moguls **1:** 130 **3:** *407, 415*
    and Muslim India **1:** 130
    sacked by the Iranians (1739) **3:** 406, 416–417
    and the Indian Mutiny **5:** 669
    British capital moved to **5:** 671
    and independence **8:** *1110, 1113*
Delors, Jacques **9:** 1196
demesnes **1:** 34
democracy
    "participatory" **9:** 1164
    liberal **9:** 1168, 1190
    triumph (1900s) **9:** 1273–1274
Democracy Wall, in China **9:** 1188
Democratic Party (U.S.) **5:** 650–651, 654
Deng Xiaoping **9:** 1184, 1185, 1186–1188
Denmark
    and the Union of Colmar **1:** 24
    and the Thirty Years' War **2:** 227–228
    religion **4:** 440
    trade (1600s) **4:** 445–446
    monarchy and national assembly (1600s) **4:** 446
    power struggle with Sweden (1600s) **4:** 446
    Norway secedes from **5:** 666
    and European union **9:** 1194, 1197
deoxyribonucleic acid (DNA) **9:** 1262
department stores **6:** 789
    first **5:** 657
Deposition, The or *Descent from the Cross* (Rubens) **2:** 257, 261
Depression Breadline, The (George Segal) **7:** *959*
Depression *See* Great Depression
des Ursins, Madame **4:** 465
Descartes, René **2:** 264, 271, *272*
Descent from the Cross or *The Deposition* (Rubens) **2:** 257, 261
Desert Campaign (1879–1880) **6:** 764
Desert Rats **8:** *1045*
de Solla Price, Derek **9:** 1253–1254
détente **8:** 1102 **9:** 1166
Detroit **7:** 949
    car industry **7:** 949 **8:** *1081*
devshirme **1:** 102, 104
Diamond, Jared **1:** 116
Dias, Bartolomeu **3:** *305,* 306, *307*
Diaz, Porfirio **6:** 742, 743
    and the Mexican Revolution **6:** 743–744
Dickens, Charles **5:** 626 **6:** 804, 806, 845
    Oliver Twist **5:** 632
    The Old Curiosity Shop **6:** 804
    Hard Times **6:** 845
    Martin Chuzzlewit **6:** 845
dictators **7:** 983
    in western Europe (1900s) *See* Hitler, Adolf; Mussolini, Benito; Stalin, Joseph
    Latin American (from 1970s) **9:** 1204–1205

1397

Volume numbers appear in **boldface type**. Page numbers in *italic type* refer to illustrations and captions.

Diderot, Denis **4:** 476, 492
    Encyclopedia **4:** 476, 477, *502*, 510, *514*
Dien Bien Phu, Battle of (1954) **8:** *1122*, 1123
Diggers (political movement) **2:** 247
Din Ilahi (Divine Faith) **3:** 412, 414
Dinwiddie, Robert **4:** 548
diplomatic revolution **4:** 469
Directory, the (France) **5:** 594, 595, 596
Discovery, Age of **3:** 303, 313
Discovery of the Interior Parts of Africa,
        Association for the **6:** 819–820
disease
    in the 1500s/1600s **2:** 247–248, 249
    discovery of microorganisms **2:** 274
    brought to the Americas from Europe **3:** 346,
        387, 390–391 **4:** 544
    in Africa **3:** 393
    brought to the Europe from the Americas **3:** 393
    in Europe (c. 1700s) **4:** 510, 522
    and scientific discovery **4:** *522* **5:** 705
    and industrialization **5:** 626, *629*
    See also plague
diseases
    in the 1800s **6:** 801
    combating (1900s) **9:** 1271–1272
dissection, human **1:** 56
Diu **3:** *325*
Divine Comedy, The (Dante) **1:** 50
Divine Faith **3:** 412, 414
Division of the North **6:** 745
divorce **9:** 1172
Djerba **2:** 193
Dmitry, False **1:** 97
DNA **9:** 1262
doctors **2:** 247–248
Dodge City **6:** 838, *839*
dollar diplomacy **6:** 835
Doll's House, A (Henrik Ibsen) **6:** 850
Dolly (sheep) **9:** 1262
domestic service, employment in **6:** *800*
Dominican Republic
    and Columbus **3:** 309, *310*
    U.S. suppression of reformist rebellion (1965)
        9: 1204
Dominicans **1:** 11, 50 **2:** 176
domino theory **8:** 1097–1098
Don Quixote (Miguel de Cervantes) **2:** *194*
Doña Marina (or La Malinche) **3:** *344*, 345
Dong Son **3:** 317
Dorgon, prince of the Manchu people **4:** 526
Dos Passos, John **7:** 968
Dostoyevsky, Fyodor M. **5:** 696 **6:** 806, 845–846
Douglass, Frederick **5:** 652 **6:** 830
Downs, Battle of the (1639) **2:** *232*, 233
Doyle, Arthur Conan **6:** 805
Drake, Francis **2:** 209
Dreadnought (ship) **7:** *875*, 876
dreadnought battleships **7:** *871*, 875, 876, 893
Dreiser, Theodore **5:** 626
Dresden **5:** 625
    elector of Saxony's court **4:** *500*
    and World War II **8:** 1063
Dreyfus, Alfred **6:** 846, *847*
Dreyfus affair **6:** 846 **7:** 990
Drogheda, storming of **2:** 241
drugs (illegal) **9:** 1178, 1208, 1277–1278
Dual Alliance **7:** 881
dualist heresy **2:** 180
Dublin **2:** 213
Duck Soup (movie) **7:** *963*
ducking stools, and witches **2:** *182*
Dudley, John, earl of Warwick and duke of
        Northumberland **2:** 210, 211
Dudley, Robert **2:** 220, 221
Dulles, John Foster **8:** 1100 **9:** 1209–1210
Duma **5:** 696 **7:** 910, 913–914
Dunant, Jean-Henri **5:** 663
Dundee, John Graham, 1st Viscount **4:** 444
Dunkirk, evacuation from **8:** 1038, *1039*
Durand, Asher **5:** 643
Dürer, Albrecht **1:** 42, 88 **2:** 255
    paintings by **1:** *46*
Durrani dynasty **3:** 406
Düsseldorf, French occupation of **7:** *956*
Dust Bowl **7:** *968*, 969, 970 **9:** 1264
Dutch East Indies *See* Indonesia

Dutch Reformed Church **2:** 224
Dutch Republic (United Provinces of the
        Netherlands) **2:** 220 **4:** 440–441
    See also Netherlands
Dutch Revolt (Revolt of the Netherlands) *See*
        Eighty Years' War
Dutch War (1672–1679) **4:** 447
Dutschke, Rudi **9:** *1162*, 1164
dyes, chemical **6:** 794
Dylan, Bob **9:** 1171
Dzerzhinski, Feliks **7:** 930

Eakins, Thomas **6:** 842
Earth, age of **5:** 698
East India Company, British **3:** 330, 403, 418
    and the American colonies **4:** 555
    and India **5:** 667, 668, 669
East India Company, Dutch **3:** 326–327, 329–330,
        362, 403 **6:** 821
East India Company, French **3:** 330
East India Company, Swedish **3:** 330
East Indies
    and the spice trade **2:** 222
    and World War II **8:** 1050, 1052
    See also Indonesia; Philippines; Spice Islands
Easter Rising **7:** 905
Eastern Orthodox Church/Christianity **1:** 10 **3:** 297
    split with the Roman Catholic Church **1:** 90
    Russian Orthodox Church **1:** 92 **4:** *481*, 530
        5: *691* **7:** 990
    and the Uniate Church **4:** 485
Ebola virus **9:** 1272
Eck, Johann **1:** 44
economics, classical political **5:** 621
economy, Pacific Rim **9:** 1209–1220
ECSC (European Coal and Steel Community)
        9: 1191–1193
Ecuador **4:** *507*
    and Simon Bolívar **6:** 753
    post-independence **6:** 760
    post–World War I **7:** 971, *977*
    producing cocaine **9:** 1208
Edgehill **2:** 239
Edirne **1:** 100
    mosque **1:** *107*
Edison, Thomas **6:** 790, 832
Edo (*later* Tokyo) **4:** 537, *538*, 540 **6:** 777, 778
education **2:** 254
    the spread of learning in Europe **1:** 49–58,
        59–62, 78
    and the rise of humanism **1:** 59–68, 80
    in the 1700s **4:** 472, 515–518
    educational reform (1800s) **6:** 800
    and segregation in the United States **8:** 1082
    See also schools; universities
EDVAC computer **9:** 1258
Edward IV, king of England **2:** 205
Edward VI, king of England **2:** 210
Edward VII, king of Great Britain **6:** *793*, 798
Edward VIII, king of Great Britain **6:** *798*
EEC (European Economic Community) **9:** *1192*,
        1193–1196
Egypt
    Mamluks **1:** 105–107 **6:** 732
    Napoleon in **5:** 596 **6:** 730, 732, 820
    independence from the Ottomans **6:** 732–733,
        735
    Suez Canal **6:** 821, *823*, 825 **7:** 887
    British control of **6:** 825
    end of the British protectorate **8:** 1024
    relationship with the Soviets (1950s) **8:** 1099,
        1135
    Suez Crisis (1956) **8:** 1127, 1133, 1135
    and the creation of Israel **8:** 1132
    war against Israel (1973) **8:** 1136–1137
    Camp David peace accords **8:** 1137 **9:** 1236,
        1237
    westernization **9:** 1232, 1235–1236
    Islamic fundamentalism **9:** 1235–1236
Eiffel Tower **6:** *841*, 846
Eighteenth Amendment, to the U.S. Constitution
        7: 948
Eighty Years' War (Revolt of the Netherlands;
        1568–1648) **1:** 44 **2:** 172, 215–224 **4:** 440
Einstein, Albert **8:** 1091–1092
Eire, dominion status (1926) **5:** 676

Eisenhower, Dwight D. **8:** *1080*, 1081–1082, 1098
    and World War II **8:** *1047*
El Alamein, Battle of (1942) **8:** 1045
El Greco, paintings by **2:** *178*
El Niño **9:** 1268
El Salvador
    post-independence **6:** 764
    internal conflict **9:** 1204, 1206
Elath **8:** 1133
Elba **5:** 604
Elbe River **1:** 42
Eldorado (mythical country) **3:** 387–388
electrical appliances, domestic **6:** 790
electricity
    discovery **5:** 704
    development of streetlamps **6:** *788*, 790
electrolysis **5:** 703, 704
electromagnetism **5:** 704–705
"Elegy Written in a Country Churchyard" (Thomas
        Gray) **5:** 638–639
elements, chemical **5:** 703–704
elements, four **2:** 266
Elizabeth I, czarina of Russia **4:** 489
Elizabeth I, queen of England **2:** 209–214, 220, 235
        3: 356
Elizabeth of York **1:** *23*
Ellis Island **6:** *834*
Emancipation Proclamation **5:** 682
Emerson, Ralph Waldo **5:** 637
Emile, or Treatise on Education (Rousseau) **4:** 478
employment, for women (late 1800s) **6:** 799–800
enclosure, of the countryside **1:** 34–35, 36 **2:** 246,
        247, 252
Enclosure Acts (late 1700s) **4:** 503–504
encomienda system **3:** 350
Encyclopedia (Diderot) **4:** 476, 477, *502*, 510, *514*
encyclopedias, Chinese (11,000 volumes) **1:** 66
Engels, Friedrich **5:** 626 **6:** 812
    The Communist Manifesto (Marx and Engels)
        5: 629–630 **6:** 811, 812–813
Engineers, Amalgamated Society of **6:** *807*
engines
    steam **4:** *509*, 510 **5:** *619*
    jet **9:** 1254–1255
England
    Hundred Years' War (1338–1453) **1:** 8, *13*, 14–15
    growth of a centralized monarchy **1:** 23
    enclosures **1:** 34–35
    migration of vagrants to towns (1500s) **1:** 36
    Protestantism and the monarchy **1:** 70–71
    common law **1:** 72
    justices of the peace **1:** 72
    Parliament **1:** 72
    Spanish Armada sails against **2:** 194, 213–214,
        221
    Tudor England **2:** 205–214
    Stuart dynasty **2:** 214, 235–244
    Civil War **2:** 235–244
    Glorious Revolution **2:** *243*, 244 **4:** 442–444,
        472, 502
    settlers in South America **3:** 348
    colonies in North America **3:** 356–360, 370–371
        4: 544–552
    the Bill of Rights and the monarchy **4:** 444
    paintings (1600s/1700s) **4:** 493–494
    See also Great Britain
English Civil War (1642–1649) **2:** 235–244
    and the Enlightenment **4:** 472
ENIAC computer **9:** 1258
"enlightened despots" **4:** 489–490
Enlightenment, the **2:** 182, 274 **4:** 471–480, 491,
        498 **5:** 610, 697
    and the monarchy **4:** 460, 476, 489
    in France **4:** 472, 492
    and religion **4:** 476
    and music **4:** 500
    Romanticism developing from **5:** 635
    and Latin America **6:** 748
Enola Gay (aircraft) **8:** 1059
Entente Cordiale **7:** 872
environmental concerns (1900s) **9:** 1263–1272,
        1274, 1282
environmental movements **9:** 1165–1166, 1271
Episcopalian church **4:** 550
Erasmus, Desiderius **1:** 54, 57–58, 65–68 **2:** 152,
        165

Dutch East Indies *See* Indonesia

Volume numbers appear in **boldface type.** Page numbers in *italic type* refer to illustrations and captions.

Erie Canal **5:** 649
Eritrea **9:** 1226
Eskimos **3:** 341
Estates General **4:** 450, 451, 452 **5:** *584,* 586
  dissolved by Louis XIII **4:** 453
Estonia **4:** 446
  independence **7:** 906
  nationalism **9:** 1248, 1249
Et in Arcadia Ego (Nicolas Poussin) **4:** *491*
ETA **9:** 1279
Ethics (Aristotle) **1:** 73
Ethiopia (*formerly* Abyssinia) **1:** 118
  crops **1:** *117*
  invasion by Mussolini (1936) **6:** 824 **7:** 987
    8: 1030
  not a European colony **6:** 826
  drought and famine (1970s/1980s) **9:** 1224, 1268
  military regime and independence movements
    (1970s) **9:** 1226
  Selassie overthrown in miltary coup (1974)
    9: 1226
ethnic cleansing **9:** 1252, 1278
EU *See* European Union
Euclid **1:** 52
Eugene, prince of Savoy **4:** 465
EURATOM (European Atomic Energy Community)
  9: *1192,* 1193
Eurocommunism **9:** 1166
Europe
  everyday life (1300s–1500s) **1:** 7–9
  transition from the medieval to the modern world
    1: 7–18, 69–78
  and the Black Death **1:** 8–9, 30, *31,* 43–44
    2: 165, 245
  everyday life (1500s/1600s) **1:** 8 **2:** 245–254
  religion in the Middle Ages **1:** 10–12 **3:** 297–298
  rise of the monarchy **1:** 12–14, 69, 70
  trade and wealth in early modern Europe **1:** 15,
    39–48
  political shape (1400s) **1:** 19–28
  map of (1400s) **1:** *20,* 22
  rise of the idea of **1:** 21–22
  nation-states **1:** 22–23, 70 **4:** 460
  population and agriculture **1:** 29–38
  inflation (1500s) **1:** 36, 48
  customs barriers **1:** 42
  bills of exchange **1:** 48
  scholasticism and universities **1:** 49–58, 94
  colonies in Africa (1800s) **1:** 118 **6:** 817–828
    7: 873–874
  Habsburg Empire **2:** 183–194, 225
  world exploration (1400s/1500s) **3:** 295–302,
    303–312
  religious unity in the Middle Ages **3:** 297–298
  trade with the East **3:** 298, 417 **4:** 524–525, 532
  Protestant northern Europe **4:** 439–448
  dynastic wars (1700s) **4:** 461–470
  the Enlightenment **4:** 471–480
  religion and superstition (1700s) **4:** 476, 520–521
  central and eastern (1600s/1700s) **4:** 481–490
  grand tour of **4:** 495–496
  cities (1700s) **4:** 508, 511–512
  everyday life (1700s) **4:** 511–522
  colonial conflicts in North America **4:** 544–549
  and Napoleon **5:** 595–604
  revolution and reform **5:** 605–614, 629–630
  spread of industrialization (1800s) **5:** 623
  immigration to the United States **5:** 650 **6:** 806,
    833, *834, 837*
  vogue for exotic art (1800s) **6:** 784–785, 799,
    824
  railroads **6:** 790, 791
  transport improvements (1800s) **6:** 790, 791–793
  emigration from (1800s) **6:** 806
  colonies after World War I **7:** 905
  post–World War I **7:** 905, 945, 951–958, 960–961
  Latin American imports (1870s–1914)
    7: 971–972
  World War II in Europe **8:** 1037–1048
  post–World War II recovery **8:** 1071–1077,
    1078–1079, 1088–1089
  welfare states **8:** 1077 **9:** 1160
  iron curtain **8:** *1084,* 1086, 1087, 1096
  and NATO **8:** *1084,* 1090, 1102, 1106 **9:** 1245
  and the Warsaw Pact **8:** *1084,* 1093–1094, 1102
    9: 1243

colonies gain independence **8:** 1117–1128
  western Europe: experiments with government
    (1960–1999) **9:** 1159–1168
  toward a united Europe **9:** 1189–1198
  single currency **9:** 1196, 1197
  fall of communism; revival of nationalism
    9: 1243–1252
  See also Holy Roman Empire
Europe, Congress of **8:** 1073
Europe, Council of **8:** 1073–1074 **9:** 1190
European Atomic Energy Community (EURATOM)
  9: *1192,* 1193
European Coal and Steel Community (ECSC)
  9: 1191–1193
European Convention for the Protection of Human
  Rights **8:** 1074
European Economic Community (EEC)
  9: *1192,* 1193–1196
European Space Agency **9:** *1192*
European Steel and Coal Community **8:** 1073
European Union (EU) **9:** 1197–1198
  flag **9:** *1189*
European Union Treaty (1991) **9:** 1196–1197
euros (currency) **9:** 1197
Eurostar train **9:** *1196*
evangelical churches, in Latin America **9:** 1208
Evans, Walker **7:** 968
Everlasting League **1:** 26
evolution, theory of **4:** 507 **5:** *697,* 698–699, 700
  and Social Darwinism **5:** 701
exclusion crisis **2:** 243–244
Executive Order 9981 **8:** 1081
Exhibition of Degenerate Art **7:** 991
Exxon *Valdez* oil spill **9:** 1268–1269
Eyck, Jan van, painting by **2:** *251*

Fabriano **1:** 60
factories **5:** 616–617, 631
  in the 1700s **4:** 510
factors, for slave procurement **3:** 382
Factory Acts (from the 1830s) **5:** 634
Fair Deal **8:** 1080
Fairfax, Sir Thomas **2:** 240
fairies **6:** 805
fairs, trading **1:** 40–41
Falconet, Etienne, statue by **4:** *486*
Falkenhayn, Erich von **7:** 894
Falklands War (1982) **9:** 1206
familiars (demons) **2:** *179,* 180, 182
families
  early modern European **1:** 76
  in the 1700s **4:** 512–513, 514–515
  middle-class (late 1800s) **6:** 798–799
  working-class (late 1800s) **6:** 799–800
famines **9:** 1275
  in early modern Europe **1:** 8, 30, 32–33 **2:** 248
  potato famine (1845) **5:** 612, 650
  in Bengal (1943) **8:** 1062, 1113
  in Sudan (1990s) **9:** 1224
  in North Korea (late 1990s) **9:** 1276
Faraday, Michael **5:** *703,* 704, *706*
Farinelli, Carlo **4:** 500
Farm Security Administration (FSA) **7:** 968
Farmers' Alliances **6:** 811–814, 833–834
farming
  in early modern Europe **1:** 16, *18,* 29–30, 32–35
    2: 247
  and trade **1:** 40
  during the reign of Henry VII **2:** 206–207
  Native American **3:** 333–334, 340
  colonies in America **3:** 349–350, *365* **4:** 505
  and the agricultural revolution **4:** 501–502, 503
  in France (1700s) **4:** *520*
  nationalization under Stalin **7:** 927–928
  collective farms in China (1960s) **9:** *1181,* 1182,
    1183
  adverse side effects of (1900s) **9:** 1264
  green revolution **9:** 1264–1265
  and pesticides **9:** 1265
  slash-and-burn **9:** *1266,* 1267
  See also famines
Farnese, Alessandro, duke of Parma **2:** 220, 221
Farnese, Cardinal **2:** 203
Farnese, Elizabeth **4:** 468
fashion *See* clothing
Fashoda **6:** 825

fatwas **6:** 729
Faust (Goethe) **5:** 638
Fawkes, Guy **2:** 236, *237*
Febrerista revolt **7:** 979
February Revolution **7:** 914
Federal Emergency Relief Administration (FERA)
  7: 967
Federal Highway Act (1921) **7:** 950
feet, binding **7:** *938,* 939
Feminine Mystique, The (Betty Friedan) **9:** 1166,
  1172–1174
feminism, and the French Revolution **5:** *588*
feminists **9:** 1166
FERA (Federal Emergency Relief Administration)
  7: 967
Ferdinand I, Holy Roman emperor **2:** 192
  before accession **1:** 93 **2:** *184,* 187, 188
Ferdinand II, Holy Roman emperor **1:** 95 **2:** 229,
  230
  as Archduke Ferdinand **2:** 226, 227
Ferdinand III, Holy Roman emperor **2:** 229
  before accession to the title **2:** 231
Ferdinand V and Isabella I, king and queen of
  Spain **2:** 24
  and the Moors of Grenada **1:** 24
  and the Spanish Inquisition **1:** 24 **2:** 179, 180
  marriage **2:** 179
  and Columbus's voyages **3:** 309
Ferdinand VII, king of Spain **6:** 749, 751
fertilizers
  from Chile **6:** 763–764
  chemical **6:** 794
feudal system **1:** 8–9, 13–14, 41
  and raising armies **1:** 27, 72
  decline **1:** 34, 35, *38*
  and the king **1:** 70
fiber-optics **9:** *1261*
fiddles, Renaissance **1:** 85
Fifteenth Amendment, to the U.S. Constitution
  6: 830–831
Fifth Coalition, War of the (1809) **5:** 601
film industry
  in the 1920s **7:** *950,* 951
  See also movies
films, of World War I **7:** *891,* 901
fin de siècle **6:** 848, 850
Finch, John **2:** 237–238
Finland **4:** 446
  struggle for independence from Russia **5:** 666
  under Russian control **5:** 688
  post–World War II **8:** 1075
firearms
  arquebus **1:** 26, *27*
  flintlock muskets **4:** 461, *466*
  pistols **4:** *462*
  in the 1800s **5:** 662–663
  breech-loading needle guns **5:** 662
  mitrailleuse **5:** 662, *663*
  American Civil War **5:** 680, *683*
  and industrial development (1800s) **6:** 794
First Balkan War (1912) **7:** 876, 879
First Indochina War (1946–1954; French-
  Vietnamese War) **8:** 1123
First International **6:** 813, 815–816
First World War *See* World War I
Fischer, Fritz **7:** 882
fish, dried **1:** 114–115
fisheries
  Atlantic **2:** 210, 248 **3:** 355, 388, 389, *390*
  Southeast Asian **3:** 316
  in colonial America **3:** *366,* 388–389, *390*
  EU quotas **9:** 1197–1198
  and El Niño **9:** 1268
  overfishing **9:** 1269
Fitzgerald, F. Scott **7:** 945, 950
Fiume **7:** 984
Five-Year Plans, of Stalin **7:** 926–927, *928*
flagpole sitting **7:** 951
flags
  Japan **8:** *1018*
  India **8:** *1113*
  European **9:** *1189*
Flanders **1:** 23 **2:** 220, 221, 252
  part of the Habsburg Empire **1:** 25
  agriculture **1:** *33*
  urbanization **1:** 40

Volume numbers appear in **boldface type**. Page numbers in *italic type* refer to illustrations and captions.

Flanders (continued)
    and the Renaissance **1:** 85
    Mercator's map of **2:** *217*
    food imports **3:** 389
    Battle of Malplaquet (1709) **4:** *461*
flappers **7:** *945, 950*
Flatford Mill (John Constable) **5:** *637*
Flaubert, Gustave **6:** 845
flight *See* aircraft
FLN (Front de Libération National) **8:** 1126
Flodden, Battle of (1513) **2:** 214
Florence
    moral renewal preached by Savonarola **1:** *10,* 11
    and the Renaissance **1:** 28, *79,* 80, 87
    humanists **1:** 64–65, 80
    churches **1:** *79, 80*
Florida **3:** 356
    Native Americans **3:** *334*
Flower of the Flock, The (painting) **6:** *805*
Flushing **2:** 219
flyboats **1:** 42, *44*
FMLN **9:** 1206
FNLA (National Front for the Liberation of Angola)
    8: 1099–1102 **9:** 1227
Fontainbleu, palace at **1:** 88 **2:** 200
food
    in Europe (1500s/1600s) **2:** 248–249, *250* **3:** 389
    in colonial America **3:** 350, *371,* 395
    brought to Europe from the Americas **3:** 389,
        392, *394,* 395–396
    and the Mogul empire **3:** 414–415
    in Europe (1700s) **4:** 522
    rationing during World War II **8:** 1068–1069
Food Administration **7:** 900
Forbidden City **1:** *128* **4:** *525* **6:** *775*
Ford, Henry **7:** 949, 991
forfeiture, powers of **2:** 206
forks, cutlery **2:** *249*
Formosa *See* Taiwan
Fort Christina **3:** 362
Fort Duquesne **4:** 548
Fort Garry **5:** *674*
Fort Necessity, Battle of (1754) **4:** 548
Fort Niagara **4:** 548
Fort Sumter, Battle of (1861) **5:** 677–678
Fort William Henry, Battle of (1757) **4:** 548
fortifications, town **1:** 73
forts, Portuguese **3:** 324, *325,* 330
fossils **5:** *697,* 698
Founders, of the American Constitution **1:** 51
Fountains Abbey, Yorkshire **2:** *209*
Four Books of the Sentences (Peter Lombard)
    1: 56–57
Fourteen Points **7:** 902–903, 906 **8:** 1024
    and China **7:** 934–935
    and India **8:** 1108
Fourteenth Amendment, to the U.S. Constitution
    6: 830
Fourth Coalition, War of the (1806–1807)
    Battle of Friedland **5:** 600
    Battle of Jena and Auerstädt **5:** 600
Foxe, John **2:** 211
Fragonard, Jean-Honoré **4:** 492, *494*
France
    Hundred Years' War (1338–1453) **1:** 8, *13,* 14–15
    rise of the monarchy **1:** 12–13
    as a nation-state **1:** 22–23
    Wars of Religion (1562–1598) **1:** 31 **2:** 161, 172,
        195–204
    monarchy and religion **1:** 70
    population increase (1400s/1500s) **2:** 196
    Grand Siècle (Great Century; 1600s) **2:** 204
    and the Thirty Years' War **2:** 232, 233 **4:** 453, 455
    Baroque style **2:** 262–263
    trade with Asia **3:** 330
    piracy **3:** 348
    colonies in North America (New France) **3:** *355,*
        360, 373–374 **4:** 545–549
    parts of North America claimed for France
        3: 355–356
    bases in India **3:** 418
    French Revolution **4:** 453, 497, 511, 521
        5: 583–594 **6:** 748
    and the War of the Spanish Succession **4:** *461,*
        464, 465
    and the Enlightenment (1700s) **4:** 472, 492

cultural dominance (1700s) **4:** 491–492
    slow development of agricultural innovation
        (1700s) **4:** 503
    economic depression (1700s) **5:** 584–585
    republic declared **5:** 592
    and Napoleon **5:** 595–604
    July Revolution (1830) **5:** *605,* 608, *610,* 655
        6: 820
    Charles X replaced **5:** 608
    liberalism **5:** 610
    nationalism (1800s) **5:** 611, 655–657
    banquet campaigns **5:** 612–613, 656
    and industrialization (1800s) **5:** 623
    Second Empire **5:** 657
    Franco-Prussian War (1870–1871) **5:** 662–663,
        664 **6:** 794 **7:** 871, 892 **8:** 1026
    colonies in Africa **6:** 732, 820, 822
    involvement in Mexico (1860s) **6:** 740–741
    railroads **6:** 791
    schooling (1800s) **6:** 800
    city homes (late 1800s) **6:** 802–803
    voting rights (1830s) **6:** 809
    foreign legion **6:** 822
    the Dreyfus affair **6:** 846 **7:** 990
    and fashion **6:** 846
    and the lead-up to World War I **7:** 871, 874
    loses Alsace-Lorraine **7:** 871
    and World War I **7:** 881, 882, 884, 890, 895, 896,
        903
    occupation of the Ruhr (1923) **7:** 953, *956*
    postwar recovery (1920s) **7:** 954–956
    and World War II **8:** 1037, 1038, *1039,* 1048,
        1067, 1068, 1071
    post–World War II **8:** 1075–1076, 1077
    decolonization of Indochina **8:** 1100, *1117,* 1122,
        1123
    French-Vietnamese War (1946–1954) **8:** 1122
    colonies lost in Africa **8:** 1125–1127, 1128
    and the Algerian War of Independence
        (1954–1962) **8:** 1126–1127
    and the Suez Crisis (1956) **8:** 1127, 1133, 1135
    labor union and student protests (1968) **9:** *1164,*
        1165
    and European union **9:** 1193–1194, 1197
Francis, duke of Anjou **2:** 203
Francis I, Holy Roman emperor, bust of **4:** *497*
Francis I, king of France **1:** *13* **2:** 187
    and the arts **1:** 88
    and Protestantism **2:** 161, 170–172, 197
    and the Council of Trent **2:** 168
    and the Habsburg Empire **2:** 188–189, 190–191
    marriage **2:** 190
    and explorers **3:** 355
Francis II, king of France **2:** 198, 199
Francis Joseph I, emperor of Austria **5:** 665
Franciscans **1:** 11, 50, *54* **2:** 166
    missionaries in Mexico **3:** 352–353
Franco, Francisco, and the Spanish Civil War
    8: 1031, 1032, 1033
Franco-Dutch War (1672–1679) **4:** 441, 457, 462
Franco-Prussian War (1870–1871) **5:** 662–663, 664
    6: 794 **7:** 871, 892 **8:** 1026
Frankenstein (Mary Shelley) **5:** 638, *639*
Franklin, Benjamin **4:** 550–551, *562*
Franklin, Rosalind **9:** 1262
Franz Ferdinand, archduke of Austria **7:** *878,*
    879–880
Frederick II, the Great, king of Prussia **4:** 466, 469,
    470, 488–489, 500, 509
    and Enlightenment thought **4:** 480
Frederick II, king of Sicily and Holy Roman
    emperor **1:** 53
Frederick II, the Wise, elector of Saxony
    2: 154–155, 156, 187, 188
Frederick III, Holy Roman emperor **2:** 183,
    184–185
Frederick III, king of Denmark **4:** 446
Frederick IV of the Palatinate **2:** 226
Frederick V of the Palatinate **2:** 227, 231
Frederick William, elector of Brandenburg **4:** 488
Frederick William I, king of Prussia **4:** 488
    army **4:** *467,* 488
Frederick William IV, king of Prussia **5:** *612,* 614,
    659–660
Fredericksburg, Battle of (1862) **5:** 682
Fredrikshamn **4:** *446*

Free Soilers **5:** 654
Freedman's Bureau **6:** 830
Freemasonry **4:** *472*
Freikorps **7:** 952, 987
French Academy **2:** 262
French Community **9:** 1222
French Company of the East Indies **3:** 330
French and Indian War (1754–1763) **3:** 368, 373,
    374 **4:** *546,* 548–549, 552 **5:** 674
French, John **7:** 888
French Republic, declared **5:** 592
French Revolution **4:** 453, 511 **5:** 583–594 **6:** 748
    heroic style **4:** 497
    and free speech **4:** 521
    legacy **5:** 594, 656
French Revolutionary Wars (1792–1802) **5:** 592,
    595–596
French-Vietnamese War (1946–1954) **8:** 1123
frescoes, Renaissance **1:** *72,* 80–81, *83,* 87
Freud, Sigmund **6:** 847, 849
Frick, Henry Clay **5:** *631*
Friedan, Betty **9:** 1166, 1172–1174
Friedland, Battle of (1807) **5:** 600
Friedman, Milton **9:** 1167
Friedrich, Caspar David, paintings by **5:** *635, 640,
    641,* 643
Fronde, the **4:** 455, *456*
frondeurs **4:** 455, *456*
Front de Libération National (FLN) **8:** 1126
Frontenac, Louis de Baude, Comte de **4:** 546
FSA (Farm Security Administration) **7:** 968
FSLN (Sandinista National Liberation Front) *See*
    Sandinista movement
fudai **4:** 534
Fugger dynasty **1:** 45, 46–47 **2:** *185,* 187
Fuji, Mount **6:** *777*
Fulton, Churchill's speech at **8:** *1086,* 1087
Funan **3:** 319
fundamentalism **9:** 1273, 1279
    Islamic fundamentalism in the Middle East
        9: 1231–1242, 1279
    Christian **9:** 1279
fur trade, in colonial America **3:** 360, 371, 374
furniture **2:** 250–251
    in the 1700s **4:** 516–517
    in colonial America **4:** *552*
    in the late 1800s **6:** 798–799
Fyodor (Theodore) I, czar of Russia **1:** 97
    lands acquired under **1:** *90*

Gadhafi, Mu'ammar **9:** 1236, 1237, *1240*
Gadsden Purchase **6:** 740
Gagarin, Yuri **9:** 1256
Gage, Thomas **4:** 556
Gainsborough, Thomas **4:** 496
Galbraith, J. K. **9:** 1159
Galen (Roman physician) **1:** 52 **2:** 247–248, 267
Galilei, Galileo (known as Galileo) **2:** *269,* 270,
    271 **4:** 471–472
galleons **3:** 302
Gallipoli **1:** 100
Gallipoli campaign (1916) **7:** *885,* 890
Galve, Lake **1:** *91*
Gama, Vasco da **3:** *303, 305,* 307, 323, 329 **5:** 667
Gandhi, Indira **8:** *1114,* 1115
Gandhi, Mohandas (*known as* Mahatma) **6:** 828
    8: *1107,* 1108–1109, 1111, 1112–1113
    9: *1175*
    assassination of **8:** 1115
Gandhi, Rajiv **8:** 1115
Gao **1:** 118
gardens, landscape **4:** 498–499
Gare St-Lazare, The (Monet) **6:** *790*
Garibaldi, Giuseppe **5:** 659, *660*
Garrison, William Lloyd **5:** 652
gas, poison **7:** 888
gas masks **7:** 888
gaslighting, domestic **6:** 790
Gates, Bill **9:** *1252*
Gates, Horatio **4:** 558
GATT (General Agreement on Tariffs and Trade)
    9: 1198
gauchos **6:** *760* **7:** *973*
Gauguin, Paul **6:** 784, 844–845
Gaulle, Charles de
    and the Algerian War of Independence **8:** 1127

Volume numbers appear in **boldface type.** Page numbers in *italic type* refer to illustrations and captions.

and France's African colonies **8:** 1127
and European union **9:** 1193–1194
gay rights **9:** *1165,* 1166
Gaza Strip **8:** 1132, 1133, 1137, 1138 **9:** 1242
gazis **1:** 99–100
Gdansk (*formerly* Danzig) **1:** 16, 93 **4:** 482 **8:** 1106
geishas **4:** 538, *541*
Gellée, Claude *See* Claude Lorrain
Gellhorn, Martha **7:** 968
gender, in the 1700s **4:** 512, 518
General Agreement on Tariffs and Trade (GATT) **9:** 1198
General Motors **7:** 949 **8:** *1081*
General Strike (1926) **7:** 958
generators, invention **5:** 704
genetics **5:** 699
Geneva
infant mortality **1:** 10
religion **2:** 160, *161,* 197
Geneva Convention (1864) **5:** 663
Genghis Khan **1:** 123, *124*
Genoa **1:** 15, 22, 28, 41, 106 **2:** 188–189
Genroku period, Japanese **4:** 540
Gentileschi, Artemisia **2:** 259
painting by **2:** *256*
Gentileschi, Orazio **2:** 259
Gentili, Antonio **2:** *168*
gentlemen **1:** 75
Geographia (Ptolemy) **1:** 65 **3:** 300
geology, and age of the Earth **5:** 698
George I, king of Britain and Ireland **4:** *444,* 445
George III, king of Great Britain, and the American colonies **4:** 556, 557
George V, king of Great Britain **6:** *798* **7:** *872*
and India **5:** *669*
Georgia (Caucasus) **5:** 691
independence **9:** *1247,* 1249
Georgia (North America) **3:** 364 **5:** *654*
Gérard, Balthazar **2:** *220*
German Confederation **5:** 660
German East Africa **7:** 887
German Workers' Party **7:** 987
Germantown, Battle of (1777) **4:** 558
Germany
Luther and the birth of Protestantism **1:** 10, 12 **2:** 151–160, 162
Hanseatic League **1:** 15, *16,* 24, 41, *42* **3:** 298
Fugger dynasty **1:** 46–47 **2:** *185,* 187
part of the Holy Roman Empire **1:** 71 **2:** 184, 190, 191–192, 225
peasant revolts (early 1500s) **2:** 156, 246
and the Thirty Years' War **2:** 225–234
immigrants to North America (c. 1700s) **3:** 371, 372
canals **4:** 509
nationalism **5:** 602, 611, *656,* 659–664
liberalism **5:** 610, 611
and the 1848 revolutions **5:** *613,* 614, 629
industrialization (1800s) **5:** 623 **6:** 794–796
Social Democratic Party **5:** 628
immigration to the United States **5:** 650
unification (1871) **5:** 664 **7:** 871
railroads **6:** 791
African colonies **6:** 796, 825
gains Alsace-Lorraine **7:** 871
and the lead-up to World War I **7:** 871–876
and World War I **7:** 880–882, 884–896
and the postwar Treaty of Versailles **7:** 903–905, 908, 952, 953, 987, 988, 993 **8:** 1026–1028, 1030–1031
civil war after World War I **7:** 952
Weimar Republic **7:** 952–953, 987 **8:** 1029
alliance with the Soviet Union (1922) **7:** 953
France occupies the Ruhr (1923) **7:** 953, *956*
hyperinflation (1923) **7:** 953–954, 988
and the rise of Hitler **7:** 987–994
and the road to World War II **8:** 1025–1036
and the Spanish Civil War **8:** 1031, 1032, 1038
and World War II **8:** 1037–1048, 1062–1063, 1066–1068
post–World War II **8:** *1072, 1073, 1074, 1075,* 1089–1090
reunification (1990) **8:** *1105* **9:** 1196, 1247–1248
Germany, East (GDR), and the Berlin Wall **8:** *1095,* 1096, *1097,* 1106 **9:** 1248

Germany, West
Social Democratic Party **9:** 1166–1167
and European union **9:** 1194
germs, discovery **5:** 701–702, 705
Geronimo **6:** 839
Gettysburg, Battle of (1863) **5:** 683, *686*
Gettysburg Address **5:** *685*
Ghana (*formerly* Gold Coast) **1:** 112, 115
decolonization **8:** 1124–1125, 1127
military coup (1966) **9:** 1225
Ghent, Pacification of (1576) **2:** 219
Ghent, Treaty of (1814) **5:** 646
Ghost Dance **6:** 839
ghulams **3:** 403
GI Bill of Rights (1944; Serviceman's Readjustment Act) **8:** 1081
Gibraltar **2:** 253
and the War of the Spanish Succession **4:** *464,* 465, 467
Gilbert Islands, Battle of Tarawa (1943) **8:** 1054, *1055*
Giorgione **1:** 84
Giotto di Bondone **1:** 81, 87
girls, education **1:** 54
Girondins **5:** 592, 593, 594
glasnost **8:** 1106 **9:** 1244, 1248
glassmaking, in Mogul India **3:** 413
global warming **9:** 1266, 1267–1268, 1271, 1274–1275
globalization **9:** 1219, 1276–1277, 1282
Glorious Revolution (accession of William and Mary) **2:** *243,* 244 **4:** 442–444, 472, 502
Gluck, Christoph Willibald **4:** 521
Goa
Portuguese colony **3:** *308,* 324, *399*
Jesuit missionaries from **3:** *411,* 412
Godunov, Boris **1:** 97
lands acquired under **1:** *90*
Goebbels, Joseph **7:** *983,* 991 **8:** 1067
Goeben (ship) **7:** *875*
Goethe, Johann Wolfgang von **4:** 500 **5:** *636,* 638, 642
Gogh, Vincent Van **6:** 844, *846*
Going Upriver at the Ming Festival (silk painting) **1:** *123*
Golan Heights **8:** 1133, 1134, 1136
gold
African **1:** 115 **6:** 826
European trade with West African gold **3:** 303, 305
from the Americas **3:** 348, *389*
California gold rush **5:** *651,* 654 **6:** 837–840
discovered in Australia **5:** 673
Klondike Gold Rush **5:** 675
Gold Coast *See* Ghana
gold standard **7:** 965, 972–973
Golden Age, Dutch **2:** 223–224
Golden Fleece, Order of the **1:** 25–26
Golden Horde, khanate of the **1:** 90
Gonçalves Zarco, Joao **3:** 304
Gone with the Wind (movie) **7:** *970*
Gonzaga, Ludovico **1:** 72
Good Hope, Cape of, rounding **3:** 305–306, *307*
Good Neighbor Policy **7:** 973, 980 **9:** 1200
Gorbachev, Mikhail Sergeyevich **8:** 1104, 1105, 1106 **9:** 1168, 1243–1244, *1245,* 1248, 1249, 1250
Gordon, Charles G. **6:** 824, 825
Gore, Al **9:** *1272*
Gosplan **9:** 926
Gothic churches **2:** 257
gothicism, and the Romantics **5:** 636
Götz von Berlichingen (Goethe) **5:** 638
Gouges, Olympe de **5:** *588*
Government of India Act (1919) **8:** 1108
Government of India Act (1935) **8:** 1112
Government of Ireland Act (1920) **7:** 957–958
governments
and trade **1:** 45
role post–World War II **8:** 1078–1079
the West's experiments with (1960–1999) **9:** 1159–1168
Gowon, Yakubu **9:** 1226
Goya, Francisco de, paintings by **2:** *175*
Graham, Billy **9:** *1177,* 1178
grain, storage **4:** *504,* 508

Gran Chaco **7:** 979
Gran Colombia **6:** 752–753, 755, 758
Granada **1:** 24
Grand Alliance
and the War of the Spanish Succession **4:** *461,* 464–465
and the War of the Austrian Succession **4:** 469
Grand Armée, of Napoleon **5:** 598–599, *603,* 604
grand tour **4:** 495–496
grand viziers **6:** 728
Grant, Ulysses S. **5:** *681,* 682, 685–686
U.S. president **6:** 830
Grapes of Wrath, The (John Steinbeck) **7:** *965*
Gravelines, Battle of (1558) **2:** *212*
Graves, Robert **7:** 895
gravity, theory of **2:** 224, 272
Gray, Thomas **5:** 638–639
Great Awakening **4:** 549–550
Second **5:** 652
Great Banda **3:** 328
Great Britain
and the War of the Spanish Succession **4:** 464, 465, 466, 467
and the Enlightenment **4:** 472, 473–475, 479–480
agricultural revolution **4:** 502, 503
society (1700s) **4:** 502
enclosures **4:** 503–504
trade with China **4:** 532
and the North American colonies **4:** 544–552, 550–552, 553–562
wars against France in North America **4:** 545–548, 553
and Napoleon **5:** 598, *599,* 600
liberal advances and reform **5:** 608
Chartist movement **5:** 612
the Industrial Revolution **5:** 615–624
industrial society (1800s) **5:** 625–634
urbanization (1800s) **5:** 625 **6:** 803
Empire **5:** 667–676
Commonwealth **5:** 676 **8:** 1120 **9:** 1190
decline in economic performance (1800s) **6:** 789
the rise of socialism **6:** 807–811
trade unions **6:** *807,* 809 **7:** 957, 958
Parliamentary democracy **6:** 809
abolition of slavery and the slave trade **6:** 819
and the lead-up to World War I **7:** 872, 873, 874, 875–876, 882
and World War I **7:** 888, 890, 894, 896, 901, 902, 903
general strike (1926) **7:** *957,* 958
post–World War I **7:** 957–958
and the road to World War II **8:** *1035,* 1036
and World War II in Europe **8:** 1037–1042, 1045–1048
and World War II in North Africa **8:** 1045, 1046
and World War II in the Pacific **8:** 1050, 1051
and World War II **8:** 1064, 1067–1068, 1069
post–World War II **8:** 1076–1077, *1078*
and the welfare state **8:** 1077
and the postwar treatment of Germany **8:** 1084–1086
and independence and partition in India **8:** 1107–1114
economic depression and India **8:** 1109
loss of the African colonies **8:** 1124–1125, 1127–1128
and the Suez Crisis (1956) **8:** 1127, 1133, 1135
and Jewish immigration to Palestine **8:** 1130
"rights politics" (1960s) **9:** 1166
swing to the political right (1980s) **9:** 1167–1168
turns to the political left (1970s) **9:** 1167
and a united Europe **9:** 1190, 1194, 1197
CJD and mad cow disease **9:** 1275
great chain of being **1:** 75
Great Depression **7:** 954, 958, 959–970 **8:** 1079 **9:** 1159
cultural effects **7:** 968–969
and Latin America **7:** 974–975
and Japan **8:** 1017–1018
Great Exhibition (1851) **5:** 615, 622, 624, 634
Great Fear **5:** 588
Great Fire of London **2:** 242–243, *244*
Great Leap Forward **9:** 1182–1183
Great Migration **3:** 359
Great Northern War (1700–1721) **4:** 447 1401

Great Plague **2:** 242–243, 247
Great Plains (North American) **3:** 341–342, 395
    9: 1264
Great Reform Act (1832) **6:** 809, 810
Great/Western Schism (papal schism; 1378–1417)
    1: 11, 20 **2:** 151, 164, *165*
Great Stink (1848) **5:** *629*, 705 **6:** 802
Great Trek (1835–1843) **6:** 821
Great Wall of China **1:** *119*, 122 **4:** 523, 526
Great War, as a name for World War I **7:** 873, 883
Great Withdrawal, in China **1:** 127–128
Great Zimbabwe **1:** 115
Greater Serbia **7:** 878
Greece
    rebellion against Ottoman rule **5:** 607, *611*
        6: 731–732
    War of Independence **5:** *611*
    and World War II **8:** 1043
    EEC membership **9:** 1195
Greece, ancient
    and humanism **1:** 17, 62, 63–64
    and learning **1:** 52–53
    influence on classicism **4:** 494–495
green parties **9:** 1271
green revolution **9:** 1264–1265
Greene, Nathanael **4:** 561
greenhouse gases *See* carbon dioxide; global
        warming
Greenpeace **9:** 1271
Gregory IX, Pope **2:** 174
Gregory XIII, Pope **2:** 202, 270
Grenada (Spain) **2:** 180
Grenada (West Indies), U.S. invasion (1983)
    9: *1205*, 1206
Grey, Edward **7:** *882*
Grey, Lady Jane **2:** 210
Grimaldi family of Genoa **1:** 46
Grimm brothers **5:** *601*, 602
Grounding for a Metaphysics of Morals
        (Immanuel Kant) **4:** 479
Group Areas Act (1950) **9:** 1228
group rights **5:** 628
Grünwald, Battle of (1410) **1:** 91
Guadalcanal, battles for (1942) **8:** 1053–1054
Guadalupe, Virgin of **3:** 353
Guam **6:** 835
    and World War II **8:** 1052, *1054*
Guanahani **3:** 309
Guatemala
    land reform program (from 1951) **9:** 1201
    destabilization of government **9:** 1201–1202
    internal conflict **9:** 1204, 1206
    overuse of pesticides **9:** 1275
Guatemalan National Revolutionary Unity (UNRG)
    9: 1203
Guayaquil **6:** 754, *755*
Guevara, Ernesto "Che" **9:** *1163*, 1164, 1203
Guevara, Fernando Niño de **2:** *178*
Gui, Bernard **2:** 176, 179
Guidobalda, duke of Urbino **1:** *45*
Guildford Court House, Battle of (1781) **4:** 561
guilds **1:** 16, 43, *44* **4:** 518
guillotines **5:** *583*, 593
Guinea **3:** 303
    independence **8:** 1127
Guise brothers **2:** *198*, 199, 200, 201
Guizot, François **5:** 612
gulags (labor camps) **7:** 927, 928
    Gulag Archipelago **7:** 932
Gulf War (1991) **9:** *1279*
    helicopters **9:** 1255
    burning oil wells **9:** *1273*
Gulhane, Edict of (1839) **6:** 733
Gulliver's Travels (Swift) **4:** 500
gunboat diplomacy **7:** 875
gunpowder **1:** 15, 26, 66 **4:** *470*
gunpowder flasks **2:** *232*
guns *See* artillery; firearms
Guomindang (Nationalist Party) **7:** *934, 935,* 936
    joins forces with the communists **7:** 936–938
Gustav III, king of Sweden **4:** *446*, 448
Gustav Adolph (Gustavus Adolphus), king of
        Sweden **2:** 225, 228, 230, 231 **4:** 446
Gutenberg, Johannes, printing press **1:** *59,* 60–61
    2: 254

Guthrie, Woody **7:** 968
Guzmán, Abimael **9:** 1206

ha-has **4:** 498
Haarlem **2:** 223 **4:** *439*
Haarlem, siege of (1573) **2:** 219
Habsburg Empire **1:** 20 **2:** 183–194, 225
    4: 485–486 **5:** *606*
    the Low Countries **1:** 25 **2:** 215–216 **5:** 590
    and Poland-Lithuania **1:** 25 **4:** *484*, 490
    and the Fugger dynasty **1:** 47
    and Hungary **1:** 93 **4:** 485–486
    and the Jagiello rulers **1:** 93
    and the Reformation **1:** 94–95
    and the Ottomans **1:** 107, 108
    in Austria **2:** 187 **4:** 460 **5:** 655
    line of succession **2:** 187
    and wealth from the Americas **3:** 348
    absolutism **4:** 460
    peasants **4:** 505
    suppressing uprisings (1848) **5:** 613–614
Habyarimana, Juvenal **9:** 1230
haciendas **3:** *349,* 350 **6:** 742
Hague, the **2:** 220
Hague, Coalition of the **2:** 228
Hague Peace Conference (1907) **6:** 765
Haida people **3:** *331*
Haifa **8:** *1129,* 1130, *1136*
Haig, Douglas **7:** 894
haikus **4:** 540
Haiphong **8:** *1122*
Haiti
    and Columbus **3:** 309, *310*
    slave revolt **3:** 386
    independence **6:** 748
Haley, Bill **9:** 1171
halles **1:** 40
Hals, Frans **2:** 261
    painting by **2:** *272*
Hamas **8:** 1138 **9:** 1242
Hamburg **2:** 188
    and industrialization **1:** 16 **5:** 612
    cholera **6:** 790
Hamburg, Treaty of (1641) **2:** 233
Hamilton, Alexander **5:** 650
Hampden, John **2:** 238
Hampton Court **2:** 207
Hampton Court Conference (1604) **2:** 236
Hancock, John **4:** 555
Hanford, Ben **6:** *815*
Hangzhou **1:** 119
Hanoi **8:** 1123
Hanover **2:** 188
Hanoverians **4:** *444,* 445
Hanseatic League **1:** 15, *16,* 24, 41, *42* **3:** 298
hara kiri **4:** 536
Hara, Takashi **8:** 1016, 1017
Hard Times (Charles Dickens) **6:** 845
Harding, Warren G. **7:** 946–947
Harijans **8:** 1111
Harlem **7:** 950
Harlequin **4:** *492*
Harmony of the Universe, The (print) **2:** *265*
harnesses **1:** 16, *18*
Harper's Bazar (later *Harper's Bazaar*) **6:** 846
harpsichords **1:** 86
Harris, Joel Chandler **6:** 804
Hats, and the Caps **4:** 448
Haussmann, Georges-Eugène **6:** 789, 790
Havana **8:** *1098*
Havel, Václav **9:** 1246
"Haw-Haw, Lord" (William Joyce) **8:** 1068
Hawaii, Pearl Harbor attacked **8:** 1025, 1042, 1049,
    1050–1051, 1053, 1067
Haydn, Joseph **4:** 500
Hayes, Rutherford B. **6:** 831
Haystack at Sunset (Claude Monet) **6:** *845*
Heath, Edward **9:** 1194
Hedvig, queen of Poland **1:** 91
Heeren Seventeen **3:** *326*
Heidelberg **8:** *1031*
helicopters, military **9:** *1254,* 1255
Hendriks, Anneken **2:** *162*
Henry I of Lorraine, duke of Guise **2:** *198,* 199,
    203

Henry II, king of France (1519–1559) **1:** *9*
    2: 191–192, 199
Henry III, king of France **2:** 198, 202, 203, 220
Henry IV, king of France, known as Henry of
        Navarre (1553–1610) **2:** 201, 202, 203–204
    4: 453
Henry VII, (Henry Tudor), king of England **1:** 23,
    71, 72 **2:** 205, 206, 214 **3:** 355
Henry VIII, king of England **1:** 71 **2:** 160, 207–209
    court painter **1:** 88
    and the Habsburg Empire **2:** 189, 190–191
    invasion of France (1544) **2:** 190
Henry the Navigator **3:** 299–300, 303–305, *306,*
    376
herbals **4:** 506
Herbst, Josephine **7:** 968
Herculaneum **4:** 495
Herder, Johann Gottfried von **5:** 602, 611
Herero people **6:** 827
heresy
    punishing *See* Inquisition
    dualist **2:** 180
Hero of Alexandria **1:** 52
Herrera, Juan de **2:** 191
Hertz, Heinrich **5:** 705
Herzl, Theodore **8:** 1129, *1131*
Hesse **2:** 188
Hesse-Kassel **5:** 660
Hessians **4:** 558
Hezbollah **9:** 1240, 1241, 1242
Hicks, Edward, painting by **3:** *365*
Hidalgo, Miguel **6:** 737, *738*
hidalgos **1:** 76
Hideyoshi **4:** 533, 539
Hildegard, abbess of Bingen **1:** 11
Hilliard, Nicholas, paintings by **2:** *205, 212*
Himeji Castle **1:** *126*
Hindenburg, Paul von **7:** 989
Hinduism/Hindus
    in Southeast Asia **3:** 317–318, 320, 322
    under the Moguls **3:** 410–411, 412, 414
    caste system in India **8:** 1109, 1111
    and independence in India **8:** 1110–1112, 1113
    and partition in India **8:** 1114
    fundamentalism in India **8:** 1116
Hine, Lewis Wickes **6:** 815, *840*
Hippocrates **1:** 52
Hirohito, emperor of Japan **8:** 1017, 1019, *1031,*
    1060
Hiroshige **4:** 540 **6:** 784
Hiroshima **8:** 1059, 1086 **9:** 1255
Hispaniola
    and Columbus **3:** 309, *310*
    slave revolt **3:** 386
    smallpox **3:** 390, 393
    See also Dominican Republic; Haiti
Hitler, Adolf **7:** 908, 958, 983, 987–994 **8:** *1025,*
    1027
    and the Jews **7:** 988, 990, 991, 993–994
    and the road to World War II **8:** *1025*–1036
    annexation of Austria (1938) **8:** *1028*
    and Mussolini **8:** *1029*
    and the Spanish Civil War **8:** 1032
    Mein Kampf **8:** 1034, 1066–1067
    and World War II **8:** 1037, 1048
Hitler Youth **7:** 992, *993* **8:** 1048
HIV (human immunodeficiency virus) **9:** 1272
Ho Chi Minh **8:** 1099, 1100, 1123 **9:** 1165
Ho Chi Minh City (*formerly* Saigon) **8:** 1099
    9: *1217*
Hobbes, Thomas **4:** 450, 473–474
hoboes **7:** 963, 969
Hogarth, William **4:** 494, 498
Hohenzollern dynasty **4:** 460, 488 **5:** 661
Hokusai **4:** 540, *542* **6:** *777,* 784
Holbein, Hans, the Younger **1:** 88
    paintings by **2:** *208, 210*
Holland **5:** 608
Hollywood **7:** 951, *963*
Holmes, Sherlock (fictional character) **6:** 805
Holocaust **7:** 991 **8:** 1129
Holstein **5:** 661
Holy Alliance **5:** 608
Holy League **1:** 108
Holy Roman emperors **1:** 20, 28, 71 **2:** 154, 225
    See also Habsburg Empire

Holy Roman Empire **1:** 28 **2:** 154, 183–184 **4:** 485
  and the Reformation **1:** 71
    Germany part of **2:** 184, 190, 191–192, 225
    and the Thirty Years' War **2:** 225–234
Holy Union (Sainte-Union) **2:** 203
Homer, Winslow **6:** 842–843
homes, middle-class (late 1800s) **6:** 798–799
Homestead **6:** *795*
Homestead Act (1862) **6:** 837
Honda **9:** 1210
Honduras, bananas **6:** *761, 763* **7:** 973
Honeker, Erich **8:** *1105* **9:** 1248
honey **3:** 390, 395, *396*
honeybees, introduced to the Americas **3:** 395, *396*
Hong Kong
  ceded to Britain **6:** 771 **9:** 1216
  returned to China (1997) **8:** 1128 **9:** 1188, 1216, 1220
  economic growth **9:** 1214–1217
Hong Taiji **4:** 526
Hooch, Pieter de **2:** 261
Hoover, Herbert **7:** 900, 946, *961–965* **8:** *1073*
Hoover Dam **7:** 967
Hormuz, Portuguese expelled from **3:** 330, 403
horses
  in Africa **1:** 114
  and colonial America **3:** 342, *387,* 394–395
  in Europe (1700s) **4:** *518,* 520
hospitals **6:** 801
  charitable **2:** *249*
House of Representatives **4:** 562
House Unamerican Activities Committee (HUAC) **8:** 1092
houses
  European (1600s) **2:** 250
  in colonial America **3:** *367*
  European (1700s) **4:** 516, 517
  in industrial London (1800s) **5:** *625*
hovercraft **9:** 1260
How the Other Half Lives (Jacob Riis) **5:** 626
Howard, Catherine **2:** 209
Howe, William **4:** 556–557, 558
Hsü Heng **1:** 125
HUAC (House Unamerican Activities Committee) **8:** 1092
Hubble Space Telescope (HST) **9:** 1256–1257
Hudson, Henry **3:** 326, 362
Hudson Bay Company **5:** 675
Hudson River School **5:** 643
Huerta, Victoriano **6:** 745
Huguenots
  and the Wars of Religion **2:** 161, 172, 195–204
  churches **2:** *196*
  in South Africa **3:** 329
  after the Wars of Religion **4:** 451, 453
  and Louis XIV **4:** 459, 462
human immunodeficiency virus (HIV) **9:** 1272
humanism/humanists **1:** 9, 17 **2:** 152, 160
  and ancient Greece and Rome **1:** 17, 62–64
  a reaction to Scholasticism **1:** 57–58
  and the spread of knowledge **1:** 59–68, 80
  in Florence **1:** 64–65, 80
  and wealth **1:** 73
  and nobility **1:** 75
  and the Bible **2:** 165
  and Latin **2:** 252
  See also Erasmus, Desiderius
humanity, science of **4:** 479
Humayun, Mogul emperor **1:** 130 **3:** *407*
Humboldt, Alexander von **4:** *507*
Hume, David **4:** 479
humors, bodily **2:** 248
Hundred Days of Reform **6:** 773
Hundred Years' War (1338–1453) **1:** 8, *13,* 14–15, 23
Hung Hsiu-ch'uan **6:** 771, 772
Hungary
  and the Habsburg Empire **1:** 93 **4:** 485–486
  and the Jagiello dynasty **1:** 93
  and the Ottomans **1:** 93, 107 **6:** 729
  nomad invasion **3:** 297
  struggle for independence from Austria **5:** 613–614
  Dual Monarchy with Austria **5:** 665
  uprising (1956) **8:** 1094
  and communism **8:** 1106

collapse of communism; rise of nationalism **9:** 1245–1246
Hunt, Henry **6:** 807
Huron (Native Americans) **3:** 335–336, 340
Hus, Jan **1:** 11, 94, *95* **2:** 152, 164, 165
Husák, Gustáv **9:** 1246
husbandry, convertible **4:** 503
hussars **4:** *466*
Hussein, Saddam **9:** 1235
Hussites **1:** 94, 95 **2:** 152
Hutten, Ulrich von **1:** 47
Hutus **9:** 1230, 1278
Huxley, T. H. **5:** 700, 705–706
Huygens, Christiaan **2:** 224
hymnbooks, Protestant **2:** *159*
Hyogo, Himeji Castle **1:** *126*
hyperinflation, German (1923) **7:** 953–954, 988

IBM **9:** 1258
Ibn Rushd (Averroës) **1:** *57*
Ibsen, Henrik **6:** 850
icons **1:** 92
Idia, mother of the king of Benin **1:** *112*
Iemitsu, shogun of Japan **4:** 537, 539
Ieyasu, shogun of Japan **4:** 533–534, *535,* 539
Ignatius of Loyola, St. **2:** 170, *171,* 257
Iguala, Plan of **6:** 738
Illiescu, Ion **9:** 1246–1247
illuminations (artwork) **1:** 60–61
IMF (International Monetary Fund) **9:** 1220
Imitation of Christ, The (Thomas à Kempis) **1:** 11 **2:** 165
Immigration Reform Act (1965) **9:** 1178
Imphal **8:** 1058
Impression: Sunrise (Claude Monet) **6:** 843
Impressionism/Impressionists **5:** 644 **6:** 843
Incas **3:** 332, 343, *389,* 391
incense **3:** 298, 315, *316*
Independence, Declaration of (1776) **4:** 480, 557, *558,* 562
Independence, War of (Greek) **5:** *611*
Independent Labour Party **6:** 816
Index of Prohibited Books **2:** 169
India
  Mogul **1:** *120,* 130 **3:** 402, 406, 407–418 **5:** 667
  rise of Muslim India **1:** 129–130
  Roman ports **3:** 298
  Portuguese discover a sea route to **3:** 307, 323
  influence on Southeast Asia **3:** 317
  and international trade **3:** 321, 324, *325,* 330
  the English in (1600s) **3:** 330
  European trade with **3:** 417
  part of the British Empire **5:** 667–671 **7:** 873
  partition **8:** 1015
  independence and partition **8:** 1107–1116
  and World War I **8:** 1107
  massacre at Amritsar **8:** 1108
  caste system **8:** 1109, 1111
  and World War II **8:** 1112–1114
  nuclear weapons **8:** 1116
  and state socialism **9:** 1161
  war with China (1962) **9:** 1186
  green revolution in farming **9:** 1265
  chemical accident at Bhopal **9:** 1270
  population (1999) **9:** 1275
India Office **8:** 1107–1108
Indian Civil Service (ICS) **5:** 669–670
Indian Mutiny **5:** 668–669
Indian National Congress **5:** 670, 671 **8:** 1107
Indian Ocean, Portuguese control of **3:** 307
Indian Removal Act (1830) **6:** 839
Indians
  North American *See* Native Americans
  Latin American **6:** *762, 764, 765*
"Indies, the"
  discovery of sea routes to **3:** 303–312
  Columbus's voyages to **3:** 307–310
Indies, Council of **3:** 347
Indies Party **8:** 1020–1021
Indo-Pakistan wars **8:** 1114
Indochina
  and France **6:** 772 **8:** 1050
  Japanese occupation (1941) **8:** 1050, 1119
  and communism (1950s) **8:** 1093

slow post–World War II economic development **9:** 1217
  See also Cambodia; Laos; Vietnam
Indochina War
  Second *See* Vietnam War
  First (1946–1954; French-Vietnamese War) **8:** 1123
Indonesia (*formerly* Dutch East Indies)
  peoples **3:** 315
  fishing **3:** *316*
  Buddhism **3:** 320
  and the Dutch **3:** 327, *328* **7:** 873 **8:** 1020, 1120–1121
  nationalism and independence **8:** 1015, 1020–1023, 1120–1121
  Japanese occupation (1942–1945) **8:** 1023, 1119, 1120
  and World War II **8:** 1023, 1050
  communist coup **8:** 1121–1122
  post–World War II economy **9:** 1217, 1218
  economic crisis (1990s) **9:** 1220
  prodemocracy demonstrations **9:** 1280
indulgences, sale of **1:** 11–12, 46, 47 **2:** 152, 153
Industrial Revolution **5:** 609–612, 615–624
  laying the basis for **4:** 501, 510
  effects on women and children **5:** *617, 629,* 631–634
  industrial development after **5:** 625–634
  and India **5:** 668
  second wave of industrialization **6:** 787–796
Industrial Revolution, "Third" **9:** 1254
industrialization
  after 1500 **1:** 33
  after the Industrial Revolution **5:** 625–634
  and Romanticism **5:** 637
  second wave of **6:** 787–796
  in Stalin's Soviet Union **7:** 926–927, 928, *929, 930*
  in China **7:** 941
  effects on the natural world **9:** 1263
industries, nationalized post–World War II **8:** 1077, 1078, 1079 **9:** 1160
inflation, European (1500s) **1:** 36, 48
influenza, post–World War I pandemic **7:** 883
Ingria **4:** 446
ink **1:** 60
ink sticks, Chinese **4:** *526*
Innocent III, Pope **1:** *54* **2:** 175
Innocent X, Pope **2:** 260
Innsbruck **2:** 192
Inquisition **2:** 174–180
  Spanish **1:** 24 **2:** 172, *175,* 179, 216–217
  Roman **2:** 167, 175, 180
  established (1231) **2:** 174
  Supreme Council of the **2:** 179
  and witches **2:** 180
  and Galileo **2:** 270
  in India **3:** 324
Institutes of the Christian Religion (John Calvin) **2:** 161
Institutional Revolutionary Party (PRI) **9:** 1206
insurance, marine **1:** 73
integrated circuits **9:** 1258
intelligentsia, Russian **5:** 695–696
intendant system, in France **4:** 453–455
International Brigades **8:** 1032
International Justice, Court of **8:** 1028
International Monetary Fund (IMF) **9:** 1220
Internationale (anthem) **6:** 815
Internationals, the **6:** *811,* 813, 815–816
Internet **9:** 1259–1260, 1277
Interpretation of Dreams, The (Freud) **6:** 849
intifada, against Israeli rule **8:** 1138
Intolerable Acts (1774) **4:** 555, 556, 557
Inuit peoples **3:** 341
IRA (Irish Republican Army) **9:** 1238, 1279
Iran
  the Safavid empire **1:** 105 **3:** 397–406 **6:** 728, 729
  arts of the Safavid dynasty **3:** 400–402, 403, *406*
  Soviet intent to occupy Azerbaijan **8:** 1086–1087
  arms sold to Iran by the U.S. **9:** 1205
  revolution (1970s) **9:** 1231, 1232–1235
  modernization under the shah (1950s–1970s) **9:** 1232–1233
  return of Ayatollah Khomeini **9:** *1233,* 1234
  U.S. embassy hostages (1979) **9:** 1234

Volume numbers appear in **boldface type**. Page numbers in *italic type* refer to illustrations and captions.

Volume numbers appear in **boldface type.** Page numbers in *italic type* refer to illustrations and captions.

Joan (Juana), wife of Philip I **2**: 185–186
Joao, Dom (John VI) **6**: 755, 756
John, surnamed Lackland, king of England **1**: 13
   and the Magna Carta **1**: *14*
John I Albert, king of Poland **1**: 93
John II, king of Portugal **3**: 305–306, 308
John III Sobieski, king of Poland-Lithuania **4**: 485
John VI (Dom João), prince regent then king of
   Portugal **6**: 755, 756
John VI Cantacuzenus **1**: 100
John of Austria, known as Don **2**: 219
John Paul II, Pope **9**: *1245*
Johnson, Andrew **6**: 829, 830
Johnson, Lyndon B. **8**: 1099, 1100, 1101 **9**: 1160,
   1173, *1174*, *1177*
Johnson-Reed Act (1924) **7**: 948
Jolliet, Louis **3**: 360
Jolson, Al **7**: 951
Jonson, Ben **2**: 209
Jordan, and the creation of Israel **8**: 1132
Joseph, Chief **6**: 839
Joseph, king of Naples **5**: 600
Joseph I, Holy Roman emperor **4**: 466
Joseph II, Holy Roman emperor **4**: 489 **5**: 590
Joseph Ferdinand, prince of Bavaria **4**: 463
journeymen **4**: 518
Joyce, William ("Lord Haw-Haw") **8**: 1068
Juana (Joan), wife of Philip I **2**: 185–186
Juárez, Benito **6**: 740, 741–743
Juchen tribe **1**: 122
Judith Slaying Holofernes (Artemesia Gentileschi)
   2: *256*
jugs
   used by Habsburg monarchs **2**: *189*
   Chinese **3**: *302*
Julie, or The New Heloise (Rousseau) **4**: 478
Julius II, Pope **1**: 11, 84
   tomb **1**: *82*, 84
July Revolution (1830) **5**: *605*, 608, *610*, 655
   6: 820
June Days (1848) **5**: 656
Jung, Carl **6**: 849
Junín **6**: 754
justices of the peace **1**: 72
Justinian, Code of **1**: 51, 52
Jutland, Battle of (1916) **7**: 876, *891*

Kaba Kangaba **1**: *114*
Kabuki theater **4**: 540
Kabul **9**: 1241
   and Babur **1**: *129*, *130*
Kádár, János **9**: 1245
Kahlo, Frida **7**: *976*
Kaifeng **1**: 122
K'aip'ing **6**: 772
Kamakura shogunate **1**: 125–126, 127
Kamenev, Lev **7**: 931
kamikaze attacks **8**: *1058*–1060
Kandinsky, Wassily **6**: 850
Kanem-Bornu **1**: 112
K'ang-hsi, emperor of China **4**: 527, 529,
   530–531
Kant, Immanuel **4**: *478*, 479
Kaohsiung **9**: *1215*
Karakorum **1**: *124*
Karanga people **1**: 115
Karim Khan, first Zand ruler of Iran **3**: 406
Karmal, Babbrak **8**: 1103
Kashmir **8**: 1114 **9**: 1278
Katanga **9**: *1223*, 1226
Kauffman, Angelica **4**: 497
Kaunda, Kenneth **9**: 1225
Kazakhstan **9**: 1248, 1249
Kedlestone Hall (England) **4**: *517*
Keiki, shogun of Japan **4**: 542
Kellogg–Briand Pact **8**: 1029
Kelly, Ned **5**: 674
Kempis, Thomas à **1**: 11 **2**: 165
Kennedy, Edward **9**: *1173*
Kennedy, Jacqueline Bouvier **9**: 1173
Kennedy, John F. **8**: 1082, 1096 **9**: 1172
   and the Cuban missile crisis **8**: 1096–1097
   and the Vietnam War **8**: 1100
   Alliance for Progress **9**: 1204
Kennedy, Robert F. **9**: 1173, 1176
Kent, William **4**: 498–499

Kenya
   a British colony **8**: 1124
   Mau Mau **8**: 1125
   independence **8**: 1128 **9**: *1221*, 1225
   tribal groups **9**: 1225
Kenyatta, Jomo **8**: 1124, 1125 **9**: *1221*, 1225
Kepler, Johannes **2**: *268*, 270
Kerbala **3**: 399
Kerensky, Aleksandr **7**: 916
Kerman **3**: 405
Kerouac, Jack **9**: 1171
Keynes, John Maynard **7**: 905, 953
Keyser, Hendrik de **2**: *260*, 261
KGB **7**: 930
Khatami, Ayatollah Seyyed Mohammad **9**: 1242
Khmelnytsky, Bohdan **4**: 485
Khmer people **3**: *318*, *319*
Khmer Rouge **8**: 1099 **9**: 1281
Khoi people **1**: 110, 117, *118*
Khoisan language **1**: 116
Khomeini, Ayatollah Ruhollah **9**: 1233, 1234, 1235,
   1241, 1242
Khorasan **3**: 399, 402
Khrushchev, Nikita **8**: 1093, 1094, *1098* **9**: 1161
   and the Cuban missile crisis **8**: 1096–1097
   and China **9**: 1186
kibbutzim **8**: *1136*
Kiel **7**: *873*, 952
Kierkegaard, Soren **5**: 702
Kiev **1**: 89, 92 **7**: 920
Kiev Rus empire **1**: 89, 90, 92
Killiekrankie, Battle of (1689) **4**: 444
Kilwa **1**: 113
Kimberley **6**: 826
Kim Il Sung **9**: *1205*
King, Martin Luther Jr. **8**: 1082 **9**: 1162, *1172*,
   1175, 1176
King Philip (Metacomet) **3**: *368* **4**: 544
King George's War (1744–1748) **4**: 546–548
King Philip's War (1675) **3**: *368* **4**: *543*, 544
King William's War (1689–1697) **4**: 545–546
King's Mountain, Battle of (1780) **4**: 561
kings *See* monarchy
Kingsley, Charles, *The Water Babies* **6**: 804, *809*
Kinshasa, population rise **9**: 1222
Kipling, Rudyard **6**: 827
Kirov, Sergey **7**: 930, *931*
Kissinger, Henry **8**: 1102, 1137
Kitchener, Horatio, 1st earl Kitchener **6**: 826
kivas **3**: 342
Klimt, Gustav **6**: 847
Klondike Gold Rush **5**: 675
knights **1**: *38*
knives, cutlery **2**: *249*
Knox, John **2**: 161, 214
Kohima **8**: 1058
Kohl, Helmut **9**: 1196
Komei, emperor of Japan **6**: 780
Koran **1**: 99
Korea
   and the Sino-Japanese War **6**: 772, 782
   annexed by Japan (1910) **6**: 783
   divided into North and South **9**: 1212
Korea, North
   and the Korean War **8**: 1093 **9**: 1212
   famine (late 1990s) **9**: 1276
Korea, South
   and the Korean War **8**: 1093 **9**: 1212
   postwar poverty followed by economic growth
      9: 1212–1213
   financial depression (1990s) **9**: 1220
Korean War (1950–1953) **7**: 944 **8**: 1081, *1092*,
   1093 **9**: 1171, 1181–1182, 1209, 1212
Kornilov, Lavr G. **7**: 916
Köse Dagh, Battle of (1243) **1**: 99
Kosovo **9**: 1252, 1278
Kosovo, Battle of (1389) **1**: 101
Kossuth, Lajos **5**: 613–614
kowtow **4**: 528
Koxinga **4**: 527
Kramer, Heinrich **2**: 180
Kremer, Gerhard *See* Mercator
Kremlin **1**: 92, *96* **7**: *932*
Kristallnacht **7**: 994
Krueger, Walter **8**: 1056

Kruger, Paul **6**: 826
Ku Klux Klan **6**: 831 **7**: 948
Kuala Lumpur, Petronas Towers **9**: 1218
Kuang-hsü, emperor of the Ching dynasty **6**: 773,
   776
"Kubla Khan" (Coleridge) **5**: 636
Kublai Khan, Mongol emperor **1**: 119, 123–124,
   125
Küçük-Kainardji, Treaty of (1774) **6**: 730, 733
kulaks **7**: 927–930
K'ung Ch'iu (Confucius) **1**: 124 **4**: 530
   See also Confucianism
Kursk, Battle of (1943) **8**: 1045
Kushka **8**: *1103*
Kuwait, Gulf War and burning oil wells **9**: *1273*
Kyoto **1**: 127 **4**: 540
   earth summit **9**: 1271

labor legislation **6**: 814
Labrador **3**: 355
La Comédie Humaine (Balzac) **6**: 846
lacquerware, Japanese **4**: *539*
Ladysmith **6**: 826
Lafayette, marquis de **4**: *560*, 561
Lagos (Nigeria), postcolonial **9**: 1222, *1223*
Lagos (Portugal) **3**: *308*, 376
laissez-faire **5**: 621, 628 **6**: 808
Lake District (England), and Romanticism **5**: 640,
   641
Lamartine, Alphonse de **5**: 613, 656
Land and Freedom party **5**: 693–694
landfill sites **9**: *1263*
landscape gardens **4**: 498–499
Landscape with a Man Bitten by a Snake
   (Nicolas Poussin) **2**: *262*
Landseer, Edwin **6**: 804–805
Lange, Dorothea **7**: 968, *969*
language
   Latin and the vernacular **1**: 49–50, 59–60, 61
   and books **1**: 61–62
Languedoc **2**: 203
Laos **3**: 314 **8**: 1099, 1101
   Japanese occupation of **8**: 1119, 1122
"la Peur" **4**: 450
La Rochelle **2**: 201, 202
   siege of (1627–1628) **4**: 453
La Salle, René Robert Cavalier, Sieur de **3**: 360
Las Casas, Bartolomé de **3**: 353
lasers **9**: 1261
Lasso, Orlando di **1**: 85, 86
Last Supper, The (Leonardo da Vinci) **1**: 81
Lateran Council, Fifth **2**: 165
La Terre (Zola) **6**: *847*
lathes **5**: 618
Latin **1**: 49–50, 52, 59–60
Latin America
   U.S. intervention in **5**: 647 **6**: 741, 766, 835
      9: 1200–1204, 1205–1206
   between the World Wars **7**: 971–982
   fight for self-determination (from 1945)
      9: 1199–1208
latitude **3**: 301
Latvia **7**: 906 **9**: 1248, 1249
Laud, William **2**: 238, 239
Laurier, Wilfrid **5**: 675, 676
Lausanne Conference (1932) **7**: 954
Lawrence, T. E. (Lawrence of Arabia) **7**: 890
Le Brun, Charles **2**: 262
Le Nôtre, André **2**: 263 **4**: 454
le Pot, Philip **1**: *25*
Le Tellier, Michel, marquis de Louvois **4**: 454, 456,
   462
League of Nations *See* Nations, League of
Lebanon
   post–World War I **7**: 905 **8**: 1023
   and the creation of Israel **8**: 1132
   Israeli invasion of (1982) **8**: 1137–1138 **9**: 1240
   and Islamic fundamentalism **9**: 1237–1241
   Palestinian refugee camps **9**: 1237–1240
   civil war (1975) **9**: 1240
   Shiite terrorists (Hezbollah) **9**: 1240, 1241, 1242
Leclerc, Georges-Louis, Comte de Buffon **5**: 698
Lee, Robert E. **5**: 681, 682–683, 686
Lee Kuan Yew **9**: 1218
Leeuwenhoek, Antonie van **2**: 224
legitimacy, principle of **5**: 606, 607

Leicester, Robert Dudley, earl of **2:** 220, 221
Leiden **3:** 358
Leiden, siege of (1574) **2:** 219
Leipzig **9:** 1248
Leipzig, Battle of (1813) **5:** 604
lend-lease, and the United States **8:** 1038–1041
Lenin, Vladimir Ilyich **7:** 930, 945 **9:** *1160, 1161*
    pre-1917 **5:** 696 **7:** 911, *913*, 918
    and the Russian Revolution (1917) **7:** 914–915, 916, 917, 918, 919
    and the Polish-Soviet War **7:** 920
    post-1917 **7:** 921–924, *925*
    and the kulaks **7:** 928
    and China **7:** 936
Leningrad *See* Saint Petersburg
Leo X, Pope **1:** 11–12 **2:** 153
Leonardo da Vinci **1:** 81, 82, 84, *85*
Leoni, Ottavio, drawing by **2:** *269*
Leopold I, king of Belgium **6:** 820, 822, 823 **7:** 873
Lepanto, Battle of (1571) **1:** 108 **2:** 194
Les Rougon-Macquart (Zola) **6:** 846
Lesczinski, Stanislas **4:** 468
Lesotho, independence **8:** 1128
Let Us Now Praise Famous Men (Evans and Agee) **7:** 968
Letter from Jamaica (Simón Bolívar) **6:** 751
Letter of Majesty **2:** 226
Leutze, Emanuel, painting by **4:** *553*
Levant, and the Ottomans **1:** 106 **3:** 298
Levellers (political movement) **2:** 247, 254
Leviathan (Thomas Hobbes) **4:** 473, 474
Levitt, Bill **9:** 1170
Lewis and Clark expedition **5:** *646*
Lexington, USS **8:** *1053*
Lexington and Concord, Battle of (1775) **4:** 556, *557*
    and Paul Revere **4:** *554*
Leyster, Judith **2:** 262–264
Leyte **8:** 1056
Leyte Gulf, Battle of (1944) **8:** 1057, 1058–1060
Li Zicheng **1:** 128, 129 **4:** 525, 526
Liao, Qidan people **1:** 120, 122
Liaodong **1:** 128
Liaotung Peninsula, and the Sino-Japanese War **6:** 772, 782
Liaoyang **4:** 525
liberal democracy **9:** 1168, 1190
Liberal Democratic Party (LDP), of Japan **9:** 1211
liberalism **5:** 609, 610–611
Liberals (Russian) **7:** 911
Liberator, The (journal) **5:** 652
Liberty Bell **4:** *562*
Liberty Leading the People (Eugène Delacroix) **5:** *605*
Liberty ships **8:** *1064*
libraries **1:** 80 **4:** 521
    and the Renaissance **1:** 80
Libya
    and terrorism **9:** 1236–1237
    and the Lockerbie bombing **9:** 1237, *1238*, 1240
Liebknecht, Karl **7:** 952
Liège, cloth guild **1:** 43
life expectancy
    in the Middle Ages **1:** 10
    in early modern Europe **1:** 31–32
Life of the Mother Teresa of Jesus (Saint Teresa of Avila) **2:** 259
light, Newton's discoveries about **2:** 272, *274*
lighting
    street **6:** *788*, 790
    domestic **6:** 790
Lima (Peru)
    and the Spanish colonies **3:** 347 **6:** 747
    and independence from Spain **6:** 754
limpieza de sangre **3:** 351
Lin Bao **9:** 1184
Lincoln, Abraham **5:** 677, 679, *685*, 686 **6:** 829
Lindbergh, Charles **7:** 951
Linnaeus, Carolus **4:** *506*, 507
lira da braccio **1:** *86*
Lisbon **3:** 324, 325 **4:** 460
    slavery in **3:** 377
    and Napoleon **5:** 600
literature, in the 1600s/1700s **4:** 497–450

Lithuania
    Poland-Lithuania **1:** 13, 25, 91–93, 98 **4:** 483–484, 485
    and the Teutonic Knights **1:** 91
    and the Jagiello dynasty **1:** 93
    Union of Lublin (1569) **1:** 98
    independence **7:** 906
    nationalism **9:** 1248, 1249
Little Bighorn, Battle of the (1876) **6:** *835*, 839
Little Ice Age **1:** 33
Little Moreton Hall, Cheshire **2:** *213*
Little Red Book (Mao Tse-tung) **9:** *1184*, 1185
Little Red Riding Hood **5:** *601*
Little Rock **8:** 1082
Little Science, Big Science (De Solla Price) **9:** 1254
Little Women (Louisa May Alcott) **6:** 804
Liu Shao-chi **9:** 1183, 1185
Liverpool, and the slave trade **3:** 382
Lives of the Artists, The (Giorgio Vasari) **1:** 87
Livingston, Philip **3:** 367
Livingstone, David **6:** 820, *821*, 824
Livonia **1:** 97 **4:** 446
Livro das Armadas (Book of Fleets) **3:** 303
Lloyd George, David **7:** 903, *904*, 957
loans, system of **1:** 45
Locarno Treaty (1925) **7:** 956, 958 **8:** 1029
Locke, John **4:** 474–475, 480, 498
Lockerbie, air disaster over **9:** 1237, *1238*, 1240
log cabins **3:** 363
Lollards **2:** 152
Lombard, Peter **1:** 56–57
Lombardy **5:** 657, 658, 659
London
    population **1:** 33 **2:** 252
    beggars (1500s) **1:** 36
    in the 1700s **4:** 508, 511–512
    industrialization and houses **5:** *625*
    Great Stink (1848) **5:** *629*, 705 **6:** 802
    and World War II **8:** 1063
    Telecom Tower **9:** *1168*
London, Treaty of (1839) **7:** 882
London Men's Working Association **6:** 811
Long, Huey P. **7:** 967
Long Drive **6:** 838
Long Island **3:** 362
Long March **7:** *934*, *940*, 941
longbows **1:** 15, 26
longhouses, Native American **3:** 335, 340, *341*
longitude **3:** 301
looms, power looms **5:** 616, 618
Lorrain, Claude **4:** *494*, 495, 498
Lorraine **2:** 192 **4:** 468
Los Angeles **8:** *1082*
    Hollywood **7:** 951, *963*
    smog **9:** *1269*
lost-wax process **1:** 113
Louis, cardinal of Lorraine **2:** *198*, 199
Louis, prince of Condé **2:** 199, 200, 201
Louis II, king of Bohemia and Hungary **1:** 93 **2:** *184*, 188
Louis IX, king of France **1:** 12–13
Louis XIII, king of France **4:** *451*, 452–453
    and Cardinal Richelieu **4:** 453–455
Louis XIV, king of France
    and arts and culture **2:** 262–263 **4:** 458, 491, 492, 496, 497, 500
    and colonies in America **3:** 360 **4:** 545, 546
    war with the Netherlands (1670s; Franco-Dutch War) **4:** 441, 457, 462
    and the rise of absolute monarchy **4:** 449–460
    army **4:** 454, 456
    as the Sun King **4:** *457*, 458, *460*
    and the War of the Spanish Succession **4:** *463*, 464, 466, 467
    See also Versailles, Palace of
Louis XV, king of France **4:** 460, 491
Louis XVI, king of France, and the French Revolution **5:** 585, 586, *589*
Louis XVIII, king of France **5:** 604
Louis-Napoleon *See* Napoleon III
Louis-Philippe, king of the French **5:** 608, *609*, 612, 613, 655, 656
Louisbourg, and colonial America **4:** 547–548
Louisbourg, Battle of (1745) **4:** 547–548
Louisiana
    Cajuns **3:** 374

and Napoleon **5:** 600–601, 646
Louvois, Michel Le Tellier, marquis de **4:** 454, 456, 462
Louvre, the **4:** *451*
Low Countries
    center of commerce **1:** 15
    the Eighty Years' War **1:** 44 **2:** 215–224
Lowell, James Russell **5:** 652
Lübeck **1:** 16, *42*
Lübeck, Treaty of (1628) **2:** 229
Lublin, Union of (1569) **1:** *98*
Ludendorff, Erich **7:** 987
Luftwaffe **8:** 1038, 1048
Lumière brothers **6:** 850
Lumumba, Patrice **9:** 1225–1226
Lusitania (ship) **7:** 894, 895
lutes **1:** 85
Luther, Martin **1:** 10, 21 **2:** 151–156, *157*, *159*, 163, 168, 170, 188
    and the sale of indulgences **1:** 12, 47 **2:** 153
    and the social order **1:** 17
    and the importance of education **1:** 55
    German translation of the Bible **1:** 62 **2:** 155
Lutheranism **1:** 12, 95 **2:** 157–160, 163, 172 **4:** 440
Lützen, Battle of (1632) **2:** *225*, *228*, 231
Luxembourg, European Parliament **9:** *1197*
Luxemburg, Rosa **7:** 952
Luzon **8:** 1051, 1057
Lvov, Georgi Evenievich **7:** 912, 913–914, 915–916
Lyell, Charles **5:** 698
Lyon **2:** 200
Lyons, poverty (1500s) **1:** 36
Lyrical Ballads (Samuel Taylor Coleridge) **5:** 639

Maastricht Treaty (1992) **9:** *1196*, 1197
Macao **3:** 324, 327 **4:** 524 **6:** 772
macaronies **4:** 496
MacArthur, Douglas **7:** *964*, 965 **8:** 1051, 1054
Macartney, George, 1st earl **6:** 767–768
McCarthy, Joseph **8:** *1091*, 1092 **9:** 1169
McClellan, George **5:** 681
Macdonald, Ramsay **7:** *956*, 957
Macedonia, taken by the Ottomans **1:** 101
Machiavelli, Niccolò **1:** 17, 65, 67, 68
machine guns **7:** 892
    Maxim **7:** *886*
Mackenzie, Alexander **5:** 675
McKinley, William **6:** 816, 835
Macmillan, Harold **8:** 1128 **9:** 1194
mad cow disease **9:** 1275
Madagascar **1:** 117 **3:** 323, 328, 330
    peoples **1:** 110, 111, 116 **3:** 315
    language **1:** 116
Madame Bovary (Gustave Flaubert) **6:** 845
Madeira **3:** 304
Maderna, Carlo **2:** *172*
Madero, Francisco **6:** 743–745
Madison, James **5:** 645, 646
Madras **3:** 330, 418 **5:** 667
Madrid **2:** 253
    monastery and palace of El Escorial **2:** *191*, 194
    in the 1700s **4:** *462*
    and the Spanish Civil War **8:** 1032, 1033
Madrid, Treaty of (1526) **2:** 189, 190
madrigals **1:** 86
Mafeking **6:** 826
Magdeburg, destruction of **2:** 230
Magellan, Ferdinand **3:** *305*, 311–312
Magellan, Strait of **3:** 312
Maghreb **1:** 110
maglev trains **9:** 1260
Magna Carta **1:** *14*
magnates **1:** 70
Magyars **1:** 89 **5:** 665
Mahdi (Sudanese ruler) **6:** 825, 826
Mahler, Gustav **6:** 847
Mahmud (Afghan ruler) **3:** *397*, 405
Mahmut II, Ottoman sultan **6:** 730–732
Maine (ship) **6:** 835
Mainz, books censored **1:** 62
Majapahit kingdom **3:** 321
Majorca **1:** 23
Malacca **3:** 322, 327 **8:** *1119*
Malagasy people **3:** 315
malaria **3:** 396 **9:** 1271–1272

Volume numbers appear in **boldface type.** Page numbers in *italic type* refer to illustrations and captions.

Malawi (*formerly* Nyasaland), independence
  8: 1128
Malaya
  and World War II **8:** 1050, 1051, 1119
  and communism (1950s) **8:** 1093
  independence **8:** 1120
Malaysia
  Indian influences **3:** 317
  independence **8:** *1119*
  arrested economic development (1950s/1960s)
    9: 1217
  economy (1990s) **9:** 1218
  financial depression (1990s) **9:** 1220
  rubber production **9:** *1266*
  deforestation **9:** 1274
Malcolm X **9:** 1175
Maldives **9:** 1268
Mali **1:** 16, 18, *109, 114*, 115–118
  neocolonialism **9:** 1222
Malinche, La (or Doña Marina) **3:** *344*, 345
Malindi **3:** 307
Mallarmé, Stéphane **6:** 844
Malleus Maleficarum (book about witches) **2:** 180
Malplaquet, Battle of (1709) **4:** *461*, 466
Malta **5:** 598
Malthus, Thomas **9:** 1264
Mamluks **1:** 105–107 **6:** 732
Manchester, and industrialization **5:** 612, 625, 626
Manchu (Ching) dynasty **1:** 128–129 **4:** 523–532
  6: 768–776
  and the Boxer Rebellion **6:** 774
Manchukuo **7:** 941–942 **8:** 1049
Manchuria **4:** 525
  Russians enter **5:** 696
  Japanese occupation of (late 1800s) **6:** 772, 783
  Japanese occupation of (by 1914) **7:** 934
  Japanese occupation of (1931) **7:** 941–942
    8: *1015*, 1018, 1019, 1031, 1049
  liberated by the Soviets for China (1945) **7:** 943
  See also Mukden
mandalas **3:** 318
Mande people **6:** 827
Mandela, Nelson **9:** 1228, 1229, 1281
Mandinka people **1:** 115
Manet, Edouard **6:** 842
Manhattan Island **3:** *360, 362, 363* **7:** *947*
Manhattan Project **8:** 1059 **9:** 1255
Manifest Destiny **5:** 654 **6:** 739, 836–837
Manila **8:** 1057
manioc **3:** 396
Manitoba **5:** 675
Mann, Thomas **6:** 850
Manon Lescaut (Prévost) **4:** 517
Manresa **2:** *170*
Mantegna, Andrea, painting by **1:** *72*
Mantua **1:** *49, 72* **5:** 596
Manutius, Aldus **1:** 61, 63
Mao Tse-tung (Mao Zedong) **6:** 785 **7:** 933,
  936–944 **8:** 1049, 1093 **9:** 1165, 1179–1185
Maoris **5:** *673, 674*
maps
  Europe's political divisions (c. 1450) **1:** *20*
  European universities (c. 1450) **1:** *50*
  eastern Europe (1300–1700) **1:** *90*
  Ottoman Empire (1400s/1500s) **1:** *100*
  African empires (900s–1300s) **1:** *110*
  Mogul India and Ming China (1500s) **1:** *120*
  Habsburg Empire under Charles V **2:** *186*
  France during the Wars of Religion **2:** *197*
  Flanders (1540) **2:** *217*
  major battles of the Thirty Years' War **2:** *227*
  England in the Civil War **2:** *240*
  Vienna **3:** *297*
  portolan charts **3:** *300*, 301
  world **3:** *300, 301, 312*
  great explorers **3:** *305*
  Southeast Asia **3:** *314*
  European trade with Africa and Asia (c. 1750)
    3: *326*
  Native American peoples (c. 1500) **3:** *336*
  Spanish America (c. 1700) **3:** *346*
  English colonies in North America **3:** *358*
  Iran's changing boundaries **3:** *400*
  Mogul India **3:** *408*
  political divisions of northern Europe (1600s)
    4: *440*

War of the Spanish Succession **4:** *464*
  Manchu dynasty **4:** *524*
  Tokugawa Japan **4:** *534*
  French and Indian Wars **4:** *546*
  American Revolutionary War **4:** *556*
  revolution and counterrevolution in France
    (post-1792) **5:** *586*
  British Empire **5:** *668*
  American Civil War battles **5:** *680*
  Russia's territorial expansion (1800s) **5:** *690*
  Mexico's changing boundaries **6:** *740*
  battles for independence in South America
    6: *750*
  South America after independence **6:** *758*
  China (1800s) **6:** *768*
  Japan (1800s) **6:** *778*
  European powers in Africa (c. 1900) **6:** *818*
  World War I **7:** *880, 886, 887, 912*
  Europe after World War I **7:** *906*
  Russian Revolution (1917) **7:** *912*
  China controlled by nationalists, communists and
    the Japanese **7:** *934*
  Japanese empire before World War II **8:** *1016*
  Hitler's Germany **8:** *1026*
  Germany and World War II **8:** *1038*
  Japanese empire (1942) **8:** *1050*
  NATO/Warsaw Pact countries in Europe **8:** *1084*
  India after partition and independence **8:** *1108*
  Asian independent states post–World War II
    8: *1118*
  Israel in 1948 and 1967 **8:** *1130*
  European integration **9:** *1190*
  Latin America since World War II **9:** *1200*
  economic growth in the Pacific Rim **9:** *1214*
  independence for African countries **9:** *1224*
  Islamic fundamentalism (1980s/1990s) **9:** *1236*
  states formed from the former Soviet Union
    9: *1244*
Maracaibo, Lake **7:** *971*
Marat, Jean-Paul **5:** *594*
Marathas **3:** 416
Marcuse, Herbert **9:** 1165
Mardi Gras **4:** 521
Marengo, Battle of (1800) **5:** *596*
Margaret, queen of Denmark **1:** 24
Marguerite de Valois **2:** 201
Maria Luisa of Orléans **4:** 463
Maria Luisa of Savoy **4:** 465, 466
Maria Teresa (wife of Louis XIV) **4:** 457
Maria Theresa, Holy Roman empress **4:** 468–469,
  488, 489
Mariana Islands **3:** 312 **8:** 1055, 1056
Marie Antoinette **4:** 497, 499 **5:** 593
market socialism, in China **9:** 1186–1187
markets **1:** 40, *94* **2:** 253
Marlborough, John Churchill, 1st duke of **4:** 465
Marne, Battle of the (1914) **7:** 884
maroons **3:** 386
Marot, Clément **2:** 201
Marquette, Jacques **3:** 360
Marranos **2:** 180
Marriage of Figaro, The (Pierre-Augustin
  Beaumarchais) **4:** 497
Marriage of Isaac and Rebecca (Claude Lorrain)
  4: *494*
marriages
  in early modern Europe **1:** *30*, 32, 77 **2:** *245*, 251
  in Europe (1700s) **4:** *515*, 520
  in Japanese society **4:** 538
Marseilles **2:** 189
  plague **4:** 522
Marshall, George C. **8:** 1072–1073, 1088–1089
Marshall, John **5:** 646
Marshall Islands, atomic tests at Bikini Atoll
  8: 1087
Marshall Plan/Marshall Aid **8:** 1072–1073, 1074,
  1076, 1088–1089
Marston Moor, Battle of (1644) **2:** 240
Martin V, Pope **1:** 84
Martin Chuzzlewit (Charles Dickens) **6:** 845
Martinet, Jean **4:** 454
Marx, Karl **6:** 812, 813 **7:** 921
  and liberalism **5:** 611
  The Communist Manifesto (Marx and Engels)
    5: 629–630 **6:** 811, 812–813 **7:** 921
  Das Kapital **6:** 812

and revolution **6:** 812 **7:** 911 **9:** 1179
  and the international movement **6:** 815
Marx Brothers **7:** *963*
Marxist Party of the Revolutionary Left (PIR)
  7: 979
Marxist People's Movement for the Liberation of
  Angola (MPLA) **8:** 1099 **9:** 1227
Mary, queen of Scots **2:** 214, 221, 236
Mary I, Tudor, queen of England **2:** 169, 207, 209,
  210–211
  marriage **2:** *190, 192*, 211
Mary of Burgundy **1:** 25 **2:** *184*
Maryland, colonial **3:** *359*, 373
Masaccio, Tommaso **1:** 81
  painting by **1:** *80*
Mashhad **3:** 405, 406
Masolino **1:** 81
Masonic lodges **4:** 472
mass transit systems **6:** 791–792
Massachuset (Native Americans) **4:** 544
Massachusetts
  Salem witch trials **2:** 182 **3:** 370, *373*
  Plymouth colony **3:** 358–359
  Massachusetts Bay Colony **3:** 359–360
Massachusetts Bay Colony **3:** 359–360
Massys, Quentin, painting by **1:** *39*
master craftsmen **4:** 518
Matthew (ship) **3:** 355, *356*
Matthias I Corvinus, king of Hungary **1:** *94*
Mau Mau **8:** 1125
Maundy Thursday **2:** *189*
Maurice, elector of Saxony **2:** 191, 192
Maurice, prince of Nassau **2:** 220–221
Mauritania, drought **9:** *1222*
Mauritius **3:** 328
Maxim machine guns **7:** *886*
Maximilian, duke of Bavaria **2:** 226
Maximilian I, Holy Roman emperor **2:** *184*, 185,
  186
  wife **1:** 25 **2:** *184*
  army **1:** *27*
  election **1:** *46*
  and the Fugger dynasty **1:** 46, 47
  education **1:** *71*
Maximilian, Ferdinand-Joseph, emperor of Mexico
  5: 657 **6:** 740–741
Maxwell, James Clerk **5:** *702*, 705
May Day **6:** *811*
May Fourth Movement (1919) **7:** 935
Maya Indians, revolt against governors **6:** 738–739
Mayan empire **3:** 332, 392
Mayflower (ship) **3:** 358
Mayflower Compact **3:** 358–359
Mazarin, Jules (*originally* Giulio Mazarini) **4:** 455,
  456
Mazzini, Giuseppe **5:** 658
Mbuti people **1:** 116–117
Mecca
  and the Ottomans **1:** 107
  Mansa Musa's pilgrimage to **1:** 118
  Wahhabi occupation of **6:** 732
  Great Mosque occupied by Shiites (1979)
    9: *1234*
Medicaid **9:** 1160
medical imaging **9:** *1262*
Medicare **9:** 1160
Medici, Catherine de' **1:** *9* **2:** 198–199, 200–201,
  202
Medici, Lorenzo de' **1:** 22, 67, 83
Medici, Marie de' **4:** 453
Medici family **1:** 68
  banking/coins **1:** *45, 48*
  and San Lorenzo Church (Florence) **1:** *79*
medicine **1:** *31* **2:** 247–248 **6:** 801
  and technology **9:** 1262
Mediterranean islands, part of Europe **1:** 21
Mehmed I, tomb commissioned by **1:** *102*
Mehmed (Mehmet or Mohammed) **I**, Ottoman
  sultan (1432–1481) **1:** 16, 101, 102, 104, *105*
Meiji, emperor of Japan **4:** 542 **6:** 780
Meiji Restoration **6:** 780
Mein Kampf (Adolf Hitler) **7:** 988 **8:** 1034,
  1066–1067
Melbourne **5:** 674
Mellon, Andrew **7:** 947, 948

1407

melodrama **6:** 805, 845
melons **4:** *520*
Menard, John W. **6:** 830
Mendel, Gregor **5:** 699
Mendeleyev, Dmitri **5:** *701*, 704
Menelik II, emperor of Ethiopia **6:** 826
Mengs, Anton **4:** 497
Mennonites **2:** 162 **3:** 372
Mensheviks **7:** 911, 915
mercantilism **4:** 550–552
Mercator (Gerhard Kremer), maps **2:** *217* **3:** 301
mercenaries **1:** 14, 72 **4:** *467*, 470
  condottiere **1:** 26
merchant bankers **1:** 44
Merchant of Venice, The (William Shakespeare)
  7: *990*
merchants **1:** 41, 44, 45, 73, *74*, 75
  Japanese **4:** 536 **6:** 778
  See also trade
mercury poisoning **9:** 1268
Merici, Angela **2:** 167
Méricourt, Anne-Josèphe de **5:** *588*
Mesopotamia
  and World War I **7:** 887, 890
  See also Iraq
Messerschmitt Company **8:** *1074*
Messina, Arab control of **1:** *101*
mestizos **3:** 351–354
  post-independence **6:** 758–759
Metacomet (or King Philip; Native American chief)
  3: *368* **4:** 544
metalworkinhg, in Africa **1:** 113
Methodists **5:** 702
métis **5:** 675
metric system, development **4:** *480*
Metternich, Klemens von **5:** 605–610, 614
Metz **2:** 192, 193
Mexican Revolution (1910–1920) **6:** 742, 743–746
  and the railroads **6:** *737*
Mexico
  under Spanish rule **3:** 346, 348, 349–350
    6: *737*
  introduction of European plants to **3:** 394
  French involvement in (1860s) **5:** 657
    6: 740–741
  and independence from Spain **5:** 665 **6:** 737–738
  Mexican Revolution (1910–1920) **6:** *737*, 742,
    743–746
  Indians (1800s) **6:** 738–739, 742
  Texan independence from **6:** 738, 739
  lands lost to the United States **6:** 739–740
  war with the United States **6:** 739
  Reform (La Reforma) **6:** 740
  Constitution of 1857 **6:** 742
  Diaz's rule (Pax Porfiriana) **6:** 743–744
  Constitution of 1917 **6:** 746
  post-independence **6:** 763, 764
  period between the World Wars **7:** 971, 973, 979,
    980
  major companies nationalized **7:** 980
  post–World War II **9:** 1199, 1206
  economic crisis (1990s) **9:** 1206–1207
  international debt **9:** 1278
  See also Aztec empire
Mexico City **3:** *343*
  and the Aztecs **3:** 344
  and the Spanish colonies **3:** 347
  uprising (1811) **6:** 737
  captured by U.S. forces (1847) **6:** 739
  and the Mexican Revolution **6:** 745
  Aprista movement **7:** 974
Mfecane **6:** 819, 821
Michelangelo **1:** 87
  sculptures by **1:** 81–82
  Sistine Chapel ceiling **1:** *83*, 84
microprocessors **9:** *1258*
microscopes **2:** 273–274
Middle Ages **1:** 80
middle class **5:** 628, 630
  in the late 1800s **6:** 797, 798–799
Middle East **1:** 106
  post–World War I **7:** 905 **8:** 1023–1024
  Israeli conflicts **8:** 1129–1138
Middle Passage **3:** 380–*381*
Midway, Battle of (1942) **8:** 1052, 1053
midwives **2:** 248

Milan **2:** 190, 193
  and mercenary soldiers **1:** 26
  city-state **1:** 28
  struggle between Habsburg and Valois monarchs
    2: 188–189
  taken by Napoleon **5:** 596
millenarian groups **2:** 241
Miller, Arthur **8:** 1092
millet **1:** *117*
millets **6:** 728
mills, cotton **4:** *501* **5:** *618*
Milosevic, Slobodan **9:** 1252
Milton, John **2:** 241
Minamata, mercury poisoning **9:** 1268
Minamoto, house (clan) of **1:** 125, 127
Minamoto Yorimoto **1:** *124*, 125–126, 127
minarets, Persian **3:** *403*
Ming dynasty **1:** 16, 18, 127–128 **4:** 523–525, 526
  map of Ming China (late 1500s) **1:** *120*
miniaturization technology **9:** 1258
mining
  in Europe **1:** *32*, 33
  silver **1:** *32* **3:** 348, 388
  salt **3:** 348
  copper **9:** *1223*
  See also coal
Minnesota, immigrants **6:** *837*
Minorca **1:** 23
  and the War of the Spanish Succession **4:** 466,
    467
Minsk **9:** 1248
Minuit, Peter **3:** 363
Minutemen **4:** 556, *557*
Mir (space station) **9:** *1257*
Miracles of Ignatius of Loyola, The (Rubens)
  2: *171*
Miranda, Francisco de **6:** 749, 750
Miss America Pageant **7:** *951*
missiles
  and the Cold War **8:** *1083*, 1094, 1096, *1102*
  intercontinental ballistic **8:** 1094
missionaries
  in Asia **3:** 324, 330, *411*, 412 **4:** 524, 528–529,
    532
  in the Spanish American colonies **3:** 352–353
  in New France **3:** 360, 374
  in China **4:** 524, 528–529, 532 **6:** 768, 771, 774,
    784
  in India **5:** 668
  in Africa **6:** *817*, 820, 828
  See also Franciscans; Jesuits
Mississippi River, exploration **3:** 360
Mississippian culture **3:** 332–333, *338*
Missouri, USS **8:** *1060*
Missouri Compromise **5:** 654
mitrailleuse **5:** 662, *663*
Mitsubishi **6:** 781
Mitterand, François **9:** 1196
Mobile Bay, Battle of (1864) **5:** 685
Mobutu, Sese Seko **9:** 1226
Mocobi people **3:** *387*
modernism **6:** 850
Modigliani, Amedeo **6:** 784, 824
Mogadishu **1:** 113
Mogul empire **1:** 16, 130 **3:** 402, 406, 407–418
    5: 667
  insularity **1:** 18
  map of (late 1500s) **1:** *120*
  culture **3:** *407*, *411*, 412–*413*, *416*
  and Akbar's syncretism **3:** 410–412
  lives of the poor **3:** 415
Mohács, Battle of (1526) **1:** 93, 107
Mohammed VI, sultan of Turkey **8:** 1023
Mohawks (Native Americans) **3:** 368
molasses, British taxes on **4:** 554
Moldova **9:** 1249
Molière **4:** 458, 460, *471*, 497
Molotov-Ribbentrop Pact (1939) **8:** *1035*, 1036
Moltke, Helmuth von **5:** 661, 663 **6:** 731, 791
    7: 880
Moluccas **3:** 315, 316, 324, *329*
  and the Dutch **3:** 327
  See also Spice Islands
Mombasa **1:** 113
Mon people **3:** 321
Mona Lisa (Leonardo da Vinci) **1:** 84, *85*

Monaco **1:** 28
monarchy
  rise in early modern Europe **1:** 12–14, 69–73
  and warfare **1:** 27
  encouraging trade **1:** 45
  and the feudal political system **1:** 70
  absolutism **4:** 439, 449–460 **5:** 583
  autocracy **4:** 460 **7:** 910
  and the Enlightenment **4:** 460, 476, 489
  and the French Revolution **5:** 583
monasteries
  dissolution under Henry VIII **1:** 38 **2:** 208, *209*
  education in **1:** 50, 54, *55*
Monastir **6:** 736
Monet, Claude **6:** 843
  paintings by **6:** *790*, 843, *845*
money
  begins to supercede barter **1:** 34
  hyperinflation in Germany (1923) **7:** 953–954,
    988
Mongolia, Karakorum **1:** *124*
Mongols **1:** 123 **4:** 523
  overrun Kiev Rus **1:** 90
  and the Ottomans **1:** 100
  conquering China **1:** 123–125
  defeated by the Chinese (1696) **4:** 527
  See also Tatars
Monkey Trial (1925) **5:** 700, 706
monkeys **4:** *507*
Monmouth, James, duke of **2:** 244
Monnet, Jean **8:** 1073 **9:** 1190–1192, 1193
Monroe, James **5:** 645, 646, 647 **6:** 741
Monroe Doctrine (1823) **5:** 607, 647 **6:** 741, 766,
    835 **7:** 973
Montagnana **1:** *28*
Montagnards/Mountain **5:** 592, 593
Montana, range wars (1880s) **6:** 839
Montcalm, Louis Joseph, marquis de **4:** 548–549
Montcontour, Battle of (1569) **2:** 201
Montenegro **6:** 734
Montepulciano **1:** *64*
Montesquieu, Charles de Secondat, baron de **4:** 476
Monteverdi, Claudio **1:** 84, 86
Montevideo **5:** *641* **7:** 979
Montgomery (Alabama), bus boycott **8:** 1082
    9: 1171
Monticello, home of Thomas Jefferson **4:** 495
Montreal
  and Cartier **3:** 356
  British assault on (1711) **4:** 546
  British assault on (1760) **4:** 549
  and the American Revolutionary War **4:** 556
Moonstone, The (Wilkie Collins) **6:** 805
Moors
  occupation of Spain **1:** 23, 24
  persecuted in Spain **2:** 180
Mopti **1:** *118*
Moral Majority **9:** 1177–1178
Moravians **3:** 372
More, Thomas **2:** 246
  and humanism **1:** 67–68
  Utopia **1:** 67–68 **3:** 376
  quoted on sheep **2:** 208
  and slavery **3:** 376
Moreau, Gustave **6:** 844
Morelos **6:** *742*, 744
Morínigo, Higinio **7:** 979
Mormons **5:** 702
Morocco
  and the lead-up to World War I **7:** 874
  and the Spanish Civil War **8:** 1032
  independence **8:** 1126
Morse, Samuel **6:** 840
Moscow
  grand principality of *See* Muscovy
  and the Orthodox faith **1:** 24, 92
  churches and cathedrals **1:** 92 **4:** *481*
  Kremlin **1:** 92, *96*
  Napoleon's retreat from **5:** *603*, 604, 688
  Russian capital **7:** 919
  buildings and architecture under Stalin **7:** 926
  Kremlin Palace **7:** 932
  May Day parades **8:** *1093*
  Red Square **9:** *1160*
mosques, Ottoman **1:** *107* **6:** *727*, *733*
Mother and Her Child (Mary Cassatt) **6:** 843

Volume numbers appear in **boldface type.** Page numbers in *italic type* refer to illustrations and captions.

motherhood, in the 1700s **4:** 512–513, *515*
motor transport, after World War I **7:** *946*, 949
motorcycles, manufacture **9:** *1210*
Mountain/Montagnards **5:** 592, 593
Mountbatten, Louis **8:** 1114
movies **6:** 850 **9:** 1171
 spy **8:** *1097*
 See also film industry
Mozambique **6:** 823, 828
Mozart, Wolfgang Amadeus **4:** 500, 521
MPLA (Marxist People's Movement for the
 Libertion of Angola) **8:** 1099 **9:** 1227
Mubarak, Hosni **9:** 1236, *1240*
Mugabe, Robert **9:** *1227*
Muhammad Ali, viceroy and pasha of Egypt
 6: 732, 820
Mühlberg, Battle of (1547) **2:** 156, 190
mujahideen **8:** 1103 **9:** *1231*, 1241
Mukden *See* Shenyang
Mukden, Battle of (1905) **5:** 696 **6:** 783
mulattos **3:** 351–354, 386
Mulla Sadra (philosopher) **3:** 403
Munch, Edvard, paintings by **6:** 850
Munich **7:** 952
 terrorism at the Olympic Games (1972) **8:** 1136
Munich Conference and Munich Agreement (1938)
 8: *1034, 1035,* 1036
Münster, Treaty of (1648) **2:** *233*
Murad II, Ottoman emperor **1:** 101–102
Murrow, Edward **8:** 1068
Murten, Battle of (1476) **1:** *26*
Musa, emperor (mansa) of Mali **1:** *109,* 115–118
Muscovy **1:** 24, 92, 96 **4:** 483
music
 Renaissance **1:** 84, 85–86
 and Protestant worship **2:** *159*
 and the Dutch Reformed Church **2:** 224
 classical **4:** 500
 in eighteenth century homes **4:** *516*
 Romantic **5:** *638,* 639, *643,* 644
 impressionism in **6:** 844
 atonal **6:** 847, 850
 and Vienna **6:** 847
 rock and roll **9:** 1171
 See also operas
music halls **6:** 806
musical instruments, Renaissance **1:** 85–86
musketeers **4:** 461
muskets, flintlock **4:** 461, *466*
Muslim Brotherhood **9:** 1232
Muslim League **8:** 1114
Muslims
 and independence in India **8:** 1110–1112, 1113
 and the partition of India **8:** 1114–1115
 fundamentalism in India **8:** 1116
 fundamentalism in the Middle East
 9: 1231–1242
 See also Islam
Mussolini, Benito **7:** 983, 984–987 **8:** 1030
 invasion of Abyssinia **6:** 824 **7:** 987 **8:** 1030
 and World War II **8:** *1025,* 1038
 and Hitler **8:** *1029*
 and the Spanish Civil War **8:** 1032
Mustafa Kemal (Kemal Atatürk) **6:** *736* **7:** 907
 8: *1022,* 1023
Mutual Economic Assistance, Council for
 (Comecon) **9:** 1243, 1249
Muybridge, Eadweard **6:** 842
Myanmar (*formerly* Burma) **3:** 314 **6:** 772
 peoples **3:** 321–322
 and World War II **8:** 1050, 1052, 1054, 1058,
 1113, 1119
 independence **8:** 1120

nabobs **3:** 417
Nader, Ralph **9:** 1271
Nadir Shah (Iranian ruler) **3:** 405–406
NAFTA (North American Free Trade Agreement)
 9: 1198
Nagasaki **4:** 540 **6:** 779 **8:** 1060, 1086 **9:** 1255
Nagorno-Karabakh **9:** 1248
Nairobi **9:** *1221*
Najaf **3:** 399
Namibia **7:** 887
Nancy **4:** 456
Nanking (Nanjing) **6:** 771

Japanese invasion of **7:** 943 **8:** 1034
Nanking, Treaty of (1842) **6:** 771
Nantes **3:** 377, 382
Nantes, Edict of (1598) **2:** *196,* 204 **4:** 451
 revoked by Louis XIV (1685) **4:** 459
Naples **5:** 658
 Spanish kingdom of **1:** 24, 28 **2:** 189
 besieged by the French (1528) **2:** 190
Napoleon I, emperor of France **5:** 595–604, 655
 and the French Revolution **5:** 591, 594, 595
 declared emperor **5:** 594, *595,* 598, 638
 and Egypt **5:** 596 **6:** 730, 732, 820
 and Beethoven **5:** 598, *638,* 639
 and India **5:** 600, 667
 and Louisiana **5:** 600–601, 646
 invasion of Portugal **6:** 749, 755
 invasion of Spain **6:** 749
Napoleon III, Louis-Napoleon Bonaparte, emperor
 of France **5:** 604, 614, 655–657, 659, 661,
 664, *665*
 and Mexico **5:** 657 **6:** 740–741
 and Paris **6:** 789
Napoleonic Code **5:** 597–598
Napoleonic Wars **5:** 599, 600, 601, 604, 646 **6:** 794
 and Russia **5:** 604, 688
 relative peace following **7:** 871
Naseby, Battle of (1645) **2:** 240
Nash, Paul, sketches by **7:** *883*
Nasser, Abdel **8:** 1099, 1133, 1135
Nasser, Gamal Abdel **9:** 1235–1236
Natal **6:** 819, 821
nation-states **1:** 22–23, 70 **4:** 460
National Assembly, French **5:** 583
National Front for the Liberation of Angola
 (FNLA) **8:** 1099–1102 **9:** 1227
National Guard (French Revolution) **5:** 587
National Health Service **8:** *1080*
National Industrial Recovery Act (NIRA) **7:** 967
National Organization for Women (NOW) **9:** 1166
national parks (American) **5:** 641 **6:** 840
National Purity Society **8:** 1018
National Recovery Administration (NRA) **7:** *966,*
 967, 970
National (Cumberland) Road **5:** 649
National Security Council (NSC) **9:** 1205
National Socialist German Workers' Party **7:** 987
National Socialist Party *See* Nazis
National Union for the Total Independence of
 Angola (UNITA) **8:** 1102 **9:** 1227–1228
nationalism **9:** 1278
 in Europe **5:** 594, 602, 609, 610–611, 655–666
 6: 730, 822 **9:** 1189–1190, 1198
 in Japan (1930s) **8:** 1018
Nationalist Party, of China *See* Guomindang
Nationalist Revolutionary Movement (MNR)
 7: 979
nationalization
 farming nationalized under Stalin **7:** 927–928
 post–World War II **8:** 1077, 1078, 1079 **9:** 1160
Nations, Battle of the (1813) **5:** 604
Nations, League of **7:** 903, 908, 956 **8:** 1026, *1027,*
 1028
 and post–World War I mandates **7:** 905 **8:** 1023,
 1024
 and the United States **7:** 945–946 **8:** *1027*
 Germany leaves **8:** 1030
 Japan leaves **8:** 1031
Native Americans **3:** 331–342 **6:** 839
 daily life **3:** 333–338, 340–342
 religion **3:** *334, 335,* 336–337
 leadership **3:** 337–340
 and colonists **3:** 350, 354, 358, 359, 368,
 373–374 **4:** 543
 as slaves **3:** 350, 380–381
 conflicts with colonists **3:** 368 **4:** 543–544,
 545–546
 and alcohol **3:** 391–393
 and European diseases **3:** 393 **4:** 544
 and horses **3:** 395
 view of the natural world **3:** 396
 displacement **5:** *653,* 654
 wars against the U.S. army (1862–1890) **6:** *835,*
 839
 and the Ghost Dance **6:** 839
NATO **8:** *1084,* 1090, 1095, 1102
 former Warsaw Pact countries in **8:** 1106 **9:** 1245

natural selection, theory of **5:** 699
natural theology **5:** 698
natural world
 viewed by Native Americans **3:** 396
 viewed in the 1700s **4:** *476,* 498, 501–510, *510,*
 512
 industrial development (1700s) **4:** 508–510
 See also rural life
nature, and Romanticism **5:** 636, 637, 639,
 640–641
Navajo (Native Americans) **3:** 335, *342*
Navarino, Battle of (1827) **6:** 732
Navarre **2:** *186*
navigation **3:** 301–302
Navigation Acts **4:** 552
Nazi-Soviet Pact (1939) **9:** 1249
Nazis **7:** 958, *983,* 989–992 **8:** 1084
 and the Holocaust **7:** 991
 uniforms **8:** *1028*
 See also Hitler, Adolf
Nea Paphos **1:** *108*
Necker, Jacques **5:** 585–586
Nehru, Jawaharlal **8:** 1112–1113, 1115
Nelson, Horatio **5:** 596, *599*
Nemours, Treaty of (1585) **2:** 203
neoclassicism **4:** 497 **5:** 621, 636 **6:** *801*
neocolonialism, in Africa **9:** 1222
Netanyahu, Benjamin **8:** 1138 **9:** 1242
Netherlands
 colonies *See* Indonesia; New Netherland
 part of the Habsburg Empire **1:** 25
 flyboats **1:** 42, *44*
 refugees from Antwerp **1:** 44
 Revolt of the (Eighty Years' War) **1:** 44 **2:** 172,
 215–224 **4:** 440
 villages **1:** *77*
 United Provinces of the **2:** 220
 a thriving culture (1600s) **2:** 222–224, 261
 4: 442
 and the Thirty Years' War **2:** 227–228, 233
 trade and empire in Asia **3:** *323,* 324–330
 Dutch settlements in Africa **3:** 328–329
 piracy **3:** 348
 religion **4:** 440
 republicanism **4:** 440–441, 442
 invasion by the French (1670s; Franco-Dutch
 War) **4:** 441, 457, 462
 decline (late 1600s) **4:** 442
 invasion by the French (1747) **4:** 442
 and the War of the Spanish Succession **4:** 464,
 465, 466
 abolition of the slave trade **6:** 819
 immigration to the United States **6:** *837*
 and World War II in Europe **8:** 1038
 and World War II in the Pacific **8:** 1050
Netherlands, Austrian *See* Austrian Netherlands
Netherlands, Spanish *See* Spanish Netherlands
Neuberg, Mariana von **4:** 463
Neuilly, Treaty of (1919) **7:** 903
New Amsterdam **2:** 244 **3:** 362
Newark (New Jersey), race riots (1967) **9:** *1174,*
 1175
New Britain **8:** 1054
New Brunswick **5:** 674, 675
Newcastle upon Tyne **2:** 238
New Deal **7:** 959, 966–970 **8:** 1079 **9:** 1160
 Second **7:** 967–970
New Delhi **8:** *1114, 1116*
 and Mahatma Gandhi **8:** *1110*
New Economic Mechanism **9:** 1245
New Economic Policy (NEP), Russia's **7:** 922–923
New England **3:** 359, 369 **4:** 552
 See also North America, colonial
Newfoundland **3:** 355 **4:** 467, 546
 fisheries **3:** 388, *390*
New France **3:** 355, 360, 373–374
 conflicts with other colonial powers **4:** 545–549
New Grenada **6:** 747–748
 Bolívar's attack on **6:** 752
New Guinea, and World War II **8:** 1052, 1053,
 1054, 1056
New Harmony **6:** 811
New Haven **3:** 360
New Jersey **3:** 361–364
New Julfa **3:** 403, 405
New Lanark, model society at **6:** *809,* 811

Volume numbers appear in **boldface type**. Page numbers in *italic type* refer to illustrations and captions.

New Mexico
  pueblos **3:** 332, *339*
  Catholic missions **3:** *352*
New Mexico, USS **8:** *1054*
New Model Army **2:** 240, 241
New Netherland **3:** 360, 361–364
New Orleans **5:** *648*
  and the Civil War **5:** 682
New Spain **3:** 346, 374, 380
newspapers **6:** 806
  in Europe (1700s) **4:** 522
New Sweden **3:** 360
Newton, Isaac **2:** 224, 271–273, *274*
New York
  iron works **6:** *795*
  suburban development **9:** 1170
New York City **2:** 244 **3:** 366
  formerly New Amsterdam **3:** 362, *363*
  Wall Street **3:** 381 **7:** *962*
  and the American Revolutionary War
    4: 556–557, 559
  and immigration **5:** 650 **6:** *834*
  railroads **6:** *791*
  Brooklyn Bridge **6:** *796*
  tenements **6:** 803
  Central Park **6:** 806 **9:** *1162*
  Triangle Shirtwaist Company fire **6:** *814*, 815
  Chrysler Building **6:** 846
  skyscrapers **7:** 947, *948*
  Harlem **7:** 950
  Fifth Avenue (1921) **7:** *960*
  and the Great Depression **7:** *962, 964*
  anti–Vietnam War demonstrations **9:** *1162*
  rich-poor divide **9:** *1178*
  World Trade Center bombed **9:** 1242, 1282
New Zealand
  peoples **3:** 315 **5:** *673*, 674
  part of the British Empire **5:** *673*, 674
  dominion status (1926) **5:** 676
  Asian influences on the economy **9:** 1218–1219
Nez Percé (Native Americans) **6:** 839
Ngo Dinh Diem **8:** 1123
Nicaragua
  bananas **6:** *761, 763* **7:** 973
  U.S. marines stationed in (1920s) **7:** 973
  U.S. intervention in (1980s) **8:** 1104
  Sandinista government and Contra rebels
    9: *1199*, 1205
  female president ousts Sandinistas **9:** 1208
Nice **2:** 190 **5:** 659
Nicholas I, czar of Russia, Russia under **5:** *688*,
  689–692
Nicholas II, czar of Russia **5:** 696 **7:** 909
  and World War I **7:** 871, *872*, 880
  and the Russian Revolution (1917) **7:** 910–911,
    913, 919
Nicoli, Nicolao **1:** 63
Nicosia **6:** *733*
Niemeyer, Oscar **9:** 1201
Nietzsche, Friedrich **6:** 850
Niger River **1:** *111, 118*
Nigeria
  Bantu language **1:** 117
  decolonization **8:** 1124–1125, 1128
  military coup (1966); Ibos massacred **9:** 1226
  the secession and return of Biafara **9:** 1226
Night of Broken Glass **7:** 994
Night of the Long Knives **7:** 992
Night Watch, The (Rembrandt) **2:** 224
Nightingale, Florence **5:** *662*
Nijinsky, Vaslav **6:** *850*
Nijmegen, Battle of (1585) **2:** *221*
Nile Valley **1:** 109–110
Nimitz, Chester **8:** 1054, 1056
Nimpuc (Native Americans) **4:** *543*
Niña (ship) **3:** 309
Nine Years' War (1689–1698) **4:** 457
NIRA (National Industrial Recovery Act) **7:** 967
Nixon, Richard **8:** *1103* **9:** 1177
  and the Vietnam War **8:** 1099, 1101
  visit to China **8:** 1102 **9:** 1186, *1187*
Nkrumah, Kwame **8:** 1124 **9:** 1221, 1225
NKVD **7:** 930
NMR (Nationalist Revolutionary Movement)
  7: 979
"no taxation without representation" **4:** 555

nobles
  and the monarchy in early modern Europe
    1: 13–14, 25, 70
  a new nobility in early modern Europe
    1: 75–76, 77–78
  in central Europe **1:** 93–94
  Russian **1:** 96, 97, 98 **4:** 482, 489–490
  Ottoman (notables) **1:** 102 **6:** 728, 729
  Swedish (1600s) **4:** 446–447
Nordhausen **8:** *1062*
Nördlingen, Battle of (1634) **2:** 231
Noriega, Manuel **9:** 1206
Normandy
  weddings (1700s) **4:** *515*
  D-Day landings in **8:** *1047*, 1048
North Africa, and World War II **8:** 1045–1046
North America
  Native Americans **3:** 331–342
  colonial life in **3:** 365–374
  frontier life **3:** 367–368
  resources and colonial exploitation **3:** 387–396
  railroads **5:** 622, *623, 649* **6:** 790–791, 792
  transport improvements (1800s) **6:** 790–793
  experiments with government (1960–1999)
    9: 1159–1168
  See also Canada; Mexico; North America,
    colonial; United States
North America, colonial
  and Native Americans **3:** 350, 354, 358, 359,
    368, 373–374 **4:** 543
  European settlement of the eastern seaboard
    3: 355–364
  life in **3:** 365–374
  population **3:** 365–366 **4:** 549
  frontier life **3:** 367–368
  conflicts with Native Americans **3:** 368
    4: 543–544, 545–546
  resources and colonial exploitation **3:** 387–396
  wars and conflicts **3:** 543–552, 553–562
  religious revival (Great Awakening) **4:** 549–550
  trade with Britain **4:** 550–552
  American Revolutionary War **4:** 553–562
  independence from Britain **4:** *554*, 557, *558, 559*,
    561–562
  and taxes **4:** 554–555
North American Free Trade Agreement (NAFTA)
  9: 1198
North Carolina **3:** 361, 371
North German Confederation **5:** 661–664
North Korea *See* Korea, North
North, Oliver **9:** 1205
Northanger Abbey (Jane Austen) **5:** 636
Northeast Passage **3:** 325–326
Northern Expedition **7:** 938–939
Northern Rhodesia (*later* Zambia), independence
  8: 1128
Northern War (1655–1660) **4:** 446
Northumberland, John Dudley, duke of and earl of
  Warwick **2:** 210, 211
Northwest Passage **3:** 326, 362
Norway
  and the Union of Colmar **1:** 24
  nationalism and independence **5:** 666
notables (Turkish nobles) **1:** 102 **6:** 728, 729
Nottingham **2:** 239
Nova Scotia **4:** 546 **5:** 674, 675
  Acadia **3:** 374 **4:** 467, 545
Novaya Zemlya **3:** 326
novels
  in the 1700s **4:** 500, 517, 521
  on the effects of industrialization **5:** 626
  Romantic **5:** 638, *639*, 642
  sentimental **6:** 804
  melodramatic **6:** 805
  thriller **6:** 805
  spy **8:** *1097*
Novgorod **1:** 89, 96
NRA (National Recovery Administration) **7:** *966*,
  967, 970
nuclear accidents **9:** 1244, 1269–1270
nuclear weapons, tests **8:** 1087 **9:** *1253*, 1271
numerals, Arabic **1:** 48
nuns, hospitals run by **2:** *249*
Nuremberg, war trials **8:** 1070
Nuremberg Laws **7:** 993–994
Nurhaci, king of the Manchu **4:** 525–526

nutmeg **3:** 316
nuts, from the Americas **3:** 396
Nyasaland, independence **8:** 1128
Nyerere, Julius **9:** 1225

Oakies **7:** 969
OAS (Organisation Armée Secrète) **8:** 1127
OAS (Organization of American States) **9:** 1200
Oates, Lawrence E. G. **5:** *676*
Oates, Titus **2:** 243
Oath of the Horatii (Jacques-Louis David) **4:** *497*
Obregon, Alvaro **6:** 746
October Revolution (1917) **7:** *909, 915*, 917
OEEC (Organization for European Economic
  Cooperation) **8:** 1073 **9:** 1190
offices, white-collar workers **6:** *802*
Ogedei **1:** 123
Oglethorpe, James **4:** 547
O'Higgins, Bernardo **6:** *748*, 753, 754, 761
Ohio, earth mounds **3:** *338*
Ohio Valley **3:** 368 **4:** *546*, 548, 553
oil spills, Exxon *Valdez* **9:** 1268–1269
Ojukwu, Chukumeka **9:** 1226
Okinawa **6:** 779 **8:** *1060*
Oklahoma, Native Americans resettled in **5:** *653*
Oklahoma City, bombing (1995) **9:** 1282
Old Curiosity Shop, The (Charles Dickens) **6:** 804
Old St. Paul's Cathedral **2:** *244*
Old Sarum, cathedral **1:** 7
Old Shepherd's Chief Mourner, The (Edwin
  Landseer) **6:** 805
Oldenbarnevelt, Johan van **2:** 220
Oliver Twist (Charles Dickens) **5:** 632
Olsen, Tillie **7:** 968
Olympia (Édouard Manet) **6:** 842
Olympic Games, Munich, terrorist attack (1972)
  8: 1136
Omdurman, Battle of (1898) **6:** 825–826
On the Chisholm Trail (Frederic Remington) **6:** *838*
On the Reason of State (G. Botero) **1:** 70
On the Right of Magistrates over their Subjects
  (Theodore Beza) **2:** 202
On the Road (Jack Kerouac) **9:** 1171
Onassis, Aristotle **9:** 1173
One-Dimensional Man (Herbert Marcuse) **9:** 1165
O'Neill, Hugh **2:** 214
open-hearth process **6:** 788
opera houses **6:** 802, *803*
operas **4:** 500, 521 **6:** 848
  of Claudio Monteverdi **1:** 84
opium, trade in **4:** 532 **6:** 769–771
Opium Wars (1839–1842; 1856–60) **4:** 541
Oppenheimer, J. Robert **8:** 1059, 1092
optical fibers **9:** *1261*
Oquendo, Antonio de **2:** 232
Orangists **4:** 441
Oratory of Divine Love **2:** 165
Order of the Golden Fleece **1:** 25–26
Oregon, Native Americans **3:** 340–341
Oregon Trail **5:** *653*
Orfeo (Claudio Monteverdi) **1:** 84
organ grinders **5:** *628*
Organisation Armée Secrète (OAS) **8:** 1127
Organization of American States (OAS) **9:** 1200
Organization for European Economic Cooperation
  (OEEC) **8:** 1073 **9:** 1190
organs, transplants **9:** 1262
Orhan, sultan of Turkey **1:** 100
Origin of Species, The (Charles Darwin) **5:** 699,
  700
Orlando, Vittorio **7:** *904*
Orléans **2:** 200
Ortega, Daniel **9:** *1208*
Ortelius, Abraham, world map **3:** *312*
Orthodox Church *See* Eastern Orthodox
  Church/Christianity
Osaka **4:** 536, 540 **6:** *782*
  siege of Osaka Castle **4:** *535*
Oscars (Academy Awards) **7:** 951
Osman I, Ottoman sultan **1:** 99–100
Osnabruck **1:** 31
ossuaries **1:** *8*
Oswald, Lee Harvey **9:** 1173
Ottoman Empire **1:** 99–108 **3:** 298
  attacking the Byzantine Empire **1:** 16–18, 19,
    100–101 **3:** 298

capture of Constantinople (1453) **1:** 16–18, 19, 26, 41, 52, 92, 99, 102, *103,* 104
and trade **1:** 40, 104, *108* **3:** 298
besieging Vienna (1529) **1:** 93, 107 **2:** 188 **3:** *297,* 298
Süleyman the Magnificent **1:** *100,* 107–108 **2:** 190 **3:** *297*
a meritocracy of slaves **1:** 104
sultans **1:** 104
encroaching on Europe (c. 1559) **2:** 193–194
conflict with the Safavid empire **3:** 399–400, 405, 406 **6:** 729
besieging Vienna (1683) **4:** 485 **6:** 729
Greek rebellion against **5:** 607, *611* **6:** 731–732
and Russia **5:** 692 **6:** 728, 730, 732, 733–734
decline of the Turkish Empire **6:** 727–736
Western influences on **6:** 729–730
and Turkish nationalism **6:** 735–736
and lead-up to World War I **7:** *877,* 878
and World War I **7:** 885, 887
post–World War I colonies **7:** 905
post–World War I **7:** 907
Israel part of **8:** 1129
Ottoman Turks
and trade **1:** 40, 104, *108* **3:** 298
besieging Vienna (1529) **1:** 93, 107 **2:** 188 **3:** *297,* 298
conflict with the Safavid empire **1:** 105 **3:** 399–400, 405, 406 **6:** 729
encroaching on Europe (c. 1559) **2:** 193–194
besieging Vienna (1683) **4:** 485 **6:** 729
Owen, Robert **5:** 619, 703 **6:** *809,* 811
Oxenstierna, Axel **2:** 231
Oxford, university **1:** 40, 51, 52, *53*
ozone layer, and CFCs **9:** 1269

Pacific Ocean
Magellan's expedition to **3:** 312
peoples **3:** 315
World War II in **8:** 1049–1060
Pacioli, Luca **1:** 45–48
paddle steamers **5:** *622*
Pagan (kingdom) **3:** 321, *322*
Paganini, Nicolò **5:** 644
Pahlavi, Reza Shah **9:** 1232–1233, 1234
Paine, Tom, *Common Sense* **4:** 557
paintings
Renaissance **1:** *80,* 81, 82, 84, *85*
perspective **1:** 81
landscape **1:** 121 **2:** *262* **5:** *637, 641,* 643
Dutch (1600s) **2:** 223–224
Baroque **2:** 256, 257–259, 261–264
still life **2:** 261–262
Romantic **5:** 641
portrait **6:** 842
abstract **6:** 850
cubist **6:** 850
Pakistan **8:** 1116
creation **8:** 1112, 1114–1115
Palace of the Facets **1:** 92
Palatinate, Spanish invasion of **2:** 227
Palembang **8:** *1021*
Palestine
and World War I **7:** 890, 905 **8:** 1023
a British mandated territory **7:** 905 **8:** 1130, 1131
and the creation of Israel within **8:** 1024, 1129–1134 **9:** 1232
Palestinian Arabs, and Israel **8:** 1134–1138 **9:** 1242
Palestinian Liberation Organization (PLO) **8:** 1134–1136, 1137, 1138 **9:** 1240
Palestrina, Giovanni Pierluigi **1:** 86
Paley, William **5:** 698
Palladio, Andrea **4:** 495
Palmach **8:** 1132
Palmer, Fanny, painting by **6:** *829*
Palmer, Mitchell **7:** 946
Pamela, or Virtue Rewarded (Samuel Richardson) **4:** *500, 513*
Pan-African Congress (1945) **8:** 1124
Pan-Islamic movement **6:** 732–733
Panama
independence **6:** 766, 835
Panama Canal **6:** 766, 835 **9:** 1200
U.S. invasion (1989) **9:** 1206
Panay (ship) **8:** 1034
Panjipat **1:** 130

pantheism, and Romanticism **5:** 636, 637
Panther (ship) **7:** 874
Papal States **5:** 658, 659
paper currency **5:** 121
papermaking **1:** 33, 60 **2:** 254
Paradise Lost (John Milton) **2:** 241
Paraguay
post-independence **6:** 760
post–World War I **7:** 971
war against Bolivia (Chaco War 1932–1935) **7:** 978–979
rule after the Chaco War **7:** 979
Paraguayan War (1865–1870) **6:** 764
parchment **1:** *33*
Paris **2:** 253
controlled by the British and Burgundians **1:** 23
pre-Versaille growth **1:** 38
University of **1:** *51*
shops **1:** *78*
in 1590 **2:** *198*
and the Wars of Religion **2:** 203, 204
Halles trading district **4:** *450*
in the 1700s **4:** 511–512
and the French Revolution **5:** 590–591, 592
Arc de Triomphe **5:** *602*
redesigned (late 1800s) **5:** 655
June Days (1848) **5:** 656
besieged by the Germans (1871) **5:** 664, *665*
declared a self-governing commune (1871) **5:** 664
urban replanning **6:** 789–790
sewers **6:** *803*
Eiffel Tower **6:** *841,* 846
a fashion center **6:** 846
and World War I **7:** 884, *888*
post–World War I **7:** 951–952
student demonstrations **9:** *1164*
Paris crowd, and the French Revolution **5:** 590–591
Paris Exhibition (1867) **6:** 794
Paris gun **7:** 893
Paris, siege of (1590) **2:** *204*
Paris, Treaty of (1763) **4:** 549, 553
Paris, Treaty of (1783) **4:** *562*
Paris, Treaty of (1951) **9:** 1192
Paris Peace Conference **7:** 903–905
Park, Mungo **6:** 820
Park Chung Hee **9:** 1212
Parks, Rosa **9:** 1171
Parlement **1:** 13
Parliament **1:** 72
development in England **1:** 23
Long **2:** 238, 242
Short **2:** 238
Catholics in **6:** 808
Parma, Alessandro Farnese, duke of **2:** 220, 221
Parr, Catherine **2:** 209
Pasha, Mehmed **7:** 877
Passchendaele (1917; Battle of Ypres) **7:** *883,* 895
Pasteur, Louis **5:** *704,* 705
Pasteur Institute **5:** 705
pasteurization **5:** 705
Patriotic Front **9:** *1227*
Patriots, Dutch **4:** 442
Patton, George **7:** 964
Paul, emperor of Russia **5:** 687
Paul III, Pope **2:** 167–168
Paul VI, Pope **2:** 180
Pavia, Battle of (1524) **2:** 189
Pax Porfiriana **6:** 743
peaches **3:** *395*
Peacock Throne **3:** 406, 417
peanuts **3:** 396
Pearl Harbor, Japanese attack on **8:** 1025, 1042, 1049, 1050–1051, 1053, 1067
Peasant Wedding, The (Brueghel the Elder) **2:** *245*
peasants
European (post–Black Death) **1:** 9, 30
European (1500s) **1:** 35–36
revolt in Germany (early 1500s) **1:** 35–36 **2:** 156
repressed in central Europe (the second serfdom) **1:** 94
revolt in Russia (1600s) **1:** 98
European (1700s) **4:** 504, 517, 519–520
in Prussia and the Habsburg empire **4:** 505
Japanese **4:** 534–536 **6:** 778–779

European (early 1800s) **5:** 609
in Russia (1800s) **5:** 687, *691,* 693, 694
and the Spanish Civil War **8:** 1032
See also serfs
Pedro I (*formerly* Dom Pedro), emperor of Brazil **6:** 755–756
Pedro II, emperor of Brazil **6:** 756, 760, 763
penicillin **9:** 1262
peninsulares **3:** 347 **6:** 748
in Mexico **6:** 737, 738
Penn, William **3:** *361,* 364 **4:** 544
Pennsylvania, colony **3:** *361,* 364, *369, 370*
"Pennsylvania Dutch" **3:** 372
Pennsylvania Gazette (newspaper) **4:** 551
peons/peonage **3:** 350 **6:** 761–762 **7:** 972
People's Action Party, of Singapore **9:** 1218
People's Council **8:** 1022
People's Party **6:** 834
Peoples of Russia, The (porcelain figurines) **4:** *482*
pepper **3:** 298, 316
Pequot War (1637) **4:** 544
perestroika **8:** 1106 **9:** 1244
periodic table **5:** *701,* 704
periodicals, in Europe (1700s) **4:** 522
Perón, Juan **7:** 977, 982 **9:** 1200, 1202
Perón, Maria Eva "Evita" **9:** 1200, 1202
Péronne, Declaration of (1585) **2:** 203
Perry, Matthew C. **4:** 541 **6:** 779
Pershing, John Joseph **6:** 746
Persia *See* Iran
personalismo **6:** 759
perspective, in paintings **1:** 81
Peru
Incas **3:** 332, 343, *389,* 391
ancient death mask **3:** *345*
a Spanish colony **3:** 349–350
moves toward independence **6:** 754–755
post-independence **6:** 760, *765*
Central Railroad **6:** *765*
post–World War I **7:** 971, 973, 974
Aprista movement **7:** 974
avoids military conflict (1930s) **7:** 978
inflation (1980s) **9:** 1199
Alvarado seizes power (1968) **9:** 1204
Shining Path guerrilla movement **9:** 1206
producing cocaine **9:** 1208
fishing and El Niño **9:** 1268
pesticides **9:** 1265, 1275
Pétain, Henri P. O. **7:** 895
Peter I, the Great, czar of Russia **4:** 486–488
Peter III, czar of Russia **4:** 489
Peterloo massacre **6:** 808
Petersburgh, Battle of (1864–1865) **5:** 685–686
Petition of Right **2:** 237
Petrarca, Francesco *See* Petrarch
Petrarch **1:** *63,* 64
Petrograd *See* Saint Petersburg
Petrograd Workers' and Soldiers' Soviet **7:** 914
petroleum industry, Russian **5:** *694*
Philadelphia **3:** 364, 366, 367
Liberty Bell **4:** *562*
Philadelphia Centennial Exposition (1876) **6:** *801*
Philip, Prince (Duke of Edinburgh) **9:** *1221*
Philip I, "the Handsome," king of Castile **2:** *184,* 185–186
Philip II, king of Spain **2:** *191,* 192–194
before accession to the title **2:** 190
marriage **2:** *190*
and the Armada **2:** 213
and the Spanish Netherlands **2:** 215, 216–217, 218, 220
and Portugal **3:** 324
and Spanish America **3:** 348
Philip IV, king of France **1:** 13
Philip IV, king of Spain **4:** 463
Philip V, duke of Anjou and first Bourbon king of Spain **4:** 462–467, 470, 500
Philippine Sea, Battle of (1944) **8:** 1056
Philippines **6:** 835
Magellan sails to **3:** 312
peoples **3:** 315
and World War II **8:** 1050, 1051, *1052,* 1054, 1056–1057, *1058,* 1119
independence **8:** 1120
and the Vietnam War **9:** 1217
green revolution in farming **9:** 1265

Volume numbers appear in **boldface type**. Page numbers in *italic type* refer to illustrations and captions.

Philosophical Dictionary, The **4:** 476
Philosophical Letters on the English (Voltaire) **4:** 476
philosophy, and Descartes **2:** 271, *272*
Phips, Sir William **4:** 546
photography **6:** *788, 789, 842–843, 844*
　color **5:** *702*
　of child laborers **6:** 815, *840*
　documentary **6:** 843
Picasso, Pablo **6:** 824, 850
Pietà (Michelangelo) **1:** 81
Pietists **5:** 702
pigs **4:** *503*
　in colonial America **3:** 394
pikes **1:** 26
Pilgrim's Progress (John Bunyan) **2:** 241, *243*
Pilsudski, Józef **7:** 920
Pinochet, Augusto **9:** *1203*, 1204
Pinochet, Gifford **6:** 840
Pinta (ship) **3:** 309
PIR (Marxist Party of the Revolutionary Left) **7:** 979
piracy **3:** 348 **4:** *547*
Pisa **1:** 28
Pisano, Andrea **1:** *31*
Pisco **6:** 754
Pissarro, Camille **6:** 843
pistols **4:** *462*
Pittsburgh **5:** 631 **6:** 832
　formerly Fort Duquesne **4:** 548
Pius V, Pope **2:** 194
Pius VII, Pope **5:** 597
Pius IX, Pope **5:** 702
Pizarro, Francisco **3:** 346
plague **4:** 522
　Black Death (1347) **1:** 8–9, 30, *31*, 43–44 **2:** 165, 245
　Great Plague (1665) **2:** 242–243, 247
plankhouses, Native American **3:** 335, 341
plantations **3:** 349, 387
　tea **4:** *531*
　cotton **5:** 647, *654*, 677
plants, European plants colonizing the Americas **3:** *394*
Plassey, Battle of (1757) **3:** 418 **5:** 667
Plate, River **3:** *347*
Plato **1:** 64–65
　and slavery **3:** 376
plays
　Romantic **5:** 638
　melodrama **6:** 805
PLO (Palestinian Liberation Organization) **8:** 1134–1136, 1137, 1138 **9:** 1240
plows **1:** 16, *18* **4:** *502*
Plymouth colony **3:** 358–359
Plymouth Rock **3:** 358
Pocahontas **3:** *357*, 358
Poe, Edgar Allan **6:** 790
poetry
　in the 1700s **4:** 500
　Romantic **5:** 636, *637*, 638–639, 640
　of Charles Baudelaire **6:** *842*
　symbolism in **6:** 844
pogroms **7:** 990
Poincaré, Raymond **7:** 955–956
Poissy **2:** 199
Pol Pot **8:** 1099
Poland
　Poland-Lithuania **1:** 13, 25, 91–93, 98 **4:** 483–484, 485, 490
　nobility **1:** 76
　and the Teutonic Knights **1:** 90–91
　and the Jagiello dynasty **1:** 91, 93
　prosperity (1400s) **1:** 93–94
　and the Reformation **1:** 95
　Union of Lublin (1569) **1:** 98
　Catholicism **2:** 172
　nomad invasion **3:** 297
　hostilities with Sweden (1600s) **4:** 446
　War of the Polish Succession **4:** 468
　and Napoleon **5:** 600, 691
　part of the Russian empire **5:** 691–692, 696
　independence (1918) **7:** 906, 956
　Polish-Soviet War (1919–1920) **7:** 920
　German invasion of (1939) **8:** 1025–1026, 1036, 1037–1038

post–World War I **8:** 1026
　population lost in World War II **8:** 1071
　Solidarity labor union **8:** 1105–1106 **9:** 1244, 1245
　collapse of communism **9:** 1244–1245
Polaris (missile) **8:** 1096
police **2:** 251
Polish Succession, War of the (1733-1738) **4:** 468
Polish-Soviet War (1919–1920) **7:** 920
politics, North America and western Europe (1960–1999) **9:** 1159–1168
Politics (Aristotle) **1:** 73
politiques (moderate French Catholics) **2:** 204
Polk, James Knox **5:** 653–654
pollution **9:** 1267, 1270, *1272*
　and global warming **9:** 1267–1268
　oil spills **9:** 1268–1269
　atmospheric **9:** 1269, *1274*
　burning oil wells **9:** *1273*
Polo, Marco **1:** 119 **3:** 296
Poltava **4:** 447
Polynesia **3:** 315
polyphony **1:** 86 **4:** 500
Pombal, Sebastien **4:** 460
Pompadour, Madame de **4:** 460, 492, *493*
Pompeii **4:** 495
Pondicherry, Battle of (1761) **3:** 418 **5:** 667
Poniatowski, Stanislaw **4:** 490
Pontiac (North American chief) **4:** 553
Pony Express **6:** 840
Poor Laws (1834) **5:** *633* **6:** 811
Poor People's Campaign (1968) **9:** *1165*
Poor Richard's Almanac (Benjamin Franklin) **4:** 551
poorhouses **5:** 632
Pope, Alexander **4:** 500
popes/papacy
　two simultaneous *See* Great/Western Schism
　and the Holy Roman Empire **1:** 20
　and Europe's secular rulers **1:** 51
　and the Renaissance **1:** 83–84
　in late Medieval (pre-Reformation) times **2:** 152
Popular Front **8:** 1032
Population Registration Act (1950) **9:** 1228
population(s)
　in early modern Europe **1:** 29, 30–31
　in France (1400s–1500s) **2:** 196
　in Europe (1600s) **2:** 234, 245–246
　shifting **2:** 254
　of colonial America **3:** 365–366 **4:** 549
　in Europe (1700s) **4:** 505–508, 511
　in postcolonial Africa **9:** 1222
　world growth (1800s–1900s) **9:** 1264, 1275
populism, in the United States **6:** 811–814, 834
porcelain, Ming **1:** *127*
Porfirio's Peace **6:** 743
Port Arthur, and the Sino-Japanese War **6:** 782
Port Arthur, Battle of (1904; Russian-Japanese War) **5:** *695*, 696 **6:** 783, *786*
Port Royal **3:** 360 **4:** 546
portolan charts **3:** *300*, 301
Portrait of a Young Man with a Medal (Sandro Botticelli) **1:** *87*
portraits **6:** 842
Portugal
　colonies and trade in Asia **1:** 41 **3:** 323–324, *325, 326, 399*
　world exploration by **3:** *295*, 302, 303–307
　slaves/slave trade **3:** 305, *308*, 376–377, 381, *383*
　New World divided for **3:** 310–311
　colonies in the New World **3:** 347–348, 354, 383
　absolute monarchies **4:** 460
　and the War of the Spanish Succession **4:** 464, 465
　trade with Japan **4:** 538
　Napoleon's invasion of (1807) **6:** 749, 755
　independence for Brazil **6:** 755–756
　African colonies **6:** 828 **8:** 1128
　African colonies lost **8:** 1128
　military coup (1974) **9:** 1166
　EEC membership **9:** 1195
possession, demonic **2:** *180*
Post-Impressionists **6:** 843–844
postal services **5:** 624 **6:** 793

posters
　World War I **7:** *902, 903*, 918
　and the Russian Revolution **7:** 918, *921*
　and the Russian Civil War **7:** *920*
　American fashion (1920s) **7:** *952*
　film **7:** *963, 970* **8:** *1097*
　Work Projects Administration **7:** *967*
　and the Great Depression **7:** *968*
　and the Spanish Civil War **8:** *1032, 1033*
　World War II **8:** *1041, 1042, 1058, 1061, 1068*
　Marshall Plan **8:** *1088*
　Vietnamese nationalist **8:** *1117*
"Potato War" **4:** 469
potatoes **3:** 350, 389, 392, *394* **4:** 504, 508
　potato famine (1845) **5:** 612, 650
potlatch ceremonies **3:** 341
Potosí **3:** 348–349, 388, 392
Potsdam Conference (1945) **8:** 1085–1086, 1089
pottery
　Chinese **1:** 121
　Wedgwood **4:** *473*, 496
Pottier, Eugène **6:** 815
Poussin, Nicolas **4:** 454, 495
　painting by **2:** *262* **4:** *491*
power looms **5:** 616, 618
Powers, Gary **8:** 1095, *1096*
Powhatan (Native American chief) **3:** 339, 358
Powhatan confederacy **3:** 544
Prague, university **1:** 94
Prague, Defenestration of **2:** 226–227
Prague, Peace of (1635) **2:** 231
Praise of Folly, The (Erasmus) **1:** 58, 67–68 **2:** 165
prayer book
　Anglican **2:** 210, 238
　for Scotland (1637) **2:** 238, *239*
Pre-Raphaelites **6:** 842
predestination **2:** 161
Presbyterian Church/Presbyterianism **2:** 161, 214 **4:** 550
　Scottish **2:** 238, *239* **3:** 371
Presley, Elvis **9:** 1171
Prester John **3:** 297–298, 299–300, 303
Prévost, Antoine-François **4:** 517
PRI (Institutional Revolutionary Party) **9:** 1206
Prince, The (Niccolò Machiavelli) **1:** 65, 67
Princip, Gavrilo **7:** *879*, 880
printing **1:** 66, 94 **2:** 267
　Gutenberg's printing press **1:** *59*, 60–61 **2:** 254
　in China **1:** 60, 121
　and the spread of Protestantism **1:** 62 **2:** 158
　in the 1700s **4:** 521
　mechanized **5:** 642
privy pails **6:** 801
processions, religious **1:** *75*
Proclamation of 1763 **4:** 553, 555
proctors **1:** *51*
Prodigal Son, The (Hieronmyous Bosch) **1:** *34*
Progressive Party (U.S.) **6:** 836
progressivism **6:** 814
Prohibition, in the United States **7:** 948
proletariat **5:** 628
Prometheus Bound (Percy Bysshe Shelley) **5:** 638
propaganda
　during World War I **7:** 901–902, 918
　during the Russian Revolution **7:** 918
　under Stalin's dictatorship **7:** 926
　during World War II **8:** *1042, 1043, 1053*, 1060, 1066–1067
　Vietnamese nationalist **8:** *1117*
prostitution **6:** 800
Protestant Union **2:** 226
Protestantism **1:** 21 **2:** 167
　in France *See* Religion, Wars of
　birth of **1:** 10 **2:** 151–162
　and the monarchy **1:** 70–71
　and the Renaissance **1:** 95–96
　name **2:** 156
　development in England (1500s) **2:** 208–209, 210
　and art **2:** 255
　and Baroque **2:** 260, 261
　Protestant northern Europe **4:** 439–448
　See also Huguenots; Reformation
Protocols of the Learned Elders of Zion **7:** 990
Proudhon, Pierre-Joseph **6:** 811
Proust, Marcel **6:** 848

Provence **1**: 23
Prussia **4**: 442
    and the Teutonic Knights **1**: 90
    Hohenzollern family **4**: 460
    under Frederick the Great **4**: *466, 469, 470,*
      488–489
    and European dynastic wars **4**: 469, 488, 489
    partition of Poland-Lithuania **4**: *484,* 490
    formation of the state of **4**: 488
    a powerful force in Europe **4**: 490
    peasants **4**: 505
    and the French Revolutionary Wars **5**: 592,
      595–596
    and German nationalism **5**: 602, *656,* 659–664
    Seven Weeks' War (1866) **5**: 661
    Franco-Prussian War (1870–1871) **5**: 662–663,
      664 **6**: 794 **7**: 871, 892 **8**: 1026
    railroads **6**: 791
    lands lost (post–World War I) **8**: 1026
psychoanalysis **6**: 849
Ptolemy
    Almagest **1**: 53
    and astronomy **1**: 53 **2**: *265,* 266, 268, 269
    Geographia **1**: 65 **3**: 300
    and the world **3**: 300–301, 304
public houses **4**: 521
Public Safety, committee for **5**: 593
Public Works Administration (PWA) **7**: 967
Pueblo Bonito **3**: 332
Pueblo Indians **3**: *339,* 342, 346
pueblos **3**: 332, 335, *339*
Puerto Rico **6**: 835
Pullman Strike (U.S.) **6**: *814*
Punjab **8**: 1114, 1115
Puritans **4**: 440
    English **2**: 236–237, 238, 241 **4**: 440
    and Oliver Cromwell's rule **2**: 241
    colonies in North America **3**: 358–359, 360, 370
Purna Swaraj resolution **8**: 1112
putting-out system **1**: 37, 77
Puyi, emperor of China **7**: 941
PWA (Public Works Administration) **7**: 967
Pym, John **2**: 238–239
Pyramids, Battle of the (1798) **5**: 596
Pyrenees mountain chain **2**: *186*

Qajar dynasty of Iran **3**: 406
Qazvin **3**: 400
Qidan people **1**: 120, 122
Qingdao **7**: 887, 935
Qizilbash tribal groups **3**: 398, 399, 400, 402
Qom **9**: 1233, 1234
quadrants **3**: 301–302
Quakers **2**: 241 **4**: 550
    and Pennsylvania **3**: *361, 364, 370*
    and New Jersey **3**: 364
Quebec (province) **5**: 674
Quebec Act (1774) **4**: 555 **5**: 674
Quebec City
    a French colonial settlement **3**: 360, 366, 373
    British assault on (1711) **4**: 546
    British capture (1759) **4**: 549
    and the American Revolutionary War **4**: 556
Queen Anne's War (1702–1713) **4**: 546
quinine **3**: 396
Quit India resolution **8**: *1112,* 1113

Rabaul **8**: 1054
rabies **5**: *704,* 705
Rabin, Yitzhak **8**: 1138 **9**: 1242
Race to the Sea (World War I) **7**: 884
Racine, Jean **4**: 497
radio
    in 1920s America **7**: 950, 951
    and World War II **8**: 1067–1068
    Japanese-manufactured **9**: *1211*
radio waves, discovery **5**: 705
railroads **4**: 509 **5**: *649*
    in the Industrial Revolution **5**: 619–620, 622, *623*
    timetables **5**: 620
    tunnels **5**: *621*
    United States **5**: 622, *623, 649* **6**: *832,* 838, 840
    Canadian transcontinental **5**: 675
    Russian **5**: *693, 694–695*
    Mexican **6**: *737, 741–743,* 746
    South American **6**: 764, *765*

European **6**: 790, 791
    underground and elevated **6**: *791,* 792
    Chinese **7**: *941*
    Indonesian **8**: *1020*
rain, acid **9**: 1269, *1270*
rain forests, deforestation **9**: 1266–1267, 1274
Rain, Steam, and Speed (Joseph M. W. Turner)
    5: *642*
Raj, age of the **5**: 669–671 **8**: 1107
Raleigh, Sir Walter **2**: 209, *214,* 236
    and North America **3**: 356
rank, social *See* class/rank, social
Ranters (religious sect) **2**: 241
Rapallo, Treaty of (1922) **7**: 953
Raphael **1**: 82
Rasputin **7**: 912, *913*
Rastadt, Treaty of (1714) **4**: 467
rationing, food, during World War II **8**: 1068–1069
rats, black **1**: 30, *31*
Ray, John **4**: 507
REA (Rural Electrification Administration) **7**: 967
Reagan, Ronald **9**: *1159,* 1166, 1167, 1168, 1177,
    1245
    and Central America **8**: 1104 **9**: 1205
    and Libya **9**: 1237
    Star Wars program **9**: 1255
realpolitik **5**: 661
Reason, Age of *see* Enlightenment, the
Reason for the Fatherland **7**: 979
"reason of state" **2**: 234
Rebel Without a Cause (movie) **9**: 1171
Reclamation, Bureau of **7**: 967
reconquista **1**: 24
Reconstruction Act (1866) **6**: 830
Reconstruction Finance Corporation **7**: 963–964
Record of Human Erosion, A (Dorothea Lange)
    7: *968*
recycling **9**: *1271*
Red Army (Chinese) **9**: *1179*
Red Army (Soviet)
    and the Russian Civil War **7**: *912,* 919, 920, 921
    8: 1084
    and World War II **8**: 1044, 1045, 1060
Red Baron **7**: 891
Red Brigades **9**: 1165, 1238
Red Cross **5**: 663
Red Guards (Russian) **7**: *909, 917,* 919
Red Guards (Chinese) **9**: 1184, 1185
Redoubtable (ship) **5**: *599*
Red Scare (1920) **7**: 946
Red Shirts (Italy) **5**: 659, *660*
reduktion policy, Swedish **4**: 447
Reform Act (1832) **5**: 608 **6**: 809, 810, 811
Reformation **1**: 12, 21, 28 **2**: 151–162, 163, 182,
    246 **4**: 440
    and education **1**: 55, 78
    effect on the monarchy **1**: 70–71
    in central Europe **1**: 94–96
    in France **2**: 197
    "Henrician" **2**: 208–209
    and the scientific revolution **2**: 267
Reformed Church, Dutch **2**: 224
refrigeration **6**: 793 **7**: 967
refuse **9**: *1263*
Reichstag **5**: 661–664
    and Hitler **7**: 989
religion
    and humanism **1**: *64,* 65
    and age of the Earth **5**: 698
    and the theory of evolution **5**: 699
Religion, Wars of (1562–1598) **1**: 31 **2**: 161, 172,
    195–204 **4**: 450
    and Philip II **2**: 194
    ended with the Edict of Nantes **2**: *196,* 204
    4: 451
Rembrandt, paintings by **2**: 224, 264
Remington, Frederic, painting by **6**: *838*
Renaissance **1**: 21, 39, 79–88 **2**: 255, 257, 267
    northern **1**: 85, 88, 94
    French **1**: 88
    and religion **1**: 95–96 **2**: 152
    and geography **3**: 300–301
Renoir, Auguste **6**: 843
Representatives, House of **4**: 562
Repton, Humphrey **4**: 498–499
Republicans, Dutch **4**: 441, 442

Requiem (Giuseppe Verdi) **5**: *658*
Resettlement Administration **7**: 968
resistance fighters, World War II **8**: *1068,* 1069
Restitution, Edict of (1629) **2**: 229, 231, 233
restoration of the monarchy **2**: 241–242
Restore Hope, Operation **9**: *1229*
Revere, Paul **4**: 554
Revolt of the Netherlands *See* Eighty Years' War
Reymersae, Marinus Van, painting by **2**: *216*
Reynolds, Sir Joshua **4**: 496
Reza Abbasi **3**: *402, 403, 406*
Reza Shah Pahlavi, shah of Iran **9**: 1232–1233,
    1234
Rhee, Syngman **9**: 1212
Rhine, Confederation of the **5**: 601
Rhineland
    post–World War I **8**: 1026
    reoccupied by Germany (1936) **8**: 1030, *1031*
Rhode Island, colonial **3**: 360, 369, 373
Rhodes, Cecil **6**: 826
Rhodesia *See* Zimbabwe
rhubarb **3**: 298
Ricci, Matteo **4**: 524, 528
rice, cultivation **1**: 121 **3**: 316–317 **4**: 524, *530*
Richard III, king of England **1**: 23 **2**: 205
Richardson, Samuel, *Pamela, or Virtue Rewarded*
    (novel) **4**: 500, *513*
Richelieu, Armand Jean du Plessis, cardinal, duc de
    4: 453–455
Richmond (Virginia), and the Civil War **5**: 678,
    679, 680, 681, 682, 685, 686
Richmond, Battle of (1865) **5**: *685,* 686
Richthofen, Manfred von **7**: 891
riding **4**: *518*
Riel, Louis **5**: 675
Riga **1**: 16, *78* **7**: *911,* 952
    siege of **4**: *447*
Right, Petition of **2**: 237
Rights, Bill of (1689) **4**: 444
rights, natural human, and Enlightenment thought
    4: 475, 480
"rights politics" **9**: 1166
Rights of Women, The (Olympe de Gouges) **5**: *588*
Riis, Jacob **5**: 626
Riksdag (Swedish parliament) **4**: 448
Rimbaud, Arthur **6**: 844
Ring of the Nibelung, The (Richard Wagner) **6**: 848
Rio de Janeiro **6**: 756 **7**: *981*
    Earth Summit (1992) **9**: 1271, *1272*
Rio Grande do Sol **7**: 981
Rite of Spring, The (Igor Stravinsky) **6**: 850
Rivera, Diego **7**: *976*
Riyadh **6**: 732
Roanoke Island, colony **3**: 356–357
robber barons **6**: 832, 834
Robespierre, Maximilien **5**: 592, 593, 594
Robinson Crusoe (Daniel Defoe) **4**: 500
rock and roll **9**: 1171
Rockefeller, John D. **6**: 834
Rocket (steam locomotive) **5**: 620
rococo style **4**: 491, 492–493
Roger II, king of Sicily **1**: 53
Roh Tae Woo **9**: *1213,* 1214
Rohlfs, Gerhard **6**: 824
Röhm, Ernst **7**: 992
Rolfe, John **3**: 358
Roman Catholics *See* Catholic Church
Romania
    independence **6**: 734 **7**: 877
    and the lead-up to World War I **7**: 877
    and World War I **7**: 895
    post–World War I **7**: 907
    collapse of communism **9**: 1246–1247
Romanov, Alexei **1**: 92
Romanov, Michael **1**: *92,* 98 **4**: 482
    lands acquired under **1**: 90
Romanov dynasty **1**: 98 **4**: 460, 482–483 **7**: 909
Romans, traders in India **3**: 315
Romanticism **4**: 500, 510, 517 **5**: 635–644 **6**: 841
Rome
    St. Peter's basilica **1**: 11–12, 84 **2**: *172*
    violence **1**: 80
    rebuilt (1400s/1500s) **1**: 84
    sacked by the Habsburg army (1527) **2**: 189
    streets **2**: 253
    and the Baroque **2**: 257, 259

Rome (continued)
    Mussolini marches on **7:** 985–986
    and World War II **8:** 1046
Rome, ancient
    and humanism **1:** 63
    influence on classicism **4:** 494–496
Rome, Treaty of (1957) **9:** *1192*, 1193
Rome-Berlin Axis **8:** *1029*, 1031, 1034
Romero, Oscar **9:** 1206
ronin **4:** 537
roofs, thatched **3:** *367*
Roosevelt, Franklin D.
    and the Great Depression **7:** 959, 965–970
    New Deal **7:** 959, 966–970 **8:** 1079
    Good Neighbor Policy **7:** 973 **9:** 1200
    and the road to World War II **8:** 1034
    and World War II **8:** 1039–1040, 1046, 1049, 1077
    and postwar Europe **8:** 1084, 1085, 1087
    and the British in India **8:** 1113–1114
Roosevelt, Theodore **6:** 766, 835–836, 840
Rosas, Juan Manuel **6:** 759, 760–761
Rosenberg, Ethel and Julius **8:** 1091
Roses, Wars of the (1455–1485) **1:** 23 **2:** 205
Rosie the Riveter (fictional character) **8:** *1061*
Rossetti, Dante Gabriel **6:** 842
Rousseau, Jean-Jacques **2:** 233 **4:** 476–478, 498, 510, 512, 513 **5:** 637 **6:** 811
Royal Academy (London) **4:** 496
Royal Academy of Painting and Sculpture (France) **2:** 262
Royal African Company of London **3:** 381, 382
Royal Society (London) **2:** 274
Royal Society for the Prevention of Cruelty to Animals **6:** 804
rubber **3:** 395 **6:** 794 **9:** 1265–1266
Rubens, Peter Paul **2:** 260–261
    paintings by **2:** *171*, *257*, 260–261
Rudolf II, Holy Roman emperor **1:** *69*, 95
Ruhr Basin, French occupation of (1923) **7:** 953, *956*
rural life
    in Europe **1:** 16 **2:** 247
    in France (1400s) **1:** *35* **2:** *195*
    in France (1700) **4:** *520*
Rurik **1:** 89
Rus **1:** 89, 90
Russia
    and the Orthodox religion **1:** 24, 92
    Kiev Rus empire **1:** 89, 90, 92
    feuds of the boyars (1500s) **1:** 96
    from the grand duchy of Moscow **1:** 96
    Ivan the Terrible **1:** 96–97 **4:** *481*
    power of the czar **1:** 96
    "Time of Troubles" (1598–1613) **1:** 97–98 **4:** 482
    expansion (1600s) **1:** 98
    Romanov dynasty **1:** 98 **4:** 460, 482–483
    wars against Sweden (1700s) **4:** 447, 448
    serfs **4:** 481, 482, 504–505 **5:** 689–690, 692–693 **6:** 809 **7:** 909
    nobles **4:** 482, 489–490
    ethnic groups **4:** *483*
    partition of Poland-Lithuania **4:** *484*, 490
    under Peter the Great **4:** 486–488
    a powerful force in Europe **4:** 490
    border with China **4:** 530
    Napoleon's invasion **5:** *603*, 604, 688
    modernization (1800s) **5:** 623, 687–696
    Decembrist revolt (1825) **5:** *688*, 689, 690
    and the Crimean War **5:** *689*, 692
    and Poland **5:** 691–692, 696
    and Ottoman Turkey **5:** 692 **6:** 728, 730, 732, 733–734, 734
    railroads **5:** *693*, 694–695
    Russian Revolution (1917) **5:** 694 **7:** 909–919 **8:** 1083–1084
    intelligentsia **5:** 695–696
    Russian-Japanese War (1904–1905) **5:** *695*, 696 **6:** 782–783, *786* **8:** 1015
    elected assembly (Duma) **5:** 696 **7:** 910, 913–914
    Russian Revolution (1905) **5:** 696 **7:** 909
    and industrialization (1800s) **6:** 796
    and the lead-up to World War I **7:** 872, 877–879, 880, 881, 882
    and the Balkans **7:** 877

    and World War I **7:** 880, 881, 882, 884, 890, 894–895, *911*
    Civil War (1918–1920) **7:** 919–920, 921 **8:** 1084, 1085
    Polish-Soviet War (1919–1920) **7:** 920
    and nationalistic uprisings in the USSR **9:** 1248–1249
    See also Russian Federation *(from 1991)*; Soviet Union *(from 1922)*
Russian Civil War (1918–1920) **7:** 919–920 **8:** 1084, 1085
Russian Federation
    and nuclear weapons **8:** 1106
    economic failure (1990s) **9:** 1250, 1251
    Chechnya invaded by Russian troops (1994) **9:** 1251
Russian Orthodox Church **1:** 92 **4:** *481*, 530 **5:** *691*
Russian Revolution (1917) **5:** 694 **7:** 909–919 **8:** 1083–1084
    October Revolution **7:** *909*, 915, 917
    February Revolution **7:** 914
    and Indonesian politics **8:** 1021
    and Indian politics **8:** 1108
Russian War (1812)
    Napoleon's retreat from Moscow **5:** *603*, 604, 688
    Battle of Borodino (1812) **5:** 604
    and the Poles **5:** 691
Russian-Japanese War (1904–1905) **5:** *695*, 696 **6:** 782–783, *786* **7:** 888 **8:** 1015
russification **5:** 696
Russo-Swedish War (1788–1790) **4:** *446*, 448
Ruth, Babe **7:** *950*, 951
Ruthenia **4:** 483
Ruysch, Rachel **2:** 262
Rwanda, civil war (1994) **9:** 1230, 1278

Saarland **8:** 1026
sabbats **2:** 180
Sacco, Nicola **7:** 946, *949*
Sacred Edict **4:** 531
Sadat, Anwar **8:** 1137 **9:** 1236, *1237*
Sadowa, Battle of (1866) **5:** 661, 662
Safavid empire **1:** 105, 108 **3:** 397–406 **6:** 728
    conflict with the Ottomans **1:** 105 **3:** 399–400, 405, 406 **6:** 729
    and trade **3:** *399*, 403–404
    and the arts **3:** 400–402, *406*
Safi, shah of Persia **3:** 404
Safi al-Din **3:** 398
sago palm **3:** 316
Sagres **3:** 304, *307*
Sahara Desert **1:** *111*, 112
Saigon *See* Ho Chi Minh City
Saint Augustine (Florida) **4:** 546, 547
Saint Bartholemew's Day Massacre **2:** *199*, *200*, 201–202, 219
Saint-Germain, Edict of **2:** 199
Saint Germain, Treaty of (1570) **2:** 201
Saint Germain, Treaty of (1919) **7:** 903
Saint Helena **5:** *603*, 604
Saint Lawrence River **3:** 356 **4:** 546, *549*
Saint Louis **5:** 650
Saint Paul (Minnesota) **9:** *1170*
Saint Peter's, Rome **1:** 11–12, 84 **2:** *172*
    Michelangelo's *Pietà* **1:** *81*
Saint Petersburg (*or* Leningrad *or* Petrograd) **5:** 688
    and Peter the Great **4:** 487
    and the Russian Revolution (1905) **5:** 696
    Winter Palace **5:** 696 **7:** *909*, 915, 916
    and the Russian Revolution (1917) **7:** *909*, 913, 916, *917*
    and World War II **8:** 1044
    after collapse of the Soviet Union **9:** *1251*
Saint Vincent, Cape of (Portugal) **3:** *306*
Saint-Simon, Henri **5:** 703
Sainte-Union **2:** 203
Saipan **8:** 1055
Sakhalin Island **8:** 1017
Salem (Massachusetts) **3:** *361*
    witch trials **2:** 182 **3:** 370, *373*
Salem (North Carolina) **3:** 372
salons **4:** 472, 521
salt
    trade in **1:** 112 **3:** 298, *299*

    cellars **3:** *301*
    mining **3:** 348
SALT (Strategic Arms Limitation Treaty) **8:** 1102, *1103*
Salvation Army **5:** *626*, 632, 702
Salvation Front **9:** 1241–1242
Samarkand **1:** 123, 130
Samoa **3:** 315
samurai warriors **1:** 127 **4:** 533–537 **6:** 777
    decline **4:** 537 **6:** 778, 780
San Francisco
    and the 1849 gold rush **5:** *651*
    anti–Vietnam War demonstrations **8:** *1101*
San Jacinto, Battle of (1836) **6:** 738
San Marino **1:** 28
San Martin, José de **5:** 665 **6:** 749, 750, 753–754, *755*
San people **1:** 117, *118*
San Salvador (Bahamas), and Columbus **3:** 309, *310*
San Salvador (Brazil)
    Portuguese settlement **3:** *347*
    Jesuits murdered **9:** *1207*
Sandinistas **8:** 1104 **9:** 1205, 1206, 1208
sanitation **2:** 249–250 **6:** 801–802
    See also sewage systems
Sankey Canal **4:** 509
sansculottes **5:** *591*, 592
Sanskrit **3:** 317
Santa Anna, Antonio López de **6:** 738, 739
Santa Fe Trail **6:** *839*
Santa Maria (ship) **3:** 309
Santiago **6:** 749, 754
Sao Paulo **9:** 1199
Saratoga, Battle of (1777) **4:** 558, *559*
Sarawak **3:** *315*, 316 **8:** *1118*
Sardinia **1:** 24 **4:** 467
Sardinia-Piedmont **5:** 658
Sarekat Islam **8:** 1020
Sargent, John Singer **6:** 842
Saskatchewan **5:** 676
satellites, artificial **8:** 1094 **9:** 1256, 1257, 1261
satyagraha movement **8:** 1109, 1110
Saudi dynasty **6:** 732
Savak **9:** 1234
Savannah, cotton exchange **5:** *647*
Savannah, Battle of (1778) **4:** 559
Savannah, Battle of (1864) **5:** 685
Savimbi, Jonas **9:** 1227–1229
Savonarola, Girolamo **1:** *10*, 11, 65
Savoy **5:** 659
    and the War of the Spanish Succession **4:** 464, 465
Saxony **2:** 188
    invasion by Prussia **4:** 469
scalawags **6:** 831
Scandinavia, Union of Colmar **1:** 24
Schall von Bell, Johann Adam **4:** 528–529
Scheldt River **2:** 222
Schlegel, August Wilhelm von **5:** 602
Schleswig **5:** 661
Schlieffen, Alfred von **7:** 881
Schlieffen Plan **7:** 880–882, 884
Schmalkaldic League **1:** 47 **2:** 156, 188, 190
Schoenberg, Arnold **6:** 847, 850
Scholasticism **1:** 57
School of Athens, The (Raphael) **1:** 82
Schoolmen **1:** 57, 58
schools **2:** *250*, 252
    cathedral **1:** 54
    grammar schools **1:** 54
    in the 1700s **4:** 518
Schubert, Franz **5:** 644
Schuman, Robert **8:** 1073
Schuman Plan **9:** *1191*, 1192
Schumann, Robert (musician) **5:** 644
science **1:** 56
    in the 1800s **5:** 697–706
    developments (1900s) **9:** 1253–1262
scientific revolution (1600s) **2:** 256, 265–274 **5:** 697–698
    and art **2:** 264
    and the Enlightenment **4:** 471–472
Scopes, John **5:** 700
Scotch-Irish, immigrants to North America (c. 1700s) **3:** 371

Volume numbers appear in **boldface type.** Page numbers in *italic type* refer to illustrations and captions.

Scotland
    Tudor **2:** 214
    and Charles I's religious reforms **2:** 238, *239*
    immigrants to North America (c. 1700s) **3:** 371
    with England as the United Kingdom **4:** 444
Scott, Robert Falcon **5:** *676*
Scott, Walter **5:** 636, 642
Scott, Winfield **6:** *739*
Scream, The (Edvard Munch) **6:** 850
scribes **1:** *49*, 60
sculpture
    Renaissance **1:** 81–82
    African **1:** *112*, 113
    Baroque **2:** 256, 259, 263
    Soviet **7:** *928*
scurvy **3:** 312, 328
SDI *See* Strategic Defense Initiative
Sea Beggars (Dutch seamen) **2:** 218–219
sea trade, Dutch (1500s/1600s) **2:** 222
seaside, vacations at **6:** 806
Secession movement **6:** 847
Second Balkan War (1913) **7:** 879
Second Coalition, War of the (1798–1800) **5:** 596
Second Empire (France) **5:** 657
Second Great Awakening **5:** 652
Second Indochina War *See* Vietnam War
Second International **6:** *811*, 816
Second New Deal **7:** 967–970
Second Treatise of Government (J. Locke) **4:** 475
Second World War *See* World War II
Sedan, Battle of (1870) **5:** 664, *665*
seed drills **4:** *502*, 503
Seekers (religious sect) **2:** 241
Sef dynasty **1:** 112
Segal, George, sculpture by **7:** *959*
Segovia **1:** *24* **2:** *189*
segregation, in the United States **6:** 831 **8:** 1082
    9: 1171
Seine River **2:** *198* **4:** *451*
sejm **1:** 13, 25, 93 **4:** 484, 485, 490
sejmiki **4:** 484
Sekigehara, Battle of (1600) **4:** 533
Selassie, Haile, emperor of Ethiopia **8:** 1030
    9: *1226*
Selective Service Act (1940) **8:** 1040, 1063
Selim I, Ottoman sultan **1:** 105–107
    Ottoman acquisitions under **1:** *100*
Selim III, Ottoman sultan **6:** *729*, 730
Seljuks **1:** 99, 103
semesters, university **1:** 40
Seminoles (Native Americans) **6:** 839
Senate **4:** 562
Sendero Luminosa **9:** 1206
Senegal **6:** 819 **9:** 1222
Senghor, Léopold **9:** 1225
sensibility, cult of **4:** 517
sentimentality, in the late 1800s **6:** 804–805
Seoul **9:** 1213
Separatists **3:** 358
sepoys **5:** 668–669
seppuku **4:** 536
Serbia
    taken by the Ottomans **1:** 101
    revolution (1804) **6:** 730
    autonomy **6:** 732, 734 **7:** 877
    and the lead-up to World War I **7:** 877, 878, 879,
        880
    and World War I **7:** 890
    attack on Albanians in Kosovo (1999) **9:** 1252,
        1278
    attack on Bosnia-Herzegovina **9:** 1252, 1278
    attack on Croatia (1991–1992) **9:** 1252
serfdom, "the second" **1:** 94
serfs
    in Europe **1:** 34, 35 **4:** 481–482, 483, 504–505
        5: 602
    in Russia **4:** 481, 482, 504–505 **5:** 689–690, 691,
        692–693 **6:** 809 **7:** 909
servants
    indentured **3:** 367
    in Europe (1700s) **4:** 513–514, 516, 520
Serviceman's Readjustment Act (1944; GI Bill of
    Rights) **8:** 1081
Sevastopol, Battle of (1854–1855; Crimean War)
    5: *689*
Seven Days' Battles (1862) **5:** 681

Seven Weeks' War (1866) **5:** 661
Seven Years' War (1756–1763) **4:** 469, 489, 548
    American involvement *See* French and Indian
        War
    in India **3:** 418
Sèvres, porcelain from **4:** 492
Sèvres, Treaty of (1920) **7:** 903, 908 **8:** 1023
sewage systems **5:** *629* **6:** 802, *803*
Sewell, Anna **6:** 805
sex *See* gender
sexual freedom (post-1960s) **9:** 1165
Seymour, Edward, 1st duke of Somerset **2:** 210
Seymour, Jane **2:** 209
Sforza, Francesco, statue of **1:** 82
Sforza, Lodovico **1:** 84
Sforza family **1:** 28
Shaanxi **7:** 941
Shah Jahan, Mogul emperor **3:** 414–415, 417
Shahjahanabad **3:** 414
Shahn, Ben **7:** *968*
Shaka, Zulu leader **6:** 819
Shakespeare, William **2:** 209
    The Merchant of Venice **7:** 990
shamans, Native American **3:** *335*
Shandong **7:** 935 **8:** 1016, 1017
Shanghai **9:** *1188*
    industrialization **6:** 772, *773*
    and the May Fourth Movement **7:** 935
    strikes (1925) **7:** 938
    Chiang Kai-shek enters (1927) **7:** 939
sharecropping **6:** 831
Sharpville, riots (1960) **9:** *1228*, 1229
sheep
    shearing **1:** *33* **2:** *246*, *247*
    and enclosure **1:** 34, 35 **2:** 246
    Thomas More quoted on **2:** 208
shell shock **7:** 889
Shelley, Mary Wollstonecraft **5:** 638, *639*
Shelley, Percy Bysshe **5:** 638
shellfish **4:** *505*
shells, cowrie **1:** 113
Shenyang (*formerly* Mukden) **1:** 128 **4:** 525 **7:** 944
    8: *1019*
Sherman, William T. **5:** *681*, 685
Shidehara Kijuro, Danshaku **8:** 1019
Shiism
    in Iran **3:** 398, 400, 406 **9:** 1233, 1234, 1237
    Lebanese Shiite terrorists (Hezbollah)
        9: 1240, 1241, 1242
Shilling, David, mother's hat **9:** *1194*
Shiloh, Battle of (1862) **5:** 682
Shimabara **4:** 539
Shimonoseki, Treaty of (1895) **6:** 772, 782
shimpan **4:** 533
Shining Path movement **9:** 1206, 1238
Shinto religion **6:** 781, 782, *783*
ships **3:** 302
    slave **3:** *375*, 380–*381*
    built in the American colonies **4:** 549
    steamships **6:** 792–793
    See also sea trade
Shiraz **3:** 406
Shirazi **1:** *113*
Shirley, William **4:** 547
Shiusky, Basil **1:** 97
Shiva **3:** *318*
Shivaji Bosle **3:** 416
shoes **2:** 251
shoguns **4:** 533 **6:** 777
shops, early modern European **1:** *73*, 77, *78*
Shunzhi, Manchu emperor **4:** 526, 527, 528
Siam *See* Thailand
Siberia, gulags (labor camps) **7:** 927, 928
Sicily **1:** *24* **5:** 658
    scholarship in **1:** 53
    and World War II **8:** 1046
siege guns **6:** 794
Siemens **6:** 790
Siemens, William **6:** 788
Sierra Leone **3:** 305 **6:** 819
Sieyès, Emmanuel **5:** 596
Sigismund, Holy Roman emperor **1:** 94
Sigismund II Augustus, king of Poland **1:** 98
Sigismund III, king of Poland **1:** 97–98
Sikandara **3:** *413*
Sikhs **3:** 416 **8:** 1108, *1109*, 1114, 1115

Silent Spring (Rachel Carson) **9:** 1265
Silesia, invasion by Prussia **4:** 469, 488, 489
silicon chips **9:** 1258
silk **3:** 298
    Iranian silk trade **3:** 403–404
    and the Depression in Japan **8:** 1017–1018
Silk Road **1:** 106
Silva Xavier, Joaquim José da (*pseudonym*
    Tiradentes) **6:** 755, *756*
silver
    mining in Europe **1:** *32*
    from the Americas **3:** 348, *350*, 388
    European silver in China **4:** 524–525
Sinai **8:** 1133, 1134, 1135, 1136
Sinan **1:** *107*
Singapore
    and World War II **8:** 1051, 1113, 1119
    independence **8:** 1120 **9:** 1218
    economic boom **9:** 1218, 1220
Single European Act (1986) **9:** 1196
Sino-Japanese War (1894–1895) **6:** 772, 782
Sino-Japanese War (1937–1945) **7:** 942–943
    8: 1019, 1025, 1034
Sioux (Native Americans) **3:** 336, 340
    Battle of the Little Bighorn **6:** *835*, 839
Sisley, Alfred **6:** 843
Sistine Chapel, ceiling **1:** *83*, 84
Sitting Bull **6:** *835*
Six-Day War (1967) **8:** 1133–1134, *1136* **9:** 1279
Sixth Coalition, War of the (1813-1815) **5:** 604
Sixtus IV, Pope **2:** 179
Sketches of British Wealth (paintings) **5:** *617*
Skimmington parties **2:** 251
skyscrapers **6:** *787*, 789 **7:** 947, *948*, 960
slave trade **5:** *678*
    Arab slave traders **3:** 375, *376* **6:** 818
    the triangular trade **3:** *379* **5:** 616
    transatlantic **3:** 380–384 **5:** 616 **6:** 817–818
    contraband slaves **5:** 684
    banned **6:** 819
slaves/slavery
    Ottoman **1:** 104
    Tatar **1:** 104
slaves/slavery
    early European slavery (1400s/1500s) **3:** 305,
        308, 376–377
    for the Dutch in Asia **3:** 327, 328 **6:** 818
    in the American colonies **3:** 348–349, 350–351,
        354, 356, 373, 377–386
    in Brazil **3:** 350, *383*, 384, *385*, 386 **6:** 758, *759*
    in the New World **3:** 375–386, 384–385
    roots **3:** 376
    daily life in the new World **3:** 384–385
    culture **3:** 385–386
    in the United States **5:** 647, 654, *678*
    abolition in the United States **5:** 651–652, 654,
        682, *683* **6:** 819, 830, 831
    slave or free states (U.S.) **5:** 654
    and the American Civil War **5:** 677, 682
    post-abolition freedmen (U.S.) **6:** 830–831
Slavophiles **5:** 690–691
Slavs **1:** 89
Slim, William **8:** 1058
Slovakia **9:** 1246
smallpox
    in the New World **3:** 346, 390–391, 393 **4:** 544
    vaccination against **4:** *522*
    eradication **9:** 1271, 1280
Smith, Adam **4:** *479*, 480 **5:** 621–624
Smith, Ian **9:** 1229
Smith, John **3:** 357, 358
Smith, Joseph **5:** 702
Smyrna **7:** 908 **8:** *1022*
soap **2:** 249–250
Sobieski *See* John III Sobieski
Social Contract, The (Jean-Jacques Rousseau)
    4: 478–479 **5:** 637
Social Darwinism **5:** 701 **6:** 820, 824
Social Democratic Party, German **5:** 628
Social Democratic Party, Russian **7:** 911, 919, 921
Social Revolutionaries, Russian **7:** 911
Social Security Act (1935) **7:** 970
social status *See* class/rank, social
socialism
    rise of (1800s–1900s) **6:** 807–816
    post–World War II **8:** 1075–1080

Volume numbers appear in **boldface type**. Page numbers in *italic type* refer to illustrations and captions.

Socialist Party, U.S. **6:** *815*
society
  divided into three estates (Middle Ages) **1:** 8
  and Enlightenment thought **4:** 474, 475, 476–478
  divided into three estates (France) **5:** 583
  Western society in the late 1800s **6:** 797–806
Society of Jesus *See* Jesuits
soda ash **6:** 794
sodbusters **9:** 1264
Sofala **3:** 306–307
soil, improvement **4:** 503
soldiers, mercenaries **1:** 14 **4:** *467*, 470
Solferino, Battle of (1859) **5:** 659, 663
Solidarity labor union **8:** 1105–1106 **9:** 1244, 1245
Solomon Islands, and World War II **8:** 1052,
    1053–1054
Somalia
  food aid hijacked by warlords (1992) **9:** *1229*,
    1230
  famine (1992) **9:** *1276*
Somerset, 1st duke of **2:** 210
Somme, Battle of the (1916) **7:** *891*, 894
Somoza, Anastasio **8:** 1104
Somoza family **9:** 1205
Son of the Sheik (film) **7:** *950*
sonatas **4:** 500
Sonderbund **5:** 612
Songhai **1:** 115–118
songs, Renaissance **1:** 86
Songs of Innocence (William Blake) **5:** *637*
Sons of Liberty **4:** 555
Sontag, Susan **9:** 1164
Sony **9:** 1210, *1211*, *1212*, *1217*
sorghum **1:** *117*
Sorrows of Young Werther (Goethe) **5:** 638
South Africa
  dominion status (1926) **5:** 676
    self-government **5:** 676
  and black Africans **6:** 828
  and independence **8:** 1127–1128
  Western support for the racist regime **9:** 1222
  subversive campaigns in Angola and
    Mozambique **9:** 1227–1229
  apartheid **9:** 1228, 1229–1230
  Sharpville riots (1960) **9:** *1228*, 1229
  end of apartheid **9:** 1229, 1230, 1281
South African Indian Congress **6:** 828
South African Native National Congress **6:** 828
South America
  named **3:** 311
  Spanish colonies in **3:** 346–354
  breaking colonial rule **6:** 747–756
  officer corps **6:** 748–749
  after independence **6:** 757–766
  between the World Wars **7:** 971–982
  and World War I **7:** 971
  rise of the military (1920s/1930s) **7:** 976–977,
    978
  emergence of democratic rule (1980s) **9:** 1168
  See also America; Latin America
South Carolina **3:** 361
South Kasai **9:** 1226
South Korea *See* Korea, South
South Pole, Scott's expedition **5:** *676*
Southern Africa
  and the Dutch **3:** 328–329 **6:** 820–821
  and the Boers **6:** 826–827 **7:** 874
  and the Cold War **9:** 1226–1227
Southern Baptist Church **9:** 1178
Southern Rhodesia (*later* Zimbabwe),
    decolonization **8:** 1124, *1125*, 1128
Southwest Africa **6:** 827
Soviet Union (USSR)
  under Lenin **7:** 921–924, *925*
  under Stalin **7:** 923–932, 936
  and China (1920s) **7:** 936
  liberates Manchuria (1945) **7:** 943 **8:** 1060
  alliance with Germany (1922) **7:** 953
  and the Spanish Civil War **8:** 1032, 1033
  nonaggression pact with Germany (Molotov-
    Ribbentrop Pact; 1939) **8:** *1035*, 1036
  and World War II **8:** *1037*, *1042*, 1043–1045,
    1048, 1061, 1062, *1067*, 1070, 1071
  invasion of Poland (1939) **8:** 1038
  rejection of post–World War II Marshall Aid
    8: *1072*, *1076*, 1089

and the Cold War (1945–1960) **8:** 1083–1094
and the Hungarian Uprising (1956) **8:** 1094
space race **8:** 1094 **9:** 1256
and the Cold War (1960–1989) **8:** 1095–*1098*,
    1102–1106
and the Cuban missile crisis **8:** 1096–1097
and war in Afghanistan (1979–1989)
    8: 1102–1104 **9:** 1167, 1241
dissolution **8:** 1106 **9:** 1196, 1198
and post–World War II colonialism **8:** 1119
communism (post-1960) **9:** 1161
insignia **9:** *1161*
and China (1950s) **9:** 1180, *1182*, 1186
and Ethiopia **9:** 1226
domination of Soviet-bloc countries **9:** 1243
reforms under Gorbachev **9:** 1243–1244
breakup **9:** 1248–1250
See also Russia; Russian Federation
soviets **7:** 914
Soweto **9:** 1229
space race **9:** 1256–1257
space shuttles **9:** 1256, *1257*
space stations **9:** 1256, *1257*
Spain
  kingdoms of Aragon and Castile **1:** 23–24
  Moorish occupation of **1:** *23*, 24
  and discovery of the New World **1:** 41
    3: 309–311
  scholarship in **1:** 53
  monarchy and religion **1:** 70
  nobility **1:** 76
  reform of the Catholic Church **2:** 165–166
  eradicating Islam from (1400s) **2:** *166*
  and Catholicism **2:** 172
  Eighty Years' War (war with the Netherlands)
    2: 172, 215–224 **4:** 440
  under Philip II **2:** 193–194
  Armada sails against England (1588) **2:** 194,
    213–214, 221
  and the Thirty Years' War **2:** 227, 231
  and Catholic Baroque **2:** 260
  New World divided for **3:** 310–311
  American colonies **3:** 343–354, 356, 374, 380
  racial purity **3:** 351, 354
  Bourbon dynasty **4:** 460 **5:** 600 **6:** 747–748
  War of the Spanish Succession **4:** *461*, 463–470
  in decline (1600s) **4:** 463
  dynastic struggles **5:** 665–666
  colonies gain independence **6:** 747–756
  Napoleon's invasion of (1808) **6:** 749
  Spanish Civil War (1936–1939) **8:** 1031,
    1032–1033
  EEC membership **9:** 1195
Spanish Civil War (1936–1939) **8:** 1032–1033
  and Germany/Italy **8:** 1031, 1032
Spanish Inquisition *See* Inquisition, Spanish
Spanish Netherlands
  rebellion against Spain (Eighty Years' War) **1:** 44
    2: 213, 215–224 **4:** 440
  and the Inquisition **2:** 180
  and art **2:** 257
Spanish Sahara **6:** 823
Spanish Succession, War of the (1701–1714)
    4: *461*, 463–470
  in North America *See* Queen Anne's War
Spanish-American War (1898) **6:** 766, 835
Spartacists **7:** 952
Spectator (periodical) **4:** 522
Spenser, Edmund **2:** 209
Spice Islands **3:** 316, *329*
  search for a route to **1:** 41 **3:** 308–312, 316, 324
    See also East Indies; Moluccas; spice trade
spice trade **2:** 222 **3:** 298, *299*, 316
  and Portugal **1:** 41 **3:** 324
  and world exploration **3:** 303–304
  and the Dutch **3:** 327
    See also Spice Islands
spinning **1:** 76
  mechanized **5:** *617*, 618
Spinoza, Baruch **2:** 224
Spiritual Exercises (Ignatius of Loyola) **2:** 170, *171*
Spotsylvania, Battle of (1864) **5:** 685
Sprenger, Jacob **2:** 180
Springtime of the Peoples **5:** 614
Sputnik (satellite) **8:** 1094 **9:** 1256
Squanto (Native American) **3:** 359

Sri Lanka (*formerly* Ceylon) **3:** 327 **9:** 1282
  independence **8:** 1120
Srivijaya **3:** 319
  trading empire **3:** 319–321
stadtholders **4:** 441
Stakhanov, Alexei **7:** 927
Stakhanovism **7:** 927
Stalin, Joseph **7:** 923–932, 936, 945, 983 **8:** 1084,
    1093 **9:** *1249*
  nonaggression pact with Germany **8:** *1035*
  and the Soviet war with Japan (1945) **8:** 1060
  and the postwar treatment of Germany **8:** 1084,
    1085–1086
  intention to occupy Azerbaijan **8:** 1086–1087
  and the British in India **8:** 1114
  and China **9:** 1180
Stalingrad, and World War II **8:** 1044–1045
Stamp Act (1765) **4:** 555
Standard Oil Company **6:** 832
Stanley, Henry Morton **6:** 820, 822
Star Wars *See* Strategic Defense Initiative
START (Strategic Arms Reduction Talks) **8:** 1104,
    1105
state, role post–World War II **8:** 1078–1079
State Domains, Ministry of **5:** 689
States General **2:** 216, 218, 220 **3:** *360* **4:** 440
stealth bombers **9:** *1255*
steam engines *See* engines, steam
steamboats **5:** *622*, 648, 649
steamships **6:** 792–793
steel
  exported to the East **3:** 298
  and industrialization **6:** 787, 788, *795*, 796
  "factories" in China (1950s) **9:** 1183
Steinbeck, John **7:** *965*, 968
Steno, Nicholaus **5:** 698
Stephenson, George **5:** 620, *706*
Stephenson, Robert **5:** *706*
Steuben, Friedrich von **4:** 559
Steuben, Adlai **8:** 1082
Stevin, Simon **2:** 224
still life paintings **2:** 261–262
Stilwell, Joseph **8:** 1058
stocks **2:** *254*
Stourbridge Lion (locomotive) **5:** *623*
Stowe, gardens **4:** *499*
Strafford, Thomas Wentworth, 1st earl of **2:** 238,
    239
strappado (instrument of torture) **2:** *176*, 177
Strasbourg
  invasion by France (1681) **4:** 462
  and the Franco-Prussian War **5:** *662*
  court of human rights **8:** 1074
  meeting of foreign ministers (1949) **9:** *1191*
Strategic Arms Limitation Treaty (SALT) **8:** 1102,
    1103
Strategic Arms Reduction Talks (START) **8:** 1104,
    1105
Strategic Defense Initiative (SDI; Star Wars)
    8: 1104 **9:** *1255*
Stravinsky, Igor **6:** 850
streetlamps, electric **6:** *788*, 790
streets, filthy **2:** 253
strike(s)
  right to **6:** 809
  Pullman Strike (U.S.) **6:** *814*
Stuart dynasty **2:** 214, 235–244
  Charles Edward, the Young Pretender **4:** *443*
Stubbs, George **4:** 496
students, protests by western students (1960s)
    9: 1162, 1163–1164, 1165
Students for a Democratic Society (SDS) **9:** 1164
stunts, in 1920s America **7:** *947*, 951
Sturm und Drang movement **5:** 638
Stuyvesant, Peter **3:** 362, 363
submarines
  World War I U-boats **7:** 890, 893, *894*, 895
  World War II **8:** 1054–1055
  and the Cold War **8:** 1096
  and nuclear missiles **9:** *1254*
suburbs **6:** 802 **9:** 1170
subways **6:** *791*, 792
Sucre, Antonio José de **6:** 752–753, 754–755
Sudan **6:** *824* **9:** 1282
  conversion to Islam in **1:** 112
  Egyptian invasion **6:** 732

Volume numbers appear in **boldface type.** Page numbers in *italic type* refer to illustrations and captions.

and the French **6:** 823–825
    an Anglo-Egyptian protectorate **6:** 825
    Britain subdues Mahdist revolt **6:** 825–826
    droughts and famines (1990s) **9:** 1224, *1225, 1280*
    guerrilla warfare (from 1956) **9:** 1226
    Ebola virus **9:** 1272
Sudetenland **7:** 993 **8:** 1034–1035, 1036
Suez Canal **6:** 821, 825
    crisis (1956) *See* Suez Crisis
    opening of **5:** 670 **6:** *823*
    and World War I **7:** 887
Suez Crisis (1956) **8:** 1127, 1133, 1135
suffragettes **7:** 898, 948
sugar **3:** 349, 390, *391*
    and the slave trade **3:** 377, *378*
Sugar Act (1764) **4:** 554
Suharto, Thojib N. J. **8:** 1121–1122 **9:** 1220, 1280
Sukarno, Achmad **8:** *1021,* 1022–1023, 1120–1121, 1122 **9:** 1217
Sukhothai **3:** 322
Sulayman, Safavid shah of Iran **3:** 404–405
Süleyman I, "the Magnificent" (1494–1566)
    1: 107–108 **2:** 190 **3:** *297*
    Ottoman acquisitions under **1:** *100*
sultans, Ottoman **1:** 104
Sumatra
    Islam **3:** 322
    and the Dutch **3:** 327 **8:** 1020, *1021,* 1022
    communist insurrection (1926) **8:** 1022
    deforestation **9:** *1277*
Summa Theologiae (Thomas Aquinas) **1:** 57
Sun King, the *See* Louis XIV, king of France
Sun Yat-sen **6:** 776 **7:** 933, 936, *937*
Sundiata **1:** *114,* 115
Sung dynasty **1:** 120–123
Sunni Islam
    and the Safavid empire **3:** 399
    in Iran **9:** 1234
superstition, in Europe (1700s) **4:** 520–521
Supper at Emmaus (Caravaggio) **2:** *256,* 259
Supremacy, Act of (1534) **2:** 208
Supreme Court (United States) **4:** 562 **5:** 646
surgery **1:** *105*
    microsurgery **9:** 1262
Suryavarman II, Khmer ruler **3:** *318*
suttee **5:** 668
swaddling **4:** 512, *513*
Swaziland, independence **8:** 1128
Sweden
    and the Union of Colmar **1:** 24
    trade and coinage **1:** 42
    and the Thirty Years' War **2:** *225,* 228, 230–231, 232, 233
    trade with Asia (1700s) **3:** 330
    colonies in North America **3:** 360, 362–363
    religion **4:** 440
    trade (1600s) **4:** 445–446
    power of the nobles (1600s) **4:** 446–447
    power struggle in the Baltic (1600s/1700s) **4:** 446, 447, 448
    reduktion policy (1600s) **4:** 447
    the crown versus parliament (1700s) **4:** 448
    everyday life (1700s) **4:** *511*
    welfare state **9:** 1160
Swift, Jonathan **4:** 500
Swing, The (Jean-Honoré Fragonard) **4:** *494*
Swiss Guards **1:** 26
Switzerland
    Everlasting League **1:** 26
    liberal constitutions **5:** 608
    Sonderbund league **5:** 612
swords **4:** *470*
    samurai **4:** *536, 537*
Sworn Confederates, Society of **6:** 776
Sydney **5:** 674
Syllabus of Errors (Pius IX) **5:** 702
symbolist movement **6:** 844
symphonies **4:** 500
syphilis **3:** 393
Syria
    castle of Krak des Chevaliers **1:** *101*
    Egyptian invasion (1831) **6:** 732
    post–World War I **7:** 905 **8:** 1023, 1024
    and the creation of Israel **8:** 1132
    war against Israel (1973) **8:** 1136–1137

Tabriz **3:** 398
Tadakuni, Mizuno **4:** 541
Taft, William Howard **6:** 836
Taft-Hartley Act (1947) **8:** 1080–1081
Tahiti **3:** 315
Tahmasp I, Safavid shah of Iran **3:** 400–403
Tahmasp II, Safavid shah of Iran **3:** 405
T'ai Tsu, emperor of China **1:** 120
Taipei **9:** *1209, 1215*
Taiping Rebellion (1850s and 1860s) **6:** 771–772, 784
Taira, house (clan) of **1:** 125
Taiwan (*formerly* Formosa) **3:** 315 **4:** 527
    becomes part of China **4:** 527
    and the Sino-Japanese War **6:** 772, 782
    Chiang Kai-shek's nationalist government in **7:** 944 **9:** 1180, 1214
    economic success (late 1900s) **9:** *1209,* 1214, 1215–1217
Taj Mahal **3:** 412, *417*
Tajikistan **9:** 1249, 1250
Tajiks **3:** 398
Talbot, William Henry Fox **6:** 842, *844*
Taleban **9:** 1241
Talleyrand, Charles Maurice de **5:** 606
Talmud **1:** 66
Tamerlane *See* Timur
Tamil (language) **3:** 317
Tanganyika (*later* Tanzania), independence **8:** 1128
Tangiers **7:** 874
tanks
    World War I **7:** 888, *892,* 893
    World War II **8:** *1043*
    Soviet **8:** *1103*
Tannenberg, Battle of (1410) **1:** 91
Tannenberg, Battle of (1914) **7:** 884
Tanzania
    Khoisan speakers **1:** 116
    German East Africa **7:** 887
    independence **8:** 1128
Tanzimat (Ottoman reform movement) **6:** 733, 734
Taraki, Nur Mohammed **8:** 1103
Tarawa, Battle of (1943) **8:** 1054, *1055*
Tartuffe (Molière) **4:** 458, 460
Tatars (Tartars) **4:** *483,* 484, 485
    and Moscovy **1:** 96
    slaves of **1:** 104
    See also Mongols
Tatler (periodical) **4:** 522
taverns **4:** 521
Tax Collector, The (Quentin Massys) **1:** *39*
taxes
    in early modern Europe **1:** *39*
    imposed on the American colonies by Britain **4:** 554–555
    on salt in India **8:** 1110
Taylor, Zachary **6:** 739
Tbilisi **9:** *1247,* 1249
tea **3:** 330 **4:** 522
    plantation in China **4:** *531*
    taxed in American colonies by Britain **4:** 554
    plantation in Sri Lanka **5:** *670*
teahouses, Japanese **4:** 540
Tehran, U.S. embassy hostages (1979) **9:** 1234
Tel Aviv **8:** *1133*
telecommunications **9:** 1261–1262
telegraphy **5:** 624 **6:** 832, 840
telephones, mobile phones **9:** *1260,* 1262
telescopes **2:** 270, *273*
    radio **9:** 1262
television **9:** 1170–1171, 1178, 1261
    satellite **9:** 1277
temperance **6:** 801
temples, Southeast Asian **3:** 317–318, 320, 321, *322*
Tennessee, USS **8:** *1051*
Tennessee Valley Authority (TVA) **7:** 967
Tennis Court Oath **5:** *585,* 586
Tenochtitlán **3:** 344, 345
tepees **3:** 333, 335, *337*
Teresa of Avila, Saint **2:** 166, *168,* 259
Terra, Gabriel **7:** 975
Terra Australis **3:** 312
Terror, the **5:** *592,* 593, 594

terrorists **9:** 1165, 1238–1239, 1279–1282
    Palestinian **8:** 1136
    Islamic **9:** 1236–1240, 1241–1242
Tet offensive **8:** 1100–1101
Tetzel, Johann **2:** 153, *154*
Teutonic Knights **1:** 90–91
Texas, independence from Mexico **6:** 738, 739
textiles, African **1:** 114
Thai people **3:** 322
Thailand (*formerly* Siam) **1:** 127 **3:** 314
    religion **3:** *317, 320*
    Mon people **3:** 321–322
    French missionaries (1660–1688) **3:** 330
    and the Vietnam War **9:** 1217
    economy (1990s) **9:** 1218, 1220
Thames, River, and the Great Stink (1848) **5:** *629,* 705 **6:** 802
Thames River, polluted (1800s) **5:** *629,* 705
Thanksgiving **3:** 359, *371*
Thatcher, Margaret **9:** 1167, 1196
theaters **6:** *803,* 806
    commedia dell'arte **4:** *492*
    Kabuki **4:** 540
Theatines **2:** 166
theocracy **6:** 728
Theodore (Fyodor) I, czar of Russia **1:** 97
    lands acquired under **1:** 90
theology **1:** 56–57, 58
theosophy **6:** 850
Third Coalition, War of the (1805) **5:** 599
    Battle of Trafalgar **5:** 598, *599*
third estate **5:** 586, *590*
Third International **7:** *931*
Third Reich **7:** 988
Thirteen Years' War (1454–1466) **1:** 91
Thirteenth Amendment, of the U.S. Constitution **6:** 830
Thirty Three Arches, Bridge of the **3:** *401*
Thirty Years' War (1618–1648) **1:** 95, 98 **2:** 172, 193, 225–234 **4:** 452, 461
    end *See* Westphalia, Peace of (1648)
    and France **2:** 232, 233 **4:** 453, 455
    and potatoes **3:** 392
    and Sweden **4:** 446
Thoreau, Henry David **5:** 637, 640–641 **9:** 1263
Thousand, the (Red Shirts) **5:** 659, *660*
Thrace **1:** 100
Three Henries, War of the (1585–1589) **2:** 203
Three Mile Island **9:** 1269
three wise monkeys **4:** *535*
thuggee **5:** 668
thunderbirds **3:** *331*
Tiananmen Square **9:** *1182*
    prodemocracy demonstrations **9:** *1187,* 1188
Tibet **4:** 527 **5:** 670
Tiepolo, Giovanni Battista **4:** 493
Tiger Hunt, The (Eugène Delacroix) **5:** *643*
Tilly, Johann t'Serclaes, baron **2:** 228–229, 231
Tilsit, Treaty of (1807) **5:** 600, 601
Timbuktu **1:** 118
Times (newspaper) **4:** 522
Timur (Tamerlane) **1:** 101
Tin Pan Alley **7:** 950
Tinian **8:** 1055
Tintoretto **1:** 84
Tipu, sultan of Mysore **5:** 667
Tiradentes **6:** 755, *756*
Titian **1:** 84
Tito (Josip Broz) **8:** *1069,* 1070 **9:** 1251, 1278
Tjokroaminoto, Omar Said **8:** 1020
Tlaxcala **3:** 345
Tlingit (Native Americans) **3:** *341*
tobacco **3:** 334, 358, 390 **4:** 543–544, *545*
Tocqueville, Alexis de **5:** 626
Togoland **7:** 885
toilets **6:** 801
Tojo, Hideki **8:** *1025*
Tokugawa clan **4:** 533–542 **6:** 777–780
Tokyo
    formerly Edo **4:** 537, *538,* 540 **6:** 777, 778
    railroad to Yokohama **6:** *784*
    and World War II **8:** 1052, 1055–1056, *1057*
    Stock Exchange **9:** *1220*
"Tokyo Rose" **8:** 1068
Toledo, Juan de **2:** 191
Tolima people **7:** *976*

Volume numbers appear in **boldface type**. Page numbers in *italic type* refer to illustrations and captions.

tolls **1:** 42
Tolstoy, Leo **1:** 106 **5:** 696 **6:** 845–846
tomatoes **3:** 396
tombs, Renaissance **1:** 82
Tonga **3:** 315
Tonkin, Gulf of **8:** 1100
Topkapi Palace **1:** *105*
Tordesillas, Treaty of (1494) **3:** 310, 311, 352, 355
Tories, and Whigs **4:** 444, 445
Torquemada, Tomás de **2:** 179–180
torture, and the Inquisition **2:** *176*, 177
Toscanelli, Paolo **1:** 65
total artwork **6:** 847–848
totalitarianism, in Europe (1900s) *See* Hitler, Adolf;
    Mussolini, Benito; Stalin, Joseph
totems **3:** *331, 340*
Toul **2:** 192, 193
Toulouse-Lautrec, Henri **6:** 784
Tournai **2:** 189
Tours **2:** 200
Toussaint-Louverture, Pierre Dominique **3:** 386
towns *See* cities and towns
Townshend, Charles **4:** 503
Toyota **9:** 1211
Toyotomi clan **4:** 533
tozama **4:** 534
trade
    Dutch (1500s/1600s) **1:** 15 **2:** 222–223
    in early modern Europe **1:** 15, 39–48, 73
    European trade with the East **1:** 15 **3:** 298, 417
        4: 524–525, 532
    and the spread of Protestantism **2:** 159–160
    during the reign of Henry II **2:** 206
    triangular **3:** *379* **5:** 616
    free trade and Enlightenment thought **4:** *479*, 480
    mercantilism and the American colonies
        4: 550–552
    Latin American trade after World War I
        7: 971–973
    See also fairs; Hanseatic League; markets;
        merchants
trade associations **4:** 518
traders, educated **2:** 254
Trades Union Council **7:** 958
Trafalgar, Battle of (1805) **5:** 598, *599*
Trail of Tears **5:** *653*, 654
trains
    Eurostar **9:** *1196*
    magnetic levitation (maglev) **9:** 1260
Trakai **1:** *91*
tramways **6:** 791
transcendentalists **5:** 640–641
Transjordan, post–World War I **7:** 905
transplants, organ **9:** 1262
transport, in early modern Europe **1:** 42
Transvaal **6:** 821, 826
    gold **6:** 826
Transylvania **1:** 93 **6:** 729 **7:** 907
trench warfare, in World War I **7:** 888, 889–890
Trent **2:** *169*
Trent, Council of (1545–1563) **2:** *163*, 167–169
Trenton, Battle of (1776) **4:** *553*, 558
Triangle Shirtwaist Company fire **6:** *814*, 815
triangular trade **3:** *379* **5:** 616
Trianon, Treaty of (1920) **7:** 903
tribalism, in Africa **9:** 1224–1225
tribes, Native American **3:** 331, 333, 335
tributary system **4:** 527–530
tricoteuses **5:** 593
tricycles **6:** *792*
Trinity College (Cambridge) **1:** *53*
Triple Alliance **7:** 872–873, 875, 887
Triple Alliance, War of the (1865–1870) **6:** 764
Triple Entente **7:** 872–873, 875, 887
Tripoli **2:** 193
trivium **1:** 52
Trollope, Anthony **6:** 806
Tromp, Maarten **2:** *232*
Trotsky, Leon **7:** 930
    and the Russian Revolution **7:** 916, 917, *919*
    and the Russian Civil war **7:** 920
    and Stalin **7:** 924, 925–926
Trouble I've Seen, The (Martha Gellhorn) **7:** 968
Troubles, Council of **2:** 217
Troubles, Time of (1598–1613) **1:** 97–98 **4:** 482
Trujillo, Rafael **9:** 1204

Truman Doctrine **8:** 1087–1088
Truman, Harry S. **8:** *1071*
    and the atomic bomb **8:** 1059, 1060
    and post–World War II America **8:** 1073,
        1077–1081
    and post–World War II Europe **8:** 1086, 1087,
        1088
trusts, in the United States **6:** 832, 836
Truth and Reconciliation Commission **9:** 1281
t'Serclaes, Johan, baron Tilly **2:** 228–229, 231
tsetse flies **1:** 110
Tsunayoshi, shogun of Japan **4:** 540, *541*
Tsushima, Battle of (1905) **6:** 783
tuberculosis **5:** 705
Tudor England **2:** 205–214
Tuileries Palace, stormed (1792) **5:** 592
Tulip Period, Ottoman **6:** 729
Tull, Jethro **4:** 503
Tunisia
    and the French **6:** 732, 820
    independence **8:** 1126
tunnels **5:** *621*
Turin, Stupinigi Palace **4:** *493*
Turkestan **1:** 123
Turkey
    Turkish nationalism under the Ottomans
        6: 735–736 **7:** 878
    and World War I **7:** *885*, 887, 890
    Turks drive Greeks from Asia Minor (1920s)
        7: 908 **8:** 1022
    under Kemal Atatürk **8:** *1022*, 1023
    lands lost after World War I **8:** 1023
    See also Ottoman Empire
turkeys **3:** 396
Turkmenistan **9:** 1249
Turks, Ottoman *See* Ottoman Turks
Turner, J. M. W., paintings by **5:** *642*, 643
turnips **4:** 503
turnpikes **4:** 509
Tuscany **4:** 460
Tutsis **9:** 1230, 1278
TVA (Tennessee Valley Authority) **7:** 967
Twa people **1:** 116–117
Tweed, William Marcy "Boss" **6:** 836
Twenty-One Demands **6:** 783–786 **7:** 934 **8:** 1016
Two Nations, Commonwealth of the **1:** 98
Two Sicilies **5:** 658
typhoid **6:** 802
Tyson, Edward **5:** 699
Tzu-hsi, dowager empress of China **6:** 773–776

U-boats
    World War I **7:** 890, 893, *894*, 895
    World War II **8:** *1040*, 1041
Uccello, Paolo, painting by **1:** *73*
Uganda
    independence **8:** 1128
    Idi Amin's rule after independence **9:** 1225
U.G.T. **8:** *1032*
uitlanders **6:** 826
Ukraine **4:** 484–485
    post–World War I **7:** 907
    and the Russian Civil War **7:** 920
    and nationalism in the USSR **9:** 1248–1249
    pollution **9:** *1274*
Ulászló II, king of Bohemia and Hungary **1:** 93
ulema **6:** 729, 730, 731
Ulster
    Protestants massacred in (1600s) **2:** 239
    post–World War I **7:** 908
Ulyanov, Vladimir Ilyich *See* Lenin, Vladimir
    Ilyich
Uncle Remus (Joel Chandler Harris) **6:** 804
Unequal Treaties (1858) **4:** 541–542
Uniate Church **4:** 485
Union, Act of (1707) **4:** 444
Union and Progress, Committee of **6:** 736
unions, labor
    after the Industrial Revolution **5:** 628, 631, 634
    in the United States **5:** 631 **6:** *814*, 833 **7:** 970
    and the rise of socialism **6:** *807*, 809, *814*
    and the British general strike **6:** *957*, 958
    Solidarity in Poland **8:** 1105–1106 **9:** 1244, 1245
UNITA (National Union for the Total Independence
    of Angola) **8:** 1102 **9:** 1227–1228
Unitarians **6:** 808

United Fruit Company **7:** 973 **9:** 1201
United Kingdom, formation **4:** 444
United Nations **8:** 1070 **9:** 1198, 1280
    Relief and Rehabilitation Administration
        (UNRRA) **8:** 1071–1072, 1073
    and the Korean War **8:** 1093
    and Israel **8:** 1129, 1131, 1133, *1134*
    and the Suez Crisis **8:** 1133, 1135
    and China **9:** 1186
    and the Congo **9:** 1226
    and Somalia **9:** *1229*, 1230
    Children's Fund (UNICEF) **9:** 1280
    UNESCO **9:** 1280–1281
    High Commission for Refugees (UNHCR)
        9: 1281
    See also World Health Organization
United Provinces of the Netherlands **2:** 220
    See also Netherlands
United States
    Monroe Doctrine (1823) **5:** 607, 647 **6:** 741, 766,
        835 **7:** 973
    cotton production **5:** 616, *622*, 647, *648*, 654,
        678
    slavery **5:** 616, 647, 654, *678*
    and industrialization (1800s) **5:** 622–623,
        630–631, 647–649 **6:** 832–833
    railroads **5:** 622, *623*, *649* **6:** *832*, 838
    labor movement **5:** 631 **6:** *814*, 833 **7:** 970
    Romanticism **5:** 640–641, 643
    national parks **5:** 641 **6:** 840
    expansion (1800–1850) **5:** 645–654
    and the War of 1812 **5:** 646–647
    American Civil War **5:** 647, 677–686 **6:** 794
    intervention in Latin America **5:** 647 **6:** 741, 766,
        835 **9:** 1200–1204, 1205–1206
    transportation revolution **5:** 649–650
    westward expansion **5:** 649, 652–654, 677
        6: 829, 836–840
    Democratic Party **5:** 650 **6:** 814
    immigration (1800–1850) **5:** 650
    abolition of slavery **5:** 651–652, 654, 682, *683*
        6: 819, 830, 831
    Manifest Destiny **5:** 654 **6:** 739, 836–837
    border with Canada **5:** 675
    Confederate States of America **5:** 677
    evolution and the Monkey Trial **5:** 700, 706
    lands gained from Mexico **6:** 739–740, 741
    Gadsden Purchase **6:** 740
    and the Mexican Revolution **6:** 744, 745
    and the Panama Canal **6:** 766, 835 **9:** 1200
    Spanish-American War (1898) **6:** 766, 835
    Theodore Roosevelt's presidency **6:** 766,
        835–836
    Farmers' Alliances **6:** 811–814, 833–834
    Jacksonian democracy **6:** 811
    populism **6:** 811–814
    antitrust laws **6:** *814*
    progressivism **6:** 814
    workers' rights **6:** 814–815
    socialism **6:** *815*, 816
    abolition of the slave trade **6:** 819
    Reconstruction after the Civil War **6:** 829–831
    post-Civil War industrialization **6:** 832–833
    trusts **6:** 832, 836
    immigration (post-1860) **6:** 833, 834, *837*
    politics at the turn of the century **6:** 834–835
    dollar diplomacy **6:** 835
    Progressive Party **6:** 836
    World War I **7:** *894*, 895–896, 899, 900, 902–903
    and the Civil War in China **7:** 944
    and the Korean War (1950–1953) **7:** 944
    post–World War I **7:** 945–951, 959–960
    Red Scare (1920) **7:** 946
    consumer boom (1920s) **7:** 948–949
    immigration from Asia (1920s) **7:** 948
    prohibition of alcohol **7:** 948
    financial aid to Germany (1920s) **7:** 954
    Great Depression **7:** 954, 958, 959–970
    stock market crash (1929) **7:** 958
    and Roosevelt's New Deal **7:** 959, 966–970
        8: 1079
    Wall Street Crash (1929) **7:** 961–963
    Dust Bowl **7:** *968*, 969, 970 **9:** 1264
    economic interest in Latin America
        (1920s/1930s) **7:** 972–973, 975–976
    Good Neighbor Policy **7:** 973, 980 **9:** 1200

Volume numbers appear in **boldface type.** Page numbers in *italic type* refer to illustrations and captions.

and the road to World War II **8:** 1034
and lend-lease **8:** 1038–1041
World War II **8:** 1038–1041, 1042–1043, 1045,
 1062, 1063–1066, 1068, 1071
World War II in the Atlantic **8:** 1042
World War II in Africa **8:** 1046
World War II in the Pacific **8:** 1049–1060
postwar aid to Europe (Marshall Plan)
 8: 1072–1073, 1074, *1076*, 1088–1089
post–World War II recovery **8:** 1077–1082
and desegregation **8:** 1081, 1082
civil rights **8:** 1082 **9:** 1162–1163, 1166, 1171,
 1174, 1175
and the Cold War (1945–1960) **8:** 1083–1094
anticommunist paranoia **8:** *1091*, 1092, 1095
 9: 1169
and the Cold War (1960–1989) **8:** 1095–1106
and the Cuban missile crisis **8:** 1096–1097
and the Vietnam War **8:** 1099, 1100–1101
 9: *1162*, 1163, 1164, 1172, 1177, 1217
and China (1960s/1970s) **8:** 1102 **9:** 1186, *1187*
and post–World War II colonialism **8:** 1119
experiments with government (1960–1999)
 9: 1159–1168
social programs under Johnson **9:** 1160, 1175
swing to the political right (1980s) **9:** 1167–1168
changes in society (1950s-1980s) **9:** 1169–1178
Watergate affair **9:** 1176–1177
Moral Majority **9:** 1177–1178
Iran-Contra Affair (Irangate) **9:** 1205–1206, 1241
and postwar Japan **9:** 1209–1210
Asian influences on the economy **9:** 1219
and Iran **9:** 1233, 1234
air strikes on Libya **9:** 1237
and Afghanistan **9:** 1241
two embassies in Africa bombed (1998) **9:** 1242
space race **9:** 1256–1257
"United States of Africa" **9:** 1221
United States Steel Corporation **6:** 832
UNIVAC computer **9:** 1258
universities
 European **1:** 40, 50–52, *53*, 58, 66, 94
 semesters **1:** 40
 North American **3:** 367
UNRRA (United Nations Relief and Rehabilitation
 Administration) **8:** 1071–1072, 1073
untouchables **8:** 1111
urbanization
 in early modern Europe **1:** 16, 33, 36, 37–38, 40,
 44, *73*, 78
 in the 1800s **5:** 625–628 **6:** 802–803
 and urban replanning (1800s) **6:** 789–790
 See also cities and towns
Ursulines **1:** 54 **2:** 166–167, 169
Uruguay
 post-independence **6:** 760, 763
 period between the World Wars **7:** 971, 979
 gauchos **7:** *973*
 military dictatorship (1933–1942) **7:** 975
 post–World War II **9:** 1199
U.S.A. (John Dos Passos) **7:** 968
Userers, The (Van Reymersae) **2:** *216*
Ussher, James **5:** 698
USSR *See* Soviet Union
usury **1:** 44, 73
Utopia (Thomas More) **1:** 67–68 **3:** 376
Utrecht, Treaty of (1713) **4:** 467, 546
Utrecht, Union of (1579) **2:** 219
Uzbekistan **9:** 1249

V-2 rockets **8:** 1063 **9:** 1255
Vacarius **1:** 51
vacations **6:** 806
vaccinations **5:** 705
 smallpox **4:** *522*
Valencia **8:** 1032
valentines **6:** *804*
Valentino, Rudolph **7:** *950*
Valley Forge **4:** 559, *560*
Valmy, Battle of **5:** 592
Valois dynasty **1:** 23 **2:** 156, 196, *197*
 and the struggle for Milan **2:** 188–189
Van Buren, Martin **5:** 647
Van Gogh, Vincent *See* Gogh, Vincent Van
Vancouver **9:** 1219
Vancouver, George **3:** 391

Vanzetti, Bartolomeo **7:** 946, *949*
Varangians **1:** 89–90
Vargas, Getúlio **7:** 977, 980–982
Varna, Battle of (1444) **1:** 102
Vasari, Giorgio **1:** 87
vases
 delftware **2:** *221*
 Iranian **3:** *404*
 Greek-style **5:** *611*
Vasily III, czar of Russia **1:** 96
 lands acquired under **1:** *90*
Vassy, Huguenots massacred at **2:** 199
Vauban, Sébastien Le Prestre de **4:** 456, *459*
Velásquez, Diego de **2:** 260
 paintings by **2:** *259*, 260
vellum **1:** 60 **2:** 254
Venetia **5:** 599, 658, 659
Venezuela
 salt mines **3:** 348
 and independence **6:** *747*, 749, 750–752
 post-independence **6:** 760, 764
 European immigration **6:** *766*
 post–World War I **7:** 971
 failed military coup (1992) **9:** 1206
Venice **2:** 188–189, *252*
 and trade **1:** 15, 18, 22, 41, *104*, 106 **3:** 298
 city-state **1:** 28
 and music **1:** 84
 and the Renaissance **1:** 84
 and the Ottomans **1:** 101–102 **6:** 727–728, 729
 paintings of **4:** 496
Veracruz **3:** 344
 attacked (1838) **6:** 738
 seized by the United States (1914) **6:** 745
Verbeek, Cornelisz, painting by **2:** *232*
Verbiest, Ferdinand **4:** *529*
Verde, Cape **3:** 305
Verdi, Giuseppe **5:** *658* **6:** 848
Verdun **2:** 192, 193 **7:** 894
Verlaine, Paul **6:** 844
Vermeer, Jan **2:** 224, 264
 paintings by **2:** *222*, 253, *261*, 264
Veronese **1:** 84
Verranzo, Giovanni da **3:** 355–356
Verrochio, Andrea del, statue by **1:** *82*
Versailles, Palace of **1:** 38 **2:** 263 **4:** 458, *459*, *460*,
 472, 491
 gardens **4:** 454, 498, 499 **5:** 635
 court of Louis XIV **4:** 458–459
 convention of the Estates General (1789) **5:** *584*
 Petit Trianon **5:** *585*
Versailles, Treaty of (1919) **7:** 903–905, *906*, *907*,
 908, 934–935, 952, 953, 956, 987, 988, 993
 8: 1026–1027
 and the League of Nations **7:** 903, 945–946
 8: 1028
 "war guilt" clause **8:** 1027
 German contradiction of **8:** 1030–1031
Vesalius **2:** 267
Vespucci, Amerigo **3:** *305*, 311
Vicksburg, Battle of (1863) **5:** 683
Victor Emmanuel III, king of Italy **7:** 986
Victor Emmanuel, king of Sardinia **5:** 659
Victoria, queen of Great Britain **6:** 798
 technology during reign of **5:** *706*
 in mourning **6:** 804
 German relatives **7:** 871
Victoria Falls **6:** *821*
Victory (ship) **5:** 599
Victory in Europe (VE) **8:** 1084
Vienna
 besieged by the Turks (1529) **1:** 93, 107 **2:** 188
 3: *297*, 298
 map **3:** *297*
 besieged by the Turks (1683) **4:** 485 **6:** 729
 in the 1700s **4:** *488*
 and Napoleon **5:** 599
 the Ringstrasse **5:** *655*
 Vienna State Opera House **6:** *803*
 and European music **6:** 847
Vienna, Congress of (1815) **5:** 605–607, 608, 609,
 691
Viet Cong movement **8:** 1099, 1100, 1123–1124
Viet Minh **8:** 1100, 1123
Vietnam **3:** 314
 and the Mongols **1:** 125

Cham people **3:** 314, *318*, 321
 art styles **3:** 317
 Indian influences **3:** 317, *318*
 part of China **3:** 317, 321
 and the Cold War **8:** 1083
 decolonization and French withdrawl from
 8: 1099, 1100, *1117*, 1122–1123
 split into North and South **8:** 1099, 1100, 1123
 Vietnam War (1959–1975) **8:** 1099, 1100–1101
 9: 1217
 reunited (1976) **8:** 1101
 Japanese occupation of **8:** 1119, 1122–1123
 French-Vietnamese War (1946–1954) **8:** 1123
 Marxist regime (1970s) **9:** 1167
 See also Annam
Vietnam War (1962–1975) **8:** 1099, 1100–1101,
 1124 **9:** *1162*, 1163, 1172, 1177
 televised **9:** 1171
 U.S. bases in Southeast Asia **9:** 1217
 helicopters **9:** 1255
View of Delft (Jan Vermeer) **2:** *222*
Vikings, Varangians **1:** 89–90
Villa, Francisco "Pancho" **6:** 742, 744, 745, 746
villages, early modern European **1:** 77, 78
Villaroel, Gualberto **7:** 979
villeins **2:** 206–207
Villiers, George **2:** 236
Vindication of the Rights of Woman, A (Mary
 Wollstonecraft) **4:** 480
viols **1:** 85
Virginia (North America)
 colonial **3:** 356, 357–358, 373 **4:** *545*, 549
 colonial conflicts in **4:** *545*
Virginia Company **3:** 358
Vishnu **3:** 317
Vitebsk **5:** *693*
Vittoria (ship) **3:** 312
Vives, Juan Luis **1:** 55
viziers **1:** 104
Volga River **1:** 21–22
Volgograd (*formerly* Stalingrad), and World War II
 8: *1044*, 1045
Volksraad **8:** 1022
Volta, Alessandro **5:** 704
Voltaire, François Marie Arouet de **4:** 475–476, 544
Vondel, Joost van den **2:** 224
Vos, Cornelius de, painting by **2:** *223*
voting rights **6:** 816
 in Britain **6:** 809
 in France **6:** 809
 of freed slaves in the United States **6:** 830–831
Vytautas, grand duke of Lithuania **1:** 91

Wagner, Richard **6:** *843*, 847–848
wagons, Conestoga **3:** *369*
Wahhabi people **6:** 732
Wake **8:** 1052
Walden, or Life in the Woods (Henry David
 Thoreau) **5:** 641 **9:** *1263*
Waldenses **2:** 174–175
Waldo, Peter **2:** 175
Waldseemüller, Martin **3:** 311
Walesa, Lech **8:** 1106 **9:** 1244, 1245
Wall Street Crash (1929) **7:** 961–963
Wallenstein (Albrecht of Valstejn) **2:** 225, 229,
 231
Walpole, Hugh **4:** 496
Walpole, Sir Robert **4:** 445
Wampanoag tribe (Native Americans) **3:** 359, *368*
 4: 544
Wandiwash, Battle of (1760) **3:** 418
war bonds **8:** 1068
War Mobilization, Office of **8:** 1064
War of 1812 **5:** 646
 and the United States **5:** 646–647
War Powers Act (1941) **8:** 1063
War Production Board **8:** 1064
warfare
 European (1400s/1500s) **1:** 26–27
 See also army/armies; artillery; firearms
Warren Commission (1964) **9:** 1173
Warsaw **4:** 485, 490
 Grand Duchy created **5:** 600, 691
Warsaw Pact **8:** *1084*, 1090, 1093–1094, 1095,
 1102 **9:** 1243
 dissolution **8:** 1106

1419

Wartburg Castle, Luther's cell **2:** *157*
Warwick, John Dudley, earl of and duke of
  Northumberland **2:** 210, 211
Washington, Native Americans **3:** 340–341
Washington, George
  and the French and Indian War **4:** 548
  and the American Revolutionary War **4:** *553,*
    556, 557–558, *560*
  president **4:** 562
Washington, D.C.
  Franklin D. Roosevelt Memorial **7:** *959*
  bonus marchers (1932) **7:** *964,* 965
  Korean War Memorial **8:** *1092*
  and Martin Luther King, Jr. **9:** *1172*
Washington Naval Conference **7:** 948
Water Carrier of Seville (Diego Velásquez) **2:** *259,*
  260
water closets **6:** 801
water filters **9:** 1257
water sellers **2:** 249
Waterbabies, The (Charles Kingsley) **6:** 804, *809*
Watergate affair **9:** 1176–1177
Waterloo, Battle of (1815) **5:** 604
Watson, James **9:** 1262
Watt, James **5:** 619
Watteau, Antoine **4:** 492
Wealth of Nations, The (Adam Smith) **4:** 480
  5: 621–624
Weathermen **9:** 1165
weaving **1:** *76,* 77
  mechanized **5:** 616
Webster, Daniel **5:** 647, 651, 654
weddings *See* marriages
Wedgwood, Josiah **5:** 620–621
  pottery **4:** *473,* 496
Weimar Republic **7:** 952–953, 987 **8:** 1029
welfare states **8:** 1077 **9:** 1160
welfare systems **8:** 1077, 1078, 1079
Welles, Gideon **5:** 679
Wellington, Arthur Wellesley, duke of **5:** 602, *604*
Wentworth, Sir Thomas **2:** 238, 239
Werther (Johann Wolfgang von Goethe) **4:** 500
West, Benjamin **4:** 497
West Bank **8:** 1132, 1133, 1134, 1136, 1138
  9: 1242
West European Union **9:** 1190
West Virginia, USS **8:** *1051*
Western Schism *See* Great/Western Schism
Westerners, the **6:** 772, 776
Westernizers **5:** 690, 691
Westinghouse **6:** 790
Westphalia, Peace of (1648) **2:** 172, 233–234
wet-nursing **4:** 512–513
What is Enlightenment? (Immanuel Kant) **4:** 479
wheat **1:** 33 **3:** 350
Whigs (England), and Tories **4:** 444, 445
Whigs (U.S.) **5:** 651, 654
White Army, and the Russian Civil War **7:** *912,*
  919, 920, 921 **8:** 1084
White Mountain, Battle of the (1620) **2:** 226, 227
White Terror **5:** 594
Whitefield, George **4:** 550
Whitney, Eli **5:** 647
Whittle, Frank **9:** 1254
wigs **5:** 642
wigwams **3:** 333, 335, 340
Wilberforce, Samuel **5:** 700, 705–706
Wilde, Oscar **6:** 848
Wilhelm II, emperor (kaiser) of Germany and king
  of Prussia **7:** 871, *872,* 874, 880, 952, 987
William I, first German emperor and king of
  Prussia **5:** 660, 664
William I, prince of Orange (William the Silent;
  1533–1584) **2:** 213, 218, 219, 220
William II, emperor of Germany and king of
  Prussia *See* Wilhelm II
William III and Mary II, king and queen of Britain
  and Ireland (William of Orange) **2:** *243,* 244
  4: 441–444, 545
  defeat of James Stuart in Ireland **4:** 445
William IV, stadtholder and captain-general of the
  Netherlands **4:** 442
Willkie, Wendell **8:** 1040
Wills, William John **5:** 673
Wilmington (*formerly* Fort Christina) **3:** 362–363
Wilmot Proviso **5:** 654

Wilson, Woodrow **6:** 745, 746, 836 **7:** 946
  and World War I **7:** 896, 902–903, *904,* 952
  and the League of Nations **7:** 908, 945–946
    8: 1028
  See also Fourteen Points
Winckelmann, Johann Joachim **4:** 497
wine **2:** 249
Winnipeg **5:** *674*
Winter Palace **5:** 696 **7:** *909, 915,* 916
Winthrop, John **3:** 360
wire, barbed **6:** 839
witches **2:** 173, *179* **3:** 366
  witch trials **2:** 181–182, 274 **3:** 370 **4:** 521
Wittenberg **1:** 28 **2:** 153, 155
Wladyslaw II Jagiello, grand duke of Lithuania and
  king of Poland **1:** 91
Wladyslaw IV Vasa, czar of Russia **1:** 97
Wöhler, Friedrich **5:** 704
Wolfe, James **4:** 549
Wollstonecraft, Mary **4:** 480, 512
Wolsey, Thomas **2:** 207, 208
women
  in early modern Europe **1:** *9,* 76–77
  and Enlightenment thought **4:** 480
  in Europe (1700s) **4:** 512–513
  in Japanese society **4:** 538, *540*
  and the French Revolution **5:** 588
  and industrialization **5:** 631–634
  middle-class (late 1800s) **6:** 798, 799
  working-class (late 1800s) **6:** 799–800
  and World War I **7:** 897–898, *899,* 945
  and the vote **7:** 898, 948
  flappers **7:** *945,* 950
  post–World War I **7:** 945
  and World War II **8:** 1064
  women's movement/rights (1960s/1970s)
    9: 1166, 1172–1174, 1177
  role in American society (1950s) **9:** 1170
  in Latin American society (late 1900s) **9:** 1208
Women's Land Army **8:** 1064
wood, gathering **1:** *35*
woodcuts, Japanese **5:** 540, *542*
Woodstock rock festival **9:** *1176*
wool
  woolen industry **1:** 35, *76* **2:** 206
  trade **1:** 40
  and the putting-out system **1:** 77
Wordsworth, William **5:** 636, 639, 640, 641
workhouses **5:** 632, *633*
working class **5:** 628
Works Progress Administration (*also* Works
  Projects Administration; 1935) **7:** *967,* 970
World Bank, and African economies **9:** 1230
World Health Organization **9:** 1271, 1280
World Trade Organization (WTO) **9:** 1198
World War I **7:** 883–896, 983
  events leading to **6:** 734, 736 **7:** 871–882
  and Latin America **6:** 766
  and socialism **6:** 816
  Battle of Jutland (1916) **7:** 876, *891*
  Schlieffen Plan **7:** 880–882, 884
  Battle of Ypres (1917; Passchendaele)
    7: *883,* 895
  Battle of the Marne (1914) **7:** 884
  Battle of Tannenberg (1914) **7:** 884
  Gallipoli campaign (1916) **7:** *885,* 890
  weapons **7:** *886,* 888–889, 892–893
  trench warfare **7:** 888, 889–890
  Battle of the Somme **7:** *891,* 894
  Battle of Cambrai (1917) **7:** 893
  social and political aftermath **7:** 897–908
  postwar treaties **7:** 903–905, 906–907, 908,
    934–935, 945, 987, 988, 993 **8:** 1026–1028
  and the Russian Revolution (1917) **7:** 912
  and China **7:** 934
  postwar America and Europe **7:** 945–958
  veterans demonstrate in the United States **7:** *964,*
    965
  and Japan **8:** 1016
  German lands lost after **8:** 1026
  German resentment after **8:** 1026
  and India **8:** 1107
World War II
  and Latin America **7:** *981* **9:** 1199
  German invasion of Poland (1939)
    8: 1025–1026, 1036, 1037–1038

  the road to **8:** 1025–1036
  in Europe **8:** 1037–1048
  and France **8:** 1037, 1038, *1039,* 1048
  and the Soviet Union **8:** *1037,* 1042, 1043–1045,
    1048
  Battle of Britain (1940–1941) **8:** 1038, *1040,*
    1047 **9:** 1255
  Dunkirk evacuation **8:** 1038, *1039*
  United States and lend-lease **8:** 1038–1041
  Battle of the Atlantic **8:** 1041–1042
  Operation Barbarossa **8:** 1043–1044
  war in the eastern Europe **8:** 1043
  Battle of El Alamein (1942) **8:** 1045
  in North Africa **8:** 1045, 1046
  liberation of Italy **8:** 1046
  D-Day landings (1944) **8:** *1047,* 1048
  Allied bombing campaign in Europe
    8: 1047–1048
  Japanese attack on Pearl Harbor **8:** 1049,
    1050–1051, 1053, 1067
  in the Pacific **8:** 1049–1060
  and Burma **8:** 1050, 1052, 1054, 1058
  and the Philippines **8:** 1050, 1051, *1052,* 1054,
    1056–1057, *1058*
  Battle of the Coral Sea (1942) **8:** 1052–1053
  victims **8:** 1055–1056, *1057,* 1059, 1060,
    1062–1063, 1071, 1131
  Battle of Leyte Gulf (1944) **8:** 1057, 1058–1060
  and the atomic bomb **8:** 1059, 1060, 1086 **9:**
    1255
  total war **8:** 1061–1070
  concentration camps **8:** *1062,* 1067
  information control in **8:** 1066–1068
  resistance fighters **8:** *1068,* 1069
  postwar trials **8:** 1070
  and the United Nations **8:** 1070
  postwar recovery in the West **8:** 1071–1082
  and India **8:** 1112–1114
  and decolonization **8:** 1117–1119
  the postwar return of Jews to Palestine **8:** 1131
  and technology **9:** 1253
World Wide Web (www) **9:** 1259
Worms, Diet of (1521) **2:** 155, *156,* 188
Worth, Charles Frederick **6:** 846
Wounded Knee, Battle of (1890) **6:** 839
Wovoka **6:** 839
Wren, Sir Christopher **2:** *244*
Wright, Frank Lloyd **6:** 784
writing, Chinese **4:** *526*
WTO (World Trade Organization) **9:** 1198
Wu Sangui **4:** 525, 526, 527
Württemberg, duchy of **2:** 234
Wuthering Heights (Emily Brontë) **5:** 636
Wycliffe, John **1:** 11 **2:** 164

Xavier, Francis **2:** 170, *171* **4:** 538–539
Xhosa **6:** 821
Xia **1:** 120

Yalta Conference (1945) **8:** 1084–1085
Yamaha **9:** 1210
Yamamoto, Isoroku **8:** 1050, *1051*
Yaqui Indians **6:** 742
Yeltsin, Boris **9:** *1248,* 1249, 1250, 1251
Yeshov, Nikolai **7:** 932
Yongzheng, emperor of China **4:** 530
Yorimoto *See* Minamoto Yorimoto
York (an African-American) **5:** 646
Yorktown, Battle of (1781) **4:** 561
Yoruba **1:** 113
Yoshimune, shogun of Japan **4:** 536, 540
Young, Brigham **5:** 702
Young, Owen D. **7:** 954
Young Ottomans **6:** 735
Young Plan (1929) **7:** 954
Young Turks **6:** 735, 736 **7:** 878, 887
Ypres, Battle of (1917; Passchendaele campaign)
  7: *883,* 895
Yuan dynasty **1:** 123–125, 127
Yuan Shih-k'ai **6:** 776 **7:** 933–934, 936
Yucatán, Maya revolt **6:** 738–739
Yugoslavia
  post–World War I **7:** 906
  D'Annunzio of Italy takes the port of Fiume
    7: 984
  and World War II **8:** 1043, *1069,* 1070 **9:** 1252

inter-republic tensions **8:** 1106 **9:** 1251–1252
  dissolution (1990s) **9:** 1198
  See also Bosnia-Herzegovina; Croatia;
  Macedonia; Montenegro; Serbia
Yung Lo **3:** 302
Yung-lo ta-tien (encyclopedia) **1:** 66
yuppies **9:** 1178

zaibatsu **6:** 781
Zaire *See* Congo, Democratic Republic of
Zambesi River **6:** *821*
Zambia (*formerly* Northern Rhodesia)
  Zulu migration to **6:** 819
  independence **8:** 1128
  copper **9:** 1224
Zand dynasty **3:** 406
Zanzibar **1:** *113*
Zapata, Emiliano **6:** 742, 744, 745, 746
Zapatistas **9:** 1206
Zaragoza **8:** 1032
Zayandeh River **3:** *401*
zemsky sobor (or land assembly) **4:** 482–483
zemstvos **5:** 692–693, 694, *695* **7:** 910
Zen Buddhism **1:** *125*, 127
zeppelins **7:** 891, 893
Zhikov, Todor **9:** 1247
Zimbabwe (*formerly* Southern Rhodesia)
  site of Great Zimbabwe **1:** 115
  and Cecil Rhodes **6:** 826
  decolonization **8:** 1124, *1125*, 1128
  independence (1980) **9:** *1227*, 1229
Zinovyev, Grigory **7:** 931
Zinzendorf, Nikolaus Ludwig von **3:** 372
Zionist World Congress, first **8:** 1129
Zionists **8:** 1129, 1130, 1132
Zola, Emile **5:** 626 **6:** 806, 844, 846, *847*
  and the Dreyfus affair **6:** 846
zouaves **7:** 884
Zulu Inkhata movement **9:** 1228
Zulus **6:** 818, 821, 826
Zurich **2:** 160
Zwingli, Huldrych **2:** 160–162

Volume numbers appear in **boldface type**. Page numbers in *italic type* refer to illustrations and captions.